The Selected Works of R.B. Zajonc

R.B. Zajonc, Editor
Stanford University

www.wiley.com/college/zajonc

Senior Editor   *Tim Vertovec*
Editorial Assistant   *Maureen Powers*
Program Assistant   *Kristen Babroski*
Marketing Manager   *Kate Stewart*
Managing Editor   *Lari Bishop*
Associate Production Manager   *Kelly Tavares*
Production Editor   *Sarah Wolfman-Robichaud*
Illustration Editor   *Benjamin Reece and Jennifer Fisher*
Cover Design   *Jennifer Fisher*

This book was set in Times by Leyh Publishing LLC and printed and bound by Courier–Westford. The cover was printed by Phoenix Color.

This book is printed on acid free paper. ∞

ISBN: 0-471-43306-3

Printed in the United States of America

10   9   8   7   6   5   4   3   2   1

I dedicate this volume to my children.

Peter, for his equanimity and clear perspective

Michael, who always knows the right way right away

Joseph, who, better than I, understands the psychology of psychology

*and to Krysia, who taught me the value of a little,
or a lot, of self-criticism*

and to my grandchildren: Jonathan, Oliver, Zoë, and Lucy Ming

Brief Contents

Contents

Chapter 12   Feeling and Facial Efference: Implications of the Vascular Theory of Emotion   197

Chapter 13   Hypothalmic Cooling Elicits Eating: Differential Effects on Motivation and Pleasure   239

Part Six The Affect–Cognition Interface

Chapter 14   Feeling and Thinking: Preferences Need No Inferences   250

Chapter 15   On the Primacy of Affect   285

Chapter 16   Affect and Cognition: The Hard Interface   297

Part Seven   Nonconscious Affect

Chapter 17   Affect, Cognition, and Awareness: Affective Priming with Optimal and Suboptimal Stimulus Exposures   324

Acknowledgements

I would like to acknowledge and also dedicate this volume to all my students, teachers, colleagues, and friends who worked with me on my problems as I sometimes worked on theirs, and whose inspirations, ideas, and critique are reflected throughout these reproduced works.

To the late Michael Argyle, Johan Barendregt, Phil Brickman, Roger Brown, Matty Chiva, Nick Cottrell, Ted Curtis, Don Dorfman, Jack French, Ruth Hamill, Hilde Himmelweit, Morris Janowitz, Joos Jaspers, Ned Jones, Dan Katz, Les Kish, J. J. Klant, Ron Lippitt, Irv Marin, Don Marquis, Jyuji Misumi, Jim Morgan, Julian Morrissette, Ted Newcomb, Michel Pecheux, Steve Sales, Stan Schachter, Ed Swanson, Henri Tajfel, Stanley Thorley, Adriana Touraine, Amos Tversky, Maria Zalewska, Al Zander, René Zazzo;

And to Bob Abelson, Verena Aebischer, Pam Adelman, S. Akeju, Toni Antonucci, Debbie Apsley, Jack Atkinson, Harry Bahlman, Mark Baldwin, Paul Baltes, Marzu Banaji, Al Bandura, John Bargh, Nancy Bellows, Michael Berbaum, Kent Berridge, Hugh Blanding, Jerry Blum, Gene Borgida, Gordon Bower, Steve Brechin, Malcolm Brenner, Bonnie Brown, Jerry Bruner, Gene Burnstein, Martha Burnstein, John Cacioppo, Nancy Cantor, Laura Carstensen, Doc Cartwright, Dave Carter, Bogdan Cichomski, Herb Clark, Kim Colwell, Rick Crandall, Dave Cross, Mary Cullen, Martha Curtis, Lou D'Alecy, Robyn Dawes, Susan DeLong, H. C. J. Duijker, Jennifer Eberhardt, Kari Edwards, Hanka Ekel, Jurek Ekel, Phoebe Ellsworth, Steve Emerick, Marv Epstein, Claude Faucheux, Norm Feather, David Featherman, Steve Fein, Leon Festinger, Susan Fiske, Claude Flament, Geoff Fong, Joe Forgas, John Forward, Benno Fricke, Ron Friedman, Nico Frijda, Stephanie Fryberg, Marty Gold, Ian Gotlib, John Greden, Janusz Grzelak, Jerry Gurin, Pat Gurin, Elaine Hatfield, Doris Hausser, Alex Heingartner, Kaaren Hanson, Frank Harary, Al Harrison, Ed Hermann, Larry Hirschfeld, Gorge Hunyady, John Innes, Martin Irle, Cal Izard, James Jackson, Marysia Jarymowicz, Judith Johnson, Lee Jussim, Sulaiman Kakli, Danny Kahnemann, Mayumi Karasawa, Sue Karp, Jurek Karylowski, Regina Karylowska, Shinobu Kitayama, Greta Klevgard, Grazyna Kochanska, Mirek Kofta, Joziek Kozielecki, Dave Krantz, Jon Krosnick, Ziva Kunda, Rick Larrick, Cpt. Bob Leatzow, Darrin Lehman, Gerard Lemaine, Wilie Lens, Mark Lepper, Maria Lewicka, Pawel Lewicki, Debbie Leyton, Ed Lichstein, Christine Linder, Gardner Lindzey, Beth Loftus, Danny McIntosh, Dick Lazarus, Dave Mande, Geroge Mandler, Mel Manis, Jean Manis, Greg Markus, Hazel Rose Markus, Margaret Matlin, Lauren Melendres, Batja Mesquita, Stasiek Mika, Dale Miller, Jennifer Monahan, Benoit Monin, Barbara Moreland, Dick Moreland, Serge Moscovici, Patty Mullally, Sheila Murphy, Tom Nelson, Paula Niedenthal, Bob Nieuwenhuijse, Dick Nisbett, Andrzej Nowak, Jeff Nuttin, Rafal Ohme, Heather Omoregie, Marysia Ostafin,

Robert Pagès, Allan Paivio, Bernard Personnaz, Rich Petty, Paula Pietromonaco, Art Platz, Michel Plon, Jean-Pierre Poitou, Carol Porter, Japp Rabbie, D. W. Rajecki, Bert Raven, Alan Reifman, David Reimer, Janusz Reykowski, Bernard Rimé, Paul Roberts, Louis van Rooijen, Lee Ross, Zick Rubin, Susan Saegert, Klaus Scherer, Grzegorz Sedek, Keith Sentis, Howard Shevrin, Yaakov Shul, Phil Shaver, Jim Sherman, Beth Shinn, Bill Siegel, Renata Siemienska, Jerry Singer, Ed Smith, Peter Smith, Alan Smithers, Bill Smoke, Alana Snibbe, Claude Steele, Dorothy Steele, Ann Stoler, Pat Suppes, Walter Swap, Carol Tavris, Shelley Taylor, Nancy Thalhoffer, Ewart Thomas, Alain Touraine, Yaacov Trope, Janusz Trzebinski, Endel Tulving. Jodie Veroff, Joe Veroff, Amiram Vinokur, Mario von Cranach, Bill von Hippel, Grazyna Wieczorkowska, Piotr Winkielman, Bill Wilson, Tim Wilson, Bogdan Wojciszke, Bob Wolosin, Myrna Wolosin, Jeff Wine, Don Wolfe, Donna Zajonc, Phil Zimbardo.

And to all those whose names I am sorry to have somehow omitted or misplaced.

About the Editor

R.B. Zajonc received his Ph.D. degree from the University of Michigan in 1955. He remained there until his retirement in 1994. During his tenure at the University of Michigan, he served as the Director of the Research Center for Group Dynamics and of the Institute for Social Research. Zajonc's research spans a number of theoretical problems, such as the nature of the relationship between cognition and communication, emotional influences, including unconscious effects, the emergence of preferences, and the aggregate pattern of intellectual performance scores as they are influenced by changing family dynamics. He is the recipient of the APA Distinguished Scientific Contribution Award, the Society for Experimental Social Psychology Distinguished Scientist Award, and Doctorates Honoris Causa from the University of Louvain and from the University of Warsaw. He is currently Professor of Psychology at Stanford University.

Introduction

Seek Out the Magician: Contrarian Tricks of Mere Simplicity Make Affect Appear and Disappear From Social Psychology

Susan T. Fiske

> People like to make sense of their world, but they also seek out the magician to be entertained by incongruity. (Zajonc, 1960a, p. 380)

The science of Zajonc possesses a magic that mesmerizes his audiences again and again, compelling them to try his tricks in their home laboratories. His work fascinates social psychologists (and wider audiences) by two brilliant lifelong techniques: a contrarian approach and mere simplicity. In the pursuit of these two strategies, Zajonc has, with a flourish, made affect appear and disappear from the stage of social psychology. Social psychologists have historically leaned toward a relative emphasis on the affective or the cognitive side of social phenomena over the 20th century, and Zajonc has pointed the way most times, his influence owing to his two hallmarks.

First, the contrarian strategy: Normally an investment strategy that entails putting money into stocks that oppose the conventional wisdom, a contrarian approach likewise profits both magic and science. In each arena, investing virtuosity where others are not currently looking simultaneously innovates and impresses the audience. Robert Zajonc dislikes too much agreement, too much consensus, because they make for dull conversation. His work always aims to go where others are not. Although he starts out alone,

---

From *Unraveling the complexities of social life: A Festschrift in honor of Robert B. Zajonc.* John A. Bargh and Deborah K. Apsley, eds. Washington, DC: American Psychological Association. Copyright © 2001 by the American Psychological Association. Adapted with permission.

the others soon follow, and then he again seeks more deserted venues. An overview of his major contributions reveals a brilliant new idea about every 5 years, just when his previous work starts to attract a crowd. He follows each idea with convincing arguments and data, but his contrarian approach keeps each project surprising anew.

In addition, his work follows "mere" simplicity as a rule. As other contributors to this volume will note, parsimony pervades Zajonc's most inspired insights. Each idea he has brought to the field can be summarized in a sentence, and not a very **[11]*** complicated sentence: Simplicity constitutes its brilliance. Zajonc explains that his work has been

> concerned with the four-letter word "mere." I happen to have used this
> seemingly innocent word on two separate occasions and on both found it
> became a source of mild controversy. There must be some well-founded
> psychoanalytic interpretation of my vulnerability to this four-letter word,
> and, most certainly, it is rooted in the deep and unsavory unconscious—as
> is true, of course, with all four-letter words. On a level more accessible to
> introspection (which we all know to be but a source of self-deception), my
> use of this word had probably something to do with a compulsion to sim-
> plify things—based, self-deceptively, on the famous hope that they indeed
> *can* be simplified. But one who simplifies runs the risk of *over*simplify-
> ing, and in our field, as in others, whereas the first is sublime, the second
> is sinful. And I must have sinned. (Zajonc, 1980a, pp. 35–36)

He goes on to describe two kinds of social psychologists, those who believe the world is "above all enormously complex" and

> then there are those ... who aren't awestricken, and perhaps not even
> much moved, by the complexity of the social world. In fact we really
> don't know whether the "real" social world is or isn't complex. We do
> believe, however, that whatever its ultimate complexity (a question to be
> decided perhaps by metaphysicians), scientific statements about it need
> not be complex. On the contrary, if at all possible they should be simple.
> Given that real life is miserably complex, why should we complicate it
> further by duplicating its complexity in our journals and books? (Zajonc,
> 1980a. pp. 35–36)

The dazzling combination of the unexpected contrarian and the mere simplicity appears most clearly in the coming and going of affect social psychology, shifts with Zajonc at their leading edge. Examining affect and cognition in the spirit of these two themes, this chapter will provide historical perspective on Zajonc's work, specifics elaborated in the chapters that follow. Viewing the pageant of social psychology from the back of the theater, this chapter takes the contrarian view that cognition did not suddenly overwhelm affect, that there was no social cognitive revolution, contrary to the popular view. Instead, each of Zajonc's mere simplicities have refocused in turn on affect or cognition.

---

*Bracketed bold numbers refer to original page numbers. Page numbers indicate where the original page ended.

A CONTRARIAN VIEW OF THE (SOCIAL) COGNITIVE REVOLUTION

The standard view holds that the social cognitive revolution, mimicking the nearby cognitive revolution, wiped affect off the social psychological itinerary (see Fiske and Taylor, 1991, for one such account). But a closer examination suggests that social psychology has always preserved cognition (Zajonc, 1980b), in the sense that it has always harbored a safe haven for mentalistic concepts and variables, even when the [12] rest of the field was at sea in a behaviorist boat. Beliefs and stereotypes, both heavily cognitive, have constituted mainstays of social psychology from its beginnings.

Moreover, even a weaker version of this argument, that the balance between cognition and affect has, since the 1970s, favored cognition, may not stay afloat. As a first approximation, we[1] searched PsycINFO abstracts for the frequency of (a) "social" plus "affect" (also plus "emotion" and "feelings," but the results are similar) and compared them with the frequency of (b) "social" plus "cogniti*" (with the asterisk presumably including both "cognition" and "cognitive"). To be conservative, we subtracted out "cognitive dissonance," as that might artificially inflate the prerevolutionary frequencies of "cogniti*"; cognitive dissonance is not typically numbered among the cognitive revolutionaries.

Over the course of Zajonc's career, the relevant historical period, the relative frequency of social cognition and social affect defies conventional wisdom. On the contrary, "affect" dominates "cogniti*" in every 6-year period, except in the 1990s, where they equal each other. As Figure 1 indicates, the relative proportion of psychological abstracts mentioning social + cognition does steadily increase, even without cognitive dissonance theory, but no sudden revolution is evident, and perhaps the rough equivalence, from 1984 on, suggests a balance of power, rather than a cognitive coup d'état.

So how has Zajonc influenced the balance between affect and cognition, if not leading a single revolutionary attack, at this strategic macro level? His impact has turned the field's attention to new themes, alternating cognition and affect with more nuanced tactics.

MERE SIMPLICITY CAPTURES THE FIELD'S ATTENTION

The major contributions of Robert Zajonc with astonishing regularity attack the dominant perspective with a simple, mere effect that shakes the field's foundations. Five themes in his contributions, discussed in the following sections, capture this pattern of a new phenomenon every 5 or so years.

Cognitive Structure

During the mid-1950s through 1960s, social psychology focused wholeheartedly on dissonance and other consistency theories (for historical perspectives, see Jones, 1998; Taylor, 1998) but neglected to examine carefully the mediating mechanisms themselves. That is, attitudes certainly changed to reduce cognitive inconsistencies, but few investigators examined the actual cognitive structure (Kiesler, Collins, and [13] Miller,

---

[1] I am indebted to Stephanie Strebel for obtaining this information.

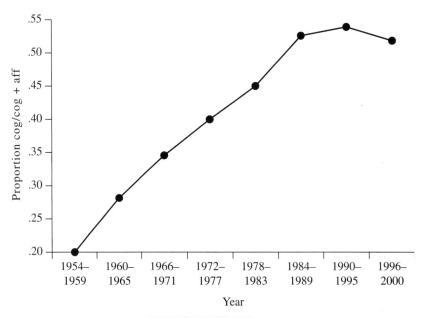

Figure 1 The proportion of psychological abstract reference to "cognition" and "cognitive" (cog) relative to total "cognition-plus-affect" (cog + aff) references, out of abstracts also using the term "social," from PsycINFO (see text), over the last half-century.

1969). Zajonc went beyond consistency to dissect the cognitive structures that undergird consistency and inconsistency. Although, as noted, the field had always been cognitive in some respects, the basic elements or building blocks had not been examined.

In Figure 2, the vertical axis makes a time line from the start of 1960, with Zajonc's publications in the first line of cognitive structure work. The cognitive balance and cognitive tuning articles appeared in 1960 (Zajonc, 1960a, 1960b). His 1968 *Handbook of Social Psychology* (2nd ed.) chapter on cognitive theory heralded, as some people would date it, the social cognitive revolution; the 1985 *Handbook of Social Psychology* (3rd ed.) cognitive perspective chapter with Hazel Markus fortified the social cognitive position. Looking at these early publications, one sees that Zajonc said it all, and the rest of us have been busy catching up ever since. A quote from the cognitive tuning article will illustrate:

> The purpose of this study is to examine the nature of cognitive structures that are activated … when persons enter into communication with others…. Cognitive structures represent organized systems whose nature depends on the various interrelations among their components. (Zajonc, 1960b, p. 159) **[14]**

This quote has aged gracefully. Indeed, the entire cognitive tuning article grapples with issues that social psychologists still struggle to understand. First, Zajonc tackles cognitive structures, or organized subsets of a person's cognitive universe. He defines

	Cognitive Structure	Social Motives	Affect & Cognition	Cognitive Intelligence	Group Hostility
1960	Cognitive tuning & balance				
1965		Social facilitation			
	Handbook: cognitive theory		Mere exposure		
1970		Cockroaches			
1975		Day-old chicks			
	Social cognition revolution			Intelligence & family configuration	
		Compresence			
1980			Preferences need no inferences	Validating confluence model	Altruism, envy, competition, & common good
			Primacy of affect		
1985	Handbook: cognitive perspective				
			Facial efference		
1990			Vascular theory		
			Nonconscious affect		
1995		Social motives redux			
				Birth order & SATs	Collective violence
			Handbook: emotions		
2000					
			2010 Affect & brain imaging coup	**2025** Social gene interaction	**2045** End group violence
Field's lag to adopt	+20	+30	+40	+50	+60

Figure 2   Time lines of five major themes in Robert Zajonc's work, as predating major trends in the field (indicated in shaded type). "Handbook" Field's lag to adopt Zajonc's theme is estimated or extrapolated in the last line of each column. Handbook = Handbook of Social Psychology.

dimensional values of stimuli (black, animated, or beautiful) as the attributes or elements of a cognitive structure. Each cognitive structure possesses degrees of differentiation, complexity, unity, and organization. When people expect to transmit information to others, as compared with receiving it, their cognitive structures become more differentiated, complex, unified, and organized. Differences between transmitters and receivers decrease when people expect to receive incongruent information, but it was the transmitter-receiver contrast in structure that captured the field's imagination. Nobody else was looking in such detail at cognitive structures. This first battle cry to investigate fine-grained cognitive structures of course then summoned others to rush into the fray, resulting in the active enterprise of social cognition that we now know.

As an assistant professor coming of professional age at a time when cognitive consistency theory was the dominant paradigm, Zajonc dared to say the unsayable. He dared to write, for example,

> Cognitive doctrines … lack specification of the conditions under which
> their predictions will hold. People like to make sense of their world, but
> they also seek out the magician to be entertained by incongruity.
> Historically the concept of consistency resembles the concept of vacuum
> in physics. A useful doctrine for organizing knowledge although full of
> exceptions and contradictions. (Zajonc, 1960a, p. 380)

Without this chutzpah, the field might never have appreciated his contrarian views.

By about 20 years after Zajonc's 1960 cognitive tuning and cognitive balance articles, the rest of the field undertook the examination of cognitive structure in earnest, debating schemas, prototypes, scripts, as well as consistency and inconsistency in memory, significantly stimulated by his cognitive contributions.

Social Motives

As consistency theories receded from center stage, with them went the interest in social motives such as consistency seeking. The field as a whole was not to return to motivational issues in earnest until recently. But way ahead of the curve, 5 years after the cognitive structure articles, Zajonc (1965) brought us modern research on social facilitation.

> Until the late 1930s, interest in social facilitation was quite active, but …
> it suddenly died. And it is truly regrettable that it died, because the basic
> questions about social facilitation, … which are, in effect, the basic questions
> of social psychology, were never solved. It is with these questions
> that this article is concerned … this nearly completely abandoned area of
> research. (Zajonc, 1965, p. 269) [16]

Again, the contrarian investment. Again, the simple idea—the mere presence of others as a motivator—made elegant by the compelling research that was to support it, including the infamous studies of cockroaches, day-old chicks, and sophomores in the "compresence" of conspecifics. The presence of others, whether audience or co-actors, enhances arousal, which in turn encourages the individual's dominant response (enhancing performance on well-practiced tasks and undermining performance on novel tasks). The rest of the field quickly followed up the revival of social facilitation (and this may be Zajonc's single most-cited article).

Nevertheless, the field neglected Zajonc's focus on specifically *social* motivations that shows so clearly in the social facilitation phenomenon. The more general issue of specifically social motives took the rest of the field nearly 30 years to catch up. Only by the 1990s would we coin the term *motivated tactician* (Fiske and Taylor, 1991), though Showers and Cantor (1985) earlier forecasted the idea of *motivated social cognition*. A full-throated chorus of social motivational effects on cognition did not arise until nearly three decades later (Pittman, 1998; Snyder and Cantor, 1998). If cognitive structures took 20 years to capture the field, and social motives 30 years, the field learning its lessons from Zajonc suggests a decelerating curve.

Affect and Emotion

Following the decelerating curve, the next 5-year plan will probably not hit the field fully for another 10 years, making a 40-year lag. In fewer than 5 years after his first social facilitation article, Zajonc rattled psychology's chain by claiming that *mere* exposure to stimuli alone could induce liking.

> It has been known for some time that social interaction enhances the attitudes of interactors toward each other. ... But it is not known just what contribution to the relationship between interaction and attitudes is made by *mere* exposure on the one hand, and by the variety of psychologically significant processes that necessarily accompany mere exposure during the course of social interaction, on the other. (Zajonc, 1968, p. 2)

In a brilliant synthesis of linguistic analyses and experimental manipulations, Zajonc showed first that positive affective connotations and positive attitudes correlate with (a) relative word frequency within antonym pairs across four languages; (b) frequency of trait adjectives; (c) frequencies of country and city names; (d) frequencies of scientific occupations; and (e) frequencies of trees, fruits, vegetables, and flowers. Next, he showed that experimental manipulation of exposure frequency increased the positive connotations of nonsense words, Chinese-like characters, and facial photographs. Finally, he argued for the logarithmic shape of the function (bigger differences at small levels of exposure) and its focus on novel stimuli.

At this time and just after, the rest of the field was trudging knee-deep in attribution and social cognition, but Zajonc's contrarian strategy dictated heavily investing in feelings, preferences, affect, and emotion. He had to hammer away at [17] this message, revealing its full implications later in a much cited, much debated 1980 *American Psychologist* article. There, Zajonc (1980b) argued that affective preferences precede and may be independent of various cognitive operations previously presumed to underlie them. Affect and cognition might be separate systems, he suggested. This challenge was followed by a decade's more of arguments for the primacy of affect over cognition (Zajonc, 1984). He also espoused the nonconscious nature of affect (e.g., Murphy and Zajonc, 1993), as well as a noncognitive, physical theory of emotion: Facial efference (expression) alters vascular configurations (i.e., blood flow) to the brain, regulating brain temperature and thereby emotion (Zajonc, 1985, 1994; Zajonc, Murphy, and Inglehart, 1989). Switching earlier allegiances, his next *Handbook of Social Psychology* (4th ed.) chapter (Zajonc, 1998) concentrates fully on emotion, with nary a cognitive perspective.

Given the resistance of the rest of the field to his brain-and-blood theory of emotion, the full development of neural imaging techniques may ultimately facilitate the field's catch-up to Zajonc. However, according to our decelerating function, the lag looks to be 40 years or so from the original mere-exposure article, predicting a conversion to his agenda by about 2010. Not an unlikely scenario!

Cognitive Intelligence

Not content with three field-shaking contributions, about 8 years after his article on mere exposure, Zajonc brought us family configurations and intelligence. Having convinced the rest of the field to take affect seriously, he kept his own cognitive options open. While the rest of social psychology had abandoned the intelligence area to genetic psychologists, Zajonc focused on a simple feature of social context: mere family configuration.

> This model … [tries] to capture the effects of the immediate intellectual environment on intellectual growth, and to specify how individual differences emerge in the social context of the family. (Zajonc, 1976, p. 227)

> [From] a substantial sample of family configurations, examined repeatedly over several years …, the relation of environmental variables that it specifies to the total IQ variance in the sample can be measured…. It would be of some interest to establish just how much can be assigned to environmental factors when the analysis begins with them. (Zajonc, 1976, p. 235)

Zajonc went on to demonstrate that, along with several other implications of his model:

- smaller families beget better intellectual performance,
- earlier-born children fare better than later-borns when the between-birth gaps are short,
- larger gaps between births enhance performance. **[18]**

Essentially, the number of intellectual marbles possessed by the parent(s) and any much older siblings are divided among the youngsters, resulting in more abundant or more sparse intellectual environments and ultimately reflected in standardized test performance. The initial article was followed by significant analyses validating the confluence model (Zajonc, 1983) and examining birth order as a predictor of SAT scores (Zajonc and Mullally, 1997).

At the field's decelerating rate of adoption of Zajonc's theories, the lag for this contribution should be about 50 years, landing us in 2025 before we fully appreciate the effects of social environmental factors on intelligence. Some of us fear it may be longer.

Group Hostility

The four best-known of Zajonc's contributions, discussed in the preceding sections, still leave room for surprises. In 1982, Zajonc authored a less-known paper on altruism, envy, competitiveness, and the common good, claiming in part:

> Justice, equity, and fairness are judgmental criteria under the control of social norms. And defying social norms may be costly. So it is in one's self-interest to be just and fair. (p. 436)

While the rest of social psychology abandoned game theory to economists and mourned the death of the group, Zajonc's contrarian strategy focused on social intent as a function of subjective, more than objective, payoffs. Justice and fairness, in the context of social norms, brought Zajonc to group-level analyses. This 1982 chapter, until recently, might be viewed as a single-shot effort, but recently Zajonc indeed has begun to tackle group-on-group conflict. If this work requires 60 years (on our decelerating curve), then the field will not truly understand group violence until 2045, when it may be too late.

A more optimistic view traces the Zajontific interest in these problems to 1950s and 1960s articles on aggression of a stranger under conformity pressure (Zajonc, 1952), cross-cultural norm conflict (French and Zajonc, 1957; Zajonc and Wahi, 1961), and cooperation, competition, and interpersonal attitudes (Zajonc and Marin, 1967). At this estimate, we might catch up to the group hostility problem somewhat sooner, or so one hopes.

CONCLUSION

The simple and contrarian magic of Robert Zajonc has molded and will continue to mold the places of affect and cognition in social psychology. The contributors in this volume pay Bob the ultimate tribute of locating their work in his spotlight. Many of us have tried to emulate his example, in our own small sideshows. Expect many more to follow his act, but none of us with the flair of the headliner. **[19]**

REFERENCES

Fiske, S.T. and Taylor, S.E. (1991). *Social cognition*. New York: McGraw-Hill.

French. J.R.P., Jr., and Zajonc, R.B. (1957). An experimental study of cross-cultural norm conflict. *Journal of Abnormal Social Psychology*, 54, 218–224.

Jones, E.E. (1998). Major developments in five decades of social psychology. In D.T. Gilbert, S.T. Fiske, and G. Lindzey (Vol. Eds.), *The handbook of social psychology* (4th ed., Vol. 1, pp. 3–57). New York: McGraw-Hill.

Kiesler, C.A., Collins, B.E., and Miller, N. (1969). *Attitude change: A critical analysis of theoretical approaches*. New York: Wiley.

Murphy, S.T. and Zajonc, R.B. (1993). Affect, cognition, and awareness: Affective priming with optimal and suboptimal stimulus exposures. *Journal of Personality and Social Psychology*, 64, 723–739.

Pittman, T.S. (1998). Motivation. In D.T. Gilbert, S.T. Fiske, and G. Lindzey (Vol. Eds.). *The handbook of social psychology* (4th ed., Vol.1, pp. 549–590). New York: McGraw-Hill.

Showers, C., and Cantor, N. (1985). Social cognition: A look at motivated strategies. *Annual Review of Psychology*, 36, 275–305.

Snyder, M. and Cantor, N. (1998). Understanding personality and social behavior: A functionalist strategy. In D.T. Gilbert, S.T. Fiske, and G. Lindzey (Vol. Eds.), *The handbook of social psychology* (4th ed., Vol. 1, pp. 635–679). New York: McGraw-Hill.

Taylor, S.E. (1998). The social being in social psychology. In D.T. Gilbert, S.T. Fiske, and G. Lindzey (Vol. Eds.), *The handbook of social psychology* (4th ed., Vol. 1, pp. 58–95). New York: McGraw-Hill.

Zajonc, R.B. (1952). Aggressive attitudes of the stranger as a function of conformity pressures. *Human Relations*, 5, 205–216.

Zajonc, R.B. (1960a). The concepts of balance, congruity, and dissonance. *Public Opinion Quarterly*, 24, 380–396.

Zajonc, R.B. (1960b). The process of cognitive tuning in communication. *Journal of Abnormal and Social Psychology*, 61, 159–167.

Zajonc, R.B. (1965). Social facilitation. *Science*, 149, 269–274.

Zajonc, R.B. (1968). Attitudinal effects of mere exposure. *Journal of Personality and Social Psychology Monograph Supplement*, 9, 1–27.

Zajonc, R.B. (1976). Family configuration and intelligence. *Science*, 192, 227–236.

Zajonc, R.B. (1980a). Compresence. In P. B. Paulus (Ed.), *Psychology of group influence* (pp. 35–60). Hillsdale, NJ: Erlbaum.

Zajonc, R.B. (1980b). Feeling and thinking: Preferences need no inferences. *American Psychologist*, 35, 151–175.

Zajonc, R.B. (1982). Altruism, envy, competitiveness, and the common good. In V.J. Derlega and J. Grzelak (Eds.), *Cooperation and helping behavior: Theories and research* (pp. 417–437). New York: Academic Press. **[20]**

Zajonc, R.B. (1983). Validating the confluence model. *Psychological Bulletin*, 93, 457–480.

Zajonc, R.B. (1984). On the primacy of affect. *American Psychologist*, 39. 117–123.

Zajonc, R.B. (1985). Emotion and facial efference: A theory reclaimed. *Science*, 228, 5–21.

Zajonc, R.B. (1994). Emotional expression and temperature modulation. In S.H.M. Van Goozen. N.E. Van De Poll, and J.A. Sergeant (Eds.), *Emotions: Essays on emotion theory* (pp. 3–27). Hillsdale. NJ: Erlbaum.

Zajonc, R.B. (1998). Emotions. In D.T. Gilbert, S.T. Fiske, and G. Lindzey (Vol. Eds.), *The handbook of social psychology* (4th ed., Vol. 1, pp. 591–632). New York: McGraw-Hill.

Zajonc. R.B. and Marin. I.C. (1967). Cooperation, competition, and interpersonal attitudes in small groups. *Psychonomic Science*, 7, 271–272.

Zajonc, R.B. and Mullally, P.R. (1997). Birth order: Reconciling conflicting effects. *American Psychologist*, 52, 685–699.

Zajonc, R.B., Murphy. S.T., and Inglehart, M. (1989). Feeling and facial efference: Implications of the vascular theory of emotion. *Psychological Review*, 96, 395–416.

Zajonc, R.B. and Wahi, N.K. (1961). Conformity and need achievement under cross-cultural change. *Human Relations*, 14, 241–250. **[21]**

Part One

The Scope and Nature of Social Psychology

Chapter 1

The Development of Social Psychology

R.B. Zajonc
University of Michigan

WHAT IS SOCIAL PSYCHOLOGY?

Scientific disciplines do not have sharp and stable boundaries. Areas of scientific endeavor very often overlap. The interests and problems of all fields continually change. Consequently, a definition of social psychology, like the definition of any other science, will at best point to the scope and to the more permanent interests in the field. The following is such a definition.

The various fields of psychology are all concerned with the analysis of behavior. If he is interested in *learning,* the psychologist studies behavior as it is influenced by past practice and by its reinforcement history. If he is interested in *perception,* the psychologist analyzes responses as they are modified by changes in physical stimuli. If he is interested in *motivation,* he analyzes responses in terms of the antecedent states of deprivation or arousal. All these psychologists would be classified in different fields, but not because they study different behaviors. On the contrary, they all may study an identical set of responses. What distinguishes these psychologists is that they analyze responses in terms of different antecedents. For instance, the rat's response of "turning left in a T-maze" may be analyzed in terms of the number of reinforced trials that have been given to the animal (the psychology of learning); or in terms of the level of the animal's hunger (the psychology of motivation); or in terms of the physical properties of the right arm of the maze as opposed to those of the left arm (the psychology of perception). If all of the above variations—reinforcement, deprivation, and physical stimulation—are held constant, and if we observe the rat's responses of "turning left in the T-maze" when there happens to be one other rat in the right arm of the maze, we become social psychologists.

Excerpt from *Social psychology: An experimental approach.* Belmont, CA: Brooks/Cole, 1996. pp 1–9.

Social psychology deals with *behavioral dependence and interdependence among individuals.* By "behavioral dependence" we mean a relation among the behavior of a number of individuals, such that a given behavior of one or more individuals is a cause or an occasion for change in the behavior of one or more other individuals. "Interdependence" simply means that the dependence is mutual and reciprocal. Note that the behaviors involved need not occur at the same time. The behavior under the influence of others need not *immediately* follow the [1]* behavior causing or precipitating it. The social psychologist may study the way in which the responses of a given individual become coordinated to the behavior of another individual when both engage in a joint task, or he may study the degree to which a particular behavior pattern depends on the sort of up-bringing the subject received—that is, how his parents, teachers, and peers behaved long in the past. Social psychology, then, asks questions about the behavioral relations of individual to individual in general, but primarily of man to man, and occasionally of animal to animal.

Social psychology is not a "kind" or a "school" of psychology. It is definitely a *branch* of psychology, and it takes full cognizance of the laws of general and experimental psychology. Its language is commensurate with the language of other fields of psychology, and its laws consistent with the laws of general psychology.

THE DEVELOPMENT OF SOCIAL PSYCHOLOGY

Around 250 B.C. the Greek astronomer Eratosthenes calculated the circumference of the earth by comparing the angles of the noon sun in Alexandria and in Aswan, which lies directly to the south on the tropic of Cancer, and where on the day of the summer solstice the angle of the noon sun is exactly 90°. His results—among the first scientific observations recorded in history—differ from the present estimates by about 180 miles, or less than 1 percent.

The velocity of light was first measured in 1675 by the Danish astronomer Ole Römer, who compared the observed eclipses of Jupiter's moons with predictions based on precise theoretical calculations. His results also agree very closely with the present ones.

The speed with which the nervous impulse is propagated was first accurately measured in 1850 by the German physicist Helmholtz. He obtained measurements by comparing delays in the muscular responses in the leg of a frog for nerves of different lengths.

The first experimental observation in social psychology was performed in 1897 by Triplett. It dealt with the effects of competition on human performance. Triplett measured the average time required to execute 150 winds on a fishing reel. His subjects performed the task while working alone and while competing in pairs against each other. Performance was found to improve when carried out in competition.

The first scientific measurement preceded the first social-psychological measurement by twenty-one centuries. Social psychology, then, is almost entirely the product of this century and of this generation. Social psychologists credited with the crucial developments in the field are still alive. The author of the first social-psychological text, William McDougall, died only in 1938. More than 90 percent of all social-psychological [2] research has been carried out during the last twenty years, and most of it during the last ten.

Why did social psychology fail to develop earlier?

---

* Bracketed bold numbers refer to original page numbers. Page numbers indicate where the original page ended.

Was the rise of social psychology inhibited by the lack of special technology? The measurements performed by Eratosthenes, Römer, and Helmholtz all required some previous knowledge and employed techniques developed earlier. Eratosthenes needed geometry, which Euclid systematized in about 300 B.C. Römer's findings could not have been possible without the telescope. The instrument he used was constructed by Father Scheiner in 1630. It contained two convex lenses and was a direct improvement of the prototype invented by Galileo in 1609. Helmholtz could not have made his observations without the work of Galvani, who was first to note the electrical properties of neural transmission in 1790 and who discovered a method of electrically stimulating a leg severed from a frog's body. In each of these examples the necessary antecedent knowledge or technique preceded the final measurement by about fifty years.

But the knowledge and technique necessary for Triplett's experiment were available at least 4,000 years ago. All he needed was (a) people who, under observation, would work alone and in groups; (b) a task that they could perform under both conditions; and (c) a means of counting units of work on this task per unit of time. Since these prerequisites were certainly present in the Egypt of the pharaohs, some other factor must explain why the development of social psychology was arrested for centuries.

Consider two alternatives. First: Social-psychological experiments were not attempted earlier because social-psychological questions were not asked until the twentieth century. Second: Social-psychological questions were asked before, but for one reason or another they were not answered before the twentieth century.

Let us first consider the former, for it can be easily rejected. Questions about human interdependence must have been asked as soon as there was the dimmest realization that men *are* interdependent. Those who built empires and those who built pyramids, coordinating the efforts of hundreds of thousands of men, must have encountered innumerable problems of human interrelationships and must have, therefore, raised some social-psychological questions. Ancient law shows clear examples of concern with these problems. Hammurabi's Code and the Old Testament attempted to regulate interpersonal relationships that were sources of problems for society. Seven of the Ten Commandments address themselves quite explicitly to the regulation of interpersonal conduct.

The social-psychological questions asked in the past were, to be sure, either about the moral nature of human interdependence, or about [3] the control and manipulation of human behavior. (Machiavelli's *Il Principe* is a splendid example of this latter interest.) Neither type of question is strictly scientific. Those of the first type are ethical; those of the second are administrative and practical. Neither type is a direct concern of social psychology, but in order to ask an ethical or moral question, some social-psychological knowledge is necessary. In analyzing the ethics of human interdependence—such as those of slavery, of incest, or of property rights—one must invariably turn toward the analysis of its *consequences*. Do these consequences, for instance, violate some religious dogma or are they consonant with some moral precepts? Or, are the consequences of human interrelationships useful or harmful to society or to the parties involved? On the other hand, questions about the control of human interdependence require the knowledge of *antecedents,* for if one is interested in producing certain effects it is always useful and often necessary to know their causes. When man asked questions about antecedents and consequences, about causes and effects, he asked *scientific* questions.

Since man was already capable of asking scientific questions, the delay in the development of social psychology becomes even more curious. But there is a possible explanation. Men may have been satisfied that they already possessed answers to social-psychological questions. In all societies there are institutional mechanisms for regulating social behavior: law, custom, religion, and etiquette. In a way these mechanisms enable the members of the given society to *explain* and to *predict* social behavior. Because of their regulatory nature, these institutional mechanisms in themselves constitute antecedents of human relationships, for to regulate is in large part to determine. In all societies such mechanisms are explicitly identified, and they provide, therefore, a ready means for the explanation of social behavior. The policeman who, after giving you a speeding ticket, declares, "I hate to do it, Mac, but it's my job," provides you not only with an apology but also with an explanation of his behavior toward you. We have been satisfied with similar explanations for centuries.

The institutional mechanisms that regulate social behavior have also another important feature in common: they produce uniformity among the members of the given society. And because they lead to uniformity of social behavior, they facilitate its prediction. By definition, uniform events are more easily predictable than heterogeneous events. It is a reasonably safe prediction that you will drive about 35 mph when the posted speed limit is 35 mph.

To the extent that law, custom, religion, and etiquette provide satisfying explanations of social behavior and enable us to predict fairly reliably, social psychology cannot contribute a great deal more. But law, **[4]** religion, custom, and etiquette have ceased to supply satisfying explanations. With the growth of civilization, man's life is regulated by these institutional mechanisms considerably less than it once was.

The Reformation introduced heterogeneity into spheres of behavior and belief governed by religious dogma. It also weakened the authority and influence of the church. Today's churches have only a fraction of the control they had in the days of the Inquisition. On the ashes of the feudal system, and in the wake of the bourgeois and industrial revolutions came freedom from institutional control in many areas of social behavior. The power of a modern employer over his workers can hardly be compared with the power of the feudal lord over his vassals. Threat and force were replaced by persuasion and advertising. Social behavior became more difficult to explain and to predict. Eventually man began to search for new explanations and for new ways of predicting events in the area of human interdependence. Social psychology is one of the developments of that search. **[5]**

SOCIAL BEHAVIOR

Many clichés undeservedly substitute for understanding. One such cliché holds that man is a social animal. The accent in this cliché is on "social," and imbedded in it are a host of mistaken implications. Calling him a "*social* animal" seemingly resolves many questions about man and about so-called "*human* nature." It has been used to explain why people live in communities, why they form groups, organizations, and societies. The implication is that because man is "social" he will behave in certain "social" ways. "Social" has been stretched to cover a variety of different, and sometimes opposite, behaviors, to explain why there is polygamy and why monogamy; why there is loyalty to the group and why treason; why there is crime and why obedience to laws; why there is marriage and why divorce; why there is altruism and why egoism.

When the accent in the cliché is shifted to "animal," then the word "social" begins to acquire innate and instinctive qualities. For instance, in *The Descent of Man,* Darwin wrote:

> As man is a social animal, it is almost certain that he would *inherit* a tendency to be faithful to his comrades, and obedient to the leader of his tribe; for these qualities are common to most social animals. He would from an *inherited* tendency be willing to defend, in concert with others, his fellow-men; and be ready to aid them in any way, which did not too greatly interfere with his own welfare or his own strong desires.[1]

In all probability Darwin was wrong about the *inherited* nature of these tendencies. In 1810, more than 60 years before Darwin published *The Descent of Man,* a not too well-known French philosopher, Helvetius, expressed himself on this point with a remarkable clarity:

> Do men seek to make dupes? They exaggerate the force of sentiment and friendship, they represent sociability as an *innate affection* or principle. Can they in reality forget that there is but one principle of this kind, which is corporeal sensibility? It is to this principle alone, that we owe our self-love, and the powerful love of independence: if men were, as it is [7] said, drawn toward each other by a strong and mutual attraction, would the heavenly Legislator have commanded them to love each other, and to honor their parents? The command to love our fathers and mothers, proves that the love of our parents is more the effect of habit and education, than of nature. Would he not have left this point to nature, which, without the aid of any law, obliges men to eat and drink when they are hungry and thirsty, to open their eyes to the light, and keep their hands out of fire?

Again, calling man a "social animal" probably does not even distinguish him from other animals. Professor Wynne-Edwards of Aberdeen University expressed himself quite succinctly on this point (1962):

> There seems to be no question of dividing the animal kingdom neatly into two camps, the one containing animals that are social and the other those that are not: rather it emerges, as might have been expected, that socialization is a general phenomenon, which from comparatively lowly and obscure beginnings has undergone progressive evolution, so that in the more advanced groups it has tended to become increasingly more conspicuous and complex. Although the extent to which social adaptations have been evolved in different animals, therefore, varies between wide extremes, the series is nevertheless a continuous one: the barnacle larva which at metamorphosis fixes itself or is inhibited from doing so, depending on the presence and number of other barnacle larvae already attached,

---

[1] Italics added.

is responding socially in a way that is not effectively different in principle from the one which animates the communal behavior of the social insects or the most highly socialized birds and mammals. In each case the behavior of the individual is conditioned by the presence and actions of other members of the population ... (p. 127).[2]

As early as 1878 the French natural scientist and philosopher Espinas claimed that sociability is not "a restricted accidental condition found only among such privileged species as bees, ants, beavers, and men, but is in fact universal."

It is unfortunate that the field being introduced to the reader bears a "social" label—which, because it means so many different things, actually means very little. But even if the label "social" *explains* nothing specifically about man, it is still necessary for us to agree on what it *denotes,* for we shall have to use the word repeatedly. Since we define social psychology as the study of behavioral dependence and interdependence among individuals, "social" will mean a property of one organism's behavior which makes the organism vulnerable to behavior of another organism. In Part I, analysis will focus on the behavior of a single individual as influenced by other individuals. The influence exercised by those others can take several forms. The forms of influence [8] selected for review in Part I correspond to the most common experimental situations employed in social-psychological research. We shall begin in Chapter 2 with the simplest case: the responses that a single individual emits in the presence of others; specifically, we shall examine changes in individual behavior produced by the presence of passive spectators. In Chapter 3 we shall look into the question of what happens to the behavior of a single individual when it occurs in the presence of others engaged in the same activity. In Chapter 4 we will be concerned with how an individual benefits from the experience of others. Finally, in Chapter 5, we shall review the processes of social reinforcement—again paying particular attention to an individual's behavior that is under the control of social rewards or punishments.

In all chapters of Part I, analysis will focus upon the behavior of a single individual, taking into account the behavior of others as an antecedent condition. The four topics differ only in the complexity of this antecedent condition. [9]

---

[2] Wynne-Edwards, 1962; reprinted with permission of author and publisher.

Chapter 2

Styles of Explanation in Social Psychology*

R.B. Zajonc
University of Michigan

INTRODUCTION

'Style' is a very subtle quality that characterizes the products or performances in such domains as art, music, literature, dance, sports, sculpture, architecture, ceramics, landscaping, clothing, jewelry, gastronomy, pastry, hair fashion, sports, and yes, science as well. 'Style' can be identified with a particular period and with a particular geographic region (Italian Baroque, German Expressionism, Heavy Metal or Cuisine Minceur), but it can also be identified with a particular individual. Chopin and Rachmaninoff had distinct styles, as did Hemingway and Proust.

There is not a universal taxonomy of stylistic properties that applies over all domains, and it is often not possible to be precise about just what is it that makes one style distinct from others in a systematic way. But given a piece by Chopin that we never heard or a painting by Modigliani that we never saw, we would have no difficulty identifying them. This subtle quality cannot be always specified, but it is a quality that can be identified with considerable agreement. It is like mustard. Few people can describe its taste, but no one will mistake it for yogurt.

There are also, of course, styles in more trivial and mundane pursuits. People walk in different styles, they eat in different styles, they have argumentative styles, conversational styles, ingratiating styles, and there are different styles of squeezing their toothpaste tubes.

While explanations differ in a variety of ways, social psychological explanations, as all scientific explanations, can also be viewed as having identifiable styles. Forms

* This work was supported by NSF Grant BNS-8505981.

European Journal of Social Psychology, 19, 345–368. R.B. Zajonc. 1989. © John Wiley & Sons Limited.
Reproduced with permission.

and [345]* types of explanation in social psychology have all the attributes of styles and are as distinct as styles in any other domain.

'Style' can be readily confused with method, even though it should be quite clear that a given method can be employed in a variety of styles and a given style can avail itself of a variety of methods. Reinforced concrete is a method of building and all sorts of stylistic variations can be achieved with reinforced concrete. But the range of variation is clearly restricted. Once we have selected reinforced concrete as the method of building, it is unlikely that Baroque or Tudor are among our stylistic options.

Some creative individuals seem to be committed to a given method in preference to a number of others that are equally available and equally satisfying for the given purposes at hand. When an individual consistently prefers one method to all others, he may be said to have chosen a 'style.' In a museum, when entering into a room of works by Marie Laurencin we expect to see mostly watercolors, and are quite sure to see oils in the next room which features Modigliani. In the same way, we can page through the contents of an issue of a recent journal and be quite sure which authors will use the ANOVA, which will display vast tables of multiple regression coefficients, and which will bless us with eigenvalues of a factor analysis. We will be able to know these facts even without knowing anything about the titles of the articles.

By 'explanation' in social psychology I will simply mean what is commonly meant by it in all other fields: a set of logically connected statements specifying the antecedents or causes of some distinct empirical phenomenon about whose existence there is consensus among the relevant scientists. Explanations then are nothing else but *theories.*

We do not tend to think of explanations as having 'style' because explanations are judged above all else for how satisfactory they are. Styles are not. Of course, explanations are satisfactory to the extent that they are valid, that is, that they agree with observable empirical data. In addition, explanations are evaluated according to the properties of all axiomatic systems, such as consistency or independence of axioms, etc. Explanations are 'satisfactory' if they allow us to understand a previously poorly understood phenomenon. They are even more satisfactory if they extend over a wider domain of phenomena and are able to make new and unexpected predictions and explanations. In any science those ideas are good that 'work'—they allow us to formulate problems in new ways, they point ways toward new solutions and new methods, they tell us how it can be determined whether the solutions are correct and useful, and they produce new knowledge that could not have been achieved without them.

Good ideas, therefore, are rich ideas. Euclid's geometry generates thousands of theorems—many non-obvious and unexpected—from a set of a two primitive terms and five axioms. Hull's *Principles of Behavior* (1943) has nearly 60 hypotheses derived from some 16 premises. Not as rich as Euclid, but quite respectable. Festinger, Riecken and Schachter's (1956) explanation of why the members of a doomsday sect, following a clear disconfirmation of the day of doom, not only continued to persevere in their beliefs but to proselytize as well, was satisfactory because it explained a poorly understood phenomenon and because, in addition, it revealed, predicted and explained many other thus far hidden phenomena.

Normally, we do not think of evaluating 'styles' for their effectiveness. Mostly, they are a matter of taste. It is certainly difficult to compare Expressionism and

---

* Bracketed bold numbers refer to original page numbers. Page numbers indicate where the original page ended.

Surrealism for their relative merits. But not all styles of explanation in social psychology are **[346]** simply a matter of taste. It is certainly the case that some stylistic debates can be ignored as inconsequential for the growth of the field. However, some stylistic elements have serious consequences for our understanding of the social aspect of the mind and of behavior. It is, therefore, important to identify those stylistic elements in social psychological explanations that have an impact on how we go about doing our research, what form of knowledge we expect these styles to generate, and how well might they be integrated with the neighboring disciplines. In this paper I have selected some stylistic elements in social psychology about which opinions differ. The elements that I discuss here have gathered supporters and opponents and sporadically occasion passionate debates over their merits. Some of these elements can and deserve to be examined for their merit. Others are indeed purely stylistic and may well be left to the idiosyncratic tastes of the producers and consumers of research.[1]

DEBATE OVER 'PROPER' STYLE

In some domains, stylistic elements are quite readily evaluated for their effectiveness. Within limits, one can certainly compare the effectiveness of a man-to-man defense in basketball to zone defense, the screwball pitch to a slider in baseball, or the toe kick to the instep kick in American football. Only two decades ago nearly all field goal kickers in American football used their toes. Today almost all use the soccer-style kick. The complete replacement of one style by the other must indicate something about the relative merits of the two styles. The fact that after nearly two decades the ethogenic approach has not spread beyond a handful of workers must reflect on its effectiveness as well. One can even compare the effectiveness of squeezing the toothpaste tube from the end and from the middle. The 'neat' style has the advantage of having the tube reduce in length as you wind the end of the tube. However, squeezing the tube from the middle has the advantage of pushing only half of the volume at a time. Thus, when you start a new tube you push four ounces and increasingly less until the first half is gone. Then you push the remaining four ounces (over a somewhat longer distance, to be sure) until the tube is empty. I am sure that precise ergonomic norms for the optimal toothpaste tube strategy could be calculated. It can also be determined (and it probably has been) what have been the percentages of successful toe kick and soccer-style field goals.

---

[1] Some expressions of epistemological malaise have been outright destructive and paralyzing for social psychology. Entirely without *heuristic* consequence has been the argument about 'social psychology as history' (e.g., Elms, 1975; Gergen, 1973; Manis, 1975). Nevertheless, the controversy has discouraged promising students from entering the field and granting agencies from increasing social psychological research budgets. One of its main contentions was that social psychology lacks temporal generality, which falls under the completeness issue. The other was that social psychology produces knowledge that will alter the very phenomena it studies. The fact that the latter contention was taken as a criticism of social psychology rather than as a mark of its success is curious in itself. After all, if vaccinations succeeded in eradicating smallpox and polio, have thereby the principles explaining bacterial and viral infections become suddenly altogether discredited? To take a social psychological example, suppose it becomes known that people work harder on simple tasks when in the presence of others, and as a result industry, business, government, the profession, and all other institutions that require some form of work, arrange their work to be done in groups rather than in solitary settings to increase output. Would social facilitation theory be discontinued? On the contrary.

Yet when comparisons among styles and elements of styles are made they must be made with caution because in most endeavors the style is confounded with talent. **[347]** Not all pitchers can throw a slider equally well. And some social psychologists have a congenital aversion to experiments. We do not really know, therefore, that the same style used by another team or another individual would be equally effective. In brief, some styles and elements of style can be evaluated with clarity, others only with some ambiguity, and still others not at all. This is true of all domains, including styles of scientific explanations.

What often seems to be an argument about the effectiveness of a style or an approach turns out to be simply a matter of taste. Consider the wisdom of arguing about some styles in comparing the assertions of two famous architects, Frank Lloyd Wright and Marcel Breuer:

First Wright (1957):

> The character of the site is always fundamental to organic design (p. 249).
> The environment and building are one (p. 227).
> Principle One: Kinship of building to ground. … in breadth, length, height and weight, these buildings [belong] to the prairie … (p. 219).
> These initial buildings were made to declare and express the affinity not only of man's life to his ground, but of the ground to the nature of the man who lived upon it (p. 202).

Contrast these assertions with Marcel Breuer's philosophy (Blake, 1949).

> A building is a man-made work, a crystallic, constructed thing. It should not imitate nature—it should be in contrast to nature. … I can see no reason at all why buildings should imitate natural, organic or grown forms (p. 38).

And again from Frank Lloyd Wright (1957):

> … to use any one material wrongly is to abuse the integrity of the whole design. (p. 229) … As the consequence of these basic principles of design, wood and plaster will be content to be and look as well as wood and plaster, and will not aspire to be treated to resemble marble (pp. 230–231).

Whereas Breuer (Blake, 1955) would have it thus:

> When wood is used in a building, it may not be "wood" in the old, traditional sense, but a new material altogether, especially if it is plywood.
> When stone is used in a wall, it is no longer some sort of rock formation, but a clear-cut slab—made of stone for the reason that stone is a good and durable and texturally pleasant material (p. 38–39).

These are two contradictory bases of quite different architectural styles, and yet neither can be regarded as wrong. One architect would never have a wooden board painted because painting it would destroy the very nature of the 'material.' The other architect considers a board to be a man-made product, having lost all claim and connection to nature, and therefore free to any sort of experiment, transformation and treatment. One architect wishes the house to be cuddled into the landscape, the other wishes the geometry of the house to stand out in stark contrast to the environment. One architect seeks to create harmony of the house with nature. The other architect views his house as testimony to the human creative genius that must dominate the environment. **[348]**

STYLE, CULTURE, AND SOCIAL SCIENCE

A few years ago a provocative article was published on cultural differences in intellectual styles. Its author, Johan Galtung (1981), identified four culturally different approaches to social science: saxonic, teutonic, gallic, and nipponic. Galtung attempted to distinguish among what he considered to be quite different ways of doing social science—ways that are peculiar to intellectual centers identified with Britain and U.S., Germany, France and Japan. What he meant by 'doing social science' was not only description and explanation of phenomena, but also the analysis of paradigms, that is, evaluating epistemological foundations and limitations, as well as the manner and method of critique and of scholarly discourse.

I cite at length his characterizations of the four styles. They are insightful and in my opinion fairly accurate of at least some proportion of social scientists in the regions dominated by the four national groupings, although there must be as many differences within a given scientific culture as there are among them. Galtung's characterizations apply to many social psychologists I know, even though they are quite an exaggeration of the majority.

Galtung asserts that

> the saxonic style fosters and encourages *debate* and *discourse,...*
> intellectuals constitute a team,... togetherness should be preserved,...
> there is a gentleman's agreement... that 'we should stick together and
> continue our debate in spite of our differences,'... the first discussant [in a
> seminar] will open his/her speech with ... 'I greatly enjoyed listening to
> Mr. X's presentation, admiring his mastery of the facts of the case as well
> as his way of marshalling the facts together, but....' The 'but' clause may
> then become quite extensive.... [In] the U.K., the 'but' clause will tend to
> be several times longer than the complimentary introductory clause,
> whereas the opposite might be the case in the U.S., particularly as one
> moves west. The U.S. professor at a graduate seminar would do his best
> to find even in the most dismal performance that little nugget which,
> when polished, might produce a credible shine (pp. 823–824).

The teutonic and gallic scholarly interactions differ substantially from their saxonic counterparts.

> [There] will be no complimentary introduction,... nobody will go out of
> his or her way to try to find that little nugget,... on the contrary, the discussants will go straight at the weakest point,... and there will be few if
> any soothing comments towards the end to put the defendant together as a
> human being; no attempt will be made to mop up the blood and put
> wounded egos together.... [Gazes] would be somewhat cold, faces somewhat stiff, and a slight element of scorn and derision might emerge from

the corners of the eyes. The paper-giving defendant would experience the situation as a victim (pp. 824–825).

In the nipponic scholarly encounter there is, according to Galtung, above all, care

> *not to harm pre-established social relations*.... There is ... respect for authority, for the master whoever he is—the respect for verticality. And then there is the sense of collectivism, of organic solidarity. ... It is much more a question of...which school do you belong to? where did you get it from? who said it first? ...*The debate is a social act rather than an intellectual one* (pp. 825–826). **[349]**

With regard to actual scientific enterprise there are differences as well. Galtung asserts that the 'British penchant for documentation is proverbial, as is U.S. love of statistics. To have thoroughly scrutinized all sources, to have put all the data together, concealing nothing, is a key criterion of scholarship.' But the saxonic social scientists are 'not very strong on theory formation,' nor are they 'known for sweeping theories, for grand perspectives.' This is in stark contrast to the teutonic and gallic intellectual who 'might not even realize that he is somewhat short on documentation to back up what he is saying. To him intellectual activity has at its very centre theory-formation. The function of the data would be to *illustrate* (italics, mine) rather than to demonstrate. A discrepancy between theory and data would be handled at the expense of the data' (p. 828).

But while both the gallic and the teutonic styles tend to be abstract and theoretical, there are some striking differences. The teutonic theory building is Euclidian. It is characterized by Galtung as purely deductive, as a construction of a pyramid in which endless theorems are derived from a few axioms, using the laws of logic. If one accepts the axioms, one may not question the conclusions (*Gedankennotwedigkeit*). Galtung, however, disparages this approach because a commitment to the deductive approach makes one 'prisoner of one's own thoughts.... It puts reality in a straight jacket' (p.830).

The gallic style in the social science, on the contrary, is not deductive. The gallic theoretical language is not dedicated to logic but to the expression of conviction, to the display of an artistic quality, where scientific argument is judged not so much for its validity as for its *elegance*. Good prose, metaphors, 'the use of bons mots, double entendres, alliterations and various types of semantic and even typographical tricks' are the valued elements of a gallic theory. The reality of an idea soon becomes the idea of reality. Galtung quotes the following review of a French book that puts the gallic expository style in a nutshell:

> This book displays once again all the distinct Foucault's traits [the book reviewed is Michel Foucault's *Surveiller et punir,* Paris: Gallimar, 1979]—a remarkable use of images; an acute sense of paradox and ambiguity; a fondness for inversion; a relentless pursuit of the multiplicity of human experience; such compelling lucidity in critical passages that the reader cannot resist persuasion and yet exasperating withdrawal into a vocabulary hermetic to the uninitiated, together with moments of undeniable self-indulgence (pp. 849–850).

The teutonic intellectual, however, differs from the gallic scholar, because he actually *believes* what he says, 'something his gallic counterpart would never really do' (p. 840). The nipponic theory, according to Galtung, is essentially a contradiction of terms. He categorically dismisses nipponic theoretical contributions to social science as virtually 'negligible' (p. 834).

Galtung summarizes the features of the four styles by looking at the question that confronts someone who offers a proposition:

Saxonic style (U.S. version):   *How do you operationalize it?*
Saxonic style (U.K. version):   *How do you document it?*
Teutonic style: *Wie können Sie das zurückführen? (How can you deduce it from your axioms?)* **[350]**
Gallic style: *Peut-on dire cela en bon français?*
Nipponic style: *Donatano monka desuka? (Who is your master?)*

Galtung's vision of the future is not optimistic. He believes that 'the teutons will continue to be irritated when the gauls become too lyrical, ... and the gauls will continue to be bored by teutonic pedantry. Both of them will be grasping for perspectives ... that will put some order into the untidy saxonic landscape of stubborn facts, and the saxons will continue to get restless when teutons and gauls speed off into outer space, leaving a thin trail of data behind' (p. 849). And it is to be expected that 'what is the virtue of one will continue to be the vice of the other.'

While Galtung's characterization may be questioned for assuming that the style differences are rooted in national and cultural predispositions, it is certainly a keen classification of social scientists within any one of these cultures. There are probably greater differences among scholars within any one country than among countries, and I have seen representatives of all four styles among my 130 colleagues here at the University of Michigan.

THE STYLISTIC ELEMENTS IN SOCIAL PSYCHOLOGICAL EXPLANATIONS

It is very difficult and not always reasonable to evaluate a style in art. This is so because we lack reasonable criteria against which to measure its success. Not everybody would agree that the sums of money spent in art auctions on paintings of a particular style could be taken as indicative of its 'true merit.' Nor would there be agreement that the number of reproductions printed is a valid indication of stylistic merit. But both of these things indicate 'something' in that direction.

Even a minor stylistic element presents a severe ambiguity if we were to judge it against others. For example, one might compare watercolors to oils. Certainly, oil painting will have a greater permanence, but the kinds of light effects that can be achieved with watercolor cannot be achieved with oil. If a painter wishes to sacrifice permanence for texture, it is certainly his choice and his privilege.

The same always applies to explanation and proof in social psychology. The choice of a particular explanatory style (or method), like any other choice, must draw a bargain between the advantages and disadvantages. No style is all perfect or all wrong. If one wishes, for example, to know whether older people are less readily influenced by propaganda than younger people, one could conduct a survey, carry out a field study, a field experiment, or a laboratory experiment. All have some advantages and some disadvantages. The survey would sample young and old people and ask them to what extent they are or were influenced by propaganda. We might get an indication about the degree to which they are influenceable without knowing how propaganda would actually affect them. But they would give us an answer that encompasses the general tendencies, covering all sorts of instances of propaganda. We could also make observations of people exposed to propaganda and of their subsequent actions. This field study method, while promising more precise and more direct results, restricts the variety of propaganda subjects that could be so analyzed. A field experiment would be even more restrictive but in turn more precise. A laboratory study could also be carried out in which there was an attempt to persuade younger and older people. This last method would be still more precise and more directly geared to answering the original problem. However, it would be most circumscribed with respect to the variety **[351]** of propaganda subjects, population, methods of 'propaganda' represented by the experimental manipulations, and its application to practical purposes.

Each of these methods strikes a bargain between precision and representativeness. In my own taste, the experimental method seems to be most appropriate, and I would readily remain ignorant about the general applicability of the finding for the sake of knowing the precise effects. But I would certainly appreciate and respect other approaches. I run experiments because I know how and avoid surveys because have not learned how to do them. It is quite obvious that one cannot always run experiments. One cannot use the experimental method in studying the relationship between birth order and intelligence. Nevertheless, there are clear preferences and for various reasons some researchers avail themselves only of one method, and as a result, are not able to study certain classes of problems that require other methods.

Style is not only a matter of expression of preference and training. It is also a matter of constraints of various kinds. Christopher Wren could not have built St. Paul's out of papier maché or reinforced concrete, and Michaelangelo could not paint in acrylic. Researchers who do not have access to a polygraph are unlikely to avail themselves of physiological measures and will not think of designing research that requires them. One cannot run studies of self schemas on rats or decortication experiments on humans.

Then there are also the constraints of the gatekeepers—the editors, publishers, the 'bishops' of the field, senior colleagues and established scholars whose opinions 'count.' They 'know' what approach is promising and who are the people with promise. An award received by a member of the field turns all the eyes in that direction. Many rush to follow the lead. Style is clearly not a matter of complete freedom and individual choice. There are many possible styles of music, painting, sculpture, or literature that never emerged or lasted for only a moment. But while style is not entirely free, it also is not entirely controlled and constrained.

STYLES IN FORMULATING PROBLEMS

Clear differences in style appear when we consider the ways different researchers formulate problems. When we formulate a problem, we already have 50 percent of the solution in mind, both in our conceptual representation and in our empirical work. Consider the following. An automobile is travelling over a hill which is 2 miles long on the way up, and 2 miles long on the way down. The automobile travels with an average speed of 30 mph on the way up. How fast must the automobile travel down hill so as to average 60 mph over the entire distance? If we formulate the problem in terms of average speeds we will never see that the downhill speed is unattainable. If we formulate it in terms of time, we will see it immediately.

Many problems are chosen for study because the researcher believes that they are solvable by him or her and that the solution is interesting. Different researchers choose different problems for study. And the choice and formulation of the problem sets constraints on the style of explanation.

Where do problems for research come from? The best answer to this question is given by Cohen and Nagel (1934). These philosophers say that the origin of a problem and the occasion for inquiry is irritation. That is, irritation exists because some needed knowledge is missing. It is irritating to know that for over 350 years, Fermat's last **[352]** theorem (that no natural numbers x, y, and z exist for which the relation $x^n + y^n = z^n$, where $n > 2$, is true) still remains unproven.[2] But the fact is not equally irritating to all mathematicians.

Irritation may also exist because there is a conflict between some findings and some other findings, or between some findings and a theory, or between two theories. These conditions cause irritation which the scientist seeks to remove. Thus, Cohen and Nagel anticipated dissonance theory.

Different researchers are irritated by different conditions. Some are irritated by a theoretical or empirical conflict, others are irritated by a condition in society that they seek to correct, and still others are irritated by some aspects of their own lives which they seek to improve or understand. But once selected, they have also different styles of formulating their problems. For example, Festinger's style is readily identifiable for certain features. In nearly all instances, the problem is formulated as an opposition of tendencies. There is always the assumption that the individual shuns each opposition and seeks to resolve it. Thus, for example, his early work on informal social communication sought to analyze the consequences of a conflict between diverse pressures toward uniformity, his work on level of aspiration contrasted performance with expectation, his work on social comparison pitted the need to know against lack of information about one's values and abilities, his work on cognitive dissonance featured the conflict among cognitions or between cognitions and behavior, and even his work on vision was also couched in terms of conflict: it examined the experience that derives from visual information when contradicted by kinesthetic sensation.

The power of this style of formulation lies in the fact that the opposing tendencies set up conceptual grounds for the motivational antecedents of people's behavior, while the nature of these opposing tendencies together with their magnitudes allow predictions about the direction of behavior. Festinger's style is then to formulate problems in a sort of 'social vector analysis.'

To some extent, problems are chosen and formulated in line with the basic beliefs psychologists hold about 'human nature' or 'the mind.' Even after decades of swings

---

[2] At the time it was unproven, but it is now.

from an emphasis on nature to an emphasis on nurture, psychology in general and social psychology in particular, have yet to settle on a firm position. The same is true of views of human rationality. Successive generations of social psychologists have alternated in attributing rationality and irrationality to the human spirit. The thirties witnessed an emphasis on human gullibility with its research on suggestibility (Lorge, 1936). The forties were dedicated to the people's search for meaning, as exemplified in the work of Helen Block Lewis (1941) and Asch, Block and Hertzman (1938). The fifties were witness to irrational perceptual defenses against trivially offensive stimuli (McGinnes, 1949), and later to the irrationality of seeking the resolution of dissonance. The sixties pictured man as a proficient analyst of variance in attributing causes of social events and intentions to people (Kelley, 1967). The seventies turned again to focus on the poverty of inferential abilities by showing the weakness of the heuristic processes (Kahneman and Tversky, 1973), and the current decade finds interest in improving and teaching the frail inference process (Nisbett and Ross, 1980). These basic beliefs and assumptions about 'human capacity' guide the way problems are formulated. They define the current fashion and research style.

Styles of explanation also differ in the assumptions one makes about the 'innateness' of social behavior. Asch (1952) had a good deal to say about it and there is no need to repeat it here, other than that social psychological problems will be [353] formulated quite differently if basic social tendencies are viewed as instinctive or learned.

THEORETICAL STYLES

I will now discuss some stylistic elements of social psychological explanation. I have selected some aspects of style that deal with theoretical and some that deal with empirical aspects of explanation. The following theoretical issues will be considered first:

1. completeness versus simplification;
2. collective versus individual focus, and
3. intuition versus inference.

For the empirical aspects, I have chosen the issues of

1. experiment and reality;
2. discrete versus continuous variation, and
3. hard versus soft measures.

Obviously, this is not an exhaustive list of stylistic elements of explanation. I have selected these particular issues because they have divided social psychologists and occasioned heated arguments. Some of these issues are debatable, some seem debatable and aren't, and some do not seem to be debatable but are.

Complexity and Completeness versus Simplification

One of the criticisms of experimental social psychology is that it represents reality in an impoverished way. According to a number of writers (Harré, 1979; Silverman, 1977; Gadlin and Ingle, 1975; Israel and Tajfel, 1972), social psychologists work under the delusion that systematic observations can be obtained by looking at factors one or few at a time. Ignoring the presence of such methods as the analysis of covariance, multiple regression, path analysis, and structural equation, Harré, for example, insists *con brio* that estimates of the effect of one or two factors while holding other factors constant are not possible and that the only valid information about social process is one that considers most of the factors at once.

It is, of course, the case that daily social life is very complex. But is it the purpose of social science to document all of the drab and boring details of our social life? Why dedicate a complex theoretical and intellectual effort to the total meaning of such episodes as 'How about a drink?' (Harré, 1979, p. 126), of which there must be billions?

Is it useful or necessary to *reproduce* the full complexity of social life in our own theories and methods? Motion, too, is very complex. There is the motion of a pebble falling down a mountain, the flight of a bird, the swing of a pendulum, the leap of an antelope, a football rolling toward a goal, an automobile speeding on a highway, a runner on a cinder track, a molecule approaching another, a planet revolving around the sun, or a moon revolving around Mars. And for each one there are millions of variants and contexts. If we were to describe all these motions and their variants in complete detail we would need an infinitely large computer and an infinite amount of time.

Completeness is not possible. No representational painting and even a succession of thousands of painters can portray *all* there is to see and to know about a given subject, however, simply. Of course, some painters seek to give a greater correspondence to [354] 'reality' than others. The completeness of a Dutch genre painting such as one by Jan Steijn or by Adriaen Brouwer's greater than of a painting by Modigliani or of a drawing by Steinberg. But even most of the super-realists of today could only choose a minute fraction of reality to detail with. A second's reflection convinces us that a *complete* representation is simply beyond reach.

Experimental social psychologists are compelled to look at a few factors at a time to gain a deeper understanding of these factors and they do so deliberately at the expense of completeness. Social psychologists whose style takes them to do surveys that cover a large number of factors are also limited by the interaction between their analytical tools and the sample size. The more variables there are the larger the sample must be to satisfy the assumptions of multivariate techniques.

One of the severe criticisms of social psychology is that its empirical findings are based mostly on data collected from American college sophomores. Clearly, as it is with different experimental environments, it would be desirable to have a sampling of different populations. But that is laborious, costly, and often quite difficult. It would be good, for example, to test the hypothesis that people seek information that confirms their biases, say on 80-year-old newspaper editors in South Africa. One might conjecture that somewhat different results might be obtained with that sample than with college sophomores. But here, too, we must compromise with what is possible and look to the fact that experimenting with the same population under the same conditions retains the standard aspects of the research. The bacterium, *Escherichia coli,* is the standard and the most popular subject in biology, biochemistry, endocrinology, genetics, biophysics, and a host of other fields. Research has accumulated that amounts to a substantial body of systematic knowledge using only that bacterium. Little is known about how results with

E. coli generalize to other forms of life. But from other knowledge and experience, it is a good guess that the basic knowledge is general.

It is a pointless procedure to rush with replications of a given finding on a variety of populations, just so that we can assess the generality of the finding. Take the Schachter and Singer study (1962), for example, which demonstrated that when the individual is in a state of arousal that cannot be readily explained, he or she will draw upon environmental cues to understand it. Once found, Schachter and Singer could have replicated the study on graduate students, bricklayers, and a sample of Kuwaiti oil executives. Or better, using the same population as in the original study, they could have gone deeper into the important phenomenon they discovered and vary some of the crucial variables of their ingenious experiment, such as the intensity and clarity of the arousal brought about by epinephrine, the source of environmental cues, attempt to induce not only happiness and anger, but other emotions as well, measure other indicators of emotion besides subjective report, etc. Which would be more useful, examining the effect over different populations or over different conditions? I believe the latter.

There are, however, problems that lend themselves to a greater emphasis on population differences. These problems are generally those that tap important individual differences. For example, the study of the self (Gergen, 1965, 1971; Markus, 1977) might very well benefit from a replication on a variety of populations that vary in success, opportunity, age, social class, or culture. It is simply a question of whether variations in the phenomenon or process under investigation are in a *crucial way* influenced by population differences, that is, whether the phenomenon is expected *a priori* to be fairly homogeneous over populations or systematically variable. One does **[355]** not need to take blood samples from 18 different populations to test if there exist a relationship between red blood cell count and blood pressure. But it is quite obvious that research seeking to identify the varieties of AIDS viruses must sample over a wide range of different populations.

Interdependence of Factors

One aspect of the style that advocates completeness as obligatory is the presupposition that all factors and all manner of things are completely interrelated and that studying one or few factors at a time is therefore misleading. Harré (1979) takes the experimental method to task just because it ignores this inter-relatedness in social life. The view is not new. The 18th century scientist Jonathan Edwards proposed to show 'how the Motion, Rest, and Direction of the *Least Atom* has an influence on the motion, rest and direction of every body in the Universe' (Edwards, 1920). That he did not succeed in giving evidence of his presupposition is today eminently obvious. And no phenomenon or set of phenomena has been studied or can be studied by looking at all of its interdependent factors. We can only know a small piece of reality at a time, and we shall never know all of it. We may well aspire to understand more and more factors and their interrelationships, but there are clearly very severe limits that are set by our grasp, methods, techniques, and instruments.

It is simply impossible to represent even a small fraction of the interdependence of factors in social behavior or in any other discipline. Consider two dentists, a complete dentist and a simpleton. The simpleton receives a patient who complains about a toothache. She assumes that there is one infected tooth and tries to locate it. She proceeds systematically and examines all 32 teeth, one at a time. Her chances of finding it are 1/32. On the average, she will locate it on the 16th probe. Now the same patient visits the complete dentist who considers not only each tooth in isolation but all the interactions among the thirty-two teeth. Now, there are $2^{32} - 1 = 4,294,967,295$ probes to be made. If the dentist takes only one minute for each probe, she would need 8171 years to check all of them. A study with 10 factors has $2^{10} - 1 = 1023$ main effects and interactions. Need more be said?

Parsimony is the enemy of completeness. It is a virtue to simplify but clearly a sin to *over*simplify. As with many other stylistic decisions, the researcher must strike a bargain between the completeness of theoretical interpretation and the simplicity of its form. There is a great deal of elegance in a simple explanation. Euclid's geometry is an elegant theory just because of the simplicity of its axioms. Beethoven's Fifth Symphony is also beautiful, among others, for the simplicity of its 'premises.' It has as its basic theme four notes, three of which are the same. Yet the work is rich in variations and derivations and elaborations based on just those four notes. Both must be considered by Galtung to be the products of a teutonic style.

Theory can be elegant without being 'true' or it can be true without being elegant. One can always make a representation simpler. For example, a ballistic trajectory can be quite accurately represented by a very simple quadratic equation. However, the accuracy would be totally uninformative about the basic factors that contribute to the nature of the process, gravity and escape velocity. The simplest and best prediction of weather is to predict for today what we had yesterday. While simple and on the whole most accurate, this method misses hurricanes, typhoons, and tornadoes. **[356]** Harré (1979) claims that 'no theory is acceptable which essentially simplifies that life form, or attempts to explain its character by reference to a single causal principle' (p.10). Of course, it is within the realm of possibilities that someone could come along one day and formulate a basic principle that goes a long way in explaining all social life. In fact, only seven pages before declaring the acceptability of a one-factor theory, Harré already asserted that 'the pursuit of reputation … is the overriding preoccupation of human life' (p. 3), and treated it throughout his volume as the basic causal principle.

Collective versus Individual Focus

The bulk of recent social psychology is concerned with social cognition, that is the representations people have of social events and the participants in these events. A great deal has been learned by the study of social cognition. However, focusing on the internal processes of individuals detracts from understanding one of the essential aspects of *social* life, namely interaction among people and the process of social influence. Studying the minds and cognitive predispositions of individuals does not lend itself to the understanding of how the contents of one mind are transmitted to another or how one mind is influenced by another.

Collective aspects of social behavior—norms, roles, institutions, social influence— exercise their effects by virtue of overt action. By focusing on the contents and processes within individual minds is not readily compatible with also observing action and interaction. Only sporadic attempts have been made to combine these two (e.g., Snyder, Tanke and Berscheid, 1977). Yet it is a strange paradox that cognition is studied in isolation of a very essential social process that is its immediate antecedent and consequence—communication (Zajonc & Adelmann, 1987). Most of our cognitions are the products of communications with others, directly or indirectly (Zajonc, 1960). And many of the cognitions that we have are eventually communicated to others. Cognition is the currency of communication. The constraints on communication and the transmission of mental content between minds, the transformations of these contents, and the resulting change in the participants, are rarely studied in the mainstream social psychology. Yet soon we will need to know about these processes if we are to understand even the contents of individual minds. For they are under serious collective influences. Moscovici's (1983) approach to the study of social representations is a step in the right direction that promises fruitful outcomes. But it must penetrate deeper into the mainstream of social psychology, especially American social psychology.

Introspection and Inference

Our own experience does not give us direct access to phenomena in the realm of molecular biology. But human beings are all fairly competent social psychologists. Our own perceptions as human beings as we participate actively in a social process give us some insight into the many social psychological processes. Should we always trust them?

On the basis of his own understanding and perception of what social life is like, Harré (1979) sought to obliterate decades of theoretical and empirical work by social **[357]** psychologists and replace it by another approach, apparently more congruent with his own private experience. He writes:

> I began this work in an attempt to clear from my mind the confusion and uncertainty I experienced when trying to reconcile *my* experience of social life with the representations of processes by which that life is created that are to be found in the writings of social scientists (p. 2; italics mine).

If we all had such keen insights into the workings of the social process there would be no need for a systematic social science. Nothing new could be discovered that is not already part of common knowledge.

We all have millions of experiences which we can retrieve and offer as systematic knowledge. However, everything that we know from the systematic study of social perception indicates that we should be very distrustful of our so-called intuitions. For example, a large number of studies have revealed a substantial self-serving bias in estimating probabilities of causal events (Kunda, 1985; Miller, 1976; Pyszczynski, Greenberg, and LaPrelle, 1985; Sicoly and Ross, 1977; Weinstein, 1983, 1984). Even though half of the marriages in the United States end in a divorce, most young people believe that they will die married to their first spouse (Lehman and Nisbett, 1985). And those who smoke do not ascribe the aggregate probability of lung cancer to their own case. People have a completely different estimate of the probabilities of events that actually did occur than about those that are about to occur. Hindsight is indeed much better than foresight (Fischhoff, 1975).

It goes without saying, however, that our own experience can be a rich source of ideas and a source of hypotheses. But taken alone it can be fatally misleading. I once gave a talk at the Bell Telephone Laboratories—an institution with more PhD's per square inch than any other I know. In the course of the presentation I showed some data on the negative relationship between family size and intelligence. During the question period a member of the audience offered the counter example that his own family is quite different; even though they are eight siblings, all of them reached important professional and scientific positions. He offered this evidence against data based on over one million observations. Surely, he must have been familiar with statistical mechanics and knew that the path of any single particle will not tell the whole story of the remaining several billion particles in an enclosed space. Yet he felt compelled to pit his own personal history against a vast aggregate result.

If we were to trust our own intuitions and observations in all fields, we would still adhere to the geocentric theory of planetary motion. How could we overcome the obvious daily experience that the sun and the moon have similar motions and that they both revolve around the earth in diurnal cycles? It was mathematical not personal insight that produced the heliocentric theory that is now accepted and which put man on the moon. Science has succeeded because it has *contradicted* the gross impressions that come from our senses and replaced these everyday impressions with basic theories. Copernican view of the planetary system is a direct contradiction of sensory experience and of a deeply established and commonly held belief. And even if most of systematic social psychology were nothing but the confirmation of the obvious, it would still be necessary and quite proper not to trust our intuitions completely. For that is what we mean by discipline.

It may be true that some problems might turn out to be tractable only by intuition and introspection, such as the nature of subjective feeling, for example. It would be **[358]** wasteful, however, if a great deal of research energy was dedicated to them alone Unless there is some semblance of a possibility that these problems are solvable by more public methods, they may well remain in the realm of philosophy, literature and the arts.

EMPIRICAL STYLES

Experiment and Reality

The most strident critique of some social psychological styles, primarily the experimental style, has as its basic argument that the experimental method misrepresents reality. Here, as I asserted earlier, we have an element of style in social psychological explanation that is as much beyond argument as it is in art.

The argument about experiment and reality is part of a broader anti-scientific attitude that has prevailed over a decade among some circles and regrettably also among social scientists. This attitude doubts all scientific endeavors and regards all science and especially social science as misguided (Roszak, 1972). Roszak asserts that 'The greatest truth mankind learned from its ancient intimacy with nature [is] the reality of spiritual being.' No psychology is possible, he contends, that ignores that truth. Silverman (1977) writes that 'The failure of social psychology to develop substance and direction has been due primarily to our misguided vision that complex social phenomena can be fruitfully studied by experimental laboratory methods' (p. 353). Harré (1979) attacks the experimental method in social psychology by decrying the impoverished environment in which experiments are run.

> Experiments take place in special places, often called social psychological laboratories, where a simplified environment consisting of undecorated walls, plain furnishings, rarely more than two chairs, the mysterious blank face of the one-way mirror, and perhaps the intrusion of the unblinking eye of the television camera (p. 106).

How many chairs to make reality? Five? Ten? And what sorts of chairs? Of course they cannot be simple metal folding or stacking chairs. Must they be Chippendale wing chairs, Louis XVI bergères? Does the absence of a third chair necessarily destroy reality? Should we serve our subjects Sprite or 1934 Armagnac?

The outcries against the experimental style in social psychology are part of a tendency that the philosopher Frankel (1973) justifiably termed as 'irrationalism.' He understands by *irrationalism*

> a studied and articulated attitude, proudly affirmed and elaborately defended which pronounces science—and not only science, but, more broadly, logical analysis, controlled observations, the norms and civilities of disciplined argument, and the ideal of objectivity—to be systematically misleading as to the nature of the universe and the conditions necessary for human fulfillment (p.927).

Why would we exclude the laboratory as part of reality? Is the barren laboratory room less of a reality to a person in that situation than a rococo boudoir? How many **[359]** chairs are required for a faithful representation of reality? Must there be brocade or damask on the walls? If a military barracks resembles a laboratory in its drabness and minimal furnishings, does it therefore cease to be 'reality?' Which is the essential reality? The bedroom? The church? The pub? The professor's office? The disco? The street? The shower? The bank? A Bloomsbury sitting room?

Social scientists had two options: They could have sampled over environments and have selected a number that would be representative of all possible and conceivable environments. Or they could have settled on one or a few 'standard' environments that would be consensually agreed upon, that would serve for comparable replications of experiments, where standard measures and standard operations could be performed under very similar conditions. Both procedures promise some cumulative progress. If social science knew how to select a representative sample and how to verify that, once selected, the sample is indeed representative, it would have been perhaps better although more costly to have such a sample. But in order to draw a representative sample of environments we have to know the universe of all possible environments. Thus far such information is not available, and although ethogeny promised some years ago to produce a taxonomy of environments, little evidence of progress has been communicated.

The basic laws of motion are also studied in standard environments—environments that are seldom found in everyday life—perfect spheres rolling over perfect surfaces that seek to approach zero friction. They are not studied by observing pebbles falling down the mountain. And acceleration is studied in vacuum—a condition so rare that our predecessors felt it to be abhorred by nature.

Compare what knowledge has been achieved using standard methods in all the sciences and by those that advertise a closer kinship to reality, such as ethnomethodology.

Experimental reality *is* 'real life' to all the participants, the experimenter and the subject alike. Experimental laboratory is just as much real life for the subject as a shoe store or the bedroom. An observation by Joseph Conrad is instructive in this respect (Author's note to *Typhoon*):

> I don't mean to say that I ever saw Captain MacWhirr in the flesh, or had ever come in contact with his literal mind and his dauntless temperament. MacWhirr is not an acquaintance of a few hours, or a few weeks, or a few months. He is the product of twenty years of life. My own life. Conscious invention had little to do with him. If it is true that Captain MacWhirr never walked and breathed on this earth (which I find for my part extremely difficult to believe) I can also assure my readers that he is perfectly authentic.

The question to examine is not whether a given procedure reveals or duplicates reality but whether the controlled and standard environments and the procedures that they employ are capable of revealing the *essential* aspects of fundamental social psychological processes. The fact that replications of laboratory experiments in the field or in free observations are seldom in contradiction with each other suggests rather that little is lost.

Discrete versus Continuous Variation

'Reality' can be represented by discrete or continuous variables. Seurat saw reality as a collection of discrete elements, for example. Some researchers formulate their **[360]** problems in terms of functions of more or less continuous variables. For example, Byrne (1971) formulated his ideas about similarity and attraction as a linear function. Anderson (1974) plots functions that describe the contributions of elements of impressions, judgments, and attitudes. Others, however, are content to deal with discrete categories that are based on continuous variables. We have thousands of experiments where the contrast is simply between a 'high' and a 'low' value of a continuous factor. There are experiments that contrast 'high' and 'low' dissonance, 'high' and 'low' ego-involvement, 'high' and 'low' competence, 'high' and 'low' self-esteem, at thousands of others factors. I am not referring to experiments that examine properly discrete categories, such as gender, ethnic group, or political party. I am referring here to studies that collapse continuous variables into discrete, usually binary, categories and construct the inevitable two-by-two design that characterizes a great deal of research in this field. These preferences are clearly a matter of style.

It is certainly wasteful to observe an entire gamut of values if the relationship between the independent and the dependent variable is previously known. If we know the function that describes their relationship, and if the function happens to be linear, two points will often suffice. But most often we do not know the function. We do not know that the preference for a selected item changes as a linear function of post-decision **[361]** dissonance. That is in fact the hypothesis to be demonstrated in a crucial experiment.

The dangers of running a two-by-two experiment when we ignore the function that relates the two continuous variables are serious. Consider the following three two-by-two tables displayed in Figure 2.1. Table A shows a solid main effect over the rows. Table B shows a clear interaction, and Table C shows two main effects as well as an interaction. These two-by-two tables present very distinct and different patterns of results. No one would dare to draw the same conclusion on the basis of these different patterns.

Now consider the graph in Figure 2.2, which shows a distribution of 60 observations around a *log* function of x describing these observations.

It just so happens that the three two-by-two tables also represent the data in the plot obtained by making different cuts of the variables into 'high' and 'low' categories (see Figures 2.3, 2.4 and 2.5).

Note that the difference between the cuts of the distributions that produce the three tables are quite minimal (Figure 2.6). Care is advised, therefore, for all those whose style is the two-by-two table. **[363]**

Hard and Soft Measures

There is among some social scientists the belief that some measures come closer to the essence of certain phenomena than others. In particular, when the research deals with affect, attitudes, predispositions, decisions, judgments, and other typical responses for which we assume some internal state, the verbal report is somehow trusted less than some other unobtrusive or physiological measures which are held in undeserved awe.

It is certainly the case that in some instances the verbal report cannot be trusted. If we wish to know whether a person is in a state of arousal there are better things to do than to ask the person about it. In fact, Zillmann (1979) has shown that verbal report cannot be trusted here. He found that following exercise and rest, the person believes to be completely rested whereas the physiological measures all indicate that he is still aroused and outcome measures also indicate that the individual must be in a state of arousal rather than in a state of rest and relaxation.

No matter how precise and refined are physiological measures, there is no way of looking at the autonomic system or the cortex or any other anatomical configuration in the brain and determine whether a person is a liberal or a conservative, democrat or republican, or how the person knows the difference between odd and even

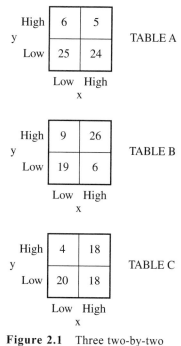

Figure 2.1   Three two-by-two tables showing divergent main effects and interactions

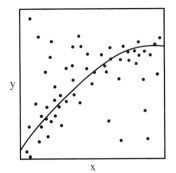

Figure 2.2 Sixty values of a variable *y* plotted as a function of variable *x*

numbers. The best procedure is to ask the person, administer some other less obtrusive verbal measure, or look up how the person voted.

A very good demonstration of the relative validity of physiological and simple verbal measures is given by Dulany and Eriksen (1959). They compared the accuracy of discrimination of brightness stimuli using verbal response and the GSR as indicators. The GSR was conditioned to a light stimulus using shock as the UCS. The accuracy criteria were equally stringent for both measures. Several intervals were presented to the subject, one of which included the conditioned stimulus. The remaining time intervals contained only noise. In this procedure the subject indicated verbally the interval containing the stimulus. For the GSR, the interval that showed the greatest change was taken as a similar indicator. For stimulus intensities that produced accuracies over the chance level (50 percent), the verbal response was consistently and considerably superior. Even when the accuracy was very low, i.e., over three weakest stimuli, the verbal response seemed to show some superiority.

It is sometimes best simply to ask the subject for a verbal response. But this is not so in all cases. As Nisbett and Wilson (1977) have demonstrated, the person has a limited access to the causes of his or her own behavior. People in fact know very little about

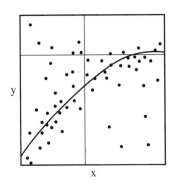

Figure 2.3 The data in Table A (Figure 2.5) superimposed on the scatterplot from Figure 2.6

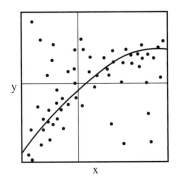

Figure 2.4 The data in Table B (Figure 2.5) superimposed on the scatterplot from Figure 2.6

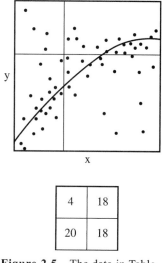

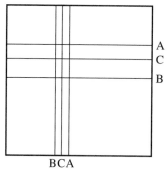

Figure 2.6   Comparison of the two-by-two splits that generated data in Tables A, B, and C in Figure 2.5

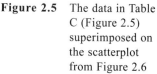

Figure 2.5   The data in Table C (Figure 2.5) superimposed on the scatterplot from Figure 2.6

themselves. Kahneman and Snell (in press) found that people are not quite able to predict their own changes in taste as a function of experience nor do they have the slightest idea how the effects of their experiences differ from those of others.

This illustration does not imply that social psychologists should reject physiological measures. It only implies that we should not use them blindly. It is becoming increasingly evident that we can no longer work in isolation of the exciting progress in neuroscience. A variety of useful information can be obtained by looking at the physiological responses of the individual, as Cacioppo and Petty (1983) have clearly shown. Attitudes, influence, judgments, impressions, memory of social events, preferences can all be better understood if the technical and theoretical sophistication in neuroscience is included in social-psychological thinking.

The progress in the behavioral sciences has been characterized by a specialization of the various fields that unfortunately promotes their isolation and segmentation from each other. A growing body of knowledge from neurochemistry, neuroanatomy, [365] and neurobiology sheds new light on the nature of emotions, motivation, conditioning, preference, association, cognition, and other basic processes that enter into social psychological processes and phenomena. We cannot ignore these findings, as neuropsychologists cannot ignore the findings of social psychology. After all, we can speak meaningfully about differences between republicans and democrats whereas the neuroscientists cannot. For our part, we need to make our concepts and our principles commensurate with the knowledge now developing in neuroscience as much as they need to pay attention to what is already known about social behavior.

CONCLUSIONS

Explanations in social psychology are in large measure a matter of style. Many styles of explanation cannot be reasonably evaluated. They remain a matter of taste. Some stylistic elements, however, can be fruitfully examined for their usefulness, heuristic value, promise, as well as for their weaknesses, disadvantages, and vulnerable features.

It is quite difficult to appreciate that a scientific method—a style of approaching certain problems—should generate an outrage such is as communicated by some writers. Why would an established philosopher find it necessary to refer to a scientific approach as the BEAST—an acronym for the British Empirical Ameliorative Sociology Tradition, or APE—the American Pragmatic Empiricism (Harré, 1979, p. 112)? APE, I suppose, is that type of crude empiricism that starts with vague definitions and poorly articulated principles, and seeks to find some useful practical applications. Group dynamics is clearly a good example of APE. It was founded by the 'American' Kurt Lewin and began its career by showing that there might be some clear differences in group performance and member satisfaction associated with different leadership styles. The ideas formed the basis of the T-Group movement, were taken quite seriously as guides to management in Japanese industry where they have now served for several decades with an apparent success. Such was the Japanese success in employing group dynamics in industry that Americans have begun introducing it in their own industry. As a result of some new management practices, including the principles of group dynamics, Ford workers received this year an average of $3700 each as a share in the company profits. The vague definitions and crude concepts seemed to have been quite effective. What then is the matter with APE? The fact that there is no polio in the world is also a product of APE.

The effectiveness of a style of explanation has many facets, and I mentioned them earlier so as not to overlook the practical applications that derive from it. In the long run we shall know better how useful the various perspectives and approaches fared. They should all continue therefore. No approach can be completely wrong, even those that seem to recruit hysterical outbursts of critique. Even a wrong explanation is useful because it has a chance of highlighting the path to a right one. A well-known scholar once walked out of a colloquium growling: 'This isn't even wrong!' A wrong explanation is certainly better than no explanation at all.

REFERENCES

Anderson, N.H. (1974). 'Cognitive algebra: Integration theory applied to social attribution.' In Berkowitz, L. (Ed.) *Advances in Experimental Social Psychology,* Vol. 7. Academic Press, New York. **[366]**

Asch, S. (1952*). Social Psychology*, Prentice-Hall, Englewood Cliffs, N.J.

Asch, S.E., Block, H. and Hertzman, M. (1938). 'Studies in the principles of judgments and attitudes: I. Two basic principles of judgment,' *Journal of Psychology*, **5**: 219–251.

Blake, P. (1949). *Marcel Breuer*, Museum of Modern Art, New York.

Byrne, D. (1971). *The Attraction Paradigm*, Academic Press, New York.

Cacioppo, J. T. and Petty, R. (1983). *Social Psychophysiology: A Sourcebook*, Guilford, New York.

Cohen, M.R. and Nagel, E. (1934) *An Introduction to Logic and Scientific Method*, Harcourt, Brace & Co., New York.

Dulany, D.E. and Eriksen, C.W. (1959). 'Accuracy of brightness discrimination as measured by concurrent verbal responses and GSRs, *Journal of Abnormal and Social Psychology*, **59**: 418–423.

Edwards, J. (1920). 'Things to be considered, or written fully about.' In: Van Doren, C. (Ed.) *Benjamin Franklin and Jonathan Edwards: Selections*, American Books, New York.

Elms, A.C. (1975). 'The crises of confidence in social psychology,' *American Psychologist*, **30**: 967–976.

Festinger, L., Riecken, H.W. and Schachter, S. (1956). *When Prophecy Fails: A Social and Psychological Study of Modern Group that Predicted the Destruction of the World*, Harper, New York.

Fischhoff, B. (1975). 'Hindsight does not equal foresight: The effects of outcome knowledge on judgment under uncertainty.' *Journal of Experimental Psychology: Human Perception and Performance*, **1**: 288–299.

Frankel, C. 'The nature and sources of irrationalism,' *Science*, **180**: 927–931.

Gadlin, H. and Ingle, G. (1975). 'Through the one-way mirror. The limits of experimental self-reflection,' *American Psychologist*, **30**: 1003–1010.

Galtung, J. (1981). 'Structure, culture, and intellectual style: An essay comparing saxonic, teutonic, gallic and nipponic approaches.' *Social Science Information*, **6**: 817–856.

Gergen, K.J. (1965). 'The effects of interaction goals and personalistic feedback on the presentation of self,' *Journal of Personality and Social Psychology*, **1**: 413–424.

Gergen, K.J. (1971). *The Concept of Self*, Holt, New York.

Gergen, K.J. (1973). 'Social psychology as history,' *Journal of Personality and Social Psychology*, **26**: 309–320.

Harré, R. (1979). *Social Being*, Basil Blackwell, Oxford.

Hull, C.L. (1943). *Principles of Behavior*, Appleton-Century-Crofts, New York.

Israel, J. and Tajfel, H. (1972). *The Context of Social Psychology: A Critical Assessment*, Academic Press, London.

Kahneman, D. and Snell, J. (1989). 'Predicting a changing taste.' In press.

Kahneman, D. and Tversky, A. (1973). 'On the psychology of prediction,' *Psychological Review*, **80**: 237–251.

Kelley, H.H. (1967). 'Attribution theory in social psychology,' *Nebraska Symposium on Motivation*, **14**: 192–241.

Kunda, Z. (1985). 'Motivation and inference: Self-serving generation and evaluation of causal theories.' PhD Thesis, University of Michigan.

Lehman, D. and Nisbett, R.E. (1985). 'Effects of higher education on inductive reasoning.' Unpublished manuscript, University of Michigan.

Lewis, H.B. (1941). 'Studies in the principles of judgments and attitudes: IV. The operation of "prestige suggestion,"' *Journal of Social Psychology*, **14**: 229–256.

Lorge, I. (1936). 'Prestige, suggestion, and attitudes,' *Journal of Social Psychology*, **7**: 386–402.

McGinnies, E.M. (1949). 'Emotionality and perceptual defense,' *Psychological Review*, **56**: 471–482.

Manis, M. (1975). 'Comments on Gergen's "Social psychology as history"', *Personality and Social Psychology Bulletin*, **1**: 450–455.

Markus, H. (1977). 'Self-schemas and processing of information about the self,' *Journal of Personality and Social Psychology*, **35**: 63–78.

Miller, D.T. (1976). 'Ego involvement and attributions for success and failure.' *Journal of Personality and Social Psychology*, **34**: 901–906.

Moscovici, S. (1983). 'Social representations and social explanations: From the "naive" to the "amateur" scientist.' In: Hewstone, M. (Ed.) *Attribution Theory: Social and Functional Extentions*, Blackwell, Oxford. **[367]**

Nisbett, R.E. and Ross, L. (1980). *Human Inference: Strategies and Shortcomings in Social Judgment*, Prentice-Hall, Englewood Cliffs, N.J.

Nisbett, E.E. and Wilson, T.D. (1977). 'Telling more than we can know: Verbal reports on mental processes,' *Psychological Review*, **84**: 231–259.

Pyszczynski, T., Greenberg, J. and LaPrelle, J. (1985). 'Social comparison after success and failure: Biased search for information consistent with self-serving conclusion,' *Journal of Experimental Social Psychology*, **21**: 195–211.

Roszak, T. (1972). *Where the Wasteland Ends*, Doubleday, New York.

Schachter, S. and Singer, J. (1962). 'Cognitive, social, and physiological determinants of emotional state,' *Psychological Review*, **65**: 379–399.

Sicoly, F. and Ross, M. (1977). 'Facilitation of ego-based attributions by means of self-serving observer feed-back,' *Journal of Personality and Social Psychology*, **35**: 734–741.

Silverman, I. (1977). 'Why social psychology fails,' *Canadian Psychological Review*, **18**: 353–358.

Snyder, M., Tanke, E.D. and Berscheid, E. (1977). 'Social perception and interpersonal behavior: on the self-fulfilling nature of social stereotypes' *Journal of Personality and Social Psychology*, **35**: 656–666.

Weinstein, N.D. (1983). 'Reducing unrealistic optimism about illness susceptibility,' *Health Psychology*, **2**: 11–20.

Weinstein, N.D. (1984). 'Why it won't happen to me: Perceptions of risk factors and susceptibility,' *Health Psychology*, **3**: 431–457.

Wright, F.L. (1957). *A Testament*, Horizon Press, New York.

Zajonc, R.B. (1960). The process of cognitive tuning in communication.' *Journal of Abnormal and Social Psychology*, **61**: 159–67.

Zajonc, R.B. and Adelmann, P.K. (1987). 'Cognition and communication: A story of missed opportunities,' *Social Science Information*, **26**: 3–30.

Zillman, D. (1979). *Hostility and Aggression*, Lawrence Erlbaum, Hillsdale, N.J. **[368]**

Chapter 3

Cognition and Social Cognition: A Historical Perspective*

R.B. Zajonc
University of Michigan

In his history of social psychology, Allport (1954) observed that "social psychologists regard their discipline as *an attempt to understand and explain how thought, feeling, and behavior of individuals are influenced by the actual, imagined, or implied presence of other human beings*" (p. 5). Few of us would find cause to disagree with this definition. The classes of phenomena which Allport regarded as significant for social psychologists, and the emphasis that he gave to these phenomena, are worth noting. According to this definition of social psychology, we wish to understand and explain *thought, feeling,* and *behavior*—in that order—with *thought* at the top of the list. And it is certainly still the case today that in the vast majority of instances our data are about thoughts. They come in the form of judgments, beliefs, opinions, preferences, expectations, guesses, or attitudes.

And according to Allport's definition, what are we to understand about thought, feeling, and behavior? We are to understand and explain *how they are influenced by the actual, imagined, or implied presence of others!* There are few social psychological experiments in which the effects of the *actual* presence of others have been studied. Rather, the bulk of our work has to do with the effects of the *implied* or *imagined* presence of others on thought, feeling, and behavior. Thus, according to Allport's **[180]**** definition of social psychology, we are cognitive on the side of the independent variables and on the side of the dependent variables as well.

---

* Portions of this chapter were presented as part of a symposium on Social Cognition and Affect at the meeting of the American Psychological Association, September 1979, New York. Preparation of this chapter was supported by a fellowship from the John Simon Guggenheim Memorial Foundation.

** Bracketed bold numbers refer to original page numbers. Page numbers indicate where the original page ended.

In fact, however, social psychology is even more cognitive than Allport's definition would imply. Cognition pervades social psychology at various levels: It enters at the level at which the problem is formulated; it provides significant components of our methods and designs; it participates at the assumptive level in theories and hypothesis building; and finally, one aspect of cognition—social cognition—represents a field of interest in its own right.

Examples of the heavily cognitive emphasis in these aspects of social psychology are easily found. Any random issue of one of the journals in the field will reveal this emphasis. I have selected the last two issues of the *Journal of Personality and Social Psychology* that arrived as this chapter was being written: No. 10 and 11 of Vol. 36 (1978), and I shall draw upon them to illustrate my point.

COGNITIVE ELEMENTS IN FORMULATING SOCIAL PSYCHOLOGICAL RESEARCH PROBLEMS

Following are specimens of problem statements from four typical articles in that issue:

1.   The present research was undertaken to test the notion that feedback of one's own autonomic activity acts as a self-awareness inducing stimulus. (Fenigstein and Carver, 1978, p. 1242)

2.   Our theory predicts that the learning interference components of experimental helplessness can be remedied by simply informing subjects that feedback was noncontingent in the past but will be contingent in the future. (Koller & Kaplan, 1978, p. 1179)

3.   What strategies do individuals actually formulate to test the hypotheses about other individuals with whom they interact? Do individuals systematically adopt confirmatory strategies and preferentially search for evidence that would confirm their beliefs? Or, do individuals systematically adopt disconfirmatory strategies and preferentially search for evidence that would disconfirm their beliefs? Or, do individuals adopt equal opportunity strategies and search for confirming and disconfirming behavioral evidence with equal diligence? We have sought answers to these questions in our empirical investigations of hypothesis-testing processes. (Snyder and Swann, 1978, p. 1203)

4.   The extent to which 4-year-old children behave in ways expected [181] of them on the basis of their gender will be related to the nature of the situations or areas in which they play. (Lott, 1978, p. 1088)

In all these examples, information processing plays a critical role. In the first experiment, self-awareness (i.e., information about the self) is related to information about the individual's psychological activity. In the second study, learning performance (i.e., the acquisition and retention of information) is related to information about feedback contingency. In the third, subjects manipulate information and make complex inferences. And in the fourth experiment, the subjects' behavior is related to the way they view their play situation (i.e., the meaning of the environmental setting).

COGNITIVE ELEMENTS IN SOCIAL PSYCHOLOGICAL RESEARCH METHODS

Social psychologists define their dependent and independent variables (when they are not manipulated), manipulate their independent variables, and create the appropriate experimental context primarily in cognitive terms and through cognitive methods.

Defining Dependent Variables

Much if not most of social psychological research relies on the verbal response. For the most part, these verbal responses are given in answer to attitude questions, or they are judgments, predictions, expectations, choices, descriptions, or recognitions. Thus, for example, in the study of conformity, subjects are asked to make judgments of lines, quality of poems, populations of cities, and others. In the study of the level of aspiration, subjects are asked to make predictions of their performance and report their confidence in these judgments. In research on the risky shift phenomenon, individuals accept or reject a hypothetical level of risk in an imaginary choice situation. In the study of group performance, measures of time to solve problems, quality of the solution, and the strategy of approach are measured. Also observed is the intermember influence process, which, of course, relies on communication which, in turn, is the product of the members' cognitions. In the study of competition and cooperation, the seemingly simple Prisoner's Dilemma paradigm requires considerable prior knowledge on the part of the subjects, and a very complex cognitive process is involved in understanding a simple 2×2 payoff matrix. It requires **[182]** subjects to make guesses about their partners' (or opponents') preferences, utilities, and estimates of probabilities and to entertain guesses about how their partners will estimate and predict their own behavior.

In the four articles from the randomly selected issues of the *Journal of Personality and Social Psychology,* the involvement of cognitive factors in the measures of the dependent variables is quite clear. In the Fenigstein-Carver paper, subjects are presented with hypothetical situations that have good or bad outcomes. They are asked to assign responsibility for these outcomes, and the final measure consists of the extent of self-attribution of responsibility. In the Koller-Kaplan article, subjects must turn off a tone by discovering a correct sequence in which to press six buttons. Measures are percent correct, latency, and errors. In the Snyder-Swann experiments, subjects are told that the experiment is concerned with the way people come to understand each other. They are provided with a list of questions and from them select those to which they would like to have answers. Their selections become the measures of the dependent variable and are used to determine whether a confirming, disconfirming, or equal-opportunity strategy is employed by the subjects in testing *their* hypotheses about the person. In the Lott study, observations are taken of children's sex role behavior. Also obtained are questionnaires on sex typing as well as ratings of children's behavior made by teachers and parents.

Even when the variables are behavioral, most often they are interpreted as indicators of some underlying cognitive processes, states, or antecedents. Thus, the level of shock which a subject administers to a learner is taken as a measure of obedience to experimental instructions (Milgram, 1963); helping a person in distress is taken as a measure of the degree to which responsibility is diffused (Darley & Latané, 1968); giving blood is taken as a measure of attitude change (Powell, 1965); contributing money for a gift to a departing secretary is taken as a measure of conformity (Blake, Rosenbaum, and Duryea, 1955); and changes in star-tracing performance are taken as a measure of evaluation apprehension (Innes and Young, 1975). All these measures, it should be noted, involve very powerful assumptions about the *connection* between the behavior measured and the cognitive state that is believed to control it. Thus, for example, in the bystander intervention research, it is assumed that the reluctance of an individual to help a victim having an epileptic fit includes complex cognitive elements that entail his or her overview of the number of other people present, the likelihood that others might help, that there might be someone [183] else who knows more about epilepsy than the subject, and so on. And it is implicitly assumed that engaging in helping behavior is directly under the control of these complex cognitive factors.

Manipulating Independent Variables

It is typical in social psychological experiments to induce the subject to engage in considerable cognitive activity in order to produce in him a desired psychological state. This state might be a belief, an expectation, an attitude, a decision, or the like.

Often complex scenarios are composed to produce these states which represent different values of the independent variable. Thus, for example, in the Fenigstein-Carver study, subjects in the experimental group are told that the study is concerned with the effects of cognitive activity on physiological processes and that the specific interest of the experimenter is in these effects on heart rate. They are given to believe that they will engage in some cognitive activity and their heartbeats will be monitored. Explanations are furnished about the workings of a plethysmograph, changes in blood volume, photocells, and other technical matters, including the fact that the impulses in the photocells are transduced into clicks that represent the heartbeat. Thus, the subjects are told that they will be hearing their own heartbeats. Of course, the heartbeats are preprogrammed.

Note that it is virtually taken for granted that the experimental manipulations will induce a cognitive activity in the subjects. This activity will produce in them a psychological state that corresponds to the experimenter's conception of the independent variables and of the latent factors which these variables are presumed to measure. For the most part, these psychological states—attitudes, expectations, inferences, attributions, preferences, etc.—are covert and not directly accessible to observation. And frequently, we know very little about the cognitive processes that might be implicated in these measures. Many experimental procedures, especially those found in complex scenarios, precede formal knowledge by years or decades. For example, in 1951 Kurt Back published a paper on the effects of cohesiveness on social influence. In one group of subjects, he manipulated cohesiveness within pairs of subjects by telling them that on the basis of a test they had previously taken, they were very similar to each other (for high cohesiveness) or very different (low cohesiveness). In turn, cohesiveness was defined in terms of mutual attraction. Thus, Back assumed that perceived similarity would produce mutual attraction. At the [184] time of his experiment, however, very little was known about this relationship, and Byrne (1961) did not publish his work on similarity and attraction until ten years later. One should not view these procedures too critically. On the contrary, they testify to the ingenuity and foresight of the author and suggest, at the same time, that the field had reached a stage of development and sophistication that allow many of its conjectures soon to turn into proven theorems.

Creating an Experimental Context

Sometimes extensive instructions are given in order to create a particular experimental context for the subjects. These instructions, of course, must be processed by the subjects, and they must produce a psychological state that we wish to create. For example, subjects are told that the experiment is concerned with psychophysical judgments of length and that accuracy is of some importance. In fact, however, judgments are given in groups and the experiment deals with conformity. Or we tell the subjects, as in the Fenigstein-Carver study, that the experiment is concerned with the effects of cognitive activity on physiological processes, expecting that they will interpret the behavior of the experimenter, the purpose of the apparatus, and the sequence of experimental procedures in just those terms. Sometimes we create a context which requires the subject to strive for accuracy, sometimes for speed of response, or a context which makes them vulnerable to the influence of others. All of these manipulations may at times require knowledge that is not available and, worse, knowledge that is sought in the experimental program. Yet, this sort of bootstrapping is common and necessary at the forefront of experimental work in new areas.

Cognition and Experimental Artifacts

Even the critique of social psychological experiments invokes cognitive psychology and is stated in cognitive terms. Experimenter effects are stated in terms of the expectations of the experimenter and their effects on the behavior that is involved in experimental procedures, measures, and observations. Demand characteristics, on the other hand, involve assumptions about the subjects' expectations. It is assumed that the experimental context leads subjects to process the available information in such a way that certain inferences about the purpose of the study become inescapable and that their behavior will be constrained by these demands. [185]

COGNITIVE ELEMENTS IN THE EXPLANATIONS OF SOCIAL PSYCHOLOGICAL PHENOMENA

Many, perhaps most, social psychological phenomena are explained by invoking various forms of cognitive mediation. Thus, for example, the self-concept is assumed to develop as a result of processing information that is supplied by the behavior and expectations of others. Some explanations of social facilitation assume that the presence of others is itself a stimulus that arouses in the subjects concerns over being evaluated. And such areas as risky shift, bystander intervention, equity, cooperation–competition, and, in fact, almost all others contain cognitive mediators in their explanations.

COGNITIVE AND PERCEPTUAL PROCESSES AS SOCIAL PSYCHOLOGICAL PROBLEMS IN THEIR OWN RIGHT

A glance at the index of any text in social psychology will immediately reveal a large number of problems that are basically problems in information processing. Some deal with encoding of social information, others with retaining or combining it, and still others deal with more complex processes that involve cognitive conflict or inference. The list will naturally include attitudes and beliefs, stereotypes, communication, rumor transmission, perceptual selectivity, self-schemas, person perception, impression formation, balance, cognitive dissonance, attribution, social inference, the sleeper effect, implicit personality theory, implicit social behavior theory, and others.

Of course, similar cognitive variables and cognitive methods are also employed in other social sciences, such as sociology, political science, or anthropology. However, it is only in social psychology that *all* the above features and aspects are so heavily dominated by cognition, and it is perhaps unique in social psychology that social cognition represents a *major* field of interest in its own right (although similar interests are now also true to a lesser extent of cognitive anthropology).

WHY DOES COGNITION DOMINATE SOCIAL PSYCHOLOGY?

Social psychology has been cognitive for a very long time. It was cognitive long before the cognitive revolution in experimental psychology—**[186]** which dates, I suppose, to Neisser's book of 1967, when experimental psychologists began slowly to suspect that the intensive study of the learning of word lists might not reveal all secrets of the mind. It is instructive to look at the popular postwar text in social psychology published by Krech and Crutchfield in 1948—roughly thirty years ago. In it one finds that there was a deep concern with the nature of cognitive representations, with the way they are organized, and with the principles that could draw upon the nature of this organization in order for us to infer the likelihood and the form of change of cognitive structures. Attitude change was, above all, cognitive change. Here is a typical quote: "How we perceive the world is a product of memory, imagination, hearsay, and fantasy as well as what we are actually 'perceiving' through our senses. If we are to understand social behavior, we must know how all perceptions, memories, fantasies are combined or integrated or organized into present *cognitive structures*" (p. 77). This was at a time when words like "cognition," "consciousness," or "mind" were purged from the vocabulary of experimental psychologists. As late as 1957, Verplanck in his *Glossary of Psychological Terms* defined "cognition" as a term which *pretends to theoretical status but which is not reducible to empirical terms and is equivalent in meaning to intuitive, literary, and conversational terms.*

And still today, Skinner (1977) holds fast to an anticognitive approach, insisting that the critical variables that control behavior are not in the head but in the environment. The associations among words or meanings are not located in the head but in the usage—out there. According to his position, children do not change their "identities"— they do not form new concepts of themselves. Children change only because the people around them change their way of behaving toward them.

There is no doubt that in a milder form this proposition is entirely defensible, and there is no arguing with Skinner that *some* portion of variance in behavior can well be explained by an appeal to environmental contingencies. We can argue with Skinner about the proportion of variance in behavior that is so controlled, but we cannot deny that *some* proportion of variance is so controlled. Whatever remains is, therefore, controlled through internal mediation—through cognitions. This proportion of unexplained variance was probably much more apparent and important to social psychologists than to experimental psychologists.

What are some of the historical reasons which promoted the preoccupation with cognitive variables among social psychologists? **[187]**

Social Behavior Is Complex

One of the popular reasons often given for the cognitive approach is that social behavior is complex. The social environment is terribly rich and complex, social stimuli are complex, and so are social responses. Somehow, the idea has emerged that reflexive behavior—behavior that is under the control of external stimuli and reinforcement schedules—must be necessarily fairly simple. Complex behavior requires more complex contingencies, and these are hard to fix by means of reinforcements and reflexes. So if it is complex, social behavior must be mediated by thought. This argument is not terribly solid because there are all sorts of complex behavior that are not controlled by thought. Take bicycle riding. Bicycle riding cannot be taught by verbal instructions alone. Verbal instructions might not even contribute a great deal to the speed of learning, which depends mainly on getting onto the bicycle and riding it.

Emphasis on Attitudes

Social psychologists' early concern with attitudes must have played a most important role in turning social psychology to cognition. This interest was immense, and three-quarters of the text *Experimental Social Psychology,* published by Murphy, Murphy, and Newcomb in 1937, was about attitudes. Of the 559 pages of the Newcomb–Turner–Converse (1965) text *Social Psychology: The Study of Human Interaction,* 201 contain references to attitudes. Attitudes were always regarded as cognitive and affective organizations that were presumed to influence behavior.

World War II

Very significant in the heavy emphasis on cognition among social psychologists must have been the war experience. The Second World War was viewed by the Allies as a war of democracy and liberalism against the forces of fascism and authoritarianism. Opposed above all was an ideology which was racist, and which extolled the virtues of "purity" of race on biological and genetic grounds. It promoted biological solutions to social and economic problems—the extermination of entire populations. At the same time, the fascist ideology was proclaiming that its ends required social control to be maintained through discipline and obedience—unquestioning blind obedience. **[188]**

The American social psychologists—Jack Atkinson, Jerry Bruner, Angus Campbell, Doc Cartwright, Al Hastorf, Nate Maccoby, Helen Peak, Sid Rosen, Ezra Stotland, and hundreds of others who took part in that war—had values that were quite opposite to the totalitarian doctrines of Nazi Germany. They believed that the perfectibility of man is not to be found in biological or genetic solutions, but in reason, in education, and in self-imposed standards of conduct and morality. Their values are clearly seen in Lewin's *Resolving Social Conflicts* (1948), Alfred Marrow's (1967) biography of Lewin, Adorno et al.'s *The Authoritarian Personality* (1950), Asch's (1952) *Social Psychology,* and many other volumes published by social psychologists during the late forties and early fifties. The American social psychologists were all immersed in the powerful ideological trend that engulfed the Allied countries as the war's end became imminent—a trend that pervaded all branches of life, that found its embodiment in the arts, literature, and the sciences, and that was ultimately reified in the formation of the United Nations Scientific, Educational, and Cultural Organization, whose pointed motto reads: "Since wars begin in the minds of men, it is in the minds of men that the defenses of peace must be constructed."

Like other intellectuals, the American social psychologists asked themselves how it was possible for a nation like Germany, with one of the richest literary, artistic, scientific, and philosophical traditions, to change so rapidly and so dramatically, to tolerate the murder of millions and the obliteration of humanist, humanitarian, and intellectual values. They were impressed, at the same time, with the powerful Nazi propaganda machine and believed that it was propaganda which succeeded in delivering the German population to Hitler and which made that population blind to unheard of atrocities. Germany was viewed as the product of a massive attitude change—a massive *cognitive* change—which was achieved by means of extremely effective propaganda.

If political, economic, and social changes of unequaled scope can take place by virtue of persuasion, through the induction of attitudes controlled by a relatively small group of people, the role of cognitive processes in social life must be exceedingly important. How then could social psychology be anything but cognitive? Add to it the fact that among those who escaped to the United States from Nazi Germany were people like Lewin, Heider, Koehler, and Wertheimer—all not only ardently humanist and liberal but at the same time deeply committed to Gestalt psychology, whose concern was mainly with the nature of perceptual and cognitive **[189]** organization and representation—and it becomes inevitable for cognition to dominate social psychology.

The heavy emphasis on cognitive functions that characterized social psychology eventually had some impact on *experimental* psychology. There were other developments in experimental psychology which laid the ground for the cognitive approach—for example, the concern with probability learning and choice behavior. The inability of explaining in purely S-R associationistic terms several memory phenomena, such as differences between recall and recognition, made experimental psychology vulnerable to new approaches. Work on human factors and decision theory also contributed to the rising trend, and the word "cognitive" finally became acceptable among experimental psychologists in 1967. Today, one even hears the words "mind" and "consciousness."

The developments in experimental cognitive psychology have been substantial, accompanied by great methodological and theoretical sophistication. What we are witnessing today in social psychology is, therefore, somewhat surprising, for we are witnessing an attempt to import the methods and concepts of cognitive psychology into social psychology—a psychology that was cognitive all along! Many social psychologists today delight in borrowing from cognitive psychology and often indiscriminately apply their ideas, concepts, and methods to the problems of cognition.

No doubt, a great deal may be gained by building upon cognitive psychology, for substantial advances have been achieved in that field. At the same time, however, it is worth asking why is it that they—the experimental cognitive psychologists—and not we, are now pursuing problems that were natural for social psychologists of the early fifties, sixties, and seventies to pursue. Why was their present work not done by us earlier? The typical experiment in cognitive psychology today can be hardly distinguished from an early experiment in social psychology. After all, the title of Bartlett's 1932 book was *Remembering: A Study in Experimental and Social Psychology.*

There is one possible reason. Social psychologists have not dedicated more effort to developing concepts and methods for the more precise study of cognitive structures, cognitive processes, and cognitive representations—as Krech and Crutchfield (1948) admonished us to do—because they encountered difficulties by which experimental psychologists were *not* burdened. Had social psychologists been satisfied with what is done today by experimental psychologists in the area of memory and cognitive representation, this work would have been done by them ten or fifteen years ago. **[190]** The very fact that social psychologists have not engaged in the precise study of cognitive processes is a hint that social perception and social cognition are not just straightforward applications of the principles of perception and cognition to social stimuli.

Social cognition has several features, unique to its own problems, which make it a very special case. These features make social cognition qualitatively so different that the lock-stock-and-barrel application of the principles and methods of modern experimental cognitive psychology may be misleading.

SPECIAL FEATURES OF SOCIAL PERCEPTION AND SOCIAL COGNITION

Lack of Stimulus Constancy

Social information processing is an integral component of social reality. Social information processing has real effects. That is, the results of social perception often have an influence on the objects perceived. When I perceive a prospective candidate for our graduate program as being likely to succeed, this will have a completely different effect on that person than when I perceive the candidate as likely to fail. The results of nonsocial perception (if such perception exists), too, have consequences on the objects perceived. If I perceive a branch blocking my driveway, I might want to cut it down; my perception of the branch will surely affect it. But there is an obvious and important difference: The branch can do very little to defend itself against the consequences of my perception, or for that matter, to *prepare* itself for this perception. People, however, do prepare themselves for such perceptions. They are able to display desirable aspects, conceal undesirable ones, and embellish others. This observation is so obvious that it hardly needs stating. And there is, of course, a great deal of social psychological literature that deals with just that aspect of social perception. The ingratiation phenomenon (Jones, 1964) and self-handicapping (Jones and Berglas, 1978), self-monitoring (Snyder, 1974), objective self-awareness (Wicklund and Duval, 1971), evaluation apprehension (Rosenberg 1965), and many other related phenomena have been studied by social psychologists for decades, and a great deal is known about these phenomena. At the same time, it is less obvious, but certainly more troublesome, that these phenomena and our knowledge about them *have not been systematically integrated into a theory of social perception.*

More generally, the lack of stimulus constancy in social perception **[191]** means that *ordinary* psychophysics does not apply, and that its methods cannot be imported without modifications. In ordinary psychophysics we must assume that stimuli do not change upon judgment. A 1000 Hz tone or a patch of monochromatic light of a given wavelength cannot do much about the fact that they are misjudged. If a subject judges a 500 Hz tone to be higher in pitch than an 800 Hz tone, neither have any recourse in the matter. Both stimuli will simply have to suffer the indignity. Nor can they prepare themselves for a future misrepresentation on the part of the same subject or on the part of a different one. People can.

I am sure that it is this feature of social perception that has prevented social psychologists from pursuing psychophysics, in spite of Stevens' (1966; 1972) admonition. The problem is, admittedly, a difficult one but certainly not insoluble. There are at least two solutions to the problem of stimulus inconstancy. One "solution" avoids the problem altogether, substituting words for their social referents. One substitutes adjectives for actual personality features of a live person. Or one supplants "live" social stimuli by pictures, films, or stories. These studies are, in fact, impervious to the confounding described earlier. An adjective is not influenced by our perception, and it cannot adjust itself so that a future perception of it would be more favorable. Of course, a great deal can be and has been learned about social perception from just such studies, and in many cases the perception of referents of words may not differ from the perception of the words themselves. But because we cannot assume a one-to-one correspondence between language and reality, we may not take it for granted that the same principles of social perception will be generated by studying words as by studying the actual social objects for which these words stand.

The second solution is to use actual social stimuli but different psychophysics—an approach that might be called "recursive psychophysics." In this form of psychophysics, several measures are obtained in succession. Thus, for instance, a measure of the *state* of the social stimulus at time $t(n)$ is taken both prior to the *judgment* of the stimulus taken at $t(n + 1)$ and following such *judgment* taken at $t(n - 1)$. The influence of the stimulus on the judgment—that is, the typical relationship observed in psychophysical functions—is obtained by the family of curves with stimuli measured at $t(n)$ and judgments at $t(n + 1)$. The influence of the judgment on the stimulus will be obtained from the family of functions relating the judgments taken at $t(n - 1)$ to the measures of the stimulus taken at $t(n)$. The families of these functions would describe both how perception **[192]** of social stimuli varies with the nature of these stimuli and how these stimuli change as a result of perception.

Independence of Stimulus Measures

There is another problem in social perception that is similar and related to the lack of stimulus constancy. Psychophysics requires not only that the stimulus be constant under judgment but that it be measured *independently* of the judgment. This often proves to be quite difficult in social perception. In typical psychophysics of sensory dimensions, the stimuli are measured in physical measurement units, their equivalents, or other countable units. There are various social phenomena that can be so measured, or that can be measured objectively and independently of judgments. Sex, age, height, weight, and other characteristics of persons and groups, and such properties of social behavior as duration and repetition, may be described objectively. And the same could be done with estimates of intelligence, such that we could write a reasonable psychophysical function relating estimates of people's intelligence to their measured IQ or SAT scores.

But when we deal with the perception of such characteristics as likeability, generosity, altruism, or honesty, the meaning of the corresponding psychophysical functions becomes ambiguous because there are no objective and independent measures of these attributes. Generally, they are described on the basis of a consensus of judgments very much like those that we seek to quantify in our psychophysical research. Hence, the measures of the stimuli are not entirely independent of the judgments of these stimuli. Since psychophysics yields as one of its products information about perceptual accuracy, a serious problem exists. How can we determine whether a subject's estimate of people's honesty is accurate if there are no independent measures of these people's honesty?

Again, we are not completely helpless here. A solution to this problem can be obtained—a solution which might be called "psychophysical triangulation." This solution entails some bootstrapping, made possible by the various techniques of path analysis and structural equations. For example, we wish to know something about the psychophysical function of honesty, and we wish to gain this knowledge in the absence of information about the validity of measures of honesty. We will require judgments of honesty and judgments of other social attributes which 1) are related to honesty [193] and 2) can be measured objectively. Thus, for example, we may obtain judgments of income and intelligence. Both of these variables have fairly reliable and valid measures. The solution would be based on six variables: the *measures* of honesty, income, and intelligence, and the *judgments* of honesty, income, and intelligence. Required are the fifteen correlation coefficients among these six variables and a model that relates the underlying constructs to each other. The models estimated in structural equation analyses distinguish between latent variables (i.e., underlying constructs) and the measures of these constructs. The solution obtained by means of simultaneous equations describes the pattern of relations among the latent variables. A reasonable model for our example might be, for example, that the latent factor of intelligence measured by IQ has an influence on the latent factor of affluence (measured by income in dollars) and the latent factor of honesty (measured by some index or test whose true validity is not known but whose test reliability can be estimated). By means of a program (such as LISREL IV; Jöreskog and Sörbom, 1978), we can estimate the coefficient relating actual honesty to the judgments of honesty. Figure 3.1 shows both the model and a fictitious correlation matrix from which it was estimated by means of LISREL IV. This

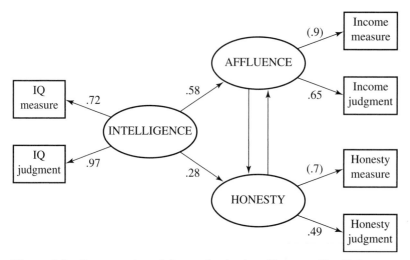

Figure 3.1 Bootstrapping of the psychophysics of honesty (Coefficients computed by Mary Grace Moore)

coefficient of .49 represents a linear relationship, whereas many psychophysical functions are of more complex forms. In order to discover the form of these functions, one could use a variety of transformations which seem reasonable and which keep the maximum residuals at their lowest values.

Once we have established an estimate of the psychophysical function for honesty in the context of its relationships to affluence and intelligence, we can get further confirmation of that psychophysical function and possibly better approximations by placing honesty in another context—with the variables of age and family size, for example. As we learn more and more about the psychophysics of honesty, the measures of honesty can be refined, and eventually honesty can be used to find psychophysical functions for other subjectively measured attributes, such as generosity or likeability. Andrews (1979) and Andrews and Crandall (1976) have employed structural equation models on survey research data in investigations of the construct validity of social indicators. Note that the problem of psychophysics for dimensions for which there is no objective measure is essentially the problem of construct validity, except that in psychophysical triangulation we are not satisfied with linear correlation coefficients but seek to establish the nature of the psychophysical functions (which are commonly power functions) more precisely. **[194]**

Affect and Cognitions

While the lack of stimulus constancy and independence are features of social cognition that derive from the particular nature of the social *stimulus,* social cognition also differs from ordinary experimental cognition in the realm of *responses.* The psychophysical judgments of a subject comparing weights or hues are for the most part dispassionate, and can be viewed as comprising primarily, or even exclusively, perceptual and cognitive elements and processes. But social perception is rarely so immaculate. In the case of social perception, responses—be they judgments or ratings—are seldom emotionally neutral. There are few social perceptions and cognitions that do not implicate affect in some significant way. The role of affect in social perception constituted one of the major concerns of the pioneer social psychologists such as McDougall and Ross. Thus, for example, McDougall (1908) gave special prominence to the *sympathetic induction of emotion* as one of the basic problems of social psychology. And the widespread concern of social psychologists with attitudes that persist unabated further testifies to the importance of affective phenomena in social psychological research.

To some extent, affect is implicated in *all* perception (Zajonc, 1979). It is difficult, for example, to look at patches of hue without experiencing some emotional reactions, and a 1000 Hz pure tone might be music to **[195]** some ears. Social perception contains affective elements because it is, above all, highly *evaluative*. There is hardly any social phenomenon—person, behavior, group, the product of some individual's work—which we perceive without at the same time having some form of reaction which can be described best on the good-bad, pleasant-unpleasant, safe-unsafe, likable-dislikable, and other such scales. To judge people as intelligent or stupid is not only to assign them to locations on the dimension of intelligence but also to make value judgments that may have profound consequences for them.

I have argued recently (Zajonc, 1979) that the affective reaction often, if not always, precedes the cognitive process. If it in fact precedes that process, affect can have extensive effects on the entire cognitive process. Affect might give it direction by diverting attention to some stimuli or some aspects of the stimuli to the exclusion of others. Affect can act selectively on the encoding of information. Thus, for example, Bower, Monteiro, and Gilligan (1979) hypnotized subjects to be in good or bad moods and found that the mood present during the learning of word lists had a distinct effect on retrieval.

Social psychologists are well aware of the detrimental effects of affect on social cognition. Stereotyping and prejudice are clearly affective phenomena which reduce the accuracy of social perception, to the clear detriment of the persons and groups so perceived. There is substantial literature on stereotyping and prejudice, and we know a great deal about the conditions under which they occur and how hard it is to eradicate them. But we know very little in this respect about the ways in which the affective components in these phenomena interact with the cognitive components to yield predispositions that are so robust.

Psychoanalytic theory also regards affect as a troublemaker. Affect pushes thoughts and impulses into the unconscious, prevents us from confronting reality, which it tends to distort, and gives us phobias and compulsions. As such, one would consider it primarily an important source of interference to efficient information processing.

But affect can also have facilitating effects on cognition. Above all, affectively charged stimuli can be discriminated at lower levels of stimulus energy than neutral stimuli, a finding which was once controversial but which is rapidly becoming much less so (Dixon, 1971; Erdelyi, 1974). For instance, when the words "happy" or "sad" are shown subliminally in association with a picture of a face, they influence the subject's perception of that face (Smith et al., 1959), a finding which was replicated recently **[196]** with words presented through the auditory channel and also subliminally (Henley, 1975).

Affective Discriminations and Cognitive Discriminations

Attitudes, stereotypes, prejudice, phobias, fixations, and related phenomena are structures combining affect and cognition. They are products of complex interactions between affective and cognitive processes. Thus, affect participates heavily in the processing of social information. The precise nature of this participation is not yet altogether clear, but that affect *is* deeply implicated in social information processing can hardly be questioned today.

The earlier writers, such as Shand (1896), McDougall (1908), and Bartlett (1932), attributed to affect an independent source of effects. Wundt (1907), too, treated affect as primary in consciousness and conjectured that it *precedes* ideational elements in both perception and retrieval. During the forties and fifties, however, affect had been treated more as a "quality" of the perceptual experience than as an independent process. Thus, for example, the work of Asch (1946) on impression formation or of Heider (1958) on the representation of affect in interpersonal relationships absorbed affect into cognitive processes. In the context of these approaches, the attractiveness of certain traits of people, the value of their actions and intentions, the appeal of certain properties of products was not regarded as being particularly distinct from such attributes as, for instance, height in the case of people, speed in the case of actions, or weight in the case of products. Yet it is becoming increasingly clear that affect may not be treated as residing in stimuli, for affect is, above all, a reaction of the organism. Affective reactions to stimuli may readily change without any changes in these stimuli. With time we become attached to some objects and bored with others, and previously neutral stimuli can be conditioned to approach or avoidance reactions by means of simple conditioning procedures.

Thus, the early versions of affect may not have been far off the mark. Recent evidence indeed suggests that affective phenomena may represent a process that is partly independent and separate from cognition (Zajonc, 1979). As such, it can interfere with cognitive processes under some conditions or make information processing more efficient under others. The independent and primary role of affect in information processing has been shown especially clearly in the context of exposure effects. These effects [197] consist of increased preference for stimuli which is generated solely as a function of repeated exposures. It has been conventionally thought, since the work of Titchener (1910), that the increased preference which is associated with familiarization through exposure occurs because of the subjective feelings of recognition. Yet a number of studies (Matlin, 1971; Moreland and Zajonc, 1977; 1979) have shown that with recognition memory held constant, the effects of repeated exposure are still quite pronounced. In an ingenious experiment, Wilson (1975; 1979) controlled for recognition experimentally. He used the dichotic listening procedure, whereby random melodies were presented several times to one ear while the subject shadowed a story read to the other ear. Under these conditions, the melodies were seldom heard, and a subsequent recognition memory test revealed that the subjects could not recognize these melodies at better than the chance level. Yet under these conditions, stimuli exposed frequently were liked significantly better than stimuli not previously encountered even though the subjects could not distinguish the former from the latter. These results were replicated in the visual mode by Kunst-Wilson and Zajonc (1980), who exposed polygons for brief intervals and later checked for recognition memory and liking. In this study, 67 percent of subjects liked objectively old stimuli better than objectively new stimuli, but only 21 percent were able to distinguish between them as being old or new at a level better than chance. Moreover, 71 percent of the subjects manifested better discrimination between the old and new stimuli using liking as their response than using "old-new" as their response. In addition, their liking responses were more reliable, and were made with greater confidence and greater speed.

Affect can also enhance memory. For example, Kleinsmith and Kaplan (1963; 1964) found that emotional words are remembered less well on immediate recall tests but show strong reminiscence effects on recall tests administered as much as one week later. Of these words, only 10 percent were recalled correctly two hours after learning, but over 40 percent in one experiment and over 30 percent in another were remembered when tests were given one week later. On the other hand, low arousal words show the typical decay function, starting with 45 percent recall two hours after learning and declining to less than 10 percent after one week. Sadella and Loftness (1972) asked subjects to form pleasant and unpleasant images in association to some words. For other words they asked them to make associations that were emotionally neutral. The recall of these words was **[198]** much better when they were accompanied by emotional imagery (good *or* bad) than when they were accompanied by neutral imagery.

Recall and recognition of words and of photographs of faces is considerably enhanced when, prior to tests, subjects are given these stimuli to view under conditions that require some affective involvement. Thus, for example, if words are judged for pleasantness, they are recalled better than when they are judged for the number of letters (Hyde and Jenkins, 1969). When photographs of faces are judged for likeability or honesty, they too are remembered better than when they are judged for sex (Bower and Karlin, 1974) or other physical attributes, such as distance between the eyes or thickness of lips (Patterson and Baddeley, 1977).

Involvement of the Self

There are few nontrivial phenomena in social cognition that do not involve the self in one way or another. Already at the turn of the century, the self was the center of social psychological inquiry and analysis. In the writings of McDougall (1908), the self-regarding sentiment was conceived of as the summit of the hierarchical organization of attitudes, and the self was equally prominent in the social psychological concepts developed by Cooley (1902) and Mead (1934). The most extensive analysis of the role of the self in social perception, however, was not undertaken until the late forties, when Combs and Snygg (1949) published their work, which regarded the self as an essential component of all perceptual and cognitive processes. Various areas of social psychological research implicated the self in many ways. For example, the research on social judgments (Sherif and Hovland, 1961) has shown powerful influences of the individual's position on attitudinal judgments, and it is customary today to attribute to the self an essential role in the experience of dissonance (Abelson et al., 1968).

Above all, social perception is highly *evaluative*. As such, it must invoke standards and comparisons. These standards and comparisons are derived from cognitive structures that comprise the self; in turn, the self is vulnerable to the individual's perception of others and others' behavior. Thus, by imposing our standards on these judgments, we necessarily implicate ourselves in the judgments. The judgments are influenced by the cognitive components comprising the self, and once made, they feed back into those components.

In general, preferences necessarily implicate the self. When stimuli **[199]** are judged for such properties as weight, pitch, or brightness, the subjects' psychophysical function orders the stimuli on what Coombs (1964) calls the I-scale. I-scales are scaled stimuli ordered with respect to some property of theirs. However, when subjects judge stimuli with respect to preferences, the scale that emerges is the so-called J-scale—a scale on which stimuli are ordered jointly with the individual's ideal point on that dimension.

When such judgments are made with respect to social attributes, the implication of the self takes on added significance. Consider judgments of intelligence or honesty, for example. When one judges the intelligence of a person, one invokes a set of values. The decision that the person is intelligent carries very different evaluative components than the judgment that the person is unintelligent. And to judge someone on the dimension of intelligence is simultaneously not only to evaluate that person but to judge and *evaluate oneself* as well. Judgments of other people on socially significant dimensions often involve some degree of invidious comparison. When a subject judges the intelligence or honesty of a group or category of persons, he or she must consider the distribution of this attribute in the population, and with this subjective impression of the distribution will also come the individual's own location on that dimension. If the cues are such as to reveal the judged persons to be of substantial intelligence, the prior impression of the distribution of intelligence may have to be revised and one's own position on it displaced. One may discover that one is less intelligent relative to the population than previously thought. Or more intelligent. The early theorizing about the risky shift phenomenon involved just such an assumption about the distribution of risk preferences and the individual's position on the dimension of risk (Brown, 1965).

Because the self is highly charged with affect, because it resists derogation and, more generally, information that may require extensive changes,[1] the judgments of others may be powerfully influenced in a variety of ways. Markus and Smith (1980) have recently reviewed the pervasive effects of self-schemas on the perception of others, revealing various categories of influence.

In the previous examples, the participation of the self in perception acts mainly to the detriment of accuracy and efficiency. But this need not be so in all instances. Like affect, the involvement of the self can also have beneficial effects on the processing of social information. Thus, **[200]** when adjectives are rated for self-reference—that is, when the subject is asked whether the adjective applies to him or to her—rather than whether it has the same meaning as some other word, for example, and recognition memory tests are administered later on these adjectives shown with an equal number of distractor adjectives, recall is much better when the prior task requires self-reference than when it requires comparison of meanings. Rogers, Kuiper, and Kirker (1977) found that more than twice as many self-reference items were recalled than meaning-comparison items under these conditions. Keenan and Bailett (1979), using recognition measures rather than recall, replicated the Rogers-Kuiper-Kirker results, adding the

---

[1] A.G. Greenwald. The totalitarian ego: Fabrication and revision of personal history. In press. *American Psychologist.*

finding that not only are self-reference items easier to recognize on later tests but that the recognition judgments are made much faster for these items than for others.

Social Perception Recruits Explanation as a Slave Process

There is an overpowering tendency to view social behavior and social phenomena as having *origins* and *causes,* and to view actors as having *intentions.* An action is not seen simply as a sequence of muscle twitches and motor movements: It is perceived as being goal directed and having its origins in some state of the individual, such as motive, intention, or habit. When perceived, all social behavior begs for explanation. When we see a man sitting quietly on a park bench, we ask ourselves, why is it that he sits so quietly? When we see a man fidgeting on a park bench, we ask ourselves with equal curiosity, why is it that he is fidgeting? Of course, we stop and pay special attention to the causes of behavior that appear strange, bizarre, or deviant. But we do not ignore the causes of *modal* behavior. Modal behavior, too, is perceived as being determined, as having underlying causes, purposes, or intentions, and these antecedents are perceived as integral parts of the actions on which we focus. People walking in the streets at 8 A.M. are not just seen walking—they are seen going to their jobs. And the same people seen walking at 5 P.M. are seen going home. Their intentions, feelings, anticipations, and purposes are seen in an entirely different light. When I see a man run, I am simultaneously aware of the direction of his progress, I am imagining his destination, and I have some awareness of where he must have come from. From the speed, manner, attire, and context, I perceive immediately and directly not just someone running, but I see a jogger, a thief escaping the police, or someone trying to catch a bus. **[201]**

There is, of course, some tendency to seek explanations for nonsocial events, too. But this tendency is much more pronounced in social cognition because the demands of everyday life make it much more important for us to know the causes of the behavior of other humans than to know the causes of the physical aspects of our environment. We can easily survive without knowing the causes of rainbows and southerly winds. But it is more difficult if we are not familiar with the causes of people's anger and rage, or with the sources of their affection.

Seeking to explain social behavior has consequences for processing social information—consequences that reveal how important this aspect of social behavior might be. In a recent study, Bower and Masling[2] gave subjects some bizarre correlations to study. Examples of these correlations are: "As the number of hockey games increases, the amount of electricity increases," or "As the number of fire hydrants in an area decreases, the crime rate increases." In one group, the subjects simply had to study these statements of correlations. In another, they were supplied with explanations of why these relationships held. And in a third group, the subjects had to discover explanations by themselves. Following this initial task, they were tested in a paired-associates manner, such that the independent variable was supplied and the subject had to recall the dependent variable and the direction of the relationship. Subjects who generated explanations by themselves were able to recall 73 percent of the statements. But the study group remembered only

[2] G.H. Bower and M. Masling. Causal explanations as mediators for remembering correlations. Unpublished manuscript, Stanford University, 1979.

39 percent of the statements, while the group that was supplied with explanations did not perform much better: they remembered 45 percent of the correlations.

Even more interesting was the fact that correlations which the subjects succeeded in explaining in the time allowed (15 sec.) were remembered considerably better than those which they tried to explain but were unable to do so: 81 versus 57 percent. So, it would appear that if we wish our students to learn psychological laws, we should allow them to prove these laws by themselves.

CONCLUSION

Upon closer examination, social perception and social cognition reveal features that make them quite distinct from their counterparts that are studied by experimental psychologists. Social perception and social cognition [202] create a social reality by affecting both the perceiver and the objects perceived. And even though not all of social reality is a function of social perception, a great deal of it is profoundly influenced by the way individuals view each other and the social world in which they live. Thus, I have argued, social perception requires equal attention on both sides: on the side of the observer or perceiver and on the side of the objects perceived. The ubiquity of affect as a companion, antecedent, and product of social cognition makes the study of social information processing as a dispassionate, computer-like activity less than an accurate representation of what is actually going on. Had these properties of social cognition been present only occasionally, it would have been most efficient simply to apply to social perception the methods and principles of cognitive psychology as they have been developed in experimental approaches, treating social perception as a special case. But the absence of object-observer interaction, the absence of affect and of the involvement of the self, are rather exceptional in social perception and cognition. It is thus more appropriate to view these phenomena as the general case and those studied by experimental psychologists as special cases in which these crucial factors and parameters have been arbitrarily set equal to zero.

The current interest among experimental cognitive psychologists in story grammars, scripts or schemas, mood effects, comprehension, artificial intelligence, and generally in the more complex forms of information processing indicates that the verbal learning tradition may have spawned oversimplified cognitive models. The perception and cognition of everyday nonsocial objects often acquire human and social qualities. The anthropomorphic metaphor is the most common one. We speak of vicious storms, fussy car engines, friendly fires, gloomy days, unruly hair, deceptive currents, and lazy rivers. David Rapaport has reminded us that "all sciences are anthropomorphic at the beginning, and all of them attempt to get away from this feature.... This is how the concept of 'forces' came about: on the basis of [man's] own experience, he knows that something can be made to happen by him if he uses force" (Gill, 1967, p. 179). Abstract line figures made into animated film sequences are seen as having intentions, goals, and conflicts (Heider and Simmel, 1944). Thus, the theoretical and empirical contradictions which appear with increasing frequency in the cognitive psychology that emerged from the verbal learning tradition are being generated, perhaps, because some critical features of information processing that cognition shares with social cognition have been ignored. The conclusion that forces itself upon us is that social perception [203] and social cognition are *not* special cases of perception and cognition. And it will simply not do, therefore, for social psychologists to apply—simply and blindly—the principles, methods, and empirical findings of experimental cognitive psychology to the problems of social perception. For social perception is not the special case. It is experimental cognition which is the special case—a case, as I said, in which the critical variables and parameters have been arranged to have zero values. It is social perception that represents the general case. Perhaps we will not understand perception fully *unless* we understand social perception.

In this respect, Simon's recent (1976) observation is interesting. He said that cognitive social psychology is simply a special case of cognitive psychology, whereas I have thought of it here the other way around. He argued his position on the grounds that "it is not plausible that the processes of the human brain that handle social situations are quite distinct from the processes that handle other situations" (p. 258). While Simon's faith in a common set of processes is entirely shared in this chapter, it must be noted at the same time that the experimental paradigms and the theoretical constructs of traditional cognitive psychology have, thus far, *not accommodated* the special needs and features of social cognition such as I described here. Those paradigms and constructs apply to a rather limited domain of information processing within which only some fairly restricted problems in social information processing can be studied. And, thus, Simon acknowledged that cognitive psychology requires some social psychological knowledge, too, although the social psychological knowledge that he sought for cognitive psychology was that of individual differences. The special dynamic features of social information processing—particularly the dependence of the objects of perception on the perceiver and their capacity to alter themselves—suggest that a general cognitive psychology requires considerably more from social psychology than information about individual differences. **[204]**

REFERENCES

Abelson, R.P., Aronson, E., McGuire, W.J., Newcomb, T.M., Rosenberg, M.J., and Tannenbaum, P. *Theories of cognitive consistency: A sourcebook*. Chicago: Rand McNally, 1968.

Adorno, T.W., Frenkel-Brunswick, E., Levinson, D., and Sanford, R.N. *The authoritarian personality*. New York: Harper & Row, 1950.

Allport, G.W. The historical background of modern social psychology. In G. Lindzey (Ed.), *Handbook of social psychology*. Vol. I., Cambridge, MA: Addison-Wesley, 1954, p. 3–56.

Andrews, F.M. Estimating the construct validity and correlated error components of the rated-effectiveness measures. In F.M. Andrews (Ed.) *Scientific productivity*, Cambridge: Cambridge University Press, 1979, pp. 405–422.

Andrews, F.M., and Crandall, R. The validity of measures of self-reported well-being. *Social Indicators Research*, 1976, **3**, 1–19.

Asch, S. *Social psychology*. Englewood Cliffs, NJ: Prentice-Hall, 1952.

Asch, S.E. Forming impressions of personality. *Journal of Abnormal and Social Psychology*, 1946, **41**, 258–290.

Back, K. The exerion of influence through social communication. *Journal of Abnormal and Social Psychology*, 1951, **46**, 9–23.

Bartlett, F.C. *Remembering: A study in experimental and social psychology*. Cambridge: Cambridge University Press, 1932.

Blake, R.R., Rosenbaum, M., and Duryea, R. Gift-giving as a function of group standards. *Human Relations*, 1955, **8**, 61–73.

Bower, G.H. and Karlin, M.B. Depth of processing pictures of faces and recognition memory. *Journal of Experimental Psychology*, 1974, **103**, 751–757.

Brown, R. *Social psychology*. New York: Free Press, 1965.

Byrne, D. Interpersonal attraction and attitude similarity. *Journal of Abnormal and Social Psychology*, 1961, **62**, 713–715.

Combs, A.W. and Snygg, D. *Individual behavior: A perceptual approach to behavior*. New York: Harper & Brothers, 1949.

Cooley, C.H. *Human nature and the social order*. New York: Scribner, 1902.

Coombs, C.H. *A theory of data*. New York: Wiley, 1964.

Darley, J.M. and Latane, B. Bystander intervention in emergencies: Diffusion of responsibility. *Journal of Personality and Social Psychology*, 1968, **8**, 377–383.

Dixon, N.F. *Subliminal perception: The nature of a controversy*. London: McGraw-Hill, 1971.

Erdelyi, M.H. A new look at the New Look: Perceptual defense and vigilance. *Psychological Review*, 1974, **81**, 1–25.

Fenigstein, A., and Carver, C.S. Self-focusing effects of heartbeat feedback. *Journal of Personality and Social Psychology*, 1978, **11**, 1241–1250.

Gill, M. *The collected papers of David Rapaport*.

Heider, F. *The psychology of interpersonal relations*. New York: Wiley, 1958.

Heider, F., and Simmel, M. An experimental study of apparent movement. *American Journal of Psychology*, 1944, **57**, 243–259.

Henley, S.H.A. Cross modal effects of subliminal verbal stimuli. *Scandinavian Journal of Psychology*, 1975, **16**, 30–36.

Hunt, P.J., and Hillery, J.M. Social facilitation in coaction setting: An examination of the effects over learning trials. *Journal of Experimental Social Psychology*, 1973, **9**, 563–571.

Hyde, T.W., and Jenkins, J.J. The differential effects of incidental tasks on the organization of recall of a list of highly associated words. *Journal of Experimental Psychology*. 1969, **82**, 472–481.

Innes, J.M. and Young, R.F. The effect of presence of an audience, evaluation apprehension and objective self-awareness on learning. *Journal of Experimental Social Psychology*, 1975, **11**, 35–42.

Jones, E.E. *Ingratiation*, New York: Appleton, Century, Crofts, 1964.

Jones, E.E., and Berglas, S. Control of attributions about the self through self-handicapping strategies: The appeal of alcohol and the role of underachievement. *Personality and Social Psychology Bulletin*, 1978, **4**, 200–206.

Joreskog, K.G. and Sorbom, D. *LISREL IV*. Chicago: National Educational Resources, Inc., 1978.

Keenan, J.M. and Bailett, S.D. Memory for personally and socially significant events. In R. S. Nickerson (Ed.), *Attention and performance VIII*. Hillsdale, NJ: Lawrence Erlbaum Associates, 1979.

Kleinsmith, L.J. and Kaplan, S. Paired associate learning as a function of arousal and interpolated interval. *Journal of Experimental Psychology*, 1963, **65**, 190–193.

Kleinsmith, L.J. and Kaplan, S. Interaction of arousal and recall interval in nonsense syllable paired-associate learning. *Journal of Experimental Psychology*, 1964, **67**, 124–126.

Koller, P.S. and Kaplan, R.M. A two-process theory of learned helplessness, *Journal of Personality and Social Psychology*, 1978, **36**, 1177–1183.

Krech, D., and Crutchfield, R. S. *Theory and problems of social psychology*. New York: McGraw-Hill, 1948.

Lewin, K. *Resolving social conflicts*. New York: Harper & Brothers, 1948.

Lott, B. Behavioral concordance with sex role ideology related to play areas, creativity, and parental sex typing of children. *Journal of Personality and Social Psychology*, 1978, **36**, 1087–1100.

McDougall, W. *Introduction to social psychology*. London: Methuen, 1908.

Markus, H., and Smith, J. The influence of self-schemas on the perception of others. In N. Cantor and J. Kihlstrom (Eds.), *Personality and cognition*. Hillsdale, NJ: Lawrence Erlbaum Associates, 1980.

Matlin, M.W. Response competition, recognition, and affect. *Journal of Personality and Social Psychology*, 1971, 295–300.

Marrow, A. *The practical theorist*.

Mead, G.H. *Mind, self and society*, Chicago: University of Chicago Press, 1934.

Milgram, S., Behavioral study of obedience. *Journal of Abnormal and Social Psychology*, 1963, **67**, 371–378.

Moreland, R.L. and Zajonc, R.B. Is stimulus recognition a necessary condition for the occurrence of exposure effects? *Journal of Personality and Social Psychology*, 1977, **35**, 191–199.

Moreland, R.L. and Zajonc, R.B. Exposure effects may not depend on stimulus recognition. *Journal of Personality and Social Psychology*, 1979, **32**, 1085–1089.

Murphy, G., Murphy, L.B. and Newcomb, T.M. *Experimental social psychology* (rev. ed.). New York: Harper, 1937.

Neisser, U. *Cognitive Psychology*. Englewood, NJ: Prentice Hall, 1967.

Newcomb, T.M., Turner, R.H., and Converse, P.E. *Social psychology: The study of human interaction*. New York: Holt, Rinehart, & Winston, 1965.

Patterson, K.E. and Baddeley, A.D. When face recognition fails. *Journal of Experimental Psychology: Human Learning and Memory,* 1977, **3**, 406–417.

Powell, F.A. Source credibility and behavioral compliance as determinants of attitude change. *Journal of Personality and Social Psychology*, 1965, **2**, 669–676.

Rogers, T.B., Kuiper, N.A. and Kirker, W.S. Self-reference and the encoding of personal information. *Journal of Personality and Social Psychology*, 1977, **35**, 677–688.

Rosenberg, J.J. When dissonance fails: On discriminating evaluation apprehension from attitude measurement. *Journal of Personality and Social Psychology*, 1965, **1**, 28–42.

Sadella, E.K. and Loftness, S. Emotional images as mediators in one-trial paired-associates learning. *Journal of Experimental Psychology*, 1972, **95**, 295–298.

Shand, A. Character and the emotions. *Mind*, 1896, **21**, 203–342.

Sherif, M. and Hovland, C.I. *Social judgment: Assimilation and contrast effects in communication and attitude change*. New Haven: Yale University Press, 1961.

Simon, H.A. Discussion: Cognition and social psychology. In J. S. Carroll and J. W. Payne (Eds.), *Cognition and social behavior*. Hillsdale, NJ: Lawrence Erlbaum Associates, 1976, pp. 253–268.

Skinner, B.F. Why I am not a cognitive psychologist. *Behaviorism*, 1977, **5**, 1–10.

Smith, G.J.W., Spence, D.P. and Klein, D.S. Subliminal effects of verbal stimuli. *Journal of Abnormal and Social Psychology*, 1959, **50**, 167–176.

Snyder, M. Self-monitoring of expressive behavior. *Journal of Personality and Social Psychology*, 1974, **30**, 526–537.

Snyder, M., and Swann, W.B., Jr. Hypothesis-testing processes in social interaction. *Journal of Personality and Social Psychology*, 1978, **11**, 1202–1212.

Stevens, S.S. A metric for social consensus. *Science*, 1966, **151**, 530–541.

Stevens, S.S. *Psychophysics and social scaling*. Morristown, NJ: Bobbs-Merrill, 1972.

Verplanck, W.S. A glossary of some terms used in the objective science of behavior. *Psychological Review*, 1957, **64**, Supplement, Part 2.

Wicklund, R.A., Duval, S. Opinion change and performance facilitation as a result of objective self awareness. *Journal of Experimental Social Psychology*, 1971, **7**, 319–342.

Wilson, W.R. Unobtrusive induction of positive attitudes. Unpublished doctoral dissertation, University of Michigan, 1975.

Wilson, W.R. Feeling more than we can know: Exposure effects without learning. *Journal of Personality and Social Psychology*, 1979, **37**, 811–821.

Wundt, W. *Outlines of psychology*. Leipzig: Wilhelm Englemann, 1907.

Zajonc, R.B. Feeling and thinking: Preferences need no inferences. Paper delivered at the meeting of the American Psychological Association, New York, September, 1979. Preparation of this work was supported by a Fellowship from the John S. Guggenheim Foundation.

REFERENCE NOTES

1. Bower, G.H., Monteiro, K.P., and Gilligan, S.G. Emotional mood as a context for learning and recall. Unpublished manuscript, Stanford, CA, 1979.

2. Wilson, W.R., and Zajonc, R.B. Affective discrimination of stimuli which cannot be recognized. Under editorial review.

3. Greenwald, A.G. The totalitarian ego: Fabrication and revision of personal history. In press.

4. Bower, G.H. and Masling, M. Causal explanations as mediators for remembering correlations. Unpublished manuscript, Stanford University, 1979.

Part Two

Social Facilitation: The Minimal Social Influence

Chapter 4

Social Facilitation

R.B. Zajonc
University of Michigan

Most textbook definitions of social psychology involve considerations about the influence of man upon man, or, more generally, of individual upon individual. And most of them, explicitly or implicitly, commit the main efforts of social psychology to the problem of how and why the *behavior* of one individual affects the behavior of another. The influences of individuals on each others' behavior which are of interest to social psychologists today take on very complex forms. Often they involve vast networks of interindividual effects, such as one finds in studying the process of group decision–making, competition, or conformity to a group norm. But the fundamental forms of interindividual influence are represented by the oldest experimental paradigm of social psychology: social facilitation. This paradigm, dating back to Triplett's original experiments on pacing and competition, carried out in 1897 (*1*), examines the consequences upon behavior which derive from the sheer presence of other individuals.

Until the late 1930s, interest in social facilitation was quite active, but with the outbreak of World War II it suddenly died. And it is truly regrettable that it died, because the basic questions about social facilitation—its dynamics and its causes— which are in effect the basic questions of social psychology, were never solved. It is with these questions that this article is concerned. I first examine past results in this nearly completely abandoned area of research and then suggest a general hypothesis which might explain them.

Research in the area of social facilitation may be classified in terms of two experimental paradigms: audience effects and co-action effects. The first experimental paradigm involves the observation of behavior when it occurs in the presence of passive spectators. The second examines behavior when it occurs in the presence of other individuals also engaged in the same activity. We shall consider past literature in these two areas separately.

AUDIENCE EFFECTS

Simple motor responses are particularly sensitive to social facilitation effects. In 1925 Travis (*2*) obtained such effects in a study in which he used the pursuit-rotor task. In this task the subject is required to follow a small revolving target by means of a stylus which he holds in his hand. If the stylus is even momentarily off target during a revolution, the revolution counts as an error. First each subject was trained for several consecutive days until his performance reached a stable level. One day after the conclusion of the training, the subject was called to the laboratory, given five trials alone, and then ten trials in the presence of from four to eight upperclassmen and graduate students. They had been asked by the experimenter to watch the subject quietly and attentively. Travis found a clear improvement in performance when his subjects were confronted with an audience. Their accuracy on the ten trials before an audience [269]* was greater than on any ten previous trials, including those on which they had scored highest.

A considerably greater improvement in performance was recently obtained in a somewhat different setting and on a different task (*3*). Each subject (all were National Guard trainees) was placed in a separate booth. He was seated in front of a panel outfitted with 20 red lamps in a circle. The lamps on this panel light in a clockwise sequence at 12 revolutions per minute. At random intervals, one or another light fails to go on in its proper sequence. On the average there are 24 such failures per hour. The subject's task is to signal whenever a light fails to go on. After 20 minutes of intensive training, followed by a short rest, the National Guard trainees monitored the light panels for 135 minutes. Subjects in one group performed their task alone. Subjects in another group were told that from time to time a lieutenant colonel or a master sergeant would visit them in the booth to observe their performance. These visits actually took place about four times during the experimental session. There was no doubt about the results. The accuracy of the supervised subjects was on the average 34 percent higher than the accuracy of the trainees working in isolation, and toward the end of the experimental session, the accuracy of the supervised subjects was more than twice as high as that of the subjects working in isolation. Those expecting to be visited by a superior missed, during the last experimental period, 20 percent of the light failures, while those expecting no such visits missed 64 percent of the failures.

Dashiell, who, in the early 1930s, carried out an extensive program of research on social facilitation, also found considerable improvement in performance due to audience effects on such tasks as simple multiplication or word association (*4*). But, as is the case in many other areas, negative audience effects were also found. In 1933 Pessin asked college students to learn lists of nonsense syllables under two conditions: alone and in the presence of several spectators (*5*). When confronted with an audience, his subjects required an average of 11.27 trials to learn a seven-item list. When working alone they needed only 9.85 trials. The average number of errors made in the "audience" condition was considerably higher than the number in the "alone" condition. In 1931 Husband found that the presence of spectators interferes with the learning of a finger maze (*6*), and in 1933 Pessin and Husband (*7*) confirmed Husband's results. The

* Bracketed bold numbers refer to original page numbers. Page numbers indicate where the original page ended.

number of trials which the isolated subjects required for learning the finger maze was 17.1. Subjects confronted with spectators, however, required 19.1 trials. The average number of errors for the isolated subjects was 33.7; the number for those working in the presence of an audience was 40.5.

The results thus far reviewed seem to contradict one another. On a pursuit-rotor task, Travis found that the presence of an audience improves performance. The learning of nonsense syllables and maze learning, however, seem to be inhibited by the presence of an audience, as shown by Pessin's experiment. The picture is further complicated by the fact that when Pessin's subjects were asked several days later to recall the nonsense syllables they had learned, a reversal was found. The subjects who tried to recall the lists in the presence of spectators did considerably better than those who tried to recall them alone. Why are the learning of nonsense syllables and maze learning inhibited by the presence of spectators? And why, on the other hand, does performance on a pursuit-rotor, word-association, multiplication, or a vigilance task improve in the presence of others?

There is just one, rather subtle, consistency in the results. It would appear that the emission of well–learned responses is facilitated by the presence of spectators, while the acquisition of new responses is impaired. To put the statement in conventional psychological language, performance is facilitated and learning is impaired by the presence of spectators.

This tentative generalization can be reformulated so that different features of the problem are placed into focus. During the early stages of learning, especially of the type involved in social facilitation studies, the subject's responses are mostly the wrong ones. A person learning a finger maze, or a person learning a list of nonsense syllables, emits more wrong responses than right ones in the early stages of training. Most learning experiments continue until he ceases to make mistakes—until his performance is perfect. It may be said, therefore, that during training, it is primarily the wrong responses which are dominant and strong; they are the ones which have the highest probability of occurrence. But after the individual has mastered the task, correct responses necessarily gain ascendancy in his task-relevant behavioral repertoire. Now they are the ones which are more probable—in other words, dominant. Our tentative generalization may now be simplified: audience enhances the emission of dominant responses. If the dominant responses are the correct ones, as is the case upon achieving mastery, the presence of an audience will be of benefit to the individual. But if they are mostly wrong, as is the case in the early stages of learning, then these wrong responses will be enhanced in the presence of an audience, and the emission of correct responses will be postponed or prevented.

There is a class of psychological processes which is known to enhance the emission of dominant responses. They are subsumed under the concepts of drive, arousal, and activation (8). If we could show that the presence of an audience has arousal consequences for the subject, we would be a step further along in trying to arrange the results of social-facilitation experiments into a neater package. But let us first consider another set of experimental findings.

CO-ACTION EFFECTS

The experimental paradigm of co–action is somewhat more complex than the paradigm involved in the study of audience effects. Here we observe individuals all simultaneously engaged in the same activity and in full view of each other. One of the clearest effects of such simultaneous action, or co-action, is found in eating behavior. It is, well known that animals simply eat **[270]** more in the presence of others. For instance, Bayer had chickens eat from a pile of wheat to their full satisfaction (9). He waited some time to be absolutely sure that his subject would eat no more, and then brought in a companion chicken that had not eaten for 24 hours. Upon the introduction of the hungry co-actor, the apparently sated chicken ate two-thirds again as much grain as it had already eaten. Recent work by Tolman and Wilson fully substantiates these results (10). In an extensive study of social-facilitation effects among albino rats, Harlow found dramatic increases in eating (11). In one of his experiments, for instance, the rats, shortly after weaning, were matched in pairs for weight. They were then fed alone and in pairs on alternate days. Figure 4.1 shows his results. It is clear that considerably more food was consumed by the animals when they were in pairs than when they were fed alone. James (12), too, found very clear evidence of increased eating among puppies fed in groups.

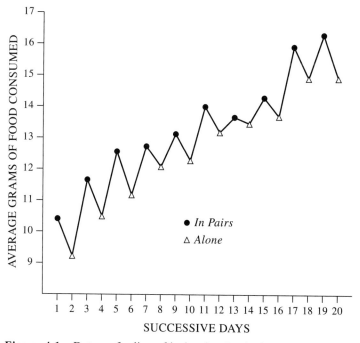

Figure 4.1   Data on feeding of isolated and paired rats. [Harlow (11)]

Perhaps the most dramatic effect of co-action is reported by Chen (*13*). Chen observed groups of ants working alone, in groups of two, and in groups of three. Each ant was observed under various conditions. In the first experimental session, each ant was placed in a bottle half filled with sandy soil. The ant was observed for 6 hours. The time at which nest-building began was noted, and the earth excavated by the insect was carefully weighed. Two days afterward, the same ants were placed in freshly filled bottles in pairs, and the same observations were made. A few days later the ants were placed in the bottles in groups of three, again for 6 hours. Finally, a few days after the test in groups of three, nest-building of the ants in isolation was observed. Figure 4.2 shows some of Chen's data.

There is absolutely no question that the amount of work an ant accomplishes increases markedly in the presence of another ant. In all pairs except one, the presence of a companion increased output by a factor of at least 2. The effect of co-action on the latency of the nest-building behavior was equally dramatic. The solitary ants of session 1 and the final session began working on the nest in 192 minutes, on the average. The latency period for ants in groups of two was only 28 minutes. The effects observed by Chen were limited to the immediate situation and seemed to have no lasting consequences for the ants. There were no differences in the results of session 1, during which the ants worked in isolation, and of the last experimental session, where they again worked in solitude.

If one assumes that under the conditions of Chen's experiment nest-building *is* the dominant response, then there is no reason why his findings could not be embraced by the generalization just proposed. Nest-building is a response which Chen's ants have fully mastered. Certainly, it is something that a mature ant need not learn. And this is

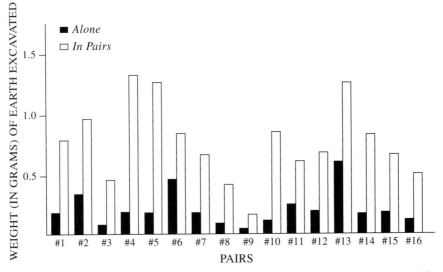

Figure 4.2   Data on nest-building behavior of isolated and paired ants. [Chen (*13*)]

simply an instance where the generalization that the presence of others enhances the emission of dominant and well-developed responses holds.

If the process involved in audience effects is also involved in co-action effects, then learning should be inhibited in the presence of other learners. Let us examine some literature in this field. Klopfer (*14*) observed greenfinches—in isolation and in heterosexual pairs—which were learning to discriminate between sources of palatable and of unpalatable food. And, as one would by now expect, his birds learned this discrimination task considerably more efficiently when working alone. I hasten to add that the subjects' sexual interests cannot be held responsible for the inhibition of learning in the paired birds. Allee and Masure, using Australian parakeets, obtained the same result for homosexual pairs as well (*15*). The speed of learning was considerably greater for the isolated birds than for the paired birds, regardless of whether the birds were of the same sex or of the opposite sex.

Similar results are found with cockroaches. Gates and Allee (*16*) compared data for cockroaches learning a maze in isolation, in groups of two, and in groups of three. They used an E-shaped maze. Its three runways, made of galvanized sheet metal, were suspended in a pan of water. At the end of the center runway was a dark bottle into which the photophobic cockroaches could escape from the noxious light. The results, in terms of time required to reach the bottle, are shown in Fig. 4.3. It is clear from the data that the solitary cockroaches required considerably less time to learn the maze than the

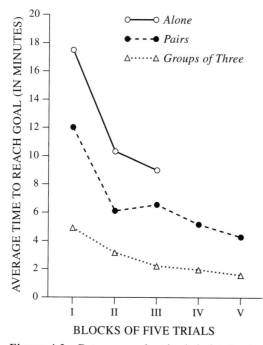

Figure 4.3   Data on maze learning in isolated and grouped cockroaches. [Gates and Allee (*16*)]

grouped animals. Gates and Allee believe that the group situation produced inhibition. They add, however (16, p. 357): "The nature of these inhibiting forces is speculative, but the fact of some sort of group interference is obvious. The presence of other roaches did not operate to change greatly the movements to different parts of the maze, but did result in increased time per trial. The roaches tended to go to the corner or end of the runway and remain there a longer time when another roach was present than when alone; the other roach was a distracting stimulus."

The experiments on social facilitation performed by Floyd Allport in 1920 and continued by Dashiell in 1930 (4, 17), both of whom used human subjects, are the ones best known. Allport's subjects worked either in separate cubicles or sitting around a common table. When working in isolation, they did the various tasks at the same time and were monitored by common time signals. Allport **[271]** did everything possible to reduce the tendency to compete. The subjects were told that the results of their tests would not be compared and would not be shown to other staff members, and that they themselves should refrain from making any such comparisons.

Among the tasks used were the following: chain word association, vowel cancellation, reversible perspective, multiplication, problem solving, and judgments of odors and weights. The results of Allport's experiments are well known: in all but the problem-solving and judgments test, performance was better in groups than in the "alone" condition. How do these results fit our generalization? Word association, multiplication, the cancellation of vowels, and the reversal of the perceived orientation of an ambiguous figure all involve responses which are well established. They are responses which are either very well learned or under a very strong influence of the stimulus, as in the word-association task or the reversible-perspective test. The problem-solving test consists of disproving arguments of ancient philosophers. In contrast to the other tests, it does not involve well-learned responses. On the contrary, the probability of wrong (that is, logically incorrect) responses on tasks of this sort is rather high; in other words, wrong responses are dominant. Of interest, however, is the finding that while intellectual work suffered in the group situation, sheer output of words was increased. When working together, Allport's subjects tended consistently to write more. Therefore, the generalization proposed in the previous section can again be applied: if the presence of others raises the probability of dominant responses, and if strong (and many) incorrect response tendencies prevail, then the presence of others can only be detrimental to performance. The results of the judgment tests have little bearing on the present argument, since Allport gives no accuracy figures for evaluating performance. The data reported only show that the presence of others was associated with the avoidance of extreme judgments.

In 1928, Travis (18), whose work on the pursuit rotor I have already noted, repeated Allport's chain-word-association experiment. In contrast to Allport's results, Travis found that the presence of others decreased performance. The number of associations given by his subjects was greater when they worked in isolation. It is very significant, however, that Travis used stutterers as his subjects. In a way, stuttering is a manifestation of a struggle between conflicting response tendencies, all of which are strong and all of which compete for expression. The stutterer, momentarily hung up in the middle of a sentence, waits for the correct response to reach full ascendancy. He stammers because other competing tendencies are dominant at that moment. It is reasonable to assume that, to the extent that the verbal habits of a stutterer are characterized by conflicting response tendencies, the presence of others, by enhancing each of these response tendencies, simply heightens his conflict. Performance is thus impaired.

AVOIDANCE LEARNING

In two experiments on the learning of avoidance responses, the performances of solitary and grouped subjects were compared. In one, rats were used; in the other, humans.

Let us first consider the results of the rat experiment, by Rasmussen (*19*). A number of albino rats, all litter mates, were deprived of water for 48 hours. The apparatus consisted of a box containing a dish of drinking water. The floor of the box was made of a metal grille wired to one pole of an electric circuit. A wire inserted in the water in the dish was connected to the other pole of the circuit. Thirsty rats were placed in the box alone, and in groups of three. They were allowed to drink for 5 seconds with the circuit open. Following this period, the shock circuit remained closed, and each time the rat touched the water he received a painful shock. Observations were made on the number of times the rats approached the water dish. The results of this experiment showed that the solitary rats learned to avoid the dish considerably sooner than the grouped animals did. The rats that were in groups of three attempted to drink twice as often as the solitary rats did, and suffered considerably more shock than the solitary subjects.

Let us examine Rasmussen's results somewhat more closely. For purposes of analysis, let us assume that there are just two critical responses involved: drinking, and avoidance of contact with the water. They are clearly incompatible. But drinking, we may further assume, is the dominant response, and, like eating or any other dominant response, it is enhanced by the presence of others. The animal is therefore prevented, by the facilitation of drinking which derives from the presence of others, from acquiring the appropriate avoidance response.

The second of the two studies is quite recent and was carried out by Ader and Tatum (*20*). They devised the following situation with which they confronted their subjects, all medical students. Each subject is told on arrival that he will be taken to another room and seated in a chair, and that electrodes will be attached to his leg. He is instructed not to get up from the chair and not to touch the electrodes. He is also told not to smoke or vocalize, and is told that the experimenter will be in the next room. That is all he is told. The subjects are observed either alone or in pairs. In the former case, the subject is brought to the room and seated at a table equipped with a red button which is connected to an electric circuit. Electrodes, by means of which electric shock can be administered, are attached to the calf of one leg. After the electrodes are attached, the experimenter leaves the room. From now on, the subject will receive 1/2 second of electric shock every 10 seconds unless he presses the red button. Each press of the button delays the shock by 10 seconds. Thus, if he is to avoid shock, he must press the button at least once every 10 seconds. It should be noted that no information was given to him about the function of the button, or about the purpose of the experiment. No essential differences are introduced when subjects are brought to the room in pairs. Both are seated at the table and both become part of the shock circuit. The response of either subject delays the shock for both.

The avoidance response is considered to have been acquired when the subject (or pair of subjects) receives less than six shocks in a period of 5 minutes. Ader and Tatum report that the isolated students required, on the average, 11 minutes, 35 seconds to reach this criterion of learning. Of the 12 pairs which participated in the experiment, only two reached this criterion. One of them required 46 minutes, 40 seconds; the other, 68 minutes, 40 seconds! Ader and Tatum offer no explanation for their curious [272] results. But there is no reason why we should not treat them in terms of the generalization proposed earlier. We are dealing here with a learning task, and the fact that the subjects are learning to avoid shock by pressing a red button does not introduce particular problems. They are confronted with an ambiguous task, and told nothing about the button. Pressing the button is simply not the dominant response in this situation. However, escaping is. Ader and Tatum report that eight of the 36 subjects walked out in the middle of the experiment.

One aspect of Ader and Tatum's results is especially worth noting. Once having learned the appropriate avoidance response, the individual subjects responded at considerably lower rates than the paired subjects. When we consider only those subjects who achieved the learning criterion, and only those responses which occurred *after* criterion had been reached, we find that the response rates of the individual subjects were, in all but one case, lower than the response rates of the grouped subjects. This result further confirms the generalization that, while learning is impaired by the presence of others, the performance of learned responses is enhanced.

There are experiments which show that learning is enhanced by the presence of other learners (*21*), but in all these experiments, as far as I can tell, it was possible for the subject to *observe* the critical responses of other subjects, and to determine when he was correct and when incorrect. In none, therefore, has the co-action paradigm been employed in its pure form. That paradigm involves the presence of others, and nothing else. It requires that these others not be able to provide the subject with cues or information as to appropriate behavior. If other learners can supply the critical individual with such cues, we are dealing not with the problem of co-action, but with the problem of imitation or vicarious learning.

THE PRESENCE OF OTHERS AS A SOURCE OF AROUSAL

The results I have discussed thus far lead to one generalization and to one hypothesis. The generalization which organizes these results is that the presence of others, as spectators or as co–actors, enhances the emission of dominant responses. We also know from extensive research literature that arousal, activation, or drive all have as a consequence the enhancement of dominant responses (*22*). We now need to examine the hypothesis that the presence of others increases the individual's general arousal or drive level.

The evidence which bears on the relationship between the presence of others and arousal is, unfortunately, only indirect. But there is some very suggestive evidence in one area of research. One of the more reliable indicators of arousal and drive is the activity of the endocrine systems in general, and of the adrenal cortex in particular. Adrenocortical functions are extremely sensitive to changes in emotional arousal, and it has been known for some time that organisms subjected to prolonged stress are likely to manifest substantial adrenocortical hypertrophy (23). Recent work (24) has shown that the main biochemical component of the adrenocortical output is hydrocortisone (17-hydroxycorticosterone). Psychiatric patients characterized by anxiety states, for instance, show elevated plasma levels of hydrocortisone (25). Mason, Brady, and Sidman (26) have recently trained monkeys to press a lever for food and have given these animals unavoidable electric shocks, all preceded by warning signals. This procedure led to elevated hydrocortisone levels; the levels returned to normal within 1 hour after the end of the experimental session. This "anxiety" reaction can apparently be attenuated if the animal is given repeated doses of reserpine 1 day before the experimental session (27). Sidman's conditioned avoidance schedule also results in raising the hydrocortisone levels by a factor of 2 to 4 (26). In this schedule, the animal receives an electric shock every 20 seconds without warning, unless he presses a lever. Each press delays the shock for 20 seconds.

While there is a fair amount of evidence that adrenocortical activity is a reliable symptom of arousal, similar endocrine manifestations were found to be associated with increased population density (28). Crowded mice, for instance, show increased amphetamine toxicity—that is, susceptibility to the excitatory effects of amphetamine—against which they can be protected by the administration of phenobarbital, chlorpromazine, or reserpine (29). Mason and Brady (30) have recently reported that monkeys caged together had considerably higher plasma levels of hydrocortisone than monkeys housed in individual cages. Thiessen (31) found increases in adrenal weights in mice housed in groups of 10 and 20 as compared with mice housed alone. The mere presence of other animals in the same room, but in separate cages, was also found to produce elevated levels of hydrocortisone. Table 4.1, taken from a report by Mason and Brady (30), shows plasma levels of hydrocortisone for three animals which lived, at one time, in cages that afforded them the possibility of visual and tactile contact and, at another time, in separate rooms.

Mason and Brady also report urinary levels of hydrocortisone, by days [273] of the week, for five monkeys from their laboratory and for one human hospital patient. These very suggestive figures are reproduced in Table 4.2 (30). In the monkeys, the low weekend traffic and activity in the laboratory seem to be associated with a clear decrease in hydrocortisone. As for the hospital patient, Mason and Brady report (30, p. 8), "he was confined to a thoracic surgery ward that bustled with activity during the weekdays when surgery and admissions occurred. On the weekends the patient retired to the nearby Red Cross building, with its quieter and more pleasant environment."

Admittedly, the evidence that the mere presence of others raises the arousal level is indirect and scanty. And, as a matter of fact, some work seems to suggest that there are conditions, such as stress, under which the presence of others may lower the animal's arousal level. Bovard (32), for instance, hypothesized that the presence of another member of the same species may protect the individual under stress by inhibiting the activity of the posterior hypothalamic centers which trigger the pituitary adrenal cortical and sympathetico-adrenal medullary responses to stress. Evidence for Bovard's hypothesis,

Table 4.1 Basal plasma concentrations of 17-hydroxycorticosterone in monkeys housed alone (cages in separate rooms), then in a room with other monkeys (cages in same room). [Leiderman and Shapiro (35, p. 7)]

Subject	Time	Conc. of 17-hydorcorticosterone in caged monkeys (μg per 100 ml of plasma)	
		In separate rooms	In same room
M-1	9 a.m.	23	34
M-1	3 p.m.	16	27
M-2	9 a.m.	28	34
M-2	3 p.m.	19	23
M-3	9 a.m.	32	38
M-3	3 p.m.	23	31
Mean	9 a.m.	28	35
Mean	3 p.m.	19	27

Table 4.2 Variations in urinary concentration of hydrocortisone over a 9-day period for five laboratory monkeys and one human hospital patient. [Leiderman and Shapiro (*35*, p. 8)]

Subjects	Amounts excreted (mg/24 hr)								
	Mon.	Tues.	Wed.	Thurs.	Fri.	Sat.	Sun.	Mon.	Tues.
Monkeys	1.88	1.71	1.60	1.52	1.70	1.16	1.17	1.88	
Patient		5.9	6.5	4.5	5.7	3.3	3.9	6.0	5.2

however, is as indirect as evidence for the one which predicts arousal as a consequence of the presence of others, and even more scanty.

SUMMARY AND CONCLUSION

If one were to draw one practical suggestion from the review of the social-facilitation effects which are summarized in this article, he would advise the student to study all alone, preferably in an isolated cubicle, and to arrange to take his examinations in the company of many other students, on stage, and in the presence of a large audience. The results of his examination would be beyond his wildest expectations, provided, of course, he had learned his material quite thoroughly.

I have tried in this article to pull together the early, almost forgotten work on social facilitation, and to explain the seemingly conflicting results. This explanation is, of course, tentative, and it has never been put to a direct experimental test. It is, moreover, not far removed from the one originally proposed by Allport. He theorized (*33,* p. 261) that "the sights and sounds of others doing the same thing" augment ongoing responses. Allport, however, proposed this effect only for *overt* motor responses, assuming (*33*, p. 274) that "*intellectual* or *implicit responses* of thought are hampered rather than facilitated" by the presence of others. This latter conclusion was probably suggested to him by the negative results he observed in his research on the effects of co-action on problem solving.

Needless to say, the presence of others may have effects considerably more complex than that of increasing the individual's arousal level. The presence of others may provide cues as to appropriate or inappropriate responses, as in the case of imitation or vicarious learning. Or it may supply the individual with cues as to the measure of danger in an ambiguous or stressful situation. Davitz and Mason (*34*), for instance, have shown that the presence of an unafraid rat reduces the fear of another rat in stress. Bovard (*32*) believes that the calming of the rat in stress which in the presence of an unafraid companion is mediated by inhibition of activity of the posterior hypothalamus. But in their experimental situations (that is, the open field test) the possibility that cues for appropriate escape or avoidance responses are provided by the co-actor is not ruled out. We might therefore be dealing not with the effects of the mere presence of others but with the considerably more complex case of imitation. The animal may not be calming *because* of his companion's presence. He may be calming *after* having copied his companion's attempted escape responses. The paradigm which I have examined in this article pertains only to the effects of the mere presence of others, and to the consequences for the arousal level. The exact parameters involved in social facilitation still must be specified.

REFERENCES AND NOTES

1. N. Triplett, *Amer. J. Psychol.* **9**, 507 (1897).
2. L.E. Travis, *J. Abnormal Soc. Psychol.* **20**, 142 (1925).
3. B.O. Bergum and D. J. Lehr, *J. Appl. Psychol.* **47**, 75 (1963).
4. J. F. Dashiell, *J. Abnormal Soc. Psychol.* **25**, 190 (1930).
5. J. Pessin, *Amer. J. Psychol.* **45**, 263 (1933).
6. R.W. Husband, *J. Genet. Psychol.* **39**, 258 (1931). In this task, the blindfolded subject traces a maze with his finger.
7. J Pessin and R.W. Husband, *J. Abnormal Soc. Psychol.* **28**, 148 (1933).
8. See, for instance, E. Duffy, *Activation and Behavior* (Wiley, New York, 1962); K. W. Spence, *Behavior Theory and Conditioning* (Yale Univ. Press, New Haven, 1956); R. B. Zajonc and B. Nieuwenhuyse, *J. Exp. Psychol.* **67**, 276 (1964).
9. E. Bayer, *Z. Psychol.* **112**, 1 (1929).
10. C. W. Tolman and G.T. Wilson, *Animal Behavior* **13**, 134 (1965).
11. H.F. Harlow, *J. Genet. Psychol.* **43**, 211 (1932).
12. W.T. James, *J. Comp. Physiol. Psychol.* **46**, 427 (1953); *J. Genet. Psychol.* **96**, 123 (1960); W. T. James and D. J. Cannon, *ibid.* **87**, 225 (1956).
13. S.C. Chen, *Physiol. Zool.* **10**, 420 (1937).
14. P.H. Klopfer, *Science* **128**, 903 (1958).
15. W.C. Allee and R. H. Masure, *Physiol. Zool.* **22**, 131 (1936).
16. M.J. Gates and W. C. Allee, *J. Comp. Psychol.* **15**, 331 (1933).

17. F.H. Allport, *J. Exp. Psychol.* **3,** 159 (1920).
18. L.E. Travis, *J. Abnormal Soc. Psychol.* **23,** 45 (1928).
19. E. Rasmussen, *Acta Psychol.* **4,** 275 (1939).
20. R. Ader and R. Tatum, *J. Exp. Anal. Behavior* **6,** 357 (1963).
21. H. Gurnee, *J. Abnormal Soc. Psychol.* **34,** 529 (1939); J. C. Welty, *Physiol. Zool.* **7,** 85 (1934).
22. See K. W. Spence, *Behavior Theory and Conditioning* (Yale Univ. Press, New Haven, 1956).
23. H. Selye, *J. Clin. Endocrin.* **6,** 117 (1946).
24. D.H. Nelson and L. T. Samuels, *ibid.* **12,** 519 (1952).
25. E.L. Bliss, A. A. Sandberg, D. H. Nelson, *J. Clin. Invest.* **32,** 9 (1953); F. Board, H. Persky, D. A. Hamburg, *Psychosom. Med.* **18,** 324 (1956).
26. J.W. Mason, J. V. Brady, M. Sidman, *Endocrinology* **60,** 741 (1957).
27. J.W. Mason and J. V. Brady, *Science* **124,** 983 (1956).
28. D.D. Thiessen, *Texas Rep. Biol. Med.* **22,** 266 (1964).
29. L. Lasagna and W. P. McCann, *Science* **125,** 1241 (1957).
30. J.W. Mason and J. V. Brady, in *Psychobiological Approaches to Social Behavior,* P. H. Leiderman and D. Shapiro, Eds. (Stanford Univ. Press, Stanford, Calif., 1964).
31. D.D. Thiessen, *J. Comp. Physiol. Psychol.* **57,** 412 (1964).
32. E.W. Bovard, *Psychol. Rev.* **66,** 267 (1959).
33. F.H. Allport, *Social Psychology* (Houghton-Mifflin, Boston, 1924).
34. J.R. Davitz and D. J. Mason, *J. Comp. Physiol. Psychol.* **48,** 149 (1955).
35. P.H. Leiderman and D. Shapiro, Eds., *Psychobiological Approaches to Social Behavior* (Stanford Univ. Press, Stanford, Calif., 1964).
36. The preparation of this article was supported in part by grants Nonr-1224(34) from the Office of Naval Research and GS-629 from the National Science Foundation. **[274]**

Chapter 5

Social Enhancement and Impairment of Performance in the Cockroach[1]

R.B. Zajonc, Alexander Heingartner, and Edward M. Herman
University of Michigan

About 35 years ago, Gates and Allee (1933) reported a study on the maze learning of isolated and grouped cockroaches in which they observed a clear inferiority of performance of the grouped subjects. Gates and Allee attributed these effects to distraction, saying that cockroaches learning in groups were responding not only to the physical topography of the maze but to the social situation as well, and that the "chemical traces introduced by one of the other roaches simultaneously occupying the maze may have acted to interfere with orientation" [Gates and Allee, 1933, p. 357]. Other studies using animal or human subjects also found a deterioration of performance under social conditions (Allee and Masure, 1936; Klopfer, 1958; Pessin and Husband, 1933). In agreement with Gates and Allee, Jones and Gerard (1967) have recently ascribed all these effects to distraction.

However, equally prevalent are data showing improvement in performance as a function of social stimuli. These socially facilitated increments in performance are usually found for behaviors that are either very well learned or instinctive. Thus, for instance, in experiments using human subjects, skilled performance on pursuit rotor (Travis, 1925), accuracy in a vigilance task (Bergum and Lehr, 1963), scores on chain-association, vowel cancellation, and multiplication tasks (Allport, 1924; Dashiell, 1930), and latency of word associations (Matlin and Zajonc, 1968) have all been shown to

[1] This research was supported by Grant GS-629 from the National Science Foundation. The authors wish to express their gratitude to Susan DeLong, Judith Johnson, and Barbara Moreland for their assistance in various phases of this research.

Zajonc, R.B., Heingartner, Alexander, and Herman, Edward M. (1968). Social facilitation in the cockroach. In E.C. Simmel, R.A. Hoppe, and G.A. Milton (Eds.), *Social facilitation and imitative behavior*. Boston: Allyn and Bacon, pp. 73–87.

improve under social conditions. Studies using animal subjects found social increments in eating (Bayer, 1929; Fischel, 1927; Harlow, 1932; Tolman and Wilson, 1965), drinking (Bruce, 1941), bar pressing (Stamm, 1961), copulating (Larsson, 1956), exploring (Simmel, 1962), nest building (Chen, 1937), and running (Scott and McCray, 1967).

It has recently been suggested (Zajonc, 1965) that these seemingly conflicting results can be reconciled if it is assumed that the presence of others is a source of general drive (D). While the presence of others can certainly be a source of specific cues, of reinforcement, and of rather specific excitation (as in mating or aggression, for example), and it can therefore *direct* behavior, it is also a source of nonspecific arousal, and, hence, acts as a general *energizer* of all responses that are likely to be emitted in the given situation. The degree of such an arousal need not be intense, of course. Nevertheless, it is assumed that its effects would be those that are predicted by the Spence-Hull drive theory (Spence, 1956). If the animal's dominant [83]* responses are appropriate from the point of view of the experimental situation, the presence of others will enhance them, and the resulting performance will appear as being improved. If these dominant responses are largely inappropriate, however, performance in the presence of others will appear as being impaired. Thus, for instance, if the given stimulus situation elicits in the animal dominant responses that are connected with eating, while the experiment "requires" the animal to delay or suppress instrumental responses leading to eating—as is the case in DRL (differential reinforcement of low rates) training—the presence of conspecifics will work against the experimental requirements, and "performance" will appear to suffer. Such an effect has indeed been obtained (Wheeler and Davis, 1967). On the other hand, if the experimenter is interested in establishing high response rates using continuous reinforcement, and if the total experimental situation also elicits dominant responses that are connected with eating, the presence of others will appear to have beneficial consequences. Hence, it is not performance but the emission of dominant responses, whatever they are, that is "facilitated" by the social stimulus.

If information about the subject's response hierarchy were available prior to the tests of social effects, the drive theory of social facilitation could be given a critical test. Such methods have been used with humans (Cottrell, Rittle, and Wack, 1967; Zajonc and Sales, 1966), and the evidence obtained was in substantial agreement with the drive theory of social facilitation. But procedures of this sort have not been employed with animal subjects.

Gates and Allee's (1933) experiment lends itself to some modifications which should generate useful information for the drive theory of social facilitation. In their experiment, Gates and Allee (1933) used an E-shaped maze suspended over water. Light served as a noxious stimulus, while an opaque bottle located in the central portion of the maze provided the subjects with the only means of escape. The procedure entailed placing the cockroach (or cockroaches) at one of the terminals of the maze and observing the time required to reach the goal bottle. Because of the many spatial alternatives available—at first, all equally inviting—many response tendencies were elicited that were not correct. In fact, of the many ways in which the cockroach could proceed in the E-maze, only one led to escape, and, hence, to what the experimenter would consider as "appropriate behavior." To the extent that the presence of conspecifics did act as a source of general drive (D), these many "inappropriate" response tendencies were energized, delaying the emission of the appropriate one.

---

* Bracketed bold numbers refer to original page numbers. Page numbers indicate where the original page ended.

If one could contrive a situation in which the cockroach's response tendencies would be largely "correct" or "appropriate," an increment rather than a decrement in performance should be obtained under social conditions. In comparison with maze performance, this situation would provide a rather stringent test of the drive theory of social facilitation. The straight runway with the noxious stimulus at the start and the means of escape at the goal can serve this purpose rather well. Such a straight runway, properly constructed, does not prompt the cockroach to turn, for if it turns, it must only face the noxious light. The entire stimulus situation is so contrived that the dominant tendencies that are elicited consist of running away from the start box and directly toward the goal box. The present paper reports two experiments in which the performance of cockroaches in a maze and in a runway was compared under various social conditions. In all these experiments, socially mediated performance decrements in the maze and socially mediated increments in the straight runway were expected.

EXPERIMENT I

This experiment had two major purposes. The first was to test the drive theory of social facilitation. To accomplish this purpose, paired and isolated cockroaches were observed as they performed in a maze and as they performed in a straight runway. As in the experiment carried out by Gates and Allee (1933), the social variable was manipulated by having the subjects traverse **[84]** the maze or the runway alone or in pairs, that is, in coaction. However, this experimental manipulation, which has been used in nearly all experiments on social facilitation with animals, may lead to a confounding of two possible effects of others' presence: its energizing effects and its directive (or cue) effects. Two animals using the same maze or runway may affect each other's behavior because they act as a source of arousal for each other, *or* because **[85]** they emit responses that may be imitated. The second purpose of the present experiment, therefore, was to determine the socially mediated effects obtained in cockroaches when the subjects could not profit from directive cues provided by companions. Hence, while the social variable in one group of subjects was manipulated by means of coaction, in the other group it was manipulated by providing an audience, in order to eliminate all cues connected with the presence of conspecifics that may have been task-relevant and may have influenced the subjects' behavioral choices rather than his response vigor. If similar socially mediated effects were obtained with an audience as with coaction, the drive theory of social facilitation would receive more unequivocal support than had these effects been obtained under the conditions of coaction alone.

Method

SUBJECTS   Seventy-two adult female cockroaches (*Blatta orientalis*) were used,[2] and for at least 1 week prior to the first experimental trial they were housed in individual mason jars supplied with screened lids. They were maintained in dark quarters with

---

[2] The authors are grateful to Louis M. Roth of the United States Army Natick Laboratory, who was kind enough to supply the subjects for the audience treatment. The subjects in the coaction treatment were obtained from the Carolina Biological Supply Company.

a relatively constant temperature of about 75 degrees Fahrenheit. The insects were fed an ad libitum diet of peeled and sliced apples.

APPARATUS The basic apparatus is shown in Figure 5.1. It consisted of a 20 × 20 × 20-inch clear plexiglass cube outfitted so as to house either a maze or a runway. A 150-watt floodlight served as a source of noxious stimulation. In the center of each vertical

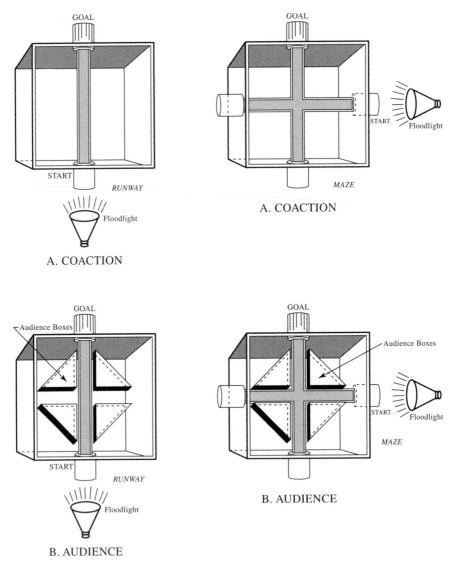

Figure 5.1 Diagrams of runways and mazes used in the coaction and in the audience treatments of Experiment I

wall of the plexiglass housing, 8 1/4 inches from the top, was a rectangular 1 3/4 × 3/4-inch opening, which could be closed by means of a guillotine gate made out of sheet metal. A set of tracks on the exterior of each opening served as a shoe for a goal box or a starting box, clamping it firmly in place against the wall opening. Both the goal box and the starting box were made of 4-inch clear plexiglass tubing. A square flange that could slide into the shoe on the vertical wall of the housing was affixed to the opening of the boxes, while the other end of the tubing was sealed with 1/4-inch clear plexiglass.

The maze and the runway could be suspended in the housing flush with the goal boxes and the starting boxes. Both the runway and the maze were made of black bakelite floor 2 inches wide, with walls made of clear plexiglass, 1 inch high. The runway and the maze were provided with clear plexiglass tops 1/8-inch thick. The runway consisted of a straight track running between two opposite vertical walls, and was 20 inches long. The maze was made of two runways, placed in the same plane and perpendicular to each other, thus forming a cross with the walls of the intersection removed. The lengths of the paths in the runway and in the maze, namely those leading from the starting box to the goal box or to a cul-de-sac, were 20 inches.

The guillotine gates that separated the starting and goal boxes from the runway or maze were made of galvanized sheet metal. To attract the roach to the goal box, an opaque cover, painted flat black on the inside, was placed over the box making its interior dark. A flat black posterboard, covering the entire 20 × 20-inch area, was hung on the wall which held the goal box. [86]

For the groups in which the social variable was manipulated by means of a passive audience, four 9 × 9 × 1-inch boxes with plexiglass sides and tops and bakelite floors were used. These boxes were placed inside the plexiglass cube housing in such a manner that their floors were flush with the floors of the runway or the maze and their sides directly contiguous with the walls of the runway or the maze. When these boxes were in position almost the entire extent of walls of the runway or maze were in direct contact with the sides of the audience boxes. Air holes in the sides of the boxes lined up with air holes in the walls of the runway and the maze to allow transmission of olfactory cues.

PROCEDURE   Before each trial, the runway (or the maze) was swabbed with alcohol which was allowed to evaporate thoroughly. The starting box and the goal box were swabbed in the same manner before each set of 10 trials. The roach was transferred from its home jar to the starting box which had been covered with an opaque container similar to that which also covered the goal box. Each trial began by removing the cover, turning on the floodlight, and removing the guillotine door separating the opening in the starting box from the runway or the maze. The floodlight was always in line with the runway or the maze and 10 inches directly behind it. No light other than that provided by the floodlight was present in the experimental room. The trial was terminated when the cockroach (or the pair of cockroaches) entered the goal box and the guillotine gate was lowered behind it (or them), or in 5 minutes—whichever was earlier. The guillotine gate was always lowered immediately after the roach's last leg crossed the entrance of the goal box. In the coaction treatment, the starting latencies and the running times were scored for each subject individually, although the gate was not lowered until the last member of the pair entered the goal box.

Thirty-two animals served in the experimental treatment involving coaction[3] and 40 in the treatment involving audience. In each treatment, half of the roaches worked in the runway and half in the maze. In addition, within each combination of treatment and task, half of the animals were run in the alone condition and half in the social condition. In the coaction treatment, the subjects were placed into starting boxes in pairs. For purposes of identification they were marked with airplane dope, one white and one blue. In the audience treatment, 10 adult female *Blatta orientalis,* which were previously housed in common quarters of the laboratory colony, were placed in each of the four audience boxes. The control group of 20 roaches, which was not to be exposed to a passive audience, worked with audience boxes in position, but empty and clean. All roaches run in the audience treatment and in their proper control conditions were run individually. Starting latencies to the nearest second and total running times to the nearest tenth of a second were recorded. Starting latency consisted of the interval beginning with the opening of the guillotine gate of the starting box and ending at the time the last part of the roach's body left the starting box. In all treatments and conditions, the subjects were given 10 consecutive trials, all separated by 1-minute intertrial intervals.

Results

Because starting latencies and running times are generally skewed, the scores subjected to the analysis of variance consisted of median times computed over the 10 trials performed by each subject. The averages reported throughout this paper are averages of these median times. Table 5.1 shows the entire results of the experiment, and Table 5.2

Table 5.1   Running Time and Starting Latency in Seconds for Subjects Tested Alone, in Coaction, and in the Presence of an Audience

	Task			
	Runway		Maze	
Treatment	Alone	Social	Alone	Social
Coaction				
Starting latency	8.25 (8)	6.88 (8)	10.56 (8)	11.19 (8)
Running time	40.58 (8)	32.96 (8)	110.45 (8)	129.46 (8)
Audience				
Starting latency	14.80 (10)	9.35 (10)	37.55 (10)	22.75 (10)
Running time	62.65 (10)	39.30 (10)	221.35 (10)	296.64 (10)
Both treatments				
Starting latency	11.89 (18)	8.25 (18)	25.56 (18)	17.61 (18)
Running time	52.84 (18)	36.48 (18)	172.06 (18)	222.34 (18)

Note: Averages of medians. Figures in parentheses indicate the number of roaches in each cell.

[3] This treatment constitutes a partial replication of a previous experiment, reported elsewhere (Zajonc, 1968).

Table 5.2 Summary of Analyses of Variance for Data in Table 5.1

Source	df	Starting latency		Running time	
		MS	F	MS	F
Alone vs. social (A)	1	603.78	< 1	5,180.48	1.962
Runway vs. maze (B)	1	2,386.25	2.650	418,826.03	158.639
Coaction vs. audience (C)	1	2,514.87	2.793	104,373.47	39.533**
A × B	1	83.42	< 1	19,977.75	7.567*
A × C	1	422.50	< 1	1,823.85	< 1.000
B × C	1	968.58	1.076	69,258.45	26.233**
A × B × C	1	143.14	< 1	5,746.66	2.183
Error	64	900.36		2,640.11	

*$p < .01$
**$p < .001$

shows the analysis of variance of these data. Above all, it is clear that, with respect to starting latencies, all effects fail to reach acceptable levels of significance. It was considered that leaving the starting box, which, it will be recalled, was the nearest to the floodlight, was a relatively simple task for the roach, comparable to traversing a straight runway. Therefore, under the coaction treatment, starting latencies should be shorter in the social condition than in the alone condition, regardless of whether the subjects are entering the maze or the runway. Under the audience treatment, however, there are no social cues in the starting box in the social as well as in the alone condition and we would, therefore, not expect strong effects associated with either treatments or conditions. While the results are not significant, we note from Table 5.1 that the task may have affected starting latencies, with the relevant F ratio nearly reaching an acceptable level of significance.

The total running times show patterns that are quite consistent with the drive theory of social facilitation. Relevant here is the significant interaction between the conditions and tasks ($F = 7.57$, $df = 1/64$, $p < .01$). Roaches running the maze in coaction required longer times than roaches running in isolation. This result replicates the findings of Gates and Allee (1933). However, the effects of coaction are reversed for the runway. Here the coacting roaches perform more quickly than the solitary subjects. And the [87] same pattern of results prevails for the audience treatment. Hence the three-way interaction was not significant.

The analysis of the results also shows that the running times and the latencies are substantially shorter in the coaction animals than in the audience groups. Unfortunately, because these subjects came from different colonies, we are unable to determine from the data alone whether these differences are due to the diverse origins of the two groups of animals, or whether they have something to do with the experimental treatments. It is a rather plausible conjecture that the differences are attributable to the former factor because of the consistently longer running times of roaches in the control groups of the audience as compared to the coaction treatment.

EXPERIMENT II

In the first experiment, it was shown that the presence of an audience of conspecifics is a sufficient condition for the enhancement of dominant responses, such that the performance of the subject in a one-alternative task is improved and the performance of the subject in a multialternative task is impaired. But the variable, "presence of conspecifics," is certainly not precise, either from a theoretical or methodological point of view. What are the essential and critical features of "presence of conspecifics" that produce these effects? What is the nature of the social stimulus that elicits these effects and has the capacity of increasing general arousal? Complete answers to these questions must await a great deal of research, not only on the nature of the social stimulation involved in social facilitation effects, but also on the nature of the arousal that is brought about by the social stimuli. But as a first step, we may inquire about the minimal conditions which are sufficient for producing social facilitation effects. Tolman (1965) found that feeding behavior of young chicks was facilitated by the presence of a companion separated from the subject by a plexiglass partition, and also by feeding the subject in front of a mirror. These increments, however, were not as impressive as those obtained with a coacting companion. Tolman (1968) regarded such socially mediated effects primarily in directive (cue) terms. Hence, he accepted as more likely the hypothesis that it is the behavior of the companion rather than its mere presence which produces increments and decrements in performance. Animal research, especially on feeding behavior, supports his contention. However, results of Experiment I with audience show that even when the conspecific companion does not emit behavior which can be used by the subject to guide the course of his action, effects which are consistent with the drive theory of social facilitation are obtained.

Experiment II attempted to determine if socially mediated effects such as those obtained in Experiment I would be produced if the immediate presence of conspecifics were somehow curtailed or reduced. Two treatments were employed. In both treatments [88] there were no other roaches besides the subject. Both dealt with some components of the presence of conspecifics; one emphasizing its cue effects, the other emphasizing its energizing (general arousal) effects. Thus, in the former, the insects ran in mazes and runways which were outfitted with mirrors alongside their vertical walls. In the second treatment, regular runways and mazes were utilized, but the animals were stimulated by the presence of olfactory cues associated with their conspecifics. These treatments were compared with one in which the insects were observed under solitary and socially neutral conditions.

Method

SUBJECTS One hundred and eighty female *Blatta orientalis* obtained from the Carolina Biological Supply Company were employed in the present experiment. All insects were housed in individual mason jars for 4 days prior to the experiment. One third of the subjects were assigned to the mirror treatment (Mi), one-third to the odor treatment (Od), and one-third to the alone treatment (Al). In each treatment, half of the subjects (30) were given tests in the straight runway and half in the maze.

APPARATUS   The apparatus from Experiment I, in which modifications were made to allow tests under the requirements of the experimental treatments, was employed. In the Mi treatment, a runway and a maze were used which were equipped with reflecting half-aluminized film affixed to the entire extent of the walls. Otherwise, the apparatus was the same as in the alone treatment of Experiment I. In the Od treatment, the regular runway and maze from the audience treatment of Experiment I were used which, it will be recalled, had holes drilled in their walls. An olfactory social stimulus was provided by placing an egg carton impregnated with the odor of conspecifics inside the housing of the apparatus and 4 inches directly beneath the maze or the runway. The egg carton was thoroughly impregnated with the odors of conspecifics by having it in the quarters of the colony for several days prior to the tests. Several cartons were kept in the quarters of the cockroach colony during the course of the experiment, and during each testing session a freshly impregnated carton was always used. The Al treatment was the same as the Od treatment except that a fresh, clean egg carton, not impregnated with cockroach odor, was placed 4 inches beneath the runway or the maze. The same procedure was used for scoring latencies and running times as in Experiment I.

Results

Table 5.3 shows the data from Experiment II. It may at first be noted that under the present experimental treatments the latencies do not differ across tasks ($F < 1$, $df = 1/174$). Such a tendency was present in Experiment I, although it also did not attain an acceptable level of significance. The latencies are also fairly uniform across treatments. The relevant F ratio did not reach an acceptable level of significance ($F = 2.681$, $df = 2/174$).

Table 5.3   Running Time and Starting Latency in Seconds for Subjects Tested Alone, with Mirror, and in the Presence of Conspecific Odor

	Task	
Treatment	Runway	Maze
Mirror		
Starting latency	27.38	28.88
Running time	77.21	160.71
Odor		
Starting latency	20.00	24.97
Running time	69.53	245.72
Alone		
Starting latency	22.67	18.33
Running time	55.67	219.63

Note: Averages of medians. These means are based on 30 independent observations in each cell.

Similarly, the interaction between treatments and tasks did not attain significance. However, with respect to total running times, both main effects and the interaction are significant ($F = 4.197$, $df = 2/174$, $p < .05$ for treatments; $F = 167.925$, $df = 1/174$, $p < .001$ for tasks; and $F = 7.117$, $df = 2/174$, $p < .001$ for the interaction between them). These effects, it seems, are due primarily to the relatively fast maze running time among the Mi subjects. In contrast to the previous experiment, running times in the straight runway are not improved in the two social treatments. Both the Mi and the Od subjects took longer times to traverse the runway than the Al subjects. Maze running seems to show a relative facilitation for the Mi treatment and an impairment for the Od treatment.

DISCUSSION

The results of Experiment I support the hypothesis that the presence of conspecifics acts as an energizer of dominant responses in the cockroach. There were rather clear indications that enhancement, as well as impairment of performance, could be obtained with [89] these insects, depending on whether a simple or a complex task was used, and, therefore, depending on whether the situation was more likely to recruit appropriate or inappropriate response tendencies. While results on starting latencies failed to generate useful information, data on running times unequivocally favored the drive theory of social facilitation.

The fact that performance in the runway was enhanced by the presence of conspecifics does damage to the distraction hypothesis proposed by Gates and Allee (1933) and reintroduced by Jones and Gerard (1967). It must be noted that the runway and the maze differed only in the number of alternative turns available to the subject at the choice point, that is, 9 inches from the starting box. The runway had only one alternative, while the maze had three. In all other respects, the two tasks and the two stimulus situations were nearly identical.[4] It would not be parsimonious, therefore, to maintain that the distraction hypothesis applies to maze performance alone, for we would have to invoke a new psychological process to account for the improvement of running times in the runway.

The results of Experiment I also eliminated the possibility that social facilitation effects depend on the specific behavioral output of the companion. In nearly all previous experiments on social facilitation with animal subjects the coaction paradigm was employed. Data from these studies could therefore be interpreted by assuming that the companion emits behavior which the subject can imitate. The fact that the results in the audience treatment show the same pattern as those in the coaction treatment indicates that specific directive cues need not be involved in socially mediated performance effects. In fact, the effects obtained in the coaction treatment were less pronounced than those found in the audience treatment. Simple effects tests on running time data from Experiment I show a strong interaction between conditions (social versus alone) and tasks (runway versus maze) for the audience treatment ($F = 9.19$, $df = 1/64$, $p < .01$), while the same interaction is only of borderline significance in the coaction treatment

---

[4] It is true, however, as the reviewer of this manuscript correctly observed, that the maze did require a right (or a left) turn of the subject, while the runway did not.

($F = 2.80$, $df = 1/64$, $p < .10$). It should be noted, at the same time, however, that in a previous experiment on coaction in cockroaches (Zajonc, 1968), using subjects as their own controls, this interaction was reliable.

Subjects in the coaction treatment did not show tendencies to crowd or to form traffic jams in the runway and in the maze. While they usually did not leave starting boxes or enter goal boxes at the same time, the openings were sufficiently wide to allow them to do so. The fact that maze performance was observed to deteriorate in the audience treatment would lead us to expect that this deterioration was socially mediated in the coaction treatment as well, rather than having been brought about by crowding or traffic jams.

Qualitative observations of the roaches did not reveal specific behaviors by virtue of which such social effects might be produced. Perhaps the only consistent pattern found was that the behavior of the subjects in the coaction treatment was devoid of tendencies to follow or to imitate. The roaches seemed to traverse the alleys of the maze and of the runway in an apparent ignorance of each other. In the audience treatment, too, there was nothing detectable in the subjects' behavior to indicate that they oriented toward the spectator roaches. But, of course, there is today only scanty information on the social significance of the various responses of the cockroach.

Another hypothesis offered to account for the effects associated with the presence of conspecifics assumes that they are not due to an increased arousal but to calming. For instance, Davitz and Mason (1955) have found that rats in an open field test reduce their fear responses when a previously habituated rat is also present. And Liddell (1950) has shown that neurotic symptoms produced in a young goat by means of a continuous noxious stimulation are attenuated when the mother goat is also present. Bovard (1959) proposed that social stimuli elicit a competing response "which inhibits, masks, or **[90]** screens the stress stimulus, such that the latter has a minimal effect" [p. 269]. Because the response of the posterior hypothalamus initiates pituitary-adrenal cortical and sympathetic-adrenal medullar activity associated with stress reactions, Bovard argued that the presence of another member of the same species must dampen the activity of the posterior hypothalamus, and thereby dampen the stress reactions of the adrenal system. It has been suggested elsewhere (Zajonc, 1965) that the reduced stress reactions may be due simply to the availability for imitation of coping responses. Hence, the experimental data associated with reduction of fear which occurs with the presence of conspecifics might be best accounted for by focusing upon the directive (cue) effects which are provided by the conspecifics. The situation in Experiment I can certainly be considered a stressful one, for the species of the cockroach used in the experiment is rather photophobic. The effects observed in the coaction and in the audience treatment are not consistent with the hypothesis that companions have a calming effect. If this were the case, we would expect an increase in the running time in the runway and a decrease in the running time in the maze—results which would be diametrically opposite to those found in Experiment I. But such an effect was found in Experiment II in the Mi treatment. In comparison with the Al treatment, these subjects took longer in the runway and were faster in the maze. The Mi treatment, it will be recalled, stresses the directive (cue) properties associated with the presence of conspecifics. But in Experiment I, there also was a treatment (coaction) in which cues were available for imitation but in which an actual companion was present. Yet this experimental situation did not produce a calming effect.

The results of Experiment II are ambiguous. One conclusion to be drawn from these results is that in order for drive effects to take place, the presence of conspecifics must be actual. Partial presence, such as the presence of olfactory traces, was not sufficient to produce effects consistent with the drive theory of social facilitation. It seemed, on the contrary, that the Od treatment generated results most consistent with the distraction hypothesis. In comparison with the Al treatment, the subjects running in the presence of the odor of conspecifics had longer times in the maze as well as in the straight runway. The question immediately arises whether social facilitation effects consistent with the drive theory of social facilitation would be obtained in the presence of an immobile audience. For instance, one could observe the runway and maze behavior of cockroaches in the presence of a dead or anaesthetized companion. The danger of such an experiment is that a dead or an immobile cockroach, while leading to an increase in the general arousal level of the subject, might also elicit specific alarm or stress responses that may interfere with task performance. The problem of what are the minimal features of the presence of conspecifics which are sufficient for social facilitation effects which the drive theory predicts is quite difficult from a methodological point of view.

Another problem associated with social facilitation effects is that concerning the nature of the arousal or drive that increases in the presence of others. Social facilitation effects obtained with human subjects can be readily interpreted as caused by a motivation to succeed, a desire to be praised and avoid blame, or, in general, by assuming that the presence of others creates in the individual the anticipation of socially positive or negative consequences and thus increases the general arousal level (Cottrell, 1968; Cottrell, Wack, Sekerak, and Rittle, 1968). Had the present been experiments using human subjects one could easily raise questions about self-disclosure, evaluation apprehension, the approval motive, etc. But one finds it rather awkward to attribute this sort of motivation to the cockroach, even though we have no idea if these seemingly spiritless creatures aren't vulnerable to some of the very same passions and weaknesses which beset our sophomore population of subjects.

REFERENCES

Allee, W.C., and Masure, R.H. A comparison of maze behavior in paired and isolated shell parakeets (*Melopsittacas undulatus,* Shaw). *Physiological Zoology,* 1936, **22,** 131–156. **[91]**

Allport, F.H. *Social psychology.* Boston: Houghton Mifflin, 1924.

Bayer, E. Beiträge zur Zweikomponentheorie des Hungers. *Zeitschrift für Psychologie,* 1929, **112,** 1–54.

Bergum. B.O., and Lehr, D.J. Effects of authoritarianism on vigilance performance. *Journal of Applied Psychology,* 1963, **47,** 75–77.

Bovard, E.W. The effects of social stimuli on the response to stress. *Psychological Review,* 1959, **66,** 267–277.

Bruce, R.H. An experimental analysis of social factors affecting the performance of white rats. I. Performance in learning in a simple field situation. *Journal of Comparative Psychology,* 1941, **31,** 363–377.

Chen, S.C. Social modification of the activity of ants in nest-building. *Physiological Zoology,* 1937, **10,** 420–436.

Cottrell, N.B. Performance in the presence of other human beings: Mere presence, audience, and affiliation effects. In E.C. Simmel, R.A. Hoppe, and G.A. Milton (Eds.), *Social facilitation and imitative behavior.* Boston: Allyn & Bacon, 1968.

Cottrell, N.B., Rittle, R.H., and WACK, D. R. Presence of an audience and list type (competitional or non-competitional) as joint determinants of performance in paired-associates learning. *Journal of Personality,* 1967, **35**, 425–434.

Cottrell, N.B., Wack, D.L., Sekerak, G., and Rittle, R. H. The social facilitation of dominant responses by the presence of an audience and the mere presence of others. *Journal of Personality and Social Psychology,* 1968, **9**, 251–256.

Dashiell, J.F. An experimental analysis of some group effects. *Journal of Abnormal and Social Psychology,* 1930, **25**, 190–199.

Davitz, J.R., and Mason, D.J. Socially facilitated reduction of a fear response in rats. *Journal of Comparative and Physiological Psychology,* 1955, **48**, 149–151.

Fischel, W. Beiträge zur Soziologie des Haushuhns. *Biologisches Zentralblatt,* 1927, **47**, 678–696.

Gates, M.G, and Allee, W.C. Conditioned behavior of isolated and grouped cockroaches on a simple maze. *Journal of Comparative Psychology,* 1933, **15**, 331–358.

Harlow, H.F. Social facilitation of feeding in the albino rat. *Journal of Genetic Psychology,* 1932, **41**, 211–221.

Jones, E.E., and Gerard, H. B. *Foundations of social psychology.* New York: Wiley, 1967.

Klopfer, P.H. Influence of social interaction on learning rates in birds. *Science,* 1958, **128**, 903–904.

Larsson, K. *Conditioning and sexual behavior in the male albino rat.* Stockholm: Almquist and Wiksell, 1956.

Liddell, H. Some specific factors that modify tolerance for environmental stress. In H. G. Wolff, S. G. Wolf, Jr., and C.C. Hare (Eds.), *Life stress and bodily disease.* Baltimore: Williams & Wilkins, 1950.

Matlin, M.W., and Zajonc, R. B. Social facilitation of word associations. *Journal of Personality and Social Psychology,* 1968, **10**, 455–460.

Pessin, J., and Husband, R.W. Effects of social stimulation on human maze learning. *Journal of Abnormal and Social Psychology,* 1933, **28**, 148–154.

Scott, J.P., and McCray, C. Allelomimetic behavior in dogs: Negative effects of competition on social facilitation. *Journal of Comparative and Physiological Psychology,* 1967, **63**, 316–319.

Simmel, E.C. Social facilitation of exploratory behavior in rats. *Journal of Comparative and Physiological Psychology,* 1962, **55**, 831–833.

Spence, K.W. *Behavior theory and conditioning.* New Haven: Yale University Press, 1956.

Stamm, J.S. Social facilitation in monkeys. *Psychological Reports,* 1961, **8**, 479–484.

Tolman, C.W. Emotional behavior and social facilitation of feeding in domestic chicks. *Animal Behaviour,* 1965, **13**, 493–502.

Tolman, C.W. The role of the companion in social facilitation of animal behavior. In E.C. Simmel, R.A. Hoppe, and G.A. Milton (Eds.), *Social facilitation and imitative behavior.* Boston: Allyn & Bacon, 1968.

Tolman, C.W., and Wilson, G.F. Social feeding in domestic chicks. *Animal Behaviour,* 1965, **13**, 134–142.

Travis, L.E. The effect of a small audience upon eye-hand coordination. *Journal of Abnormal and Social Psychology,* 1925, **20**, 142–146.

Wheeler, L., and Davis, H. Social disruption of performance on a DRL schedule. *Psychonomic Science,* 1967, **7**, 249–250.

Zajonc, R.B. Social facilitation. *Science,* 1965, **149**, 269–274.

Zajonc, R.B., and Sales, S.M. Social facilitation of dominant and subordinate responses. *Journal of Experimental Social Psychology,* 1966, **2**, 160–168.

Zajonc, R.B. Social facilitation in the cockroach. In E.C. Simmel, R.A. Hoppe, and G.A. Milton (Eds.), *Social facilitation and imitative behavior.* Boston: Allyn & Bacon, 1968.

(Received January 24, 1969) **[92]**

Part Three

The Effects of Mere Exposure: The Minimal Source of Attitude Formation

Chapter 6

Attitudinal Effects of
Mere Exposure

R.B. Zajonc
University of Michigan

On February 27, 1967, the Associated Press carried the following story from Corvallis, Oregon:

> A mysterious student has been attending a class at Oregon State
> University for the past two months enveloped in a big black bag. Only his
> bare feet show. Each Monday, Wednesday, and Friday at 11 A.M. the Black
> Bag sits on a small table near the back of the classroom. The class is
> Speech 113—basic persuasion.... Charles Goetzinger, professor of the
> class, knows the identity of the person inside. None of the 20 students in
> the class do. Goetzinger said *the students' attitude changed from hostility
> toward the Black Bag to curiosity and finally to friendship* [italics added].

This monograph examines the general hypothesis implied by the above phenomenon: mere repeated exposure of the individual to a stimulus is a sufficient condition for the enhancement of his attitude toward it. By "mere exposure" is meant a condition which just makes the given stimulus accessible to the individual's perception.

Even though the hypothesis seems to be in conflict with such celebrated laws as *familiarity breeds contempt* and *absence makes the heart grow fonder*, it is not particularly original or recent (Fechner, 1876, pp. 240–243; James, 1890, p. 672; Maslow, 1937; Meyer 1903; Pepper, 1919). The foremost proponent of this hypothesis, the advertising industry, has always attributed to exposure formidable advertising potential. But—apparently, in respect for the law of enhancement by association—it seldom dared to utilize *mere* exposure. The product, its name, or its hallmark is always presented to the public in contiguity with other and always attractive stimuli, commonly females, exposed more boldly than the product itself. At the same time, however, the advertising

Zajonc, R.B. (1968). Attitudinal effects of mere exposure. *Journal of Personality and Social Psychology, Monograph Supplement*, 9, 1–27. Copyright © 1968 by the American Psychological Association. Reprinted with permission.

industry also likes to warn against *over*exposure, relying, it would appear, on the law of familiarity (Erdelyi, 1940; Wiebe, 1940).

It isn't altogether clear just what evidence supports these advertising principles. And **[1]*** direct evidence that attitudes are enhanced by *mere* exposure or *mere* contact with the stimulus object is scant. Moreover, it is the product of antiquated methods, and almost all of it concerns music appreciation (Downey and Knapp, 1927; Krugman, 1943; Meyer, 1903; Moore and Gilliland, 1924; Mull, 1957; Verveer, Barry, and Bousfield, 1933; Washburn, Child, and Abel, 1927). The problem of attitudinal effects of social contact and interaction has also been of some interest in the study of interracial attitudes (Cook and Selltiz, 1952). But these studies have invariably examined the effects not of *mere* perceptual exposure of people to each other, but of processes considerably more complex: prolonged social interaction, group interdependence, cooperation, etc. (Deutsch and Collins, 1951; Kramer, 1950; MacKenzie, 1948; Wilner, Walkley, and Cook, 1952). Although the independent variables in these studies have generally been featured under the labels "contact" and "exposure," the effects they report cannot, because of confounding with a multitude of other events (and with reinforcement in particular), be regarded as produced alone by contact or exposure. Thus, it has been known for some time that social interaction enhances the attitudes of interactions toward each other (Bovard, 1951; Festinger, 1951; Homans, 1961; Newcomb, 1963). But it is not known just what contribution to the relationship between social interaction and attitudes is made by *mere* exposure on the one hand, and by the variety of psychologically significant processes that necessarily accompany mere exposure during the course of social interaction, on the other.

The main empirical support for the exposure hypothesis comes, therefore, not from work on interaction, interracial attitudes, or attitudes in general, but from an entirely different and seemingly unrelated area of research. It comes from some recent work on word frequencies. This recent research shows that there exists an intimate relationship between word frequency and meaning. And this relationship, in my opinion (for which I shall later present support), may be a special case of the more general relationship between mere exposure and attitude enhancement.

The strength and pervasiveness of the relationship between word frequency and meaning—the *evaluative* aspect of meaning, in particular—is truly remarkable. For, if there is any correspondence between the frequency with which words are used and the actual preponderance of the things and events for which these words stand, then we may congratulate ourselves on living in a most happy world. According to the Thorndike-Lorge count (1944), the word "happiness" occurs 761 times, "unhappiness" occurs only 49 times. "Beauty" is to be found at least 41 times as often as "ugliness," and "wealth" outdoes "poverty" by a factor of 1.6. We "laugh" 2.4 times as often as we "cry"; we "love" almost 7 times more often than we "hate"; we are "in" at least 5 times more often than we are "out"; "up" twice as often as we are "down"; much more often "successful" than "unsuccessful"; and we "find" things 4.5 times more often than we "lose" them—all because most of us are "lucky" (220) rather than "unlucky" (17).

We have all the reasons in the world to be "happy" (1449) and "gay" (418) rather than "sad" (202) and "gloomy" (72), for things are 5 times more often "good" than "bad," almost 3 times more often "possible" than "impossible," and about five times

---

* Bracketed bold numbers refer to original page numbers. Page numbers indicate where the original page ended.

more "profitable" than "unprofitable." That is, perhaps, why "boom" and "prosperity" outdo "recession" by a factor of just about 30, "abundance" outdoes "scarcity" by at least 3:1, and "affluence" is 6 times more prevalent than "deprivation." Catering to our corporeal sensibilities, things are 3 times more often "fragrant" than they are "foul," 12 times more often "fresh" than "stale," and almost 7 times more often "sweet" than "sour," and everything that can be filled is three times as often "full" as it is "empty." If we have anything, we have "more" of it 6 times more often than we have "less" of it,[1] and 3 times more often "most" of it than "least" of it. And those things that we have so frequently more of are 5 times more often "better" than they are "worse," 6 times more often "best" than "worst," and 4 times more often "superior" than "inferior." Still, [2] they "improve" at least 25 times as often as they "deteriorate."

These examples suffice to convince one that the world represented by a one-to-one correspondence with word frequencies is as unreal as it is spectacular. Bitterly aware of it, Sartre (1964) confessed in his autobiography, "… as a result of discovering the world through language, for a long time, I took language for the world." [p. 182]

But, while they are unfaithful in representing reality, word frequencies are extraordinarily accurate in representing real values: words that stand for good, desirable, and preferred aspects of reality are more frequently used.

It isn't entirely clear who discovered this remarkable relationship between word frequency and the evaluative dimension of word meaning. Postman (1953) seems to be one of the early workers to note its generality, while Howes and Solomon (1950) observed in their critique of McGinnies' (1949) perceptual defense experiment that the so-called "taboo" words he used as stimuli are particularly infrequent. However, the first systematic research effort that demonstrates the word frequency-word-value relationship is due to Johnson, Thomson, and Frincke (1960). These authors were the first, I believe, to collect empirical data showing that words with "positive" meaning have higher frequency counts than words with "negative" meanings. They have also gathered experimental evidence showing that the repeated use of a nonsense word tends to enhance its rating on the good-bad scale of the semantic differential. Johnson, Thomson, and Frincke (1960) have not tried to explain either of these two aspects of the frequency-value relationship, being primarily concerned with its implications for the study of word-recognition thresholds.

This paper examines the frequency-value relationship, proposing that it is considerably more pervasive and general than implied by the Johnson–Thomson–Frincke results, and that it is, moreover, a special case of a broader and more basic phenomenon: the enhancement of attitudes by mere repeated exposure. I shall first review evidence on the correlation between word frequency and word value, and between stimulus frequency and attitude. Experimental evidence on these two relationships, and on the likely causal direction, will then be examined.

WORD FREQUENCY-WORD VALUE: CORRELATIONAL EVIDENCE

Johnson, Thomson, and Frincke (1960) obtained correlations of .63, .40, and .38 between the L-count (Thorndike and Lorge, 1944) and the good-bad scale values for

---

[1] N.B. The more-less ratio in this text is 7:1 up to now.

three samples of randomly chosen words. In a further attempt, they constructed 30 pairs, each consisting of one frequent and one infrequent word. These pairs were given to a group of subjects with the instructions to "encircle the most pleasantly toned word of each pair." In 87% of the pairs, the majority of subjects endorsed the more frequent word. Finally, 64 nonsense syllables of low, medium, and high association were rated by a group of subjects on the good-bad scale of the semantic differential. Johnson, Thomson, and Frincke reported a clear relationship between association value and "goodness" ratings. The rationale of this study invoked the assumed relationship between association of the given nonsense syllable and the probability of occurrence of the corresponding letter combination in meaningful words (Underwood, 1959).

In an attempt to examine the generality of this phenomenon, we studied the evaluations of 154 antonym pairs. First, a large pool of antonym pairs was amassed. From this pool, all symmetric[2] pairs were chosen in the following manner. For each antonym pair, 10 judges, 1 at a time, were asked to give the antonym of one member of the pair. Ten other judges—independently of the first 10—were asked to give the antonym of the other [3] member of the pair. Only those pairs were retained about which the 20 judges showed unanimous agreement with the dictionary sources. A list of 154 antonym pairs was thus obtained. These were given to 100 subjects, all college students, for judgments as to which member had "the more favorable meaning, represented the more desirable object, event, state of affairs, characteristic, etc." A different random order of the antonym pairs was given to each subject, and the lateral positions of the members of each pair were reversed at random for half of the group.

Table 6.1 shows the list of these 154 antonym pairs, together with the "desirability" and the frequency data (the Thorndike-Lorge L-count). The preferred member of each pair is always listed first. The "desirability" figures are simply the percentages of subjects choosing the left member of the pair as the preferred alternative.

It is of some interest, however incidental, that there is considerable agreement about desirability of the meanings. On half of the items, the agreement exceeded 95%. Agreement is high even for words which are not genuinely evaluative. For instance, 97 of the 100 students preferred "on" to "off," 98 preferred "add" to "subtract," 96 "above" to "below," and 92 "upward" to "downward."

For the overwhelming majority of the items, the preferred word is also the more frequent one. Only 28 of the 154 antonym pairs (18%) show a negative relationship between frequency and desirability. Moreover, these "reversals" occur primarily for antonym pairs on which there is relatively little agreement. For pairs with agreement greater than 95% (i.e., the upper half of the list), there are only six reversals out of the 77 possible. It is significant, moreover, that in three of these six antonym pairs, the less desirable member (which in these cases is the more frequent one) has more meanings

---

[2] One finds in the course of this endeavor that the antonymic relation is seldom symmetric. According to the standard sources, if Y is listed as the antonym of X, then chances are that not X but Z is listed as the antonym of Y. For instance, in the 1960 edition of Webster's New Collegiate Dictionary, "extend" is given as the antonym of "contract." Looking up "extend" we find, however, that its antonym is "reduce." The antonym of "reduce," on the other hand, is "increase." The antonym of "increase" is "decrease," the antonym of "decrease" is "amplify," the antonym of "amplify" is "condense," and the antonym of "condense" is "expand." We can ultimately close the circle, because "contract," according to this source, is the antonym of "expand."

Table 6.1   Semantic Preference and Frequency of 154 Antonym Pairs

% agree-ment	Preferred alternative (a)	Nonpreferred alternative (b)	Fre-quency of (a)	Fre-quency of (b)	% agree-ment	Preferred alternative (a)	Nonpreferred alternative (b)	Fre-quency of (a)	Fre-quency of (b)
100	able	unable	930	239	96	active	passive	186	29
100	attentive	inattentive	49	4	96	early	late	1,022	2,859
100	better	worse	2,354	450	96	front	back	1,094	6,587
100	encourage	discourage	205	147	96	full	empty	1,129	395
100	friendly	unfriendly	357	19	96	live	die	4,307	1,079
100	honest	dishonest	393	41	96	presence	absence	277	163
100	possible	impossible	1,289	459	96	probable	improbable	64	14
99	advance	retreat	452	105	96	rational	irrational	33	9
99	best	worst	1,850	292	96	reasonable	unreasonable	155	56
99	clean	dirty	781	221	96	resolutely	irresolutely	30	4
99	comfortable	uncomfortable	348	112	96	strong	weak	770	276
99	favorable	unfavorable	93	25	96	succeed	fail	264	620
99	good	bad	5,122	1,001	96	superior	inferior	166	40
99	grateful	ungrateful	194	13	96	timely	untimely	27	6
99	peace	war	472	1,118	95	accept	reject	667	51
99	present	absent	1,075	65	95	direct	indirect	416	23
99	pure	impure	197	4	95	include	exclude	533	38
99	responsible	irresponsible	267	30	95	increase	decrease	781	86
99	reward	punishment	154	80	95	most	least	3,443	1,259
99	right	wrong	3,874	890	95	practical	impractical	340	12
99	smile	frown	2,143	216	95	regularly	irregularly	122	5
99	tolerant	intolerant	42	13	95	rich	poor	656	857
99	victory	defeat	118	166	95	wealth	poverty	243	146
98	add	subtract	2,018	6	94	approve	disapprove	171	45
98	advantage	disadvantage	404	41	94	conscious	unconscious	299	116
98	agreeable	disagreeable	58	43	94	leader	follower	373	45
98	capable	incapable	176	30	94	obedient	disobedient	70	4
98	desirable	undesirable	160	42	94	together	apart	1,835	276
98	find	lose	2,698	593	93	agreement	disagreement	143	21
98	fortunate	unfortunate	136	108	93	certain	uncertain	800	107
98	forward	backward	736	139	93	first	last	5,154	3,517
98	friend	enemy	2,553	883	93	major	minor	366	83
98	high	low	1,674	1,224	93	normal	abnormal	335	43
98	honorable	dishonorable	58	8	93	regular	irregular	340	44
98	kind	unkind	1,521	34	93	unselfish	selfish	32	137
98	legal	illegal	180	34	93	upwards	downwards	9	40
98	life	death	4,804	815	93	wide	narrow	593	391
98	love	hate	5,129	756	92	more	less	8,015	1,357
98	mature	immature	91	17	92	now	then	7,665	10,208
98	moral	immoral	272	19	92	up	down	11,718	5,534
98	pleasant	unpleasant	457	114	92	upward	downward	111	27
98	polite	impolite	115	3	92	visible	invisible	110	74
98	reliable	unreliable	78	9	92	yes	no	2,202	11,742
98	success	failure	573	262	91	always	never	3,285	5,715
98	valid	invalid	22	56	91	familiar	unfamiliar	345	39
98	voluntary	involuntary	28	26	91	maximum	minimum	43	86
97	adequate	inadequate	95	59	91	optimism	pessimism	28	11
97	competent	incompetent	69	23	90	agree	disagree	729	38
97	found	lost	2,892	1,074	90	necessary	unnecessary	715	107
97	important	unimportant	1,130	40	90	over	under	7,520	2,961
97	likely	unlikely	364	25	90	sweet	sour	679	102
97	on	off	30,224	3,644	90	whole	part	1,663	1,585
97	patience	impatience	139	39	89	light	dark	2,387	1,005
97	patient	impatient	392	79	88	deep	shallow	881	104
97	patiently	impatiently	85	82	88	smooth	rough	346	294
97	popular	unpopular	418	12	86	white	black	2,663	1,083
97	positive	negative	92	28	85	in	out	75,253	13,649
97	profitable	unprofitable	57	12	85	independent	dependent	134	18
97	promote	demote	90	2	84	fast	slow	514	434
97	remember	forget	1,682	882	83	comedy	tragedy	126	189
97	satisfactory	unsatisfactory	154	32	83	fasten	unfasten	142	16
97	willingly	unwillingly	66	13	79	day	night	4,549	3,385
96	above	below	941	529	78	dry	wet	592	319

(continued)

Table 6.1   Semantic Preference and Frequency of 154 Antonym Pairs *(continued)*

% agree-ment	Preferred alternative (a)	Nonpreferred alternative (b)	Fre-quency of (a)	Fre-quency of (b)	% agree-ment	Preferred alternative (a)	Nonpreferred alternative (b)	Fre-quency of (a)	Fre-quency of (b)
78	long	short	5,362	887	63	answer	question	2,132	1,302
78	unshaken	shaken	6	83	63	men	women	3,614	2,552
77	usually	unusually	718	91	61	different	same	1,194	1,747
74	upstairs	downstairs	314	226	59	inward	outward	43	54
72	inner	outer	143	97	59	man	woman	7,355	2,431
72	interior	exterior	185	48	58	husband	wife	1,788	1,668
70	near	far	1,338	1,835	58	usual	unusual	516	273
70	unlimited	limited	43	67	57	offense	defense	86	223
68	inside	outside	656	921	55	hot	cold	1,006	1,092
68	wrap	unwrap	293	17	55	import	export	86	88
67	infinite	finite	71	2	55	inwardly	outwardly	32	33
67	internal	external	36	26	54	inconspicuous	conspicuous	33	59
65	coming	going	1,486	4,623	52	play	work	2,606	2,720
64	informal	formal	64	166	51	mortal	immortal	54	26

and linguistic uses than the more desirable one. "Invalid" means both "not valid" and "cripple," but "valid" is just "valid." "Yes" is an adverb, but "no" is an adverb *and* an adjective. And "front" is a noun, a verb, and an adjective, while "back" is all that and an adverb to boot.

Toward the end of the list, where the desirability preferences are divided fairly evenly between the two members of the antonym pairs, the frequencies of the two antonyms often are nearly the same. "Play" is preferred to "work" only by a majority of two (a curious commentary on the contemporary college population!), and the respective frequency counts of these antonyms are 2606 and 2720. The "hot-cold" preference is 55 to 45 and their frequency counts 1006 and 1092. The "husband-wife" preference is 58 to 42 and their respective frequencies, 1788 and 1668.

Three antonym items about which agreement was complete or nearly complete show a curious pattern of results. They are "good-bad" (5122:1001), "better-worse" (2354:450), and "best-worst" (1850:292). Since "better" is presumably better than "good," "worse" worse than "bad," and since "best" is presumably better than "better," and "worst" worse than "worse," we would expect [5] the greatest separation between the frequencies of "best" and "worst," smallest between the frequencies of "good" and "bad," and medium between the frequencies of "better" and "worse." Since absolute differences are deceiving, we best take the ratios of the frequencies, which are 6.34, 5.23, and 5.12 for "best-worst," "better-worse," and "good-bad," respectively. It is indeed the case that the frequency ratios increase from "good-bad" to "best-worse." However, if frequency reflects "desirability," we would also expect the frequency of "best" to exceed the frequency of "better," and that of "better" to exceed the frequency of "good." In fact, however, "good" is more frequent than "better," and "better" more frequent than "best!" But *is* "better" better than "good?" In an extensive study of meanings, Mosier (1941) found that "good" was consistently rated as better than "better."

> Startling as this may appear to grammarians, it is psychologically sound, since GOOD is a positive assertion, whereas BETTER implies comparison with some standard which might, in many cases, be itself unfavorable.

Compare the often heard comment, "He is getting better, but he is still far from good" [p.134].

For purposes of comparison, the frequencies of French, German, and Spanish equivalents of some of the antonyms examined are given in Table 6.2. Systematic data on indigenous desirability ratings are unfortunately not available, but it would be surprising if the French, German, and Spanish judgments differed from those obtained in the United States. An informal inquiry among foreign visitors marshalled a good deal of support for his conjecture. Comparing the data in Tables 1 and 2, the agreement is rather striking. In 15 out of the 44 cases, the frequency relation in the antonym pairs is the same in the three foreign languages as in English: the more favorable item is more frequent, a result exceeding chance expectation by a large margin. The results in Table 6.2, furthermore, give a ready expression to our favorite ethnic prejudices. The relatively low frequency of the two Romance equivalents of "early" and the high frequency of these equivalents of "late," a comparison to the Germanic counterparts, make generalizations about national character tempting, as does the relatively low frequency of the German equivalent of "reward." The foreign equivalents of answer-question, hot cold, import-export, peace-war, etc., however, show patterns of differences that may reflect more than superficial linguistic idiosyncrasies.

Several questions can immediately be raised about the results. First, are these figures up-to-date? The Thorndike-Lorge count is based on samples of material published during the late twenties and the early thirties. The German equivalents come from a source dating to the late 19th century (Käding, 1898). The French count was published in 1929 (Van der Beke, 1929), and the Spanish in 1927 (Buchanan, 1927). Secondly, do these results reflect general verbal habits? Word counts are based on printed material alone. Do people show the same linguistic predilections in ordinary speech as they do in writing? Admittedly, both questions indicate caution in generalizing from the results. But this caution needn't be excessive. Howes (1954) has recently asked Harvard and Antioch undergraduates to estimate the probabilities of various words. The correlations between the students' estimates of several word samples and the L-count of the Thorndike-Lorge source varied around .80. There is also evidence from word association studies showing that word counts do reflect general verbal habits of the population. A word which has a high frequency of occurrence in print is also a highly probable associate. The association norms to 200 words were recently collected by Palermo and Jenkins (1964) from a sample of 4,500 school children and college students in Minneapolis. The list of the 200 stimulus words represents a systematic sample of verbs, nouns, pronouns, adverbs, adjectives, participles, etc., all having fairly high frequency on the Thorndike-Lorge counts. Since in the word association task each subject makes one response to each stimulus word, Palermo and Jenkins collected from their subjects 900,000 word responses. Among them, "good" occurred 4890 times, "bad" only 1956. The response "right" was given 477 times, the response "wrong" only 100 times. "Full" was found 431 times among the associations, "empty" only 62 times. "Strong" was given 557, "weak" 96 times. "Together" occurred 575 times, "apart" **[6]** 29 times. "Light" was a response 8655 times (N.B., some subjects must have given it more than once), "dark" 4274 times. But, as in the case of the Thorndike-Lorge count, "front" occurred 22 times, while "back" occurred 265 times; "rich" was given 36 times,

Table 6.2   Frequency Ranks of English, French, German, and Spanish Antonym Pairs

English	French	German	Spanish
able (3)	capable (3)	fähig (4)	capaz (3)
unable (9)	incapable (4)	unfähig (11)	incapaz (7)
accept (3)	accepter (2)	annahmen (2)	acceptar (3)
reject (9)	rejecter (5)	ablehnen (5)	rechazar (5)
active (6)	actif (6)	tätig (5)	activo (6)
passive (14)	passif (?)	untätig (?)	passivo (10)
answer (2)	résponse (4)	Antwort (3)	respuesta (4)
question (3)	question (2)	Frage (2)	pregunta (4)
better (2)	meilleur (2)	besser (2)	mejor (2)
worse (4)	pire (5)	schlechter (9)	peor (2)
certain (2)	certain (2)	sicher (2)	cierto (2)
uncertain (9)	incertain (10)	unsicher (9)	incierto (9)
clean (3)	propre (2)	sauber (9)	limpio (3)
dirty (7)	sale (7)	schmutzig (12)	sucio (6)
comedy (9)	comédie (6)	Komödie (9)	comedia (4)
tragedy (9)	tragédie (9)	Tragödie (11)	tragedia (8)
comfortable (5)	à l'aise (4)	bequem (5)	cómodo (7)
uncomfortable (11)	incomfortable (9)	unbequem (10)	incómodo (10)
day (2)	jour (2)	Tag (2)	día (2)
night (2)	nuit (2)	Nacht (2)	noche (2)
direct (3)	direct (6)	direkt (3)	directo (4)
indirect (12)	indirect (12)	indirekt (8)	indirecto (8)
dry (3)	sec (3)	trocken (5)	seco (3)
wet (4)	mouillé (5)	nass (9)	mojado (6)
early (2)	tôt (3)	früh (2)	temprano (4)
late (2)	tard (2)	spät (2)	tarde (2)
fast (2)	vite (2)	schnell (2)	pronto (2)
slow (3)	lent (4)	langsam (3)	lento (4)
find (2)	trouver (2)	finden (2)	encontrar (2)
lose (3)	perdre (2)	verlieren (2)	perder (2)
friend (2)	ami (2)	Freund (2)	amigo (2)
enemy (3)	ennemi (2)	Feind (2)	enemigo (2)
full (2)	plein (2)	voll (2)	lleno (2)
empty (4)	vide (4)	leer (4)	vacio (4)
good (2)	bon (2)	gut (2)	buen (2)
bad (2)	mauvais (2)	schlecht (3)	mal (2)
high (2)	haut (2)	hoch (2)	alto (2)
low (2)	bas (2)	niedrig (4)	bajo (2)
hot (2)	chaud (3)	heiss (5)	caliente (5)
cold (2)	froid (3)	kalt (3)	frío (2)
husband (3)	mari (3)	Mann (2)	esposo (2)
wife (3)	femme (2)	Frau (2)	esposa (2)
import (7)	importation (11)	Einfuhr (11)	importación (?)
export (11)	exportation (10)	Ausfuhr (12)	exportación (13)
increase (3)	augmentation (10)	Vermehrung (6)	aumento (5)
decrease (8)	reduction (11)	Verminderung (11)	diminución (13)
independent (6)	indépendent (7)	selbstständig (4)	independiente (5)
dependent (14)	dépendent (?)	abhängig (6)	dependiente (9)
life (2)	vie (2)	Leben (2)	vida (2)
death (2)	mort (2)	Tod (2)	muerte (2)
light (2)	clair (3)	hell (4)	claro (2)
dark (2)	sombre (3)	dunkel (3)	obscuro (2)

(continued)

Table 6.2   Frequency Ranks of English, French, German, and Spanish Antonym Pairs *(continued)*

English	French	German	Spanish
live (2)	vivre (2)	leben (2)	vivir (2)
die (2)	mourir (2)	sterben (2)	morir (2)
long (2)	long (2)	lang (2)	largo (2)
short (2)	court (3)	kurz (2)	corto (3)
love (2)	aimer (2)	lieben (2)	amar (2)
hate (4)	haïr (6)	hassen (6)	odiar (7)
more (2)	plus (2)	mehr (2)	más (2)
less (2)	moins (2)	weniger (2)	menos (2)
near (2)	près (3)	nah (2)	cerca (2)
far (2)	loin (2)	fern (2)	lejos (2)
peace (3)	paix (3)	Friede (3)	paz (3)
war (2)	guerre (3)	Krieg (2)	guerra (2)
positive (9)	positif (6)	positiv (8)	positivo (7)
negative (11)	negatif (11)	negativ (11)	negativo (7)
possible (3)	possible (2)	möglich (2)	posible (2)
impossible (5)	impossible (3)	unmöglich (3)	imposible (2)
presence (4)	présence (2)	Anwesenheit (9)	presencia (3)
absence (7)	absence (5)	Abwesenheit (9)	ausencia (4)
reward (6)	récompense (6)	Anerkennung (5)	premio (4)
punishment (6)	punition (12)	Strafe (4)	castigo (4)
right (2)	juste (2)	richtig (2)	justo (3)
wrong (3)	faux (3)	falsch (3)	mal (2)
strong (2)	fort (2)	stark (2)	fuerte (2)
weak (3)	faible (3)	schwach (3)	debil (4)
sweet (2)	doux (2)	süss (4)	dulce (2)
sour (9)	amer (4)	sauer (9)	amargo (4)
together (2)	ensemble (2)	zusammen (2)	junto (2)
apart (4)	séparé (2)	getrennt (3)	separado (3)
victory (5)	victoire (4)	Sieg (4)	victoria (5)
defeat (7)	défaite (8)	Niederlage (8)	derrota (9)
wealth (4)	richesse (5)	Vermögen (4)	riqueza (3)
poverty (7)	pauvreté (12)	Armut (10)	pobreza (5)
white (2)	blanc (2)	weiss (2)	blanco (2)
black (2)	noir (2)	schwartz (3)	negro (2)
wide (2)	large (2)	breit (4)	ancho (3)
narrow (3)	étroit (3)	schmal (6)	angosto (8)

Note: The figures in brackets indicate frequency ranks: (1) means that the word is among the 500 most frequent words, (2) that it is among the 1,000 most frequent words, (3) that it is among the 1, 500 most frequent words, etc. The source of these counts is Eaton (1940).

while "poor" was a response 95 times. "Near" was given 981 times, "far" 1218. "Coming" was given 166 times, "going" 714 times. And, as in L-count, "play" and "work" showed 791 and 957 occurrences, respectively.

However, the best evidence about the relationship between the individual's verbal habits and the evaluative aspect of meaning is found in a recent study by Siegel,[3] although it wasn't the purpose of her study to explore this relationship. Siegel's experiment dealt with the effects of verbal reinforcement on the emission of words differing in affective connotation and in frequency. Eighteen six-letter words of known frequencies and previously judged on the good-bad and the pleasant-unpleasant scales were selected

---

[3] Siegel, Felicia S. Effects of word frequency and affective connotation on verbal responding during extinction. (Mimeo)

from a larger [8] sample. Six of these words were of high frequency (100 and more in 1 million), six of medium (20 to 30), and six of low frequency (1 to 5). Within each frequency class, two words were previously judged to be good, two neutral, and two bad. Three groups of subjects, other than those involved in the affective judgments, participated in the experiment, each having to deal with six words of the same frequency. The procedure consisted of presenting the subject with the list of six words, all high, medium, or low in frequency, depending on the condition in which he was in, and giving him at the same time a stack of cards on which appeared illegible six-letter "words." Ostensibly, each card contained one of the six words in the subjects' list. Actually, the "words" consisted of random sequences of six letters, printed over several thicknesses of paper and one carbon. Their legibility was further reduced by placing each card in an onionskin paper envelope. The subjects' task was to "read" or to guess what word appeared on each card. Of interest for the present purposes are the first 50 trials which served to establish operant rate, and during which, of course, no reinforcement of any sort was given. Table 6.3 shows data on the guessing behavior of Siegel's subjects as a function of word frequency and affective connotation. Reported in each cell is the average number of times a word of a given frequency and affective value was used as a guess during the 50 operant trials. Since there are six words to choose from, 8.33 represents a chance response rate. It is clear, however, that both frequency and affective connotation displace response rate away from the chance level. High frequency seems to result in overcalling, and low frequency in undercalling. But it is striking to discover that affective connotation had an even stronger effect on response emission, the marginals for that variable showing a somewhat greater range of differences.

Some words in the language have primarily an evaluative function. These words should show the frequency-value relationship with particular clarity. Several instances of this relationship are examined.

Let us first consider the scales of the Semantic Differential (Osgood, Suci, and Tannenbaum, 1957). We have chosen only those scales which have high and relatively pure loadings on one of the three main factors: *evaluation, potency,* and *activity.* Table 6.4 shows the polar opposites of these scales, together with their frequencies according to the Thorndike-Lorge L-count. The left-hand polar opposites in the three columns are the favorable, potent, and active ends of the scales. It is significant that, among the 19 evaluative scales, the favorable polar opposite has always higher frequency than the

Table 6.3   Free Response Emission as a Function of Word-Frequency and Word Value*

| Word value | Word frequency | | | |
	Low	Medium	High	$\bar{X}$
Good	7.43	9.43	9.68	8.85
Medium	6.28	8.57	8.71	7.85
Bad	6.28	5.86	7.71	6.61
$\bar{X}$	6.66	7.95	8.70	

*From Siegel, 1960.

unfavorable opposite. For the scales which do not load high on the evaluative factor, the high frequencies are divided fairly evenly among the potent and nonpotent opposites. In 9 of the 15 potency scales, the highly potent end of the scale is more frequent. In 3 of the 8 activity scales, the active polar opposite is more frequent.

There are two other instances of a high correlation between frequency and value for adjectives. The first comes from the work by Gough (1953). Gough has given the items of his Adjective Checklist to 30 judges who rated each adjective for favorability. The most favorable and the least favorable quartiles of Gough's checklist are reported in his publication. The average word frequency of the upper quartile is 140, and of the lower quartile 48. The second illustration comes from data collected by Anderson (1964). A list of 555 adjectives was recently used by Anderson in his work on impression formation. The list was constructed out of a large sample of items. The 555 selected items were given by Anderson to a group of 100 subjects with the instructions to rate on a 7-point scale "how much you yourself would like the person described by that word." We have simply computed the correlation between these likeability [9] ratings and the logarithm of the Thorndike-Lorge L-count.[4] Figure 6.1 shows this relationship graphically, where means of log frequencies are plotted for six categories of adjectives in increasing order of favorability. Considering that the reliabilities of the Thorndike-Lorge count and of Anderson's favorability ratings are less than perfect, the coefficient of correlation of .83 is particularly impressive.

Miller, Newman, and Friedman (1958) have shown that word frequency is a negative function of word length. The problem immediately arises, therefore, as to which of

Table 6.4   Polar Opposites of the Semantic Differential and Their Frequencies

Evaluative factor			
beautiful	ugly	987	178
clean	dirty	781	221
fair	unfair	561	59
fragrant	foul	66	39
good	bad	5,122	1,001
grateful	ungrateful	194	13
happy	sad	1,449	202
harmonious	dissonant	26	9
honest	dishonest	393	41
kind	cruel	1,521	165
nice	awful	630	370
pleasant	unpleasant	457	114
positive	negative	92	28
reputable	disreputable	23	21
sacred	profane	102	13
successful	unsuccessful	352	14
sweet	sour	679	102
true	false	1,711	209
wise	foolish	420	223

Potency factor			
bass	treble	28	17
brave	cowardly	216	26
deep	shallow	881	104
hard	soft	1,909	549
heavy	light	680	1,005
large	small	1,697	1,818
masculine	feminine	54	40
mature	youthful	91	99
rough	smooth	294	346
rugged	delicate	37	248
severe	lenient	119	9
strong	weak	770	276
tenacious	yielding	22	7
thick	thin	443	646
wide	narrow	593	391

Activity factor			
active	passive	514	434
bright	dark	645	1,005
excitable	calm	7	267
fast	slow	514	434
heretical	orthodox	2	21
hot	cold	1,006	1,092
rash	cautious	37	48
sharp	dull	324	289

---

[4] Items for which there was no frequency information in the Thorndike-Lorge count were not included in computing this coefficient. These items were primarily of the hyphenated form, such as open-minded, good-humored, well-spoken, fault-finding, ultra-critical, wishy-washy, etc.

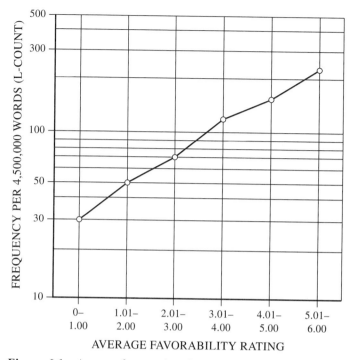

Figure 6.1   Average frequencies of 555 adjectives rated for favorability (Based on data
from Anderson, 1964)

these two variables is critical for word value and word meaning. In order to examine
this possible confounding between frequency and word length, the correlation was
recomputed holding the number of letters constant. No appreciable change in the previously obtained coefficient was observed.

The relationship between word frequency and word length is generally explained
in terms of the principle of least effort. Words that require considerable effort in writing and in speech are less likely candidates for use. In an attempt to control for effort,
Frincke and Johnson (1960) have asked subjects to choose the "most pleasantly toned
word" from each of 108 homophone pairs. The greatest majority of these pairs consisted
of words of the same length, and all pairs, of course, consisted of words that required
the same effort in uttering them. Out of 3,132 possible choices, [10] the more frequent
member of the pair was chosen 1,836 times.

Dixon and Dixon (1964) have given a list of 200 verbs (in past-tense form) to 60
female and 60 male judges who rated them on an 11-point good-bad scale. The instructions were to rate what "kind of impression the subject thought a psychologist would
get of him when he used each verb in a sentence." These impression ratings have correlations with log frequencies (the Thorndike-Lorge L-count) equal to .48 for females
and to .50 for males. But it must be pointed out that these coefficients represent correlations severely attenuated by unreliability of the frequency variable. The Thorndike-
Lorge count lists verbs in the present-tense form. If an adjectival form of the verb exists,

then it is also listed. In our own research, in computing correlation coefficients, only the present-tense frequencies were used.

Miron (1961) had American and Japanese subjects rate a sample of three-element phonetic combinations on various scales of the Semantic Differential. The subjects also rated these stimulus materials for their familiarity. It is interesting that the correlations between familiarity and the composite of evaluative scales were .59 and .50 for the American and the Japanese samples, respectively. But the correlations of familiarity with the composites of the potency and activity factors were low and negative.

As a final example of the relationship between word frequency and the evaluative aspect of meaning, two poems by William Blake are called to the reader's attention:

Infant joy
"I have no name:
I am but two days old,"
What shall I call thee?
"I happy am,
Joy is my name."
Sweet joy befall thee!
Pretty joy!
Sweet joy but two days old,
Sweet joy I call thee:
Thou dost smile,
I sing the while,
Sweet joy befall thee!

Infant Sorrow
My mother groaned! My father wept;
Into the dangerous world I leapt;
Helpless, naked, piping loud,
Like a fiend hid in a cloud,
Struggling in my father's hands,
Striving against my swadling bands,
Bound and weary I thought best
To sulk upon my mother's breast.

In these two poems, expressing opposite qualities of affect, the frequencies of the critical words (i.e., words which convey the major content, and, hence, not articles, pronouns, or auxiliary verbs) were averaged. The average frequency of *Infant Joy* is 2,037. The average for *Infant Sorrow* is 1,116. Two formally similar verses, one by Browning and the other by Shelley, show the same pattern:

Song. R. Browning
The year's at the spring,
And day's at the morn;
Morning's at seven;
The hillside's dew-pearled;
The lark's on the wing;

The snail's on the thorn;
God's in his Heaven—
All's right with the world.

Dirge. P. B. Shelley
Rough wind, that moanest loud
Grief too sad for song;
Wild wind, when sullen cloud
Knells all the night long;
Sad storm, whose tears are in vain,
Bare woods, whose branches strain,
Deep caves and dreary main—
Wail, for the world's wrong.

The average word frequency of Browning's poem is 1,380. The poem by Shelley—which comes to a rather different and sadder conclusion—has an average frequency of 728.

STIMULUS FREQUENCY-ATTITUDE: CORRELATIONAL EVIDENCE

We may now turn to the more general question of the effect of exposure on attitude, still limiting ourselves to correlational studies. Here, less evidence exists, and the evidence which is available is often indirect. But the [11] results are quite similar to those just reviewed. For instance, Alluisi and Adams (1962) found a correlation of .843 between the preference subjects expressed for the appearance of letters and their frequency in the language. Strassburger and Wertheimer (1959) had subjects rate for "pleasantness" nonsense syllables varying in association value. Higher association values consistently received higher "pleasantness" ratings. Wilson and Becknell (1961) and Braun (1962) successfully replicated these results. Braun also found that eight-letter pseudo-words, varying in their order of approximation to English (Miller, 1951), show the same pattern. These two studies differ from the similar ones by Johnson, Thomson, and Frincke, discussed earlier, in that subjects in the former ones were asked to judge how pleasant were the stimuli themselves, or how much subjects liked them (Wilson and Becknell, 1961), while in the latter, whether they *meant* something close to "good" or close to "bad."

In 1947, the National Opinion Research Center conducted an extensive survey on the "prestige" of various occupations and professions. Nearly 100 occupational categories were rated for "general standing." Twenty-four of these occupations are labeled by single words, such as "physician," "scientist," "janitor," etc. The remainder is described less economically: "owner-operator of a printing shop," or "tenant farmer—one who owns live stock and machinery and manages the farm." Thus, one is able to determine the frequency of usage for only a part of this list—the 24 single-word occupations. The correlation between rated occupational prestige of these 24 items and the log of frequency of usage is .55.

Similar to the ratings of occupational prestige are the social distance ratings of ethnic and racial groups, first developed by Bogardus (1925) over 30 years ago. Recent replications show that these social distance ratings enjoy remarkable stability (Bogardus, 1959). The correlation between the so-called "racial-distance quotients," which are numerical equivalents of these ratings, and the log frequency of usage of these ethnic labels is .33.

In order to explore relationships of this sort further, I have selected 10 countries whose names are found in the Thorndike-Lorge L-count, and whose frequencies can be arranged in increasing order in approximately constant log units. These countries were then given to high school students with the instructions to rank-order them in terms of liking. Table 6.5 shows the average rank each country received and its frequency of usage according to the L-count. There seems to be little question about the frequency-attitude relationship. The same relationship is found with American cities. Selected were 10 cities that (a) are listed in the Thorndike-Lorge L-count, and (b) can be arranged in increasing order of frequency in approximately constant log units. University students were asked how much they would like to live in each of these 10 cities. Their task, specifically, was to rank-order these cities according to their preferences "as a place to live." The average ranks, together with frequency counts of these 10 cities, are shown in Table 6.5.

Other subjects, also high school students in the Midwest, were asked to rate on a 7-point scale how much they liked various trees, fruits, vegetables, and flowers. In each case, 10 items were selected which were listed in the Thorndike-Lorge count and which could be ordered according to a constant log frequency unit. Table 6.6 shows both the average ratings (0 = dislike; 6 = like) and the frequency counts for the four types of items. The rank correlations between the frequency and average attitude are .89, .85, .84, .81, .85, and .89, for countries, cities, trees, fruits, vegetables, and flowers, respectively. [12]

Of course, word counts do not faithfully represent the frequencies with which one encounters the items. And it is difficult to discover precisely how often the average Midwestern high school student encounters a yew, a cowslip, or a radish. But a fair

Table 6.5   Preference Ranks and Frequency Counts for 10 Countries and 10 Cities

Countries			Cities		
Country	Frequency	Average Preference Rank	City	Frequency	Average Preference Rank
England	497	2.67	Boston	255	2.75
Canada	130	3.33	Chicago	621	3.08
Holland	59	3.42	Milwaukee	124	3.83
Greece	31	4.00	San Diego	9	4.25
Germany	224	4.92	Dayton	14	5.75
Argentina	15	6.08	Baltimore	68	6.08
Venezuela	9	6.58	Omaha	28	7.08
Bulgaria	3	7.75	Tampa	5	7.08
Honduras	1	7.92	El Paso	1	7.50
Syria	4	8.34	Saginaw	2	7.58

Table 6.6   Preference Rating of Trees, Fruits, Vegetables, and Flowers, and Their Corresponding Frequencies

Trees	f	APR	Fruits	f	APR	Vegetables	f	APR	Flowers	f	APR
pine	172	4.79	apple	220	5.13	corn	227	4.17	rose	801	5.55
walnut	75	4.42	cherry	167	5.00	potato	384	4.13	lily	164	4.79
oak	125	4.00	strawberry	121	4.83	lettuce	142	4.00	violet	109	4.58
rosewood	8	3.96	pear	62	4.38	carrot	96	3.57	geranium	27	3.83
birch	34	3.83	grapefruit	33	4.00	radish	43	3.13	daisy	62	3.79
fir	14	3.75	cantaloupe	1.5	3.75	asparagus	5	2.33	hyacinth	16	3.08
sassafras	2	3.00	avocado	16	2.71	cauliflower	27	1.96	yucca	1	2.88
aloes	1	2.92	pomegranate	8	2.63	broccoli	18	1.96	woodbine	4	2.87
yew	3	2.83	gooseberry	5	2.63	leek	3	1.96	anemone	8	2.54
acacia	4	2.75	mango	2	2.38	parsnip	8	1.92	cowslip	2	2.54

index of frequency of exposure can be found in farm production data. For seven of the vegetables in Table 6.6, farm production figures for 1963 are available, and they are shown here in thousands of tons:

corn (4.17)	2,340.9
potatoes (4.13)	13,777.1
lettuce (4.00)	1,937.6
carrots (3.57)	843.8
asparagus (2.33)	187.8
cauliflower (1.96)	123.4
broccoli (1.96)	123.9

Included also (in brackets) are average preference ratings of these seven vegetables. The rank correlation between the production figures and the average preference ratings is .96.

Of course, this impressive correlation coefficient, like those we observed earlier, may not reflect the effect of frequency on attitude but the effect of attitude on frequency. Thus, it can be argued that many roses are grown because people like roses. But it can also be argued that people like roses because there are many roses growing. There is less ambiguity, however, with regard to the correlation between frequency of letters and the preference for their appearance (Alluisi and Adams, 1962). There aren't so many e's in English just because we like the way e's look. Still, until there is experimental evidence, the question of which is the cause and which the effect remains a matter of conjecture. We shall now turn, therefore, to such experimental evidence.

EXPOSURE—MEANING: EXPERIMENTAL EVIDENCE

Experiment I

The first experimental study on the relationship between exposure and word meaning was carried out by Johnson, Thomson, and Frincke (1960). These authors first asked subjects to rate a number of nonsense words on the good-bad scale of the semantic differential. The subjects were then instructed that "this is an experiment concerning the effectiveness of repetition in learning to pronounce strange words correctly." Some of these words were shown once, others twice, 5 times, or 10 times. Subjects were required to look at these words and to pronounce them on each presentation. Following this training procedure, the words were again rated on the good-bad scale. A significant exposure effect was obtained, with the words shown frequently increasing on the evaluative scale. Strangely, however, words which were seen only once in training were judged afterwards not quite as "good" as before training. Thus, as a result of 2, 5, and 10 exposures, words improved in meaning, and as a result of but 1 exposure, they deteriorated. This finding, however, may be an artifact of the before-after procedure used by Johnson, Thomson, and Frincke. Moreover, frequencies and stimuli were fully confounded in their study.

Our experiment used the same stimuli which, incidentally, came from the familiar experiment by Solomon and Postman (1952) on the effects of word frequency on recognition threshold, but our design differed from the one used by Johnson, Thomson, and Frincke in several respects. In the Johnson-Thomson-Frincke experiment, the same words always appeared in the same frequencies to all subjects. Thus, the word "jandara," for instance, was given 10 times to each subject, and the word "mecburi" was given once to each subject. It is possible that the effects these authors obtained are not due to the [13] frequency manipulation alone, but that they depend on the stimulus material with which the frequency variable was fully confounded. In our study, words and training frequencies were, therefore, counterbalanced in a Latin-square design. Because words and the number of exposures were counterbalanced, an after-only design could be employed, requiring no premeasures. The effects of repeated exposure could be observed for each word by comparing the favorability rating it received after having been exposed during training once, twice, five times, etc. Eliminating premeasures also eliminated for each stimulus one full exposure that necessarily preceded, and therefore accompanied, the frequency manipulation.

The present experiment differs from that of Johnson, Thomson, and Frincke (1960) in several other respects which are less critical for the interpretation of results. The procedure of this experiment, therefore, is described in some detail. Except for some specific changes, the same general methodology is followed throughout this series of studies.

Twelve seven-letter "Turkish" words, shown in Figure 6.3, were counterbalanced against six frequencies (0, 1, 2, 5, 10, and 25) in six replications of the experiment. Seventy-two subjects were run, one at a time, 12 subjects in each replication. The initial instructions informed the subject that the experiment dealt with "pronouncing foreign words." He was told that he would be shown some foreign words, hear the experimenter pronounce them, and that he would be required to pronounce them himself. The words were typed on 3 × 5-inch cards. On each trial, a card was shown to the subject for approximately 2 seconds. Simultaneously, the experimenter pronounced the word, requiring the subject to follow him. Since each frequency class contained two word-stimuli, there were 86 trials altogether. The position of a given stimulus in the sequence of these 86 trials was determined at random. Following the frequency training, subjects were told that the words they had just learned to pronounce were, in fact, Turkish adjectives, and that their next task would be to guess what they meant. The experimenter told the subject that he realized how nearly impossible this task was, and he therefore did not require him to guess the word meanings exactly. Instead, it would suffice if the subject indicated on a 7-point (0 to 6) good-bad scale whether each word meant something good or something bad and to what extent, because these Turkish adjectives all meant something good or bad. These ratings were made of the 10 stimuli which the subject received during the frequency training, and of 2 additional ones previously never seen by him.

The results of the experiment are shown in Figure 6.2 and in Figure 6.3. In Figure 6.2 are shown the ratings of "goodness" averaged for each of the six frequencies, and plotted on a log scale. Each point in that curve is based on 144 observations, and it is clear that a strong exposure effect was obtained ($F = 5.64$; $df = 5/355$; $p < .001$). Figure 6.3 shows the exposure effect for each of the 12 words separately. The ratings of "goodness" were averaged for each word when it was given during training with the lower frequencies of 0, 1, and 2 (hatched bars), and when it was given with the higher frequencies of 5, 10, and 25 (solid bars). This was possible because each word was used in each frequency equally often but for different subjects. It is evident from Figure 6.3 that some words are rated as having more positive meaning than others, and this effect is indeed significant ($F = 8.35$; $df = 11/781$; $p < .001$). Apparently, some of these words "sound better" than others. But independently of word content, subjects consistently rated the given word to mean something "better" if they had seen it (and had said it) more often. This is true for all the 12 words used in the experiment, a result that has a chance likelihood equal to .00024.

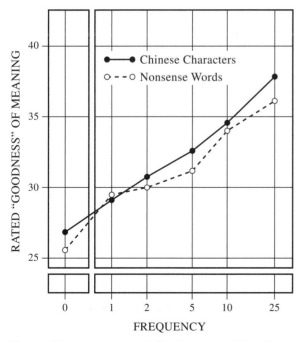

Figure 6.2 Average rated affective connotation of nonsense words and Chinese-like characters as a function of frequency of exposure

Experiment II

Since the hypothesis proposed holds that it is *mere* exposure that is a sufficient condition of attitude change, the procedure used in Experiment I is not optimal for testing its validity. Subjects In Experiment I were required to pronounce the nonsense words during training, and it is possible that a decrease in difficulty in pronouncing the words associated with successive presentations was responsible for the results. In other words, subjects rated the frequent stimuli more favorably because they found them easier to pronounce than stimuli which they saw and pronounced only once or twice. And, there were stimuli which they never pronounced and, in fact, did not really know how to pronounce. Wilson and Becknell (1961) suggested that the evaluative ratings of nonsense syllables of high association value are higher than of low association [14] value because they are easier to pronounce. In order to follow up their suggestion, a group of 22 University of Michigan subjects were given the "Turkish adjectives" with the instructions to rate them accord-

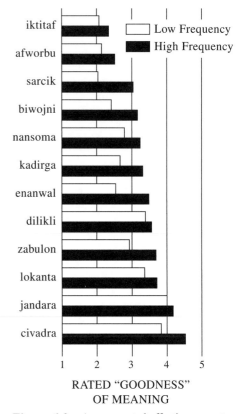

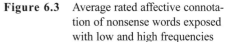

RATED "GOODNESS"
OF MEANING

Figure 6.3   Average rated affective connotation of nonsense words exposed with low and high frequencies

ing to "how easy or difficult it is to pronounce" them. Using a 7-point scale, a significant item-effect was revealed by an analysis of variance ($F = 14.28$; $df = 11/263$; $p <$ .001), showing that there are, indeed, differences among the nonsense words in the ease with which they can be pronounced upon their first presentation. The Wilson-Becknell conjecture is supported by a correlation of .46 between the average ease of pronouncing the words and the evaluative scores obtained in Experiment I. These latter scores were obtained by averaging for each word the rating it obtained in all frequencies.

These results, however, in themselves do not preclude a relationship between exposure and evaluative rating. With ease of pronouncing held constant, the exposure effect may still be obtained. This expectation is strengthened by the results of a study described earlier (Frincke and Johnson, 1960) in which homophone pairs differing in word-frequency were rated for "pleasantness." Since homophones do not differ in pronunciation, the obtained frequency effects show that ease of pronouncing may be a sufficient factor in affecting evaluative ratings but not a necessary one. In order to eliminate the pronunciation factor and to reduce the subjects' active participation while exposure is being manipulated, the following experiment was carried out.

To meet the requirements of the definition of "mere exposure," Chinese characters were substituted for the nonsense words. These stimuli were taken from Hull's (1920) concept formation study, and I am told that not only are most of them meaningless, but that they are also far from the absolutely minimal standards of Chinese calligraphy. Nevertheless, they were quite adequate for our experimental purposes. The subjects were again told that the experiment dealt with the learning of a foreign language, but now they were not required to pronounce the characters. Nor were they able to pronounce them subvocally. They were simply instructed to pay close attention to the characters whenever they were exposed to them. In all other respects, the experiment was identical to the one employing nonsense words. Now, too, following training, subjects were told that the characters stood for adjectives, and that their task was to guess their meaning on the good-bad scale. Characters and exposures were again counterbalanced. Figures 6.2 and 6.4 show the results, and it is obvious that the exposure-favorability relationship previously found with nonsense words obtains ($F = 4.72$; $df = 5/335$; $p <$ .001) even if the individual's exposure to the stimulus consists of his passively looking at it for a period of about 2 seconds. Figure 6.4 shows that the exposure effect is found for all stimuli but one.

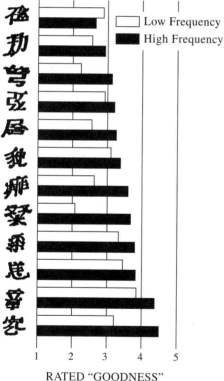

RATED "GOODNESS"
OF MEANING

Figure 6.4   Average rated affective connotation of Chinese-like characters exposed with low and high frequencies

The results add strength to the hypothesis that mere exposure is a sufficient condition for attitude enhancement. But, again, the last experiment did not succeed in completely eliminating a learning factor from the exposure manipulation, for it is possible that this manipulation is now confounded with the ease of recognition. This danger of confounding, however, is probably minimal because at no time were the subjects ever required to recognize or discriminate the idiograms.

The results of Experiments I and II are in an apparent conflict with results reported by Amster and Glasman (1966). These researchers report a negative result using a procedure similar to that employed by Johnson, Thomson, and Frincke (1960). The experiment was similar in all respects except that meaningful English words were substituted for the nonsense stimuli. No exposure effect was observed by Amster and Glasman for these meaningful words. But this finding is not at all surprising. Nor is it especially significant for the understanding of exposure effects. Adding one more occasion (or even 10 more occasions) to see and say a perfectly well known English word to all the times this word had been seen and uttered by the individual in the past—a figure often in the thousands—really shouldn't have much effect on the meaning he attributes to it. The expectation of a change in the evaluative aspect of meaning as a function of a few additional exposures becomes even less reasonable when we consider that [15] the change in affective connotation is a linear function of the logarithm of frequency, as we noted in Figures 6.1 and 6.2. If n is the frequency of the subject's pre-experimental exposure to the word, then the comparisons made by Amster and Glasman involved the following four frequencies: $n +1$, $n + 2$, $n + 5$, and $n + 10$. Since n is large, perhaps as large as 1000, the differences in exposures amounted to fractions of 1%.

WORD-FREQUENCY—WORD-VALUE RELATIONSHIP AS A SPECIAL CASE OF THE EXPOSURE-ATTITUDE RELATIONSHIP

In the first section of this paper, some evidence was presented suggesting that words with positive affective connotations are used more frequently (both in print and in speech) than words with negative affective connotations. In the second section, evidence was given to suggest that the affective connotation of a word improves with their repeated use. Because the second item of evidence rests on experimental proof, in which the frequency of usage was systematically and independently manipulated, one cannot question the causal direction implied in these data. But finding that the frequency of usage affects meaning needn't necessarily preclude the possibility that meaning determines the frequency of usage. It is necessary, therefore, to examine more closely the results on the correlational evidence between word-frequency and word value.

Why are positive words used more frequently? Besides the rather wistful and unlikely explanation that there are more positive than negative referents (i.e., we live in a paradise), one real possibility suggests itself. The evidence reviewed so far deals only with usage *per word*. The totality of "good" and "bad" usage, however, depends on the numbers of different "good" and "bad" words in the language. It is entirely possible, therefore, that the superiority of "good" words in frequency *per word* exists side by side with the superiority of "bad" words in their greater variety. This possibility receives some support from the fact that, in English (and in a host of other languages), prefixes and suffixes that serve to negate or reverse meaning, such as anti, de, im, in, ir, less, un, etc., are most commonly attached to words having a positive connotation. Once attached to a word, they almost universally form a word with a negative affective connotation. Positive words with these prefixes or suffixes are exceptional: unselfish, independent, are some examples.

It would appear, therefore, that there are indeed more negative than positive words. And if there are more different negative words, the usage *per word* would naturally be attenuated for these words, because the total usage would be distributed among a larger universe of items.

Norman[5] has asked a group of students to separate a large sample of adjectives into "good" ones and "bad" ones. On the average, 2.31 more items were placed in the "bad"

---

[5] Warren T. Norman, personal communication, 1965.

pile than in the "good" pile. The frequency figures in Table 6.1 show a pattern consistent with Norman's independent finding. [16] The average frequency of the preferred antonyms is 2.3 times larger than the average frequency of the non-preferred antonyms! Therefore, for the material considered here, the ratio of total positive and negative usage is equal to unity.

If repeated usage enhances the affective meaning of words, a relatively large supply of negative words would, in fact, be needed. It would be equally reasonable to expect that there exist devices in language protecting words from a deterioration of meaning. It is entirely possible that the prefixes and suffixes discussed earlier serve this function. Because the negative qualities of these prefixes and suffixes are independent of their referents, because they are essentially abstract, and because they derive their negativity from the semantic function they perform, words formed by means of these prefixes and suffixes are perhaps better able than root words to resist an enhancement of affective connotation as a result of repeated usage. I was unable to find evidence corroborating this point-of-view, although there is a good deal of philological literature on both positive changes in meaning (see, for instance, Van Dongen, 1933) and negative changes in meaning (see, for instance, Schreuder, 1929). Most of the sources, however, consider changes in meaning of root words only.

If there are many remaining doubts that frequency of words is a function of the value of their referents, then the following frequencies of a few well-chosen but significant words should, once and for all, dispel them:

Psychologist	36
Chemist	32
Economist	32
Sociologist	14
Astronomer	12
Geologist	9
Physicist	8
Geographer	7
Botanist	6
Biologist	5

EXPOSURE-ATTITUDE RELATIONSHIP: EXPERIMENTAL EVIDENCE

Experiment III

In all of the experiments, the question asked of the subjects in rating the stimuli following exposure dealt with the evaluative aspect of their meaning. The subjects were never required to say just how much they liked the nonsense words or "Chinese" characters. In all probability, the results would have been the same if they were asked directly to stale their altitude toward these words and characters, and the Wilson-Pecknell (1961), results support this conjecture. But because their stimuli were essentially verbal, subjects' answers could in these studies be strongly influenced by semantic factors. This would have been less likely, of course, in the case of Chinese characters than in the case of nonsense words.

As was pointed out earlier, there is some direct evidence on the attitudinal effects of mere exposure, dealing almost exclusively with music appreciation. Meyer (1903), for example, played to his students oriental music 12 to 15 times in succession. In most cases, the students' introspective protocols indicated a better liking for the pieces on the last than on the first presentation. One of the students who took part in Meyers' experiment (H.T. Moore), and who showed enhancement effects of repeated exposure ("I liked the last time better than the first, because I became more used to the successive chords"), followed up this work in a study of his own 20 years later. Moore and Gilliland (1924) played to their students jazz and classical records once a week for 25 weeks. Liking for classical records increased, but no change was found for jazz music. Similar results are reported by other writers (Krugman, 1943; Verveer, Barry, and Bousfield, 1933; Washburn, Child, and Abel, 1927). Downey and Knapp (1927) played to 33 students a variety of musical selections (e.g., Tschaikowsky's *Marche Slave,* Massenet's *Meditation* from "Thais," *Columbia, The Gem of the Ocean,* etc.) once a week for five weeks. All pieces of music except one (*Columbia, The Gem of the Ocean*) became better liked at the close of the sessions. Alpert (1953) presented subjects with sounds having unfamiliar rhythms. His subjects found these sounds at first unpleasant. After repeated presentations, however, the liking for them increased. Additional exposures of subjects to the tones resulted in increasing indifference on the part of the listeners. More recently, Mull (1957) found that, upon repeated exposure to their music, subjects enjoyed Schoenberg and Hindemith more.

In the area of visual arts, Pepper (1919) found that repeated exposure resulted in more positive aesthetic judgments of unusual color combinations. Krugman and Hartley (1960), however, using famous paintings, could only find ambiguous results. Maslow (1937) projected for 4 days in succession 15 paintings of great masters. Six days following the last presentation, the 15 paintings were presented once again, and interspersed among them were 15 others (matched for the artist) which the subjects had never seen. The results indicated a greater liking for the familiar paintings. Maslow (1937) also made tests of preference, frequently with similar results, for other familiar and unfamiliar objects, such as rubber bands, paper clips, [17] blotters, pens, pencils, etc. A similar experiment to the one with paintings, but using instead Russian girls' names, showed the same results. The same subjects were used in all these studies and the sessions took place in the same room, the subjects always sitting in the same chairs. Toward the end of the testing program, Maslow asked if anyone would like to change seats. No one did, preferring, apparently, to remain in the familiar one.

Although the results of the studies are fairly consistent, the conditions under which they were carried out make their conclusions somewhat less than compelling. In the majority of instances, the circumstances of the repeated exposure were quite ambiguous. The experiments were usually conducted in classes, the instructor serving as the experimenter. Subjects often responded aloud, thus being able to influence each other's judgments and opinions. Prior to the sessions, the experimenter often expressed his own preferences. The stimuli, repeatedly shown, were not always exposed under the same conditions, and the material, exposures, and sequences were seldom counterbalanced. But in all of these experiments, a pattern of results emerges showing that the frequency manipulation has more pronounced attitude effects for stimuli that are novel, unfamiliar, or unusual than for familiar stimuli. This pattern is, of course, consistent with the observation that attitude enhancement is a function of the logarithm of frequency.

Becknell, Wilson, and Baird (1963) have recently reported more convincing support for the exposure-attitude hypothesis. Slides of nonsense syllables were presented with different frequencies (1, 4, 7, and 10). Following this exposure training (which also included interspersed presentations of slides with landscapes and with ads), female subjects were given pairs of boxes containing nylon stockings, and they were asked to choose the "brand" they preferred. These "brands" corresponded to the nonsense syllables previously shown, and they were printed on the boxes. Each subject received two different pairs of boxes for comparison. The paired-comparison data showed a tendency of subjects to prefer the box marked by the more frequent syllable. Again, however, the semantic component is not excluded from the effects obtained in these two studies.

There is one more item of evidence, somewhat indirect, on the problem of the effects of exposure. In a study by Munsinger (1964), subjects were given the opportunity to present to themselves CVC trigrams whose association value, evaluation scale value, and prepotency score (Mandler, 1955) were previously assessed. By pressing a response key, the subject would expose in a small window a trigram which he would then have to spell. The rate at which he key-pressed constituted the dependent measure. In one of Munsinger's experimental groups, subjects could expose to themselves, by means of that key response, trigrams that were matched for association and prepotency. All these trigrams, however, previously scored low on the evaluative scales of the semantic differential. After subjects reached an asymptotic key-pressing rate, the experimental conditions changed such that now the subjects' response would expose trigrams that were high in evaluation, although they were still matched for association and prepotency. A significant increase in key-pressing rates is reported by Munsinger following the change in the affective value of the trigrams. Again, however, the semantic component is not entirely excluded from the effects obtained in these two studies.

Because they are less a matter of semantic factors, we have chosen to manipulate interpersonal attitudes by means of exposure. Using the same experimental design as with the Chinese characters, faces of men (photographs of graduating Michigan State University seniors taken from the MSU Yearbook) were employed as attitude objects. The experiment was introduced to subjects—all students at the University of Michigan—as dealing with the problem of "visual memory." Following the exposure manipulation, which consisted of presenting each photograph a different number of times for a period of 2 seconds, subjects were asked to rate on a 7-point scale how much they might like the man on each photograph. The results of this study are shown in Figures 6.5 and 6.6. While the exposure effect is not as clear as previously (only 9 of the 12 stimuli show it), it is still rather impressive ($F = 9.96$; $df = 5/355$; $p < .001$).

THE EXPOSURE-ATTITUDE HYPOTHESIS AND
RELATED THEORETICAL ISSUES

The previous results raise a series of empirical and theoretical questions. Are all attitudes [18] enhanced by mere repeated exposure? Is there a number of repetitions beyond which attitude begins to become negative? Does this number vary systematically across attitude

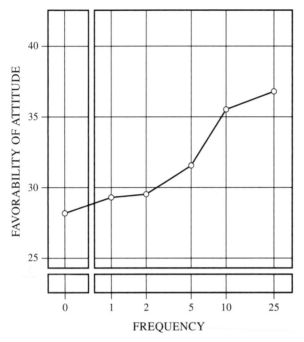

Figure 6.5   Average attitude toward photographs as a function of frequency of exposure

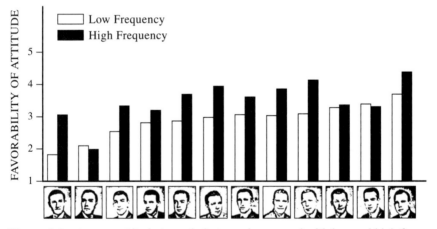

Figure 6.6   Average attitude toward photographs exposed with low and high frequencies

objects? Are these effects stable? These and similar questions can only be answered by further empirical work. On a theoretical level, these questions address themselves primarily to those psychological processes that mediate exposure effects.

Let us first consider a possible biological significance of an exposure-enhancement mechanism. A stimulus presented for the first time evokes in the organism an instinctive fear reaction. Lorenz (1956) noted that a young raven,

> confronted with a new object, which may be a camera, an old bottle, a
> stuffed polecat, or any thing else, first reacts with escape responses. He
> will fly up to an elevated perch, and, from this point of vantage, stare at
> the object literally for hours. After this he will begin to approach the
> object very gradually ...

Bühler, Hetzer, and Mabel (1928) observed that human infants reacted to a strange sound by crying out with fear. Upon the second exposure of the sound stimulus, movement and vocalization that indicated displeasure were observed. On the third exposure, the infants listened to the sound showing some signs of attention, but did not seem to show any displeasure. On the fourth exposure, they looked in the direction of the sound with detectable interest. These facts, of course, are borne out by common observation. Hunt (1965) reported that young infants he observed preferred a familiar mobile to a new one. And the "Black Bag" story cited in the introduction represents another example of phenomena in this category. At the outset, the "Black Bag," in fact, attracted a good deal of hostility. Cairns (1966) has recently presented a very convincing argument that the affiliative behavior and social attachments among animals are solely determined by the animals' exposure to one another. Examining evidence on affiliative preferences of animals observed under conditions of inter- and intraspecific cohabitation and of animals deprived of social contact, Cairns concluded that such affiliative preferences vary directly with the length of the association and with the importance of the cues which are generated in the course of the association. Cairns, moreover, did not limit his conclusion to inter-animal social attachments, but proposed that "animals tend to remain in the presence of [any] objects to which they have been continually exposed." [p. 409].

The survival value of an avoidance reflex to a novel stimulus is obvious. But there is no direct evidence that all organisms are equipped with an avoidance reaction occurring upon the encounter of a novel stimulus. However, if we assume that they are, then the exposure-attitude hypothesis becomes more [19] reasonable. The first encounter with the novel stimulus produces fear reaction. If no negative consequences are associated with this first encounter, the avoidance reaction upon the second encounter will naturally be weaker. If such encounters continue, and if no other events—negative in their consequences for the organism—accompany these encounters, then the organism's attitude toward the stimulus must improve. To be sure, the hypothesis does not deny or preclude the effects of reinforcement. The exposure of a stimulus coupled with reward will strengthen the animal's approach behavior; and the exposure of stimulus coupled with a noxious event will strengthen his avoidance reactions. But in the absence of reward or punishment, mere exposure will result in the enhancement of the organism's attitude toward the given stimulus object.

If novel stimuli evoke fear, conflict, or uncertainty, one should be able to detect these states, and to observe their dissipation upon repeated exposure. To the extent that GSR measures arousal that is associated with the above states, we would expect greater GSRs upon the presentation of novel stimuli than upon the presentation of familiar ones, and we would also expect a drop in GSR reactivity to be the consequence of repeated stimulus exposure.

Experiment IV

Changes in affective arousal that occur as a result of repeated exposure of a novel stimulus were examined in an independent experiment. Fifteen subjects were presented with nonsense words (the same as in Experiment I) in a series of 86 trials. Two words appeared 25 times, two 10 times, two 5 times, two twice, and two once. The position of a word in the series of trials was determined by a random device. Words were counterbalanced against frequencies in three experimental replications. Due to a mechanical failure of the apparatus, data for one subject could not be used, and were not included in the analysis.

On a given trial, the stimulus word was projected onto a screen for a period of 2 seconds, and the subject's GSR was recorded. The interstimulus interval was 20 seconds. GSR was measured only during the first 10 seconds following stimulus onset, and all GSRs occurring during the last 12 seconds of the interstimulus interval were treated as artifacts. The Kaplan-Hobart technique of GSR measurement (Kaplan and Hobart, 1964), which requires current of only 10 microamperes, was employed. Zinc-zinc sulphate electrodes (Kaplan and Fisher, 1964; Lykken, 1959) were applied to the forefinger and the middle finger of the subject's nonpreferred hand.

The results of the experiment are shown in Figure 6.7 and Figure 6.8. In Figure 6.7, changes in conductance are plotted for each successive presentation of the stimulusword. For purposes of clarity, data for only one stimulus are graphed in each frequency class. The results for the other set of stimuli are the same. It can be seen that, in general, successive presentations result in a lower autonomic reactivity. After about seven or eight exposures, a stable asymptote is reached. Hence, only stimuli shown 25 and 10 times attain an asymptote. Words shown five times, twice, or once generate greater changes in conductance even on their last exposure. This effect is seen better in Figure 6.8 in which GSRs on the last exposure of the stimuli were plotted. As prior frequency

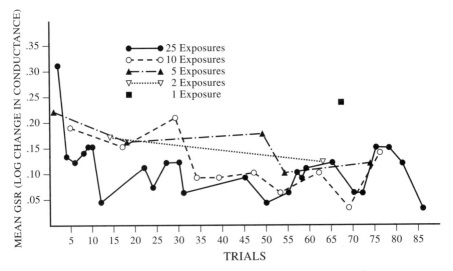

Figure 6.7   GSR obtained upon repeated exposures of nonsense words

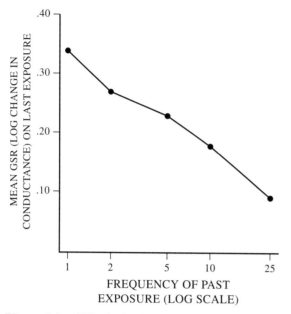

Figure 6.8   GSR obtained on the last exposure of nonsense words exposed with various frequencies

of exposure increases, there is a **[20]** lesser change in conductance upon stimulus presentation. This effect is significant at the .05 level ($F = 4.01$; $df = 4/117$).

These results cannot be due to an overall adaptation that may be occurring as the series of the 86 trials progresses. It is clear that the stimulus shown just once generated a substantial GSR, although it occurred as late as on the 67th trial. As a matter of fact, its GSR does not differ from the GSR obtained for the *first* presentation of the other stimuli. The last presentation of the stimulus word that had just one prior exposure also resulted in a substantial GSR, although it occurred on the 64th trial. And on the whole, although there is variability over trials, at any one point during the series, GSR's are higher for stimuli with infrequent prior exposures than for stimuli previously seen by the subject many times. It seems, therefore, that with increased exposure there is a genuine reduction in stimulus-evoked arousal. These findings are in agreement with those reported by Berlyne, Craw, Salapatek, and Lewis (1963). In their study, subjects were shown visual patterns differing in complexity and in incongruity. The patterns were presented for 3 seconds on three successive occasions. A significant drop in GSR was obtained between the first and the second presentation. But no significant GSR effects were associated with complexity or incongruity.

DISCUSSION

While the bulk of the results presented and reviewed in this monograph supports the hypothesis that repeated exposure is a sufficient condition of attitude enhancement, there are findings and theoretical formulations which appear to be in conflict with the hypothesis. The most pronounced source of ostensibly contradictory results is in the area of exploration and curiosity. There is impressive evidence today that in a free situation, the subject (human or animal) will turn toward a novel stimulus in preference to a familiar one (e.g., Berlyne, 1960). If such orienting and exploratory "approach" behavior is a symptom of a favorable attitude toward the stimulus object, the wealth of data on exploration and orienting behavior (Berlyne, 1950, 1955; Berlyne and Slater, 1957; Dember and Millbrook, 1956; Montgomery, 1953; Thiessen and McGaugh, 1958; Thomson and Solomon, 1954) stands in clear contradiction to those reported in this monograph.

But there is, at present, no direct evidence to support the assumption. And, on the contrary, it is more likely that orienting toward a novel stimulus in preference to a familiar one may indicate that it is less liked rather than it is better liked. Ordinarily, when confronted with a novel stimulus, the animal's orienting response enables it to discover if the novel stimulus constitutes a source of danger. It need not explore familiar stimuli in this respect. Novelty is thus commonly associated with uncertainty and with conflict—states that are more likely to produce negative than positive affect. Most recent work by Harrison (1967) indicates quite clearly that exploration and favorable attitudes are, in fact, negatively related. Using nonsense words, Chinese characters, and photographs of men's faces, Harrison obtained measures of liking from one group of subjects and measures of exploration from another group. The correlations between exploration and liking were −.69, −.69, and −.60 for nonsense words, characters, and photographs, respectively. If the function of orienting behavior is eventually to change the novel stimulus into a familiar one, it is also its consequence to render the stimulus object eventually more attractive (or perhaps merely less repulsive).

In his research, Harrison also obtained data on the behavioral consequences of exposure, and, in particular, on response conflict that novelty seems to arouse. It is a truism, of [21] course, to assert that novel stimulus is one to which *no* specific response, beside orienting, has as yet been attached. But the novel stimulus cannot fail being similar to an entire host of other stimuli that the individual had encountered in the past, and to which he had attached specific responses. And it is entirely likely that some of these generalized response tendencies that the novel stimulus simultaneously excites are mutually incompatible; that is, they cannot all be emitted at the same time. This antecedent condition is what makes response conflict (of some, however small, magnitude) a necessary concomitant of novelty.

Using latency of free associations as a measure of response conflict, Harrison was able to demonstrate that response conflict is markedly reduced upon repeated exposure of a novel stimulus. Chinese ideographs were shown to a group of subjects once, twice, 5 times, 10 times, and 25 times, in a manner similar to that used in other experiments described earlier. Following this exposure manipulation, Harrison presented each stimulus once again requiring the subject to respond "with the first thing that came to mind." Included now were also Chinese ideographs that the subject had never seen. The latency of these free associations was obtained on each such trial, and the results revealed a systematic and significant drop in latencies as a function of the frequency of prior exposure.

Another set of data which may also be of some consequence for the exposure-attitude hypothesis is to be found in the area of semantic satiation. In a typical semantic-satiation experiment, the subject is asked to repeat words, two or three per second, for a period of 15 seconds. The general findings in this area indicate that following this sort of rapid repetition, the word seems to "lose" its meaning (for a review of the literature see Amster, 1964). Loss of meaning is measured by a departure from polarity on semantic differential scales, such as good-bad, strong-weak, etc. (Lambert and Jakobovits, 1960).When repeated in rapid succession and rated on some semantic differential scale, immediately thereafter the words tend to be placed neither toward one (e.g., good) nor the other (e.g., bad) end of the scale, but are rated toward the neutral point of the scale. While several studies have demonstrated a reduction of polarization following rapid repetition of a word (Das, 1964; Kanungo and Lambert, 1963a, 1963b; Messer, Jakobovits, Kanungo, and Lambert, 1964), there is an equal amount of conflicting evidence (Amster and Glasman, 1965; Floyd, 1962; Reynierse and Barch, 1963; Schulz, Weaver, and Radtke, 1965). Yelen and Schulz (1963) attribute satiation findings to a regression artifact. A reduction of polarity of *positive* words as a result of repetition would indeed be embarrassing for the exposure-attitude hypothesis. A reduction of polarity of *negative* words (i.e., words with a semantic score below the neutral point) would, of course, be entirely in agreement with the present results, for they would simply be showing an enhancement effect along the evaluative dimension. It should be noted that all our stimuli initially received negative ratings, that is, below the neutral point, 3, on the 0–6 good-bad scale. Given no exposure at all, the evaluative ratings for the Turkish nonsense words, Chinese-like characters, and photographs were 2.56, 2.67, and 2.79, respectively. In terms of polarity, these averages are –.44, –.33, and –.21. Contrary to the semantic satiation hypothesis, absolute polarities increased after 25 exposures, for they were +.61, +.78, and, +.61, respectively. Admittedly, the controversy within semantic satiation literature may have to be resolved before clear implications for the exposure effect can be drawn. Parenthetically, it should be noted, however, that the form of exposure used in the semantic satiation paradigm (i.e., 30 to 45 repetitions in 15 seconds) is not what has been defined as the sufficient condition of attitude enhancement. Moreover, in semantic satiation studies, the stimulus is commonly a verbal response made by the subject himself. Whether such a response-produced stimulus should constitute what is meant by mere exposure is a matter of some doubt.

The hypothesis and data seem to be consistent with the theory of reinforcement recently proposed by Premack (1959). This new and engaging approach to reinforcement effects, for which a good deal of impressive **[22]** evidence has already been accumulated (Premack, 1961, 1962, 1963, 1965; Premack and Bahwell, 1959; Premack and Collier, 1962), holds that if the emission of one response, A, is made contingent upon the emission of another response, B, and if A occurs with greater frequency than B, B will gain in the rate of emission. A can, therefore, be considered as having positive reinforcement value which seems to depend alone upon its frequency of occurrence. Contingencies between responses can be introduced by controlling manipulanda or the availability of goal objects. Thus, for instance, in studying these effects in Cebus monkeys, Premack (1963) used four manipulanda: a plunger, a hinged door, a vertically operated lever, and a horizontally operated lever. It was possible to make any manipulandum inoperable at any time, and to make it operable only in the case of a prior manipulation of another manipulandum. Thus, each manipulandum could serve for the reinforc*ing* or for the reinfor*ced* response. After establishing for each monkey the probabilities of operating each item under free access to all, contingencies were arranged between pairs of items, such that, for instance, the vertical lever could not be operated unless the animal pulled the plunger, or the hinged door remained locked unless the subject pressed the horizontal lever, etc. The introduction of these contingencies resulted in the predicted effects. In general, responses that were less probable increased in the rate of emission when more probable responses were made contingent upon them. When two responses were equal in probability of emission, little or no change in response rates was observed.

Viewed in the present context, the individual's response probabilities can be taken as an indication of his "attitudinal liking" or "attraction" to the goal objects of these responses, or to the instrumental stimuli associated with them. To the extent that the reward value of a given response, A, which is contingent upon another response, B, is a direct function of A's probability of emission, then increasing its probability of emission will increase its reward value. Premack (1961) was able to demonstrate such an effect in rats for licking and bar pressing. Changing the language somewhat, it may be said that the individual's "attitudinal liking" for the goal object of the response A increases with the individual's exposure to the goal object of A. In Premack's work, continuous reinforcement schedules are used and, hence, the individual's frequency of exposure to the goal object of A is equal to the frequency of emission of A.

There are important differences between the phenomena observed by Premack and those reported in the present paper. In most of his experiments, the frequency of occurrence of responses results from an independent, perhaps genetically given or previously acquired, response preference of the subject. In the experimental work on attitudinal effects of exposure, the frequency of occurrence of the stimulus-object is deliberately manipulated. Moreover, the subject usually does not have a prior preference for the stimulus exposed. On the contrary, he may often manifest avoidance tendencies. But the parallel is compelling.

While there is a great deal in common between Premack's work on reinforcement and the research on attitudinal effects of exposure, a clear understanding of the implications of one for the other requires a systematic de termination of what "reinforcement value" and "attitudes" have in common that makes them both equally vulnerable to simple frequency effects.

CONCLUSION

The balance of the experimental results reviewed and reported in this paper is in favor of the hypothesis that mere repeated exposure of an individual to a stimulus object enhances his attitude toward it. But, as yet, the account books cannot be closed. Further research must examine the boundary conditions of the exposure-attitude relationship, for it is possible that the neat linear log-frequency-attitude relationship, repeatedly observed here, may well break down under some conditions. This future research must, in particular, concentrate on the effects of large frequencies of exposure, on duration of exposure, on interexposure intervals, and on [23] many other similar parameters of mere exposure. This research must also assess the applicability of the exposure-attitude relationship to a greater variety of stimulus objects. The question of generalization of specific exposure effects is of equal theoretical importance. Does repeated exposure to a given stimulus result in the enhancement of attitudes toward similar or related stimuli?

Because the effects seem to be a function of the *logarithm* of frequency of exposure, they are more apparent and more pronounced for differences among small frequencies than for differences among large frequencies. For the same reason, attitudinal enhancement produced by means of exposure will be more readily affected for novel objects than for familiar ones. It is likely that exposure effects for very familiar objects are absent completely, or are so small that they cannot be detected at all by methods now available. As we have seen earlier, Amster and Glasman (1966) failed to obtain the exposure effect for common English words. It will be important for future research, therefore, to determine the range of familiarity for which the exposure effect is obtained.

Mere exposure is a necessary precondition of a vast variety of experimental manipulations. For example, in attempts to change attitudes by means of persuasive communications, the attitude object is mentioned repeatedly, regardless of whether the attempt is directed toward making the attitude more favorable or toward making it less favorable. Making attitudes more favorable should, therefore, be easier than making them less favorable. It is interesting that studies on the effectiveness of persuasion in attitude change seldom try to effect a negative change, and almost never compare the relative success of a pro-persuasion with the success of a con-persuasion. In an attitude-change study, Tannenbaum and Gengel (1966) have recently obtained only positive shifts, although both a positive as well as a negative manipulation were employed.

The partial reinforcement manipulation, too, is subject to possible confounding with the number of stimulus presentations. Erlebacher and Archer (1961), for instance, reported the curious result that, at the completion of training, greater numbers of correct responses were associated with smaller percentages of reinforcement. However, in the various conditions of reinforcement, subjects worked until they performed in succession a predetermined number of correct responses, the same for all percentages of reinforcement. Therefore, percentage of reinforcement was, in this study, completely confounded with the number of stimulus exposures (and also with the number of reinforcements). Although many authors have tried to cope with this confounding in one way or another (e.g., Festinger, 1961; Kanfer, 1954; O'Connell, 1965), the methodological difficulties have not been completely overcome. None of the four variables that are associated with the partial reinforcement effect—percentage of reinforced trials, number of trials, number of positive reinforcements, number of nonreinforcements—can be studied independently of the others.

REFERENCES

ALLUISI, E.A., and ADAMS, O.S. Predicting letter preferences: Aesthetics and filtering in man. *Perceptual and Motor Skills,* 1962, **14**, 123–131.

ALPERT, R. Perceptual determinants of affect. Unpublished master's thesis, Wesleyan University, 1953.

AMSTER, H. Semantic satiation and generation: Learning? Adaptation? *Psychological Bulletin,* 1964, **62**, 273–286.

AMSTER, H., and GLASMAN, L.D. Verbal repetition and connotative change. *Journal of Experimental Psychology,* 1966, **71**, 389–395.

ANDERSON, N.H. *Likeableness ratings of 555 personality-trait adjectives.* Los Angeles: University of California, 1964. (Mimeo)

BECKNELL, J. C., JR., WILSON, W.R., and BAIRD, J. C. The effect of frequency of presentation on the choice of nonsense syllables. *Journal of Psychology,* 1963, **56**, 165–170.

BERLYNE, D.E. Novelty and curiosity as determinants of exploratory behavior. *British Journal of Psychology,* 1950, **41**, 68–80.

BERLYNE, D.E. The arousal and satiation of perceptual curiosity in the rat. *Journal of Comparative and Physiological Psychology,* 1955, **48**, 232–246.

BERLYNE, D.E. Conflict, curiosity, and exploratory behavior. New York: McGraw-Hill, 1960.

BERLYNE, D.E, CRAW, M.A., SALAPATEK, P.H., and LEWIS, J.L. Novelty, complexity, incongruity, extrinsic motivation, and the GSR. *Journal of Experimental Psychology,* 1963, **66**, 560–567.

BERLYNE, D.E., and SLATER, J. Perceptual curiosity, exploratory behavior, and maze learning. *Journal* **[24]** *of Comparative and Physiological Psychology,* 1957, **50**, 228–232.

BOGARDUS, E.S. Measuring social distance. *Journal of Applied Sociology,* 1925, **9**, 299–308.

BOGARDUS, E.S. *Social distance.* Yellow Springs, Ohio: Antioch Press, 1959.

BOVARD, E.W., JR. Group structure and perception. *Journal of Abnormal and Social Psychology,* 1951, **46**, 398–405.

BRAUN, J.R. Three tests of the McClelland discrepancy hypothesis. *Psychological Reports,* 1962, **10**, 271–274.

BUCHANAN, M.A. *Graded Spanish word book.* Toronto: Toronto University Press, 1927.

BÜHLER, C., HETZER, H., and MABEL, F. Die Affektwirksamkeit von Fremdheitseindrücken im ersten Lebensjahr. *Zeitschrift für Psychologie,* 1928, **107**, 30–49.

CAIRNS, R.B. Attachment behavior of mammals. *Psychological Review.* 1966, **73**, 409–426.

COOK, S.W., and SELLTIZ, C. *Contact and intergroup attitudes: Some theoretical considerations.* New York: Research Center for Human Relations, 1952.

DAS, J.P. Hypnosis, verbal satiation, vigilance, and personality factors: A correlational study. *Journal of Abnormal and Social Psychology,* 1964, **68**, 72–78.

DEMBER, W.N., and MILLBROOK, B.A. Free choice by the rat of the greater of two brightness changes. *Psychological Reports,* 1956, **2**, 465–467.

DEUTSCH, M., and COLLINS, M.E. *Interracial housing: A psychological evaluation of a social experiment.* Minneapolis: University of Minnesota Press, 1951.

DIXON, T.R., and DIXON, J.F. The impression value of verbs. *Journal of Verbal Learning and Verbal Behavior,* 1964, **3**, 161–165.

DOWNEY, J.E., and KNAPP, G.E. The effect on a musical programme of familiarity and of sequence of selections. In M. Schoen (Ed.), *The effects of music.* New York: Harcourt, Brace, 1927.

EATON, H.S. *An English, French, German, Spanish word frequency dictionary.* New York: Dover, 1940.

ERDELYI, M. The relation between "Radio Plugs" and sheet sales of popular music. *Journal of Applied Psychology,* 1940, **24**, 696–702.

ERLEBACBER, A., and ARCHER, E.J. Perseveration as a function of degree of learning and percentage of reinforcement in card sorting. *Journal of Experimental Psychology,* 1961, **62**, 510–517.

FECHNER, G.T. *Vorschule der Aesthetik.* Leipzig: Breitkopf and Härtel, 1876.

FESTINGER, L. Group attraction and membership. *Journal of Social Issues,* 1951, **7**, 152–163.

FESTINGER, L. The psychological effects of insufficient reward. *American Psychologist,* 1961, **16**, 1–11.

FLOYD, R.L. Semantic satiation: Replication and test of further implications. *Psychological Reports,* 1962, **11**, 274.

FRINCKE. G., and JOHNSON, R.C. Word value and word frequency in homophone pairs. *Psychological Reports,* 1960, **7**, 470.

GOUGH, H.G. *Reference handbook for the Gough Adjective Check List.* Berkeley: University of California Institute of Personality Assessment and Research, April 1955. (Mimeo)

HARRISON, A.A. Response competition and attitude change as a function of repeated stimulus exposure. Unpublished doctoral dissertation. University of Michigan, 1967.

HOMANS, G.C. *Social behavior: Its elementary forms.* New York: Harcourt, Brace, 1961.

HOWES, D. On the interpretation of word frequency as a variable affecting speed of recognition. *Journal of Experimental Psychology,* 1954, **48**, 106–112.

HOWES, D.H., and SOLOMON, R.L. A note on McGinnies' "Emotionality and perceptual defense." *Psychological Review,* 1950, **57**, 229–234.

HULL, C.L. Quantitative aspects of the evolution of concepts. *Psychological Monographs,* 1920, **28** (1, Whole No. 123).

HUNT, J. McV. Traditional personality theory in the light of recent evidence. *American Scientist,* 1965, **53,** 80–96.

JAMES, W. *The principles of psychology.* Vol. 2. New York: Holt, 1890.

JOHNSON, R.C., THOMSON, C.W., and FRINCKE, G. Word values, word frequency, and visual duration thresholds. *Psychological Review,* 1960, **67,** 332–342.

KÄDING, F.W. Häufigkeitswörterbuch der deutschen Sprache. Berlin: Mittler, 1948.

KANFER, F.H. The effect of partial reinforcement in acquisition and extinction of a class of verbal responses. *Journal of Experimental Psychology,* 1954, **48,** 424–432.

KANUNGO, R.N., and LAMBERT, W.E. Paired-associate learning as a function of stimulus and response satiation. *British Journal of Psychology,* 1963, **54,** 135–144 (a).

KANUNGO, R.N., and LAMBERT, W.E. Semantic satiation and meaningfulness. *American Journal of Psychology,* 1963, **76,** 421–428 (b).

KAPLAN, S., and FISHER, G.R. A modified design for the Lykken zinc electrodes. *Psychophysiology,* 1964, **1,** 88–89.

KAPLAN, S, and HOBART, J.L. A versatile device for the measurement of skin resistance in rats and humans. *American Journal of Psychology,* 1964, **77,** 309–310.

KRAMER, M. Residential contact as a determinant of attitudes toward Negroes. Unpublished doctoral dissertation, University of Chicago, 1950.

KRUGMAN, H.E. Affective response to music as a function of familiarity. *Journal of Abnormal and Social Psychology,* 1943, **38,** 388–392.

KRUGMAN, H.E, and HARTLEY, E.C. The learning of tastes. *Public Opinion Quarterly,* 1960, **24,** 621–631.

LAMBERT, W.E., and JAKOBOVITS, L.A. Verbal satiation and changes in the intensity of meaning. *Journal of Experimental Psychology,* 1960, **60,** 376–383.

LORENZ, K. *L'instinct dans le comportement de l'animal et de l'homme.* Paris: Masson, 1956. **[25]**

LYKKEN, D.T. Properties of electrodes used in electrodermal measurements. *Journal of Comparative and Physiological Psychology,* 1959, **52,** 629–634.

MacKENZIE, B.K. The importance of contact in determining attitudes toward Negroes. *Journal of Abnormal and Social Psychology,* 1948, **43,** 4.

MANDLER, G. Associative frequency and associative prepotency as measures of response to nonsense syllables. *American Journal of Psychology,* 1955, **68,** 662–665.

MASLOW, A.H. The influence of familiarization on preference. *Journal of Experimental Psychology,* 1937, **21,** 162–180.

McGINNIES, E. Emotionality and perceptual defense. *Psychological Review,* 1949, **56,** 244–251.

MESSER, S., JAKOBOVITS, L.A., KANUNGO, R.N, and LAMBERT, W.A. Semantic satiation of words and numbers. *British Journal of Psychology,* 1964, **55,** 156–163.

MEYER, M. Experimental studies in the psychology of music. *American Journal of Psychology,* 1903, **14,** 456–476.

MILLER, G.A., NEWMAN, E.B., and FRIEDMAN, E.A. Length-frequency statistics for written English. *Information and Control,* 1958, **1,** 370–398.

MIRON, M.S. A cross-linguistic investigation of phonetic symbolism. *Journal of Abnormal and Social Psychology.* 1961, **62,** 623–630.

MONTGOMERY, K.C. Exploratory behavior as a function of "similarity" of stimulus situations. *Journal of Comparative and Physiological Psychology,* 1953, **46,** 129–133.

MOORE, H.T., and GILLILAND, A.R. The immediate and long time effects of classical and popular phonograph selections. *Journal of Applied Psychology.* 1924, **8,** 309–323.

MOSIER, C.I. A psychometric study of meaning. *Journal of Social Psychology,* 1941, **13,** 123–140.

MULL, H.K. The effect of repetition upon enjoyment of modern music. *Journal of Psychology,* 1957, **43,** 155–162.

MUNSINGER, H.L. Meaningful symbols as reinforcing stimuli. *Journal of Abnormal and Social Psychology,* 1964, **68,** 665–668.

National Opinion Research Center. Jobs and occupations: A popular evaluation. In R. Bendix and S.B. Lipsit (Eds.), *Class, status, and power: A research in social stratification.* Glencoe, Ill.: Free Press, 1953.

NEWCOMB, T.M. Stabilities underlying changes in Interpersonal attraction. *Journal of Abnormal and Social Psychology,* 1963, **66,** 376–386.

O'CONNELL, D.C. Concept learning and verbal control under partial reinforcement and subsequent reversal and non-reversal shifts. *Journal of Experimental Psychology,* 1965, **69,** 144–151.

OSGOOD, C.E., SUCI, G.J., and TANNENBAUM, P.H. *The measurement of meaning.* Urbana: University of Illinois Press, 1957.

PALERMO, D.S., and JENKINS, J.J. *Word association norms—grade school through college.* Minneapolis: University of Minnesota Press, 1964.

PEPPER, S.C. Changes of appreciation for color combinations. *Psychological Review,* 1919, **26,** 389–396.

POSTMAN, L. The experimental analysis of motivational factors in perception. In J. S. Brown (Ed.), *Current theory and research in motivation.* Lincoln: University of Nebraska Press, 1953.

PREMACK, D. Toward empirical behavior laws: I. Positive reinforcement. *Psychological Review,* 1959, **66,** 219–233.

PREMACK, D. Predicting instrumental performance from the independent rate of the contingent response. *Journal of Experimental Psychology,* 1961, **61,** 163–171.

PREMACK, D. Reversibility of the reinforcement relation. *Science,* 1962, **136,** 255–257.

PREMACK, D. Rate differential reinforcement in monkey manipulation. *Journal of the Experimental Analysis of Behavior,* 1963, **6,** 81–89.

PREMACK, D. Reinforcement theory. *Nebraska Symposium on motivation,* 1965, **13,** 123–180.

PREMACK, D., and BAHWELL, R. Operant-level lever pressing by a monkey as a function of interest interval. *Journal of the Experimental Analysis of Behavior,* 1959, **2,** 127–131.

PREMACK, D, and COLLIER, G. Joint effects of stimulus deprivation and intersession interval: Analysis of nonreinforcement variables affecting response probability. *Psychological Monographs,* 1962, **76,** (5, Whole No. 524).

REYNIERSE, J.H., and BARCH, A.M. Semantic satiation and generalization. *Psychological Reports,* 1963, **13,** 790.

SARTRE, J.P. *Words.* New York: Braziller, 1964.

SCHREUDER, H. *Pejorative sense development.* Groningen: Noordhoff, 1929.

SCHULZ, R.W., WEAVER, G.E., and RADTKE, R.C. Verbal satiation?? *Psychonomic Science,* 1965, **2,** 43–44.

SOLOMON, R.L, and POSTMAN, L. Usage as a determinant of visual duration thresholds of words. *Journal of Experimental Psychology,* 1952, **43,** 195–201.

STRASSBURGER, F., and WERTHEIMER, M. The discrepancy hypothesis of affect and association value of nonsense syllables. *Psychological Reports,* 1959, **5,** 528.

TANNENBAUM, P.H, and GENGEL, R.W. Generalization of attitude change through congruity principle relationships. *Journal of Personality and Social Psychology,* 1966, **3,** 299–304.

THIESSEN, D.D, and McGAUGH, J.L. Conflict and curiosity in the rat. Paper presented at the meeting of the Western Psychological Association, Monterey, California, 1958.

THOMSON, W.R., and SOLOMON, L.M. Spontaneous pattern discrimination in the rat. *Journal of Comparative and Physiological Psychology,* 1954, **47,** 104–107.

THORNDIKE, E.L, and LORGE, I. *The teacher's wordbook of 30,000 words.* New York: Teachers College, Columbia University, 1944. **[26]**

UNDERWOOD, B.J. Verbal learning and the educative process. *Harvard Educational Review,* 1959, **29,** 107–117.

VAN DER BEKE, G.E. *French word book.* New York: Macmillan, 1929.

VAN DONGEN, G.A. *Amelioratives in English.* Rotterdam: De Vries, 1933.

VERVEER, E.M, BARRY, H., JR., and BOUSFIELD, W.A. Change in affectivity with repetition. *American Journal of Psychology,* 1933, **45,** 130–134.

WASHBURN, M.F., CHILD, M.S., and ABEL, T.M. The effects of immediate repetition on the pleasantness or unpleasantness of music. In M. Schoen (Ed.), *The effects of music.* New York: Harcourt, Brace, 1927.

WIEBE, G. The effects of radio plugging on students' opinions of popular songs. *Journal of Applied Psychology,* 1940, **24,** 721–727.

WILNER. D.M., WALKLEY, R.P., and COOK, S.W. Residential proximity and intergroup relations in public housing projects. *Journal of Social Issues,* 8, **1,** 1952.

WILSON, L.R., and BECKNELL, J.C. The relation between the association value, pronounciability, and affectively of nonsense syllables. *Journal of Psychology,* 1961, **52,** 47–49.

YELEN, D.R., and SCHULZ, R.W. Verbal satiation? *Journal of Verbal Learning and Verbal Behavior,* 1963, **1,** 372–377. **[27]**

Chapter 7

Affiliation and Social Discrimination Produced by Brief Exposure in Day-Old Domestic Chicks

R.B. Zajonc, William Raft Wilson, and D.W. Rajecki
University of Michigan

Interaction among members of a given social grouping differs markedly from interaction with outsiders. Group members maintain proximity, agonistic confrontations are infrequent, beneficial responses (e.g., grooming, feeding, playing, etc.) are prevalent, and the exploitation of scarce resources is relatively conflict-free. At the same time, "strangers" are shunned, repelled or attacked. This study is concerned with the early development of social discrimination as it emerges in the context of a communal experience. One-day-old chicks that had been exposed to one another are observed for their ability to discriminate between companions and "strangers." Research on the domestic fowl shows that when strange hens are introduced into flocks they immediately become targets of aggression (Schjelderup-Ebbe, 1935; Guhl and Allee, 1944). However, it is not known at what age domestic chicks begin recognizing companions and distinguishing them from strangers. The emergence of this form of social discrimination is not understood fully, but it is probable that factors that are implicated in the formation of affiliative bonds are also implicated in the development of social discrimination. Hence, procedures that are successful in establishing affiliation (approach behavior, following and other forms of preference for the given target) should simultaneously establish avoidance and rejection of other objects. In some cases, the antecedents of affiliation are remarkably simple. In the imprinting of precocial hatchlings, for example, the

Reprinted from *Animal Behavior*, 23, R.B. Zajonc, W.R. Wilson, and D.W. Rajecki, "Affiliation and social discrimination produced by brief exposure in day-old chicks" 131–138, Copyright © 1975, with permission from Elsevier.

repeated exposure of an object is sufficient for the formation of strong preference for that object (Bateson, 1966; Sluckin, 1965; Zajonc, 1971).

Inferences about social behavior among adult hens, especially in the areas of affiliation and dominance, are made readily from observations of pecking (Murchison, 1935; Ratner, 1961). Pecking also serves as an index of ingroup/outgroup discrimination, but quantitative data in this specific area are scarce for adult hens (e.g., Craig, Biswas and Guhl, 1969) and are not available for hatchlings. It is not known at present how soon pecking begins to play a significant part in the social life of the hatchling, how soon after hatching mutual social discriminations are made, or whether they are revealed in pecking interactions. The majority of imprinting research relies on reactions of single individuals to inanimate objects in situations that preclude social interactions. Of the imprinting studies with chicks that are concerned with social choices among conspecifics rather than among inanimate objects, only two measured the effects of social experience for day-old chicks (Kilham, Klopfer and Oelke, 1968; Rajecki and Lake, 1972). The remaining studies observed these effects on chicks already several days old (Pattie, 1936; Smith, 1957; Salzen and Cornell, 1968) or even several weeks old (Howells and Vine, 1940). Without exception, these studies employ confined targets and do not allow, therefore, for inferences about the emergence of social preferences in the context of social interaction. **[131]***

The present experiments seek to establish whether the same minimal conditions that are sufficient for the formation of early affiliative bonds, namely brief communal exposures, are also sufficient for the emergence of social discriminations. The main focus is on early exposure and its consequence: the discriminability of individuals. In contrast to imprinting research in which the attainment and maintenance of spatial proximity serve as the primary measure, observations are made of social pecking at companions and at strangers. Generalization of the effects of imprinting to objects not initially exposed is rather limited (Jaynes, 1956, 1958; Bateson, 1964). We would expect, therefore, that exposure alone should be sufficient in generating social discrimination.

EXPERIMENT I

In the first experiment, 1-day-old chicks were observed in a series of pairwise pecking bouts; each chick was matched in some way against its companion and in others against strangers. The role of visual information in establishing and maintaining social discrimination, revealed in differential pecking, was explored by varying supplementary cues in the form of artificially induced pre-hatch coloring. In one condition the coloring of the subjects was designed to facilitate discriminations between "strangers" and "companions," in another condition it was irrelevant to this discrimination, and in a third it was designed to have confounding consequences.

Methods

SUBJECTS   All subjects used in experiment I and in experiment II were of the DeKalb (White Leghorn variety) hybrid stock. In the first experiment, 168 chicks were hatched in visual and tactile isolation of each other. Between day 11 and day 13 of incubation,

---

* Bracketed bold numbers refer to original page numbers. Page numbers indicate where the original page ended.

the eggs were injected with commercial food coloring (2.5 percent solution of U.S. certified color in water and propylene glycol). Half of the embryos were dyed green and half red. The procedure suggested by Evans (1951) and modified by Rajecki and Lake (1972) was followed. The narrow end of the egg was swabbed with alcohol and punctured with a 20-gauge needle, about 1.25 cm from the top. Approximately 0.7 ml of the preparation was injected with a 25-gauge needle. Following injection, the puncture was wiped with alcohol and sealed with a small fragment of adhesive tape.

The resulting coloring of the hatched chicks' plumage approximated the 5R 1/12 Munsel red chip and 2.5G 6/8 Munsel green chip. No physiological or behavioral side effects are known to be associated with the procedure, and none were observed in this experiment.

APPARATUS   The subjects were dark-hatched in a Jamesway 252B incubator that maintained a constant temperature of 38°C and 61 percent relative humidity. After hatching, birds were housed in 22 × 28 × 20-cm cages. The side walls were made of sheet metal. The door and the back wall were made of wire mesh. The back was covered with Lucite. Visual and tactile contact was not possible between birds housed in different cages. The ambient temperature of the housing units was 29° to 32°C and illumination was provided by two 25-W lamps placed directly behind the rear wall of the housing unit, 3 cm behind the Lucite. Behavioral observations were of subjects placed in a 20 × 45 × 25-cm deep box constructed of masonite and lined with absorbent paper that was changed after each test. Two identical boxes were constructed since two pairs of birds were observed at one time.

PROCEDURE   No earlier than 12 hr. and not later than 24 hr. after hatching, the hatchlings were placed in exposure cages for a period of 16 to 18 hr. Forty-eight green and forty-eight red chicks were housed in pairs of like coloring. Forty-eight chicks, half green and half red, were housed in pairs of unlike coloring. An additional twenty-four hatchlings, also dyed red or green, were housed in isolation for the same period of time.

All testing was carried out in "tournaments" of tetrads. For each pair of companion chicks, one other pair of companion chicks was selected to form a tetrad. In each experimental condition, therefore, there were twelve such tetrads, and in the control condition (chicks housed in isolation), there were six tetrads. Within each tetrad, one pair of companions was always designated *A* and *B,* and the other *X* and *Y.* Prior to the tournament, all chicks were marked with a water-soluble marker to allow identification of individuals.

For each tetrad, the tournament involved observing each individual in several pecking bouts against the remaining three, according to a specified order. These pairwise bouts took place in the masonite boxes described above and lasted 3 min. each. The first bout of each tournament would begin with two birds being **[132]** placed at opposite ends of the masonite box under opaque cylinders, 14.8 cm in diameter and 31.3-cm high. One minute was allowed to elapse and the opaque cylinders were removed simultaneously. The birds were given 2 min. of adaptation, after which all pecks were counted for a period of 3 min., with each minute scored separately. The second and subsequent bouts did not include the 2-min. adaptation period.

In each tournament, there were four ingroup and four outgroup bouts. Each bird of the tetrad had two bouts with its companion and one bout each with the two strangers. Hence, in each tournament, there were the following eight bouts: AB_1, AB_2, AX, AY, BX, BY, XY_1 and XY_2, where subscripts $_1$ and $_2$ stand for the first and second ingroup bout, respectively. At any one time, two of the eight bouts were observed simultaneously, each by a different observer, and in a separate box. While one observer might have observed bout AB_1, the other would be necessarily observing bout XY_1. If, in the subsequent bout, the first observer would, according to schedule, observe the AX bout, the second observer would score the BY bout, etc., until all eight bouts were completed.

In each condition, there were six different orders of bouts. Birds in different tetrads encountered their companions and strangers in different sequences of bouts. Since two bouts of a given tournament were run at the same time, and since both had to be either ingroup or outgroup encounters, the six orders were IIOO, IOIO, IOOI, OOII, OIOI, OIIO, where I means ingroup and O means outgroup bout.

The starting position of the bird in the observation box and the number of transfers from one box to the other were randomized within each order of bouts. Each of the two ingroup encounters within each tetrad was observed by a different observer. Thus, for example, for the order IOIO, if one observer scored AB_1 as his first ingroup bout, he would score XY_2 as his second ingroup bout. Pecks to all portions of the birds' bodies were counted and tabulated for each minute separately. A reliability check disclosed an acceptable level of agreement (0.98).

DESIGN   Twelve tetrads were of the same color within pairs and of the same color between pairs (HOM–HOM); hence, all chicks in the given tetrad were either green or red (see Table 7.1). Twelve tetrads were of the same color within pairs but of unlike color between pairs (HOM–HET). Twelve pairs composed of one green and one red chick were matched against twelve similar unlike-color pairs (HET–HOM). The six tetrads of isolates were yoked in color and order of bouts to six tetrads selected from among the socially reared chicks.

Table 7.1   Pairing, During Exposure and in Test Bouts

Experimental condition	Cohabitation	Test bouts	
		Ingroup	Outgroup
HOM–HOM	Red with red (24 chicks) or Green with green (24 chicks)	Red vs. red or Green vs. green	Red vs. red or Green vs. green
HOM–HET	Red with red (24 chicks) or Green with green (24 chicks)	Red vs. red or Green vs. green	Red vs. green
HET–HOM	Red with green (28 chicks)	Red vs. green	Red vs. red, Red vs. green, and Green vs. green

Results

All data were computed from the number of pecks per min. per bird. Because the pecking behavior of one bird within a given tetrad is not independent of the pecking of another, analysis of variance was performed using not individual subjects, but, instead, entire tetrads as data points. Conditions (three levels) and orders (six levels) were between-subject factors, while bouts (four levels) and minutes (three levels) were within-subject factors, with ingroup-outgroup effects (two levels) nested in bouts.

Figure 7.1 shows pecking rates for each of the thirty-six tetrads as well as the average peck **[133]** rates for each of the three experimental conditions. It is evident that there is considerably more pecking among "strangers" than among companions ($F = 178.01$; $df = 1/198$; $P < 0.001$). There is also a significant discriminability effect, with the HOM–HET condition showing the sharpest differences in peck rates ($F = 19.93$; $df = 2/198$; $P < 0.001$). The HOM–HET tetrads are those in which the greatest differentiation would, in fact, be expected, since the two pairs are unfamiliar to each other

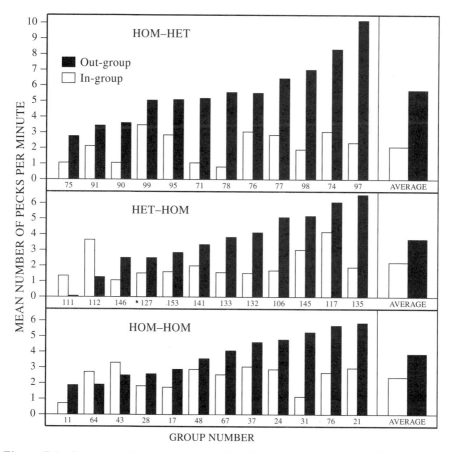

Figure 7.1   Ingroup and outgroup pecking for chicks of the same and of different coloring

because of lack of common experience, and because in the encounter between strangers their coloring is mutually unfamiliar as well.

While differences in coloring facilitate discrimination (see data for the HOM–HET condition), they are neither necessary nor sufficient for the emergence of differential ingroup/outgroup pecking. That color differences are not necessary is evident from the contrast between ingroup and outgroup pecking found in the HOM–HOM condition in which the four birds were of the same coloring ($F = 24.65$; $df = 1/198$; $P < 0.001$). It is not always possible, by means of prehatch dye injections, to produce completely uniform coloring in all hatchlings. Hence, there is some, however limited, possibility that these slight differences in coloring served as discriminable cues in the HOM–HOM condition. However, data from experiment II (see Figure 7.1), in which uncolored chicks were used, will support further the conclusion that reliable social discrimination can develop without differences in coloring.

That color differences are not in themselves sufficient is evident from data of the HET–HOM and of the isolate conditions. In the HET–HOM condition, the members of the cohabiting pairs are of different coloring. Each bird has one bout with a stranger of the same coloring and one with a stranger of a different coloring than his own. If color differences between individual subjects were alone capable of inducing differences in pecking, we would expect (a) that the ingroup peck rate of the HET–HOM condition would be higher than in the other two experimental conditions, (b) that ingroup peck rate of the HET–HOM birds would be higher than their outgroup peck rate, and (c) that they would peck more at the stranger of different coloring than at the stranger of their own coloring. In fact, the opposite is true in each case. The data relevant to (a) and (b) can be seen in Fig. 7.1. As for (c), the mean peck rate at a like-color stranger was 4.00 and unlike-color stranger 3.32. The relatively high peck rate in bouts with a like-color stranger is due to unfamiliarity of the coloring, because the social experience of the HET–HOM subjects was primarily (and if we exclude experience with self, exclusively) with individuals of coloring different from their own. With respect to the isolates which were all strangers to one another, the sufficiency argument would lead us to expect more pecking in unlike pairs than in like pairs. No difference, however, was found between these two types of pairs among the isolated subjects ($t = 0.435$; $df = 34$). At the same time, the overall peck rate of the isolates was higher than the highest experimental outgroup peck rate (8.43 versus 5.74; $t = 2.81$; $df = 34$; $P < 0.01$).

Because of the short time of the tournaments, we may not consider their outcomes as stable social structures (peck orders), but it is possible to examine the tournaments for their consistency. Within each tournament, the outcomes of bouts (i.e., which of the two birds pecks more) can be examined for their transitivity. Therefore, if A > B (meaning "A beats B") and B > C, transitivity exists if A > C. There are three such transitivities possible in each tournament, and their presence was assessed by means of coefficients of consistency (Kendall and Smith 1940). The average coefficients of consistency in the HOM–HET, HET–HOM and HOM–HOM groups were respectively 0.96, 0.97 and [134] 0.98, almost complete transitivity in each case. Furthermore, by comparing the peck-orders of birds within tetrads generated by each successive minute of the tournament, we can, within these limits, assess the temporal stability of these social relationships using Kendall's W. The coefficients of concordance (W's) over the

3 min. for the HOM–HET, HET–HOM and HOM–HOM conditions were 0.82, 0.65 and 0.65; again, quite high (Siegel, 1956).

Murchison's (1935) Social Reflex No. 1 (that is, the time and distance traversed by each of two contestants toward each other) was observed in a restricted form. For each bout, the observation was made as to which of the two chicks made the first move toward the other. When we compare these figures against the probability of "winning" the bout, i.e., pecking more than the opponent, it appears that the tendency to "start" has some power in predicting the outcome. Of those birds that made the first move, 61.3, 61.4 and 58.7 percent "won" their bouts in the HOM–HET, HET–HOM and HET–HOM conditions, respectively. Among isolates, the starters had an almost equal chance of winning their bouts (52.0 percent). This difference between the experimental and isolated birds might be explained by assuming that birds raised socially may have had experience in similar social encounters, and that some of them were reinforced negatively by counter-attacks that followed such "starts." This experience would tend to inhibit the tendency to move first. Ratner (1961) has shown that adult White Leghorns are quite capable of learning responses appropriate to subordinate social rank. Since isolates did not have the benefit of experience with conspecifics, probable winners and probable losers were both likely starters.

Behavioral reciprocity can only be evaluated indirectly and was done in the following manner. Separate determination was made for reciprocity among strangers and among companions. (Since each chick has two separate 3-min. bouts with two different strangers, we can determine from which of the two strangers it received the greater number of pecks and can inquire whether the pecks delivered vary as a positive or as an inverse function of pecks received.) In each tournament, two independent determinations of outgroup reciprocation can be made. Therefore, if $AX > BX$ and $XA > XB$, we have an instance of reciprocity, and if $AX > BX$ and $XA < XB$, we have an instance of complementarity, where AX means all the pecks delivered by A to X, and XA all the pecks delivered by X to A. If $AX = BX$ or $XA = XB$, no determination can be made. Using this method of assessing reciprocation of pecking, there were fourteen, fourteen and sixteen reciprocations in the HOM–HET, HOM–HOM and HET–HOM conditions, respectively. Also, respectively, there were six, six and five complementarities, and four, four and three indeterminate encounters as far as outgroup pecking is concerned. Across conditions, then, there were forty-four reciprocating, seventeen complementary and eleven indeterminate encounters.

Ingroup pecking, too, can be assessed for reciprocity by comparing the first with the second ingroup bout. Therefore, if $AB_1 > AB_2$ and $BA_1 > BA_2$ (or if $AB_1 < AB_2$ and $BA_1 < BA_2$), there would be reciprocation, for as one bird increases pecking, so does the other. If $AB_1 > AB_2$ and $BA_1 < BA_2$, there is again complementarity. If $AB_1 = AB_2$ or $BA_1 = BA_2$, no determination can be made. (According to this procedure, there were eleven, ten and eleven reciprocated encounters in the HOM–HET, HOM–HOM and HET–HOM conditions, five, eight and eight complementary encounters, and eight, six and five indeterminate encounters, for a total of thirty-two reciprocated, twenty-one complementary and nineteen indeterminate encounters.) The large number of indeterminate outcomes among the ingroup triads is due to a preponderance of passive encounters where no pecking at all occurred. Also, it appears that there is less reciprocation in ingroup than in outgroup encounters. Overall, reciprocity occurs about twice as often as complementarity.

EXPERIMENT II

In thirty-two of the thirty-six tetrads of experiment I, there was clearly more outgroup than ingroup pecking, and in the HOM–HET condition, there was nearly three times as much outgroup as ingroup pecking. The maximal differences in ingroup/outgroup pecking were obtained for different-colored pairs, but there were significant differences in pecking even for those pairs that could not distinguish between companions and strangers on the basis of color. To approach the minimal conditions necessary for the occurrence of social discrimination, we have tried in experiment II to eliminate or to reduce factors that favor differential pecking rates. **[135]**

Four modifications were introduced to impose these restrictions. (a) Subjects were not colored. (b) Observations were made of four-way bouts, in which all four birds (previously housed in pairs) were observed for their pecking behavior. Under these conditions, social discrimination is more difficult to achieve, since each subject must discriminate among three individuals, two of whom are strangers, and one its companion. (c) Some pairs were housed, as previously, in cages that afforded visual, auditory and tactile contact, but other birds were housed in cages equipped with wire partitions that prevented social pecking during the exposure phase. (d) Time of exposure was varied, the shortest being 1 hr.

Methods

One hundred and ninety-two undyed chicks were hatched as previously and transferred to exposure cages at ages ranging from 12 to 23 hr.

Exposure was again in pairs but a third of the chicks were exposed to each other for just 1 hr., a third for 4 hr. and a third for 16 hr. Termination of exposure always coincided with the 24th hr. of the subject's life. Ninety-six birds were housed as in experiment I, and ninety-six were housed in similar cages that provided for separation between the two members of the pair by means of a wire partition extending the entire depth and height of the cage.

Testing again was done at the completion of the exposure phase and was carried out in an open field, 45 × 45 × 16-cm high for a period of 5 min. The bouts were recorded on videotape; all pairwise pecking was tabulated from the tapes.

Results

Entire tetrads, and not individual subjects, again served as units of analysis. Data were corrected for the availability of targets. That is, since each bird had the opportunity of pecking at two strangers but at only one companion, for purposes of analysis, his peck rate at strangers was divided by two. Figure 7.2 shows peck rates (pecks per min. per subject) for the six experimental groups. The presence of partition during exposure makes a pronounced contribution to the incidence of pecking. Birds

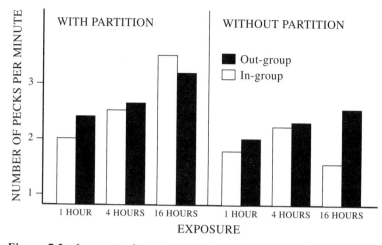

Figure 7.2 Ingroup and outgroup pecking as a function of duration of prior exposure for birds housed with and without partition.

housed in partitioned cages peck at each other significantly more than birds housed as in the previous experiment ($F = 5.38$; $df = 1/42$; $P < 0.05$). Moreover, there seems to be no difference between ingroup and outgroup pecking for birds housed in partitioned cages and, hence, deprived of an opportunity to peck each other freely. For those birds housed in undivided cages, only the 16-hr. group attained significance. The appropriate interaction term was significant at the 0.05 level, and the difference between ingroup and outgroup peck rates for the nonpartitioned 16-hr. group was significant at the 0.001 level ($F = 11.81$; $df = 1/42$).

DISCUSSION

The early social life of the chick hatchling appears to be quite sophisticated. Other research has shown that the hatchling exhibits a rich repertoire of social behavior (Andrew, 1966; Evans, 1967), and the present studies have demonstrated that it is able to acquire socially significant discriminations very rapidly. Evidence of reliable discrimination between individual strangers and companions was obvious as early as the first minute of the encounter ($F = 46.07$; $df = 1/193$; $P < 0.001$). The two experiments taken together show that pecking is useful in revealing social differentiation that is established by virtue of early exposure.

Interest in pecking behavior as a form of social interaction has emphasized either its agonistic (Evans, 1967) or dominance-related aspects (see, for example, Craig, Biswas and Guhl, 1969, or Murchison, 1935). While some pecking observed in the present experiments could be categorized as aggressive according to Evans' (1967) criteria, for the most part, its character was rather exploratory and not distinct in topography from pecks delivered at the physical segments of the chick's environment, such as the walls or the floors of the enclosures. A number of the present results suggest that pecking is a [136] vehicle of social exploration. They show that social pecking is highly sensitive to variations in the novelty of the target, which is the primary stimulus for exploratory behavior. Pecking was consistently elevated whenever the encounter involved a novel element: (a) pecking was greater among strangers than among companions; (b) pecking was greater among strangers of unfamiliar coloring than among strangers of familiar coloring; the HOM–HET condition showed the highest rate of outgroup pecking, and in the HET–HOM condition, there was more outgroup pecking at the stranger whose coloring was different from the subject's companion than at the stranger whose coloring was the same; (c) chicks raised in isolation, and for whom another chick was a totally novel stimulus, exhibited the highest amount of pecking; and (d) in experiment II, birds housed in partitioned cages manifested more overall pecking than did birds housed without this constraint. In agreement with these observations are those of Craig, et al., (1969) who found an increase in social interaction in groups of adult hens containing strangers, and of Guiton and Sluckin (1969) and Dimond (1970) who observed more overall social pecking among dark-reared than among light-reared chicks.

Even though the directly observable quality of early pecking among chick hatchlings is exploratory, it nevertheless seems to have pronounced social consequences. Under some circumstances, it may familiarize specific individuals with one another, laying ground for affiliation and attachment. Possibly through repeated pecking contact, the reciprocal reactions of two particular individuals assume predictable and recognizable patterns. For instance, the approach and the exploratory posture of each individual may be in some measure unique and identifiable, and so may be the reactions of those to whom it is addressed. The fact that birds housed in partitioned cages did not show discrimination between strangers and companions suggests that pecking might contribute to and facilitate the identification of particular individuals.

Under other circumstances, and perhaps entirely accidentally, exploratory social pecking develops into a chain of agonistic reactions. For example, a given exploratory peck is directed accidentally at a vulnerable or an injured part of the target's body; if it produces pain, the target might avoid the explorer in future encounters. Or, retaliatory pecking may be elicited, escalating into a higher level of aggression.

Little fear (freezing, jumping, etc.) was observed in encounters between birds, including those without any prior social experience. If fear manifested itself in ways that were not readily detectable, it did not seem to depress pecking. This seems to be in contrast with the observation that novel stimuli and novel environments depress food pecking—a phenomenon explained by invoking the inhibitory effects of fear of novel environment (Hogan, 1965; Wilson, 1968). It is possible that in these studies food pecking was reduced because other targets, being novel, elicited exploratory pecking that competed successfully with pecking for food. However, our findings are consistent with results showing that fear responses do not emerge until chicks are somewhat older than 24 hr.

Because the behavior observed in the present experiments involved reciprocation and mutuality, certain aspects of social phenomena were revealed with greater clarity than is usually the case in imprinting experiments. Interindividual pecking, never used previously in the study of early avian social behavior and imprinting, seems to be an efficient and reliable measure. Above all, it is very easy to quantify. Because a large sample of pecking can be obtained within relatively short observations, unlike choice behavior, for example, it attains high levels of reliability that are determined readily. The high level of reliability of social pecking is quite apparent in the high coefficients of consistency and of concordance reported above. Pecking seems to be less vulnerable to extraneous fluctuations than, for instance, first choice, the latency of choice or maintenance of proximity.

Future research should determine the permanence of social bonds established by means of early exposures and contact, and whether social discrimination is maintained through interindividual pecking once the hatchlings begin to feed. The vulnerability of social bonds to subsequent separations and isolation should also be explored. **[137]**

REFERENCES

Andrew, R.J. (1966). Precocious adult behavior in the young chick. *Anim. Behav.*, **14**, 485–500.

Bateson, P.P.G. (1964). Effect of similarity between rearing and testing conditions on chicks' following and avoidance responses. *J. comp. physiol. Psychol.* **57**, 100–103.

Bateson, P.P.G. (1966). The characteristics and context of imprinting. *Biol. Rev.*, **41**, 171–220.

Craig, J.V., Biswas, D.K. and Guhl, A.M. (1969). Agonistic behavior influenced by strangeness, crowding and heredity in female domestic fowl (*Gallus gallus*). *Anim. Behav.*, **17**, 498–506.

Dimond, S.J. (1970). Visual experience and early social behavior in chicks. In: *Social Behavior in Birds and Mammals* (Ed. by J.H. Crook), pp. 441–466. New York: Academic Press.

Evans, C.D. (1951). A method of color marking young waterfowl. *J. Wildl. Mgmt.*, **15**,101–103.

Evans, R.M. (1967). Early aggressive responses in domestic chicks. *Anim. Behav.*, **16**, 24–28.

Guhl, A.M. and Allee, W.C. (1944). Some measurable effects of social organization in flocks of hens. *Physiol. Zoöl.*, **17**, 320–347.

Guiton, P. and Sluckin, W. (1969). The effects of visual experience on behavioral development in neonatal domestic chicks. *Br. J. Psychol.*, **60**, 494–507.

Hogan, J.A. (1965). An experimental study of conflict and fear: An analysis of behavior of young chicks toward a mealworm. *Behaviour*, **25**, 45–97.

Howells, T.H. and Vine, D.O. (1940). The innate differential in social learning. *J. Abnorm. Soc. Psychol.*, **35**, 537–548.

Jaynes, J. (1956). Imprinting: The interaction of learned and innate behavior: I. Development and generalization. *J. comp. physiol. Psychol.*, **49**, 201–206.

Jaynes, J. (1958). Imprinting: The interaction of learned and innate behavior: IV. Generalization and emergent discrimination. *J. comp. physiol. Psychol.*, **51**, 238–242.

Kendall, M.G. and Smith, B.B. (1940). On the method of paired comparisons. *Biometrika*, **31**, 324–345.

Kilham, P., Klopfer, P.H. and Oelke, H. (1968). Species identification and color preferences in chicks. *Anim. Behav.*, **16**, 238–244.

Murchison, C. (1935). The time function in the experimental formation of social hierarchies of different sizes in *Gallus domesticus*. *J. Soc. Psychol.*, **7**, 3–18.

Pattie, F.A. (1936). The gregarious behavior of normal chicks and chicks hatched in isolation. *J. comp. Psychol.*, **21**, 161–178.

Rajecki, D.W. and Lake, D. (1972). Social preference in chicks as a function of own color and rearing condition. *Rev. Comp. Anim.*, **6**, 151–155.

Ratner, S.C. (1961). Effect of learning to be submissive on status in the peck order of domestic fowl. *Anim. Behav.*, **9**, 34–37.

Salzen, E.A. and Cornell, J.M. (1968). Self-perception and species recognition in birds. *Behaviour*, **30**, 44–65.

Schjelderup-Ebbe, T. (1935). Social behavior in birds In: Murchison's *Handbook of Social Psychology*. Worcester: Mass.: dark University Press, 947–972.

Siegel, S. (1956). *Non-parametric Statistics for the Behavioral Sciences.* New York: McGraw-Hill.

Sluckin, W. (1965). *Imprinting and Early Learning.* Chicago: Aldine.

Smith, W. (1957). Social "learning" in domestic chicks. *Behaviour*, **11**, 40–55.

Wilson, G. (1968). Early experience and facilitation of feeding in domestic chicks. *J. comp. physiol. Psychol.*, **66**, 800–802.

Zajonc, R.B. (1971). Attraction, affiliation, and attachment. In: *Man and Beast: Comparative Social Behavior* (Ed. by J.F. Eisenberg and W.S. Dillon), pp. 143–179. Washington, D.C.: Smithsonian Institution Press. **[138]**

Part Four

Cognition

Chapter 8

The Process of Cognitive Tuning in Communication

R.B. Zajonc
University of Michigan

Considerable evidence is now available on selective and directive effects in perception and cognition. The earliest explanation of these effects was advanced by the Würzburg School in their postulation of a determining tendency that arises from the subject's (*S's*) task assignment (*Aufgabe*), and acts as a steering mechanism in information-seeking behavior (Ach, 1905; Lewin, 1922a, 1922b; Watt, 1905). The specific effects of determining tendencies were shown to be intimately related to the nature of the *Aufgaben* (Chapman, 1932; Kulpe, 1904).

The effects of *Aufgaben* are readily detected in communication. Each person is daily a source and a destination of numerous messages, and strong selective and directive effects should result when the individual's role in the communication process is manipulated. Hovland and his associates (Hovland, Janis, and Kelley, 1953) have shown in extensive studies that the characteristics of the communicator and the circumstances of the communication influence the attitudinal and cognitive impact of communications. Zimmerman and Bauer (1956), on the other hand, have demonstrated that communicators themselves are influenced by their audiences. The purpose of this study is to examine the nature of cognitive structures that are activated or "tuned in" when persons enter into communication with others.

For the purposes of this research, a set of formal properties were defined for the description and measurement of cognitive structures. Since it is generally agreed that cognitive structures represent organized systems whose nature depends on the various interrelations among their components (Asch, 1946; French, 1947), the main emphasis was placed on morphological description. The properties defined are to some extent based on Lewin's (1951) analysis of the life space and on French's (1947) work on sentiments. Two experiments were conducted in which measures of the cognitive dimensions were obtained and the effects of "tuning" to receive and transmit information were analyzed.

Zajonc, R.B. (1960). The process of cognitive tuning in communication. *Journal of Abnormal Social Psychology*, 61, 159–168. Copyright © 1980 by the American Psychological Association. Reprinted with permission.

PROPERTIES OF COGNITIVE STRUCTURES[1]

It is assumed that objects and events are perceived and discriminated on the basis of psychological dimensions. By a psychological dimension is understood the organism's capacity to respond to stimuli in such a way that, given a set of stimuli and a set of responses made to them, the stimuli and responses form two ordered sets with a determinate correspondence between the elements of each set. From the person's responses one can infer the values of which psychological dimensions consist. An act of perceiving or discriminating may be thought of in terms of "projecting" the given stimulus on some psychological dimensions, and thereby attributing to it values taken from these dimensions. The values thus assigned to stimuli constitute the elements of cognitive structures and are called attributes. They are the qualities or characteristics that individuals "assign" to objects and events.

An attribute, then, is a concept (or a category) in its simplest form, since a value from a given psychological dimension generally characterizes an entire class of objects. More complex concepts are formed, as Bruner, Goodnow, and Austin (1956) suggest, by conjunctive and disjunctive combinations of attributes. The larger and the more inclusive the set of objects (class) denoted by a concept, the more general is the concept. For instance, all sorts of objects are "black," "animal," or "beautiful." Only a few are "76 ft. 4 5/32 ins. long."

A person has at his disposal a large number of concepts or attributes by means of which he can identify and discriminate objects and events in his environment. The set of all such attributes is called his cognitive universe. Let a cognitive structure then be defined as an organized subset of the given cognitive universe in terms of which the individual identifies and discriminates a particular object or event. The morphological properties of cognitive structures describe various relationships among attributes. Those defined here are differentiation, complexity, unity, and organization.

Degree of Differentiation

Given a universe of, let us say, m alternative attributes, by means of which a given [159]* person is capable of identifying and discriminating objects and events, he can construct a maximum of 2^m distinct cognitive structures. The number (n) of attributes constituting a given cognitive structure is taken to reflect its degree of differentiation.

Degree of Complexity

The attributes constituting a given cognitive structure may come from a single class or category of discriminanda, or they may represent many categories. For instance, a painting may be perceived exclusively in terms of its objective qualities, such as size, object matter, color, type of frame, etc. Or, it may be looked upon partly in terms of its objective qualities, partly in terms of its formal properties (period, style, symmetry, harmony, etc.), and partly in terms of its impact on the subjective experience of the viewer. Such attribute groupings may be further subdivided into smaller classes, and the extent of such subdivision may be used in defining the complexity of cognitive structures.

---

* Bracketed bold numbers refer to original page numbers. Page numbers indicate where the original page ended.

[1] For a more detailed exposition of the descriptive model, see Zajonc (1954).

Let us denote the level of inclusion of a given class by r, such that if the class K_i does not include another subclass, $r = 1$; when K_i includes some subclasses, which, in turn, do not include other subdivisions, $r = 2$; when K_i includes subclasses which themselves contain other indivisible subclasses, $r = 3$, etc. The degree of complexity of a given cognitive structure may be obtained by weighting each attribute by the level of inclusion of its class membership and summing the weighted scores thus obtained. Thus:

$$\text{com} = \sum_{r=1}^{n} rn_r$$

where n_r is the number of attributes in the rth level of inclusion.

Degree of Unity

The structural components of a whole may depend on each other to a greater or lesser extent. The more attributes depend on each other, the more the cognitive structure is unified. If we define the dependence of the attribute A_i on the attribute A_j as equal to 1 when a change in A_j produces a change in A_i and as equal to 0 when change in A_j does not produce a change in A_i, then a dependency matrix can be constructed for all attributes of a given cognitive structure, and the total dependency of each attribute may easily be obtained by summing the entries in the appropriate row. To compare the unity of structures of different degrees of differentiation, the measure of unity must be normalized. Given a structure with n attributes, the maximum dependency of a given attribute, $\text{dep}(A_i)^{\text{max}}$, is equal to $n - 1$, and the maximum sum of dependencies in the cognitive structure to $n(n - 1)$. Unity then can be defined as:

$$\text{uni} = \frac{\sum_{i=1}^{n} \text{dep}(A_i)}{n(n-1)}$$

where $\text{dep}(A_i)$ is the total dependency of the ith attribute.

Degree of Organization

Lewin (1951) thought of degree of organization of a whole in terms of the existence of a guiding force or principle that controls its parts. To the extent that one part or a cluster of parts dominates the whole, the whole is said to be highly organized. On the basis of this view, the degree of organization can be readily defined. From the dependency matrix, the degree to which a given attribute, A_i, depends on others can be computed, as well as the degree to which it determines others. This value is obtained by summing the entries in the appropriate column of the matrix. Taking the determinance of the strongest attribute, $\text{det}(A_i)^{\text{max}}$, and dividing it by unity of the cognitive structure, we obtain a measure that reflects the degree to which the interdependence among the attributes is concentrated around a single core. Thus:

$$\text{org} = \frac{\text{det}(A_i)^{\text{max}}}{\text{uni}}$$

Empirical measures of the dimensions defined above can be obtained with the aid of various well-known methods that analyze the S's perception or conception of a given stimulus in terms of its characteristics or properties: adjective check lists, rating scales, the semantic differential, Q sort, and the like. The method used in the present series of studies required the S to describe a stimulus object, namely, another person, by freely listing the qualities and attributes that characterized him. The number of such qualities enumerated constituted the measure of differentiation. Complexity was measured by having the S organize the attributes he listed into meaningful groupings and subgroupings, which served as a basis for assigning weights reflecting the respective levels of inclusion. Both unity and organization were computed from Ss' ratings of dependencies among attributes they listed. Unity was scored by summing the dependency ratings among pairs of attributes, and, as required by the definition, dividing the sum by the possible sum of dependencies. Organization was measured by finding for the given cognitive structure the attribute on which the greatest number of other attributes depended, taking its determinance score (i.e., simply the number of attributes that were rated as depending on it) and dividing it by unity.

The scope of this paper does not allow the discussion of the interrelations among the cognitive dimensions, either as these arise from the formal properties of the definitions, or as they were observed in empirical results. An extended analysis of this problem is given elsewhere (Zajonc, 1954). **[160]**

EXPERIMENT I

Although a person is capable of activating a large number of cognitive structures, at any one time, only a few can operate. Specific conditions must therefore exist under which cognitive structures become activated, and the specification of these conditions should enable one to predict the nature of the structures that are activated. It is assumed that a cognitive structure relevant to a particular object or event is activated primarily when the person expects to deal with information about that object or event. Such anticipation constitutes one of the most fundamental occasions for the activation of cognitive structures. Casual observation reveals that messages exchanged between communicators at the onset of communication generally indicate what the communication is going to be about, and thus allow the activation of appropriate cognitive structures. One has merely to scan the opening paragraphs of articles in this journal to observe the tendency. The structure of language also shows such a propensity. Sentences generally begin with the subject. Placing the subject at the beginning of the sentence indicates what cognitive structures should be activated so that the information contained in the predicate can be meaningfully received.

If it is assumed that cognitive structures are activated in the anticipation of dealing with information, it follows that not only the subject matter of anticipated communication, but also the person's role in the communication process determines the kind of cognitive structure that he activates. Two basic ways of dealing with information may be distinguished: receiving and transmitting. When a person primarily anticipates receiving information, he may be expected to activate a cognitive structure capable of admitting the incoming information. Concomitant with the anticipation of receiving information is the anticipation of cognitive change. On the other hand, anticipation of transmitting information should activate structures that may serve as a source of potential messages.

These two processes may be termed receiving and transmitting tuning. The purpose of this study is to examine the differences in the properties of cognitive structures activated under receiving and transmitting tuning.

Method

SUBJECTS   The Ss used in this study were recruited on a voluntary basis from the AFROTC at the University of Michigan. Altogether, 45 Ss participated in the experiment.

PROCEDURE   After assembling in a classroom, the Ss in all conditions were issued the following verbal instructions by E:

> This is a study on how groups operate under certain conditions. I will tell you more about it later. Before, however, I will distribute copies of a real letter which was written by one individual to another. I want you to skim over this letter and get a general idea of what sort of person the writer is. Just try to imagine what kind of individual he is, and what are some of the things which are characteristic of him. But, please do not try to memorize the letter. This is not an experiment on memory. Just try to get a general picture of the individual who wrote the letter. You will have two minutes to read it.

At this point, the letter was distributed face down; then a signal was given to begin reading the letter. After 2 minutes, a signal was given to turn the letter face down again. The copies of the letter were then collected.

The letter used in the experiment was written to a potential employer by a job applicant. It contained some of the qualifications of the applicant and information regarding his background.

INDUCTION OF COGNITIVE TUNING   Twenty Ss received induction intended to produce transmitting tuning, and 25 received induction intended to produce receiving tuning. After the copies of the letter were collected, the transmitters received the following instructions:

> I said that we are trying to discover how groups operate under certain conditions. We are especially interested in the process of communication.
> At this very moment there is another group in the building. Your responsibility will be to communicate the information you have obtained about the person who wrote the letter to the members of the other group. You will have to describe this person to the other groups, so that they can know him as well as you do now.
> But before we begin to transmit this information to the other group, we will put down the things we learned about the writer from his letter. I will now distribute forms which you will fill out according to the instructions written on each page. **[161]**

The receivers were issued the same instructions except the second and third paragraphs were changed to read:

At this very moment there is another group in the building. They have detailed information on the individual who wrote the letter, and they will communicate this information to you. We want to see how well they can convey to you all the information they have.

But before we begin to receive this information from the other group, we will put down the things we learned about the writer from his letter. I will now distribute forms which you will fill out according to the instructions written on each page.

MEASUREMENT OF THE PROPERTIES OF COGNITIVE STRUCTURES   To obtain measures of the properties of cognitive structures, the following procedure was used. *S*s were issued instruction booklets to which were attached stacks of 52 blank cards marked from A to ZZ. The *S*s' first task was outlined on the first page of the booklets:

Detach the stack of cards from this booklet.

On each card *separately* write *one* characteristic which describes the applicant. You can put down whatever comes to your mind, since there is no one list of characteristics that can be considered as either "correct" or "incorrect." Everyone of us sees things in a slightly different way.

You may have too many or too few cards, but this shouldn't bother you. Put down as many characteristics as you feel are necessary to describe the applicant adequately. Work rapidly.

The number of characteristics attributed to the applicant constituted the degree of differentiation in each case.

To determine complexity, the *S*s were required to:

Lay out in front of you all the cards you used for listing the characteristics of the applicant. Look over them carefully and notice whether they fall into some broad natural groupings. If they do, arrange them into such groups.

After arranging the cards into groupings, the *S*s were issued the following instructions:

Now, look at your groups one by one and see whether these can't be broken down into subgroups. If they can, separate the cards accordingly. It is also possible that these subgroups can be broken down further, and so on.

When you arrange *all* cards into groups and subgroups, list your groupings on the sheet below as if they were points and subpoints of an outline. First, give names or titles to your groups and subgroups. Then in the right-hand column list the letters of all the characteristics that belong into the respective groups and subgroups.

The groupings and subgroupings were used to determine the levels of inclusion of the attributes, the basis for computing complexity scores. The *S*s were instructed to proceed as follows for the last task:

It is possible that some of the characteristics are related to one another. They may depend on one another in such a way that if one changes, the other ones would change too. Suppose the table in front of you were bigger than it is now. Then it would also become heavier. This means that the weight of the table depends on its size. The relationships between the characteristics you put down may not be so obvious and so simple, but try to decide whether such relationships exist nevertheless. To do this lay out the cards in front of you in alphabetical order, and follow the procedure below:

List all the characteristics which would change if Characteristic *A* were changed, absent, or untrue of the applicant; list all the characteristics which would change if Characteristic *B* were changed, absent, or untrue of the applicant, etc.

On the basis of the above responses, dependency matrices were constructed and measures of unity and organization computed.

After the *S*s completed the booklets, they were told with an apology that the experiment was over.

Results and Discussion

DEGREE OF DIFFERENTIATION   The overall results are shown in Table 8.1, which shows a significantly higher degree of differentiation for transmitters. The transmitters listed, on the average, 7.90 attributes; the receivers 5.12. It was assumed that the components of cognitive structures activated under tuning for reception act as *receiving categories,* whereas those activated under tuning for transmission act as *potential units of transmittable information.* The relevant difference between these two types of attributes is along the dimension of specificity-generality. Attributes whose function is to admit all possible types of information must be sufficiently broad and general. Since they are to serve as "codes" or "files" in terms of whichever new units of information are admitted, they must be sufficiently comprehensive so that all possible information can be appropriately categorized.

When the components of the cognitive structure are to serve as potential units of transmittable information, they are more likely to be specific. A "message" is composed of specific units alone, whereas general units constitute skeletons that organize the substantive

Table 8.1   Differences in the Properties of Cognitive Structures between Transmitters and Receivers

Property	Mean Score for Transmitters	Mean Score for Receivers	*t*
Differentiation	7.90	5.12	5.67***
Complexity	17.80	9.32	6.83***
Unity	0.309	0.222	2.19*
Organization	13.75	8.40	2.94**

  * $p < .05$
 ** $p < .01$
*** $p < .001$

and specific units of the message. Since specific units require more detail, their essential difference from general units lies in the coarseness of their "grain." Cognitive representations made in specific terms normally require a larger number of attributes than representations made primarily in broad and general [162] terms. If it is assumed that, other things equal, differentiation is a function of the level of specificity of a given cognitive structure, and if tuning for transmission results in a tendency toward greater specificity than tuning for reception, transmitters should indeed show higher differentiation. Thus, if it can be demonstrated that the transmitters, in fact, employ a higher proportion of specific attributes than the receivers, then the differences in the degree of differentiation are better understood.

The attributes of all Ss were coded for specificity by two independent judges, assigning each attribute to either specific or general categories. The general category included such items as "intelligent," "shiftless," "immature," "he does not seem to be ambitious." The specific category included attributes like, "didn't finish college because of financial problems," "he has never worked as a mail clerk." The reliability measured in percent agreement was 82%. The results indicate that the transmitters' cognitive structures had on the average 57.6% specific attributes, while those of the receivers, only 32.6%. This difference was significant at the .001 level.

DEGREE OF COMPLEXITY   The results show a higher degree of complexity for transmitters. Two factors may account for this finding. First, it would appear that the larger proportion of specific attributes, the more likely should the attributes fall into equivalence classes and subclasses. Furthermore, the results have indicated a higher degree of differentiation on the part of the transmitters. From the definition of complexity, it is evident that a high degree of differentiation increases the probability of high complexity. Both factors work to enhance complexity on the part of the transmitters.

DEGREE OF UNITY   From the concept of cognitive tuning, it would follow that receiving tuning corresponds to the anticipation of a cognitive change in one's own cognitive structure, whereas transmitting tuning corresponds to the anticipation of inducing changes in cognitive structures of other persons. A person who anticipates the occurrence of cognitive change is very likely to "unfreeze" his cognitive structure or to make it more susceptible to the anticipated changes. Susceptibility and resistance to change may be thought of in terms of the strength of forces necessary to induce changes in a given cognitive structure. In order to change a highly unified structure, a strong force is necessary because the components of the structure depend on one another to a great degree. Thus, a change in one attribute should result in changes in other attributes. In order to change a single attribute of a highly unified cognitive structure, a force must be applied which is capable of overcoming the resistance of not only the given attribute, but of all the other attributes on which it depends. To produce a similar change in an unified structure, a force is required that is capable of overcoming the resistance of the given component alone. If cognitive structures activated under receiving tuning are more susceptible to change than those activated under transmitting tuning, then they must be less well unified than the latter. The results indicate that this, in fact, is the case.

DEGREE OF ORGANIZATION   The dynamics of receiving tuning are of such nature that a high degree of structure and elaboration should deter the smooth reception of information. Rather, the situation calls for unstructured and loosely integrated cognitive structures, so that all possible types of changes could easily be introduced. The receiver does not know what specific information is to be imparted to him, and he cannot focus his cognitive processes on any single aspect of the matter, but must think in general terms. Degree of organization, it will be recalled, was defined in terms of the extent to which the cognitive structure is organized around such one specific aspect. Receiving tuning should therefore result in a relatively low degree of organization.

Transmitting tuning, however, represents a different psychological state. The transmitter is aware of the specific units of information to be transmitted, and his thinking revolves around them, with a certain focus of attention. He should therefore show a relatively higher degree of organization.

One should also expect a higher degree of organization for transmitters on other grounds. Predominance of specific attributes requires a structure into which the attributes can be ordered. The specific attributes are organized by means of general ones. Since the transmitters were shown to employ fewer general **[163]** attributes, their cognitive structure should be organized around fewer foci than those of the receivers.

The results show that the degree of organization was significantly higher for transmitters than for receivers. It should be noted that this result was obtained independently of the differences in unity. From the definition, it follows that, other things being equal, degree of organization actually decreases with higher unity. The higher degree of organization found for the transmitters was obtained despite their higher unity.

EXPERIMENT II

In the previous experiment, lower degrees of differentiation, complexity, unity, and organization were obtained under receiving than under transmitting tuning. These results were assumed to derive from the fact that the receivers tune in flexible cognitive structures, readily susceptible to changes, and having few specific attributes, while the transmitters' cognitive structures are characterized by a considerable resistance to change and a larger proportion of specific attributes. If resistance to change and degree of specificity account for the differences arising under receiving and transmitting tuning, they should also account for data obtained under other conditions involving these two factors. Suppose that persons expect to enter into communication with others who hold opinions opposite to or incongruent with their own. In the case of receiving tuning, there should be more resistance to accepting information that is contrary to the person's own beliefs than to accepting information that supports them. Since resistance to cognitive change has been assumed to be reflected in increased unity, we expect the receivers to show a relatively higher degree of unity when dealing with incongruent information than when dealing with congruent information. Furthermore, if they are to protect themselves from unwanted changes, receivers of incongruent information should eliminate from their cognitive structures components that make them vulnerable to change. If they have committed themselves to a positive opinion, they should ignore or omit negative attributes, and if they have committed themselves to a negative opinion, the opposite should be the case. Jones and Kohler (1958) have recently shown that Ss tend to recall plausible arguments that support their opinion and implausible arguments that question it, and to forget the converse. Simultaneously, the commitment to an opinion places a requirement on specificity. Thus, the first factor, because of its *selective* effects should tend to reduce differentiation for receivers of incongruent information, while the second should tend to increase it. If the two factors are equal in magnitude, the degree of differentiation should remain the same for receivers regardless of whether they deal with congruent or incongruent information. Similar consequences should follow for transmitters. The differences in the degree of differentiation between receivers and transmitters when incongruent information is involved should depend therefore on the relative increments of specificity and selectivity in both groups. If we assume that both groups select all those and only those attributes which are consistent with their position, then, because the number of such attributes is held constant for both groups, no differences in specificity should appear, and, consequently, the groups should not manifest any differences in differentiation. If receivers and transmitters increase in specificity and selectivity when confronted with incongruent information, with these increments being more pronounced for receivers, we should expect a lowering of differentiation for transmitters and a heightening for receivers. The differences in complexity should show the same pattern as differences in differentiation. Degree of organization, on the other hand, should increase for both groups, since now there is a core around which cognitive components may readily become organized—namely, the commitment to a positive or a negative position. But, again, this increase should be relatively more pronounced for the receivers, resulting in approximately equal levels of organization for both groups. The purpose of the second experiment is to examine these predictions.

Method

SUBJECTS   The Ss were sophomore and junior women enrolled at the University of Michigan. Altogether, 92 Ss took part in the experiment.

PROCEDURE   Four groups of 23 Ss each were assigned [164] randomly to four experimental groups: Transmitters of Congruent Information (T), Receivers of Congruent Information (R), Transmitters of Incongruent Information (TI), and Receivers of Incongruent Information (RI). The stimulus materials and the measurement method were the same as in Experiment I. Also, the procedure for the T and R groups was the same as in Experiment I, except that, for the present purposes, the induction of tuning preceded the reading of the letter. The TI and RI groups were issued the following instructions after assembling in the experimental room:

> The main point of this study is to find out something about the process of communication. I will give you a letter to read. This letter was written by an individual who is applying for a job. After you have read this letter and have gotten some idea about its author, each one of you will decide for herself whether or not he should be hired. Let me tell you something else. Right now there is another group in the building. They have the same information about the applicant, and each of them is also making a decision whether or not the individual should be hired. After you have decided whether or not to hire the applicant, every one of you will be paired with a member of the other group. What is more, you will be paired up with someone who decided differently from you. In other words, if a member of this group had decided to hire him, she will be paired with someone who has decided not to hire him, and vice versa.

Both the TI and the RI groups were given these initial instructions, and, afterwards, transmitting and receiving tuning was induced in the same manner as it was in Experiment I. The procedure for collecting data was the same as in the previous experiment.

Results

It was assumed that anticipation of dealing with incongruent information and commitment to an opinion result in an increased proportion of specific attributes, especially for the receivers. The average percentages of specific attributes for the T, R, TI, and RI groups, respectively, were 52.0%, 39.8%, 72.3%, and 70.7%. The analysis of variance (using the arc sin $\sqrt{\%}$ transformation) presented in Table 8.2 shows significant effects for both tuning and congruence. It will be noted that under conditions that involve anticipation of dealing with incongruent information, both receivers and transmitters increase the proportion of specific attributes markedly, with the increase being somewhat larger for the receivers. It is also clear from the data that when persons anticipate dealing with contrary information, the differences in the proportion of specific attributes between the groups disappear. The difference in the proportion of specific components between the R and the T groups was significant at the .01 level, and not significant between the RI and TI groups.

DEGREE OF DIFFERENTIATION   The increment in specificity alone would lead to the expectation that the degree of differentiation should be greater for both groups that dealt with incongruent information. The receivers of contrary information should show a more pronounced increase, such that they reach the level of differentiation equal to that of the TI group. However, it was assumed that a factor operates simultaneously that tends to reduce differentiation, namely, the tendency to select attributes consistent with one's position. If this factor operates equally for both groups, as was assumed above, the TI groups should show a decrement and the RI group an increment. The results for all the properties, as summarized in Table 8.3, follow just this pattern. The analysis of variance, presented in Table 8.4, shows significant main effects deriving from tuning as well as a significant T × C interaction. The overall mean differentiation scores are somewhat higher than when Ss deal with congruent information, but this difference is not significant. The differences between transmitters and receivers are significant only when congruent information is involved ($p < .001$). **[165]** It appears, therefore, that there must exist strong

Table 8.2   Summary of Analysis of Variance for the Proportion of Specific Attributes

Source	df	MS	F
Tuning (T)	1	3,885.61	5.85*
Congruence (C)	1	8,068.15	12.14***
T × C	1	1,585.74	2.39
Error	88	664.27	

   * $p < .05$
*** $p < .001$

Table 8.3   Differences in the Properties of Cognitive Structures between Transmitters and Receivers Dealing with Congruent and Incongruent Information

	Transmitters		Receivers	
Property	Congruent	Incongruent	Congruent	Incongruent
Differentiation	11.39	9.26	6.65	7.70
Complexity	27.09	20.83	14.35	16.48
Unity	0.265	0.269	0.226	0.300
Organization	15.54	22.13	10.41	19.48

Table 8.4   Summary of Analyses of Variance for Data in Table 8.3

		Differentiation		Complexity		Unity		Organization	
Source	df	MS	F	MS	F	MS	F	MS	F
Tuning (T)	1	228.53	30.92***	1678.79	21.15***	.027	1.35	568.13	7.12**
Congruence (C)	1	6.79	<1.00	198.10	2.50	.035	1.75	1034.51	12.97***
T × C	1	64.72	9.13***	304.88	3.48*	.001	<1.00	151.33	1.90
Error	88	7.39		79.36		.020		79.75	

* $p < .05$ level
** $p < .01$ level
*** $p < .001$ level

selective effects, as well as increments in specificity when persons deal with contrary information, and that these two factors result in the equalization of differentiation.

DEGREE OF COMPLEXITY   The results for complexity are essentially the same as for degree of differentiation. The effects of tuning on complexity were significant ($p < .001$), as was the T × C interaction ($p < .05$). The degree of complexity of the transmitters shows a drop when they anticipate dealing with contrary information. The difference between the T and the TI group is significant at the .01 level. The decrement in complexity on the part of the transmitters is due to the selective effects of commitment to a position. Since they abandon those aspects that may weaken their position, their cognitive structures lose in elaboration. The receivers show a slight but insignificant increment in complexity, and a significant T × C interaction is thus obtained. It should be noted, however, that the TI group shows a higher degree of complexity than the RI group, this difference being significant at the .05 level. Apparently, the effects of tuning are sufficiently strong here to be maintained despite the selectivity and the specificity factors.

DEGREE OF UNITY   While there is some increase in the degree of unity in the "incongruent" condition, the overall effects of congruence do not reach an acceptable level of significance. The strongest difference appears to be that between the R and the RI group. This was the only significant result with respect to unity ($p < .05$). It may be assumed, therefore, that when dealing with incongruent information, receivers protect themselves from unwanted changes by increasing unity, while transmitters because of their already high unity need not increase it.

DEGREE OF ORGANIZATION As expected, degree of organization shows pronounced effects of both tuning and congruence. For both receivers and transmitters, there are significant increments in organization when contrary information is involved (both differences are significant at the .01 level). The commitment to a position, therefore, because it leads to the selection of a particular type of material—selection that is quite systematic—provides a strong core around which the components of the cognitive structure may become readily organized. Even though the receivers showed an increase in unity when dealing with contrary information, they manifest a significant, almost twofold, increment in degree of organization. The effects of the anticipation of dealing with incongruent information are therefore stronger for the receivers than for transmitters.

SUMMARY

The cognitive effects of the person's role in the communication process were examined in two experiments. A systematic method for the description of cognitive structures was developed, and, in the first experiment, persons expecting to transmit information were compared with others expecting to receive information for the extent of differentiation, complexity, unity, and organization. The results show that transmitters activate cognitive structures which are more differentiated, complex, unified, and organized than those activated by receivers.

The second experiment involved the anticipation **[166]** of dealing with incongruent information, and in comparison with groups dealing with congruent information, those expecting to deal with incongruent information generally showed decreased differences between transmitters and receivers. These results were accounted for by an increase in the proportion of specific cognitive components and in the tendency to reject material inconsistent with the person's own opinion.

REFERENCES

Ach, N. *Ueber die Willenstätigkeit und das Denken.* Gottingen: Yandenhoeck and Ruprecht, 1905.

Asch, S.E. Forming impressions of the personality. *J. abnorm. soc. Psychol.*, 1946, **41**, 258–290.

Bruner, J.S., Goodnow, J., and Austin, G. *A study of thinking.* New York: Wiley, 1956.

Chapman, D.W. Relative effects of determinate and indeterminate Aufgaben. *Amer. J. Psychol.*, 1932, **44**, 163–174.

French, V. The structure of sentiments. *J. Pers.*, 1947, **15**, 247–280.

Hovland, C.I., Janis, I.L., and Kelley, H.H. *Communication and persuasion: Psychological studies of opinion change.* New Haven: Yale Univer. Press, 1953.

Jones, E.E., and Kohler, R. The effects of plausibility on the learning of controversial statements. *J. abnorm. soc. Psychol.*, 1958, **67**, 315–320.

Kulpe, O. Versüche über Abstraction. *Ber. I. Kongr. Exp. Psychol.*, 1904, 56–68.

Lewin, K. Das Problem der Willenmessung und das Grundgesetz der Assoziation. *Psychol. Forsch.*, 1922, **1**, 191–302. (a)

Lewin, K. Das Problem der Willenmessung und das Grundgesetz der Assoziation. *Psychol. Forsch.*, 1922, **2**, 65–140. (b)

Lewin, K. *Field theory in social science.* New York: Harper, 1951.

Watt, H.J. Experimentelle Beiträge zur einer Theorie des Denkens. *Arch. ges. Psychol.*, 1905, **4**, 289–436.

Zajonc, R.B. Cognitive structure and cognitive tuning. Unpublished doctoral dissertation, University of Michigan, 1954.

Zimmerman, Claire, and Bauer, R.A. The effect of an audience upon what is remembered. *Publ. opin. Quart.*, 1956, **20**, 238–248.

Chapter 9

The Concepts of Balance, Congruity, and Dissonance

R.B. Zajonc
University of Michigan

Common to the concepts of balance, congruity, and dissonance is the notion that thoughts, beliefs, attitudes, and behavior tend to organize themselves in meaningful and sensible ways.[1] Members of the White Citizens Council do not ordinarily contribute to NAACP. Adherents of the New Deal seldom support Republican candidates. Christian Scientists do not enroll in medical schools. And people who live in glass houses apparently do not throw stones. In this respect, the concept of consistency underscores and presumes human *rationality*. It holds that behavior and attitudes are not only consistent to the objective observer, but that individuals try to appear consistent to themselves. It assumes that inconsistency is a noxious state setting up pressures to eliminate it or reduce it. But in the *ways* that consistency in human behavior and attitudes is achieved, we see rather often a striking lack of rationality. A heavy smoker cannot readily accept evidence relating cancer to smoking;[2] a socialist, told that Hoover's endorsement of certain political slogans agreed perfectly with his own, calls him a "typical hypocrite and a liar."[3] Allport illustrates this irrationality in the following conversation: **[280]***

> Mr. X: The trouble with Jews is that they only take care of their own group.
> Mr. Y: But the record of the Community Chest shows that they give more generously than non-Jews.
> Mr. X: That shows that they are always trying to buy favor and intrude in Christian affairs. They think of nothing but money; that is why there are so many Jewish bankers.
> Mr. Y: But a recent study shows that the percent of Jews in banking is proportionally much smaller than the percent of non-Jews.
> Mr. X: That's just it. They don't go in for respectable business. They would rather run night clubs.[4]

* Bracketed bold numbers refer to original page numbers. Page numbers indicate where the original page ended.

Public Opinion Quarterly, 24, "The concepts of balance, congruity, and dissonance," 380–396, The University of Chicago Press. © 1960 by Princeton University. All rights reserved.

Thus, while the concept of consistency acknowledges man's rationality, observation of the means of its achievement simultaneously unveils his irrationality. The psychoanalytic notion of rationalization is a literal example of a concept which assumes both rationality and irrationality—it holds, namely, that man strives to understand and justify painful experiences and to make them sensible and rational, but he employs completely irrational methods to achieve this end.

The concepts of consistency are not novel. Nor are they indigenous to the study of attitudes, behavior, or personality. These concepts have appeared in various forms in almost all sciences. It has been argued by some that it is the existence of consistencies in the universe that made science possible, and by others that consistencies in the universe are a proof of divine power.[5] There is, of course, a question of whether consistencies are "real" or mere products of ingenious abstraction and conceptualization. For it would be entirely possible to categorize natural phenomena in such a haphazard way that instead of order, unity, and consistency, one would see a picture of utter chaos. If we were to eliminate one of the spatial dimensions from the conception of the physical world, the consistencies we now know and the consistencies which allow us to make reliable predictions would be vastly depleted.

The concept of consistency in man is, then, a special case of the concept of universal consistency. The fascination with this concept led some psychologists to rather extreme positions. Franke, for instance, wrote, "... the unity of a person can be traced in each instant of his life. There is nothing in character that contradicts itself. If a person who is known to us seems to be incongruous with himself that is only an indication of the inadequacy and superficiality of our previous observations."[6] This sort of hypothesis is, of course, incapable of either **[281]** verification or disproof and therefore has no significant consequences.

Empirical investigations employing the concepts of consistency have been carried out for many years. Not until recently, however, has there been a programmatic and systematic effort to explore with precision and detail their particular consequences for behavior and attitudes. The greatest impetus to the study of attitudinal consistency was given recently by Festinger and his students. In addition to those already named, other related contributions in this area are those of Newcomb, who introduced the concept of "strain toward symmetry,"[7] and of Cartwright and Harary, who expressed the notions of balance and symmetry in a mathematical form.[8] These notions all assume inconsistency to be a painful or at least psychologically uncomfortable state, but they differ in the generality of application. The most restrictive and specific is the principle of congruity, since it restricts itself to the problems of the effects of information about objects and events on the attitudes toward the source of information. The most general is the notion of cognitive dissonance, since it considers consistency among any cognitions. In between are the notions of balance and symmetry, which consider attitudes toward people and objects in relation to one another, either within one person's cognitive structure, as in the case of Heider's theory of balance, or among a given group of individuals, as in the case of Newcomb's strain toward symmetry. It is the purpose of this paper to survey these concepts and to consider their implications for theory and research on attitudes.

THE CONCEPTS OF BALANCE AND STRAIN TOWARD SYMMETRY

The earliest formalization of consistency is attributed to Heider,[9] who was concerned with the way relations among persons involving some impersonal entity are cognitively experienced by the individual. The consistencies in which Heider was interested were those to be found in the ways people view their relations with other people and with the environment. The analysis was limited to two persons, labeled P and O, with P as the focus of the analysis and with O representing some other person, and to one impersonal entity, which could be a physical object, an idea, an event, or the like, labeled X. The object of Heider's inquiry was to discover how relations among P, O, and X are organized in P's cognitive structure, and whether there exist recurrent and systematic tendencies in the way these relations are experienced. Two types of relation, liking (L) and so-called U, or unit, relations [282] (such as possession, cause, similarity, and the like) were distinguished. On the basis of incidental observations and intuitive judgment, probably, Heider proposed that the person's (P's) cognitive structure representing relations among P, O, and X are either what he termed "balanced" or "unbalanced." In particular, he proposed, "In the case of three entities, a balanced state exists if all three relations are positive in all respects or if two are negative and one positive." Thus, a balanced state is obtained when, for instance, P likes O, P likes X, and O likes X; or when P likes O, P dislikes X, and O dislikes X; or when P dislikes O, P likes X, and O dislikes X (see Figure 9.1). It should be noted that within Heider's conception a relation may be either positive or negative; degrees of liking cannot be represented. The fundamental assumption of balance theory is that an unbalanced state produces tension and generates forces to restore balance. This hypothesis was tested by Jordan.[10] He presented subjects with hypothetical situations involving two persons and an impersonal entity to rate for "pleasantness." Half the situations were by Heider's definition balanced and half unbalanced. Jordan's data showed somewhat higher unpleasantness ratings for the unbalanced than the balanced situations.

Cartwright and Harary[11] have cast Heider's formulation in graph theoretical terms and derived some interesting consequences beyond those stated by Heider. Heider's concept allows either a balanced or an unbalanced state. Cartwright and Harary have constructed a more general definition of balance, with balance treated as a matter of degree, [283] ranging from 0 to 1. Furthermore, their formulation of balance theory extended the notion to any number of entities, and an experiment by Morrissette[12] similar in design to that of Jordan obtained evidence for Cartwright and Harary's derivations.

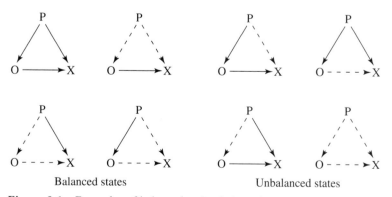

Figure 9.1   Examples of balanced and unbalanced states according to Heider's definition of balance. Solid lines represent positive, and broken lines negative, relations.

A notion very similar to balance was advanced by Newcomb in 1953.[13] In addition to substituting A for P, and B for O, Newcomb took Heider's notion of balance out of one person's head and applied it to communication among people. Newcomb postulates a "strain toward symmetry" which leads to a communality of attitudes of two people (A and B) oriented toward an object (X). The strain toward symmetry influences communication between A and B so as to bring their attitudes toward X into congruence. Newcomb cites a study in which a questionnaire was administered to college students in 1951 following the dismissal of General MacArthur by President Truman. Data were obtained on students' attitudes toward Truman's decision and their perception of the attitudes of their closest friends. Of the pro-Truman subjects, 48 said that their closest friends favored Truman and none that their closest friends were opposed to his decision. Of the anti-Truman subjects, only 2 said that their friends were generally pro-Truman and 34 that they were anti-Truman. In a longitudinal study, considerably more convincing evidence was obtained in support of the strain-toward-symmetry hypothesis. In 1954, Newcomb set up a house at the University of Michigan which offered free rent for one semester for seventeen students who would serve as subjects. The residents of the house were observed, questioned, and rated for four to five hours a week during the entire semester. The study was then repeated with another set of seventeen students. The findings revealed a tendency for those who were attracted to one another to agree on many matters, including the way they perceived their own selves and their ideal selves, and their attractions for other group members. Moreover, in line with the prediction, these similarities, real as well as perceived, seemed to increase over time.[14]

Newcomb also cites the work of Festinger and his associates on social communication[15] in support of his hypothesis. Festinger's studies on communication have clearly shown that the tendency to influence other group members toward one's own opinion increases with the degree of attraction. More recently, Burdick and Burnes reported two experiments **[284]** in which measures of skin resistance (GSR) were obtained as an index of emotional reaction in the presence of balanced and unbalanced situations.[16] They observed significant differences in skin resistance depending on whether the subjects agreed or disagreed with a "well-liked experimenter." In the second experiment, Burdick and Burnes found that subjects who liked the experimenter tended to arrange their opinions toward greater agreement with his, and those who disliked him, toward greater disagreement. There are, of course, many other studies to show that the attitude toward the communicator determines his persuasive effectiveness. Hovland and his co-workers have demonstrated these effects in several studies.[17] They have also shown, however, that these effects are fleeting; that is, the attitude change produced by the communication seems to dissipate over time. Their interpretation is that over time subjects tend to dissociate the source from the message and are therefore subsequently less influenced by the prestige of the communicator. This proposition was substantiated by Kelman and Hovland,[18] who produced attitude changes with a prestigeful communicator and retested subjects after a four-week interval with and without reminding the subjects about the communicator. The results showed that the permanence of the attitude change depended on the association with the source.

In general, the consequences of balance theories have, up to now, been rather limited. Except for Newcomb's longitudinal study, the experimental situations dealt mostly with subjects who responded to hypothetical situations, and direct evidence is scarce. The Burdick and Burnes experiment is the only one bearing more directly on the assumption that imbalance or asymmetry produces tension. Cartwright and Harary's mathematization of the concept of balance should, however, lead to important empirical and theoretical developments. One difficulty is that there really has not been a serious experimental attempt to *disprove* the theory. It is conceivable that some situations defined by the theory as unbalanced may, in fact, remain stable and produce no significant pressures toward balance. Festinger once inquired in a jocular mood if it followed from balance theory that since he likes chicken, and since chickens like chicken feed, he must also like chicken feed or else experience the tension of imbalance. While this counterexample is, of course, not to be taken seriously, it does [285] point to some difficulties in the concepts of balance. It is not clear from Heider's theory of balance and Newcomb's theory of symmetry what predictions are to be made when attraction of both P and O toward X exists but when the origin and nature of these attractions are different. In other words, suppose both P and O like X but for different reasons and in entirely different ways, as was the case with Festinger and the chickens. Are the consequences of balance theory the same then as in the case where P and O like X for the same reasons and in the same way? It is also not clear, incidentally, what the consequences are when the relation between P and O is cooperative and when it is competitive. Two men vying for the hand of the same fair maiden might experience tension whether they are close friends or deadly enemies.

In a yet unpublished study conducted by Harburg and Price at the University of Michigan, students were asked to name two of their best friends. When those named were of opposite sexes, subjects reported they would feel uneasy if the two friends liked one another. In a subsequent experiment, subjects were asked whether they desired their good friend to like, be neutral to, or dislike one of their strongly disliked acquaintances, and whether they desired the disliked acquaintance to like or dislike the friend. It will be recalled that, in either case, a balanced state obtains only if the two persons are negatively related to one another. However, Harburg and Price found that 39 percent desired their friend to be liked by the disliked acquaintance, and only 24 percent to be disliked. Moreover, faced with the alternative that the disliked acquaintance dislikes their friend, 55 percent as opposed to 25 percent expressed uneasiness. These results are quite inconsistent with balance theory. Although one may want one's friends to dislike one's enemies, one may not want the enemies to dislike one's friends. The reason for the latter may be simply a concern for the friends' welfare.

OSGOOD AND TANNENBAUM'S PRINCIPLE OF CONGRUITY

The principle of congruity, which is, in fact, a special case of balance, was advanced by Osgood and Tannenbaum in 1955.[19] It deals specifically with the problem of *direction* of attitude change. The authors assume that "judgmental frames of reference tend toward maximal simplicity." Thus, since extreme "black-and-white," "all-or-nothing," judgments are simpler than refined ones, valuations tend to move toward extremes or, in the words of the authors, there is "a continuing pressure toward polarization." Together with the notion of maximization of simplicity is the assumption of identity as being less complex than the discrimination [286] of fine differences. Therefore, related "concepts" will tend to be evaluated in a similar manner. Given these assumptions, the principle of congruity holds that when change in evaluation or attitude occurs, it always occurs in the direction of increased congruity with the prevailing frame of reference. The paradigm of congruity is that of an individual who is confronted with an assertion regarding a particular matter about which he believes and feels in a certain way, made by a person toward whom he also has some attitude. Given that Eisenhower is evaluated positively and freedom of the press also positively, and given that Eisenhower (+) comes out in favor of freedom of the press (+), congruity is said to exist. But given that the *Daily Worker* (–) is evaluated negatively, and given that the *Daily Worker* (–) comes out in favor of freedom of the press (+), incongruity is said to exist. Examples of congruity and incongruity are shown in Figure 9.2. The diagram shows the attitudes of a given individual toward the source and the object of the assertion. The assertions represented by heavy lines imply either positive or negative attitudes of the source toward the object. It is clear from a comparison of Figures 9.1 and 9.2 that, in terms of their formal properties, the definitions of balance and congruity are identical. Thus, incongruity is said to exist when the attitudes toward the source and the object are similar and the assertion is negative, or when they are dissimilar and the assertion is positive. In comparison, unbalanced states are defined as having either one or all negative relations, which is, of course, equivalent to the above. To the extent that the person's attitudes are congruent with those implied in the assertion, a stable state exists. When the attitudes toward the person and the [287] assertion are incongruent, there will be a tendency to change the attitudes toward the person and the object of the assertion in the direction of increased congruity. Tannenbaum obtained measures on 405 college students regarding their attitudes toward labor leaders, the *Chicago Tribune,* and Senator Robert Taft as sources, and toward legalized gambling, abstract art, and accelerated college programs as objects. Some time after the attitude scores were obtained, the subjects were presented with "highly realistic" newspaper clippings involving assertions made by the

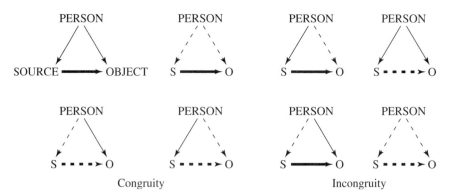

Figure 9.2   Examples of congruity and incongruity. Heavy lines represent assertions, light lines attitudes. Solid heavy lines represent assertions which imply a positive attitude on the part of the source, and broken heavy lines negative attitudes. Solid light lines represent positive, and broken light lines negative, attitudes.

various sources regarding the concepts. In general, when the original attitudes toward the source and the concept were both positive and the assertion presented in the newspaper clippings was also positive, no significant attitude changes were observed in the results. When the original attitudes toward the source and the concept were negative and the assertion was positive, again no changes were obtained. As predicted, however, when a positively valued source was seen as making a positive assertion about a negatively valued concept, the attitude toward the source became less favorable, and toward the concept more favorable. Conversely, when a negatively valued source was seen as making a positive assertion about a positively valued concept, attitudes toward the source became more favorable and toward the concept less favorable. The entire gamut of predicted changes was confirmed in Tannenbaum's data; it is summarized in Table 9.1, in which the direction of change is represented by either a plus or a minus sign, and the extent of change by either one or two such signs.

A further derivation of the congruity principle is that incongruity does not invariably produce attitude change, but that it may, at times, lead to incredulity on the part of the individual. When confronted by [288] an assertion which stands in an incongruous relation to the person who made it, there will be a tendency not to believe that the person made the assertion, thus reducing incongruity.

There is a good deal of evidence supporting, Osgood and Tannenbaum's principle of congruity. As early as 1921, H.T. Moore had subjects judge statements, for their grammar, ethical infringements for their seriousness, and resolutions of the dominant seventh chord for their dissonance.[20] After two and one-half months, the subjects returned and were presented with judgments of "experts." This experimental manipulation resulted in 62 percent reversals of judgments on grammar, 50 percent of ethical judgments, and 43 percent of musical judgments. And in 1935, in a study on a similar problem of prestige suggestion, Sherif let subjects rank sixteen authors for their literary merit.[21] Subsequently, the subjects were given sixteen passages presumably written by the various authors previously ranked. Although, in actuality, *all* the passages were written by Robert Louis Stevenson, the subjects were able to rank the passages. Moreover, the correlations between the merit of the author and the merit of the passage ranged

Table 9.1   Change of Attitude toward the Source and the Object When Positive and Negative Assertions Are Made by the Source

Original Attitude Toward the Source	Positive Assertion about an Object Toward Which the Attitude is		Negative Assertion about an Object Toward Which the Attitude is	
	Positive	Negative	Positive	Negative
	CHANGE OF ATTITUDE TOWARD THE SOURCE			
Positive	+	− −	− −	+
Negative	+ +	−	−	+ +
	CHANGE OF ATTITUDE TOWARD THE OBJECT			
Positive	+	+ +	− −	−
Negative	− −	−	+	+ +

from between .33 to .53. These correlations are not very dramatic, yet they do represent some impact of attitude toward the source on attitude toward the passage.

With respect to incredulity, an interesting experiment was conducted recently by Jones and Kohler in which subjects learned statements which either supported their attitudes or were in disagreement with them.[22] Some of the statements were plausible and some implausible. The results were rather striking. Subjects whose attitudes favored segregation learned plausible pro-segregation statements and implausible anti-segregation statements much more rapidly than plausible anti-segregation and implausible pro-segregation statements. The reverse was of course true for subjects whose attitudes favored desegregation.

While the principle of congruity presents no new ideas, it has a great advantage over the earlier attempts in its precision. Osgood and Tannenbaum have formulated the principle of congruity in quantitative terms allowing for precise predictions regarding the extent and direction of attitude change—predictions which, in their studies, were fairly well confirmed. While balance theory allows merely a dichotomy of attitudes, either positive or negative, the principle of congruity allows **[289]** refined measurements using Osgood's method of the semantic differential.[23] Moreover, while it is not clear from Heider's statement of balance in just what direction changes will occur when an unbalanced state exists, such predictions can be made on the basis of the congruity principle.

FESTINGER'S THEORY OF COGNITIVE DISSONANCE

Perhaps the largest systematic body of data is that collected in the realm of Festinger's dissonance theory. The statement of the dissonance principle is simple. It holds that two elements of knowledge "… are in dissonant relation if, considering these two alone, the obverse of one element would follow from the other."[24] It further holds that dissonance "… being psychologically uncomfortable, will motivate the person to try to reduce dissonance and achieve consonance" and "… in addition to trying to reduce it, the person will actively avoid situations and information which would likely increase the dissonance."[25] A number of rather interesting and provocative consequences follow from Festinger's dissonance hypothesis.

First, it is predicted that all decisions or choices result in dissonance to the extent that the alternative not chosen contains positive features which make it attractive also, and the alternative chosen contains features which might have resulted in rejecting it. Hence, after making a choice, people seek evidence to confirm their decision and so reduce dissonance. In the Ehrlich experiment cited by Cohen in this issue, the finding was that new car owners noticed and read ads about the cars they had recently purchased more than ads about other cars.[26]

Post-decision dissonance was also shown to result in a change of attractiveness of the alternative involved in a decision. Brehm had female subjects rate eight appliances for desirability.[27] Subsequently, the subjects were given a choice between two of the eight products, given the chosen product, and after some interpolated activity (consisting of reading research reports about four of the appliances) were asked to rate the products again. Half the subjects were given a choice between products which they rated in a similar manner, and half between products on which the ratings differed. Thus, in the first case, higher dissonance was to be expected than in the second. The prediction from **[290]** dissonance theory that there should be an increase in the attractiveness of the chosen alternative and decrease in the attractiveness of the rejected alternative was, on the whole, confirmed. Moreover, the further implication was also confirmed that the pressure to reduce dissonance (which was accomplished in the above experiment by changes in attractiveness of the alternatives) varies directly with the extent of dissonance.

Another body of data accounted for by the dissonance hypothesis deals with situations in which the person is forced (either by reward or punishment) to express an opinion publicly or make a public judgment or statement which is contrary to his own opinions and beliefs. In cases where the person actually makes such a judgment, or expresses an opinion contrary to his own as a result of a promised reward or threat, dissonance exists between the knowledge of the overt behavior of the person and his privately held beliefs. Festinger also argues that, in the case of noncompliance, dissonance will exist between the knowledge of overt behavior and the anticipation of reward and punishment.

An example of how dissonance theory accounts for forced-compliance data is given by Brehm.[28] Brehm offered prizes to eighth-graders for eating disliked vegetables and obtained measures of how well the children liked the vegetables. Children who ate the vegetables increased their liking for them. Of course, one might argue that a simpler explanation of the results is that the attractiveness of the prize generalized to the vegetable, or that, even more simply, the vegetables increased in utility because a reward came with them. However, this argument would also lead one to predict that the increment in attraction under such conditions is a *direct* function of the magnitude of the reward. Dissonance theory makes the opposite prediction, and, therefore, a test of the validity of the two explanations is possible. Data collected by Festinger and Carlsmith[29] and by Aronson and Mills[30] support the dissonance point of view. In Festinger and Carlsmith's experiment, subjects were offered either $20 or $1 for telling someone that an experience which had actually been quite boring had been rather enjoyable and interesting. When measures of the subjects' private opinions about their actual enjoyment of the task were taken, those who were to be paid only $1 for the false testimony showed considerably higher scores than those who were to be paid $20. Aronson and Mills, on the other hand, tested the effects of negative incentive. They invited college women to join a group requiring them to go through a process of **[291]** initiation. For some women, the initiation was quite severe; for others it was mild. The prediction from dissonance theory that those who had to undergo severe initiation would increase their attraction for the group more than those having no initiation or mild initiation was borne out.

A third set of consequences of the theory of dissonance deals with exposure to information. Since dissonance occurs between cognitive elements, and since information may lead to change in these elements, the principle of dissonance should have a close bearing on the individual's commerce with information. In particular, the assumption that dissonance is a psychologically uncomfortable state leads to the prediction that individuals will seek out information reducing dissonance and avoid information increasing it. The study on automobile-advertising readership described above is a demonstration of this hypothesis.[31] In another study, Mills, Aronson, and Robinson gave college students a choice between an objective and an essay examination.[32] Following the decision, the subjects were given articles about examinations presumably written by experts, and they were asked if they would like to read them. In addition, in order to vary the intensity of dissonance, half the subjects were told that the examination counted 70 percent toward the final grade, and half that it counted only 5 percent. The data were obtained in the form of rankings of the articles for preference. While there was a clear preference for reading articles containing positive information about the alternative chosen, no significant selective effects were found when the articles presented arguments against the given type of examination. Also, the authors failed to demonstrate effects relating selectivity in exposure to information to the magnitude of dissonance, in that no significant differences were found between subjects for whom the examination was quite important (70 percent of the final grade) and those for whom it was relatively unimportant (5 percent of the final grade).

Festinger was able to account for many other results by means of the dissonance principle, and, in general, his theory is rather successful in organizing a diverse body of empirical knowledge by means of a limited number of fairly reasonable assumptions. Moreover, from these reasonable assumptions, dissonance theory generated several nontrivial and nonobvious consequences. The negative relationship between the magnitude of incentive and attraction of the object of false testimony is not at all obvious. Also not obvious is the prediction of an increase in proselytizing for a mystical belief following an event that clearly contradicts it. Festinger, Riecken, and Schachter studied a group of [292] "Seekers"—people who presumably received a message from outer space informing them of an incipient major flood.[33] When the flood failed to materialize on the critical date, instead of quietly withdrawing from the public scene, as one would expect, the "Seekers" summoned press representatives, gave extended interviews, and invited the public to visit them and be informed of the details of the whole affair. In a very recent study by Brehm, a "nonobvious" derivation from dissonance theory was tested.[34] Brehm predicted that, when forced to engage in an unpleasant activity, an individual's liking for this activity will increase more when he receives information essentially berating the activity than when he receives information promoting it. The results tended to support Brehm's prediction. Since negative information is said to increase dissonance, and since increased dissonance leads to an increased tendency to reduce it, and since the only means of dissonance reduction was increasing the attractiveness of the activity, such an increase would, in fact, be expected.

CONCLUSIONS

The theories and empirical work dealing with consistencies are mainly concerned with intra-individual phenomena, be it with relationships between one attitude and another, between attitudes and values, or information, or perception, or behavior, or the like. One exception is Newcomb's concept of "strain toward symmetry." Here, the concern is primarily with the interplay of forces among individuals which results in uniformities or consistencies among them. There is no question that the concepts of consistency, and especially the theory of cognitive dissonance, account for many varied attitudinal phenomena. Of course, the various formulations of consistency do not pretend, nor are they able, to account completely for the phenomena they examine. Principles of consistency, like all other principles, are prefaced by the *ceteris paribus* preamble. Thus, when other factors are held constant, then the principles of consistency should be able to explain behavior and attitudes completely. But the question to be raised here is just what factors must be held constant and how important and significant, relative to consistency, are they.

Suppose a man feels hostile toward the British and also dislikes cricket. One might be tempted to conclude that if one of his attitudes were different, he would experience the discomfort of incongruity. But there are probably many people whose attitudes toward the British and cricket are incongruent, although the exact proportions are not known [293] and are hardly worth serious inquiry. But if such an inquiry were undertaken, it would probably disclose that attitudes depend largely on the conditions under which they have been acquired. For one thing, it would show that the attitudes depend, at least to some extent, on the relationship of the attitude object to the individual's needs and fears, and that these may be stronger than forces toward balance. There are, in this world, things to be avoided and feared. A child bitten by a dog will not develop favorable attitudes toward dogs. And no matter how much he likes Popeye, you can't make him like spinach, although according to balance theory he should.

The relationship between attitudes and values or needs has been explored, for instance, in *The Authoritarian Personality,* which appeared in 1950.[35] The authors of this work hypothesized a close relationship between attitudes and values on the one hand, and personality on the other. They assumed that the "... convictions of an individual often form a broad and coherent pattern, as if bound together by a mentality or spirit." They further assumed that "... opinions, attitudes and values depend on human needs and since personality is essentially an organization of needs, then personality may be regarded as a determinant of ideological preference." Thus, the *Authoritarian Personality* approach also stresses consistency, but while the concepts of congruity balance, and dissonance are satisfied with assuming a general tendency toward consistency, the *Authoritarian Personality* theory goes further in that it holds that the dynamic of consistency is to be found in personality, and it is personality which gives consistency meaning and direction. Attitudes and values are thus seen to be consistent among themselves and with one another because they are both consistent with the basic personality needs, and they are consistent with needs because they are determined by them.

The very ambitious research deriving from the *Authoritarian Personality* formulation encountered many difficulties and, mainly because of serious methodological and theoretical shortcomings, has gradually lost its popularity. However, some aspects of this general approach have been salvaged by others. Rosenberg, for instance, has shown that attitudes are intimately related to the capacity of the attitude object to be instrumental to the attainment of the individual's values.[36] Carlson went a step further and has shown that, if the perceived instrumentality of the object with respect to a person's values and needs is changed, the attitude itself may be modified.[37] These studies, while not assuming [294] a general consistency principle, illustrate a special instance of consistency, namely that between attitudes and utility, or instrumentality of attitude objects, with respect to the person's values and needs.

The concepts of consistency bear a striking historical similarity to the concept of vacuum. According to an excellent account by Conant,[38] for centuries the principle that nature abhors a vacuum served to account for various phenomena, such as the action of pumps, behavior of liquids in joined vessels, suction, and the like. The strength of everyday evidence was so overwhelming that the principle was seldom questioned. However, it was known that one cannot draw water to a height of more than 34 feet. The simplest solution of this problem was to reformulate the principle to read that "nature abhors a vacuum below 34 feet." This modified version of *horror vacui* again was satisfactory for the phenomena it dealt with, until it was discovered that "nature abhors a vacuum below 34 feet only when we deal with water." As Torricelli has shown, when it comes to mercury "nature abhors a vacuum below 30 inches." Displeased with the crudity of a principle which must accommodate numerous exceptions, Torricelli formulated the notion that it was the pressure of air acting upon the surface of the liquid which was responsible for the height to which one could draw liquid by the action of pumps. The 34-foot limit represented the weight of water which the air pressure on the surface of earth could maintain, and the 30-inch limit represented the weight of mercury that air pressure could maintain. This was an entirely different and revolutionary concept, and its consequences had drastic impact on physics. Human nature, on the other hand, is said to abhor inconsistency. For the time being, the principle is quite adequate, since it accounts systematically for many phenomena, some of which have never been explained and all of which have never been explained by one principle. But already today there are exceptions to consistency and balance. Some people who spend a good portion of their earnings on insurance also gamble. The first action presumably is intended to protect them from risks; the other to expose them to risks. Almost everybody enjoys a magician. And the magician only creates dissonance—you see before you an event which you know to be impossible on the basis of previous knowledge—the obverse of what you see follows from what you know. If the art of magic is essentially the art of producing dissonance, and if human nature abhors dissonance, why is the art of magic still flourishing? If decisions are necessarily followed by dissonance, and if nature abhors dissonance, why are decisions ever made? Although it is true that those decisions which would ordinarily [295] lead to great dissonance take a very long time to make, they are made anyway. And it is also true that human nature does not abhor dissonance absolutely, as nature abhors a vacuum. Human nature merely avoids dissonance, and it would follow from dissonance theory that decisions whose instrumental consequences would not be worth the dissonance to follow would never be made. There are, thus far, no data to support this hypothesis, nor data to disprove it.

According to Conant, *horror vacui* served an important purpose besides explaining and organizing some aspects of physical knowledge. Without it, the discomfort of "exceptions to the rule" would never have been felt, and the important developments in theory might have been delayed considerably. If a formulation has then a virtue in being wrong, the theories of consistency do have this virtue. They do organize a large body of knowledge. Also, they point out exceptions, and, thereby, they demand a new formulation. It will not suffice simply to reformulate them so as to accommodate the exceptions. I doubt if Festinger would be satisfied with a modification of his dissonance principle which would read that dissonance, being psychologically uncomfortable, leads a person to actively avoid situations and information which would be likely to increase the dissonance, except when there is an opportunity to watch a magician. Also, simply to disprove the theories by counterexamples would not in itself constitute an important contribution. We would merely lose explanations of phenomena which had been explained. And it is doubtful that the theories of consistency could be rejected simply *because* of counterexamples. Only a theory which accounts for all the data that the consistency principles now account for, for all the exceptions to those principles, and for all the phenomena which these principles should now but do not consider, is capable of replacing them. It is only a matter of time until such a development takes place. **[296]**

FOOTNOTES

1. The concepts of balance, congruity, and dissonance are due to Heider, Osgood and Tannenbaum, and Festinger, respectively. (F. Heider, "Attitudes and Cognitive Organization," *Journal of Psychology,* Vol. 21, 1946, pp. 107–112. C. E. Osgood and P. H. Tannenbaum, "The Principle of Congruity in the Prediction of Attitude Change," *Psychological Review,* Vol. 62, 1955, pp. 42–55. L. Festinger, *A Theory of Cognitive Dissonance,* Evanston. III., Row, Peterson, 1957.) For purposes of simplicity, we will subsume these concepts under the label of consistency.
2. Festinger, *op.cit.,* pp. 113–156.
3. H.B. Lewis, "Studies in the Principles of Judgments and Attitudes: IV, The Operation of 'Prestige Suggestion'," *Journal of Social Psychology,* Vol. 14, 1941, pp. 229–256.
4. G.W. Allport, *The Nature of Prejudice,* Cambridge, Mass., Addison-Wesley, 1954.
5. W.P. Montague, *Belief Unbound,* New Haven, Conn., Yale University Press, 1930, pp. 70–73.
6. R. Franke, "Gang und Character," *Beihefte, Zeitschrift für angewandte Psychologie,* No. 58, 1931, p. 45.
7. T.M. Newcomb, "An Approach to the Study of Communicative Acts," *Psychological Review,* Vol. 60, 1953, pp. 393–404.
8. D. Cartwright and F. Harary, "Structural Balance: A Generalization of Heider's Theory," *Psychological Review,* Vol. 63, 1956, pp. 277–293.
9. Heider, *op.cit.*
10. N. Jordan, "Behavioral Forces That Are a Function of Attitudes and of Cognitive Organization," *Human Relations,* Vol. 6, 1953, pp. 273–287.
11. Cartwright and Harary, *op.cit.*
12. J. Morrissette, "An Experimental Study of the Theory of Structural Balance," *Human Relations,* Vol. 11, 1958, pp. 239–254.
13. Newcomb, *op.cit.*
14. T.M. Newcomb, "The Prediction of Interpersonal Attraction," *American Psychologist,* Vol. 11, 1956, pp. 575–586.
15. L. Festinger, K. Back, S. Schachter, H.H. Kelley, and J. Thibaut, *Theory and Experiment in Social Communication,* Ann Arbor, Mich., University of Michigan, Institute for Social Research, 1950.
16. H.A. Burdick and A. J. Burnes, "A Test of 'Strain toward Symmetry' Theories," *Journal of Abnormal and Social Psychology,* Vol. 57, 1958, pp. 367–369.
17. C.I. Hovland, I.L. Janis, and H.H. Kelley, *Communication and Persuasion: Psychological Studies of Opinion Change,* New Haven, Conn., Yale University Press, 1953.
18. H.C. Kelman and C.I. Hovland, "'Reinstatement' of the Communicator in Delayed Measurement of Opinion Change," *Journal of Abnormal and Social Psychology,* Vol. 48, 1953, pp. 327–335.
19. Osgood and Tannenbaum, *op.cit.*
20. H.T. Moore, "The Comparative Influence of Majority and Expert Opinion," *American Journal of Psychology,* Vol. 31, 1921, pp. 16–20.
21. M. Sherif, "An Experimental Study of Stereotypes," *Journal of Abnormal and Social Psychology,* Vol. 29, 1935, pp. 371–375.
22. E.E. Jones and R. Kohler, "The Effects of Plausibility on the Learning of Controversial Statements," *Journal of Abnormal and Social Psychology,* Vol. 57, 1958, pp. 315–320.
23. C.E. Osgood, "The Nature and Measurement of Meaning," *Psychological Bulletin,* Vol. 49, 1952, pp. 197–237.
24. Festinger, *op.cit.,* p. 13.
25. *Ibid.,* p. 3.

26. D. Ehrlich, I. Guttman, P. Schönbach, and J. Mills, "Post-decision Exposure to Relevant Information," *Journal of Abnormal and Social Psychology,* Vol. 54, 1957, pp. 98–102.

27. J. Brehm, "Post-decision Changes in the Desirability of Alternatives," *Journal of Abnormal and Social Psychology,* Vol. 52, 1956, pp. 384–389.

28. J. Brehm, "Increasing Cognitive Dissonance by a *Fait Accompli,*" *Journal of Abnormal and Social Psychology,* Vol. 58, 1959, pp. 379–382.

29. L. Festinger and J.M. Carlsmith, "Cognitive Consequences of Forced Compliance," *Journal of Abnormal and Social Psychology,* Vol. 58, 1959, pp. 203–210.

30. E. Aronson and J. Mills, "The Effect of Severity of Initiation on Liking for a Group," *Journal of Abnormal and Social Psychology,* Vol. 59, 1959, pp. 177–181.

31. Ehrlich *et al., op.cit.*

32. J. Mills, E. Aronson, and H. Robinson, "Selectivity in Exposure to Information," *Journal of Abnormal and Social Psychology,* Vol. 59, 1959, pp. 250–253.

33. L. Festinger, J. Riecken, and S. Schachter, *When Prophecy Fails,* Minneapolis, University of Minnesota Press, 1956.

34. J.W. Brehm, "Attitudinal Consequences of Commitment to Unpleasant Behavior," *Journal of Abnormal and Social Psychology,* Vol. 60, 1960, pp. 379–383.

35. T.W. Adorno, E. Frenkel-Brunswik, D.J. Levinson, and R.N. Sanford, *The Authoritarian Personality,* New York, Harper, 1950.

36. M.J. Rosenberg, "Cognitive Structure and Attitudinal Affect," *Journal of Abnormal and Social Psychology,* Vol. 53, 1956, pp. 367–372.

37. E.R. Carlson, "Attitude Change through Modification of Attitude Structure," *Journal of Abnormal and Social Psychology,* Vol. 52, 1956, pp. 256–261.

38. James B. Conant, *On Understanding Science,* New Haven, Conn., Yale University Press, 1947.

Part Five

Emotion, Emotional Expression, and Affect

Chapter 10

Perception, Drive, and Behavior Theory[1]

R.B. Zajonc
University of Michigan

Donald D. Dorfman
San Diego State College

In his last book, Hull (1952) wrote:

> Perhaps one of the reasons why the failure to distinguish sharply between
> stimulation and perception does not interfere any more markedly with the
> validity of the present deductions is that the elements of both stimulation
> and generalization are explicitly included in the system. [p. 354]

The distinction between perception and stimulation has, in fact, been regarded as unnecessary in behavior theory for many years. There is, however, a growing body of literature never directly associated with behavior theory, which might question this position. This body of literature, generally referred to under the rubric of sensory inter-action, contains a fair amount of evidence that perceived magnitudes of stimuli impinging on a given sense modality are often markedly influenced by the simultaneous (or near-simultaneous) stimulation to another sense modality. The causes of sensory interaction effects are far from well understood, and the effects are by no means universal or unequivocal. But one can hardly question the fact that sensory interaction

[1] Studies reported here were part of a research program supported jointly by Grants AF-49(638)367 and G-4951 from the Air Force Office of Scientific Research and the National Science Foundation, issued to the Research Center for Group Dynamics.

Zajonc, R.B., & Dorfman, D.D. (1964). Perception, drive, and behavior theory. *Psychological Review*, 71, 273–290. Copyright © 1964 by the American Psychological Association. Reprinted with permission.

effects do occur.[2] Viewed in the light of the Hullian position, the results of sensory interaction research have potentially significant implications for behavior theory. The present paper attempts to examine some of these implications and to demonstrate that the failure to distinguish between stimulation and [273]* perception does, in fact, interfere with the deductions of behavior theory.

SENSORY INTERACTION AND STIMULUS GENERALIZATION

The sensory interaction literature has a direct relevance for Postulate XI: Afferent stimulus interaction (Hull. 1952. p. 11). Reviews and summaries of this literature (Carter, 1962; Dufy, 1962; Gilbert, 1941; London, 1954; Ryan, 1940) seem to indicate that in the majority of instances, the simultaneous or near-simultaneous extraneous stimulation results in the lowering of sensory thresholds. Also, when subjects are required to estimate stimulus magnitudes presented at supraliminal levels, simultaneous extraneous stimulation results in the overestimation of these magnitudes. In a small number of cases, one also finds absolute threshold increase or magnitude underestimation. About a third of the experiments show no effects.

While these threshold and estimation effects are probably manifestations of the same perceptual consequences of the extraneous stimulation, in that the obtained threshold changes reflect changes in the perceived or "effective" stimulation, rather than improvement or deterioration of the sensory capacity,[3] it is the stimulus magnitude over- and underestimation that has a more direct bearing upon the afferent stimulus interaction postulate. The postulate reads as follows:

> All afferent impulses (s's) active at any given instant, mutually interact converting each other into s's which differ qualitatively from the original $\check{s}$'s so that a reaction potential ($_s E_R$) set up on the basis of some afferent impulse (s) will show a generalization fall to $_{\check{s}} E_R$ when the reaction (R) is evoked by the other afferent impulse ($\check{s}$) [Hull, 1952, p. 11].[4]

---

[2] The reader can easily observe a sensory interaction effect some quiet evening by lifting his telephone receiver, listening to the dial tone, fixating at a light bulb, and having someone switching it on and off in rapid succession. The amplitude of the dial tone will appear to oscillate in phase with the light. For best results no other light source should be present.

* Bracketed bold numbers refer to original page numbers. Page numbers indicate where the original page ended.

[3] The effects of factors such as extraneous stimulation or drive on absolute threshold and magnitude judgments are subjects of a separate problem. It might be pointed out in passing, however, that when we observe a lowering of absolute threshold which obtains as a consequence of some manipulation, such has increased drive level for example, the results cannot always be interpreted as an "improvement" in perception. The same manipulation introduced when the subject is making magnitude judgments of these stimuli, supraliminally presented, may result in the overestimation of these magnitudes. Overestimation can hardly be interpreted as an "improvement," since it represents a decrement in accuracy.

[4] As paraphrased by Hilgard (1956), the afferent stimulus interaction postulate reads more clearly:

When a response has been conditioned to a stimulus (S_1) and one or more previously neutral stimuli (S_2, S_3, ...) are presented along with S_1, the afferent impulses from this combination of stimuli interact to yield a new molar impulse (s). This new impulse is equivalent to a stimulus at a greater or less distance from S_1 on a qualitative continuum. The resulting generalized reaction potential to s will be smaller than to S_1, depending upon their remoteness from each other.

While the postulate assumes a *qualitative* change in the molar impulse which arises when the original stimulus is presented together with previously neutral stimuli, it certainly must, as a special case, subsume *quantitative* changes. For in the last analysis, a qualitative change is nothing but a cluster of quantitative changes too complex to be conveniently described in quantitative terms. Allowing the postulate to deal with quantitative changes in the molar impulse will enable us, on the basis of sensory interaction literature, to derive some new implications.

Consider a given sensory interaction effect on stimuli lying on a particular intensity continuum, A. Stimulus intensities on this continuum are known to be overestimated when judged in the presence of some extraneous stimulation, B. Low magnitudes of the extraneous stimulation, [274] B_1, result in minimal overestimation, and high magnitudes, B_2, result in a larger overestimation of the A stimuli. Suppose further that a response is conditioned to a particular A stimulus when the latter is presented together with B_1. Following training, this A stimulus is again presented, but now together with B_2, and performance is observed. Since the perceived or "effective" intensity of the A stimuli is known to increase in the presence of B_2, performance to the particular CS will show a generalization fall when the extraneous stimulus intensity is increased. Thus far, the prediction is entirely in agreement with the afferent stimulus interaction postulate. However, since we are dealing with presumably known quantitative changes in the "effective" stimulation, we are also in a position of making specific predictions about generalized responses to A stimuli other than the particular CS; for instance, CS $- a$, CS $- 2a$, CS $- 3a$, ..., CS $+ a$, CS $+ 2a$, CS $+ 3a$, ..., where a is a magnitude on the A dimension, expressed perhaps in log units to satisfy Postulate X (Hull, 1952, p. 11).

The generalization fall in performance to the CS had been obtained because its perceived intensity increased when it was presented together with B_2. But other A stimuli will also be perceived as more intense in the presence of B_2 than in the presence of B_1. Since CS $- a$, CS $- 2a$, ..., would in the presence of B_2 appear more intense, they would become effectively *more similar* to the trace of the CS maintained from training, where it was presented in the company of the weaker extraneous stimulation, B_1. Let us, for the purposes of argument, assume that the psychophysical change in the perception of the A stimuli occurring when B_1 is replaced by B_2 is equivalent to one a unit, and that such changes are more or less uniform for the range of values employed in the generalization test, such that any given stimulus intensity on the A continuum, S_{Ai}, when presented with B_1 is perceptually equivalent to $S_{Ai} + a$, when B_1 is replaced by B_2. Thus, generalized responses to CS $- a$, CS $- 2a$, ..., will be more probable (or stronger) when obtained in the presence of B_2 than when obtained in the presence of B_1. Responses to CS $- a$ obtained in the presence of B_2 might be as probable as responses to the CS itself when the latter is presented in the company of B_1. Responses to CS $- 2a$ obtained in the presence of B_2 will be as probable as those obtained to CS $- a$ in the presence of B_1, etc.

Since CS $+ a$, CS $+ 2a$, ..., would in the presence of B_2 also increase in their perceived intensity by one a unit, they would become less similar to the trace of the original CS, and the generalized responses elicited by them would be weaker than when observed in the presence of B_1. Consequently, for the stimulus continuum employed in the test, we obtain not a fall in the generalization gradient, but a lateral displacement of the gradient toward the lesser stimulus intensities of the A continuum, with mode at CS $- a$.

These predictions conflict with ones derived from Postulate XI. Consider only two stimuli, the CS and CS $- a$, which, for the purpose of simplicity, we will now refer to as

S_1 and S_2, retaining the relation $S_1 > S_2$. Since the original training occurs in the presence of B_1, the trained response is attached to the compound S_1B_1. Above, we predicted that the generalized reactions to stimuli *weaker* than the CS will be more probable when obtained under increased extraneous stimulation than when obtained under **[275]** constant extraneous stimulation, or in Hullian terms, that $_{S_2B_2}E_R > _{S_2B_1}E_R$. Essentially then we are predicting that in the case of a two-dimensional stimulus generalization, a test stimulus which differs from the CS on one dimension will produce a lower reaction potential than a test stimulus which differs from the CS to an equal extent on that dimension, but which also differs from the CS on one other dimension!

But we are dealing here with stimulus-intensity continua and, therefore, considerations deriving from stimulus-intensity dynamism (V) may complicate matters. A more critical examination of the Hullian prediction is therefore called for. If drive (D) and incentive (K) are held constant, we have the generalized reaction potential to S_2, obtained when extraneous stimulation remains the same from training to test, $_{S_2B_1}E_R = _{S_1B_1}E_R \times 10^{-jd_S} \times V_{2B_1}$, where j is an empirical generalization constant, d_S the difference between S_1 and S_2 in log units, and V_{2B_1} the stimulus-intensity dynamism of the combined S_2 and B_1 stimulation. The generalized reaction potential to the same test stimulus but obtained under increased extraneous stimulation can be written as follows: $_{S_2B_2}E_R = _{S_2B_1}E_R \times 10^{-id_B} \times V_{2B_2}$, where i is another empirical generalization constant, d_B the difference between B_1 and B_2 in log units, and V_{2B_2} the stimulus-intensity dynamism of the combined S_2 and B_2: stimulation. To obtain the prediction based on sensory interaction effects from Hullian theory, we must prove that $_{S_2B_2}E_R > _{S_2B_1}E_R$, or $_{S_2B_1}E_R \times 10^{-id_B} \times V_{2B_2} > _{S_2B_1}E_R$. But since both 10^{-id_B} and V_{2B_2} are equal to or smaller than unity, the above relation is false according to Hull's theory.

When a response is trained to an A stimulus in the presence of the stronger extraneous stimulation, B_2, and generalization tests are performed in the presence of the weaker extraneous stimulation, sensory interaction effects suggest that a mirror image of the former prediction will be obtained. Now the generalization gradient will show a lateral displacement toward the greater stimulus intensities with the peak of the gradient at CS + a. Under these conditions, the responses to stimuli stronger than the CS will increase in probability when extraneous stimulation is decreased during generalization testing. Here, the Hullian model is even less likely to predict an increment in generalized reaction potentials as a consequence of the decrement in extraneous stimulation. Now the difference between the CS and the testing stimulus, as well as the reduction in the total stimulus-intensity dynamism, both act to reduce $_SE_R$.

In an experiment whose attempt was to examine the above predictions (Dorfman, 1961a), the training CS and the generalization stimuli were slight electric shocks (from $-.38$ to $-.02$ log milliampere) of 1-second duration. The extraneous stimulation was a 45-decibel tone for B_1 and a 96-decibel tone for B_2, both at 1,000 cps, occurring also for a 1-second duration and simultaneously with the electric shocks. The distance between the stimuli selected for the generalization test ($-.06$ log milliampere) was established on the basis of a previous psychological investigation (Dorfman, 1961b) in which there were indications that a change from B_1 to B_2 resulted in an overestimation of shock intensities of approximately that order.

One group of subjects were trained under low extraneous stimulation, and another group under high extraneous stimulation. In order to avoid the **[276]** problem of asymmetrical generalization gradients, a procedure developed by Brown, Clarke, and

Stein (1958) was employed. One verbal response (WIN) was reinforced to the −.20 log milliampere shock, and another (LOSE) to the shock of the lowest (−.38 log milliampere) and to the shock of the highest intensity (−.02 log milliampere).[5] The three training stimuli were presented one at a time in 15-second intervals, and simultaneously with either B_1 or B_2, depending on the experimental condition. In both groups, subjects were given 12 training trials to the middle stimulus, and 7 training trials to each of the two extreme stimuli. The subjects were reinforced for correct responses by the experimenter saying "right," and for incorrect responses by the experimenter's saying "wrong."[6] In the generalization test, each of the seven stimuli was presented six times: three times

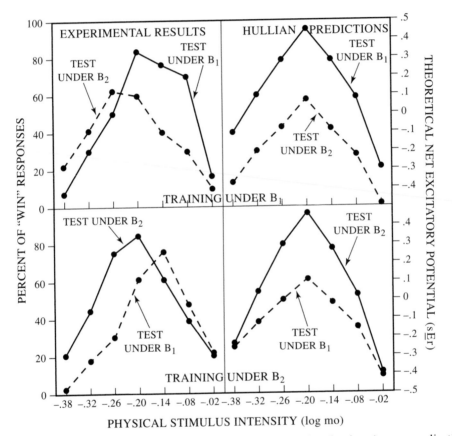

Figure 10.1   The effect of change in extraneous stimulation (loudness) on generalization along the shock dimension: Experimental results and theoretical predictions from Hull.

---

[5] This experiment was also performed using a conventional generalization procedure involving only one response, and essentially the same results were obtained (Karp, 1961).

[6] There were fewer than 10% of incorrect responses during the initial training, the discrimination performance reaching 100% accuracy toward the end of the training.

with B_1 and three times with B_2 in a random sequence. During test, no reinforcement was given, however, interspersed among the testing trials were six reconditioning trials. The data for this experiment are reproduced in Figure 10.1, where it is clear that a lateral displacement of the gradients occurred when the extraneous stimulation was changed from training to test. When subjects are trained in the presence of low extraneous stimulation, the modes and the medians of their generalization gradients are at significantly lower shock intensities for tests taken in the presence of strong extraneous stimulation than for tests taken in the presence of weak extraneous stimulation. Conversely, when training occurs under high extraneous stimulation, and when the test is given in the presence of the weaker tone, the modes and medians of the gradients are displaced toward higher shock intensities. When extraneous stimulation is increased, generalized reactions to stimuli weaker than the CS gain in probability of emission, and when it is decreased, reactions to stimuli stronger than the CS gain in probability. These effects were uniform throughout the course of the generalization tests. For purposes of comparison, the Hullian predictions for this $- + -$ training procedure were computed, assuming the usual constants for generalization and for V (Hull, 1952), and using a formula suggested by Hull (1951, p. 94) for computing the combined V, involving both the S and the B intensities. These predictions are shown alongside the empirical results, and it is clear that the results are in disagreement with the implications of the Hullian model.

DRIVE AND STIMULUS GENERALIZATION

There has always been some ambiguity in predicting the effects of drive shift upon generalization. The energizing component of drive (D) leads to one set of predictions and the stimulus component of drive (S_D) to another. Because of the multiplicative laws, $E = D \times H$ and $E = D \times \overline{H}$, one would expect increments in generalized responses and in the generalization slope when drive is increased following training, and decrements when drive is decreased. No displacement of the modal values of the generalization gradients would be expected. In support of this prediction, Spence (1958) reports an experiment by Newman (1955) who observed **[277]** generalization along the size dimension for rats whose hunger level was either increased or decreased following training.

From the point of view of the drive stimulus, S_D, however, one would expect a decrement in response strength regardless of whether drive is increased or decreased following training. Since increments as well as decrements in drive represent changes in the molar impulse, the law of afferent stimulus interaction applies, predicting that any change in the molar impulse produces a generalization fall. It seems that Hull must have given more weight to the role of S_D, for in Corollary XI he states:

> When a habit is set up in association with a given drive intensity and its strength is tested under a different drive intensity, there will result a falling gradient of $_S\overline{H}_R$ and $_S\underline{E}_R$. [Hull, 1951. p. 90]

Apparently, this corollary was established solely on the basis of empirical **[278]** results such as those of Yamaguchi (1952), for one aspect of the corollary seems to contradict the formal model. The corollary is consistent with the model with respect to the prediction of a falling $_S\overline{H}_R$ gradient. However, it is difficult to see that the model can also predict a falling $_S E_R$ gradient. Consider a reaction potential set up under a given drive level, D_1, and a subsequent test under an increased drive, D_2. The corollary predicts that $_{SS_{D_1}} E_R > _{SS_{D_2}} E_R$, where S_{D_1} and S_{D_2} are the two drive stimuli. Expanding, we have: $_{SS_{D_1}} H_R$ $\times D_1 \times V_1 > _{SS_{D_1}} H_R \times 10^{-bds_D} \times D_2 \times V_1$, where b is an empirical generalization constant, and d_{S_D} the difference between the drive stimuli. The above relation simplifies to $D_1 > 10^{-bds_D} \times D_2$. Fixing D_1 at 1.0 and assuming that S_D is equal to log D, we obtain the result that the empirical generalization constant b must be smaller than -1.0 for the relation to hold. Since the empirical results on generalization consistently indicate that the constant is seldom smaller than $-.15$, the corollary cannot be justified. Moreover, the corollary conflicts with the data reported by Newman (1955). On the other hand, working with the stimulus sampling model and treating drive as a set of irrelevant stimulus elements, Estes (1958) arrived at a prediction for generalization gradients obtained after a drive shift. Contrary to the above inferences, increments in drive following training were predicted by him to result in a shallower gradient with response probability somewhat depressed at the CS, while decrements in drive in a steeper gradient, also with a depressed response probability at the CS.

If, in the case of drive shift, the most significant aspect of drive is, as Estes argues, its stimulus element, S_D may be viewed simply as an extraneous stimulus such as we dealt with in the above experiment by Dorfman (1961a). If as such S_D leads to the overestimation of other stimulus magnitudes, then an increment in drive following training should result in a lateral displacement of the generalization gradient in the direction of lower stimulus magnitudes, and a decrement in drive in the direction of higher stimulus magnitudes. We would thus expect essentially the same effects whether we manipulate some irrelevant extraneous stimulation of irrelevant drive. It should be noted that neither the inference based on S_D effects, nor one based on the multiplicative law predict a lateral displacement of the generalization gradient following a drive shift.

In the present program of research, some experiments dealt with this problem (Carter and Zajonc, 1962; Matlin, 1960; Platz, 1962; Platz and Zajonc, 1961; Zajonc and Cross, 1964). In one of the experiments (Platz, 1962), subjects were first given differential fear conditioning in a series of 29 trials in which one of two lights was followed by a fairly strong electric shock. The duration of the light was .5 second, and its separation from the shock offset varied randomly from zero to five seconds for each subject. The shock intensity was set according to the tolerance of each subject, found prior to the fear conditioning. Measures of GSR were taken to assess the relative effectiveness of the differential fear conditioning. Following this fear conditioning, essentially the same procedure as that in Dorfman's experiment (1961a) was employed. A particular verbal response (HIT) was reinforced over a series of 15 trials to a 45-decibel tone, and another verbal response (MISS) was reinforced to a 42.5-decibel and to a 50.0-decibel [279] tone over a series of 12 trials each. In one group of subjects, the middle and the extreme stimuli were presented together with the previously shocked light (with the shock now absent), and in another group, the three training stimuli were presented with the previously nonshocked light. As in Dorfman's experiment, following the $- + -$ training, Platz observed the proportion of HIT responses to seven test stimuli ranging from 42.5 to 50.0 decibels. All auditory stimuli were given at 1,000 cps. The test stimuli were given in a random order in 15-second intervals. The shock (or nonshock) light was of .5-second duration, and it preceded the tone stimulus by one second. On half of the trials, the test stimuli were presented together with the shocked light (but without the shock), and on the other half in the presence of the nonshocked light. Interspersed among the generalization trials were also some reconditioning trials to maintain the differential fear reaction to the two lights. On each generalization trial, GSR measures were taken.

Figure 10.2 shows the results of the drive shift upon the proportion of generalized HIT responses. A lateral displacement similar to that found when extraneous stimulation was manipulated is observed. When drive is increased from training to test, the [280] curve is displaced toward the weaker tones. When drive is decreased, however, the gradients show a displacement in the direction of the louder tones. But Platz's results, although at an acceptable level of significance,[7] seem to be less pronounced than those of Dorfman. When drive is manipulated, the peaks of the gradients did not shift, as was the case when extraneous stimulation was manipulated. There is, however, a basic difference between

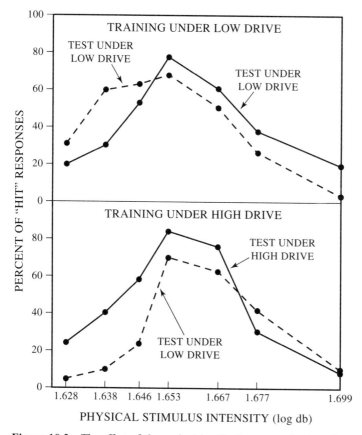

Figure 10.2   The effect of change in drive (fear) on generalization along the loudness dimension.

---

[7] The average median of the gradient of the group trained under high drive was displaced in the direction of higher stimulus intensities by .68 decibel when the test stimuli were given with the nonshock light, while the group trained in the nonshocked light was displaced in the direction of lower intensities by .77 decibel when the stimuli were given in the presence of the shocked light. This effect was significant at .001 level ($F = 36.85$, $df = 1/38$).

the two [281] manipulations. In Dorfman's experiment, the difference in the levels of extraneous stimulation were constant for all subjects. In the experiment manipulating drive, the differences in conditioned fear depended on the success of the previous differential fear conditioning and its extinction status during the training and testing of responses to the auditory stimuli. Individuals who conditioned well, in that their GSRs to the shocked and nonshocked lights reached and maintained a relatively large difference, would necessarily be under the influence of a relatively greater drive shift than individuals whose psychogalvanic reactions to the two lights were not very different. The subjects in the study were accordingly separated into "good" and "poor" conditioners, and their results are shown in Figure 10.3. It is immediately clear that the generalization displacement occurring as a function of drive shift obtains primarily for "good" conditioners.

Another related finding was obtained in Platz' study, which is of some interest. If a subject emits the response which was originally trained to the CS when a *weaker* tone is presented, he is essentially "mistaking" it for the CS. His response is HIT while it should have been MISS. One could argue that such "mistakes" are facilitated when the

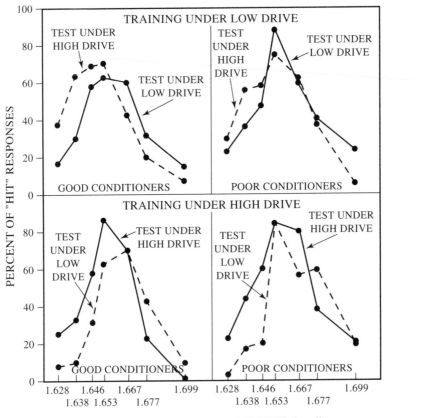

PHYSICAL STIMULUS INTENSITY (log db)

Figure 10.3   The effect of change in drive (fear) on generalization along the loudness dimension for "good" and "poor" conditioners.

drive-produced stimulation present at the moment is relatively high. Here, the high drive-produced stimulation increases the apparent or "effective" intensity of the weak tone, and thus makes it more similar to the CS. On the other hand, HIT responses to stimuli *louder* than the CS will occur when the drive-produced stimulation is relatively low. Here, the low drive-produced stimulation decreases the apparent intensity of the test stimulus, and thereby makes it similar to the CS. To the extent that the GSR measures the intensity of this drive-produced stimulation, we would expect that the GSR obtained when the subject emits a HIT response should *decrease* with the intensity of the test stimulus. The level of GSR observed when HIT responses were given by subjects to the seven auditory stimuli are shown in Figure 10.4. The relation expected from the sensory interaction point of view is clearly evident. This effect is of particular significance because, other factors held constant, normally we obtain an *increase* in GSR with an increase in stimulus intensity.

In other experiments with pigeons, using hunger (Zajonc and Cross, 1964) or electric shock (Carter and Zajonc, 1962) as the drive-producing stimulus, or with human subjects, using dynamometer tension as the drive-producing stimulus (Matlin, 1960), significant lateral displacements of generalization gradients were also found as a consequence of drive shift.

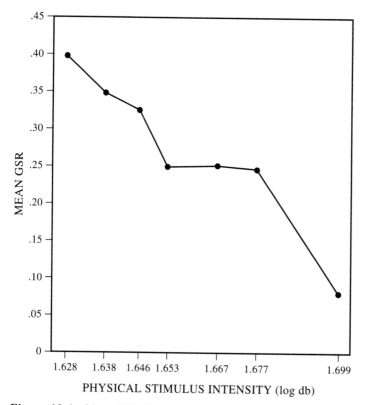

Figure 10.4   Mean GSR (in micromhos) accompanying "hit" responses as a function of stimulus intensity.

SENSORY INTERACTION AND DISCRIMINATION BEHAVIOR

The experiments reported earlier used with human subjects a generalization procedure often involving discrimination learning. Another series of experiments in the present research program examined some implications of sensory interaction and drive effects upon discrimination learning and performance in their own right.

Consider two stimuli, S_1 and S_2, slightly different in intensity, with $S_1 < S_2$. Suppose that in a successive discrimination learning procedure, S_1 is associated with one response, R_1, such as pressing one button, and S_2 with another response, R_2, such as pressing another button. Suppose further that S_1 and S_2 are always [282] presented together with some extraneous stimulation B_1, low in intensity. Correct responses to the stimuli are rewarded and incorrect punished. The pairs S_1B_1 and S_2B_2 occur in a random sequence and equally often over a series of trials. Interspersed among these trials, however, are also trials on which the two stimuli, S_1 and S_2, one at a time, are presented simultaneously with extraneous stimulation, B_2, considerably more intense than B_1. These trials occur in a random sequence and as often as those accompanied by B_1. Whenever S_1B_2 or S_2B_2 are presented, neither positive nor negative reinforcement is administered, although the subjects are still required to select one of the two responses. We are concerned with the prediction of discrimination performance with respect to the nonreinforced pairs, S_1B_2 and S_2B_2.

Since we are dealing with discrimination learning, the critical element of the situation is the distance between S_1 and S_2. It was noted above that sensory interaction effects lead to changes in the perceived intensities of stimuli, and we must therefore consider not the physical, but the "effective" or the perceived distance between stimuli. The assumption that extraneous stimulation increases the perceived intensities of S_1 and S_2 leads us to predict that the "effective" distance from S_2B_1 will be greater for the reinforced S_1B_1 than for the nonreinforced S_1B_2. The change in the "effective" distance obtains because the perceived intensity of S_1 [283] increases when it is accompanied by B_2. Consequently, performance to S_1B_2 will suffer. However, from the same assumption it follows that the "effective" distance from S_1B_1 will be smaller for the reinforced S_2B_1 than for the nonreinforced S_2B_2. The effect obtains because the perceived intensity of S_2 increases when it is presented in the company of B_2. Consequently, the performance to the pair S_2B_2 will gain. Assuming that the reaction potentials for the training pairs S_1B_1 and S_2B_1 are about equal, we obtain the prediction that the proportions of correct responses should be ordered as follows: $S_2B_2 > S_2B_1 \approx S_1B_1 > S_1B_2$. This prediction holds that the highest proportion of correct responses should obtain for a stimulus compound, S_2B_2 to which responses were never reinforced! And it is again in conflict with one derived from the Hullian system.

It suffices to show that at least one of the inequalities of the above relation cannot be derived from Hull's postulates. Let us examine the ability of the Hullian model in predicting $_{S_2B_1}\dot{E}_{R_2} < {}_{S_2B_2}\dot{E}_{R_2}$, where $_S\dot{E}_R$ is the net discriminatory reaction potential. In terms of the Hullian law of discrimination learning (Hull, 1952, pp. 85–92), we have the net discriminatory reaction potential for S_2B_1:

$$_{S_2B_1}\dot{E}_{R_2} = {}_{S_2B_1}E_{R_2} \dot{-} {}_{S_2B_1}E_{R_1}$$

Assuming that the product $D \times K$ is constant:

$$_{S_2 B_1} \dot{E}_{R_2} =_{S_2 B_1} E_{R_2} \dot{-}_{S_1 B_1} H_{R_1} \times V_{1 B_1} \times V_{2 B_1} \times 10^{-b d_S}$$

where the first subscript for V refers to the discriminanda S_1 and S_2, and the second to the extraneous stimuli, B_1 and B_2 (V being the stimulus-intensity dynamism of the combined S and B stimulation), b is an empirical generalization constant, and d_S the distance between S_1 and S_2. We also have:

$$\begin{aligned}
_{S_2 B_2} \dot{E}_{R_2} &=_{S_2 B_2} E_{R_2} \dot{-}_{S_2 B_1} \dot{E}_{R_1} \\
&=_{S_2 B_2} \overline{H}_{R_2} \times V_{2 B_2} \dot{-}_{S_2 B_2} \overline{H}_{R_1} \times V_{2 B_2} \\
&=_{S_2 B_1} H_{R_2} \times V_{2 B_1} \times 10^{-a d_B} \\
&\times V_{2 B_2} \dot{-}_{S_2 B_1} \overline{H}_{R_1} \times V_{2 B_1} \times 10^{-a d_B} \times V_{2 B_2} \\
&=_{S_2 B_1} H_{R_2} \times V_{2 B_1} \times 10^{-a d_B} \\
&\times V_{2 B_2} \dot{-}_{S_1 B_1} H_{R_1} \times V_{1 B_1} \\
&\times 10^{-b d_S} \times V_{2 B_1} \times 10^{-a d_B} \times V_{2 B_2}
\end{aligned}$$

where a is another empirical generalization constant, and d_B the distance between B_1 and B_2. Let us assume that the training was sufficiently long such that $_{S_1 B_1} H_{R_1}$ and $_{S_2 B_1} H_{R_2}$ are equal to unity.

Dividing both sides of the inequality under examination by $V_{2 B_1} \times 10^{-a d_B} \times V_{2 B_2}$ we have:

$$\frac{1 \dot{-} V_{1 B_1} \times 10^{-b d_S}}{V_{2 B_2} \times 10^{-a d_B}} < 1 \dot{-} V_{1 B_1} \times 10^{-b d_S}$$

Since the denominator of the left side of the inequality must be smaller than unity, the inequality is false.

Consider further a situation where the reinforcement is administered only in the presence of the stronger extraneous stimulation, and we are concerned with the prediction of performance to the nonreinforced pairs, $S_1 B_1$ and $S_2 B_1$. Since a decrease in extraneous stimulation results in the "effective" weakening of S_1 and S_2 when they are presented with B_1, the distance between the pairs $S_1 B_2$ and $S_2 B_2$ will be smaller than between $S_1 B_1$ and $S_2 B_2$, and greater than between the pairs $S_1 B_2$ and $S_2 B_1$. Here, then, we predict that the highest percentage of correct responses will obtain for the nonreinforced pair $S_1 B_1$. Thus, when reinforcement is given only in the presence of B_2, the [284] net discriminatory reaction potentials are ordered as follows: $_{S_1 B_1} \dot{E}_{R_1} > {}_{S_1 B_2} \dot{E}_{R_1} \approx {}_{S_2 B_2} \dot{E}_{R_2} > {}_{S_2 B_1} \dot{E}_{R_2}$. It can be shown, as above, that the Hullian model predicts $_{S_1 B_1} \dot{E}_{R_1} < {}_{S_1 B_1} \dot{E}_{R_1}$.

Several experiments using the above paradigm were recently carried out, and their results seem rather consistent with expectations. In each experiment, one group of subjects were reinforced only in the presence of weak, and another only in the presence of strong extraneous stimulation. In all experiments, the discriminanda were presented for a 1-second duration and simultaneously with the extraneous stimuli. In one of the experiments (Dorfman, Platz, and Zajonc, 1962), mild electric shocks (.92 and 1.32 milliampere) served as the discriminanda, and tones of weak and strong intensities as extraneous stimuli. In another, two stimuli slightly differing in loudness (51 and 55 decibels, 1,000 cps) were used as the discriminanda, and two levels of illumination provided extraneous stimulation. In a third experiment, two similar levels of brightness of a patch of light were used as discriminanda, and two levels of auditory stimulation served as B_1 and B_2. On each trial, one of the four S_iB_i combinations occurred, all equally often and in a random sequence over a series of 128 trials. Always, in one group of subjects, reinforcement was given in the presence of B_1 only, and in another in the presence of B_2 only. The percentage of correct responses to the S_iB_i pairs found in these three experiments is summarized in the upper portions of Figure 10.5. The two first experiments clearly show the expected pattern of response probabilities. The results of the third experiment are somewhat weaker, although the same trend is still to be

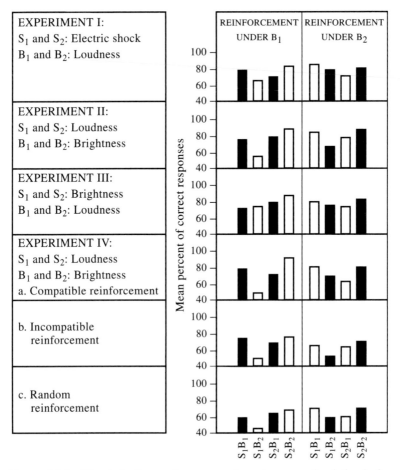

Figure 10.5 Discrimination performance under extraneous stimulation in four experiments.

observed. In the second experiment (where auditory stimuli served as the discriminanda and illumination as the extraneous stimulation, and when reinforcement was administered under B_1), the difference in correct responses between the nonreinforced pairs S_1B_2 and S_2B_2 is over 30%, with correct responses to S_1B_2 being only slightly better than chance, and those to S_2B_2 reaching almost 90%. It should be noted that the above response measures are based always on the entire set of trials, including early blocks when performance to all four S_1B_1 combinations does not exceed the chance level.

It might be argued that in the present series of discrimination experiments, the subjects may have used the irrelevant extraneous stimulation as an additional, albeit improper, cue. That is, for instance a subject who is only reinforced in the presence of the weaker stimulus, and is asked to choose between R_1 and R_2 when the pair S_1B_2 is presented, might, when uncertain, be tempted to select R_2 rather than the correct R_1, simply because the extraneous component of the pair is clearly strong, and because R_2 was always reinforced to the stronger of the two stimuli, namely S_2. Performance to S_1B_2 would therefore suffer. When presented with S_2B_2 and also uncertain, he might also choose R_2 in preference to R_1 for the same reason. This tendency, however, would benefit the performance to S_2B_2. The opposite tendencies may obtain when reinforcement is given only in the presence of B_2. Here, performance to S_1B_1 would benefit and to S_2B_1 suffer. To examine these possibly confounding effects, the second of the previous discrimination experiments was repeated using the same two auditory stimuli as S_1 and S_2, and the same two levels of illumination as B_1 and [285] B_2, and the following preexperimental procedure. Before the experiment proper and before introducing S_1 and S_2 at all, the subjects were trained to respond to B_1 and B_2 in the absence of the discriminanda. In one group (Compatible Reinforcement), the response which was later to be associated with the weaker S_1 was reinforced to B_1, and the response to be later associated with the stronger S_2 to B_2. In another group (Incompatible Reinforcement), the response to be later associated with the weaker S_1 was reinforced to B_2, and that to be later associated with S_2 to B_1. In a third group (Random Reinforcement), half of the R_1 responses was randomly reinforced to B_1 and half to B_2, and similarly for the R_2 responses. This training was carried out for 60 trials. In the second part of the experiment, a discrimination learning procedure identical to that in Discrimination Experiment II was used.

In all groups, the effect found previously was observed. As can be seen in the lower portion of Figure 10.5, the pattern of differences between the proportions of correct responses is most pronounced for the Compatible Reinforcement group, showing that in the original experiments at least a part of the effect may be attributed to the tendency of responding on the [286] basis of extraneous stimulation when a discrimination with respect to S_1 and S_2 is difficult. However, the presence of the differential response percentages to the four S_iB_i pairs, consistent with previous findings and found for all three groups, strengthens the conclusion that the effects previously obtained were, in large part, due to a sensory-interaction influence.

CONCLUSIONS

The results of the experiments presented above seem to argue for an increased role of perception in Behavior Theory. In particular, they argue for an increased role of the afferent stimulus interaction postulate, although the postulate may have to be somewhat modified. Afferent impulses (s's) present at a given time do seem to interact and seem to convert one another. But it is also apparent that, at least with respect to the continua used in the above research, they convert one another into $š$'s which are not qualitatively but quantitatively different from the original s's. Consequently, while the prediction of the fall in reaction potential ($_{š}E_R$) resulting when the response is elicited by $š$ is correct, one cannot readily extend this prediction to the generalized reaction potential, $_{š}\bar{E}_R$. Depending upon the nature of the afferent interaction, the test stimulus, and the levels of extraneous stimulation present during training and testing, $_{š}\bar{E}_R$ may either show a fall or a rise. Exact predictions of $_{š}E_R$ and $_{š}\bar{E}_R$ would therefore require exact knowledge of the specific sensory-interaction effects which obtain for the particular eliciting and extraneous stimuli under consideration. Unfortunately, there are, at the moment, no systematic principles governing such sensory-interaction effects. For each pair of stimuli, specific previous knowledge of interaction effects must be available.

The afferent stimulus interaction postulate holds specifically that $_{š}E_R = {_s}E_R \times 10^{-jd}$, where j is an empirical generalization constant, and d the difference between s and $š$ (Hull, 1951, p. 94). The only modification required is the addition of the qualification that, at times, a generalization gain obtains when responses are made to $š$, and that d be considered in terms of "effective" or perceived rather than in terms of physical distance.

The increased significance of the afferent stimulus interaction postulate may have wider implications. Perceptual constructs and variables have never played important roles in Behavior Theory. Among the formal principles of Behavior Theory, only the afferent-stimulus-interaction and the stimulus-intensity-dynamism postulates might be "perceptual" or "quasi-perceptual" in nature. Of these two, the former remained largely idle, while the latter was shown to be in conflict with experimental results (Nygaard, 1958), and ultimately unnecessary for the explanation of the data which prompted its introduction (Champion, 1962; Logan, 1954; Perkins, 1953). The idleness of the afferent stimulus-interaction postulate placed the eliciting stimulus in a rather enviable position among other variables. We began to view it as a stable and dependable component of the system. When experimental variables popular in behavioral research, and in particular drive, are manipulated, they are conventionally viewed as leaving the eliciting stimulus untouched. Rather, the principal attention is directed to how these variables affect the output side. Sensory-interaction data indicate that the same [287] stimulus administered under two different background conditions is simply not the same stimulus. At least, it is not perceived or reacted to as if it were the same stimulus.

A further implication follows from the research presented in this paper. It is quite well established that the strength of learned responses is markedly influenced by drive (Spence, 1956). It is also rather well established that, with drive level held constant, the intensity of the eliciting stimulus influences the strength of learned responses in very much the same way. Estes (1958) made this observation in a somewhat different context. The former effect has been commonly dealt with by means of the multiplicative law. The latter effect, on the other hand, has been originally treated in terms of stimulus-intensity dynamism, and later by means of the discrimination principle elaborated by Perkins (1953) and Logan (1954). In the light of the results presented here, the communality of drive and stimulus-intensity effects need not remain simply accidental. The high rate of responding under high drive need not be entirely due to the energizing force of D. These effects might, in some degree, reflect the increased perceived intensity of the eliciting stimulus, which derives from its interaction with the drive-stimulus. Although the problem is more complex for acquisition, here, too, the possibility exists that stimulus intensity and drive can be "traded off" for one another *because* the latter increases the "effective" intensity of the eliciting stimulus. Thus, the effects of stimulus intensity and drive on acquisition and performance may prove to be equivalent not only in their consequences, but, in part, also in their immediate antecedents.

The possibility that the drive stimulus may produce sensory interaction effects is strengthened by recent neurophysiological evidence. On the one hand, Steller (1954) argued that the state of drive of the organism is directly correlated with the amount of activity in the hypothalamus. Hebb (1955) and Lindsley (1957) also view general level of motivation as reflected in cortical arousal. On the other hand, many studies show perceptual effects due to neural activation. As a matter of fact, afferent stimulus interaction was, at first, presented under the label of afferent *neural* interaction. Fuster (1958), for instance, reports that discrimination is facilitated by a mild stimulation of the brain stem, and Boswell (1958) that recognition thresholds are lowered when obtained during the excitatory phase of the alpha rhythm. Thus, to the extent that drive, as well as extraneous stimulation, produce increased neural activity, and to the extent that such arousal interacts with other sensory inputs, drive, extraneous stimulation, and the eliciting stimulus intensity might all show equivalent effects.

The equivalent effects of drive and extraneous stimuli on stimulus reception and transmission may also have some implications for the work which, since the classical Bruner-Goodman experiment (1947) on the estimation of coin sizes, has concentrated on demonstrating motivational effects in perception. Although the role of motivational influences in perception is constantly being challenged by response-oriented interpretations, the argument presented here would certainly support the possibility of motivational effects in perception, such as accentuation of stimulus magnitudes and the lowering of sensory thresholds under increased motivation. **[288]** But a departure from the New Look formulation is also indicated. Traditionally, the general hypothesis that motivational factors influence perception requires that, in order for a motivational state to exert some effect upon the perception of a stimulus, the stimulus must in some relevant, perhaps instrumental, way be related to the manipulated drive. The above restriction, which is essential to the New Look interpretation of motivational effects in perception, may be quite unnecessary. Any drive, provided its S_D interacts with the judged stimulus may exercise such effects as magnitude over- or underestimation and changes in recognition threshold. This latter thought is perhaps less enchanting from a clinical point of view, but, on the other hand, there is little reason to doubt it. Differential perceptual performance associated with personality differences need not be interpreted in terms of the differential psychological relation of the different personalities to the stimulus object. Rather, it can be viewed as a consequence of differences in arousal, drive, or sensitivity to sensory-interaction effects. It is still possible that when the judged stimulus has instrumental significance for the motivational state in question, some special effects might be obtained. It is more likely, however, that these effects would be limited to influences upon processes peripheral to what might be called "immaculate" perception, such as orienting, attending, and the like.

REFERENCES

Boswell, R.S. An investigation of the phase of the alpha rhythm in relation to visual recognition. Unpublished doctoral thesis, University of Utah, 1958.

Brown, J.S., Clarke, F.R., and Stein, L.A new technique for studying spatial generalization with voluntary responses. *J. exp. Psychol.*, 1958, **55**, 359–362.

Bruner, J.S., and Goodman, C.D. Value and need as organizing factors in perception. *J. abnorm. soc. Psychol.*, 1947, **42**, 33–44.

Carter, D.E. Some effects of inter-sensory stimulation and drive on psychophysical responses. Unpublished report. Ann Arbor: Research Center for Group Dynamics, 1962.

Carter, D.E., and Zajonc, R.B. Studies on drive and incentive in perception: VI. Some effects of drive produced by electric stimulation on generalized responses to loudness. Technical Report No. 16, AF-49(638)367, G-4951. Ann Arbor: Research Center for Group Dynamics, 1962.

Champion, R.A. Stimulus-intensity effects in response evocation. *Psychol. Rev.*, 1962, **69**, 428–449.

Dorfman, D.D. Some effect of drive on the effective intensity of a stimulus. *Psychol. Rep.*, 1961, **9**, 87–98. (a)

Dorfman, D.D. Some effects of drive on the perceived intensity of a stimulus. Unpublished doctoral thesis, University of Michigan, 1961. (b)

Dorfman, D.D., Platz, A., and Zajonc, R.B. Studies on drive and incentive in perception: VII. Some effects of extraneous sound and manifest anxiety on discrimination behavior. Technical Report No. 17, AF-49(638)367. Ann Arbor: Research Center for Group Dynamics, 1962.

Dufy, E. *Activation and behavior.* New York:Wiley, 1962.

Estes, W.K. Stimulus-response theory of drive. In M.R. JONES (Ed.), *Nebraska symposium on motivation: 1958.* Lincoln: Univer. Nebraska Press, 1958. Pp. 35–68.

Fuster, J.M. Effects of stimulation of brain stem on tachistoscopic perception. *Science,* 1958, **127**, 150.

Gilbert, G.M. Inter-sensory facilitation and inhibition. *J. gen. Psychol.*, 1941, **24**, 381–407.

Hebb, D.O. Drives and the C.N.S. (conceptual nervous system). *Psychol. Rev.*, 1955, **62**, 243–253.

Hilgard, E. *Theories of learning.* New York: Appleton-Century-Crofts, 1956.

Hull, C.L. *Essentials of behavior.* New Haven: Yale Univer. Press, 1951.

Hull, C.L. *A behavior system.* New Haven: Yale Univer. Press, 1952.

Karp, S.E. Studies on drive and incentive in perception: III. Some effects of drive on stimulus generalization obtained with a revised training procedure. Technical Report No. 8, AF-49(638)367, G-4951. Ann Arbor: Research Center for Group Dynamics, 1961. **[289]**

Lindsley, D.C. Psychophysiology and motivation. In M. R. Jones (Ed.), *Nebraska symposium on motivation: 1957.* Lincoln: Univer. Nebraska Press, 1957. Pp. 44–105.

Logan, F.A. A note on stimulus intensity dynamism (V). *Psychol. Rev.*, 1954, **61**, 77–80.

London, I.D. Research on sensory interaction in the Soviet Union. *Psychol. Bull.*, 1954, **51**, 531–568.

Matlin, A.H. Studies on drive and incentive in perception: II. The effect of drive produced by proprioceptive stimulation on generalized responses to loudness and pitch. Technical Report No. 6, AF-49(638)367, G-4951. Ann Arbor: Research Center for Group Dynamics, 1960.

Newman, J.R. Stimulus generalization of an instrumental response under high and low levels of drive. *Amer. Psychologist,* 1955, **10**, 459–461.

Nygaard, J.E. Cue and contextual stimulus intensity in discrimination learning. *J exp. Psychol.*, 1958, **55**, 195–199.

Perkins, C.C., JR. The relation between conditioned stimulus intensity and response strength. *J. exp. Psychol.*, 1953, **46**, 225–231.

Platz, A. Some effects of conditioned fear on stimulus generalization. Unpublished doctoral thesis, University of Michigan, 1962.

Platz, A., and Zajonc, R.B. Effects of change in drive on stimulus generalization. Paper read at Midwestern Psychological Association, Chicago, May 1961.

Ryan, T.A. Interrelations of the sensory systems in perception. *Psychol. Bull.*, 1940, **37**, 659–608.

Spence, K.W. *Behavior theory and conditioning.* New Haven: Yale Univer. Press, 1956.

Spence, K.W. Behavior theory and selective learning. In M.R. Jones (Ed.), *Nebraska symposium on motivation: 1958.* Lincoln: Univer. Nebraska Press, 1948.

Steller, E. The physiology of motivation. *Psychol. Rev.*, 1954, **61**, 5–22.

Yamaguchi, H.E. Gradients of drive stimulus (S_D) intensity generalization. *J. exp. Psychol.*, 1952, **43**, 298–304.

Zajonc, R.B. and Cross, D.V. Stimulus generalization as a function of drive shift. *J. exp. Psychol.*, 1964, **69**, 363–368.

Chapter 11

Emotion and Facial Efference: A Theory Reclaimed

R.B. Zajonc
University of Michigan

Nearly 80 years ago a book appeared in Paris under the title *Physionomie Humaine: Son Mécanisme et son Rôle Social* (1). The book, written by Israel Waynbaum, a physician, offered a radical theory of emotional expression, defying all previous ones, including Darwin's dominant theory. It clarified, for the first time, the function of emotional expression in the emotional process—the foremost problem in the study of emotions at the turn of the century. Yet Waynbaum's book received no attention and it has remained unknown until now. Neither the author nor his idea are to be found in the *Science Citation Index* or in numerous reviews of research on emotion or facial expression. In this article I review Waynbaum's theory, compare it with Darwin's, bring it up to date, and show that it forms a promising basis for a comprehensive theory of the emotions.

Waynbaum's analysis led him first to question the term "emotional *expression*." He feared that referring to facial movements as "expressions," the standard term since Aristotle, reinforced by Darwin's classic work (2), implicitly fixed their role in the emotional process, and "solved" the problem by definition. The term "expression" specifies a priori the causal sequence among emotional correlates, placing the efferent process at the terminus. As such, therefore, "expression" cannot be the cause of any other aspect of the emotional process. The term "expression" also implies the existence of an antecedent internal state which "expression" externalizes, manifests, and displays. It implies further that the antecedent internal state seeks externalization that forces itself onto the surface, Hence, there also exists the term "suppression." In many cases the behavioral output may well "express" an internal state, and some reactions are indeed suppressed. But it is by no means established that all facial gestures that are classified as expressions are caused by internal subjective states. It may be [15]* best, therefore,

---

* Bracketed bold numbers refer to original page numbers. Page numbers indicate where the original page ended.

---

to refer to these phenomena as "emotional efference"—a term that has fewer a priori implications. Of course, the term "expression" is consistent with all current theories of emotion; only Lange and James (3) questioned the assumption that feeling precedes efference, but they failed to provide an explanatory and conceptual framework, and their argument was soon rejected. Waynbaum's first contribution was to question these 19th-century views—views that still dominate current thinking about emotion.

According to Andrew (4, p. 1034), facial expression has evolved "to communicate information about the probable future behavior of the displaying animal." By expressing its emotions, one animal could signal its intentions to another. But why should humans, who have such a powerful means of communication—language—be the one animal to have also developed the most complex repertoire of facial movements? Do we need, in addition to speech, some 80 facial muscles merely to broadcast our intentions?

Moreover, why should we project our intentions on our faces in the first place? It is perhaps reasonable to suppose that baring teeth and growling in rage might cause an intruder to retreat, and thus prevent violence. But what purpose might be served by displaying one's own fear to an enemy, or one's own surprise to an intruder? No doubt some evolutionary explanations might be suggested, but such explanations depend on conjecture, and it is difficult to imagine the evolutionary process whereby they could have become universal. Hardly any theory of emotion and facial expression challenges or even questions this critical aspect of Darwin's theory.

In contrast to all contemporary theories of emotion, Waynbaum offered the hypothesis that emotional responses have as their principal function the auxiliary control of cerebral blood flow (CBF). Noting that all overt emotional responses (blushing, sobbing, weeping, frowning, and so forth) are closely tied to vascular processes, Waynbaum proposed that the musculature of the face is capable of compressing veins and arteries of the face and thus controlling facial blood flow, which he thought could act as a safety valve for CBF. Blood circulation was also implicated in the actions of the diaphragm that arise in sobbing or laughing, or in tears shed when weeping or laughing. Waynbaum did not take issue with the display function of facial movements, but he considered this function to be derivative and incapable of explaining them.

To fully appreciate Waynbaum's contribution, however, one must put it in the context of Darwin's work.

DARWIN'S THEORY OF EMOTIONAL EXPRESSION

To explain emotional expression, Darwin wrote, one must understand "why different muscles are brought into action under different emotions; why, for instance, the inner ends of the eyebrows are raised, and the corners of the mouth depressed, by a person suffering from grief or anxiety" (2, p. 3). However, Darwin's theory of emotional expression does not begin to answer his own question.

Darwin seems, by his empirical method, to have been less interested in explicating emotional expressions than in using these phenomena to substantiate the evolutionary hypothesis for behavior as he did for structure. He did not seek to specify the ongoing process of emotional expressions, nor to understand their mechanisms. Instead, he solicited observations about emotions from remote parts of the world to establish the universality of expressions. His book closes with the assertion that his "theory of expression confirms to a certain limited extent the conclusion that man is derived from some lower animal form" (2, p. 365). Most subsequent research on emotions has followed Darwin's interest in universality and taxonomy (5). This research supports the hypothesis of the innate basis of expression, but it does not address Darwin's "why" question.

Darwin's theory consists of three principles. The first—that of serviceable habits— holds that some actions relieve the organism's wants, gratify its needs and desires, and guide it in reacting to sensations and to internal states. These serviceable actions will be repeated by force of habit, especially when they have done so "during a long series of generations" (2, 6). The second principle holds that for many actions there exist antithetical actions elicited by the opposite stimulus conditions. Darwin gives the example of a dog mistaking a familiar person for a stranger, and upon discovery of its error changing from a threatening posture to the antithetical posture of submission and affection. The third principle—that of the direct action of the nervous system—concerns behavior that occurs independently "of the Will, and independently to a certain extent of Habit" (2). Tears, trembling, rage, and changes in heart rate are such direct products of the nervous system.

Thus, Darwin's three basic principles are a heuristic schema that directs the researcher interested in knowing "why different muscles are brought into action under different emotions" to conjure up any reasonable function that the given expression could have played at some point of evolution. If such a function cannot be hypothesized, then the researcher must look for a function of an opposite expression. If both fail, then the expression must be elicited by the direct action of the nervous system. But we are not told by Darwin how or where to look for these functions, and it is not obvious what are "opposite" actions. Thus, the baring of teeth is viewed as a threat signal, even though teeth are also displayed in the grin (4). Therefore, Darwin's principles cannot be falsified. Darwin revolutionized the thinking on emotional expression by placing it in the context of adaptive processes, and he was an outstanding observer who amassed a wealth of data. But it would be false to credit him with a general theory of emotional expression.

WAYNBAUM'S VASCULAR THEORY OF EMOTIONAL EXPRESSION

In contrast to Darwin, Waynbaum refused to view muscular movements as the terminal stage of the emotional process. He attributed to them a much more significant internal regulatory role. Waynbaum's thinking was based on a number of converging facts. (i) The supply of blood to the brain and to the face derives from one source, the common carotid artery. (ii) The supply of cerebral blood must be stable. There can be no sudden changes even if the rest of the circulatory system undergoes violent variations. (iii) Although the bony [16] structure of the face is mostly rigid, the face has an inordinate number of muscles. Why? (iv) The facial artery, a major branch of the external carotid, is rich in muscular tissue. Again, why?

Waynbaum argued that all emotional reactions produce circulatory perturbations. Either they mobilize considerable energy, or, as in depression, they remove energy demands. They may thus produce a disequilibrium in CBF. Since the external and internal carotid have a common origin, equilibrium in the CBF can be maintained by directing more blood to the face and skull or by diverting it toward the brain.

Because facial muscles, when contracting, push against the bony structure, they can act as tourniquets on arteries and veins and thus regulate facial blood flow. By modulating flow in the external carotid and in the facial veins, they regulate CBF, reducing or complementing it. The same is true of other expressive acts, such as those controlled by glandular secretion or the diaphragm. For example, the lachrymal gland is supplied by the lachrymal artery which branches off from the internal carotid by way of the ophthalmic artery. Therefore, an augmented blood flow in the lachrymal artery should reduce the flow in the internal carotid, decreasing CBF, and hence causing momentary anesthesia of the corresponding regions of the nervous system.

If Waynbaum's theory is correct, it can answer Darwin's "why" question more directly than the evolutionary theory of expression. Why are smiling and laughing the major gestures of happiness and joy? Waynbaum asserted that moderate brain hyperemia is associated with healthy and positive affective tonus, whereas the opposite—temporary brain anemia or ischemia—is associated with negative affect, depressive moods, and unsound physical condition. But he also asserted that the subjective experience of elation follows the smile, not the other way around. The laughing person approaches a state of congestion. A hard laugh makes the face quite red, and sometimes even violet. The return circulation is impeded by the contracted cervical skin muscles that press on the jugular veins. Thus, more blood remains in the brain. The function of tears that are often shed during hard laughter is to relieve the rising pressure of cerebral blood. These tears always come at the very end of a laughing bout, and, as in crying, they lead to a local anesthesia.

Why is the zygomatic muscle involved in smiling and in happiness? The contraction of the major zygomatic muscle, asserted Waynbaum, has a congestive cerebral circulatory function. The proof is simple. Pull the corners of your mouth apart by contracting the major zygomatic muscle, as if in intense exaggerated smile. After several seconds, the frontal vein will be gorged with blood. Thus, claims Waynbaum, the zygomatic muscle acts as a ligature on the branches of the external carotid and the slave action of the corrugator blocks the return blood. Cerebral blood is thus momentarily retained causing temporary intracerebral hyperemia, which in turn leads to a surge of subjectively felt positive effect.

Waynbaum offered the opinion that, given its beneficial circulatory effects, laughing must be healthy. It is like taking an oxygen bath. The cells and tissues receive an increased supply of oxygen, causing a feeling of exuberance. The conversion of venous blood into arterial blood is accelerated and, because of the spasmodic action of the diaphragm, the lungs oxygenate at a more rapid pace. In contrast, sadness produces disoxygenation of tissues and attenuates vital processes. Happiness leaves the face young because it involves only one major muscle—the zygomatic. In sadness, many muscles are contracted: the elevators, orbicularis oculi, orbicularis oris, corrugator, frontalis, pyramidal, and others. Hence, frequent crying results in a prematurely wrinkled face.

Why do we furrow our forehead when we concentrate? The frontalis contracts and the forehead becomes furrowed by transverse wrinkles. The eyeball is swollen and pupils dilated. The eyes are often closed, and the orbicularis oris, as well as the masseter, are contracted to make the jawbone project forward. By putting a tourniquet on the external carotid and on facial veins, all these actions, at the cost of facial circulation, send more blood to the brain. More cerebral blood means better brain work. After 60 years, this hypothesis received empirical support (7). A host of other mannerisms, universal in all cultures, are recognized as revealing internal mental states, such as thinking, problem-solving, trying to remember, or making decisions. They are rubbing one's chin, scratching one's head, licking lips, pressing one's ocular region, passing the hand over the forehead, frowning, biting fingernails or pencils, and pulling one's earlobes or eyebrows. If facial musculature can to some extent control CBF, we would have an explanation for phenomena that seem otherwise bizarre and for which no explanation has thus far been offered. While these efferents are peripheral to the emotional process, they show the pervasive role of the vascular system in mental phenomena.

HAD WAYNBAUM WORKED TODAY

Waynbaum developed his theory nearly 80 years ago, and he necessarily made some assumptions now known to be false. Had Waynbaum worked in a modern laboratory he would have known, for example, that the blood supply to the brain does not derive from a single source but that it is distributed through the circle of Willis, which is supplied by a large network of vessels, and that the interdependence between the internal and facial flow is much more limited than he suspected. He would also have known that neural circulatory controls, the profusion of arteries and veins, and the presence of resistance beds create a redundancy in blood supply that can keep CBF constant in a variety of ways, in spite of various muscular acts. But muscle action could be more significant with respect to return circulation because veins are more readily controlled by muscles. (Hence one notes the gorged frontal veins when straining excessively or when in rage.) Because blood from the brain drains through the forehead and face, the muscular action in the face can briefly delay the outflow of blood from the brain. Thus, Waynbaum might have focused more on the influence of muscles on veins than on arterial flow, especially since arteries abound in neural circulatory controls (vasoconstrictors and vasodilators), while veins do not. This new knowledge about the vascular system, nevertheless, does not preclude [17] Waynbaum's basic hypothesis. The stability of CBF, being of crucial importance, may well be maintained by partially redundant systems. Alterations in CBF that are under different time constraints may be controlled by more than one mechanism. Facial action also has a direct effect on CBF. CBF supplies blood to those regions that are active, and those areas of the motor cortex that correspond to a particular group of facial muscles that are activated receive increased flow. Thus CBF can be regulated by facial musculature, but not necessarily through facial blood flow.

Had Waynbaum worked today, he would not have suspected CBF changes to be the direct antecedents of mood and emotional effects. Rather, he may have drawn a connection between emotion and brain temperature. Before entering the brain, the internal carotid passes through the cavernous sinus. One function of this structure, the only one in the body in which the artery is located inside a vein, is thermoregulation of arterial blood before it enters the brain. In desert ungulates such as the camel, for example, the internal artery is divided into numerous small vessels, creating a radiator pattern. The brain, which in the resting adult organism produces one-fifth of the body's heat, is cooled by arterial blood (8).

Temperature is important because it is likely to influence the biochemical action of neurotransmitters and enzymatic pathways. Thus a particular pattern of regional blood flow, together with local rise and fall of brain temperature, might enhance or impair the release and synthesis of different neurotransmitters and thereby produce different subjectively felt states. These subjective states are distinctive because different emotional muscular patterns can alter temperature in different brain regions in different ways. Not only different brain regions and different temperatures may be produced by different muscular patterns, but different quantities of neurotransmitters (serotonin, enkephalin, and so forth) may be synthesized and released selectively.

Variations in the external flow cause corresponding complementary variations in the internal flow (9), effects achieved by direct ligatures on the external carotid. It has not been shown that facial musculature, by action on external flow, can affect CBF. If it can, the effect is likely to be limited. Nevertheless, Waynbaum's hypothesis of facial efference having subjective pleasurable consequences by affecting CBF, might be true for reasons that he could not have suspected. For if facial action instigates localized regional CBF, not by peripheral but central processes, and if there are concomitant effects on venous flow, the obtained temperature change may act on the release and synthesis of neurotransmtters (10).

Migraine headaches are caused by a vascular dysfunction. Migraine sufferers make a variety of unusual mouth movements, such as licking lips and biting the inside of their cheeks, and the external carotid flow rises during headache (11). These previously ignored facial movements may therefore play some role in reducing external vasodilation.

Although Waynbaum was right in many ways, his theory was necessarily incomplete because he lacked knowledge that became available only decades later. He constructed his theory piece by piece, creating a coherent and elegant structure of assumed processes, about which he could no more than make intelligent guesses. Waynbaum's theory is a product of a superior imagination that conceptualized the nature of emotional processes almost entirely by the force of logical necessity, for Waynbaum had no special training other than in medicine and never did research in a laboratory.

Tests of the Vascular Theory of Expression

The vascular theory answers Darwin's "why" question of emotional expression directly and it is directly falsifiable. Modern methods of measuring blood flow, for example after xenon-133 is inhaled (12), or thermography can be applied to determine whether emotional expressions influence blood flow and CBF. It can now also be determined whether changes in CBF and brain temperature have the effects on emotion and mood that Waynbaum hypothesized. Many hypertensive drugs that produce significant circulatory changes often have serious depressive side effects, and profound mood changes are associated with cerebral vascular disease and with stroke (13).

The stability of CBF, suspected by Waynbaum nearly 80 years ago, has also been demonstrated. Globus *et al.* (14) found increases in heart rate, breathing, and blood pressure during heavy 10-minute exercise, yet there was no change in CBF over the same time interval. These findings need not contradict the vascular theory because different measures of time are probably involved. The sort of stability found in CBF by Globus *et al.* is obtained by comparing intervals of several minutes. Therefore, these data could conceal local changes in CBF that occur within seconds and dissipate rapidly. Little is known today about the effects of brain temperature on the release of neurotransmitters, although it would be surprising if the optimum temperature for their synthesis and release were not confined to a narrow range, perhaps a fraction of a degree.

TOWARD AN INTEGRATED THEORY OF EMOTIONAL EXPRESSION

Waynbaum's most significant contribution was to examine the role of facial movements apart from their expressive consequences. His analysis provides some answers to the controversial problem raised by Lange and James (3) about the relative positions of muscular output and subjective feeling in the causal structure of the emotional process. Both Waynbaum and Lange, however, begged the question of what causes bodily emotional movements in the first place. The antecedents of facial muscular movements, glandular secretions, arrested breathing, or diaphragmatic spasms are numerous.

1. Since several of these actions can be produced at will, whatever moves a person to perform them—desire to please or frighten another individual, craving for affection, need for help, playful imitation, caprice—is a candidate for an antecedent condition for what might be perceived as "emotional expression." These voluntary acts can be performed even though no emotion, or an emotion other than the one displayed, is experienced by the individual.

2. Among the involuntary antecedents are fixed action patterns—instinctual reactions that occur spontaneously, such as fear reactions to strangers, withdrawal of an injured limb, or retreat from a rapidly looming object.

3. Expressive movements might be elicited as conditioned responses that have been acquired in the past. A dog that withdraws its leg in response to a shock that had been preceded by a bell comes to withdraw the leg on hearing the bell alone.

4. Expressive acts can arise in mimicry either as instinctive reactions or as responses established by previous reinforcement. For example, if a child's smile is a response to the father's smile and the child, as a result, receives affection, the child's likelihood of returning smiles (and other expressions) is heightened.

5. A class of antecedent conditions for emotional bodily movements derives [18] from the organisms's orienting reactions. The theories of Piderit and of Gratiolet (15) specified these conditions. According to Piderit, emotional expressions derive from the sensory and peripheral activity elicited by emotional stimuli and from the hedonic reactions to these stimuli. Piderit assumed that sensory events give rise not only to peripheral orienting muscular acts but also to consequent acts that are occasioned by their hedonic effects. Orienting acts, such as squinting, drawing up one's nostrils, or licking one's lips, optimize sensory receptivity. The consequent reactions, however, depend on the hedonic nature of the stimulation. When a bitter solution is placed in the mouth, a person tends to make expelling motions. Piderit thus assumed that some sensory events are in themselves pleasurable, and so are the representations that derive from these events. These pleasurable events evoke approaching and accepting actions. Sensations and representations that are disagreeable evoke rejecting actions.

Muscular reactions can occur not only to sensory events but to the memories of these events, to imaginary events, and, through generalization, to emotional excitation.

When we imagine biting into a lemon, we may form a rejecting buccal motion, and similar facial gestures express disdain for a silly idea. Gratiolet noted that bowlers contort their bodies to "correct" the paths of their bowling balls. We smile in joy because, by generalization, the mouth makes movements that are homologous to those when the individual tastes a savory morsel. Language is replete with sensation-emotion metaphors. We speak of "bitter enemies," "dark thoughts," and the "pain of separation." And there are "honey," "sweetie, "sugar," "tootsie," "buttercup," among endearments whose etymology lies in gustatory pleasures.

Whatever the antecedents of these facial and bodily movements, they are critical for Waynbaum in affecting CBF and thereby changing the affective tonus and subjective hedonic experience of the individual. A subjective state might exist immediately before what came to be known as expressive movements, or these movements could also be executed automatically and without a prior subjectively felt experience. And if Waynbaum is correct, there is necessarily one afterward. For the most part, for example, the onset of withdrawal and alarm reactions often occurs before pain is actually felt. Writhing, weeping, and thrashing of limbs bring relief. Frey (16) reported finding enkephalin in tears, which suggests that tears may act to relieve pain. The entire emotional process can therefore be conceptualized as being triggered by an internal sensory or cognitive event that leads to peripheral muscular, glandular, or vascular action that, in turn, results in a change of the subjective hedonic tone.

In this sense, the facial movements associated with emotion are no different from sneezing, coughing, and yawning. The universality of emotional expression is therefore no more surprising than the universality of yawning and sneezing. All have clear biological bases and can be ascribed to corresponding neuroanatomical structures and neurophysiological processes. What distinguishes them from emotions is that they are regarded as having no psychological instigating causes (although this cannot be always said of yawning). Moreover, being constant and universal, they can readily acquire communicative and symbolic significance.

Empathy

The expressions of basic emotions can be universally recognized by conspecifics through an empathic process. In case of fear expressions, for example, "the eyes and mouth are widely opened, and the eyebrows raised" (2, p. 289). Since opening of the eyes and mouth allows greater blood flow into the facial artery, lower CBF, and a more vigorous draining from the brain, a temporary rapid rise in brain temperature is allowed. As a consequence, the organism may experience momentary dysphoria. An animal in close proximity will notice the terrified neighbor because its change in posture is conspicuous. The attention of the neighbor turns into mimicry by virtue of the empathic process, and the neighbor, too, experiences some dysphoria in association with its own altered brain temperature.

Empathy is an important social mechanism whereby the feelings of one individual are transmitted and partially experienced by another. It is not entirely clear how such transmission takes place (17). The vascular theory, however, suggests a hypothesis that makes the puzzle of empathy less mystifying. If muscular movements of the face, by virtue of their effects on CBF and on the release of particular neurotransmitters, are sufficient to induce

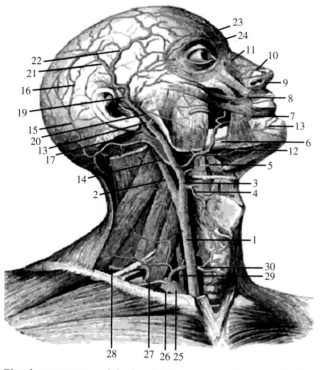

Circulatory system of the head. The arteries of interest for Waynbaum's theory are (1) the common carotid, (2) the internal carotid, and (3) the external carotid. [Reproduced from P. Sappey, *Traité d'Anatomie Descriptive* (Delahaye Lecrosnier, Paris, 1888/89).]

changes in hedonic tone and result in changed subjective states, then reproducing the expression of another may well produce in the onlooker a similar emotional state. Of course, the feeling is not experienced equally. But this might be so only because the movements are not all faithfully reproduced. The question of why should one imitate others' emotional expressions remains, and the answer may come from the theory of evolution. Mimicry has been shown in 11-day-old infants (18), and it is generally viewed as part of the innate behavioral repertoire of many species. **[19]**

THEORETICAL CONSEQUENCES OF AN EXPANDED VASCULAR THEORY

Once Waynbaum's hypothesis that expressive acts have positive and negative hedonic and subjective consequences is verified, a number of phenomena associated with emotion can be explicated and the theory of emotional processes enriched.

Blushing and Pallor

Blushing and pallor are emotional phenomena that are relatively involuntary and uncontrollable. Noting that "women blush much more than men" (2, p. 310), Darwin concluded that blushing occurs because attention is focused on part of one's own body. Since blushing occurs "in relation to the opinion of others" (2, p. 325), it affects primarily the exposed parts of the body. These vascular phenomena had a different meaning for Waynbaum. Blushing occurs in the case of emotions that are intense, often sending a sudden surge of blood through the main artery. Hence a great deal of energy is deployed without a possibility of efferent output. The person is ashamed, wishes to flee, hide, conceal a previous act, or confound someone's possible deprecating attribution. But in situations that cause blushing, there is little that the individual can usefully do. The mobilized energy has no outlet and, as in suppressed rage, facial blood flow takes up the surplus. Thus, blushing relieves CBF. The face blushes, according to Waynbaum, not because it is exposed but because the facial artery is a branch of the external carotid.

The same is true of pallor. Pallor occurs in temporary cerebral anemia, and the contraction of the facial capillaries remedies it by increasing CBF. These actions are possible because the facial artery is rich in muscular tissue and can contract and expand rapidly. Pallor brought about in pain is caused by the peculiar pain grimace of the major muscles around the mouth and eyes that diminish facial blood flow, and redirect it to the brain to ease suffering. Waynbaum's faith in his theory led him to assert that if the main carotid branched off not at the neck but at the shoulders, we would express our emotions with our arms, and blush with our shoulders.

Facial Feedback

The facial feedback theory (19) holds that feedback from facial musculature provides information for the subjective experience of emotion. The facial feedback hypothesis differs from Waynbaum's theory in that this feedback only furnishes information about what the individual must have previously felt. Feedback does not cause hedonic subjective experiences—those are assumed to have taken place beforehand.

Ekman et al. (20) have thrown a light on the problem. Subjects (some of them professional actors) were instructed to form their muscles, one by one, into six classical emotional expressions. The results showed striking changes in heart rate associated with the various expressions, even though the connection between their muscular movements and emotions was not disclosed to the subjects. The muscular pattern that conveys disgust, for example, reduced heart rate, whereas that related to sadness accelerated it. Ekman et al. suggested that the activity of the facial muscles triggers the autonomic reactions directly, either by means of facial feedback or through the direct excitation of the hypothalamus by the motor cortex.

Neither the evolutionary theory of emotional expression nor the sensory theory have much to contribute to the facial feedback hypothesis or to the understanding of the Ekman et al. data. But the vascular theory may be useful here. To the extent that facial muscles modulate arterial and venous facial blood flow, thereby controlling CBF, heart rate may have to respond to these changes. In expressions of disgust, cerebral blood supply is augmented by increased flow through the internal carotid and reduced draining because the instructed subject places a "tourniquet" on the branches of the facial artery and on the veins around the mouth and forehead. Brain blood, receiving new supply that passed through the cavernous sinus, is thus momentarily cooled. In sad expression, the same facial muscles are relaxed allowing a greater flow in the facial artery, lesser CBF, and more profuse return. Brain temperature is thus allowed to rise since metabolic processes continue while there is no cooling (21).

Physiognomics

Since Aristotle, numerous scholars attempted to relate individual differences in temperament to appearance, especially the face (22). In fact, much of the early work on emotional expression is closely allied to physiognomics, but because no plausible explanatory principles were proposed, interest in physiognomics died. A reasonable and testable physiognomic theory can be derived from Waynbaum's ideas.

Substantial individual differences exist in facial musculature. For example, in some people the risorius muscle, which extends the angle of the mouth, is absent altogether. If the facial muscles play a significant role in CBF and the resulting neurotransmitter effects, and if muscles differ among people, then individual differences in expression may emerge. If some facial muscle configurations can modulate brain temperature to optimize the action of neurotransmitters that are differentially involved in moods and emotions, and others cannot, then different affective dispositions correlated with facial expression should be found.

This conjecture is strengthened if we consider that voluntary and spontaneous emotional expressions are controlled by different neural pathways (23). Spontaneous emotional expressions use the extrapyramidal motor system, whereas "acted" facial expressions receive their impulses from the cortical motor strip, passing through the corticobulbar projections. The social value of a well-functioning voluntary expressive control is as important as spontaneous expression since both are powerful communicators of internal states and both influence the behavior of others. Inability to smile "sincerely" invites, throughout one's lifetime, social reactions that produce a different personality predisposition than the capacity to break into a "sparkling smile."

Emotional Expression and Mental Health

Since emotions are central phenomena of mental health, the vascular theory of expression can be examined for its usefulness. For example, if brain temperature can influence moods by facilitating the release of particular neurotransmitters, and if facial musculature can modify brain temperature, then thermal biofeedback should be useful in teaching anxious or depressed patients to control the appropriate facial muscles to induce more favorable affective states. Yoga and various forms of meditation are based in part on such an assumption (24). The effectiveness of such treatments, however, depends on whether voluntary movements of facial muscles have the same CBF effects as spontaneous ones and if patients can be trained to reproduce the spontaneous ones sufficiently well. Perhaps the study of other affective disorders and vascular diseases may draw upon Waynbaum's theory for new research directions.

Postscript

It remains for historians of science to discover why Waynbaum's original ideas have been so completely ignored for so long. Of course his theory, ostensibly implausible, is not congruent with what is known today about the vascular system, and it was already doubted when Waynbaum first presented it at a meeting of the Societé de Psychologie Expérimentale et Comparée. He was then struck down by such rising luminaries as Henri Piéron and Georges Dumas (25), the former alluding [20] to serious physiological difficulties, and both arguing his functional explanations. Yet his basic idea is ingenious and rich in consequences; when modified in the light of what is known and assumed today about these processes, it organizes an array of divergent facts. It therefore deserves to be reclaimed.

REFERENCES AND NOTES

1. L Waynbaum, *La Physionomie Humaine; Son Mécanisme et son Rôle Social* (Alcan, Paris, 1907).
2. C.R. Darwin. *The Expression of the Emotions in Man and Animals* (Univ. of Chicago Press, Chicago, 1965).
3. C.G. Lange and W. James, *The Emotions* (Williams &. Wilkins, Baltimore, 1922).
4. R.J Andrew, *Science* 142, 1034 (1963). Andrew's interpretation of Darwin's principles has to be taken with care in the light of Darwin's passing disclaimer that there is any muscle that "has been developed or even modified exclusively for the sake of expression" (2, p. 354).
5. See, for example, R. Plutchik and H. Kellerman, Eds., *Emotion: Theory, Research, and Experience* (Academic Press, New York, 1980).
6. Note the Lamarckian touch in this interest of Darwin.
7. D.H. Ingvar and J. Risberg, *Exp. Brain Res.* 3, 195 (1967).
8. D. Minard and L. Copman, in *Temperature: Its Measurement and Control in Science and Industry.* C.M. Herzfeld, Ed. (Reinhold, New York, 1963), vol. 3, part 3, p. 527.
9. K.M.A. Welch, P.J. Spira, L. Knowles, J.W. Lance, *Arch. Neurobiol.* 37, 253 (1974).
10. R.W. Ross Russell, Ed., *Brain and Blood Flow* (Pitman, London, 1971). Studies that demonstrated increased regional CBF in the motor cortex that corresponds to the action of particular muscle groups used measures that register at best within 6 millimeters of the brain surface; deeper flow dynamics escape these measures. In emotional facial movement, CBF effects may reach deeper into the brain and perhaps touch upon structures such as the limbic system that are involved in emotional processes.
11. M.D. O'Brien, *Headache* 10, 139 (1971).
12. W.D. Obrist. H.K. Thompson, C.H. King, H.S. Wang, *Circ. Res.* 20, 124 (1967).
13. D.S. Bell, *Med. J, Aust.* 2, 829 (1966); R.G. Robinson *et al. Stroke* 14, 736 (1983).
14. M. Globus *et al. J. Cereb. Blood Flow Metab.* 3, 287 (1983).
15. T. Piderit, *Grundzuege der Mimik und Physiognomik* (Vieweg, Braunschweig, 1858); P. Gratiolet, *De la Physionomie et des Mouvements d'Expression* (Hetzel, Paris, 1865).
16. W.H. Frey, II, D. DeSota-Johnson, C. Hoffman, *J. Ophrhalmol.* 92, 559 (1981).
17. M.L. Hoffman. in *Emotions, Cognition, and Behavior*, C.E. Izard *et al.,* Eds. (Cambridge Univ. Press, Cambridge, 1984), p. 103.
18. A.N. Meltzhoff and M.K. Moore, *Science* 198. 75 (1977).
19. C.E. Izard, *Human Emotions* (Plenum, New York, 1977); S,S. Tomkins, *Affect, Imagery. Consciousness,* vol. 1. *The Positive Affects* (Springer, New York, 1962); J.D. Laird. *J. Pers. Soc. Psychol.* 24, 475 (1974); J.T. Lanzetta and S.P. Orr, *ibid,* 39, 1081 (1980).
20. P. Ekman. R.W, Levenson, W.V. Friesen, *Science* 221, 1208 (1983). A similar, more extensive experiment, was carried out by M.N. Rusalova, C.E. Izard, and P.V. Simonov [*Aviat. Space Environ. Med.* 46, 1132 (1975)].
21. Heart rate is not reduced to avoid flooding the internal artery, but rather to decrease arterial pressure outside the brain. When cerebral spinal fluid pressure reaches that of arterial pressure, CBF is generally decreased if that arterial pressure remains constant. With freely varying arterial pressure, the increase of intracranial pressure triggers the Cushing reflex, that is, a conspicuous increase in arterial blood pressure. As a consequence, heart rate is reduced to attenuate arterial blood pressure outside of the brain.
22. M. Stanton, *The Encyclopaedia of Face and Form Reading* (Davis, Philadelphia, 1924).
23. G.H. Monrad-Krohn, *Brain* 47, 22 (1924).
24. G.E. Schwartz, *Am. Sci.* 3, 314 (1975).
25. I. Waynbaum, *J. Psychol. Norm. Pathol.* 3, 467 (1906).
26. Supported by NSF Brant BS-8117977. I thank P. Adelmann, L.G. D'Alecy, J.F. Greden, J.T. Hoff, C.E. Izard, and H. Markus for their valuable suggestions, and M. Waynbaum for information about his father. [21]

Chapter 12

Feeling and Facial Efference: Implications of the Vascular Theory of Emotion*

R.B. Zajonc, Sheila T. Murphy, and Marita Inglehart
University of Michigan

Photographers ask us to say *cheese* because that word transforms facial muscles into a facsimile of a spontaneous smile. It is reasonable to inquire whether such a "smile" is merely an outward appearance or whether it also contains some genuine emotional elements. No definitive answer to this question presently exists. Among theories of emotion, only facial feedback theories (Izard, 1977; Tomkins, 1962) regard facial expression as an important determinant of the subjective feeling state. In cognitive appraisal theories (Arnold, 1960; Averill, 1983; Lazarus, Averill, and Opton, 1970; Mandler, 1984; Roseman, 1984; Smith and Ellsworth, 1985, 1987), facial expression does not figure as a significant process that modifies or induces feeling states. According to cognitive appraisal theories, subjective feeling derives from and follows a prior cognitive appraisal. Facial expression is regarded as the terminal link of the emotional episode and, as such, could not be expected to contribute systematically to the subjective experience. Yet another approach to the understanding of emotions, the one offered by the classic Schachter and Singer (1962) theory, assumes as a necessary condition the presence of a subjectively felt arousal that, when ambiguous, seeks cognitive elaboration. The ensuing cognitive construal specifies the arousal's particular meaning and is thereby capable of altering certain qualities of the subjective state that the person experiences.

These diverse views provide different answers to the significant questions about emotion: What occasions the subjective feeling state? Which elementary processes

---

* This research was supported by National Science Foundation Grant BS-8117977.

We wish to thank Stanley Schachter, who suggested that we demonstrate the affective effects of temperature directly. Hence, he inspired Study 5. We also wish to thank Louis D'Alecy, Arndt Von Hippel, and Pamela K. Adelmann for their useful suggestions.

Zajonc, R.B., Murphy, S.T., & Inglehart M. (1989) Feeling and facial efference: Implications of the vascular theory of emotion. *Psychological Review*, 96, 395–416. Copyright © 1989 by the American Psychological Association. Reprinted with permission.

cause or constitute what is known as *feeling?* Where in the chain of causal events lies the emergent feeling of fear, euphoria, or rage? Is expression of emotion invariably the terminal link in the process, or can it, on its own, engender subjective feeling? What is it that we *feel* when we feel sad, angry, or happy? What are the more fundamental processes that underlie the experience of pleasure or disgust? This article addresses certain aspects of these problems. Specifically, it seeks to determine whether facial muscular movements alone are capable of altering subjective feeling states, and it proposes a physiological process making such effects possible.

THEORIES OF EMOTIONAL EXPRESSION

James (Lange and James, 1922/1967) contradicted the view of his predecessors and contemporaries that "bodily disturbances [occasioned by an emotion] are said to be the 'manifestation' of these…emotions, their 'expression' or 'natural language'" (p. 12–13). Rather, he argued,

> *the bodily changes follow directly the* PERCEPTION *of the exciting fact,
> and… our feeling of the same changes as they occur* IS *the emotion.*
> Common sense says, we lose our fortune, are sorry and weep; we meet a
> bear, are frightened and run; we are insulted by a rival, are angry and strike.
> The hypothesis here to be defended says that this order of sequence is incor-
> rect, that the one mental state is not immediately induced by the other, that
> the bodily manifestations must first be interposed between, and that the
> more rational statement is that we feel sorry because we cry, angry because
> we strike, afraid because we tremble, and not that we cry, strike, or tremble,
> because we are sorry, angry, or fearful as the case may be. (p. 13)

For James (1890), *feeling* was the very essence of emotion, without which the concept was vacuous. After having asserted that "*every one of the bodily changes whatsoever it be, is* FELT, *acutely or obscurely, the moment it occurs*" (p. 1066), James goes on to say that "If we fancy some strong emotion, and then **[395]*** try to abstract from our consciousness of it all the feelings of its bodily symptoms, we find we have nothing left behind" (p.1067). Facial feedback theories revived one aspect of James' assertion, namely, that "*the bodily manifestations must first be interposed between*" the eliciting event and emotional expression. But, rather than including all bodily changes, facial feedback theories focused primarily on the face. According to facial feedback theories, the subjective experience of emotion derives from the sensory (cutaneous or proprioceptive) feedback of facial motor action (Buck, 1980; Cupchik and Leventhal, 1974; Izard, 1971, 1977, 1981; Kraut, 1982; Laird, 1974; Tomkins, 1962, 1979, 1981; Zuckerman, Klorman, Larrance, and Spiegel, 1981).

"Strong" and "weak" versions of the facial feedback hypothesis have been distinguished, but these distinctions have not always been consistent. For example, according to Rutledge and Hupka (1985), the strong version considers facial feedback "sufficient to induce and specify emotion," whereas the weak version calls only for an intensification of any emotion that was previously elicited by other causes. This latter form of the weak version dates to Darwin (1955), who proposed that expression intensifies emotion,

---

* Bracketed bold numbers refer to original page numbers. Page numbers indicate where the original page ended.

whereas suppression "softens" it (p. 22). In fact, a recent study by McCanne and Anderson (1987) has demonstrated just that. Winton's (1986) definition of the strong version of facial feedback is the same as that of Rutledge and Hupka (1985). However, he attributed to the weak version more than simply the capacity of intensifying an otherwise elicited emotion. Even at its weakest, facial expression, according to Winton, has the capacity of producing global hedonic effects, that is, feelings of positivity or negativity, liking or disliking, and tendencies of avoidance or approach, independently of what emotion is present at the time. Both strong and weak versions of the facial feedback hypothesis hold, nevertheless, that subjective feeling is a consequence of facial movement.

Critics of the facial feedback hypothesis claim that the evidence offered in support of the hypothesis is, at best, ambiguous. Matsumoto (1987) performed a meta-analysis of facial feedback studies and concluded that there is only a modest effect. It is, indeed, reckless to suppose that facial efference is the main, let alone the only, factor in *all* subjective feelings. Clearly, in the more complex emotions, such as jealousy or pride, most of the variance in the subjective experience derives from a prior cognitive process. However, such an observation does not in itself preclude facial efference from having subjective consequences of its own.

The most serious criticism of studies seeking to document that subjective feeling states derive from muscular action is that subjects can make inferences about the subjective feelings that they "should be" experiencing under the experimental manipulations. Thus, in the typical facial feedback experiment, subjects are asked to imagine an emotional situation, arrange their facial musculature to conform to classical emotional expressions, or emotions are induced directly by presenting emotional stimuli (Colby, Lanzetta, and Kleck, 1977; Cupchik and Leventhal, 1974; Duncan and Laird, 1977; Ekman, Levenson, and Friesen, 1983; Kotsch, Izard, and Walker, 1978; Laird, 1974; Laird and Crosby, 1974; Lanzetta, Cartwright-Smith, and Kleck, 1976; Leventhal and Mace, 1970; McArthur, Solomon, and Jaffe, 1980; McCaul, Holmes, and Solomon, 1982; Tourangeau and Ellsworth, 1979; Zuckerman et al., 1981). As a result, these manipulations contain emotional elements based on subjects' common knowledge about the relation between feeling and expression and, as such, constitute ambiguous evidence that facial muscular movement *alone* can have objective or subjective emotional aftereffects. Besides the aforementioned criticism, Rutledge and Hupka (1985) listed no less than 12 additional experimental artifacts that characterize facial feedback research.

In an ingenious experiment that addresses the most serious of these criticisms, Strack, Martin, and Stepper (1988) prevented subjects from drawing a connection between facial action and emotion by having them hold a pen either in their teeth (simulating a smile) or in their lips (requiring the opposite muscular action) while exposing them to affective material (humorous cartoons). These authors found support for the facial feedback hypothesis in their studies. However, effort could have played a significant role in their subjects' reactions because it is considerably more effortful to hold a pen by its tip in one's lips than in one's teeth.

At the theoretical level, some ambiguity exists as well for the concept of facial feedback. It is not yet clear, for example, why cutaneous and proprioceptive feedback should be either necessary or sufficient for the emotional experience, nor how it fits in the entire physiological and behavioral process that constitutes emotion. For Buck (1985), facial feedback is a matter of self-perception. The person feels his or her teeth clench and infers, "Oh, I must be angry." An earlier theorist (Tomkins, 1962), on the other hand, attributed to facial feedback a more active causal and compelling role. Moreover, some researchers have emphasized the role of musculature (e.g., Izard, 1977), whereas others have looked on facial skin (Tomkins, 1979) as the major source of feedback. Clearly, a fully developed statement of a facial feedback process requires the specification of mechanisms that link facial movement to feeling.

The fact that there may exist a theoretical conflict between facial feedback theories and appraisal theories over the temporal location of the subjective affective state in the causal chain of emotion has been largely ignored. Simply stated, in the former theories, cognitive appraisal is not considered a necessary precondition for the emergence of the subjective emotional state because such a feeling state can be achieved by muscular facial action alone. The latter theories, however, regard appraisal as a strictly necessary factor in all emotional experience (Lazarus, 1982). Dialogue between the two schools of thought regarding the role of facial expression has been scarce, and consequently, experimental confrontation between the cognitive and feedback theories of emotion has been equally scarce. Appraisal theories formulate their experimental paradigms entirely within the confines of cognitive processes. Consequently, cognitive appraisal research is unlikely to determine the contribution of expressive elements to the emotion experience because data on expressive output are almost never collected. Likewise, feedback theories are seldom concerned with appraisal and instead induce emotions by methods in which appraisal is either taken for granted or ignored. Evidence bearing on the resolution of the theoretical conflict is, therefore, lacking.

VASCULAR THEORY OF EMOTIONAL EFFERENCE

A novel idea, albeit one that has been in abeyance for more than 80 years, is to be found in the vascular theory of emotional [396] efference (VTEE) proposed by Israel Waynbaum (Zajonc, 1985). Waynbaum (1907) argued that facial gestures in general, and emotional gestures in particular, have regulatory and restorative functions for the vascular system of the head. He first observed that all emotional experiences entail a considerable and rapid disequilibrium of the vascular process. For example, blood is redistributed to supply skeletal muscles to meet the demands of an incipient activity. Noting the intimate relation between facial and cerebral blood flow (CBF), Waynbaum suggested that facial muscular movements contribute to the regulation of CBF by pressing against facial veins and arteries and, thus, shunting blood to the brain when needed, or diverting it away when the brain is threatened with excess. The main carotid artery is divided at the neck into two arteries—the internal, which supplies the brain, and the external, which supplies the face and skull—a curious configuration that prompted Waynbaum to search for a particular function that would justify it. This vascular arrangement exists, Waynbaum conjectured, to allow the facial branch of the main carotid artery to act as a safety valve for the brain, where blood supply can vary only within narrow limits. Waynbaum also suggested that these regulatory muscular actions of the face have subjective consequences, such that changes in CBF caused by facial motor movement are reflected as changes in feeling states. He did not disagree with Darwin (1955) that the function of emotional facial gestures is to communicate the individual's internal states to those around him, but, rather, that they do not in themselves have hedonic consequences. Waynbaum's focus on these consequences was more in line with the thinking of James (1890), who wrote

> Smooth the brow, brighten the eye, contract the dorsal rather than the ventral aspect of the frame, and speak in a major key, pass the genial complement, and your heart must be frigid indeed if it does not gradually thaw! (pp. 1067–1068)

The VTEE was based on physiology of the turn of the century. It is not surprising, therefore, that several of Waynbaum's (1907) assumptions are questionable and other are outright wrong (Burdett, 1985; Fridlund and Gilbert, 1985; Izard, 1985; Zajonc, 1986). For instance, arterial flow is unlikely to be much affected by muscular action of the face because it is under the control of so many other central factors that the periphery can have only negligible direct effects. However, much of Waynbaum's thinking can be useful (Zajonc, 1986) and can actually be correct, albeit for the wrong reasons. For instance, facial muscles might not have a significant effect on arteries, but they can affect venous flow. More important, facial action might alter temperature of blood entering the brain by interfering or facilitating cooling. Such a process may, in turn, have subjective effects through its impact on the neurochemical activity in the brain. We develop this point more extensively later.

Independent of the validity of the *particular* physiological processes that could be involved in producing subjective effects, the basic principle that facial efferents may have regulatory functions, and thereby subjective consequences, has a great deal of plausibility and, if true, profound theoretical importance. If true, VTEE organizes diverse findings such as biofeedback, placebo effects, unconscious preferences and aversions, the growth of preference with repeated exposure, empathy, and such actions as fingernail biting or scratching one's forehead (Zajonc, 1986). It moreover offers a better understanding of the universality of emotional expression and of its recognition across cultures and species. The *particular* neurophysiological and neurochemical processes are yet to be specified by empirical investigations. Useful speculations about such processes that would guide future research, however, can be made now.

A testable hypothesis that follows from VTEE is that facial efferents can produce changes in brain blood temperature, which, in turn, have significant hedonic consequences (Stellar, 1982). Hedonic consequences are obtained for a variety of reasons. For instance, subjective changes can be obtained because changes in brain temperature can facilitate and inhibit the release and synthesis of a variety of neurotransmitters. Thus, if a certain action of facial muscles results in changing the temperature in a particular brain region that is active in releasing norepinephrine, for example, then norepinephrine might be either partially blocked or released, and the individual might experience calming or excitation. Not all neurochemicals that have subjective effects are region-specific. Peptides, for example, are found in profusion throughout the brain, and a change in temperature might change the threshold of the enzymatic action that releases them.

To be sure, the conjecture that changes in brain temperature can influence the release and synthesis of neurohormones and neuroenzymes that are associated with subjective emotional states still needs empirical documentation, but it is consistent with the fact that all biochemical processes are affected by temperature. The Q_{10} law describes the proportional change in the rate of a reaction over a 10°C interval. Within the range of human body temperature, the value of Q_{10} for many processes is about 3, which means that a rise of 10°C increases a given reaction by as much as 300% (Precht, Christophersen, Hensel, and Larcher, 1973). Values of Q_{10} that are much smaller and much larger than the typical, however, are quite common. In the immune system, these values vary over a very wide range, with some reactions requiring minute temperature changes. For example, thymus-dependent antigens have Q_{10} values as high as 1,000 to 5,000, whereas thymus-independent antigens have Q_{10} values of only 2 (Jampel, Duff, Gershon, Atkins, and Durum, 1983; Miller and Clem, 1984). Less is known about the temperature dependence of the neurotransmitters implicated in emotional reactions. But there are indications that these, too, as do most neurochemical processes, vary with regional cerebral temperature. For instance, a decrease in the neuronal accumulation of adrenaline by a factor of 3.6 was found when the spleen temperature of the Atlantic cod (*Gadus morhua*) was lowered by 10°C to 14°C (Ungell, 1984).

It suffices for present purposes to note that (a) brain temperature is partially regulated by the cavernous sinus, a venous structure that surrounds the internal carotid as it enters the brain (see Figure 12.1), (b) that the cavernous sinus receives cooled blood from some facial veins, and (c) that facial action can cool the blood in these veins by direct mechanical action on the veins (such as Waynbaum, 1907, proposed) or by allowing greater air flow of ambient temperature into the nasal cavity. Finally, we will make the plausible assumption that some temperature changes of the brain are correlated with hedonic states.

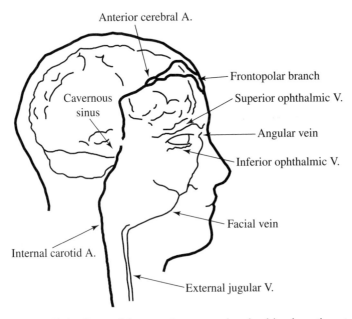

Figure 12.1   Parts of the vascular system involved in phonetic output and homologous emotional expressions.

Thermoregulation of the brain is controlled mainly by the [397] anterior hypothalamus and preoptic area (Satinoff, 1964). Numerous findings (e.g., Corbit, 1969, 1973; Dib and Cabanac, 1984) show that hypothalamic cooling is a rewarding event of considerable incentive value.

Behavioral aspects of thermoregulation, such as shivering, panting, or vasodilating, are controlled by the anterior and the lateral hypothalamus (Satinoff and Shan, 1971). It is significant that these behaviors can be elicited not only by changes in temperature but by emotional stimuli as well. In general, there is a close link, both at the behavioral and the physiological level, between thermoregulation and emotion. For example, the bilateral lesion of the anterior hypothalamus-preoptic area in the snake disturbs equally courtship behavior and thermoregulation (Krohmer and Crews, 1987). Also, it has been shown recently (Hori, Kiyohara, Shibata, and Oomura, 1986) that thermosensitive neurons in the preoptic area show a significant change in activity in response to emotional stimuli.

Cooling of the brain is a crucial physiological function. The brain, which is a heat producer many times more active than any other tissue, is also an organ that cannot tolerate temperature variations as readily as do other organs. In the upper limits, the human brain can tolerate temperatures up to about 40.5°C, whereas the trunk often reaches much higher temperatures. For example, trunk temperature during marathon running goes as high as 42°C (Cabanac, 1986; Caputa, 1981). The temperature of the human brain depends on the rate of heat production in its cells, cerebral blood flow, and the temperature of the blood that supplies the brain. The cooling of the brain relies heavily on heat exchange, whereby venous blood cooled by evaporation exchanges heat with arterial blood that enters the brain. In addition, brain temperature is controlled conductively by the temperature of venous blood that reaches the cavernous sinus, a venous configuration enveloping the internal carotid just before the latter enters the brain. This structure, which is the only one in the body in which an artery passes in the interior of a vein, participates actively in the regulation of brain temperature (Figure 12.1). The cavernous sinus is able to perform this function because its veins (that drain blood from nasal and oral mucosa) are air cooled in the course of normal breathing. In an elegant experiment, Kluger and D'Alecy (1975) demonstrated the role of breathing in the cooling of the hypothalamic temperature via the cavernous sinus. Using a reversible tracheal canula, they were able to observe rabbits that were either breathing normally or directly through the trachea, thus bypassing the upper nasal passage and, therefore, also the cavernous sinus. Measures of hypothalamic temperature revealed an increase when the cavernous sinus was bypassed. When the rabbits were breathing normally, the hypothalamic temperature was 0.3°C lower than rectal temperature. When the rabbits were breathing directly through the trachea, their brain temperature rose to the level of rectal temperature. Parallel results are reported for dogs by Baker, Chapman, and Nathanson (1974).

It is here that contact can be made between the kind of speculation that Waynbaum (1907) offered and what we now know about brain blood processes, thermoregulation, and facial efference. In several emotional expressions, the muscles of the face press against facial veins that empty into the cavernous sinus. And more important, breathing pattern is altered, enhancing or impeding nasal air intake. Both the rate of ambient air intake and the venous flow to the cavernous sinus may have significant roles in altering brain temperature. In a thorough review of research on brain cooling, Baker (1982) described the anatomy and the vascular thermoregulation process in ways that make the VTEE hypothesis quite plausible:

> The cavernous sinus receives venous blood from the nasal mucosa and the skin of the face. Anteriorly, the nasal mucosal veins empty into veins of the palate and into the subcutaneous dorsal and lateral nasal veins, which also drain the skin of the face. Blood in these veins can enter the cavernous sinus via the angularis oculi and ophthalmic veins …or can flow into the facial vein and then into the external or internal jugular, bypassing the cavernous sinus. This pattern of venous drainage appears to be similar in most mammals studied …, including humans. Since there are no valves in the angularis oculi vein, flow in this vessel can be in either direction. … Magilton and Swift (1969) found that the dorsal nasal, angularis oculi, and facial veins in the dog had thick muscular walls and suggested that flow could be diverted either to the cavernous sinus or to the external jugular vein by constriction of one or the other pathways. The direction and rate of blood flow in the angularis oculi vein in humans is dependent upon the thermal state of the subject (Caputa, Perrin, and Cabanac, 1978). Blood flow was low and directed toward the face in cool subjects. In subjects with elevated deep body temperatures, blood flow was higher and directed away from the face toward the cavernous sinus. (pp. 86–87)

Thus, when brain temperature is elevated, blood can be cooled by evaporation on the face and directed toward the cavernous sinus. In some forms of facial emotional efference, the zygomatic muscle, for example, presses against the deep facial vein that receives blood from the angular vein whose tributaries are the supraorbital and the supratrocheal veins (see Figure 12.1). Constricted at the same time are the superior and the inferior [398] ophthalmic veins. All of these veins empty into the cavernous sinus that cools the internal carotid artery as it enters the brain.

The role of the cavernous sinus is indeed important, and perhaps unique, in thermoregulation. Baker and Hayward (1968) concluded "that the changes in brain temperature which we observe in conscious mammals are not due to changes in local cerebral blood flow or in local neuronal metabolism" and wrote that they "have never observed temperature changes in the brains of conscious animals which were not due to changes in temperature of the arterial blood perfusing the brain" (p. 576). Cooling cannot occur by a reaction that lowers the level of local metabolic activity because it would disturb the ongoing brain processes and the life functions they control. The same can be said about local cerebral blood flow. Although local temperature could be changed by a flow of cooler blood to warmer regions, a change of blood flow for cooling purposes alone would also disrupt vital functions. Thus, the brain must be cooled by an external source and process, and if the arterial blood passing through the cavernous sinus does not change its temperature, hypothalamic temperature will not change either.

Winquist and Bevan (1980) have demonstrated bidirectionality of blood flow in the facial vein of the rabbit, finding that it is extremely sensitive to minute changes in temperature. An increase of only 1°C produced a 100% increase in the vascular myogenic tone of the facial vein. More important, with respect to the relationship between thermoregulation and the emotions, Winquist and Bevan pointed out that the buccal segment of the facial vein shows an unusual preponderance of β-adrenergic receptors. Therefore, if it is true that altered brain temperature can influence the neurochemistry of the brain, then if we can influence the cooling capacity of the cavernous sinus, we will succeed in altering subjective feeling state. One clue to this process can be found in the discomfort we experience during the common cold and profuse nasal congestion. Under these conditions, the cooling action of the cavernous sinus is severely restricted, and as a result, we feel distinct discomfort. Likewise, individuals with a deviated septum, a condition that impairs efficient air cooling of the angularis occuli and the ophthalmic veins, often suffer recurrent headaches. At the extreme end of the continuum, many patients who, for various reasons, must breathe through tubes inserted directly into the trachea, and thus bypassing the cavernous sinus, experience severe emotional shock (Bendixen, Egbert, Hedley-Whyte, Laver; and Pontoppidan, 1965).

In some cases of severe chronic nose bleeding, a procedure is performed that consists of packing the nose with gauze tampon. The pack is so tight that no ambient air reaches the nasal mucosa, and the patient feels essentially incapable of taking any air through the nose. The procedure can result in a violent emotional reaction, quite often that of severe panic. On removal of the pack, the patient experiences exceptional relief. Monkeys whose nasal airways were packed developed severe distress symptoms, and to some rats this procedure is fatal after only a few hours (P. S. Vig, personal communication, November 1988).

The role of the cavernous sinus in these surgical procedures has never been explored. The nasal-pulmonary syndrome, which has as one of its features the panic felt by the patient, is attributed to hypoxia. However, research indicates no differences in oxygen desaturation for patients with and without nose packing (Taasan, Wynne, Cassisi, and Block, 1981). There is after all, sufficient air intake through the mouth. More likely is the possibility that the failure of cooling the cavernous sinus is responsible for the panic attacks that the patients suffer.

It has also been supposed that individuals who are mouth-breathers prefer air intake through the mouth because of some nasal obstruction or difficulty. The supposition is based on the least effort hypothesis, which holds that because there are two sources of air intake, the individual will use the one that requires least effort. However, research by Vig (1985) and his colleagues (e.g., Drake, Keall, Vig, and Krause, 1988; Spalding and Vig, 1988) that examined the least effort hypothesis consistently failed to find changes in the proportion of total air breathed nasally as a function of changes in nasal resistance. That is, even when breathing through the nose is made very difficult and effortful, the proportion of nasal breathing is largely unaffected. This must mean that nose breathing serves another function besides taking in air, very likely that of cooling the cavernous sinus.

If facial efference occurring in the course of an emotional experience has an influence on the cavernous sinus, then it, too, will cause altered subjective feeling states. Stellar (1982) noted quite explicitly that "an operantly produced change in temperature on the skin or in the brain is a highly rewarding hedonic process" (p. 390). From experiments on thermoregulation cited earlier (e.g., Corbit, 1969, 1973), we would expect a slight cooling of the brain to be rewarding and a rise above normal to be noxious.

THEORETICAL VIEWS OF THE SOURCES OF SUBJECTIVE STATES

The two large divisions among theories of emotion, the feedback view and the cognitive appraisal view, assign roles to facial efference that differ in significance. The feedback position regards facial action as virtually necessary to the subjective emotional experience, whereas cognitive appraisal theory has no specific predictions to make about the subjective effects of facial action.

This article is mainly concerned with two aspects of the emotional process—facial efference and subjective state. It seeks to determine if there is a causal path from the first to the second, and what are the specific links in this process. In Figures 12.2 and 12.3, we diagram the basic concepts of the theories of emotion just discussed. We show only those factors with which we are concerned here, facial efference and subjective slate. We then diagram the process hypothesized by VTEE that links facial efference to feeling.

Note that, in general, facial feedback theories do not require extensive computation of the stimulus as a necessary prerequisite for either facial efference or feeling—nor does VTEE, as shown in Figure 12.4.

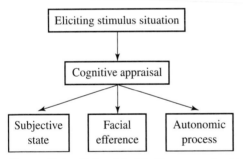

Figure 12.2   Role of facial efference and subjective feeling in cognitive appraisal theories.

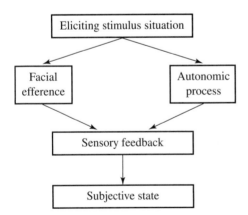

Figure 12.3   Role of facial efference and subjective feeling in facial feedback theories.

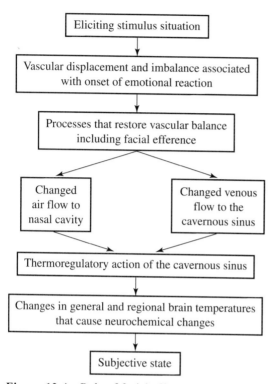

Figure 12.4   Role of facial efference and subjective feeling in the vascular theory of emotional efference.

Specificity of Emotions

Cannon (1927) and James (1890) represent the opposing views on the question of specificity of emotions. For Cannon, there was virtually no physiological specificity, whereas for James, physiological specificity was a necessary basic premise. [399] Nearly 100 years of research has shown that the sort of specificity of emotions that exists at the level of semantic labels is not paralleled in the fundamental correlates of emotion—the subjective, the physiological, and the efferent. Thus, although the distinction between guilt and shame is quite clear at the semantic level, it is otherwise obscure.

More than 30 years ago. M.A. Wenger and Cullen (1958) took measures of nine autonomic nervous system (ANS) variables in reaction to 14 stimulus situations, such as an injection, cold pressor, and electric shock. Of course, different stimuli elicited different ANS patterns. However, nothing systematic was learned from the experiment because one could not connect the reactions to the stimuli in a meaningful way.

There are good reasons why this is so. First, there is no one-to-one correspondence at the afferent point of the emotional process, that is, between the eliciting stimulus and emotion. Even for the same individual, the same stimulus will often evoke different emotions on different occasions, habituation being only one among a host of factors that introduce changes in emotional reaction to the same stimulus.

The sensory quality of the eliciting stimulus plays an important role as well. The fear of receiving a failing grade on an exam and the fear of snakes, of loud noises, or of punishment are all types of fear. But the sensory processes in these emotional reactions are quite different, and because these sensory processes are integrated into the physiological reaction, emotions evoked by different sensory and cognitive events will have different physiological responses.

Second, there is *no* one-to-one correspondence at the efferent point of the emotional process either. Many, but not all, emotions originate a chain of motivated action. Often, this action is initiated even before the sensory signal is consciously registered, as for example, in the case of pain reactions. Hence, emotional expressions often overlap with instrumental acts.

Physiological changes take place not only in the course of instrumental action, but even in the anticipation of such action. Obviously, different physiological demands are placed on the angry organism that lurches in blind fury than on the organism that remains immobile and freezes.

More important, some emotions require no instrumental acts at all. The positive emotions, such as joy, pleasure, or happiness, for example, do not instigate instrumental behavior following the emotion because there is nothing to correct or adjust. Generally, although the positive emotions may instigate instrumental action to gain an emotional experience later, the negative emotions elicit instrumental acts afterward to remove the distress. Fear, anger, rage, and disgust, as soon as they had been experienced, motivate complex and often vigorous behavior. Happiness and pleasure do not. Because the negative emotions place substantial energy demands on the organism (e.g., preparation for flight or fight), different autonomic reactions should be expected than from positive emotions. But the differences in these reactions derive not from differences in expressive aspects of the emotions but in their instrumental consequences.

Anger that is repressed and contained will evoke a different physiological response than anger that is expressed in a furious [400] attack. Ax (1953) reported an increase in diastolic blood pressure under conditions of manifested anger, but suppressed anger was found to be associated with a decrease in diastolic pressure by Funkenstein, King, and Drolette (1957). Escape from a threatening stimulus must be associated with a very different ANS pattern than freezing.

Not only are the three components weakly intercorrelated, these correlations must surely vary from individual to individual. Take facial efference as an example. There are significant differences in skeletal and muscular structure of the face. The *risorius Santorini* shows enormous range of variation (Gray, 1985, p. 445), as do other muscles and skeletal structures of the face. There are also differences in the reinforcement history of an individual's display behavior. Some children are lavished with rewards for their first smile; others may be ignored. Societies differ in the degree to which emotional efference is permitted to surface as an outward signal, and the display rules that relate facial efference to particular eliciting events differ as well. Moreover, they differ depending on the audience that might be present (Ekman, 1984). It clearly follows that there will be significant individual differences in expressive facial acts.

Despite the disagreement on the taxonomic boundaries of emotion labels, there is virtually full agreement about one important fact—emotions can be discriminated from each other quite reliably according to their positive-negative hedonic polarity. Many theorists consider this polarity to be a fundamental feature of all emotions (Plutchik, 1984; Russell and Bullock, 1986; Tomkins, 1962, to name only a few). The significance of the positive-negative polarity has been underscored by theoretical and empirical work claiming asymmetrical structures for the two polarities (e.g., Davidson, 1984). Consequently, the empirical work presented here focuses exclusively on this fundamental hedonic polarity and does not aspire to shed light on emotion specificity.

EMPIRICAL EVIDENCE ON THE LINK BETWEEN FACIAL EFFERENCE AND SUBJECTIVE STATE

Most aspects of the basic questions we raised earlier in the article cannot be resolved without further empirical work. We are not yet in a position of designing critical experiments that would definitively establish the causes of subjective feeling states in emotion, mainly because subjective states and facial action cannot be manipulated independently of one another. So far, no method exists whereby a subjective emotional state can be induced while final action is arrested. Even if we were to use patients suffering facial paralysis, we could not be entirely sure that all muscular facial impulses, especially those of low amplitude, were absent. And in these patients, the cavernous sinus action is not critically deficient. But we are in a much better position in attempting to elicit facial efference in the absence of *prior* emotional arousal. If facial efference can *by itself* induce positive or negative affect, then, according to VTEE, natural facial gestures having no apparent tie with emotions, but which have a similar muscular and cutaneous topography, must also produce such effects. The following studies offer data showing that facial movement alone, elicited not by emotional stimuli but by conditions unrelated to emotion, is capable of producing a subjectively felt hedonic experience. The studies must not be understood to claim that facial efference is a *necessary condition* for the elicitation and modification of subjective feeling states, nor that its effects are very powerful. What will be claimed, however, is that facial efference in itself can produce altered subjective feeling states.

To examine the hypothesis that facial action, unrelated to emotion, can in itself produce subjective feelings, a naturally occurring facial action was examined for its affective consequences. Consider the following example. The French vowel *u* (as in *sur*) or the German vowel *ü* (as in *für*), require a vigorous action of muscles around the mouth. Benguerel and Cowan (1974) have demonstrated that the upper lip protrusion that accompanies pronunciation of the French *u* begins four to six phonemes in advance of its actual production. The zygomatic muscle, which is contracted in smiling, is extended in uttering *ü*. whereas the corrugator performs the same action in various negative emotions and in uttering *ü*. In addition, the nostrils are constricted, reducing air flow to cool veins draining into the cavernous sinus. If facial action alone can induce subjective feeling changes, either by virtue of some form of facial feedback or by the causal chain that is suggested here, then uttering certain phonemes, whose pronunciation requires muscle movements analogous to those in emotional expressions, should reveal objective and subjective emotional effects.

STUDY 1

Method

SUBJECTS   A total of 26 native German speakers, who were either exchange students, visiting scholars, or University of Michigan professors and who spoke German daily, were solicited to participate in the following study. They ranged in age from 20 to 65 years. The ostensive purpose of this and of the following four studies was that they dealt with language acquisition.

MATERIALS   Four short (approximately 200 words) stories were written in German for the purposes of Study 1. Of the four stories, two contained a high frequency of the vowel *ü,* whereas the remaining two contained no words at all with the vowel *ü.* Two sets of stories were compiled, each consisting of one *ü* story and one no-*ü* story. One set of stories involved young boys, Peter and Jürgen (in the no-*ü* story and in the *ü* story, respectively), who wished for their birthdays either dogs and cats (Hunde und Katzen) or foxes and hens (Füchse *und* Hühner). The second set of stories were written in the style of newspaper articles, depicting Peter Meier, who excelled in shot put (Kugelstosser), and Günter Müller, a promising young hurdler (Hürdenläufer). Within each set, every attempt was made to match the *ü* and no-*ü* stories for emotional tone and semantic content.

PROCEDURE   Each subject was asked to read aloud one set of two stories: one half of the subjects read an *ü* story first followed by a no-*ü* story, and one half read the stories in the opposite order. To obtain an indication of cerebral temperature changes, thermographic images of subjects' faces were collected using an AGA infrared Thermographic 782M system. The argon-cooled thermographic camera takes an infrared television image that generates isotherms of surface temperature variations. Depending on the range of temperature variations investigated, different absolute degrees of resolution can be obtained. For our purposes, a range of variation was selected that generated a resolution of 0.5°C, which was found adequate at the aggregate level. After a 10-min. habituation period that stabilized facial temperature, baseline images were collected from each subject prior to reading each story. Subsequent images were taken immediately after subjects read each of the four paragraphs of a story. **[401]**

After reading both stories aloud, subjects completed a questionnaire probing both their affective reactions to the stories and their recall of the information conveyed. The affect questions asked the subject to make pairwise comparisons of the two stories regarding the suitability of each story for children, their relative resemblance to a fable, the quality of the German prose, the formality of the language, which story was more interesting, and most important, which of the two was more pleasant and which the subject liked better. Free recall questions for the animal stories asked for the names of the protagonists, the color of a truck that brought the animals, which birthday was being celebrated, and what animals the children wished for and received. Similar items were asked in the sports stories.

Results

Two points on the subject's forehead, midway between the eyebrows and the hairline and directly above the pupil of the eye, were measured for surface temperature. These points are on or near the frontopolar branch of the anterior cerebral artery, which issues from the internal carotid as it enters the brain. Hence, the distance of these arteries from the cavernous sinus is small, and the locations give reliable estimates of changes in brain temperature.[1] Individual change scores were calculated by subtracting each subject's baseline temperature from their subsequent temperature at the same two points on the forehead following the first, second, third, and fourth paragraphs. These change scores were then subjected to a 2 × 2 × 2 × 4 (Phoneme × Story Set × Lateral Position × Paragraph) mixed-design repeated measures analysis of variance (ANOVA).

The two forms (one from each set) of the *ü* stories did not differ from one another either in thermographic measures or in subjective ratings. The same was true of the two forms of the no-*ü* stories. Also, no differences were detected in temperature changes between the left and the right frontal locations. However, forehead temperatures changed markedly when subjects read the *ü* stories. The mean rise for the reading of the *ü* stories was +0.30°C, whereas there was virtually no temperature change (+0.02°C) for the no-*ü* stories. This difference was significant at the .001 level, $F(1, 24) = 18.16$. Also, the rise for the *ü* stories was significantly different from each subject's baseline, $t = 5.55, p < .001$, and not significant for the no- *ü* stories, $t = 0.45$. Figure 12.5 indicates that the change in temperature observed for the *ü* stories was not gradual, but, rather, it rose sharply during the first paragraph and remained elevated for the remainder of the *ü* stories.

At the subjective level, the no-*ü* stories were liked significantly better than the *ü* stories by 78% of the subjects ($p < .005$), and 81% ($p < .001$) found the no-*ü* stories more pleasant. No differences were found between the *ü* and no-*ü* stories in how interesting they were, which was written in better or more formal German, which was more like a fairy tale, and which was more suitable for children. The accuracy of recall was quite high, and no differences between stories were obtained. Hence, differences in the ease of processing apparently did not contribute to the obtained differences.

STUDY 2

Elevated negative affect, which, in the first study, was manifested by elevated forehead temperatures and the lower pleasantness and liking ratings, was attributed to the muscular movements made in reading material containing the frequent occurrence of the phoneme *ü*. But a possibility remains that the muscular movements were not actually necessary for the physiological and subjective changes that we found in association with uttering the phoneme *ü*. If there was a quality in the semantic patterns, for

---

[1] Typically, brain temperature in humans is estimated from tympanic membrane (Baker, Stocking, and Meehan, 1972; Benzinger, 1969). However, these measures are intrusive; for instance, one of the criterion for a proper placement of the probe against the membrane is the subject's affirmation of an acute pain (Brinnel and Cabanac, in press). As we noted above, in several veins of the head that are implicated in the thermoregulation of the brain, blood flows in both directions. This is true of the ophthalmic veins (Caputa, Perrin, and Cabanac, 1978), of the angularis oculi (Baker, 1982), and of the mastoid and parietal emissary veins (Cabanac and Brinnel, 1985). When the brain temperature is elevated, flow in these veins is from the surface toward the brain. But in the case of hypothermia, the flow is away from the brain and toward the surface of the skin. Hence, some surfaces of the face and head are a good indication of the thermal status of the brain. The forehead represents such an area. Although forehead temperature cannot be used to estimate absolute levels of brain temperature, it is a good estimate of *changes* in brain temperature (see, e.g., Germain, Jobin, and Cabanac, 1987; McCaffrey, McCook, and Wurster, 1975).

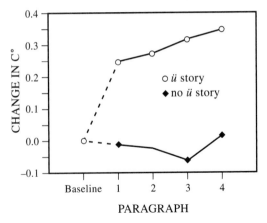

Figure 12.5 Changes in facial temperature for reading *ü* and *o* stories.

example, that made the *ü* stories less pleasant independent of the subjects' facial muscular involvement, and if the subjective experience deriving from this quality (and established perhaps by some form of interoceptive conditioning) acted to increase facial temperature, then it cannot be claimed that facial muscular movement is a sufficient condition for change in subjective affective state.

It is the case that beyond differences in liking and pleasantness ratings, the stories were not judged to be different in their quality of German, interestingness, or suitability for children. Nor were there any recall differences. But there could have been other unmeasured properties of the stories that were responsible for the obtained differences. For example, it might be possible that *ü* is semantically associated with generally negative affect. This is unlikely, however, because a vast number of positive words contain the phoneme *ü* in German. Many German nouns that in the first syllable contain *u* change it into *ü* in their plural form. This would mean that if *ü* is associated with negative [402] affect, the same must hold for *u*. More important, however, such nouns also change *u* into *ü* in their diminutive form (e.g., *Mutter-Mütterchen, Bruder-Brüderlein*), and the diminutive form is clearly a mark of particularly positive affect. Nevertheless, an experiment was carried out for the purposes of further control, using subjects who could not process the semantic content; that is, Americans who could not speak or understand German, and whose native language does not contain the phoneme *ü*.

If some form of conditioning takes place in the German subjects' early linguistic experience whereby negative affect is conditioned to the sound *ü*, such conditioning is not possible for American subjects because these subjects have virtually never been exposed to the sound *ü* as a conditioned stimulus, nor have they ever learned to produce the response *ü*. Even for Germans, it is quite unlikely that *ü* could have become *uniquely* conditioned to negative affect, inasmuch as words containing *ü* are likely to have positive as well as negative valence.

Nevertheless, new insights can be gained by comparing a population that has access to the semantic content of the stories with one that does not. Because of the obvious constraints in Study 2, therefore, subjects did not read the stories, but they listened to them instead. This aspect of the experiment makes the comparison between native

Germans and Americans especially informative, because if both the German and the American subjects show negative affect that is equal in strength to that obtained as a result of uttering the phoneme *ü*, then we would conclude that facial muscular action is not necessary for the elicitation of negative subjective feelings.

Method

SUBJECTS A total of 20 native German and 20 American subjects who spoke no German participated in this study. The American subjects were recruited from the University of Michigan subject pool and they received credit in an introductory psychology course for their participation. Of the German subjects, 12 had participated in the previous study; the remaining 8 were recruited from the same population as in Study 1. The stories presented to the German subjects who participated in the previous research were never those that they had been exposed to in Study 1.

PROCEDURE Subjects listened to one of the two sets of stories used in Study 1, including one *ü* story and one no-*ü* story. The stories were played aloud. Baseline thermographic images were collected following habituation but before subjects listened to the stories. Because in Study 1, the major changes in temperature were evident after the first paragraph and no other temporal trends in forehead temperature were detected, changes in temperature were now observed by taking measures only before and after listening to the stories. Finally, subjects were asked to report subjective information similar to that gathered in Study 1. The German subjects were also asked to recall factual information as in Study 1. No recall data were collected from the American subjects.

Results

Data from 2 American subjects were excluded because of head movement artifacts. Data collected from the remaining American subjects revealed no significant shifts in temperature between listening to the *ü* and no-*ü* stories. Both story types resulted in small but insignificant elevations from subjects' baseline temperature, +0.07°C, $t(17) = 0.30$, $p < .24$, for the *ü* stories, and +0.03°C for the no-*ü* stories, $t(17) = 0.2$, $p < .77$.

German subjects from whom free recall data were collected showed no differences in recall of the two stories. Although German subjects experienced somewhat greater deviations from their baseline temperatures, +0.10°C for the *ü* stories and –0.22°C for the no-*ü* stories, these shifts were likewise insignificant, $t(19) = 0.54$, $p < .59$, and $t(19) = 1.80$, $p < .09$. Together with data from Study 1, this result indicates that motor involvement, such as was present in reading the stories, contributes in a significant degree to temperature change. The fact that German subjects show a somewhat greater, albeit nonsignificant, temperature change than do American subjects is probably due to the fact that they understand the stories. Therefore, they respond more uniformly to particular phrases and particular features than do the American subjects. These reactions may also involve some facial actions, such as smiles, frowns, surprise expressions, and raised eyebrows. Americans, too, may have made some minimal facial responses in listening to the stories, but, because they do not understand the content, their reactions are likely to vary randomly from subject to subject, preventing systematic effects.

In fact, a breakdown by story reveals that what appears to be a marginally significant drop in temperature of –0.22°C for Germans listening to the no-*ü* stories is primarily due to a significant reduction in temperature of approximately –0.30°C associated with a particular no-*ü* story entitled "Hunde und Katzen" or "Dogs and Cats," $t(9) = 2.25, p < .05$. Listening to the alternate no-*ü* story "Kugelstosser," about Peter Meier, a man who excelled in shot put, resulted in a much smaller (less than –0.10°C) and insignificant shift in temperature among the German subjects, $t(9)$ 0.56, $p < .59$. No parallel differences for stories were found among the American subjects.

The suspicion that one version of the no-*ü* stories ("Hunde und Katzen") aroused positive feelings among the German subjects who appreciated its content and therefore responded accordingly with an appropriate facial action, is supported by subjective evidence. Of German subjects listening to the "Hunde und Katzen" story, 80% liked it better and rated it as more pleasant and less formal than they did the corresponding *ü* story. These differences were significant at the .05 level for each of the three ratings. Germans listening to the alternate set of stories showed no systematic preference between the *ü* and no-*ü* stories.

Parallel findings were obtained in Study 1. The "Katzen und Hunden" story was perceived as more pleasant than the "Kugelstosser" story in that study as well. However, no corresponding significant differences were found in temperature changes.

As noted, no significant differences between story sets was found for American subjects in Study 2. These subjects, however, did show a marginally significant preference for the no-*ü* stories, as 70% of these subjects reported liking the no-*ü* stories better and finding them more pleasant ($p < .06$) than the *ü* stories. American subjects also found the *ü* stories more interesting, whereas German subjects found the no-*ü* stories somewhat more interesting. This interaction is significant at the .02 level. The other subjective measures showed no significant main effects or differences between Germans and Americans.

The results of Study 2 support the proposition that facial [403] movement contributes significantly to altered subjective feeling. It does not rule out the possibility, however, that changes in subjective feeling may occur for other reasons. In Study 2, facial movement was not eliminated; it was merely reduced. If there was any facial action at all, it was now elicited when subjects reacted to the semantic content of the stories. Temperature associated with positive subjective reaction to a particular story suggests that content of the stimulus materials may have induced some facial movement and may have therefore constituted a source of confounding in the first two studies. The studies that follow seek to exclude any such confounding effects deriving from semantic content.

STUDY 3

Study 3 seeks to examine the affective reactions to a naturally occurring muscular movement that is free from virtually any semantic or affective content. Semantic content, except for phonetic symbolism, was eliminated as completely as possible by having subjects utter phoneme sounds. The task, thus, consisted simply of repeatedly pronouncing the phoneme *ü* and a control phoneme *o*. If differences are now obtained in forehead temperature and in subjective ratings, there is less suspicion that the stories in Study I varied along dimensions that we did not measure but that nevertheless contributed to the obtained effects. There is also stronger support for the hypothesis that muscular movement of the face has objective and subjective affective consequences and that its effects are revealed in altered facial temperature. A comparison between German and American subjects would again be informative.

Method

SUBJECTS   A total of 20 native German speakers and 20 Americans served as subjects. The subjects were the same as in Study 2.

PROCEDURE   Both German and American subjects repeated aloud after a tape-recorded voice the vowel sounds *ü* and *o* 20 times each, at 3-s intervals. In the course of uttering the vowel phonemes, thermographic readings were taken before the vowel session (baseline) and after the 5th, 10th, 15th and 20th repetition of each vowel sound. Finally, subjects rated the two sounds on 7-point scales according to how pleasant, familiar, and difficult they were to produce, and how much they liked each sound.

Results

Data from 1 German and 2 American subjects were excluded from the analysis because of head movement artifacts. A 2 × 2 × 2 × 4 (Phoneme × Native Language × Lateral Position × Trial Blocks) mixed-design repeated measures ANOVA revealed significant temperature effects when subjects uttered the vowel sounds *ü* and *o* (Figure 12.6).

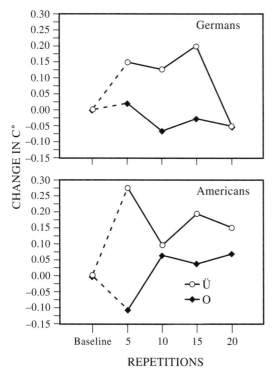

Figure 12.6   Changes in facial temperature for *ü* and *o* vowels.

The phoneme o had no apparent effect on forehead temperature, producing a change of only +0.02°C. In response to the phoneme $ü$, however, there was a rise of +0.14°C, $F(1, 35) = 4.40, p < .04$. The differences in temperature appeared to be slightly greater for the American speakers (+0.17°C and –0.02°C for the $ü$ and o, respectively) than for the German speakers (+0.11°C and –0.03°C). However, this interaction did not reach an acceptable significance level.

As seen in Figure 12.7, both German and American subjects liked the o sound better than the $ü$ sound and rated it as more pleasant, $t(36) = 7.70$, and $t(36) = 6.37, p < .001$, respectively, for liking and pleasantness for both groups together. It is interesting that the less the German subjects liked the vowel $ü$, the greater was their average rise in temperature across the 20 repetitions ($r = -.45, p < .05$). For the American subjects, however, this correlation was not significant.

American subjects, *but not the German subjects,* rated the $ü$ sound as less familiar, $t(17) = 4.51, p < .001$, and more difficult **[404]** to produce, $t(17) = 2.61, p < .02$, than the o sound. For the German speakers, o and $ü$ were equal in difficulty. Because we have here two samples showing similar affect ratings and similar temperature changes, and because one found the phoneme $ü$ difficult and the other found it easy, we can eliminate the possibility that o was perceived as more pleasant than $ü$ just because it was more familiar or easier to produce. The German subjects who found the two sounds equally familiar and equally difficult nevertheless had a decidedly more positive affective reaction to the o phoneme than to the $ü$ phoneme, $t(18) = 5.08, p < .001$. This preference for the phoneme o, although somewhat weaker, was also true for Americans, $t(18) = 3.83$, $p < .001$), for whom the phoneme $ü$ is strange and difficult.

To determine whether temperature change has an independent effect on liking, a set of multiple regression analyses were carried out in which liking was regressed on temperature change, familiarity, and difficulty ratings (see Table 12.1). Pleasantness ratings were not included in these analyses because they were very highly correlated with liking. As

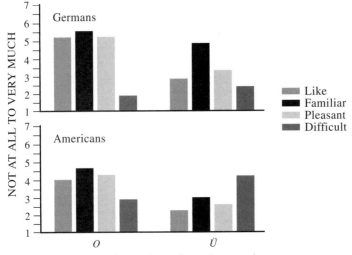

Figure 12.7 Subjective ratings of o and $ü$ vowels.

Table 12.1   Standardized regression coefficients for liking regressed on temperature change, familiarity, and difficulty in response to uttering *ü* and *o* phonemes.

Subjects/ condition	R^2	Temperature change	Familiarity	Difficulty
Germans				
o	.17	−.13	.37	−.09
ü	.61***	−.50***	.64***	.03
Americans				
o	.38	.10	.58**	−.09
ü	.50**	−.40*	.66***	−.02

* $p < .06$ ** $p < .02$ *** $p < .01$

shown in Table 12.1, the multiple regressions are significant and substantial for the *ü* conditions and not significant for the *o* condition. This is so because there was virtually no temperature effect for the phoneme *o,* and, hence, hardly any variance. The standardized regression coefficients are significant for the phoneme *ü,* both among the German as well as the American subjects. The data, therefore, can be taken as indicating that the subjective feeling associated with uttering phonemes is directly related to temperature change, even when other factors are held statistically constant.

DISCUSSION

The results of these studies indicate that muscular movement of the face, analogous to that involved in emotional expression, is a sufficient condition for the induction of affective reactions. At the level of the physiological measure used, as well as on the basis of subjective affect ratings, consistent results indicate that facial efference plays a significant role in generating affect.

In the aforementioned studies, we were able to eliminate artifacts due to task difficulty, affective reactions based on semantic content, and most important, artifacts that derive from the subjects making inferences about the relation between their own facial action and emotions such as are present in many studies of facial feedback. When the subjects were questioned after the experiment, none guessed that affect was of any interest in the study. Furthermore, none of the German subjects in the reading study spontaneously mentioned that the two stories differed in the frequency of the *ü* phoneme, although a few acknowledged it when this difference was pointed out to them. Finding similar results in Study 3 in subjective affect and objective measures for both German and American subjects eliminated the possibility that semantic symbolism played a role in the subjective and objective reactions. One cannot rule out, however, unconscious cognitive appraisal such as is postulated by Leventhal and Scherer (1987). But the influence of unconscious cognitive factors can be neither proven nor falsified (Zajonc, 1984) under the conditions of the present experiments, nor can it be specified what aspect of the stimulus or the situation was being appraised.

STUDY 4

Studies 1–3 succeeded only in generating negative affect by means of phonetic utterance. If we are to approximate emotional expressions by muscular action associated with phonetic utterance, it is useful to discover if positive affect can also be so generated. Study 4 examined subjective and objective reactions over seven vowel sounds—*i, e, o, a, ü, ah,* and *u*—in an attempt to discover if some of them produce positive affect. A priori, we would expect that the phoneme *e,* having facial action similar to a smile, and the phoneme *ah,* which is similar in muscular pattern to that in pleasant surprise, might have such effects. We would further expect that positive affect is associated with a drop in temperature. If so, then temperature will have become a new physiological measure, besides heart rate (Winton. Putnam, and Krauss, 1984) and brain asymmetry (Davidson, 1984) to discriminate affective polarity.

Method

SUBJECTS   A total of 26 male introductory psychology students at the University of Michigan participated in this study in partial fulfillment of a course requirement.

PROCEDURE   Subjects arrived separately and were informed that the experimenter would be with them momentarily. A 10-min. habituation period that stabilized facial temperature was necessary to ensure that subjects, who had been exposed to varying weather conditions, returned to a normal range of temperature. After this time elapsed, subjects were told that they would be involved in a study of language acquisition and were given a copy of the following instructions:

> The first segment of this experiment requires that you repeat seven vowel
> sounds aloud twenty times each following a tape-recorded voice. Please try
> to repeat each sound as accurately as possible even though several vowels
> may sound unfamiliar. Because you will be photographed periodically
> throughout these repetitions, it is extremely important that you do not move
> your head. Following each series of twenty repetitions you will be asked sev-
> eral questions about that particular vowel sound. Do you have any questions?

Subjects then repeated aloud after a tape-recorded voice the first vowel sound 20 times, at 3-s intervals. Thermographic readings were collected, as previously, prior to the vowel session (baseline) and following the 5th, 10th, 15th and 20th repetitions. After the 20 repetitions, subjects were asked to rate the sounds on 7-point scales according to how pleasant, familiar, and difficult it was to produce, as well as how **[405]** much they liked the sound and whether it put them in a good or bad mood. This procedure was repeated for the remaining six vowel sounds.

To control for possible order effects, one half of the subjects were presented with the seven vowel sounds in one order (*i, e, o, a, ü, ah, u*) and one half in another order (*i, ü, o, a, e, ah, u*). Note that only the phonemes that are of focal interest, namely *e* and *ü,* change places to control for position effects. The positions of the other phonemes remained constant.

Results

Two points on the subject's forehead, midway between the eyebrows and the hairline and directly above the pupil of the eye, were again measured for surface temperature, and as previously individual change scores were calculated by subtracting each subject's baseline temperature, taken immediately prior to a set of 20 repetitions from their subsequent temperature after the 5th, 10th, 15th, and 20th repetition of each vowel.

The mean of these change scores for each vowel was subjected to a 2 × 2 × 7 (Order × Lateral Position × Vowel Sound) mixed-design repeated measures ANOVA. This analysis revealed no significant differences in surface temperature between the left and right frontal locations. Likewise, the order in which subjects repeated the vowels appeared to have no effect on temperature. However, there was a significant temperature effect for the various vowel sounds, $F(6, 144) = 2.40, p < .05$.

Collapsing across order and right and left frontal location, the mean change scores for each of the vowel sounds are shown in Figure 12.8.

Tests revealed that the vowel sound $\ddot{u}$ resulted in a significant increase in forehead temperature from baseline, $t(25) = 2.24, p < .05$, whereas the sounds ah and e both resulted in a marginally significant decrease in temperature, $t(25) = 1.86, p < .07$, and $t(25) = 1.83, p < .08$, respectively.

In general, the subjective ratings are consistent with the changes in temperature. The phoneme that was associated with the highest rise in forehead temperature ($\ddot{u}$) was liked least and put the subjects in the worst mood, whereas the phonemes that were associated with the greatest decrease in forehead temperature (ah and e) were liked best, $t(25) = 3.45$, and $t(25) = 3.46$, respectively, $p < .01$, for both, and put subjects in the best mood, $t(25) = 2.41, p < .05$, and $t(25) = 1.58, p < .12$, respectively; see Figure 12.9A and 12.9B. Because order was counterbalanced for $\ddot{u}$ and $e,$ we can be fairly certain that the differences are due primarily to the muscular movements associated with pronouncing these phonemes.

Thus, the present study, along with previous results, confirms that the phoneme $\ddot{u}$ raises forehead temperature and receives the most negative affective ratings. But also, and more important, we found that some vowel phonemes are capable of decreasing

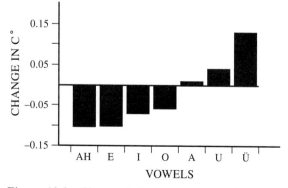

Figure 12.8 Changes in facial temperature for vowel phonemes.

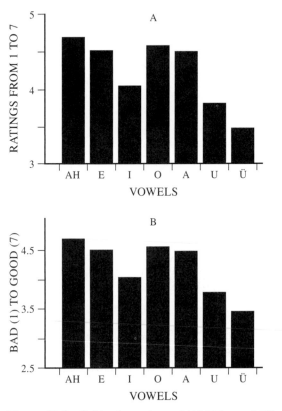

Figure 12.9   Subjective ratings of (A) liking and (B) mood for vowel phonemes.

temperature and eliciting positive subjective affect. This data represents a clear instance in which a physiological measure discriminated systematically between hedonic polarities. These findings, then, are in clear contrast to those that are generally obtained with such physiological measures as blood pressure and galvanic skin response (GSR) that discriminate only among hedonic intensities, and fail to discriminate between positive and negative affect. Thus far, there are only two such measures, recently discovered, heart rate (Winton et al., 1984) and brain asymmetry (Davidson, 1984).

It is important to note that both positive and negative reactions were obtained in association with different vowel sounds, and that these positive and negative reactions were highly consistent with changes in temperature, both at the aggregate and **[406]** at the individual level. For instance, even though forehead temperature increased for *ü* and decreased for *e* for both of these phonemes, the standardized regression coefficients for temperature change, when liking was regressed on temperature change, familiarity, and difficulty, were negative (–.36 and –.23 for *ü* and *e,* respectively). It is of interest that the results in the present study closely parallel the results in Study 3, in which we obtained a correlation of –.45 between liking and temperature change for the phoneme *ü.* Here, this correlation was –.43 for the phoneme *ü.* Thus, a hypothesis that seeks to explain affective ratings of vowel sounds on the basis of other factors, such as phonetic symbolism, familiarity, or effort would stop short of accounting for the correlated changes in temperature, obtained with these other factors held constant.

DISCUSSION

Taken together, Studies 1–4 strongly suggest that facial muscular action is capable of inducing positive and negative subjective feeling states. The data agree with the theoretical expectations based on VTEE in showing correlated changes in forehead temperature. The precise details of the process, of course, still need to be documented and described. However, in fundamental aspects, especially those that involve the role of the cavernous sinus in cooling the brain and its vulnerability to facial action, VTEE seems to be supported. In other words, because the pronunciation of *ü* restricts nasal respiration, restraining cooled blood before it reaches the cavernous sinus, brain temperature is likely to be elevated. The phonemes *e* or *ah,* on the other hand, expand nasal air access. Facial muscles constrict the veins carrying blood to the cavernous sinus in *u* and *ü,* but in uttering *e* or *ah,* these vessels are apparently free to carry blood unimpeded.

Still, more direct evidence is needed in exploring the role of temperature in subjective states. In a preliminary experiment on the role of nasal cooling of the cavernous sinus in humans, we observed forehead temperature in 6 subjects who placed a swimmers' clip on their noses, thus restricting nasal breathing. Measures were taken during a 1-min. baseline period (at onset and then after each of four 15-s intervals) and a 2-min. experimental period (at onset and after each of eight 15-s intervals). There was an average of 0.25°C difference between this experimental condition and the no-nose-clip control condition in temperature rise.

STUDY 5

If it is indeed the case that the cooling and warming of the cavernous sinus[2] plays a significant role in affective experiences, then we should be able to see these effects in reaction to a more direct manipulation. We might simply allow air that is slightly cooled or slightly warmed to enter the nasal cavity and observe the subsequent facial temperature and subjective state Baker and Hayward (1968) reported that when air at 25°C is blown over the nasal mucosa of the sheep, there is a precipitous temperature drop in the cavernous sinus, at the cerebral arteries, and in the brain. However, Baker and Hayward did not vary air temperature. An experiment with human subjects, similar to theirs but using ambient, cooled, and warmed air, would further strengthen the supposition that the temperature of the blood entering the brain has a great deal to do with subjective state.

The nose-clip study only dealt with temperature rise, but that effect could have been occasioned by a different process than the one we assumed to operate, because restricting airflow to the nasal arch may have a variety of confounding effects. Hence, it is desirable also to observe affective reactions when the cooling process is promoted. Note that other theories of emotional expression, such as facial feedback, are not able to predict whether cooling should be associated with pleasant or unpleasant subjective

---

[2] Some authors have recently questioned the cooling efficiency of the cavernous sinus in humans (C.B. Wenger, 1987).

state. Neither can the cognitive appraisal theory. A theory involving subcortical factors in the emotional subjective state has no means of making such a prediction either. However, VTEE makes the prediction that warm air intake should be unpleasant, whereas cool air intake should be experienced as pleasant.

Method

SUBJECTS   A total of 20 male introductory psychology students at the University of Michigan participated in this study in partial fulfillment of a course requirement.

PROCEDURE   In order to conceal the purpose of the experiment and to eliminate any possible connection to emotion, the experiment was presented as dealing with reactions to olfactory stimulation. Subjects arrived separately and were informed that the experimenter would be with them momentarily. A 10-min. habituation period that stabilized facial temperature was necessary to ensure that subjects, who had been exposed to varying weather conditions, returned to a normal range of temperature. After this time elapsed, subjects were told that they would be involved in a study of reactions to olfactory stimulation and given a copy of the following instructions:

> The experiment you will be participating in today involves individual differences in the perception of smell. You will be asked to smell several different scents, all of which are organic and totally harmless, and rate each on a variety of dimensions. During the two minute period in which you are evaluating a particular scent you will be photographed periodically. It is extremely important, therefore, that you find a comfortable position and do not move during the trials. Do you have any questions?

Air used in the three trials was generated by a heating and cooling unit, similar to that of a hair dryer, that was not visible to the subject. During the warm-air trial, the air was heated to 32.2°C (note that this is less than normal body temperature by about 5°C). Air temperature in the cool air trial was 18.9°C. During the oregano trial, air of 22.2°C was slightly scented using a porous sachet of oregano. The ambient room temperature varied between 20.0°C and 21.1°C, the same as in all previous experiments.

The air was funneled at a rate of 111 ml/s through a 156-cm length of Norton Tryon plastic tubing, 0.64 cm in diameter, with a 2.56-cm-long removable tip that was replaced for each subject for sanitary purposes. Subjects held the tip of the tubing immediately below their right nostrils throughout the 2 min. of a trial. The position of the tubing was justified to subjects on the grounds that otherwise they might miss some subtle scents. Even though there were substantial differences in air flow temperatures, no subject after debriefing indicated any awareness that the trials involved differing temperatures, perhaps because the trials were separated by approximately 3-min. intervals. **[407]**

To monitor cerebral blood temperature, thermographic readings were collected prior to each of the three trials (baseline), and every 15-s for the 2-min. duration of the trial. After each of the three trials, subjects were asked to rate the "scent" on 7-point scales, according to how pleasant, familiar, and sweet it was, as well as how much they liked it and whether they thought that smelling this scent for a prolonged period would be more likely to put them in a good mood or in a bad mood.

To control for possible order effects, one half of the subjects were presented with warm air on the first trial, then with oregano, and then with cool air on the last trial, whereas the remaining subjects received the cool air first and the warm air last.

Results

As before, two points on the subject's forehead, midway between the eyebrows and the hairline and directly above the pupil of the eye, were measured for surface temperature. Individual change scores for each of the three trials (warm air, oregano, cool air) were calculated by subtracting subjects' baseline temperature taken immediately prior to a given trial from their subsequent temperature at the same two points on the forehead from the eight subsequent readings taken at 15-s intervals during a trial.

The means of these change scores for the three trials (warm air, oregano, cool air) were subjected to a 2 × 2 × 3 (Order × Lateral Position × Trial) mixed-design repeated measures ANOVA. This analysis revealed no significant differences in surface temperature due to the order in which the warm and cool air were presented. Also, no significant differences in temperature between the left and right frontal locations emerged. However, there was a significant temperature effect for the air presented, $F(3, 54) = 4.75, p < .01$. The mean change scores for each of the trials are shown in Figure 12.10, collapsed across order and right and left frontal location.

Pairwise t tests reveal that during the warm-air trial, subjects' facial surface temperature rose significantly, $t(19) = 4.14, p < .01$. Conversely, during the cool-air trial, subjects showed a marginally significant decrease in temperature, $t(19) = 1.84, p < .08$. Although surface temperature rose slightly during the oregano trial, this increase was not significant.

Subjective ratings across the three trials are shown in Figure 12.11. Subjects liked the "scent" that was ostensibly introduced with the warm air significantly less than that with both oregano and cool air, $t(19) = 6.29$, and $t(19) = 3.80, p < .01$, for both. (Of course, as noted in the Method section, no scent accompanied the warm and cool-air trials.) This same trend was evident in subjects' ratings of how pleasant they found each of the trials, with the warm-air "scent" once again being given a significantly lower rating than both

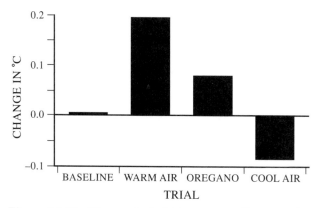

Figure 12.10   Changes in facial temperature for warm-air, oregano, and cool-air trials.

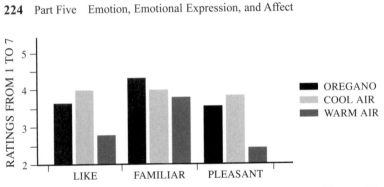

Figure 12.11 Rating of liking, familiarity, and pleasantness of "scents" in warm-air, oregano, and cool-air trials.

the oregano and the cool-air "scent," $t(19) = 6.29$, and $t(19) = 2.92$, $p < .01$, for both. No significant differences were found for familiarity or for the sweet-sour dimension.

The preceding findings show stronger effects for warm air than cool air, both in temperature change and in affective ratings. The increase in forehead temperature that was associated with warm air was greater than the drop associated with cool air, and liking ratings paralleled the temperature data. This result is entirely consistent with the differences between ambient air temperature and air that was introduced into the subjects' nasal cavities. Recall that ambient temperature of the laboratory room was kept at 20°C to 21°C. Thus, for warm air, the difference was +11.2°C to +12.2°C, whereas for cool air it was only –1.1°C to –2.1°C. It should not be surprising that our effect mirrors these differences with warm air, causing a more dramatic shift in both temperature and liking. For the same reason, oregano trials generated effects similar to cool-air trials. These differences between air introduced into the nasal cavities and ambient air were kept minimal in order to conceal from the subjects that temperature was a critical factor in the experiment. In fact, no subject became aware of temperature differences.

Table 12.2 shows the results of three multiple regression analyses in which liking ratings were regressed on temperature change [408] and familiarity. As previously, the standardized beta coefficients for the relation between liking and temperature change were significant, and in the case of warm air, in which the most pronounced temperature change occurred, they were quite substantial.

Table 12.2 Standardized Regression Coefficients for Liking Ratings Regressed on Temperature Change and Familiarity in Three Conditions of Air Induction

Condition	R^2	Temperature change	Familiarity
Cool air	.12	–.35	.06
Oregano	.31	–.29	.51*
Warm air	.36*	–.69**	.19

* $p < .02$ ** $p < .01$

Subjects' predictions as to whether smelling a particular scent for a prolonged period of time would be more likely to put them in a good mood or in a bad mood yielded similar results. Of the 20 subjects, 17 reported that the "scent." which they ostensibly smelled when warm air was introduced would induce a bad mood, departing significantly from chance ($p < .05$). In contrast, only 7 of the 20 subjects in both the cool-air and oregano trials suggested that this scent would result in a bad mood. If our assumptions are correct, these results may now be interpreted to mean that if facial efference results in subjective affective reactions, it does so by virtue of its influence over brain temperature. This is so because, in the absence of facial movement, the direct physical manipulation of the temperature reaching the cavernous sinus also results in affective changes, with cooling being felt positively and warming being felt negatively. Thus, Study 5 shows temperature once again to be a measure capable of discriminating between hedonic polarities.

GENERAL DISCUSSION

It appears, therefore, that muscular facial actions may have an independent influence over the individual's subjective feeling state. To the extent that pronouncing the phoneme *ü* constricts angular and ophthalmic veins and reduces air intake into the nasal cavity, cooling by the cavernous sinus is impeded and the blood entering the brain is not sufficiently cooled. Such a state is felt as discomfort, and subjects, in turn, rate the phoneme *ü* negatively. On the other hand, the more open phonemes *ah* and *e* do not restrict venous flow to the cavernous sinus and enhance free passage of ambient air (which, of course, is considerably cooler than venous blood) into the nasal cavity, thus cooling the venous blood in the ophthalmic veins that feed the cavernous sinus. In fact, *e* requires some distension of the nostrils. The uttering of the phoneme *e,* as in *cheese,* has a great topographical similarity to the muscular movement of a smile inasmuch as both require the contraction of the major zygomatic muscle. There is no reason to doubt that muscular movements elicited in the course of emotional episodes have similar effects. And the similarity of the phoneme *ah* to the facial actions often seen in delight and pleasant surprise, would lead one to expect low temperatures and positive subjective ratings for that phoneme as well.

The mediating role of cerebral temperature in the link between facial efference and subjective state is supported by a variety of facts. First, we did obtain a significant correlation between blood temperature and liking—the less the item was liked, the higher was the subject's rise in forehead temperature. A similar relation between temperature and emotion has been found in other contexts. Cohen, Izard, and Simons (1986) recently found forehead temperature to differentially track heart rate changes in 4 1/2-month-old infants expressing sadness or anger. Ekman et al. (1983) used finger temperature to distinguish between fairly specific emotions. Finger temperature, more often, is commonly used as a cue in biofeedback treatment of migraine headaches, which are typically associated with cerebral vascular disturbances (Mathew et al., 1980).

But there is also another line of research that has a bearing on the link between brain temperature and emotion and that can benefit from the concepts of VTEE. The metaphors *hot-head, boiling mad, hot under the collar,* and *cool as a cucumber* are not altogether accidental, and the present study is not the first to measure head temperature change in response to an emotional episode. More than 100 years ago, Lombard (1879) made just such measurements. More recently, extensive research has shown that aggression and negative affect occur more readily when ambient temperature is high (Baron, 1977). For example, one study demonstrated that when placed in high ambient temperature, subjects reported feeling more aggressive and rated a stranger in more hostile terms (Griffitt, 1970; Griffitt and Veitch, 1971). Significantly, aggression in the form of rape, murder, and assaults was also found to increase with elevated ambient temperature (Anderson and Anderson, 1984; Cotton, 1981; Harries and Stadler, 1988; Rotton and Frey, 1985), Reifman, Larrick, and Fein (1988) have found that in major-league baseball, the batter's likelihood of being hit by a pitched ball increases with ambient temperature. These studies simply assert that a relation exists between elevated temperature and negative affect, but they do not explain why. The concepts of VTEE that implicate the role of the cavernous sinus offer a plausible explanation.

The question about the role of facial efference in the experience of emotion, which is a fundamental problem for a theory of emotions, can now be better answered. There is now clearer evidence that facial movement *alone* is capable of inducing changes, albeit small, in the subjective feeling of the individual. And there is some suggestive information about how such effects are generated, which means that we are beginning to understand some of the processes underlying the experience of positive and negative affect.

To be sure, the process postulated here is complex, and many of its components remain to be investigated. But the theory is falsifiable, and the direction of future research is clear. Specific questions both at the behavioral and at the neurochemical level can be readily formulated. We assume that the process whereby emotional efference generates changes in subjective feeling state is essentially the same as one that we observe in more elementary phonetic action. We further assume that it consists of two links. First, muscular activity in uttering different phonemes changes brain blood temperature. Second, this change in temperature is sufficient to alter the individual's subjective state, which is probably due to the effects of changed temperature on neurochemical activity of the brain.

Each of these two links has an unknown probability of being true. The results of our experiments suggest that these probabilities are decidedly greater than zero. It is, indeed, somewhat of a surprise that muscular movement and nasal breathing can affect temperature to an extent sufficient to produce a subjectively felt affective reaction. The internal carotid carries a large volume of blood to the brain, and it carries it at a considerable rate. A significant drop in its temperature would require, it would seem, a large ambient change. Cabanac (1986) concluded that the cavernous sinus can keep the hypothalamus 1°C or more below trunk temperature. The data of Kluger and **[409]** D'Alecy (1975) show systematic changes in hypothalamic temperature when the cavernous sinus is not cooled by air breathed through the nose—changes that have very short latencies. Our data show similar changes. Ekman et al. (1983) observed a 0.15°C rise in finger temperature with emotional expression of anger held for only 10-s. Thus, the link between facial movements and brain temperature is now more than a mere hypothesis. But it requires more direct evidence.

The second assumption that temperature changes in the brain cause subjective changes is also supported (Stellar, 1982). The further supposition that the subjective changes derive from neurochemical effects brought about by brain temperature change is clearly speculative. There is considerable evidence, however, that neurochemical activity has dramatic effects on temperature (Brown, 1982; Clark and Bernardini, 1982; Hawkins and Avery, 1983; Kavaliers, 1982; Lee and Lomax, 1983; Lin and Pivorun, 1986; Morley, Elson, Levine, and Shafer, 1982; Thornhill and Saunders, 1984; Yehuda and Sheleff, 1985). For example, neurotensin, a peptide found primarily in the anterior hypothalamus—a structure important in thermoregulation—and in the nucleus accumbens—a structure implicated in emotional reactions—has pronounced hypothermic effects. A dose of 30 μg neurotensin was found to reduce rectal temperature in mice by as much as 17°C (Bissette, Nemeroff, Loosen, Prange, and Lipton, 1976). Note that neurotensin is known to produce excitation and, when injected centrally, to reduce aversion to painful stimuli (Cooper, Bloom, and Roth, 1986). Thus, because neurotensin produces both hypothermia *and* affective consequences, it is quite reasonable to suppose that the manipulation of hypothalamic temperature, achieved by any method, might also have affective consequences.

Because, according to the Q_{10} law, a 10°C drop reduces the rate of reactions threefold, such a profound temperature change must have widespread biochemical consequences. Systematic knowledge about temperature effects on neurochemical activity is scant, but not altogether absent. It has been demonstrated, for instance, that the adrenergic system is temperature dependent (e.g., Corwin, Malvin, Katz, and Malvin, 1984; Gandhi and Ross, 1987; U'Prichard and Snyder, 1977), as are some peptides (Zachary and Rosengurt, 1987). Often, the effects require very minimal changes in temperature (see Jampel et al., 1983, and Miller and Clem, 1984). Bode and Molinoff (1988) have found very substantial changes in the plasma membranes of cells with small temperature changes. The finding is important because the physical properties of cell membranes control neurotransmitter activity across the synapse.

One can certainly question the likelihood that differences in temperature as small as we obtained may have neurochemical effects and ensuing subjective influences.[3] Two observations apply here. First, the temperature changes were measured on the skin of the forehead as proxies for brain temperature changes, which may be considerably greater. Similar procedures resulted in greater changes in tympanic membrane temperature in our calibration and validation tests. Second, one would not expect strong neurochemical effects with small temperature changes if one takes as an anchor studies based on animal models. In these studies, the effects are observed on the basis of gross behavioral output. However, the effects we observed are in the form of subjective reports and are considerably more sensitive to even slight differences than are gross behavioral measures. Thus, both assumptions have substantial probabilities of being true, and each is readily falsifiable. More important, if correct, they lead to very important implications.

---

[3] The results we obtained here can be readily verified by the reader on the occasion of a mild headache. When such a headache arises, simply relax in a chair for a few seconds. Take 10 slow, deep breaths through the nose, and exhale through the mouth. Relax for 2 min. Take 5 breaths through the nose, exhaling through the mouth. A noticeable relief will be felt. We have administered the procedure to 50 headache sufferers. Except for severe sinus and migraine cases, the procedure was effective in reducing the discomfort by a considerable degree, and it acted much faster than aspirin—virtually in an instant. For control purposes, the reader may try inhaling and exhaling through the mouth. One could speculate that the hedonic effects obtained here may be mediated or accompanied by an analgesia coming from the action of endorphins that might be released more readily in lower brain temperatures.

The link between temperature change and the release of neurochemicals is not necessary for our purposes, inasmuch as the only part of the assumption required is that temperature change be capable—by any process—of altering hedonic tone. Nevertheless, it is a supposition that is highly plausible, given the systematic dependence of biochemical processes on temperature, and it is a supposition that, for many reasons, would be worthwhile to substantiate empirically.

It is significant that we did not obtain lateral differences in forehead temperature in any of the studies. These lateral differences have been repeatedly found (Fox and Davidson, 1986), although the hypothesis that the hemispheres perform distinct functions does not enjoy complete consensus (LeDoux, 1982). Absence, in the present research, of lateral differences in forehead temperature may be due to the communication between the left and the right supratrocheal veins through the transverse nasal arch before each drains into the supraorbital vein. The cavernous sinuses that form the circular sinus are also joined. The VTEE would thus not predict lateral differences, whereas a subcortical explanation of the results would suggest lateral differences. This, again, should not be construed to mean that, in general, subcortical processes play no role in the subjective experience.

It should be clear that we do not regard the vascular mechanisms that mediate subjective states to be unique or to act alone. Certainly, other physiological processes and systems are equally capable of influencing them. The amygdala has been demonstrated to play a major role in the elicitation of emotion by integrating sensory inputs (see Aggleton and Mishkin, 1986; Geschwind, 1965; LeDoux, in press; Rolls, 1986, for other hypotheses about the origin of the subjective experience). The bulk of theoretical and empirical work in the neurobiology of emotion indicates that *isotelesis*—the principle that any one function is reserved by several structures and processes—applies to emotion as it applies to thermoregulation, for example (Satinoff, 1982).

UNIVERSALITY OF EMOTIONAL EFFERENCE

Charles Darwin regarded his work on emotional expression as a crowning achievement of the theory of evolution. For, if emotional expression is subject to the forces of natural selection, [410] then the laws of evolution are even more general than one would originally expect. Now, it could be said that these laws apply not only to morphological character and physiological process, but to behavior as well. Darwin's theoretical argument on the evolutionary origins of emotional expressions was based on their adaptive value. His empirical argument was based on their universality among cultures and among species. It was this universality of emotional expressions that Darwin (1896/1955) used as proof that "man evolved from some lower animal form" (p. 365). And it should be noted in this context that Darwin's principal interest was probably more in marshaling new evidence for the theory of evolution than in explicating the emotions. His contemporary Piderit (1888, pp. 7–8), a scholar chiefly dedicated to the study of emotions, wrote "Darwin ne cherche içi, comme dans tous ses autres travaux, qu'à découvrir de nouveaux documents en faveur de sa théorie de l'évolution" (Here, as in all of his other studies, Darwin is only searching for new evidence to support his theory of evolution).

The evolution of emotional expression was based on their function. The language of Darwin's (1896/1955) entire volume leads one to view emotional expression as having for its *primary* function the broadcasting of information about the animals' internal states. By displaying their internal states—their fears, their appetites, and their intentions—animals communicate to others the probabilities of incipient behaviors—a process that has an important adaptive value. The universality of emotional expressions was documented to some extent by Darwin, and later research has shown him to be quite right (e.g., Ekman, 1972; Ekman and Friesen, 1971). However, not until the closing pages of his book does Darwin disclaim, albeit partially, the evolutionary primacy of expression (Adelmann and Zajonc, 1989). He stated explicitly, although belatedly, that "there are no grounds, as far as I can discover, for believing that any muscle has been developed or even modified exclusively for the sake of expression" (Darwin, 1896/1955, p. 354). It is interesting that Darwin implicated the respiratory and the vascular system. He said, in fact, that "If the structure of our organs of respiration and circulation had differed in only a slight degree from the state in which they now exist, most of our expressions would have been wonderfully different" (p. 363). Note that he only disallows the evolutionary primacy of particular morphological features as having been selected for expressive functions. But there is no doubt that he thought of expressive behavior as having been selected for its communicative value. This is clear from the fact that he regarded expression as a genetically transmitted "serviceable associated habit" (p. 28) that has "evolved like an instinct" (p. 30).

Darwin (1896/1955) does not consider seriously the possibility that facial actions might have direct hedonic consequences. For if they did, such consequences would promote their repeated occurrence and, hence, exert selective influence in their own right. It is in this sense that the evolutionary theory of emotional expression and VTEE differ. The VTEE proposes that facial muscular movements, above all else, serve a restorative function: that they help regulate blood flow to the brain and brain temperature. Only as a secondary, fortuitous bonus might they be used to communicate internal states. In this sense, they are no different from sneezing, which too serves a restorative function in the respiratory organs (and fortuitously broadcasts to others that there is a respiratory obstruction), or vomiting, which has a gastric restorative function (and reveals unambiguously that there are some problems of the digestive tract). Sneezing evolved primarily to serve the respiratory system, and vomiting, the gastro-intestinal system. Both are universally understood among humans and probably among animals as well. But people don't sneeze or vomit to inform those around them of their internal difficulties. At a formal level, one would be hard put to distinguish sneezing and vomiting from a pain grimace made in response to a stomach ache, which might indeed be classified as an expression of emotion. And more relevant to the present studies, piloerection and shivering, for example, serve both thermoregulation and emotional expression. In fact, the parallels may be even more striking: The effector mechanisms that serve cooling (panting, sweating, vasodilation) are very often those that are also associated with positive emotional experiences such as sexual excitation, whereas those that serve warming (shivering and vasoconstriction) are often associated with negative emotional experiences, such as fear or anger. Fusco, Hardy, and Hammel (1961) cooled and heated the anterior hypothalamus of dogs obtaining vasoconstriction and shivering, or vasodilation and panting, respectively, under unchanged ambient temperature. It is a matter for further empirical research to demonstrate that an appropriate stimulation of the amygdala that is assumed to control emotional expressions would also produce similar effector outputs without changes in hypothalamic temperature.

Darwin (1896/1955) formulated the problem of emotional expression by asking why is it that "different muscles are brought into action under different emotions; why, for instance, the inner ends of the eyebrows are raised, and the corners of the mouth depressed by a person suffering from grief or anxiety" (p. 3). It is now clear after 100 years of research that there is nothing particular in each of the expressions that would explain its topography as compellingly displaying one emotion rather than another. There are no a priori grounds to suppose that the corrugator muscle must be contracted in anger and the zygomatic in pleasure. The expressions are not onomatopoeic. The semantics of emotional expression are as arbitrary as the semantics of the verbal language. But we know that they are fairly universal and universally understood. Why? VTEE may offer an answer to Darwin's question by examining the particular vascular, thermoregulatory, and neurochemical consequences of a particular facial action. If these vascular/thermoregulatory/neurochemical patterns are systematically associated with particular subjective states, the answer will have been found, for they will indeed be in the same class as sneezing and coughing.

But with respect to emotional efference, there remains still the question of which function dominated selective pressures of the evolutionary process. If the evolution of emotional efference were in its later stages dominated by their communicative function, there would be as much variation in emotional expressions across cultures as there is in language. But the similarities among the members of completely diverse linguistic communities in the display of emotions are enormous (Ekman, 1980; Ekman et al., 1987). People from remote parts of the, globe, who have no comprehension of each other's languages at all, can understand each other's emotions with great ease.

It is the case, of course, that the understanding and the expression [411] of specific emotions as they are connected to their eliciting conditions, are influenced by learning and conditioning. This should not deter us from entertaining the idea that the facial actions themselves can act as restoratives and regulators of CBF and brain blood temperature, and, as such, are no different than sneezing, coughing, yawning, or vomiting. Treating emotional expressions in the light of VTEE, as serving primarily restorative vascular functions, makes their evolutionary basis less Lamarckian, their universality better understood, and their ultimate origins considerably more plausible.

In light of the preceding discussion, it is quite clear that the processes that emerge in emotion are governed not only by isotelesis, but by the principle of *polytelesis* as well. The first principle holds that many functions, especially the important ones, are served by a number of redundant systems, whereas the second holds that many systems serve more than one function. There are very few organic functions that are served uniquely by one and only one process, structure, or organ. Similarly, there are very few processes, structures, or organs that serve one and only one purpose. Language, too, is characterized by the isotelic and polytelic principles; there are many words for each meaning and most words have more than one meaning. The two principles apply equally to a variety of other biological, behavioral, and social phenomena. Thus, there is no contradiction between the vascular and the communicative functions of facial efference; the systems that serve these functions are both isotelic and polytelic.

EFFECTS OF FACIAL EFFERENCE AND COGNITIVE APPRAISAL

If we accept simple affective polarities as fundamental dimensions of emotions, then the evidence cited here shows that a prior cognitive appraisal is not a necessary condition for subjective emotional experience. In our experiments, neither an emotional stimulus nor a cognitive appraisal of that stimulus was a necessary condition for the observed changes in subjective feeling state. We can now more fully appreciate that preferences and aversions can emerge without and prior to cognitive activity (Zajonc, 1980), and how they can emerge without the person's awareness (Kunst-Wilson and Zajonc, 1980; Seamon, Brody, and Kauff, 1983a, 1983b). Of course, more complex emotional experiences, such as pride, disappointment, jealousy, or contempt obviously require extensive participation of cognitive processes. We would not expect someone who has just learned that he has cancer to turn his grief into joy by the mere contraction of the zygomatic muscle. Likewise, the complete emotion of fear must recruit a cognitive process of some form because it is elicited by a specific stimulus that needs to be encoded to a level sufficiently articulated so as to become integrated with other sensory associations that make that stimulus aversive. Anxiety, however, because it may not always need the participation of a specific eliciting stimulus, might be precognitive.

It is unlikely that all emotions have the same etiology, are characterized by the same affective and cognitive processes, exhibit the same sequencing of these component processes, or have the same underlying neuroanatomical structure and neurochemical action. Thus, certain subjective feelings emerge early and determine the ensuing course of the emotional process, whereas others develop much later. For some emotions, cognitive appraisal is a necessary precondition, whereas for others it is not necessary. LeDoux (1987) has shown that aversive reactions can be demonstrated as having identifiable correlates at the subcortical level. The careless child withdraws a burned hand before experiencing the aversive hedonic state. A subtle pun, on the other hand, may not be appreciated nor reacted to with laughter unless it has been extensively processed.

The answer to the question of where in the chain of emotional links lies the subjective state, therefore, is that it can be pre- as well as postcognitive. A theory of emotion needs to be a theory of emotions. Such a theory will need to classify the sequential topography of the various emotional patterns, describe the transitional contingencies, and specify the conditions that produce them. Moreover, it would appear that a taxonomy of the emotions cannot at this time designate any one set of criteria as primary, be they muscular patterns, linguistic labels, forms of cognitive appraisal, introspective accounts of subjective states or autonomic, peripheral, or subcortical reactions. There is no theory thus far developed that has procedures for identifying boundaries between emotions that are consistent across the above criteria, and the correlations between these criteria are disappointingly low. According to Russell and Bullock (1986), emotions are best described as "fuzzy concepts" occupying overlapping regions of a two-dimensional space, whose axes are pleasure-displeasure and arousal-quiescence. The boundaries between emotions must, therefore, be explored by empirical methods that look for convergence of the diverse emotional correlates and indicators, and a focus on the one dimension about which there is general consensus—hedonic polarity—might well be the most fruitful research strategy at this time.

VASCULAR THEORY OF EMOTIONAL EFFERENCE AND FACIAL FEEDBACK

It could be argued that the muscular patterns associated with the phonemes are far removed from typical emotional expressions, and, hence, the present results have little bearing on the facial feedback hypothesis. This argument, however, must be taken in the light of the criticism of facial feedback theories that facial movement has no subjective consequences whatsoever. Because we found subjective consequences with muscular action that resemble emotional efference, actions that are implicated in *actual* emotional experiences should have even better chances of having significant subjective consequences.

The present studies, together with the conjectured theoretical explanation, go beyond facial feedback conceptions of the nature and antecedents of subjective feelings in emotions. They are consistent with the facial feedback theory and its weak version, that is, that facial movement has generalized and polarized affective impact, differentiated at the level of the positive-negative or approach-avoidance polarity. As such, these studies are among the few that show a clear discrimination by a physiological measure between positive and negative affect.

Nevertheless, nothing in the present study precludes the possibility of more specific affective effects that are produced by emotion-free facial movements, be they spontaneous or deliberate. It is entirely possible that more specific and identifiable dynamic patterns of temperature change and affective feelings might be associated with different facial patterns, and that some [412] of these patterns fall within the range of emotional expressions distinguished by Ekman and Friesen's (1978) FACS or Izard's (1979) MACS classification systems. Perhaps there exist some phonetic patterns, consisting of two or three phonemes, that resemble quite closely some specific emotional facial action patterns. An investigation of the subjective reactions following these patterns together with other physiological measures, including not only hypothalamic temperature but measures of the activity of the autonomic nervous system, such as heart rate or GSR, will generate more precise information about the role of facial movement in the emotional experience.

The relations that we have found and theorized about in this article prompt several conclusions. First, the vascular system, especially the one that supplies the face and the brain, must play an important role in generating the subjective feeling state. Second, facial action is not a process that serves only or even primarily the display function; rather, it is a process that, among other processes, participates in the maintenance and regulation of the vascular system of the head and of its thermoregulation. It follows that more knowledge about the relation between subjective feeling states and facial action can be gleaned with a stronger focus on vascular processes. Third, thermoregulation of hypothalamic blood offers a significant clue to the study of emotion, for it bridges peripheral processes to brain neurochemistry. Fourth, it is unlikely that emotion specificity is to be found at all levels of emotion analysis—the subjective, behavioral, and physiological. Given existing knowledge, close interrelations among these three aspects of emotional processes may be found only if distinctions among emotions do not go beyond hedonic polarities. Fifth, forehead temperature is a reliable psychophysiological measure found to discriminate reliably between positive and negative hedonic experiences.

REFERENCES

Adelmann, P.K., and Zajonc, R.B. (1989). Facial efference and the experience of emotion. *Annual Review of Psychology*, **40**, 249–280.

Aggleton, J.P., and Mishkin, M. (1986). The amygdala: Sensory gateway to the emotions. In R. Plutchik and H. Kellerman (Eds.), *Emotion: theory, research and experience: Vol. 3, Biological foundations of emotion* (pp. 281–299). New York: Academic Press.

Anderson, C.A., and Anderson, D.C. (1984). Ambient temperature and violent crime: Tests of the linear and curvilinear hypotheses. *Journal of Personality and Social Psychology*, **46**, 91–97.

Arnold, M. (1960). *Emotion and personality*. New York: Columbia University Press.

Averill, J.R. (1983). Studies on anger and aggression: Implications for theories of emotion. *American Psychologist*, **38**, 1145–1160.

Ax, A.F. (1953). The psychological differentiation between fear and anger in humans. *Psychosomatic Medicine*, **15**, 433–442.

Baker, M.A. (1982). Brain cooling in endotherms in heat and exercise. *Annual Review of Physiology*, **44**, 85–96.

Baker, M.A., Chapman, L.W., and Nathanson, M. (1974). Control of brain temperature in dogs: Effects of tracheostomy. *Respiration Physiology*, **22**, 325–333.

Baker, M.A., and Hayward, J.N. (1968). The influence of the nasal mucosa and the carotid rete upon hypothalamic temperature in sheep. *Journal of Physiology*, **198**, 561–579.

Baker, M.A., Stocking, R.A., and Meehan, J.P. (1972). Thermal relationship between tympanic membrane and hypothalamus in conscious cat and monkey. *Journal of Applied Physiology*, **32**, 739–742.

Baron, R.A. (1977). *Human aggression*. New York: Plenum Press.

Bendixen, H.H., Egbert, L.D., Hedley-Whyte, J., Laver, M.B., and Pontoppidan, H. (1965). *Respiratory care*. St. Louis, MO: Mosby.

Benguerel, A., and Cowan, H.A. (1974). Coarticulation of upper lip protrusion in French. *Phonetica*, **30**, 41–55.

Benzinger, T. (1969). Clinical temperature. *Journal of the American Medical Association*, **209**, 1200–1206.

Bissette, G., Nemeroff, C.B., Loosen, P.T., Prange, A.J., Jr., and Lipton, M.A. (1976). Hypothermia and intolerance to cold induced by intracisternal administration of the hypothalamic peptide neurotensin. *Nature*, **262**, 607–609.

Bode, D.C., and Molinoff, P.B. (1988). Effects of chronic exposure to ethanol on the physical and functional properties of the plasma membrane of S49 lymphoma cells. *Biochemistry*, **27**, 5700–5707.

Brinnel, H., and Cabanac, M. (in press). Tympanic temperature is a core temperature in humans. *Journal of Thermal Biology*.

Brown, M.R. (1982). Bombesin and somatostatin related peptides: Effects on oxygen consumption. *Brain Research*, **242**, 243–246.

Buck, R. (1980). Nonverbal behavior and the theory of emotion: The facial feedback hypothesis. *Journal of Personality and Social Psychology*, **38**, 811–824.

Buck, R. (1985). Prime theory: An integrated view of motivation and emotion. *Psychological Review*, **92**, 389–413.

Burdett, A.N. (1985). Emotion and facial expression. *Science*, **230**, 608.

Cabanac, M. (1986). Keeping a cool head. *News in Physiological Sciences*, **1**, 41–44.

Cabanac, M., and Brinnel, H. (1985). Blood flow in the emissary veins of the human head during hyperthermia. *European Journal of Applied Physiology*, **54**, 172–176.

Cannon, W.B. (1927). The James-Lange theory of emotion: A critical examination and an alternative theory. *American Journal of Psychology*, **39**, 106–124.

Caputa, M. (1981). Selective brain cooling, an important component of thermal physiology. In S. Szelenyi and M. Szekely (Eds.), *Contributions of thermal physiology: Proceedings of a Satellite Symposium of the 28th International Congress of Physiological Sciences, Budapest 1980* (pp. 183–192). New York: Pergamon.

Caputa. M., Perrin G., and Cabanac, M. (1978). Écoulement sanguin réversible dans la veine ophthalmique: Mécanisme de refroidissement sélectif du cerveau human [Reversible cooling of the blood in the ophthalmic vein: Mechanism of selective recooling in the human brain]. *Comptes Rendues d'Academie des Sciences, Paris,* **287,** 1011–1014.

Clark, W.G., and Bernardini, G.L. (1982). Depression of learned thermoregulatory behavior by central injection of opioids in cats. *Pharmacology, Biochemistry, and Behavior,* **16,** 983–988.

Cohen, B., Izard, C.E., and Simons, R.F. (1986). *Facial and physiological indices of emotions in mother-infant interactions.* Paper presented at the 26th Annual Meeting of the Society for Psychophysiological Research, Montreal.

Colby, C.Z., Lanzetta, J.T., and Kleck, R.E. (1977). Effects of expression of pain on autonomic and pain tolerance responses to subject-controlled pain. *Psychophysiology,* **14,** 537–540.

Cooper, J.R., Bloom, F.E., and Roth. R.H. (1986). *The biochemical basis of neuropharmacology.* New York: Oxford University Press.

Corbit, J.D. (1969). Behavioral regulation of hypothalamic temperature. *Science,* **166,** 256–258.

Corbit, J.D. (1973). Voluntary control of hypothalamic temperature. *Journal of Comparative and Physiological Psychology,* **83,** 394–411.

Corwin, E., Malvin, G.M., Katz. S., and Malvin, R.L. (1984). Temperature sensitivity of the renin-angiotensin system in *Ambystoma trigrinum. American Journal of Physiology,* **246,** 510–515.

Cotton, J.L. (1981, April/May). *Ambient temperature and violent* [413] *crime.* Paper presented at the Midwestern Psychological Association convention, Detroit, MI.

Cupchik, G., and Leventhal, H. (1974). Consistency between expressive behavior and the evaluation of stimuli: The role of sex and self-observation. *Journal of Personality and Social Psychology,* **30,** 429–442.

Darwin, C.R. (1955). *The expression of emotions in man and animals.* New York: Philosophical Library. (Original work published 1896.)

Davidson, R.J. (1984). Hemisphere asymmetry and emotion. In K. Scherer and P. Ekman (Eds.), *Approaches to emotion* (pp. 39–57). Hillsdale, NJ: Erlbaum.

Dib, B., and Cabanac, M. (1984). Skin or hypothalamus cooling: A behavioral choice by rats. *Brain Research,* **302,** 1–7.

Drake, A.F., Keall, H., Vig, P.S., and Krause, C.J. (1988). Clinical nasal obstruction and objective respiratory mode determination. *Annals of Otology, Rhinology and Laryngology,* **97,** 397–402.

Duncan, J., and Laird, J.D. (1977). Cross-modality consistencies in individual differences in self-attribution. *Journal of Personality,* **45,** 191–206.

Ekman, P. (1972). Universals and cultural differences in facial expression of emotion. In J. K. Cole (Ed.), *Nebraska Symposium on Motivation* (pp. 207–283). Lincoln: University of Nebraska Press.

Ekman, P. (1980). *The face of man: Expressions of universal emotions in a New Guinea village.* New York: Garland STPM Press.

Ekman, P. (1984). Expression and the nature of emotion. In K. R. Scherer and P. Ekman (Eds.), *Approaches to emotion* (pp. 319–343). Hillsdale, NJ: Erlbaum.

Ekman, P., and Friesen, W.V. (1971). Constants across cultures in the face and emotion. *Journal of Personality and Social Psychology,* **17,** 124–129.

Ekman, P., and Friesen, W.V. (1978). *Facial action coding system.* Palo Alto, CA: Consulting Psychologists Press.

Ekman, P., Friesen, W.V., O'Sullivan, M., Diacoyanni-Tarlatzis, I., Krause, R., Pitcairn, T., Scherer, K., Chan, A., Heider, K., LeCompte, W.A., Ricci-Bitti, P.E., and Tomota, M. (1987). Universals and cultural differences in the judgments of facial expressions of emotions. *Journal of Personality and Social Psychology,* **53,** 712–717.

Ekman, P., Levenson, R.W., and Friesen, W.V. (1983). Autonomic nervous system activity distinguishes among emotions. *Science,* **221,** 1208–1210.

Fox, N.A., and Davidson, R.J. (1986). Taste-elicited changes in facial signs of emotion and the asymmetry of brain electrical activity in human newborns. *Neuropsychologia,* **24,** 417–422.

Fridlund, A.J., and Gilbert, A.N. (1985). Emotion and facial expression. *Science,* **230,** 607–608.

Funkenstein, D.H., King, S.H., and Drolette, M.E. (1957). *Mystery of stress.* Cambridge, MA: Harvard University Press.

Fusco, M.M., Hardy, J.D., and Hammel, H.T. (1961). Interaction of central and peripheral factors in physiological temperature regulation. *American Journal of Physiology,* **200,** 572–580.

Gandhi, V.C., and Ross, D.H. (1987). Alterations in alpha-adrenergic and muscarinic cholinergic receptor binding in rat brain following nonionizing radiation. *Radiation Research,* **109,** 90–99.

Germain, M., Jobin, M., and Cabanac, M. (1987). The effect of face fanning during recovery from exercise hyperthermia. *Journal of Physiological Pharmacology,* **65,** 87–91.

Geschwind, N. (1965). Disconnexion syndromes in animals and man (Pt 1). *Brain,* **88,** 237–294.

Gray, H. (1985). *Anatomy of the human body.* Philadelphia. PA: Lea and Febiger. (Original work published 1858)

Griffitt, W. (1970). Environmental effects on interpersonal affective behavior: Ambient effective temperature and attraction. *Journal of Personality and Social Psychology,* **15,** 240–244.

Griffitt, W., and Veitch, R. (1971). Hot and crowded: Influence of population density and temperature on interpersonal affective behavior. *Journal of Personality and Social Psychology,* **17,** 92–98.

Harries, K.D., and Stadler, S.J. (1988). Heat and violence: New findings from Dallas field data, 1980–1981. *Journal of Applied Social Psychology,* **18,** 129–138.

Hawkins, M.F., and Avery, D.D. (1983). Effects of centrally-administered bombesin and adrenalectomy on behavioral thermoregulation and locomotor activity. *Neuropharmacology,* **22,** 1249–1255.

Hori, T., Kiyohara, T., Shibata, M., and Oomura, Y. (1986). Responsiveness of monkey preoptic thermosensitive neurons to non-thermal emotional stimuli. *Brain Research Bulletin,* **17,** 75–82.

Izard, C.E. (1971). *The face of emotion.* New York: Appleton-Century Crofts.

Izard, C.E. (1977). *Human emotions.* New York: Plenum.

Izard, C.E. (1979). *The maximally discriminative facial movement cooling system.* Newark: University of Delaware.

Izard, C.E. (1981). Differential emotions theory and the facial feedback hypothesis of emotion activation: Comments on Tourangeau and Ellsworth's "The role of facial response in the experience of emotion." *Journal of Personality and Social Psychology,* **40,** 350–354.

Izard, C.E. (1985). Emotion and facial expression. *Science,* **230,** 608.

James, W. (1890). *Principles of psychology.* New York: Dover Publications.

Jampel, H.D., Duff, G.W., Gershon, R.K., Atkins, E., and Durun, S.K. (1983). Fever and immunoregulation: III. Hyperthermia augments the primary in vitro humoral immune response. *Journal of Experimental Medicine,* **157,** 1229–1238.

Kavaliers, M. (1982). Pinealectomy modifies the thermoregulatory effects of bombesin in goldfish. *Neuropharmacology,* **21,** 1169–117.

Kluger, M.J., and D'Alecy, L.B. (1975). *Journal of Applied Physiology,* **38,** 268–271.

Kotsch, W.E., Izard, C.E., and Walker, S.G. (1978). *Experimenter-manipulated patterning of the facial musculature and the experience of emotion.* Unpublished manuscript, Vanderbilt University, Nashville, TN.

Kraut, R.E. (1982). Social presence, facial feedback, and emotion. *Journal of Personality and Social Psychology,* **42,** 853–863.

Krohmer, R.W., and Crews, D. (1987). Temperature activation of courtship behavior in male red-sided garter snake (*Thamnophis sirtal parietalis*): Role of the anterior hypothalamus-preoptic area. *Behavioral Neuroscience,* **101,** 228–236.

Kunst-Wilson, W.R., and Zajonc, R.B. (1980). Affective discrimination of stimuli that cannot be recognized. *Science,* **207,** 557–558.

Laird, J.D. (1974). Self-attribution of emotion: The effects of expressive behavior on the quality of emotional experience. *Journal of Personality and Social Psychology,* **29,** 475–486.

Laird, J.D., and Crosby, M. (1974). Individual differences in self-attribution of emotion. In H. London and R. Nisbett (Eds.), *Cognitive alteration of feeling states* (pp. 44–59). Chicago: Aldine-Atherton.

Lange, C.G., and James, W. (1967). *The emotions.* New York: Hafne (Original work published 1922)

Lanzetta, J.T., Cartwright-Smith, J., and Kleck, R.E. (1976). Effect of nonverbal dissimulation of emotional experience and autonomic arousal. *Journal of Personality and Social Psychology,* **33,** 354–370.

Lazarus, R.S. (1982). Thoughts on the relations between emotion and cognition. *American Psychologist,* **37,** 1019–1024.

Lazarus, R.S., Averill, J.R., and Opton, E.M. (1970). Towards a cognitive theory of emotion. In M. B. Arnold (Ed.), *Feelings and emotions* (pp. 207–232). New York: Academic Press.

LeDoux, J.E. (1982). Neuroevolutionary mechanisms of cerebral asymmetry in man. *Brain, Behavior, and Evolution,* **20,** 196–212.

LeDoux, J.E. (1987). Emotion. In F. Plum (Ed.), *Handbook of physiology—The nervous system* (Vol. 5, pp. 419–459). Washington, DC, American Physiological Society. [414]

LeDoux, J.E. (in press). Plasticity in the neural computation of stimulus values. In M. Gabriel and J. Moore (Eds.), *Neurocomputation and learning: Foundation and adaptive networks.* Cambridge, MA: MIT Press.

Lee, R.J., and Lomax, P. (1983). Thermoregulatory, behavioral and seizure modulatory effects of AVP in the gerbil. *Peptides,* **4,** 801–805.

Leventhal, H., and Mace, W. (1970). The effect of laughter on evaluation of a slapstick movie. *Journal of Personality,* **38,** 16–30.

Leventhal, H., and Scherer, K. (1987). The relationship of emotion to cognition: A functional approach to semantic controversy. *Cognition and Emotion,* **1,** 3–28.

Lin, L.H., and Pivorun, E.B. (1986). Effects of intrahypothalamically administered norepinephrine, serotonin and bombesin on thermoregulation in the deermouse (*Peromyscus maniculatus*). *Brain Research,* **364,** 212–219.

Lombard, J.S. (1879). *Experimental researches on the regional temperature of the head.* London: H. K. Lewis.

Mandler, G. (1984). *Mind and body.* New York: Norton.

Matsumoto, D. (1987). The role of facial response in the experience of emotion: More methodological problems and a meta-analysis. *Journal of Personality and Social Psychology,* **52,** 769–774.

Mathew, R.J., Largen, J.W., Dobbins, K., Meyer, J.S., Sakai, F., and Claghorn, J.L. (1980). Biofeedback control of skin temperature and cerebral blood flow in migraine. *Headache,* **20,** 19–28.

McArthur, L.Z., Solomon, M.R., and Jaffe, R.H. (1980). Weight differences in emotional responsiveness to proprioceptive and pictorial stimuli. *Journal of Personality and Social Psychology,* **39,** 308–319.

McCaffrey, T. V., McCook, R.D., and Wurster, R.D. (1975). Effect of head skin temperature on tympanic and oral temperature in man. *Journal of Applied Physiology,* **39,** 114–118.

McCanne. T.R., and Anderson, J.A. (1987). Emotional responding following experimental manipulation of facial electromyographic activity. *Journal of Personality and Social Psychology,* **52,** 759–768.

McCaul, K.D., Holmes, S.D., and Solomon, S. (1982). Voluntary expressive changes and emotion. *Journal of Personality and Social Psychology,* **42,** 145–152.

Miller, N.W., and Clem, L.W. (1984). Temperature-mediated processes in teleost immunity: Differential effects of temperature on catfish *in vitro* antibody responses to thymus-dependent and thymus-independent antigens. *Journal of Immunology,* **133,** 2356–2359.

Morley, J.E., Elson, M.K., Levine, A., and Shafer, R.B. (1982). The effects of stress on central nervous system concentrations of opioid peptide, dynorphin. *Peptides,* **3,** 901–906.

Piderit, T. (1888). *La mimique et la physiognomie* [The face and its action]. Paris: Alcan.

Plutchik, R. (1984). Emotions: A general psychoevolutionary theory. In K. R. Scherer and P. Ekman (Eds.), *Approaches to emotion* (pp. 197–219). Hillsdale, NJ: Erlbaum.

Precht, H., Christophersen, J., Hensel, H., and Larcher, W. (1973). *Temperature and life.* New York: Springer-Verlag.

Reifman, A.S., Larrick, R.P., and Fein, S. (1988, September). *The heat-aggression relationship in major-league baseball.* Paper presented at the 1988 Annual Convention of the American Psychological Association, Atlanta.

Rolls, E.T. (1986). A theory of emotion, and its application to understanding the neural basis of emotion. In Y. Omura (Ed.), *Emotions: Neural and chemical control* (pp. 325–344). Basel, Switzerland: Karger.

Roseman, I.J. (1984). Cognitive determinants of emotions: A structural theory. In P. Shaver (Ed.), *Review of personality and social psychology: Vol. 5, Emotions, relationships, and health* (pp. 11–36). Beverly Hills, CA: Sage.

Rotton, J., and Frey, J. (1985). Air pollution, weather, and violent crimes: Concomitant time-series analysis of archival data. *Journal of Personality and Social Psychology,* **49,** 1207–1220.

Russell, J.A., and Bullock, M. (1986). Fuzzy concepts and the perception of emotion in facial expression. *Social Cognition,* **4,** 309–341.

Rutledge, L.L., and Hupka, R.B. (1985). The facial feedback hypothesis: Methodological concerns and new supporting evidence. *Motivation and Emotion, 9,* 219–240.

Satinoff, E. (1964). Behavioral thermoregulation in response to local cooling of the rat brain. *American Journal of Physiology, 206,* 1389–1394.

Satinoff, E. (1982). Are there similarities between thermoregulation and sexual behavior? In D. W. Pfaff (Ed.), *The physiological mechanisms of motivation* (pp. 217–251). New York: Springer-Verlag.

Satinoff, E., and Shan, S. (1971). Loss of behavioral thermoregulation after lateral hypothalamic lesion in rats. *Journal of Comparative and Physiological Psychology, 77,* 302–312.

Schachter, S., and Singer, J.E. (1962). Cognitive, social, and physiological determinants of emotional state. *Psychological Review, 69,* 379–399.

Seamon, J.J., Brody, N., and Kauff, D.M. (1983a). Affective discrimination of stimuli that are not recognized: Effect of shadowing, masking and cerebral laterality. *Journal of Experimental Psychology: Learning, Memory, and Cognition, 9,* 544–555.

Seamon, J.J., Brody, N., and Kauff, D.M. (1983b). Affective discrimination of stimuli that are not recognized: II. Effect of delay between study and test. *Bulletin of the Psychonomic Society, 21,* 187–189.

Smith, C.A., and Ellsworth, P.C. (1985). Patterns of cognitive appraisal in emotion. *Journal of Personality and Social Psychology, 48,* 813–838.

Smith, C.A., and Ellsworth, P.C. (1987). Patterns of appraisal and emotion related to taking an exam. *Journal of Personality and Social Psychology, 52,* 475–488.

Scalding, P.M., and Vig, P.S. (1988). Respiration characteristics in subjects diagnosed as having nasal obstruction. *Journal of Oral and Maxillofacial Surgery, 48,* 189–194.

Stellar, E. (1982). Brain mechanisms in hedonic processes. In D. W. Pfaff (Ed.), *The physiological mechanisms of motivation* (pp. 377–407). New York: Springer-Verlag.

Strack, F., Martin, L.L., and Stepper, S. (1988). Inhibiting and facilitating conditions of facial expressions: A nonobtrusive test of the facial feedback hypothesis. *Journal of Personality and Social Psychology, 54,* 768–777.

Taasan, V., Wynne, J.W., Cassisi, N., and Block, A.J. (1981). The effect of nasal packing on steep-disordered breathing and nocturnal oxygen desaturation. *Laryngoscope, 91,* 1163–1172.

Thornhill, J.A., and Saunders, W.S. (1984). Thermoregulatory (core, surface and metabolic) responses of unrestrained rats to repeated POAH injections of b-endorphin or adrenocorticotropin. *Peptides, 5,* 713–719.

Tomkins, S.S. (1962). *Affect, imagery, consciousness: I. The positive affects.* New York: Springer-Verlag.

Tomkins, S.S. (1979). Script theory: Differential magnification of affects. In H. E. Howe, Jr. and R. A. Dienstbier (Eds.), *Nebraska Symposium on Motivation* (Vol. 26, pp. 201–236). Lincoln: University of Nebraska Press.

Tomkins, S.S. (1981). The role of facial response in the experience of emotion: A reply to Tourangeau and Ellsworth. *Journal of Personality and Social Psychology, 40,* 355–357.

Tourangeau, R., and Ellsworth, P.C. (1979). The role of facial response in the experience of emotion. *Journal of Personality and Social Psychology, 37,* 1519–1531.

Ungell, A.L. (1984). Temperature effects on catecholamine accumulation in neuronal and extraneuronal compartments of the cod spleen. *Acta Physiologica Scandinavica, 126,* 589–592.

U'Prichard, D.C. and Snyder, S.H. (1977). Binding of ^{3}H-catecholamines [415] to α-noradrenergic receptor sites in calf brain. *Journal of Biological Chemistry, 252,* 6450–6463.

Vig, P.S. (1985). Respiration, nasal airway, and orthodontics: A review of current clinical concepts and research. In L.E. Johnston (Ed.), *New vistas in orthodontics* (pp. 76–102). Philadelphia: Lea and Febiger.

Waynbaum, I. (1907). *La Physionomie humaine: Son mécanisme et son rôle social* [The human face: Its mechanism and social function]. Paris: Alcan.

Wenger, C.B. (1987). More on "Keeping a cool head." *News in Physiological Sciences, 2,* 150.

Wenger, M.A., and Cullen, T.D. (1958). ANS response patterns to fourteen stimuli. *American Psychologist, 13,* 423.

Winquist, R.J., and Bevan, J.A. (1980). Temperature sensitivity of tone in the rabbit facial vein: Myogenic mechanism for cranial thermoregulation? *Science, 207,* 1001–1002.

Winton, W..M. (1986). The role of facial response in self-reports of emotion: A critique of Laird. *Journal of Personality and Social Psychology, 50,* 808–812.

Winton, W.M., Putnam, L.E., and Krauss, R.M. (1984). Facial and autonomic manifestations of the dimensional structure of emotion. *Journal of Experimental Social Psychology,* **20,** 195–216.

Yehuda, S., and Sheleff, P. (1985). The effects of MIF-I, b-endorphin and a-MSH on d-amphetamine induced paradoxical behavioral thermoregulation: Possible involvement of the dopaminergic system. *Peptides,* **5,** 975–992.

Zachary, I., and Rosengurt, E. (1987). Internalization and degradation of peptides of the bombesin family in Swiss 313 cells occurs without ligand-induced receptor down-regulation. *European Molecular Biology Organisation Journal,* **6,** 2233–2239.

Zajonc, R.B. (1980). Feeling and thinking: Preferences need no inferences. *American Psychologist, 35,* 151–175.

Zajonc, R.B. (1984). On the primacy of affect. *American Psychologist, 39,* 151–175.

Zajonc, R.B. (1985). Emotion and facial efference: A theory reclaimed. *Science, 228,* 15–21.

Zajonc, R.B. (1986, January). *The face as a primary instrument of social process.* Paper presented at the symposium on "Social Psychology and the Emotions," Maison des Sciences de l'Homme, Paris.

Zuckerman, M.. Klorman, R., Larrance, D., and Spiegel, N. (1981). Facial, autonomic, and subjective components of emotion: The facial feedback hypothesis versus the externalizer-internalizer distinction. *Journal of Personality and Social Psychology, 41,* 929–944.

Chapter 13

Hypothalamic Cooling Elicits Eating: Differential Effects on Motivation and Pleasure

Kent C. Berridge and R.B. Zajonc
University of Michigan

Human evaluations of pleasure and attractiveness can be manipulated by minute changes in cephalic temperature (Adelmann and Zajonc, 1989; Zajonc, Murphy, and Inglehart, 1989). Small decreases in the temperature of cephalic blood measured at the forehead, for example, heighten the pleasantness ratings given by persons to odors or speech sounds (Zajonc, Murphy, and Inglehart, 1989). Such changes in cephalic temperature may originate in ordinary life from activation of facial musculature patterns that restrict the flow of ascending blood through the cavernous sinus (a large network of channels beneath the brain that mixes venous blood returning from the brain and face), from alterations in the temperature of air inhaled into the nasal mucosa that cools the cavernous sinus, or from changes in breathing patterns.

These studies of human pleasantness ratings were guided by a hypothesis proposed by Zajonc, which relates subjective pleasure to the temperature of blood within the venous cavernous sinus (Zajonc, 1985). The relationship between pleasure and cephalic temperature is suggested by an early theory of emotion and facial efference originally put forth by Waynbaum (1907). The hypothesis proposes that pleasure may be controlled in an inverse direction by transient thermal fluctuations within the cavernous sinus. Increase of the blood temperature within the cavernous sinus is posited to induce an aversive state; decrease of blood temperature within the sinus is posited to induce a pleasurable state (Zajonc, 1985). Thermal fluctuations can be caused naturally by sources ranging from arterial constriction to facial expression and breathing pattern. The mechanism by which temperature fluctuations within the cavernous sinus might

Berridge, K.C. & Zajonc, R.B. (1991). Hypothalamic cooling elicits eating: Differential effects on motivation and pleasure. *Psychological Science*, 2, 184–189.

cause the modulation of pleasure that was reported by subjects in the studies above has remained unclear, but several candidates are conceivable.

One especially promising candidate arises from the anatomical position of the cavernous sinus beneath the hypothalamus. The temperature of the hypothalamus is influenced by heat exchange with the cavernous sinus (Kluger and D'Alecy, 1975), and the flow of blood through the cavernous sinus is actively regulated during changes in deep body temperature (Baker, 1982; Caputa, Perrin, and Cabanac, 1978). The hypothalamus itself is temperature-sensitive and plays a major role in thermoregulation. Local changes in hypothalamic temperature exert far-reaching effects on physiology and behavior: Homeostatic adjustments by autonomic reflexes, behavioral adjustments to preserve body temperature, etc. (see Satinoff, 1983). Even small, localized changes in the temperature of the hypothalamus can be detected by animals (Cabanac and Dib, 1983; Corbit, 1973; Satinoff, 1964). For example, rats will learn to perform an instrumental response in order to turn off a probe that heats the hypothalamus by approximately 3° to 6°C (Corbit and Ernits, 1974; Dib and Cabanac, 1984), a finding that is consistent with the Zajonc–Waynbaum hypothesis relating effect to brain temperature as well as with the homeostatic hypothesis that guided its original interpretation.

Does cooling of the hypothalamus enhance a pleasurable or appetitive state? This proposition may be tested by cooling the hypothalamus directly via a hypothalamic thermode implanted permanently in the brain, and examining the influence of temperature fluctuations on reactions to natural elicitors of pleasure and appetitive behavior, such as food. Because this experiment is suitable only for animal subjects, it requires reliable animal measures of food *attractiveness* and of food *pleasure*. A food's *attractiveness* may be reflected by the propensity of an animal to approach and eat it. Food *pleasure* and *aversion* can be assessed in rats through an analysis of hedonic and aversive patterns of affective facial reactions, which are elicited naturally by palatable or noxious tastes respectively (Figure 13.1), and which can be assessed using an ethologically based technique (see Grill and Berridge, 1985, for

Hedonic
Actions

Adversive
Actions

Figure 13.1   Affective reactions to taste. Hedonic reactions (top) are elicited by sweet sucrose and other palatable tastes. Hedonic reactions include rhythmic midline tongue protrusion, nonrhythmic lateral tongue protrusion, and paw lick. Aversive reactions (bottom) are elicited by bitter quinine and other noxious tastes. Aversive reactions include gape, head shake, face wash, and forelimb flail.

review). A procedure for eliciting and measuring these natural reactions was developed by Grill and Norgen (1978a) using direct infusion of taste solutions into the mouth and a frame-by-frame video analysis of hedonic and aversive reaction patterns.

In this study, thermodes for cooling or heating the hypothalamus directly were permanently implanted in the brains of rats. After the rats had recovered from surgery, we examined the effect of changes in hypothalamic temperature on reactions to the sight of food and to sweet, bittersweet, or neutral tastes. **[184]***

METHODS

Subjects and Surgery

Seventeen male rats (Sprague-Dawley, 300 g) were anesthetized (100 mg/kg ketamine; 10 mg/kg xylazine) and implanted with sterile hypothalamic thermodes, each consisting of two lengths of hypodermic steel tubing (33 gauge) that were connected together at the tip. The tubing was encased in both a steel inner sheath and a plastic outer sheath for insulation (1.1 mm total outside diameter) except at the bare tip (0.67 mm diameter), which was exposed to the brain. A thermistor recording wire at the tip of the hypothalamic thermode detected the hypothalamic temperature at the outer steel skin of the thermode, and relayed the signal to a digital thermometer. Each hypothalamic thermode was implanted so that its tip lay at the anterior border of the medial hypothalamus (on the midline 0.3 mm anterior to bregma; 8.5 mm below skull surface). Thermodes were anchored into place with skull screws and acrylic cement. Each rat was implanted with two chronic oral cannulae in order to permit taste reactivity testing (Grill and Norgen, 1978b). These cannulae did not disturb normal behavior or interfere with eating. The oral cannulae entered the mouth just lateral to the first maxillary molar. The cannulae tubing ascended beneath the zygomatic arch on each side to the top of the head, and were anchored together next to the external ends of the hypothalamic thermode.

Behavioral testing began after a 10-day recovery period. Rats were housed individually with free access to food and water. Anatomical placement of hypothalamic thermodes was confirmed histologically at the end of the experiment.

Temperature Control

Rats were housed and tested at an ambient temperature of 20°C to 22°C. To cool or heat the hypothalamus, the external ends of a hypothalamic thermode were connected to a length of tubing filled with water, which flowed through the thermode at a rate of 3 to 6 ml/min. The normal hypothalamic temperature at the tip of the thermode was 37.1 ± 0.6°C (mean ± standard error). To cool the hypothalamus, the temperature of the water flow was reduced until the temperature at the tip of the probe fell 2.5°C below the rat's baseline temperature. For hypothalamic heating, the temperature of the water was raised until the temperature at the tip of the probe rose 2.5°C above baseline.

---

* Bracketed bold numbers refer to original page numbers. Page numbers indicate where the original page ended.

EXPERIMENT 1

Initial Screening for Elicitation of Feeding

A screening procedure, similar to the type used in studies of electrical stimulation of the lateral hypothalamus to identify "positive" feeders, was carried out in two phases, an initial habituation phase that lasted 10 days and a test phase that lasted 6 days. In both phases, a rat was placed once per day in a transparent chamber and its hypothalamic thermode was connected to the water flow. Small food pellets (75 mg each) were scattered across the floor, and a water drinking spout was available. For a 10-min period, the hypothalamic thermode was cooled by 2.5°C in alternating On/Off bins of 15 sec each.

During the test phase, behavior was videotaped for subsequent analysis of time spent eating and drinking. Cooling was delivered on days 1, 3, and 5 of the test phase. On days 2, 4, and 6, the behavioral test was run but the hypothalamus was not cooled. Several rats showed enhanced feeding during hypothalamic cooling, and this effect appeared to grow with repetition. Cooling-bound drinking was not observed. The criterion for a rat to qualify as a "cooling-bound feeder" during test phase was to eat at least twice as much on trials when it received hypothalamic cooling as when it did not. Seven of the 17 rats met this criterion (a proportion roughly similar to the proportion of rats that feed during electrical stimulation of the hypothalamus under similar conditions (Berridge and Valenstein, 1991). These rats were considered to be "cooling-bound feeders."

Confirmation of Hypothalamic Cooling-Elicited Feeding

In a separate confirmation of the ability of hypothalamic cooling to elicit feeding, hypothalamic *cooling* was compared to hypothalamic *heating* and to normal hypothalamic temperature for the seven cooling-bound feeders that had tested positive in screening. After at least six days of additional habituation to the new procedure, elicited behavior was videotaped. An A-B-B-A design for cooling and heating was used on consecutive days for this 8-min test: The hypothalamic thermode was cooled or heated by 2.5°C in 15-sec On/Off alternating bins during the middle 4 min (min 3–6) but not during the first 2 min or the last 2 min (min 1–2 and 7–8). Control trials were administered on two other days inserted at random in the series, in which the hypothalamus [185] was left at its normal temperature. Videotapes were analyzed for the consumption of food pellets and the occurrence of food-related and other actions. Behavioral categories were: Lick or eat food, lift food, carry food, lick object (nonfood), groom, and walk or rear up. Actions were recorded each time they occurred; continuous actions were counted in 5-sec bins.

RESULTS

Elicitation of Feeding by Hypothalamic Cooling

More feeding was elicited during trials when the hypothalamus was cooled than when it was either heated or left at its normal temperature (Figure 13.2). More food pellets were consumed on trials when cooling was delivered than on control days or trials when heating was delivered (ANOVA $F(2, 12) = 23.6$, $p < 0.01$). On trials when cooling was

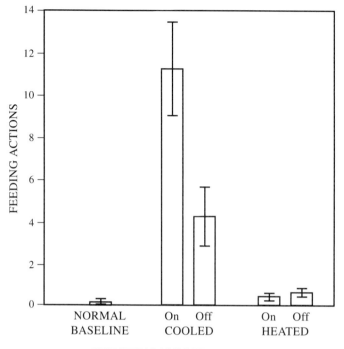

Figure 13.2   Feeding actions (lick, lift, carry, and eat food) elicited by food during trials in which the hypothalamus either remained at normal baseline temperature, was cooled by the hypothalamic thermode, or was heated by the hypothalamic thermode. *On* denotes the 4-min portion of the trial during which the hypothalamus was cooled or heated. *Off* denotes the 4-min portion of the trial during which no thermal manipulation occurred. Feeding was elevated during the On portion of cooling trials compared to the Off portion, and compared to all other conditions (bars show mean ± standard error of each mean). Feeding during the Off portion of cooling trials remained slightly elevated over the Off portion of heating or control trials, perhaps reflecting a "spillover" due to delay in heat dissipation.

delivered, more food pellets were consumed during the 4-min period when the hypothalamus was actually cooled (7.7 ± 1.8 pellets) than during the 4-min period when cooling was not delivered (4.3 ± 1.5 pellets; $F(1, 6) = 13.5$, $p < 0.02$). A similar result was obtained when categories of behavior emitted by each rat, rather than simply the number of food pellets eaten, were considered (Figure 13.2). More feeding actions (lick, lift, carry, or eat food) were shown during cooling trials than during control or heating trials (Figure 13.2; ANOVA $F(2, 12) = 21.3$, $p < 0.01$) for rats that had tested positive during screening. Trial type (cooled, heated, or normal hypothalamus) and hypothalamic thermode activation (thermal fluctuation [cool/heat] versus thermode off) interacted to control feeding actions (ANOVA $F(2, 12) = 11.2$, $p < 0.01$). On cooling trials, there were more feeding actions during the portion of the trial when the hypothalamic thermode was activated (min 3–6) than when it was not activated (min 1–2 and 7–8; Figure 13.2, $F(1, 6) = 18.3$, $p < 0.01$). Whether measured in terms of consumption or related behavior, feeding during hypothalamic heating did not differ from eating during normal trials, in which the hypothalamus was neither cooled nor heated. It should be noted in this context that no category of nonfeeding action (e.g., grooming, locomotion, object licking) was changed significantly by hypothalamic cooling or heating.

EXPERIMENT 2

Hedonic and Aversive Reactions to Taste

The hypothalamic thermode of each of the 17 rats was connected to the water flow as above, and its oral cannula was connected to an infusion delivery tube. A mirror suspended beneath the transparent floor of the test chamber reflected a view of the mouth and face into the closeup lens of a videocamera. An infusion into the mouth of either 0.03 M pure sucrose solution, a sucrose/quinine mixture (0.2 M sucrose/0.0003 M quinine HCI), or distilled water was made in random order through the oral cannula over a 1-min period (1 ml volume). Rats received a single infusion per day.

For 50% of trials, the thermode was Off from 0–20 sec, and was either cooled or heated by 2.5°C from 20–60 sec. As a counterbalance, the Off/On order was reversed for remaining trials: The probe was activated and the desired temperature **[186]** attained before the oral infusion began. The thermode remained cooled or heated during sec 0–20, and was switched off during sec 20–60. Each rat was tested in each condition with every taste. A transition period of several seconds followed onset or termination of cooling/heating before a new stable temperature was reached at the tip of the probe. The desired cooling or heating stable state was always reached before sec 40; this allowed comparison of a stable off state during sec 0–20 to a stable on (cool or heat) state during sec 40–60, and vice versa during reverse-order trials.

RESULTS

Hypothalamic Cooling Fails to Enhance Taste Hedonics

Hedonic reactions to sucrose, quinine/sucrose, or water were not altered by hypothalamic cooling or heating (Figure 13.3; ANOVA $F(1, 6) = 1.71$, $p > .1$) even for those rats that ate during hypothalamic cooling in Experiment 1 (hedonic and aversive reactions from the seven cooling-bound feeders were representative of all 17 rats; only data from cooling-bound feeders are presented here). Activation of the thermode from off to on or vice versa did not change hedonic reactions ($F(1, 6) = 1.92$, $p > .1$), and there was no interaction between thermode activation and cooling versus heating (two-way interaction $F(1, 6) = 1.55$, $p > .1$), nor between thermode activation, temperature direction, and taste (three-way interaction $F(2, 12) = 0.97$, $p > .1$) for hedonic reactions. Similarly, aversive reactions were not changed by hypothalamic cooling or heating (Figure 13.3; $F(1, 6) = 0.47$, $p > .1$). Aversive reactions remained unaltered by thermode activation ($F(1, 6) = 1.86$, $p > .1$), and no interaction was found between thermode activation and

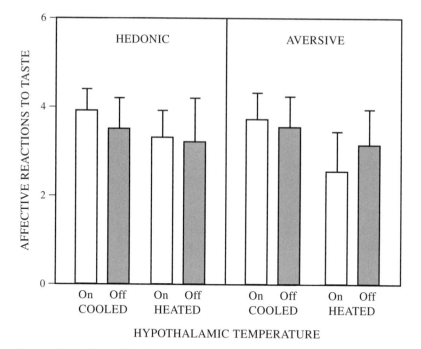

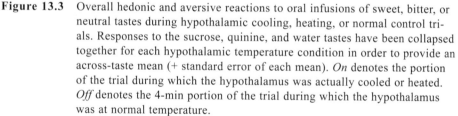

Figure 13.3   Overall hedonic and aversive reactions to oral infusions of sweet, bitter, or neutral tastes during hypothalamic cooling, heating, or normal control trials. Responses to the sucrose, quinine, and water tastes have been collapsed together for each hypothalamic temperature condition in order to provide an across-taste mean (+ standard error of each mean). *On* denotes the portion of the trial during which the hypothalamus was actually cooled or heated. *Off* denotes the 4-min portion of the trial during which the hypothalamus was at normal temperature.

temperature direction (two-way interaction $F(1, 6) = 1.09, p > .1$), or thermode activation, temperature direction, and taste (three-way interaction $F(2, 12) = 0.55, p > .1$) for aversive reactions. In short, manipulation of hypothalamic temperature by 2.5°C failed to change hedonic or aversive reactions to sucrose, sucrose/quinine, or water, regardless of whether feeding was elicited by hypothalamic cooling.

DISCUSSION

Cooling of the hypothalamus by an implanted thermode elicited feeding consistently from "positive" rats. Only cooling of the hypothalamus elicited feeding; heating by the same hypothalamic thermode had no effect. A *reduction* of hypothalamic temperature appears to be uniquely able to induce this motivational state.

The induction of feeding by hypothalamic cooling did not enhance hedonic reactions to sweet or bittersweet tastes. Unlike the induction of feeding by a 48-hr fast, by depletion of body sodium, or by the administration of benzodiazepines, all of which enhance hedonic reactions to sweet, bittersweet, or salty tastes (Berridge, in press; Berridge, Flynn, Schulkin, and Grill, 1984; Berridge and Treit, 1986; Breslin and Grill, 1988; Grill and Norgen, 1978b), eating elicited by hypothalamic cooling appears not to involve an enhancement of basic taste pleasure. Instead, hypothalamic cooling appears to elicit eating through the activation of a psychological process that is separable from basic pleasurable or aversive reactions to food.

Feeding elicited by hypothalamic cooling is similar in this respect to that elicited by electrical stimulation of the lateral hypothalamus (Berridge and Valenstein, in press). Both a hypothalamic thermode, which cools the hypothalamus, and a depolarizing electrode, which stimulates nearby cells and axons, elicit feeding without inducing a hedonic enhancement of taste. An additional feature shared by hypothalamic cooling and by electrical stimulation is that animals will work to gain both, at least under some conditions (although it is not yet known whether brief hypothalamic cooling [187] may be reinforcing to a nonheated animal), yet usually will work to escape from the prolonged experience of either (Cabanac and Dib, 1983; Corbit, 1973; Corbit and Ernits, 1974; Satinoff, 1964; Valenstein and Valenstein, 1964).

The similarity between the behavioral effects of hypothalamic cooling and electrical stimulation is striking. At first sight, the similarity may seem paradoxical. Electrical stimulation is known to induce excitatory potentials (depolarization) and release of synaptic neurotransmitters. Cooling of neural tissue, conversely, suppresses synaptic transmission between neurons (e.g.. Bullock, 1948). The suppression of synaptic transmission is so effective that extreme local cooling has been used as a technique to temporarily deactivate brain regions. More moderate cooling of brain tissue, however, can facilitate some aspects of neuronal activity, such as the summation of graded and action potentials (Andersen, Gjerstad, and Pasztor, 1972; Ritchie and Straub, 1956). A hypothalamic thermode that induces only moderate cooling may in this way have both excitatory and inhibitory effects on different neuronal functions—as may a stimulating electrode (Ranck, 1975). It is at least conceivable that the behavioral similarities of hypothalamic cooling and electrical stimulation are mediated by shared effects on neuronal function.

A major psychological question is: How do hypothalamic cooling and electrical stimulation elicit feeding, if they do not do so by enhancing the hedonic palatability of food? Although further work is necessary, an intriguing preliminary answer is that these manipulations might directly potentiate the attractiveness or incentive salience of external stimuli and their representations without activating intermediary pleasure. In other words, hypothalamic stimulation and cooling might potentiate "wanting" for a food without heightening "liking" for its taste (see Berridge and Valenstein, 1991 for discussion of this distinction). The separation of wanting from liking finds support also from examples of converse dissociations, such as the reduction of wanting without change in liking after avoidance training or brain dopamine depletion (Parker, 1988; Pelchat, Grill, Rozin, and Jacobs, 1983; Berridge, Venier, and Robinson, 1989), and such as differences in liking (hedonic/aversive reactions) for stimuli that are equally wanted or chosen (Grill and Berridge, 1985).

A related psychological question is: Why do human subjects report that their liking for odors and sounds is changed by manipulations of cephalic temperature, when the hedonic and aversive reactions of rats to taste appear not to be influenced by hypothalamic temperature? It may be that temperature reductions other than 2.5°C would enhance hedonic reactions to taste. It may be that blood temperature controls human pleasure via thermal transducers that lie outside of the hypothalamus. It may be that there are important differences between rat and human species in the relation of hypothalamic systems to emotion. Finally, it may be that a human subject who experiences a change in the incentive salience of a stimulus mistakenly *interprets* the changed attractiveness of the stimulus to be a change in hedonic pleasure; in other words, when made to *want* a stimulus more, a person might infer and report that the stimulus is also more *liked,* regardless of any change in fundamental processes of pleasure. The report of change in basic hedonic experience in such instances may be a confusion due to limitations of access between cognitive schemas of self-representation and the basic psychological processes of emotion, perception, memory, etc., that are interpreted by introspection (Booth, 1987; Nisbett and Wilson, 1977; Schachter and Singer, 1962).

In conclusion, cooling of the hypothalamus (but not heating) elicits eating in a relatively unique fashion. Elicited eating does not involve the enhancement of hedonic reactions to taste that accompanies many homeostatic appetites. This effect may reflect the direct activation of a motivational incentive component of appetite—rather than a pleasure component—by hypothalamic cooling.

Acknowledgments—We are grateful to Elliot Valenstein and Neil Grunberg for helpful comments on a manuscript of this paper. We are also grateful to Tarek El-Alayli, John Kim, and Buda Martonyi for assistance with the experiments. This work was supported by a grant from the NIH to K.B. (NS-23959) and from the NSF to R.Z. (BNS-8919734).

REFERENCES

Adelmann, P.K., and Zajonc, R.B. (1989). Facial efference and the experience of emotion. *Annual Review of Psychology, 40*, 249–280.

Andersen, P., Gjerstad, L., and Pasztor, E. (1972). Effect of cooling on synaptic transmission through the cuneate nucleus. *Acta Physiologica Scandinavica, 84*, 433–447.

Baker, M.A. (1982). Brain cooling in endotherms in heat and exercise. *Annual Review of Physiology, 44*, 85–96.

Berridge, K.C. (in press). Modulation of taste affect by hunger, caloric satiety, and sensory-specific satiety. *Appetite.*

Berridge, K.C., Flynn, F.W., Schulkin, J., and Grill, H.J. (1984). Sodium depletion enhances salt palatability in rats. *Behavioral Neuroscience, 98*, 652–660.

Berridge, K.C., and Treit, D. (1986). Chlordiazepoxide directly enhances positive ingestive reactions in rats. Pharmacology, Biochemistry, Behavior, 24. 217–221.

Berridge, K.C., and Valenstein, E.S. (1991). What psychological process mediates feeding evoked by electrical stimulation of the lateral hypothalamus? *Behavioral Neuroscience, 105*, 3–14.

Berridge, K.C., Venier, I.L., and Robinson, T.E. (1989). A taste reactivity analysis of 6-OHDA induced aphagia: Implications for arousal and anhedonia hypotheses of dopamine function. *Behavioral Neuroscience, 103*, 36–45.

Booth, D.A. (1987). Cognitive experimental psychology of appetite. In R.A. Boakes, D.A. Popplewell, and M.J. Burton (Eds.), *Eating habits* (pp. 175–209). New York: Wiley.

Breslin, P., and Grill, H. (1988). A stimulus-response analysis of ingestive taste reactivity. *Neuroscience Abstracts, 14*, 360.

Bullock, T. (1948). Properties of a single synapse in the stellate ganglion of squid. *Journal of Neurophysiology, 11*, 343–364.

Cabanac, M., and Dib, B. (1983). Behavioural responses to hypothalamic cooling and heating in the rat. *Brain Research, 264*, 79–87.

Caputa, M., Perrin, G., and Cabanac, M. (1978). Écoulement sanguin réversible dans la veine ophthalmique: Mécanisme de refroidissement sélectif du cerveau human. *Comptes Rendues d'Academie des Sciences, Paris, 287*, 1011–1014.

Corbit, J.D. (1973). Voluntary control of hypothalamic temperature. *Journal of Comparative and Physiological Psychology, 83*, 394–411.

Corbit, J.D., and Emits, T. (1974). Specific preference for hypothalamic cooling. *Journal of Comparative and Physiological Psychology, 86*, 24–27.

Dib, B., and Cabanac, M. (1984). Skin or hypothalamus cooling: A behavioral choice by rats. *Brain Research, 302*, 1–7.

Grill, H.J., and Berridge, K.C. (1985). Taste reactivity as a measure of the neural control of palatability. In J.M. Sprague and A.N. Epstein (Eds.), *Progress in psychobiology and physiological psychology*, Vol. II. Orlando, FL: Academic Press.

Grill, H.J., and Norgen, R. (1978a). The taste reactivity test I: Mimetic responses to gustatory stimuli in neurologically normal rats. *Brain Research, 143*, 263–279.

Grill, H.J., and Norgen, R. (1978b). Chronic decerebrate rats demonstrate satiation but not bait-shyness. *Science, 201*, 267–269.

Kluger, M.J., and D'Alecy, L.B. (1975). Brain temperature during reversible upper respiratory bypass. *Journal of Applied Physiology, 38*, 268–271.

Nisbett, R. E., and Wilson, T.D. (1977). Telling more than we can know: Verbal reports on mental processes. *Psychological Review, 84*, 231–259. **[188]**

Parker, L. (1988). A comparison of avoidance and rejection responses elicited by conditionally and unconditionally aversive tasting solutions. *Learning and Motivation, 19*, 1–12.

Pelchat, M.L., Grill, H.J., Rozin, P., and Jacobs, J. (1983). Quality of acquired responses to tastes by *Rattus norvegicus* depends on type of associated discomfort. *Journal of Comparative Psychology, 97*, 140–153.

Ranck, J.B. (1975). Which elements are excited in electrical stimulation of mammalian central nervous system: A review. *Brain Research, 98*, 417–440.

Ritchie, J.M., and Straub, R.W. (1956). The effect of cooling on the size of the action potential of mammalian non-medulated fibres. *Journal of Physiology, 134*. 712–717.

Satinoff, E. (1964). Behavioral thermoregulation in response to local cooling of the rat brain. *American Journal of Physiology, 206*, 1389–1394.

Satinoff, E. (1983). A reevaluation of the concept of the homeostatic organization of temperature regulation. In E. Satinoff and P. Teitelbaum (Eds.), *Handbook of behavioral neurobiology*, Vol. 6: *Motivation* (pp. 443–472). New York: Plenum Press.

Schachter, S., and Singer, J.E. (1962). Cognitive, social, and physiological determinants of emotional state. *Psychological Review, 69*, 379–399.

Valenstein, E.S., and Valenstein, T. (1964). Interaction of positive and negative reinforcing systems. *Science, 145*, 1456–1458.

Waynbaum, I. (1907). *La Physionomie humaine: Son mécanisme el son rôle social*. Paris: Alcan.

Zajonc, R.B. (1985). Emotion and facial efference: A theory reclaimed. *Science, 228*, 15–21.

Zajonc, R.B., Murphy, S.T., and Inglehart, M. (1989). Feeling and facial efference: Implications of the vascular theory of emotion. *Psychological Review, 96*, 395–416.

Part Six

The Affect–Cognition Interface

Chapter 14

Feeling and Thinking: Preferences Need No Inferences*

R.B. Zajonc
University of Michigan

The intellectual contact between psychology and poetry is scarce and, when it takes place, often tends to be exploitative. If we happen to come across a poem that appears to support one of our favorite generalizations, we are tempted to cite it (not as evidence, of course, but more in the form of a testimonial). Or we might confer upon it the status of an epigraph in one of our forthcoming chapters (commonly, to the detriment of both the poem and the chapter). But when poetry disagrees with us we are apt to ignore the conflict altogether. Nevertheless, this paper begins with a poem by E.E. Cummings (1973), the first stanza of which affirms a premise tacitly rejected by psychology many decades ago:

> since feeling is first
> who pays any attention
> to the syntax of things
> will never wholly kiss you (p. 160)

In it, Cummings takes for granted that feelings are primary and, by implication, that they are fundamental. They are precedent to the intellective qualities and elements of experience, and they are nearer to its essence: They are nearer to an inner "truth."

In contrast, contemporary psychology regards feelings as last. Affect is postcognitive. It is elicited only after considerable processing of information has been accomplished (see Figure 14.1). An affective reaction, such as liking, disliking, preference, evaluation, or the experience of pleasure or displeasure, is based on a prior cognitive process in which a variety of content discriminations are made and features are identified, examined for their value,

---

* This article was the Distinguished Scientific Contribution Award address given at the meeting of the American Psychological Association, New York, New York, September 2, 1979. It was prepared with the support of a John Simon Guggenheim Fellowship.

I benefited greatly by discussing these ideas with several people, and I am very indebted to them. I am especially grateful to Hazel Markus, Phoebe Ellsworth, Allan Paivio, and Robyn Dawes, who all made extensive and helpful comments on an earlier draft.

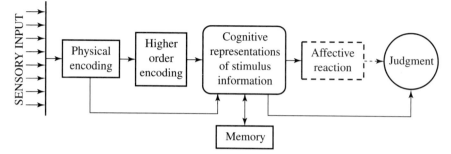

Figure 14.1   Typical information-processing model of affect.

and weighted for their contributions. Once this analytic task has been completed, a computation of the components can generate an overall affective judgment. Before I can like something I must have some knowledge about it, and in the very least, I must have identified some of its discriminant features. Objects must be cognized before they can be evaluated.

Most of us will not be deeply distressed by discovering that our current theories are in conflict [151]* with a controversial poet of the 1920s. But contemporary psychology not only contradicts Cummings, it also contradicts one of its very own founding fathers. Thirty years before Cummings published his poem on feelings, Wundt (1907) wrote in a similar vein:

> When any physical process rises above the threshold of consciousness, it is
> the affective elements which as soon as they are strong enough, first become
> noticeable. They begin to force themselves energetically into the fixation
> point of consciousness *before anything is perceived of the ideational
> element*[1].... They are sometimes states of pleasurable or unpleasurable char-
> acter, sometimes they are predominantly states of strained expectation....
> Often there is vividly present ... the special affective tone of the forgotten
> idea, although the idea itself still remains in the background of conscious-
> ness.... In a similar manner ... the clear apperception of ideas in acts of cog-
> nition and recognition is always preceded by feelings. (pp. 243–244)

Whatever happened to Wundt's affective primacy idea? Is there compelling evidence to reject it?[2] Or to accept it, for that matter? Strictly speaking, we have no better evidence today than Wundt had in 1896. Perhaps a bit better.

---

* Bracketed bold numbers refer to original page numbers. Page numbers indicate where the original page ended.

[1] The italics are mine. The original is even more to the point "Affective elements" were "Gefühlselemente," and the italicized part of the citation was "ehe noch von den Vorstellungselementen irgend etwas wahrgenommen wird" (Wundt, 1905, p. 262).

[2] It is a fact that only 12 years after the first edition of Wundt's *Grundriss* was published, Nakashima (1909a; 1909b) tested Wundt's assertion by collecting reaction times of psychophysical (pitch, hue, temperature, etc.) and affective (preference) judgments made on the same sets of stimuli. He did not find shorter reaction times for judgments of preference than for judgments of pitch, hue, temperature, etc., and thus disagreed with Wundt with regard to the primacy of feelings. But his study alone could not have buried Wundt's idea. Actually, Nakashima's data were rather inconclusive, since he failed to control for levels of discriminability associated with the two types of judgments. Thus, for example, subjects can detect very small differences in hue yet feel quite indifferent in their preference for stimuli that differ so little. Since reaction times for comparisons vary with the size of the difference, these times can be compared meaningfully only if the stimuli are preselected so that difference thresholds for the two types of judgments are the same.

In part, my concern in this paper is with Wundt's assertion. More specifically, building on the scanty evidence we now have, I have tried to develop some notions about the possible ways in which affect is processed as part of experience and have attempted to distinguish affect from processing of information that does not have affective qualities. This article is confined to those aspects of affect and feeling that are generally involved in preferences. These aspects are reflected in the answers to such questions as "Do you like this person?" "How do you feel about capital punishment?" "Which do you prefer, Brie or Camembert?" "Are you pleased with the review your recent book received?" In short, I deal with some hot cognitions (as Abelson [1963] christened them) and try to distinguish them from the cold ones. The class of feelings considered here is that involved in the general quality of behavior that underlies the approach-avoidance distinction. Thus, for the present purposes, other emotions such as surprise, anger, guilt, or shame, which have been identified in the literature and extensively analyzed by Tomkins (1962, 1963), Izard (1977), and others, are ignored.

Unlike experimental psychologists,[3] social psychologists are deeply concerned with affect and with hot cognitions. The extensive work on attitudes, research on cognitive dissonance and cognitive [152] balance, the Schachter and Singer (1962) studies on emotion, and Heider's (1958) attempts to describe the cognitive representation of

---

[3] Contemporary cognitive psychology simply ignores affect. The words *affect, attitude, emotion, feeling,* and *sentiment* do not appear in the indexes of any of the major works on cognition (Anderson, 1976; Anderson and Bower, 1973; Bobrow and Collins, 1975; Crowder, 1976; Kintsch, 1974; Lachman, Lachman, and Butterfield, 1979; Norman and Rumelhart, 1975; Schank and Abelson, 1977; Tulving and Donaldson, 1972). Nor do these concepts appear in Neisser's (1967) original work that gave rise to the cognitive revolution in experimental psychology. And in the six volumes and the 2,133 pages of the *Handbook of Learning and Cognitive Processes* (Estes, 1975–1978), there is only one entry for *affect* and only one for *attitude*. It is worth noting that both of these entries are in Volume 3 in a contribution written by a social psychologist. In the last three volumes—those principally devoted to cognition—there are no references to affect whatsoever.

The notable exceptions are Mandler's (1975) work on thought and emotion, Neisser's 1976 essay, and Miller and Johnson-Laird's (1976) recent volume on language and perception from which the following revealing quotation is taken:

> The information-processing system that emerges from these remarks is fearfully cognitive and dispassionate. It can collect information, remember it, and work toward objectives, but it would have no emotional reaction to what is collected, remembered, or achieved. Since, in this respect, it is a poor model of a person, we should add at least one more predicate to this list of those that take "person" as their first argument. We will use *Feel* (person, *x*) to indicate that people have feelings as well as perceptions, memories, and intentions. It might be possible to subsume *Feel* under *Perceive* on the grounds that our feelings are a special class of perception of inner states. Or we might discuss feelings under *Remember;* the recognition that some word or object is familiar, is, after all, a matter of feeling a certain way about it. Or, since we have already recognized that there is a strong affective component to our intentions, we might link *Feel* to *Intend*.... All these considerations testify to the systematic importance of this psychological predicate. Nevertheless, we will have little to say about *Feel* in the following pages. (pp. 111–112)

Thus, Miller and Johnson-Laird explicitly acknowledge the significance of feelings as part of experience, yet they decide to devote minimal attention to them. Their decision is noteworthy in the light of their belief that "*Feel* is an indispensable predicate for any complete psychology and that it probably lies much closer *than Perceive, Remember,* and *Intend* to the basic sources of energy that keep the whole system running" (p. 112).

Beyond these volumes there are some isolated theoretical attempts directed toward the understanding of the role of motivational and emotional factors in perception and cognition (Broadbent, 1977; Erdelyi, 1974; Posner and Snyder. 1975a).

affect that characterizes interpersonal relationships are all clear manifestations of this concern.[4] There are practically no social phenomena that do not implicate affect in some important way. Affect dominates social interaction, and it is the major currency in which social intercourse is transacted. The vast majority of our daily conversations entail the exchange of information about our opinions, preferences, and evaluations. And affect in these conversations is transmitted not only by the verbal channel but by nonverbal cues as well—cues that may, in fact, carry the principal components of information about affect. It is much less important for us to know whether someone has just said "You are a friend" or "You are a fiend" than to know whether it was spoken in contempt or with affection. Argyle and his colleagues (Argyle, Salter, Nicholson, Williams, and Burgess, 1970) found that 22 times more variance is accounted for by the tone of one's voice than by the content of the utterance when people are asked to interpret utterances. In fact, even when the content of recorded utterances is nearly completely obliterated by means of electronic masking, filtering, or random splicing of the tape, subjects still can encode the emotions expressed in these utterances quite reliably (Dawes and Kramer, 1966; Scherer, Koivumaki, and Rosenthal, 1972). And we have no difficulty in identifying emotions expressed by members of unknown cultures speaking unknown languages. In a recent volume on person perception, Schneider, Hastorf, and Ellsworth (1979) noted that "inferences based on nonverbal cues are primarily inferences about relationships and feelings, and thus are among the most important inferences we make" (p. 142). One cannot be introduced to a person without experiencing some immediate feeling of attraction or repulsion and without gauging such feelings on the part of the other. We evaluate each other constantly, we evaluate each others' behavior, and we evaluate the motives and the consequences of their behavior. And you have already made up your mind about this paper!

Nor is the presence of affect confined to *social* perception. There are probably very few perceptions and cognitions in everyday life that do not have a significant affective component, that aren't hot, or, in the very least, tepid. And perhaps all **[153]** perceptions contain some affect. We do not just see "a house": we see "a *handsome* house," "an *ugly* house," or "a *pretentious* house." We do not just read an article on attitude change, on cognitive dissonance, or on herbicides. We read an "exciting" article on attitude change, an "important" article on cognitive dissonance, or a "trivial" article on herbicides. And the same goes for a sunset, a lightning flash, a flower, a dimple, a hangnail, a cockroach, the taste of quinine, Saumur, the color of earth in Umbria, the sound of traffic on 42nd Street, and equally for the sound of a 1000-Hz tone and the sight of the letter Q.[5]

---

[4] While such studies as those of Byrne (1961), Berscheid and Walster (1978), or Rubin (1973), which deal with interpersonal attraction, also have a concern with affect, they do not contain specific analyses of how affect is represented as part of experience. And in studies that compare the effects of conditions that differ on the affective dimension (such as self- vs. nonself-relevance, ego-involvement), it is generally not the affective quality per se in these conditions that is examined as the major source of variation.

[5] This conjecture probably does not apply to incidental perceptions where the attentive processes are at minimum, although it is not inconceivable that the traces of these incidental perceptions still might recruit affect upon retrieval and thus become hot. In fact, Izard (1979) assumes that some emotion is *always* present in consciousness. Normally, it is the emotion of "interest" that dominates behavior. This emotion, which directs and sustains attention and exploration, is absent only when other emotions such as distress or anger "achieve consciousness" (p. 165).

FEELING AND THINKING

According to the prevalent models for affect (e.g., Figure 14.1), preferences are formed and expressed only after and only as a result of considerable prior cognitive activity. How fully and completely must objects be cognized before they can be evaluated? I argue, along with Wundt and Cummings, that to arouse affect, objects need to be cognized very little—in fact, minimally.

In order to consider this possibility more specifically it is important to distinguish between thoughts and feelings. At the genotypic level, this distinction is not an easy one to make, for it hovers dangerously near the mind-body duality. Some conceptual elements of this distinction, however, may be identified for purposes of clarity. While feelings and thoughts both involve energy and information, the first class of experiences is heavier on energy, whereas the second is heavier on information (e.g., Inhelder and Piaget, 1958; pp. 347–348). In the pure case, the analysis of feelings attends primarily to energy transformations, for example, the transformation of chemical or physical energy at the sensory level into autonomic or motor output. In contrast, the analysis of thoughts focuses principally on information transformations. In nearly all cases, however, feeling is not free of thought, nor is thought free of feelings. Considerable cognitive activity most often accompanies affect, and Schachter and Singer (1962) consider it a necessary factor of the emotional experience. Thoughts enter feelings at various stages of the affective sequence, and the converse is true for cognitions. Feelings may be aroused at any point of the cognitive process: registration, encoding, retrieval, inference, etc. But this converse relation is not totally symmetrical. I will later argue for Wundt's conjecture that affect is *always* present as a companion to thought, whereas the converse is not true for cognition. In fact, it is entirely possible that the very first stage of the organism's reaction to stimuli and the very first elements in retrieval are affective. It is further possible that we can like something or be afraid of it before we know precisely what it is and perhaps even *without* knowing what it is. And when we try to recall, recognize, or retrieve an episode, a person, a piece of music, a story, a name, in fact, anything at all, the affective quality of the original input is the first element to emerge. To be sure, the early affective reaction is gross and vague. Nevertheless, it is capable of influencing the ensuing cognitive process to a significant degree. Needless to say, after some cognitive activity has been executed, there may be new feeling to the stimulus. But the fact that cognitions *can* produce feelings—as in listening to a joke, for example, where affect comes at the end with a punch line or as a result of post-decision dissonance—need not imply that cognitions are necessary components of affect. What I want to argue is that the form of experience that we came to call feeling accompanies *all* cognitions, that it arises early in the process of registration and retrieval, albeit weakly and vaguely, and that it derives from a parallel, separate, and partly independent system in the organism.

At the phenotypic level, we can support Wundt's conjecture by spelling out in somewhat greater detail some of the ways in which affective judgments and reactions, or hot cognitions, differ from their cold cognitive counterparts, keeping in mind that the first category is represented by the prototype "I like Joe," and the second by "Joe is a boy."

Affective Reactions Are Primary

Wundt and Cummings are joined by Bartlett and Osgood in the view that feelings come first. Bartlett (1932) observes in his book on remembering, **[154]**

> Attitude names a complex psychological state or process which it is very hard to describe in more elementary psychological terms. It is, however, as I have often indicated, very largely a matter of feeling, or affect.... [When] a subject is being asked to remember, very often the first thing that emerges is something of the nature of attitude. The recall is then a construction, made largely on the basis of this attitude, and its general effect is that of a justification of the attitude. (pp. 206–207)

In his analysis of environments as perceptual targets, Ittelson (1973) asserts that "the first level of response to the environment is affective. The direct emotional impact of the situation, perhaps largely a global response to the ambiance, very generally governs the directions taken by subsequent relations with the environment. It sets the motivational tone and delimits the kinds of experiences one expects and seeks" (p. 16). Preferences influence language comprehension and language production as well (Premack, 1976). Osgood (1962) was impressed with the primacy of affect in a different way:

> First, I must confess that, when we began this research over ten years ago, I had the expectation that the major factors of the semantic space would represent the ways in which our sensory apparatus divides up the world— e.g., would parallel Boring's "dimensions of consciousness." ... The accumulating data have proved my expectation wrong ... the dominant factors of *evaluation, potency* and *activity* that keep appearing certainly have a response-like character, reflecting the ways we can react to meaningful events rather than the ways we can receive them.
>
> But these major factors also seem to have an *affective* as well as a response-like character. As a matter of fact, the similarity of our factors to Wundt's (1896) tridimensional theory of *feeling*—pleasantness-unpleasantness, strain-relaxation, and excitement-quiescence—has been pointed out to me." (pp. 19–20)

It is significant also that at least three social-psychological conceptions labeled "cognitive" consistency theories focus not on consistency of content but on the consistency of affect (Abelson and Rosenberg, 1958; Heider, 1958; Osgood and Tannenbaum, 1955).

Decisions are another area where thought and affect stand in tension to each other. It is generally believed that *all* decisions require some conscious or unconscious processing of pros and cons. Somehow we have come to believe, tautologically, to be sure, that if a decision has been made, then a cognitive process must have preceded it. Yet there is no evidence that this is indeed so. In fact, for most decisions, it is extremely difficult to demonstrate that there has actually been *any* prior cognitive process whatsoever. One might argue that these are cases in which one alternative so overwhelmingly dominates all the others that only a minimum of cognitive participation is required and that that is why the cognitive involvement preceding such decisions is so hard to detect.

But this argument must confront the observation that if all decisions involve the evaluation of alternatives, then when choices appear quite lopsided to the decision maker, it is even more important to scrutinize the alternatives that appear inferior, for it is entirely possible that one of them possesses some hidden but overriding virtue. It is therefore not without merit to suppose that in many decisions affect plays a more important role than we are willing to admit. We sometimes delude ourselves that we proceed in a rational manner and weigh all the pros and cons of the various alternatives. But this is probably seldom the actual case. Quite often "I decided in favor of X" is no more than "I liked X." Most of the time, information collected about alternatives serves us less for making a decision than for justifying it afterward. Dissonance is prevalent just because complete and thorough computation is not performed before the decision (Festinger, 1964). We buy the cars we "like," choose the jobs and houses that we find "attractive," and then justify those choices by various reasons that might appear convincing to others who never fail to ask us, "Why this car?" or "Why this house?" We need not convince ourselves.[6] *We* know what we like.

In a study of consumer behavior, Quandt (1956) found that buyers often do not attend to the features of the article that they consider criterial for their decisions and often base their choices on features that they previously dismissed as irrelevant. And Kahneman and Tversky (1979) have demonstrated that numerous axioms of decision theory that give decisions their rational flavor are blatantly contradicted by experimental results. **[155]**

Affect Is Basic

In one of her last books, which bears the provocative title of *Mind: An Essay on Human Feeling*, Susan K. Langer (1967) tried to show "that the entire psychological field— including human conception, responsible action, rationality, knowledge—is a vast and branching development of feeling" (p. 23). Affect is the first link in the evolution of complex adaptive functions that eventually differentiated animals from plants. And unlike language or cognition, affective responsiveness is universal among the animal species. A rabbit confronted by a snake has no time to consider all the perceivable attributes of the snake in the hope that he might be able to infer from them the likelihood of the snake's attack, the timing of the attack, or its direction. The rabbit cannot stop to contemplate the length of the snake's fangs or the geometry of its markings. If the rabbit is to escape, the action must be undertaken long before the completion of even a simple cognitive process—before, in fact, the rabbit has fully established and verified that a nearby movement might reveal a snake in all its coiled glory. The decision to run must be made on the basis of minimal cognitive engagement.

It is thus significant that, in categorizing facial expressions, about 50% of the variance is explained by the pleasant-unpleasant dimension (Abelson and Sermat, 1962; Hastorf, Osgood, and Ono, 1966), and the same value is obtained for the multidimensional scaling of similarities among photographs of faces (Milord, 1978). Similarly, it

---

[6] Phoebe Ellsworth (Note 1) illustrates the role of affect in her own recent decision experience. In trying to decide whether to accept a position at another university, she says, "I get half way through my Irv Janis balance sheet and say, 'Oh hell, it's not coming out right! Have to find a way to get some pluses over on the other side.'"

is a typical result in semantic differential studies that among the three factors Evaluation, Potency, and Activity, all of which Osgood considers to be affective components of meaning, it is the first that accounts for about 50% of the variance.[7] And it is no accident, according to Osgood (1969), that these three factors of the semantic space are found repeatedly among diverse sets of concepts:

> In my opinion, it is the innateness of the emotional reaction system of the human animal that underlies the universality of the affective E-P-A component of meaning. In other words, the "innateness" of E-P-A ... is really the pan-humanes of emotional reactions, and these obviously have evolutionary significance for the survival of any species. Organisms without other specialized adaptive mechanisms (e.g., armor, coloration, poisons, etc.) which were unable to represent for themselves the good versus bad implications of things (antelope versus saber-toothed tiger), the strong versus weak of things (saber-toothed tiger versus mosquito), and the quick versus slow of things (saber-toothed tiger versus quicksand) would have little chance of survival. In the human species these "gut" reactions to things appear as the affective meaning system (the E-P-A components of total meaning), and it is these components which provide us with what might most appropriately be called the "feeling-tones" of concepts as a part of their total meaning. (p.195)

Affective Reactions Are Inescapable

Unlike judgments of objective stimulus properties, affective reactions that often accompany these judgments cannot always be voluntarily controlled. Most often, these experiences occur whether one wants them to or not. One might be able to control the expression of emotion but not the experience of it itself. It is for this very reason that law, science, sports, education, and other institutions of society keep devising ever new means of making judgments "objective." We wish some decisions to be more independent of these virtually inescapable reactions.

We may completely fail to notice a person's hair color or may hardly remember what it was shortly after meeting the person. But we can seldom escape the reaction that the person impressed us as pleasant or unpleasant, agreeable or disagreeable, as someone to whom we were drawn or someone by whom we were repelled. And these affective reactions—and, more important, the retrieval of affect—occur without effort. In contrast, some cognitive judgments require substantial effort. Chess contestants typically lose several pounds of their weight in the course of a tournament.

Because affective judgments are inescapable, they cannot be focused as easily as perceptual and cognitive processes. They are much more influenced by the context of

---

[7] It is therefore something of a paradox that so little attention is paid to affect in information-processing studies. Most of the tasks in experiments on information processing are verbal. Most of them involve some forms of *semantic* memory. If the semantic space is primarily an *affective* space, as Osgood argues, then the affective components and qualities of information need to be given as much attention as their phonemic, graphemic, lexical, semantic, conceptual, or pictorial counterparts.

the surround, and they are generally holistic. Affective reactions are thus less subject to control by attentive processes.[8] **[156]**

Affective Judgments Tend to Be Irrevocable

Once a cognitive judgment has been made—for example, that at the forthcoming social hour there will be more scotches drunk than bourbons—one can still be persuaded that it may turn out otherwise. It can be pointed out, say, that the distribution of ages of the guests is different than that we *really* like scotch better than bourbon, is greater than the supply of scotch. We can readily accept the fact that we can be wrong. But we are never wrong about what we like or dislike. Hot cognitions are seldom subjectively false. It would be much harder to persuade us that we *really* like scotch better than bourbon, given that we feel otherwise. Once formed, an evaluation is not readily revoked. Experiments on the perseverance effect, the strong primacy effects in impression formation, and the fact that attitudes are virtually impervious to persuasion by communication all attest to the robust strength and permanence of affect. Affect often persists after a complete invalidation of its original cognitive basis, as in the case of the perseverance phenomenon when a subject is told that an initial experience of success or failure has been totally fabricated by the experimenter (Ross, Lepper, and Hubbard,1975).

The reason why affective judgments seem so irrevocable is that they "feel" valid. We are not easily moved to reverse our impression of a person or of a piece of music. We trust our reactions, we believe that they are "true" and that they accurately represent an internal state or condition. Perhaps the subjective validity of affective judgments and reactions and our confidence in these judgments derive from the Cartesian tradition[9] that allows us to doubt everything except our own feelings, especially the feelings of doubt. Perhaps it reflects a basic reality.[10]

Affective Judgments Implicate the Self

When we evaluate an object or an event, we are describing not so much what is in the object or in the event, but something that is in ourselves. Cognitive judgments deal with qualities that reside in the stimulus: "This cat is black," "Camembert and Brie are soft-ripened cheeses." These judgments are made on I-scales that are orders of stimuli (Coombs, 1964). Affective judgments, however, are made on I-scales, that is, scales on which are located jointly the various stimuli as well as the ideal preference point of the

---

[8] The existentialists (e.g., Sartre, 1947) ascribe a substantial voluntary component to emotion. "The existentialist does not believe in the power of passion. He will never agree that a sweeping passion is a ravaging torrent which fatally leads a man to certain acts and is therefore an excuse. He thinks that man is responsible for his passion" (pp. 27–28). Because of the participation of sensory, cognitive, and motor processes, the argument that emotions have some voluntary component is not without basis.

[9] Hume (1898), too, held that emotions (passions) cannot be false. "A passion must be accompanied with some false judgment, in order to its being unreasonable; and even then 'tis not the passion properly speaking, which is unreasonable, but the judgment" (p. 196).

[10] Because nonverbal cues exchanged in social interaction are dominated by affect, they are perceived as having such properties as trustworthiness and freedom from voluntary control (Schneider. Hastorf, and Ellsworth, 1979, pp. 123–127).

person. "I dislike this black cat" or "I prefer Camembert to Brie" are judgments on J-scales. Thus, affective judgments are *always* about the self. They identify the state of the judge in relation to the object of judgment.

Affective Reactions Are Difficult to Verbalize

The remarkable aspect of first impressions of persons is their immediacy. When we meet a stranger, we know within a fraction of a second whether we like the person or not. The reaction is instantaneous and automatic. Perhaps the feeling is not always precise, perhaps we are not always aware of it, but the feeling is always there. If our later experience with the stranger conflicts with the first impression, we are terribly surprised. We consider it an exception. Paradoxically, this subjective validity of affective reaction, this certainty that we "know what we like," is often accompanied by our inability to verbalize the reasons for our attraction or repulsion to the person.[11] When asked why we like someone, we say that we like the person because he or she is "nice," "pleasant," or "interesting." But these adjectives describe our reactions to the person, not the person. There simply aren't very effective verbal means to communicate why we like people and objects or what it is that we like about them.

The communication of affect, therefore, relies much more on the nonverbal channels (Ekman and Friesen, 1969; Schneider, Hastorf, and Ellsworth, 1979). Yet it is remarkably efficient. And it is in the realm of nonverbal expression of feelings that their basic nature is again revealed. The universality of emotional expression strongly suggests our evolutionary continuity with other species and the fundamental nature of affect. The facial expressions of humans upon biting into a **[157]** sour apple and their expressions of surprise, anger, delight, or serenity are remarkably similar across all cultures and are not far removed from the expressions of the great apes. Perhaps we have not developed an extensive and precise verbal representation of feeling just because in the prelinguistic human this realm of experience had an adequate representation in the nonverbal channel.

The role of affective communication is particularly significant in the social interaction among animals. The effectiveness of communication of affect and the accuracy of recognition of affective expression are illustrated by the results of Pratt and Sackett (1967). They raised rhesus monkeys in conditions that allowed complete contact with peers, in conditions that allowed only visual and auditory access, and in complete isolation. The monkeys were then examined for the kinds of animals they preferred to approach. Those raised under the same conditions preferred each other twice as much as those raised under different conditions, even when the stimulus animals were total strangers to the test monkeys. While it could not be determined what sorts of cues allowed the animals to make these fine discriminations, it is very likely that the three groups developed during the course of their previous experience distinct patterns of emotional responding to new stimuli and to strange individuals, and that the animals

---

[11] Mandler (1975), Neisser (1967), and Nisbett and Wilson (1977) pointed out that individuals have no access to the cognitions that occasion, mediate, or cause their actions, that are parts of their attitudes, or that determine their preferences. On the basis of an extensive review of the social psychological literature, Nisbett and Wilson (1977) concluded that introspective reports about influences on the subjects' evaluations, decisions, and actions were so unreliable as not to be trusted.

raised under the same conditions found each other more attractive because of the familiarity of these emotional patterns.

The reliance of affect on nonverbal means of communication has, I believe, implications for the way it is processed. For if affect is not always transformed into semantic content but is instead often encoded in, for example, visceral or muscular symbols, we would expect information contained in feelings to be acquired, organized, categorized, represented, and retrieved somewhat differently than information having direct verbal referents. Recent electromyographic research provides strong 'evidence for the participation of muscular activity in the imagination, recall, and production of emotional states (Lang, 1979; Schwartz, Fair, Salt, Mandel, and Klerman, 1976). In light of these intuitions, it is not unreasonable to speculate that the processing of affect is closer to the acquisition and retention of motor skills than of word lists.

Affective Reactions Need Not Depend on Cognition

At the turn of the century, Nakashima (1909a, 1909b) tried to find support for Wundt's affective-primacy conjecture by comparing reaction times for psychophysical judgments and for preferences. He failed. But he did find evidence that judgments of pleasantness were independent of sensory qualities and that these judgments could not have been mediated by these qualities. Similar independence, based on multidimensional scaling, has been reported more recently, for example, in studying the perceptions of and preferences for soft drinks. Cooper (1973) found that similarity scaling yielded a space dominated by a "cola-ness" dimension, whereas preference scaling generated a space dominated by popularity of the drinks. Generally, it appears that similarity judgments predict preferences only when the similarity judgments are themselves highly evaluative, as in the case of admissions officers judging college candidates (Klahr, 1969) or art-trained students judging paintings (Berlyne, 1975; O'Hare, 1976). Osgood (1962) took it as a given that the affective reaction system "is independent of any particular sensory modality" (p. 21).

If there is indeed a separation between affect and cognition, then it is not surprising that research on preferences, attitudes, attractions, impressions, aesthetic judgments, and similar affective responses—research that commonly has invoked cognitive mediators—has not been terribly successful. If overall preferences were simply a matter of calculating the combination of weighted component preferences, and if component preferences were nothing more than cognitive representations of object features marked with affect, then the problems of predicting attitudes, decisions, aesthetic judgments, or first impressions would have been solved long ago. After all, these problems have been around for nearly a century. Yet except for trivial cases or cases in which the responses are highly cognitive (e.g., Yntema and Torgerson's [1961] study of judgments of ellipses), the cognition-based solutions to these problems have rarely predicted more than 20% of the total variance.

The dismal failure in achieving substantial attitude change through various forms of communication or persuasion is another indication that affect is fairly independent and often impervious to cognition. If attitudes consist of information units that have affect or utilities attached to them, then to change an individual's attitude, what could be simpler than providing the individual with alternative information units that have the same sort [158] of affect as that attached to the desired attitude? If a person believes that Candidate A is honest, we can simply give the person information proving that A is not honest. Or, we could change the centrality or the weight of honesty. Yet this approach has been the least successful in attitude change. Even the most convincing arguments on the merits of spinach won't reduce a child's aversion to this vegetable. Direct persuasion effects have been so weak that researchers have instead turned to more pernicious avenues of attitude change, such as insufficient justification, persuasion through distraction, the foot-in-the-door technique, or the bogus pipeline.

It is unlikely that calculations based on discriminable component features and their affective values will reliably predict our overall affective reactions to objects and events. These reactions do not seem to be composites of such elements. An affective reaction to a person we meet emerges long before any of these features can be identified, let alone evaluated. The assumption that component affect, utilities, or values attach themselves *to the very same* features that the subject attends to in a typical detection, recognition, discrimination, or categorization task is likely to be wrong.[12] The analysis of preferences is not simply an analysis of cold cognitive representations that have become hot, that is, cognitive representations that have some affect attached to them.[13] The stimulus features that serve us so well in discriminating, recognizing, and categorizing objects and events may not be useful at all in evaluating these objects. If this is indeed the case, then there must exist a class of features that can combine more readily with affect and thereby allow us to make these evaluations, to experience attraction, repulsion, pleasure, conflict, and other forms of affect, and to allow us to have these affective reactions quite early after the onset of the sensory input. These features might be quite gross, vague, and global. Thus, they might be insufficient as a basis for most cognitive judgments—judgments even as primitive as recognition, for example. In order to distinguish this class of features from simple discriminanda, I call them *preferenda* (Zajonc, Note 2).

I cannot be very specific about preferenda. If they exist they must be constituted of interactions between some gross object features and internal states of the individual—states that can be altered while the object remains unchanged, as, for example, when liking for a stimulus increases with repeated experience. Color preferences are a case in point. Similarity scaling of color yields three dimensions—brightness, hue, and saturation—that explain almost all of the variance in similarity judgments. But on the basis of Nakashima's (1909a) research and according to unpublished work of Premack and Kintsch (Note 3), the scaling of color for preference would not reveal these three factors. If we did not know from other sources that brightness, hue, and saturation exhaust the entire range of differences among colors, then we would not discover them by means of preference scaling. Abstract preferences for color and color preferences for classes of objects, such as hair, cars, or houses, are still more problematic if we insist on using brightness, hue, and saturation in quantifying them. And the same applies to

---

[12] I did not have the slightest doubt of this assumption, however, when I wrote my dissertation (Zajonc, 1955), which employed it without question.

[13] The term *hot cognition* has been used fairly indiscriminately, although it generally refers to cases when affect *accompanies* or *qualifies* information. "I have a malignant tumor" is a hot cognition. However, the emotional experience of listening to one's favorite piece of music performed by one's favorite artist is less likely to receive the label of *hot cognition*. It is even less meaningful to speak of *hot cognitions* when affect becomes separated from the original cognitions.

face recognition: Physical features do not serve as discriminanda for faces (Milord, 1978; Patterson and Baddeley, 1977). It is therefore an interesting problem to discover what it is in color that "holds" affect if it isn't brightness, hue, and saturation and what it is in a face that "holds" affect if it isn't physical features. The answer to this problem is probably that *some* physical aspects, perhaps vague, gross, or configural, are involved, but not alone. Preferenda must consist of an interaction of these global features with some internal state or condition of the individual.

Affective Reactions May Become Separated from Content

It sometimes happens that we are reminded of a movie or of a book whose contents we are unable to recall. Yet the affect present when leaving the movie or our general impression of the book are readily accessible. Or we are reminded of an interpersonal conflict of long ago. The cause of the conflict, the positions taken, the matter at issue, who said what, may have all been forgotten, and yet the affect that was present during the incident may be readily retrieved. Such experiences, together with such clinical phenomena [159] as free-floating anxiety, hysteria, or posthypnotically induced moods, all point to the possibility that some aspects of affective processes might well be separate and partly independent of cold cognitions. Occasions when they are not include those when an affective experience has been communicated to someone else or when it has been thought of a great deal. On such occasions an elaborate cognitive representation of affect occurs that may be processed very much like any other type of information. It is important to observe, however, that not all affective experiences are accompanied by verbal or other cognitive representations and that when they are, such representations are imprecise and ambiguous.

PREFERENCES NEED NO INFERENCES: EMPIRICAL EVIDENCE

The prevalent approach to the study of preferences and related affective phenomena holds that affective reactions follow a prior cognitive process: Before I can like something I must first know what it is. According to this prevalent view, therefore, such cold cognitive processes as recognition or categorization are primary in aesthetic judgments, in attitudes, in impression formation, and in decision making: They come first. If we say, for example, that we like John *because* he is intelligent, rich, and compassionate, it follows that we must have gained some impression of John's intelligence, wealth, and compassion, and combined them, before we formed an attraction to him. This must be especially so in the case of judgments of novel stimuli before the component units become fused into an integrated structure. Thus, if the complexity of polygons is an important basis of their attractiveness, then polygons that are judged pleasing (or displeasing) must have previously been somehow examined for their complexity. Otherwise, the calculus of preferences makes little sense.[14]

---

[14] Affective reactions to objects that have been encountered and evaluated many times may become automated, thus gaining some independence from the component processes (Shiffrin and Schneider, 1977). As such, they may have different properties than *first* reactions. It is those first affective reactions (that is, those elicited when individuals are asked to evaluate objects totally novel to them) that I wish to consider at this point.

The first indication that affect may not require extensive participation of cold cognitive processes appeared in studies of the exposure effect, that is, the phenomenon of increasing preference for objects that can be induced by virtue of mere repeated exposure (Harrison, 1977; Zajonc, 1968). While the empirical results that established the phenomenon were quite consistent, their explanation continues to be very elusive. Theories that attempted to account for the mere exposure effect, such as Harrison's (1968) response competition hypothesis or Berlyne's (1970) optimal arousal theory, treated affect as resulting from a prior cognitive process. Both theories contained the remnants of Titchener's (1910) thesis on familiarity. In explaining the preference for familiar objects, Titchener attributed a critical role to recognition, which he thought gave the individual a "glow of warmth, a sense of ownership, a feeling of intimacy" (p. 411). The majority of subsequent findings bearing on the explanation of the exposure effect, however, have revealed that recognition must play a relatively minor role, as must the subjective feeling of recognition.

Matlin (1971) was the first to discover that the role of recognition in the exposure effect may have been overstated. During an initial experimental session, she presented Turkish-like words either three times or six times. Subsequently, these words, together with others that were not shown at all, were rated for liking and also for familiarity. That is, for each word the subjects had to decide whether they saw it previously in the exposure series and to report how much they liked it. Table 14.1 shows Matlin's results. Liking is averaged as a function of objective familiarity and as a function of subjective familiarity. Note that there is an effect due to subjective familiarity, that is, when the subjects thought a stimulus was old they rated it more positively than when they thought it was new. However, the *objective* history of the individual's experience with the stimulus is just as effective in influencing liking. Stimuli **[160]** that the subjects had actually seen were liked better than stimuli not seen, independently of whether the subjects thought of them as "old" or "new."

Similar results were obtained recently by Moreland and Zajonc (1977, 1979), using Japanese ideographs. Subjects were given 0, 1, 3, 9, and 27 prior exposures, counterbalanced, of course, with the stimuli. Following these exposures, the subjects made a variety of recognition and liking judgments. A number of findings are of interest. Many stimuli shown in the first series, some of them 27 times, were not recognized as familiar when shown later. Taking only those stimuli that were so judged, and relating the

Table 14.1   Average stimulus affect ratings as a function of objective familiarity (old-new) and subjective familiarity ("old"-"new").

Objective familiarity	"Old"	"New"	M
Old	4.90	4.20	4.47
New	4.20	3.90	4.01
M	4.55	4.05	

Note: Data are from Matlin (1971).

rated attractiveness of these stimuli to their actual number of exposures, we obtained correlations of .43 in one experiment and of .50 in another. An objective history of exposure influenced liking of stimuli for which the subjects could not have felt a "glow of warmth" or a "sense of ownership."

We also performed another type of analysis. Because we had a sufficient number of measures, we were able to use linear structural equation analyses to evaluate various causal models of our data. We used the LISREL III program (see Jöreskog and Sörbom, 1977) to calculate maximum likelihood estimates for causal models that assign different roles to the recognition factor. The program distinguishes between latent variables (constructs) and their observed indicators (measures). By estimating the unknown coefficients in a system of simultaneous equations for any particular model, the program describes the pattern of relations among the latent variables, distinguishing causal effects from unexplained variation in each case.

The results of this analysis are shown in Figure 14.2. Latent variables are shown in ellipses, while measures of those variables are shown in rectangles. The coefficients linking the ellipses with the boxes represent the validities with which particular latent variables were assessed by their measures. Path coefficients linking the latent variables to each other represent causal relations. Unexplained variation in the latent variables (V_1

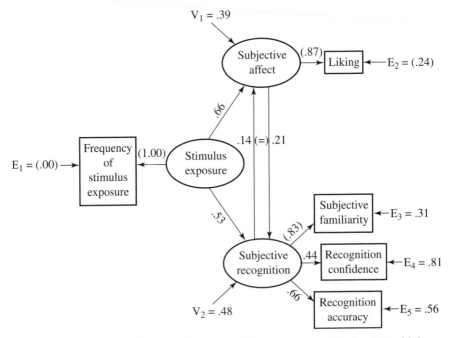

Figure 14.2 Causal model for independent affect; goodness of fit is $x^2(5) = 39.0$.
V = variable; E = error.

SOURCE: From "Exposure Effects May Not Depend on Stimulus Recognition" by R.L. Moreland and R.B. Zajonc, *Journal of Personality and Social Psychology*, 1979, *37*, 1085–1089. Copyright 1979 by the American Psychological Association. Reprinted by permission.

and V_2) and error in the various measures (E_1 through E_5) are also shown. Some parameters (shown in parentheses) had to be set equal to some a priori value in the maximum likelihood solution so that variance in all of the latent variables could be identified.

The first model tested was one postulating that stimulus exposure has two mutually independent effects, one cognitive and one affective, or one cold and one hot. We supposed that under the **[161]** impact of repeated exposure, people gain an increasing ability to recognize the stimulus—they achieve a feeling of subjective familiarity and an awareness of recognition, which authors since Titchener have thought to be the necessary conditions for an increased positive affect toward the stimulus. This is the purely cold effect that is capable of generating the eventual "glow of warmth." However, we wanted to know as well whether, quite independently of this cold cognitive effect, there is also an affective change, or hot effect—that is, whether subjects acquire a more positive attitude toward the object as exposure increases, independently of recognition. They do. While the path coefficient from stimulus exposure to subjective recognition is substantial (.53), indicating that recognition improves with exposure, there also is a hot effect: There is a strong path from stimulus exposure to subjective affect that is *independent of recognition* (.66).

We can compare this model with one that is entirely cold, that is, with one that requires the entire process to be mediated by cognitive factors, by the discriminanda. This model, shown in Figure 14.3, says essentially that whatever affective changes take place as a result of exposure are entirely mediated by stimulus recognition. The result of requiring affect to be mediated by recognition is a substantial reduction in the efficiency of prediction. The x^2 in the previous model was 39.0 ($df = 5$) and in this model is 83.6 ($df = 6$), generating a significant ($p < .01$) difference between the two models of $x^2(1) = 44.6$.

The experiments just described all involved presentation of stimuli under optimal conditions; that is, there was nothing to prevent the subjects from registering what was shown and from memorizing the information presented to them. Subjective recognition and the likelihood of recognition were controlled by statistical techniques. And the

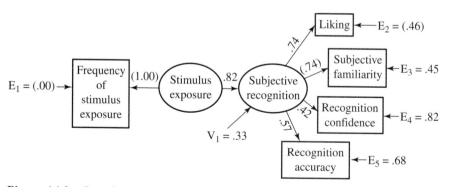

Figure 14.3   Causal model for mediated affect; goodness of fit is $x^2(6) = 83.6$.
V = variable; E = error.

SOURCE: From "Exposure Effects May Not Depend on Stimulus Recognition" by R.L. Moreland and R.B. Zajonc, *Journal of Personality and Social Psychology,* 1979, *37,* 1085–1089. Copyright 1979 by the American Psychological Association. Reprinted by permission.

results showing that stimulus recognition was not a necessary condition for the exposure effect were correlational.

Much firmer evidence, however, that hot cognition is quite short on cognition was collected by W.R. Wilson (1975), who controlled for recognition experimentally by means of an ingenious technique. He employed the method of dichotic listening in order to reduce recognition to a chance level. Random sequences of tones, such as those constructed by Vitz (1964), were presented to one ear, and a story was simultaneously presented to the other. Subjects were asked to track the story on a written page to verify whether what they heard corresponded to the printed text. The melodies were played five times each. The subjects were subsequently given a recognition memory test in which the earlier melodies and other melodies that they had never heard were played. But now there was no interference from the other channel, and no other task was required of the subject. The subjects also rated all the melodies for liking, some subjects giving their recognition memory judgments before, others after, the ratings for liking. The procedure succeeded in reducing recognition memory nearly to the chance level. The accuracy of recognition was 59% in one experiment and only 53% in another.

Table 14.2 shows the results of these experiments. Again, as in the case of previous results, liking varies with subjective recognition. But apart from this effect, liking also varies with the objective history of stimulus exposure. With recognition reduced nearly to the chance level, differential affective reaction to the stimuli is obtained as a consequence of mere repeated exposure. Random melodies [162] presented five times were liked better than melodies never heard, even though the subjects could not discriminate the former from the latter for familiarity.

In a follow-up of these studies, Kunst-Wilson (who is the same person as W.R. Wilson) and I tried to reproduce the effect in a visual mode (Kunst-Wilson and Zajonc, 1980). Random polygons were constructed and presented for an extremely brief time interval—in fact, only 1 millisecond. Subsequently, the subjects rated the polygons for

Table 14.2   Average stimulus affect ratings as a function of objective familiarity (old-new) and subjective familiarity ("old"-"new").

	Subjective familiarity		
Objective familiarity	"Old"	"New"	*M*
Old			
Experiment I	4.20	4.03	4.12
Experiment II	3.51	3.85	3.66
New			
Experiment I	3.75	3.07	3.30
Experiment II	3.03	3.02	3.03
M			
Experiment I	4.02	3.52	
Experiment II	3.29	3.40	

Note: Data are from Wilson (1975).

liking and were tested for their recognition memory. Judgments were made in paired comparisons to avoid possible response bias. Again, recognition was at a chance level: 48%. However, of the stimuli that were liked, 60% were old and 40% were new. Sixteen of 24 subjects liked objectively old stimuli better than new stimuli, but only 5 of 24 recognized them as such at better than chance level. And of the 24 subjects, 17 showed better discrimination between objectively old and objectively new stimuli in their affective judgments than in their recognition responses, while only 4 showed such superiority of recognition over affective judgments. Thus, the subjects were able to distinguish between the old and new stimuli if they used liking as their response, but they were not able to distinguish between them if they had to identify them as "old" or "new." This result may be taken as evidence that a class of features (preferenda) exists that allows individuals to experience affect toward objects but does not allow them to accomplish cognitive tasks as simple as those in recognition memory tests.

These experiments establish, I believe, that affective reactions to a stimulus may be acquired by virtue of experience with that stimulus even if not accompanied by such an elementary cold cognitive process as conscious recognition. Thus, a theory that assumes that subjective experiences of novelty and familiarity mediate the affective response acquired during the course of exposures must contend with the results showing that with the subjective experience of novelty held constant, systematic variations in affect can be obtained just by means of an objective manipulation of exposure.

However, one should not assume that no form of recognition occurred. Obviously, some discrimination, however primitive or minimal, must have taken place, even though it must have been at a level not accessible to the subject's awareness. It is somewhat surprising that any effect at all was obtained with exposures as short as 1 millisecond, but it should be noted that the stimuli were high contrast (black on white) and that no mask was used. Detectable effects with 1-millisecond exposures were also obtained by Shevrin and Fritzler (1968) and by Shevrin, Smith, and Fritzler (1971). These authors reported differential evoked potentials and word associations to critical and control stimuli presented for 1 millisecond—stimuli that the subject could neither recognize nor identify. Even more pertinent is the work of Marcel (Note 4). He presented over a large number of trials either a single word or a blank always followed by a mask. The exposure duration of the word was varied. The subjects were then asked whether anything had been presented before the mask. If they answered yes, two words were then presented to them under optimal conditions. The subjects were then asked which of these two words was more *visually* similar to the one shown before the mask. Finally, they were asked which of these same two words was more *semantically* similar to the stimulus shown before the mask. With decreasing stimulus exposure, all three types of judgments tended to become less accurate, and eventually all three reached the chance level. But the first to become totally unreliable were judgments regarding the actual presence of the stimulus words. The second type of judgment to be reduced to a chance level by the decreasing exposures was that concerned with physical similarity. And when the subjects were totally unable to rise above chance in comparing [163] physical similarities of the words, they were still judging their semantic similarities quite reliably.

Marcel's results are reminiscent of those reported by Broadbent and Gregory (1967), who found that unpleasant words (such as "blood") were more often misperceived as other unpleasant words (such as "death") than as equally probable neutral words. Marcel's results, moreover, are of particular interest if we consider the consistent findings from the semantic differential literature showing that meaning is very highly saturated with affect. If it is indeed affect that allows subjects to make a semantic match in the absence of conscious recognition, then deciding which of two given words is *emotionally* more similar to a stimulus word should be at least as easy as deciding which is semantically more similar. This experiment, in fact, is now being carried out by Moreland and myself.

Another consequence derives from the prevalent approach to affect and cognition. Prevalent theories, especially the one developed by the late Daniel Berlyne (1967), generally assume that the affective reaction occurs in response to the level of arousal, which in turn is mediated by collative variables such as complexity, novelty, or congruity. If complexity, congruity, and novelty mediate liking, in that objects and events are liked just because they are optimally complex or simple, novel or familiar, then the judgments of objects along these dimensions should, in general, be more stable, more consistent, and made sooner than affective judgments. At the very least, these judgments should not be slower, more inconsistent, unstable, or inefficient than affective ratings. In particular, we would expect that recognition judgments, for example, which reflect the operation of the collative variable of novelty, should be made with greater confidence than liking judgments. Figure 14.4 shows the results from our previous study with Kunst-Wilson using 1-millisecond exposures. The results show that compared to liking judgments, recognition judgments are made with much less confidence. The differences are, in fact, huge—more than 6 times their standard errors. Even if we take only the recognition judgments on which the subject was correct, this effect remains true.[15]

One more bit of data. According to the prevalent view, attending to discriminanda alone should be easier and quicker than attending to discriminanda tagged with values. Since the latter involve more information, more detail must be attended to, and the subject would consequently **[164]** require more processing time. If familiarity mediates the affective reaction generated as the result of repeated exposures, then judgments of familiarity should be made quicker than judgments of liking. If anything, however, our results showed the opposite. Although of only borderline significance, affective judgments of polygons were made faster than recognition judgments.

---

[15] We suspected that these results may be due to the fact that the subjects knew they could be wrong on the old-new judgments, and awareness of this fact might have induced caution in them. But they could not be "wrong" on their liking judgments. These latter judgments express opinions, and people generally feel free to hold any opinions whatsoever. We tried, therefore, to "objectify" affective judgments and to "subjectify" recognition judgments in order to determine whether the confidence ratings would be reversed. To obtain "objectified" affective ratings, subsequent to stimulus exposures, we asked subjects in another experiment to rate the polygons for their "aesthetic value." We told them also in this connection that our polygons had all been rated for aesthetic value by art critics. To obtain "subjectified" recognition judgments, we told the subjects that one of the two polygons in each slide might appear more "familiar" than the other and asked the subjects to indicate which one did, in fact, appear more familiar. Thus, the subjects could now be "wrong" in their affective judgments, whereas recognition became much more a matter of subjective impression. The results did not change a great deal. Confidence was a little greater for subjective familiarity judgments than for the old-new judgments and a little weaker for aesthetic judgments than for judgments of outright liking. But these differences were quite small. The means were 2.01 and 2.41 for familiarity and aesthetic judgments, whereas they were 1.60 and 2.29 for recognition and liking.

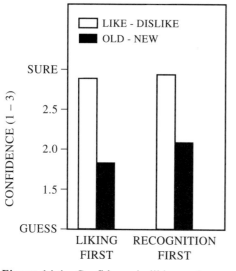

Figure 14.4   Confidence in liking and recognition judgments.

SOURCE: Drawn from data reported by Kunst-Wilson and Zajonc, 1980.

FEELING AND THOUGHT: TWO SYSTEMS?

About 10 years ago, Hyde and Jenkins (1969) carried out an experiment in which subjects were tested for recall of word lists to which they were exposed under different conditions. Some subjects were simply exposed to the words with the instruction to pay close attention. Of three other groups, one was instructed to count the number of letters in each word, another to report the presence of the letter E, and a third to rate each word for pleasantness. In some groups the subjects were warned that they would be tested for recall; in others they were not warned. Hyde and Jenkins's results were quite strong. Among both the subjects who were warned about a future recall test and those who were not warned, those asked to rate pleasantness showed the best recall. Hyde and Jenkins took their data to mean that items are "arranged" differently in storage depending on the context prevailing during acquisition. The superior performance of subjects who rated the words for pleasantness was due to the fact that these subjects acquired the words as "units of meaning" and could therefore recruit for them supportive components of associative structures. When words are examined for number of letters or the presence of the letter E, such "structures are not activated and the recall is unorganized" (Hyde and Jenkins, 1969, p. 480).

Since, as we have seen earlier, the semantic content of verbal material is saturated with affect, the facilitation that occurred as a result of prior pleasantness ratings in the Hyde and Jenkins experiment could have strong affective components. Two conditions of a recent experiment by Rogers, Kuiper, and Kirker (1977) are of particular interest in this respect. In all conditions, their subjects were tested for recall of previously shown adjectives. In one condition, the subjects had to check the adjectives to see if they were printed in the same or different type as a sample print (structural), and in another whether they rhymed with comparison words (phonemic). But in two conditions the subjects were required to engage in extensive semantic processing of the adjectives: In one they checked the adjectives to see if they meant the same as comparison words (semantic) and in another to see whether they described the subject (self-reference). Note that while these last two conditions both activate semantic structures within which the adjectives are imbedded, the self-reference condition brings the subject into a cognitive domain greatly charged with affect. Rogers, Kuiper, and Kirker's findings are especially significant in view of the virtual discontinuity of the self-reference effects. Of the 10 self-reference adjectives, 2.84 were correctly recalled. In contrast, only .34, .68, and 1.33 adjectives were correctly recalled in the structural, phonemic, and semantic treatments, respectively.

Another group of similar studies that used recognition memory rather than recall also suggests strong participation of affect in information processing. Formulating their experimental problem in depth-of-processing terms (Craik and Lockhart, 1972), Bower and Karlin (1974) showed photographs of faces to subjects with instructions to judge the photographs for gender, honesty, or likeability. Following exposures, subjects were tested for recognition memory in two experiments. The hit rate was higher when the subjects rated photographs for honesty or likeability than when they reported gender. Strnad and Mueller (1977) replicated Bower and Karlin's results in a between-subjects design, and Warrington and Ackroyd (1975) found parallel effects when comparing these effects for faces and words, also in a between-subjects design. According to Bower and Karlin (1974), deeper processing facilitates recognition because it forces the subject to attend to a greater variety of detail. "Judgment of honesty of face would appear to require comparison to an idiosyncratic set of vague prototype criteria regarding the patterning of features such as distance between the eyes, size of pupils, curvature of the mouth, thickness of lips, and so on" (p. 756). They went on to say that "if you want. to remember a person's face, try to make a number of difficult personal judgments about his face when you are first meeting him" (pp. 756–757). Patterson and Baddeley (1977) asked subjects to do just that: In one condition their subjects rated photographs of faces for the length of nose, distance between the eyes, roundness of face, or fullness of lips. In another condition the ratings [165] were vague and less detailed but much more likely to recruit affect: nice-nasty, reliable-unreliable, intelligent-dull, and lively-stolid. Recognition memory, as reflected by d' and by hit- and false-alarm rates, was clearly superior for what Patterson and Baddeley called "personality" ratings. Patterson and Baddeley (1977) thus disagreed with Bower and Karlin and concluded that their own "results clearly did not implicate analysis of facial features as a critical or optimal basis for face recognition" (p. 411). Instead, they believed that should they "ever find an optimum strategy for encoding of faces, analysis of individual features is unlikely to be its focus" (p. 417).

There seems to be general agreement that when judgments of pleasantness are made of faces or of adjectives, individuals engage in forms of deeper information processing. What is not agreed upon is the type of content that is accessed at these deeper levels. Patterson and Baddeley (1977) doubt that face recognition is based on the sorts of discriminanda that we would intuitively suspect of serving recognition. But if these discriminanda are not the basis of face recognition, what is? Is face recognition, then, based on preferenda? Recall in this respect that the scaling of faces for similarity yields pleasantness as the major factor, explaining about 50% of the variance, whereas physical features play a relatively minor role. Clearly, the contribution of affect to face recognition has been underestimated. Early face discrimination is based primarily on affective reactions. Infants smile at an approaching face as early as 10 weeks of age, and at 12 weeks they smile differently at familiar and unfamiliar faces (Izard, 1978).

Curiously enough, none of the above studies mention the possible role of affect in processing face information. And none of the studies on recognition memory of faces collected reaction time data to verify whether the assumed deeper processing was accompanied by longer response latencies. However, in one recent study, Keenan and Bailett (1979) used methods similar to those of Rogers, Kuiper, and Kirker (1977) but instead administered recognition memory tests. They report results that have an important bearing on the form of information processing that may emerge when affect is involved. As in the previous studies, a number of adjectives were presented, and the subjects were required to check them against a number of criteria. For example, subjects were asked whether the given adjective described themselves, a best friend, a parent, another friend, a teacher or boss, a favorite TV character, or Jimmy Carter. Also asked for some adjectives was a semantic encoding question: "Means the same as ————?" Following the initial series, subjects were given a recognition memory task in which the original adjectives were interspersed among an equal number of similar distractor items. Keenan and Bailett's results are very clear. Self-reference generated by far the highest recognition performance (over 90%), whereas reference to Jimmy Carter produced a recognition rate of less than 65%. The other recognition rates were arranged according to the social significance that the target had for the subject: best friend, parent, friend, and teacher.

If the superior recognition memory for the self-reference items was due to deeper processing, one would expect that response times for these items would be longer than response times for items processed at shallow levels. However, the results were quite the opposite and very strikingly so. Encoding times for self-reference items were by far the shortest. The longest reaction time was found for items referred to Jimmy Carter (note that the experiment was run in 1977 when Carter was not quite as well known as he is now). Moreover, the other targets had response times that varied directly with the proportion of correct recognitions.

Keenan and Bailett (1979) attempt a variety of cognitive interpretations, but at the conclusion of what is truly a valiant effort, they offer the possibility that in the course of processing self-referent information, "the crucial dimension underlying memory is not what the subject knows or the amount of knowledge that is used in encoding the item, but rather what the subject feels about what he knows" (p. 25). It is no longer clear that deeper processing necessarily requires more time. Structures that are highly integrated and that have been frequently "tuned in" may process information quite rapidly. The relation between reaction time and depth of processing cannot be predicted, therefore, for all tasks (Baddeley, 1978). Keenan and Bailett's study may be taken as evidence against the levels-of-processing approach. But it may also be taken as evidence that the participation of affect in processing information of some types may increase efficiency to a remarkable degree. The beneficial role of [166] affect in memory is dramatically illustrated in a paired-associates study in which Sadalla and Loftness (1972) asked subjects to form pleasant, unpleasant, and nonemotional images for each pair and found considerably poorer performance for the neutral pairs than for either the pleasant or the unpleasant pairs.

It is this type of result that suggests the possibility of some separation between affect and cognition. Consider the task in those experiments where the subject is asked to verify if a given adjective, say "honest," describes him or her. It is most unlikely that the process of this verification involves checking the item for its presence in a list, as some information-processing models would have it. For one thing, no evidence suggests even vaguely that the self is represented as a list of trait adjectives (Markus, 1977). For another, the question is probably not interpreted by the subject to mean "Is the trait 'honest' true of you?" but more likely to mean "Is the trait 'honest' consistent with your perception of yourself?" If this is indeed the interpretation that the subject imposes upon the task, then we must inquire what may be meant by "consistent with your perception of yourself?" To some extent this consistency may involve absence of content that is mutually contradictory; for example, the person could not be both tall and short. But more important, some form of affective consistency is probably involved. That is, the self as used in this task is probably some global and general impression suffused with affective quality. What is matched is primarily the affective quality of the item with the affective quality of the impression. Of course, the shorter processing times for self-referent items may be due to the fact that we have more integrated and better structured impressions of ourselves and of people who are important to us. But it is equally true that the self is a target charged with strong, widespread, and clear affect, and an emotional match would therefore be quite easy for the subject to verify. There is a need in these studies to separate the elaboration and integration of the cognitive structure from the affect that pervades it, but such a control procedure is difficult, for the two properties are highly correlated.

That the affective qualities in impression formation are processed differently and perhaps separately from the cognitive content that "carries" that impression is shown both by Anderson and Hubert (1963) and by Posner and Snyder (1975b). In a typical impression formation task, the first authors found strong primacy effects for impressions (i.e., the overall affective rating of the person was influenced more by early trait adjectives in the list) and an equally strong recency effect for the recall of the adjectives. Anderson and Hubert (1963) suggested that "the impression response is based on a different memory system than that which underlies the verbal recall" (p. 388). They did not go on to specify how these two systems might differ except to say that "as each adjective is received, its meaning is extracted and combined with the current impression, thus yielding a changed impression. Once this is done, memory for the adjective *per se* is no longer necessary for the impression process" (pp. 390–391).

Dreben, Fiske, and Hastie (1979) found similar order effects for impressions, and Hamilton, Katz, and Leirer (in press) obtained better recall when subjects organized items into an impression of a person than when subjects regarded these items as discrete units. More important for the dual-process hypothesis, however, is the finding of Dreben, Fiske, and Hastie that the weights calculated for the adjectives did not predict their recall. That is, the adjectives assumed to be contributing the most to impression are not necessarily also the ones that are best recalled. Following his cognitive response theory, Greenwald (1980) suggested that cues effective in helping the individual retrieve content may not be the same ones that are effective in helping retrieve the evaluative aspects of the content. It is not unreasonable to suppose that the major difference between these two types of cues may be the difference between discriminanda and preferenda. And it is perhaps the difference between these cues that is also involved in the perseverance effect (Ross, Lepper, and Hubbard, 1975), in that details of initial information about success (or failure) are used only to construct an overall impression of one's own task competence and are soon discarded. Thus, in debriefing, when the experimenter tells the subjects that their success (or failure) was rigged, this new information may no longer be capable of making contact with the original input (which by then has been recoded and discarded) and may therefore have little effect on its original affective consequences.

Posner and Snyder (1975b) also argue for a dual memory. In their experiments, subjects are shown a sentence such as "James is honest, loyal, [167] and mature," and in a subsequent display a probe word such as "foolish" is flashed. Two tasks are studied. In one the subject is asked to verify if the word itself was among those in the preceding sentence. In another, the required match is between the emotional tone of the word and that of the preceding sentence. The interesting result these authors obtain is that, as the length of the list increases, reaction times increase for word matching and decrease for emotional tone matching. Posner and Snyder (1975b) agree with Anderson and Hubert about the two memory systems for the component adjectives and for the overall impression, but they doubt that the "emotional information concerning impression is handled in any different way than other semantic dimensions in the memory system" (p. 80). Their doubts should be weakened by a recent impression-formation experiment in which the pattern of recall of individual adjectives was effectively manipulated in the hope of thereby affecting the primacy of impressions. Riskey (1979) was able to change the recall of adjectives, but the primacy of impressions nevertheless remained unchanged.

While these authors propose separate systems, it is always separate *cognitive* systems that they propose. In contrast, the separation being considered here is between an affective and a cognitive system—a separation that distinguishes between discriminanda and preferenda and that takes us back to Wundt and Bartlett, who speculated that the overall impression or attitude has an existence of its own, independent of the components that contributed to its emergence. The question that cannot be answered with the data thus far collected is whether the affect-content separation is simply a matter of separate storage (as Anderson and Hubert, on the one hand, and Posner and Snyder, on the other, have proposed) or whether there isn't some separation already at the point of registration and encoding. The rapid processing times of affect suggest a more complete separation of the two processes at several junctures.

One is necessarily reminded in this context of the dual coding hypothesis proposed by Paivio (1975) for the processing of pictures and words. Paivio (1978a) suggested a number of differences between the processing of these types of content, for example, that representations of pictures emerge as perceptual isomorphs or analogs (imagens), whereas parallel units in the verbal system are linguistic components (logogens). He also proposed that pictorial information is organized in a synchronous and spatially parallel manner, whereas verbal information is discrete and sequential. Finally, he suggested that the processing of pictures is more likely to be the business of the right-brain hemisphere, whereas the processing of words is the business of the left. Paivio's proposal for a dual coding theory kindled a controversy of some vigor. While Anderson (1978) has recently argued that the controversy cannot be resolved with what we now know about these processes, it has nevertheless stimulated some exciting empirical and theoretical work (e.g., Banks and Flora, 1977; Kerst and Howard, 1977; Kosslyn and Pomerantz, 1977; Paivio, 1978b; Pylyshyn, 1973; Shepard, 1978).

Most relevant for my discussion, however, is Paivio's (1978c) finding that reaction times for pleasant-unpleasant ratings are faster for pictures than for words. Paivio takes this result to indicate that "the analog information involved in pleasantness and value judgments is more closely associated with the image system than with the verbal system" (p. 207). This

> analog pleasantness information is "carried by" affective and motor processes that are closely associated with visual memory representations of things. Such processes presumably originate as reactions to things and persist as affective or motor memories that can be activated by pictures of the referent objects, or, more indirectly, by their names when accompanied by the appropriate contextual cues. More specifically, pleasantness and value judgments might be based on continuously variable interoceptive reactions and approach or avoidance tendencies that are activated jointly by the comparison stimuli and the task instructions. (p. 207)

However, the specific responses of the autonomic nervous system are not readily discriminable, since there are not many receptors to register the fine changes in autonomic processes (Averill, 1969; Mandler, Mandler, Kremen, and Sholiton, 1961). Moreover, interoceptive process and motor memories are slower than the affective responses they are presumed to activate.

It is a fact, of course, that *all* sorts of judgments are faster and more efficient for pictures than for words, and this may be so just because pictures are able to evoke an affective reaction more directly and faster than words. An affective reaction aroused early in the encoding process—earlier than it is possible for the interoceptive and motor memories to become effective—might facilitate a complex cognitive encoding sequence by an initial categorization along affective lines, which, **[168]** as we have seen, requires minimal stimulus information. Such facilitation through early affective sorting that relies not only on discriminanda but on preferenda as well may also induce a constructive process that can more readily recruit stored content by searching for congruent affective tags.[16]

---

[16] Another area of research in which affect may be implicated (although it had not been so suspected) is the frequency-judgment paradigm. Typically, in these experiments subjects are shown stimuli in different frequencies, and two types of judgments are collected afterwards. In one condition, the subjects are shown the old stimuli interspersed among new ones and are asked to report for each item whether it is new or old. In the other condition, the subjects must say how often each stimulus occurred. It turns out that the frequency judgment generates greater accuracy than the binary recognition memory judgment (e.g., Proctor, 1977; Proctor and Ambler, 1975).

Two findings are of interest in the present context. First, subjects have remarkable confidence in their frequency judgments (Howell, 1971). Second, warning the subjects that they will be estimating frequencies of events (vs. simply recalling them) and varying the length of the list both influence free recall but have little, if any, effect on frequency estimation (Howell, 1973). It thus appears that frequency judgments behave like affective judgments. It is possible, therefore, that frequency estimation is more likely to invoke an underlying affective reaction (which accrues from repeated stimulus exposures) than the binary recognition memory task. It may be hotter. Since frequency judgment makes exposure effects salient and since it requires finer discrimination than recognition memory, it may recruit affect as an auxiliary source of information. In fact, it has been suggested that recognition memory responses and frequency estimation are not made from the same sources of information (Wells, 1974), although what these sources are and how they differ from each other is not altogether clear (Hintzman, 1976).

This review suggests that a separation between affect and cognition may well have a psychological and a biological basis.[17] Recall that in contrast with cold cognitions, affective responses are effortless, inescapable, irrevocable, holistic, more difficult to verbalize, yet easy to communicate and to understand. Consider also that the processing of affect is probably an even stronger candidate for the right hemisphere than the processing of pictures (Carmon and Nachson, 1973; Dimond, Farrington, and Johnson, 1976; Ley and Bryden, 1979; Milner, 1968; Safer and Leventhal, 1977; Schwartz, Davidson, and Maer, 1975). In the context of this review it is especially interesting (a) that face recognition is superior when the stimuli are presented in the left visual field (De Renzi and Spinnler, 1966; Moscovitch, Scullion, and Christie, 1976), and (b) that the recognition of emotional expressions shows the same right-brain superiority (Suberi and McKeever, 1977).

It has also been suggested to me by Richard J. Katz (Note 5) that there exists a network in the central nervous system, the *locus coeruleus,* which is ideally suited for the kind of partially independent processing of affect that I have suggested here. The potential sensitivity of the locus coeruleus to preferenda can be inferred from a number of interesting properties and features of this system. Above all, it is excited differently by novel and by familiar stimuli. Second, self-stimulation studies have demonstrated that the locus coeruleus is sensitive to incentives. It is further known that it is capable of innervating sensory areas (such as the colliculi and geniculate bodies), emotional areas (the amygdala and hypothalamus), mnestic areas (the hippocampus), and the cerebral cortices. Most important, however, is the fact that the locus coeruleus is capable of very fast responding. Finally, Katz also noted that the enkephalenergic system, which controls the action of enkephalins (naturally occurring opiates) and is situated at the locus coeruleus, is also involved in reinforcement and in different reactions to novelty and familiarity. All of this means, at the very least, that what I have proposed about the processing of affect is not inconsistent with recent knowledge about the relevant neurophysiological mechanisms. It means that the organism is equipped with a neurochemical apparatus capable of telling the new from the old and the good from the bad, of remembering the old, the good, and the bad, and of making all these decisions rapidly without having to wait for the slow feedback from the autonomic system.

Affective reactions are primary in ontogeny. The infant knows to cry and to smile long before it acquires any semblance of verbal skills (Izard, 1978, 1979). Meltzoff and Moore (1977) report that human infants can imitate emotional expressions at 12 days of age, long before they acquire language. And good-bad is one of the very first discriminations that children learn.

More important, however, affect is clearly primary in philogeny. Affect was there before we evolved language and [169] our present form of thinking. The limbic system that controls emotional reactions was there before we evolved language and our present form of thinking. It was there before the neocortex, and it occupies a large proportion of the brain mass in lower animals. Before we evolved language and our cognitive capacities, which are so deeply dependent on language, it was the affective system alone upon which the organism relied for its adaptation. The organism's responses to the stimuli in its environment were selected according to their affective

---

[17] Multiple processing systems and multiple channel conceptions are today more the rule than the exception in the study of sensory processes (Graham and Nachmias, 1971; Trevarthen, 1968).

antecedents and according to their affective consequences. Thus, if the most recent version of homo sapiens specifies that affective reactions are mediated by prior cognitive processes—as contemporary cognitive views would have it—then at some point in the course of evolution, affect must have lost its autonomy and acquired an intermediary in the form of cold cognition. This scenario seems most unlikely. When nature has a direct and autonomous mechanism that functions efficiently—and there is no reason to suppose that the affective system was anything else—it does not make it indirect and entirely dependent on a newly evolved function. It is rather more likely that the affective system retained its autonomy, relinquishing its exclusive control over behavior slowly and grudgingly. At most, the formerly sovereign affective system may have accepted an alliance with the newly evolved system to carry out some adaptive functions jointly. These conjectures make a two-system view more plausible than one that relegates affect to a secondary role mediated and dominated by cognition.

Because it is so heavily rooted in verbal skills, the cognitive system in humans has properties that are quite distinct from those of affect. Above all, the cognitive system is infinitely more diverse and flexible than the affective system. Anything at all can be said and thought with various degrees of precision, and these things can be said and thought in an infinite variety of ways. But there are only a handful of emotions and feelings that can be felt, and they can be felt only in some few, very constrained ways. And for reasons that must be rooted in the partial separation of the two systems, affect can be communicated much more efficiently and accurately than thought in spite of the fact that its vocabulary is quite limited. It was a wise designer who provided separately for each of these processes instead of presenting us with a multiple-purpose appliance that, like the rotisserie-broiler-oven-toaster, performs none of its functions well.

CONCLUSION

It is too early to write a model for affect and for the various ways that it interacts with cold cognitions. The important pieces of evidence are still missing. However, we can begin to specify the facts that such a model must accommodate. Figure 14.5 summarizes these facts by schematizing the time course of the stimulus together with the ensuing sensory process, the affective response, and some simple aspects of the cognitive process (recognition and feature identification). A stimulus is presented for a fixed time interval. The stimulus triggers a number of processes that can vary in their onset times and offset times. I have shown these processes as ranges of their onset times, ignoring the offset times altogether for the present purposes. (I have also ignored the fact that under some conditions, stimulus onset can be anticipated by the response process.) The onset times of these four processes are influenced by stimulus conditions and by subject states (e.g., previous experience with stimuli of the given class, exposure to immediately preceding stimuli that may generate contrast or assimilation, knowledge, mood states, priming, or expectation. [170]

Note that a variety of temporal relations holds among affect, recognition, and feature identification. Of course, sensory process must have the earliest onset. Its onset times, too, differ depending on the stimulus, level of attention of the organism, the peripheral processes that are activated, context, etc. Also, an affective reaction always

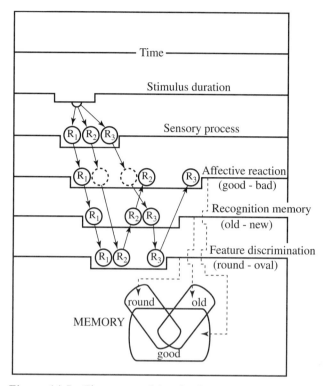

Figure 14.5   Time course of the stimulus, sensation, affect, and cold cognitions (R = response).

directly follows the sensory input. In R_1 this reaction is strong and salient, and it might dominate the ensuing cognitive process. In R_2 and R_3, affect (shown in broken circles) is also aroused immediately following the sensory process, but it is weak and does not significantly influence the subsequent stages of the cognitive process. But for affect, recognition, and feature discrimination, all combinations are possible. I have given examples of three of the six possible response patterns. In R_1, affect is first, recognition occurs later, and feature discrimination is last. The primacy of affect over recognition in R_1 reflects our own data (Kunst-Wilson and Zajonc, 1980) and the results of typical subliminal perception experiments (e.g., Blum and Barbour, 1979; Shevrin and Fritzler, 1968). The difference between recognition and feature discrimination that favors the former reflects the results of Patterson and Baddeley (1977), who, it will be recalled, found that subjects could recognize photographs better when they judged them on "personality" characteristics than when they judged them on specific physical features. The results of Marcel (1976) and of Keenan and Bailett (1979) also suggest that recognition can precede feature identification.[18]

R_2 presents the case typically considered by information-processing models: The cognitive process begins with the individual first discriminating a critical feature that

---

[18] Similar effects are obtained in vision (e.g., Graham and Nachmias, 1971).

allows recognition. And finally it is recognition that gives rise to the affective response. In R_3, recognition precedes feature identification, as is the case when letters that form words are recognized better than letters that do not form words (Johnston and McClelland, 1974) or when meaning is apprehended while the word itself cannot be identified, as in the paralexic response of certain aphasic patients (Marshall and Newcombe, 1966).

Figure 14.5 shows the lower temporal limits of these reactions. Except for the sensory process, affect is assumed to be capable of the earliest onset. How can that be?

Perhaps the following analysis, speculative to be sure, may point to some possible answers. Decisions about affect require the least information and are often based on a different decision scheme than either recognition or feature identification. Each of the three, affect, recognition, and feature identification, is a form of categorization. Affective reactions of the type considered here are for the most part unidimensional and sometimes just binary: safe-dangerous, good-bad, or nice-nasty. Such binary decisions can, under some circumstances, be made quite reliably, even in the absence of reliable bases. Moore and Shannon (1956) have shown that reliable circuits can be constructed using arbitrarily unreliable relays, provided the relays form parallel circuits that are mutually redundant. Zajonc and Smoke (1959) applied this principle to group performance, and Smoke and Zajonc (1962) to group decisions. That is, given certain group decision processes, groups can make judgments much more reliably than the average group member. An analogous situation may well exist for affect where the stimulus triggers several parallel responses and the decision scheme can well be a minimal quorum.[19] Recognition, however, even though it also constitutes a binary choice (old-new), does not have a similar advantage because the redundancy of the component criteria (e.g., features of configural properties) is seldom as high as in the case of affect. Moreover, minimal quorum is seldom a decision basis. In fact, in experimental work on recognition memory, great care is taken to assure that criterial features are fairly independent of each other. Just because a photograph shows the face of a male is not sufficient for calling it "old" or rejecting it as "new," unless previous exposures have shown only female faces.

Each of the responses in Figure 14.5 can facilitate the ones succeeding it. An affective reaction can thus act to precategorize the stimulus for the subject trying to decide whether it is "old" or "new." And recognition may facilitate feature identification by a similar prior selection process. Each operation reduces the universe of alternatives for the next choice. It is therefore entirely possible for stimuli that have a strong effective potential to evoke affective reactions rapidly, to be recognized sooner than neutral stimuli, and to be remembered better. Thus, Figure 14.5 also shows [171] the representations in memory that are left by the three processes (affect, recognition, and feature identification). To the extent that these traces are redundant, the likelihood of a later retrieval would be facilitated.

I began this paper with a quotation from Wundt, and it must be apparent that another spirit has emerged as I have developed my arguments—that of Freud. The separation of affect and cognition, the dominance and primacy of affective reactions, and their ability to influence responses when ordinary perceptual recognition is at chance

---

[19] In the case of decisions or parallel signalling circuits such as may be involved in affective reactions, the minimal quorum is equivalent to a veto decision or its inverse.

level are all very much in the spirit of Freud, the champion of the unconscious. In terms of my formulation, there seem to be at least two different forms of unconscious processes. One emerges where behavior, such as that occurring in discrimination among stimuli, is entirely under the influence of affective factors without the participation of cognitive processes. Included here are such phenomena as perceptual defense and vigilance, subliminal perception and discrimination, state dependent recall, and mood and context effects. Another form of unconscious process is implicated in highly overlearned, and thus automated, sequences of information processing; this form includes cognitive acts but has collapsed them into larger molar chunks that may conceal their original component links (cf. Shiffrin and Schneider, 1977). And there may be other forms of process in which the separation between affect and cognition prevents the individual from apprehending the potential connection between them.

Because the language of my paper has been stronger than can be justified by the logic of the argument or the weight of the evidence, I hasten to affirm that one of my purposes was to convince you that affect should not be treated as unalterably last and invariably postcognitive. The evolutionary origins of affective reactions that point to their survival value, their distinctive freedom from attentive control, their speed, the importance of affective discriminations for the individual, the extreme forms of action that affect can recruit—all of these suggest something special about affect. People do not get married or divorced, commit murder or suicide, or lay down their lives for freedom upon a detailed cognitive analysis of the pros and cons of their actions. If we stop to consider just how much variance in the course of our lives is controlled by cognitive processes and how much by affect, and how much the one and the other influence the important outcomes in our lives, we cannot but agree that affective phenomena deserve far more attention than they have received from cognitive psychologists and a closer cognitive scrutiny from social psychologists.

REFERENCE NOTES

1.   Ellsworth, P. Personal communication, May 13, 1979.
2.   Zajonc, R.B. *Preferenda and discriminanda: Processing of affect*. Paper presented at the First Ontario Symposium on Personality and Social Psychology, London, Ontario, Canada, August 1978.
3.   Premack, D., and Kintsch, W. Personal communication, July 1979.
4.   Marcel, J. *Unconscious reading: Experiments on people who do not know that they are reading*. Paper presented to the British Association for Advancement of Science, Lancaster, England, 1976.
5.   Katz, R.J. Personal communication, February 1979.

REFERENCES

Abelson, R.P. Computer simulation of "hot cognitions." In S. Tomkins and S. Mesick (Eds.), *Computer simulation of personality*. New York: Wiley, 1963.

Abelson, R.P., and Rosenberg, M.J. Symbolic psychologic: A model of attitudinal cognition. *Behavioral Science*, 1958, *3*, 1–13.

Abelson, R.P., and Sermat, V. Multidimensional scaling of facial expressions. *Journal of Experimental Psychology*, 1962, *63*, 546–554.

Anderson, J.R. *Language, memory, and thought*. Hillsdale, N.J.: Erlbaum, 1976.

Anderson, J.R. Arguments concerning representations for mental imagery. *Psychological Review*, 1978, *85*, 249–277.

Anderson, J.R., and Bower, G.H. *Human associative memory*. Washington, D.C.: Winston, 1973.

Anderson, N.H., and Hubert, S. Effects of concomitant verbal recall on order effects in personality impression formation. *Journal of Verbal Learning and Verbal Behavior*, 1963, *2*, 379–391.

Argyle. M., Salter, V., Nicholson. H., Williams, M., and Burgess, P. The communication of inferior and superior attitudes by verbal and non-verbal signals. *British Journal of Social and Clinical Psychology*, 1970, *9*, 222–231.

Averill, J.R. Autonomic response patterns during sadness and mirth. *Psychophysiology*, 1969, *5*, 399–414.

Baddeley, A.D. The trouble with levels: A re-examination of Craik and Lockhart's framework for memory research. *Psychological Review*, 1978, *85*, 139–152.

Banks. W.P., and Flora, J. Semantic and perceptual processes in symbolic comparisons. *Journal of Experimental Psychology: Human Perception and Performance*, 1977, *3*. 278–290.

Bartlett, F.C. *Remembering: A study in experimental and social psychology*. Cambridge, England: Cambridge University Press, 1932.

Berlyne, D.E. Arousal and reinforcement. In D. Levine (Ed.), *Nebraska Symposium on Motivation* (Vol. 15). Lincoln: University of Nebraska Press, 1967.

Berlyne. D.E. Novelty, complexity, and hedonic value. *Perception and Psychophysics*, 1970, *8*, 279–286.

Berlyne, D.E. Dimensions of perception of exotic and pre-renaissance paintings. *Canadian Journal of Psychology*, 1975, *29*, 151–173. **[172]**

Beracheid, E., and Walster, E. *Interpersonal attraction*. Reading, Mass.: Addison-Wesley, 1978.

Blum, G.S., and Barbour, J.S. Selective inattention to anxiety-linked stimuli. *Journal of Experimental Psychology: General*, 1979, *108*, 182–224.

Bobrow, D.G., and Collins, A. *Representation and understanding*. New York: Academic Press, 1975.

Bower, G.H., and Karlin, M.B. Depth of processing pictures of faces and recognition memory. *Journal of Experimental Psychology*, 1974, *103*, 751–757.

Broadbent, D.E. The hidden preattentive processes. *American Psychologist*, 1977, *32*, 109–118.

Broadbent, D.E., and Gregory, M.H.P. The perception of emotionally toned words. *Nature*, 1967, *215*, 581–584.

Byrne, D. Interpersonal attraction and attitude similarity. *Journal of Abnormal and Social Psychology*, 1961, *62*, 713–715.

Carmon, A., and Nachson, I. Ear asymmetry in perception of emotional non-verbal stimuli. *Acta Psychologica*, 1973, *37*, 351–357.

Coombs, C.H. *A theory of data*. New York: Wiley, 1964.

Cooper, L.G. A multivariate investigation of preferences. *Multivariate Behavioral Research*, 1973, *8*, 253–272.

Craik, F.I.M., and Lockhart, R.S. Levels of processing: A framework for memory research. *Journal of Verbal Learning and Verbal Behavior*, 1972, *11*, 671–684.

Crowder, R.G. *Principles of learning and memory*. Hillsdale, N.J.: Erlbaum, 1976.

Cummings, E.E. *Complete poems* (Vol. I). Bristol, England: McGibbon and Kee, 1973.

Dawes, R.M., and Kramer, E. A proximity analysis of vocally expressed emotion. *Perceptual and Motor Skills*, 1966, *22*, 571–574.

De Renzi, E., and Spinnler H. Facial recognition in brain-damaged patients. *Neurology*, 1966. *16*, 145–152.

Dimond, S.J., Farrington, L., and Johnson, P. Differing emotional response from right and left hemisphere. *Nature*, 1976, *261*, 690–692.

Dreben, E.K., Fiske, S.T., and Hastie, R. The independence of evaluative and item information: Impression and recall order effects in behavior-based impression formation. *Journal of Personality and Social Psychology*, 1979, *37*, 1758–1768.

Ekman. P. and Friesen, W.V. The repertoire of nonverbal behavior: Categories, origins, usage, and coding. *Semiotica*, 1969, *1*, 49–98.

Erdelyi, M.H. A new look at the New Look: Perceptual defense and vigilance. *Psychological Review*, 1974, *81*, 1–25.

Estes, W.K. (Ed.). *Handbook of learning and cognitive processes* (Vols. 1–6). Hillsdale, N.J.: Erlbaum, 1975–1978.

Festinger, L. *Conflict, decision, and dissonance*. Stanford, Calif.: Stanford University Press, 1964.

Gainotti, G. Emotional behavior and hemispheric side of the lesion. *Cortex*, 1972, *8*, 41–55.

Graham, N., and Nachmias, J. Detection of grating patterns containing two spatial frequencies: A comparison of single-channel and multiple-channels models. *Vision Research*, 1971, *11*, 251–259.

Greenwald, A.G. Cognitive response analysis: An appraisal. In R.E. Petty, T.M. Ostrom, and T.C. Brock (Eds.), *Cognitive responses in persuasive communication*. Hillsdale, N.J.: Erlbaum, 1980.

Hamilton, D.L., Katz, L.B., and Leirer, V.O. Organizational processes in impression formation. In R. Hastie, T. Ostrom, E. Ebbesen, R. Wyer, D. Hamilton, and D. Carlston (Eds.), *Person memory*. Hillsdale, N.J.: Erlbaum, in press.

Harrison, A.A. Response competition, frequency, exploratory behavior, and liking. *Journal of Personality and Social Psychology*, 1968, *9*, 363–368.

Harrison, A.A. Mere exposure. In L. Berkowitz (Ed.), *Advances in experimental social psychology* (Vol. 10). New York: Academic Press, 1977.

Hastorf, A.H., Osgood, C.E., and Ono, H. The semantics of facial expressions and the prediction of the meanings of stereoscopically fused facial expressions. *Scandinavian Journal of Psychology*. 1966, *7*, 179–188.

Heider, F. *The psychology of interpersonal relations*. New York: Wiley, 1958.

Hintzman, D.L. Repetition and memory. In G.H. Bower (Ed.), *The psychology of learning and motivation* (Vol. 10). New York: Academic Press, 1976.

Howell, W.C. Uncertainty from internal and external sources: A clear case of overconfidence. *Journal of Experimental Psychology*, 1971, *89*, 240–243.

Howell, W.C. Representation of frequency in memory. *Psychological Bulletin*, 1973, *80*. 44–53.

Hume, D. *A treatise on human nature* (Vol. 2). London: Longmans, Green, 1898.

Hyde, T.W., and Jenkins J.J. The differential effects of incidental tasks on the organization of recall of a list of highly associated words. *Journal of Experimental Psychology*, 1969, *82*, 472–481.

Inhelder, B., and Piaget, J. *The growth of logical thinking from childhood to adolescence*. New York: Basic Books, 1958.

Ittelson, W.H. Environment perception and contemporary perceptual theory. In W.H. Ittelson (Ed.). *Environment and cognition*. New York: Seminar Press, 1973.

Izard, C.E. *Human emotions*. New York: Plenum Press, 1977.

Izard, C.E. On the development of emotions and emotion-cognition relationship in infancy. In M. Lewis and L. Rosenblum (Eds.), *The development of affect*. New York: Plenum Press, 1978.

Izard, C.E. Emotions as motivations: An evolutionary-developmental perspective. In R. Dienstbier (Ed.), *Nebraska Symposium on Motivation* (Vol. 27). Lincoln: University of Nebraska Press, 1979.

Johnston, J.C., and McClelland, J.L. Perception of letters: Seek not and ye shall find. *Science*, 1974, *184*, 1192–1194.

Jöreskog, K.G., and Sörbom, D. Statistical models and methods for analysis of longitudinal data. In D.J. Aigner and A.S. Goldberger (Eds.), *Latent variables in socio-economic models*. Amsterdam: North-Holland, 1977.

Kahneman, D., and Tversky, A. Prospect theory: An analysis of decision under risk. *Econometrica*, 1979, *47*, 263–291.

Keenan, J.M., and Bailett, S.D. Memory for personally and socially significant events. In R.S. Nickerson (Ed.), *Attention and performance VIII*. Hillsdale, N.J.: Erlbaum, 1979.

Kerst, S.M., and Howard, J.H., Jr. Mental comparisons for ordered information on abstract and concrete dimensions. *Memory and Cognition*, 1977, *5*, 227–234.

Kintsch, W. *The representation of meaning in memory*. Hillsdale, N.J.: Erlbaum, 1974.

Klahr, D. Decision making in a complex environment: The use of similarity judgments to predict preferences. *Management Science*, 1969, *15*, 595–618. **[173]**

Kosslyn, S.M., and Pomerantz, J.R. Imagery, propositions, and the form of internal representations. *Cognitive Psychology*, 1977, *9*, 52–76.

Kunst-Wilson, W.R., and Zajonc, R.B. Affective discrimination of stimuli that cannot be recognized. *Science*, 1980, *207*, 557–558.

Lachman, R., Lachman, J.L., and Butterfield, E.C. *Cognitive psychology and information processing*. Hillsdale, N.J.: Erlbaum, 1979.

Lang, P.J. A bio-informational theory of emotional imagery. *Psychophysiology*, 1979, *16*, 495–512.

Langer, S.K. *Mind: An essay on human feeling* (Vol. 1). Baltimore. Md.: Johns Hopkins University Press, 1967.

Ley, R.G., and Bryden, M.P. Hemispheric differences in processing emotions and faces. *Brain and Language,* 1979, *7,* 127–138.

Mandler, G. *Mind and emotion.* New York: Wiley, 1975.

Mandler, G., Mandler, J.M., Kremen, I., and Sholiton, R.D. The response to threat: Relations among verbal and physiological indices. *Psychological Monographs,* 1961, *75* (9, Whole No. 513).

Markus, H. Self-schemata and processing of information about the self. *Journal of Personality and Social Psychology,* 1977, *35,* 63–78.

Marshall, J.C., and Newcombe, F. Syntactic and semantic errors in paralexia. *Neuropsychologia,* 1966, *4,* 169–176.

Matlin, M.W. Response competition, recognition, and affect. *Journal of Personality and Social Psychology,* 1971, *19,* 295–300.

Meltzoff, A.N., and Moore, M.K. Imitation of facial and manual gestures by human neonates. *Science,* 1977, *198,* 75–78.

Miller. G.A., and Johnson-Laird, P.N. *Language and perception.* Cambridge, Mass.: The Belknap Press of Harvard University Press, 1976.

Milner. B. Visual recognition and recall after right temporal-lobe excision in man. *Neuropsychologia,* 1968, *6,* 191–209.

Milord, J.T. Aesthetic aspects of faces: A (somewhat) phenomenological analysis using multidimensional scaling methods. *Journal of Personality and Social Psychology,* 1978, *36.* 205–216.

Moore. E.F., and Shannon, C.E. Reliable circuits using less reliable relays. Part I. *Journal of the Franklin Institute,* 1956, *262,* 191–208.

Moreland, R.L., and Zajonc, R.B. Is stimulus recognition a necessary condition for the occurrence of exposure effects? *Journal of Personality and Social Psychology,* 1977, *35,* 191–199.

Moreland, R.L., and Zajonc, R.B. Exposure effects may not depend on stimulus recognition. *Journal of Personality and Social Psychology,* 1979, *37,* 1085–1089.

Moscovitch, M., Scullion. D., and Christie, D. Early versus late stage of processing and their relation to functional hemispheric asymmetries in face recognition. *Journal of Experimental Psychology: Human Perception and Performance,* 1976, *2,* 401–416.

Nakashima, T. Contribution to the study of the affective processes. *American Journal of Psychology,* 1909, *20,* 157–193. (a)

Nakashima, T. Time-relations of the affective process. *Psychological Review,* 1909, *16,* 303–339. (b)

Neisser, U. *Cognitive psychology.* Englewood Cliffs, N.J.: Prentice-Hall, 1967.

Neisser, U. *Cognition and reality.* San Francisco: Freeman, 1976.

Nisbett. R.E., and Wilson, T.D. Telling more than we can know: Verbal reports on mental processes. *Psychological Review,* 1977, *84,* 231–259.

Norman, D.A., and Rumelhart, D.E. *Explorations in cognition.* San Francisco: Freeman, 1975.

O'Hare, D. Individual differences in perceived similarity and preference for visual art: A multidimensional scaling analysis. *Perception & Psychophysics,* 1976, *20,* 445–452.

Osgood, C.E. Studies on the generality of affective meaning systems. *American Psychologist,* 1962, *17,* 10–28.

Osgood, C.E. On the whys and wherefores of E, P, and A. *Journal of Personality and Social Psychology,* 1969, *12,* 194–199.

Osgood, C.E., and Tannenbaum, P.H. The principle of congruity in the prediction of attitude change. *Psychological Review,* 1955, *62,* 42–55.

Paivio, A. Perceptual comparisons through the mind's eye. *Memory and Cognition,* 1975, *3,* 635–647.

Paivio, A. Dual coding: Theoretical issues and empirical evidence. In J.M. Scandura and C.J. Brainerd (Eds.). *Structural/process models of complex human behavior.* Leiden, The Netherlands: Nordhoff, 1978. (a)

Paivio, A. Images, propositions, and knowledge. In J.M. Nicholas (Ed.), *Images, perception, and knowledge. The Western Ontario Series in Philosophy of Science* (No. 8). Dordrecht, The Netherlands: Reidel, 1978. (b)

Paivio, A. Mental comparisons involving abstract attributes. *Memory and Cognition.* 1978, *3,* 199–208. (c)

Patterson, K.E., and Baddeley, A.D. When face recognition fails. *Journal of Experimental Psychology: Human Learning and Memory,* 1977, *3,* 406–417.

Posner, M.I., and Snyder, C.R.R. Attention and cognitive control. In R.L. Solso (Ed.), *Information processing and cognition: The Loyola Symposium.* Hillsdale, N.J.: Erlbaum, 1975. (a)

Posner, M.I., and Snyder, C.R.R. Facilitation and inhibition in the processing of signals. In P.M.A. Rabbitt and S. Dornic (Eds.), *Attention and performance V*. New York: Academic Press, 1975. (b)

Pratt, C.L., and Sackett, G.P. Selection of partners as a function of peer contact during rearing. *Science*, 1967, *155*, 1133–1135.

Premack, D. *Intelligence in ape and man*. Hillsdale, N.J.: Erlbaum, 1976.

Proctor. R.W. The relationship of frequency judgments to recognition: Facilitation of recognition and comparison to recognition-confidence judgments. *Journal of Experimental Psychology: Human Learning and Memory*, 1977, *3*, 679–689.

Proctor, R.W., and Ambler, B.A. Effects of rehearsal strategy on memory for spacing and frequency. *Journal of Experimental Psychology: Human Learning and Memory,* 1975, *1*, 640–647.

Pylyshyn, Z.W. What the mind's eye tells the mind's brain: A critique of mental imagery. *Psychological Bulletin*, 1973, *80*, 1–24.

Quandt, R.E. A probabilistic theory of consumer behavior. *Quarterly Journal of Economics*, 1956, *70*, 507–536.

Riskey, D.R. Verbal memory process in impression formation. *Journal of Experimental Psychology: Human Learning and Memory*, 1979, *5*, 271–281.

Rogers. T.B., Kuiper, N.A., and Kirker, W.S. Self-reference and the encoding of personal information. *Journal of Personality and Social Psychology*, 1977, *35*, 677–688.

Ross. L., Lepper, M.R., and Hubbard, M. Perseverance in self-perception and social perception: Biased attributional processes in the debriefing paradigm. *Journal of Personality and Social Psychology*, 1975, *32*, 880–892.

Rubin, Z. *Liking and loving*. New York: Holt, Rinehart & Winston, 1973. **[174]**

Sadalla, E.K., and Loftness, S. Emotional images as mediators in one-trial paired-associates learning. *Journal of Experimental Psychology*. 1972, *95*, 295–298.

Safer, N.A., and Leventhal, H. Ear differences in evaluating emotional tones of voice and verbal content. *Journal of Experimental Psychology: Human Perception and Performance*. 1977, *3*, 75–82.

Sartre, J.P. *Existentialism*. New York: Philosophical Library. 1947.

Schachter, S., and Singer, J. Cognitive, social, and physiological determinants of emotional state. *Psychological Review*, 1962, 65, 379–399.

Schank, R.C., and Abelson, R.P. *Scripts, plans, goals, and understanding*. Hillsdale, N.J.: Erlbaum, 1977.

Scherer. K.R., Koivumaki, J., and Rosenthal, R. Minimal cues in the vocal communication of affect: Judging emotions from content-masked speech. *Journal of Psycholinguistic Research*, 1972, *1*, 269–285.

Schneider, D.J.. Hastorf, A.H., and Ellsworth, P.C. *Person perception*. Reading, Mass.: Addison-Wesley, 1979.

Schwartz, G.E., Davidson, R.J., and Maer, F. Right hemisphere lateralization for emotion in the human brain: Interactions with cognition. *Science*, 1975, *190*, 286–288.

Schwartz. G.E., Fair, P.L., Salt, P., Mandel. M.R., and Klerman, G.L. Facial muscle patterning to affective imagery in depressed and nondepressed subjects. *Science*, 1976, *192*, 489–491.

Shepard, R.N. The mental image. *American Psychologist*, 1978, *33*, 125–137.

Shevrin, H., and Fritzler, D.E. Visual evoked response correlates of unconscious mental process. *Science*, 1968, *161*, 295-298.

Shevrin, H., Smith, W.H., and Fritzler, D.E. Average evoked response and verbal correlates of unconscious mental processes. *Psychophysiology*, 1971, *8*, 149–162.

Shiffrin, R.M., and Schneider, W. Controlled and automatic human information processing: II. Perceptual learning, automatic attending, and a general theory. *Psychological Review*, 1977, *84*, 127–190.

Smoke, W.H., and Zajonc, R.B. On the reliability of group judgments and decisions. In J. Criswell, H. Solomon, and P. Suppes (Eds.), *Mathematic methods in small group process*. Stanford, Calif.: Stanford University Press, 1962.

Strnad, B.N., and Mueller, J.H. Levels of processing in facial recognition memory. *Bulletin of the Psychonomic Society*, 1977, *9*, 17–18.

Suberi, M., and McKeever, W.F. Differential right hemispheric memory storage of emotional and non-emotional faces. *Neuropsychologin* 1977. 15, 757–768.

Titchener. E.B. *A textbook of psychology*. New York Macmillan, 1910.

Tomkins, S.S. *Affect, imagery, consciousness: Vol. 1. The positive affects*. New York: Springer, 1962.

Tomkins, S.S. *Affect, imagery, consciousness: Vol. 2. The negative affects*. New York: Springer, 1963.

Trevarthen, C.B. Two mechanisms of vision in primates. *Psychologische Forschung*, 1968, *31*, 299–337.

Tulving, E., and Donaldson, W. *Organization of memory*. New York: Academic Press, 1972.

Vitz. P.C. Preferences for rates of information presented by sequences of tones. *Journal of Experimental Psychology*, 1964, *68*, 176–183.

Warrington, E.K., and Ackroyd. C. The effect of orienting tasks on recognition memory. *Memory and Cognition* 1975, *3*, 140–142.

Wells, J.E. Strength theory and judgments of recency and frequency. *Journal of Verbal Learning and Verbal Behavior*, 1974,*13*, 378–392.

Wilson. W.R. *Unobtrusive induction of positive attitudes*. Unpublished doctoral dissertation, University of Michigan. 1975.

Wilson, W.R. Feeling more than we can know: Exposure effects without learning. *Journal of Personality and Social Psychology*, 1979, *37*, 811–821.

Wundt, W. *Grundriss der Psychologie*. Leipzig: Wilhelm Engelmann, 1905.

Wundt, W. *Outlines of psychology*. Leipzig: Wilhelm Englemann, 1907.

Yntema. D.B., and Torgerson, W.S. Man-computer cooperation in decision requiring common sense. *IRE Transactions of the Professional Group on Human Factors in Electronics 1961*, Vol. HRE-2, No. 1, 20–26.

Zajonc, R.B. *Cognitive structure and cognitive tuning*. Unpublished doctoral dissertation, University of Michigan, 1955.

Zajonc, R.B. Attitudinal effects of mere exposure. *Journal of Personality and Social Psychology Monograph*, 1968, *9* (2, Part 2, 1–28).

Zajonc, R.B., and Smoke, W.H. Redundancy in task assignment and group performance. *Psychometrika*, 1959, *24*, 361–369. **[175]**

Chapter 15

On the Primacy of Affect*

R.B. Zajonc
University of Michigan

Only a few years ago I published a rather speculative article entitled "Feeling and Thinking" (Zajonc, 1980). The title also included the provocative subtitle "Preferences Need No Inferences," deliberately suggesting an occasional independence of emotion from cognition. In this article I tried to appeal for a more concentrated study of affective phenomena that have been ignored for decades, and, at the same time, to ease the heavy reliance on cognitive functions for the explanation of affect.

The argument began with the general hypothesis that affect and cognition are separate and partially independent systems and that, although they ordinarily function conjointly, affect could be generated without a prior cognitive process. It could, therefore, at times precede cognition in a behavioral chain. I based this proposition on a number of diverse findings and phenomena, none of which alone could clinch the argument, but all of which taken together pointed to a clear possibility of an affective independence and primacy. This idea was first advanced by Wundt (1907) and later reiterated by others (e.g., Izard, 1984). Lazarus (1982) takes a very strong issue with all of this and almost categorically rejects the likelihood of the independence of affect of cognition, let alone the possibility of an affective primacy. In this article, I will review Lazarus's position and contrast it with mine.

Lazarus employs two definitions, one for emotion and one for cognition. All of his inferences are based on these two definitions. Lazarus's definition of emotion (which requires cognition as a necessary precondition) is central to his position. On the basis of this definition alone, therefore, the argument is unassailable. If Lazarus insists on his definition, as he has the right to do, we must agree that affect cannot be independent of cognition because *by definition* cognition is a necessary precondition for affective arousal.

For Lazarus, cognition is an ever-present prior element of affect, and since the presence of cognitive functions cannot always be documented, a rather special definition of cognition is required. Thus, Lazarus's definitions of cognition and of cognitive appraisal also include forms of cognitive appraisal that cannot be observed, verified, or documented.

* This work was supported by Grant BS-8117477 from the National Science Foundation. I wish to thank Pam Adelmann and James L. Olds for drawing my attention to the literature on retinohypothalamic tract.

Because the emotional reaction is *defined* as requiring cognitive appraisal as a crucial precondition, it must be present whether we have evidence of it or not. Even if cognitive appraisal of a given emotional excitation cannot be documented, according to the definition it must have nevertheless taken place, albeit at an unconscious level or in the form of most primitive sensory registration. Therefore, Lazarus's proposition cannot be falsified.

Perhaps because the argument is circular, more need not be said. However, there are important reasons to say more. Whether cognitive appraisal is always necessary for emotion or not should not be settled by definitions alone. Empirical facts should contribute to the formulation of these definitions, and if we wish to understand how cognition and emotion interact, it is important to know what is true. Assuming that cognitive appraisal is always a necessary precondition of emotion preempts research on the matter. My preference is to leave the question of cognitive appraisal open for empirical research, postponing the task of precise and extensive definitions of both processes until we know more about them. Solving problems by definition is not an incentive for further study. It is a useful maneuver that allows us to proceed with our work for awhile, pretending that one aspect of our problem had already been solved. But we can pretend just so long. At some point of theoretical development, we must look to the empirical side of the problem and confront our assumptions and definitions with empirical reality [117]* and examine our theoretical consistency. I believe that this point of theoretical development has now been reached. Of course, the question contested here cannot be *fully* resolved unless we have a full understanding of consciousness. Such an understanding is, at the moment, beyond our reach. But we have learned just about enough about cognition and emotion to move beyond definitional disputes. Conflicting results that I pointed out in my earlier article (Zajonc, 1980) need to be integrated. Questions about the independence and primacy of affect can now be seriously asked at the empirical level. I offered the notion of affective independence and primacy as a hypothesis to be empirically verified, not as a definition to be disputed. Above all, however, defining affect as heavily dependent on cognition should make it rather clumsy to study the interaction of cognition and emotion, and especially those forms of emotion in which the latter influences cognition (for example, in phobia and prejudice).

"WIDESPREAD MISUNDERSTANDING"

Lazarus (1982) bemoans "widespread misunderstandings of what it means to speak of cognition as a causal antecedent of emotion" (p. 1019). According to Lazarus, "Cognitive appraisal means that the way one interprets one's plight … is crucial to the emotional response" (p. 1019). But "cognitive appraisal" need not be a deliberate, rational, or conscious process (p. 1022). We "do not have to have complete information to react emotionally to meaning" (p. 1021). Perceptions that are "global or spherical" (p. 1020) will suffice. In this respect, however, Lazarus mistakenly assumes that I equated intention, rationality, and awareness with cognition *in general,* or with cognitive appraisal *in particular.* This is not so. I selected some examples in which deliberate, rational, or conscious processes could be shown to be clearly unnecessary for the generation of affect. I selected these examples on purpose. If Lazarus and I could agree that

---

* Bracketed bold numbers refer to original page numbers. Page numbers indicate where the original page ended.

these forms of cognition are not necessary for an emotional arousal, then part of our problem would be solved. Now we would only need to determine whether the forms of cognition that are hidden from the cognizer are necessary antecedents of emotion. Only the requirement for an unconscious cognitive appraisal remains to be analyzed, because Lazarus and I agree that cognitive processes which are unintentional and irrational but conscious are unnecessary for emotional arousal. My definition of cognition (Zajonc, 1980, p. 154) required some form of transformation of a present or past sensory input. "Pure" sensory input, untransformed according to a more or less fixed code, is not cognition. It is just "pure" sensation. Cognition need not be deliberate, rational, or conscious, but it must involve some minimum "mental work." This "mental work" may consist of operations on sensory input that transform that input into a form that may become subjectively available, or it may consist of the activation of items from memory.

The essence of the question can be stated as follows. If there is a detectable emotional response, but there is, at the same time, no detectable antecedent cognitive process, did such a cognitive process take place nevertheless, albeit at the unconscious level? Lazarus's position is that it was there but we could not document it. Lazarus asks, "Are there any exceptions?" (p. 1201). "I think not," he answers himself.

Now, a host of theories, within and outside of psychology, assume entities and processes that cannot be observed given current observational capabilities. These unobservable processes are postulated because otherwise explanation of the phenomena under investigation would be impossible. Moreover, they are postulated only when they do not conflict with empirical evidence. This is not true of emotions. Many emotional phenomena can be explained and have been explained without invoking cognitive processes of any kind (e.g., Izard, 1977; Tomkins, 1962), and conflict with empirical reality is, in fact, created if we assume a cognitive appraisal for every emotion. The facial feedback theory of emotion (Darwin, 1955; Izard, 1971; Tomkins, 1962), which is gaining increasing empirical support (Duncan and Laird, 1977; Laird, 1974; Laird, Wegener, Halal, and Szegda, 1982; Lanzetta and Orr, 1980; Rhodewalt and Comer, 1979; Zuckerman, Klorman, Larrance, and Spiegel, 1981), requires no assumptions about prior cognitive appraisal, and appraisal of the kind Lazarus postulates would play havoc with the opponent process theory of affect (Solomon, 1980).

For Lazarus (1982), "cognitive appraisal (of meaning or significance) underlies and is an integral feature of all emotional states" (p. 1021). Thus, all three aspects of emotional reaction—bodily processes, overt behavioral expression, and subjective experience—need cognitive appraisal as a necessary precondition. I believe that this is not so, and I shall try to show why not.

EMPIRICAL BASIS OF AFFECTIVE PRIMACY

There are various phenomena that cannot be ignored when one questions the independence of affect from cognition. At the moment, the best single explanation for these phenomena is the assumption that affect can be aroused *without* the participation of cognitive [118] processes and that it may therefore function independently for those circumstances. This is true provided we mean by "cognition" something more than pure sensory input. I have reviewed some of this evidence elsewhere (Zajonc, 1980; Zajonc,

Pietromonaco, and Bargh, 1982). However, it did not impress Lazarus. I will now briefly summarize these and some previously unmentioned findings and phenomena. These findings need comment from theoreticians who assume all of affect to be always post-cognitive and always depending on appraisal.

1. *Affective reactions show phylogenetic and ontogenetic primacy.* Izard (1984) reviewed the evidence on ontogenetic primacy of emotion, and the picture that emerges from his extensive examination of the literature is quite convincing. Thus, if emotion precedes cognition at some level of the individual's development, then at that level of development no cognitive appraisal is necessary (or even possible) for the arousal of an affective reaction. In my 1980 article, I hypothesized the *independence* of affect *of* cognition. At the formal level, therefore, affect could be simultaneous or secondary and still independent of cognition. Proving this hypothesis requires no demonstration that affect is primary. Nor must affect be *always* primary. If evidence can be uncovered about the primacy of affect in only one situation, the independence hypothesis would be confirmed.

2. *Separate neuroanatomical structures can be identified for affect and cognition.* For example, Izard (1984) wrote,

> The case for considering emotions as a separate system seems fairly well established at the neurophysiological-biochemical level. At this level it is well known that some brain structures, neural pathways, and neurotransmitters are relatively more involved than others with emotion expression, emotion experience or feelings, and emotion-related behaviors. The limbic system is sometimes referred to as the "emotional brain," and the fact that at least one limbic structure, the hippocampus, has been strongly implicated in information processing (Simonov, 1972) and memory (O'Keefe and Nadel, 1979) suggests the existence of brain mechanisms specially adapted for mediating emotion-cognition interactions. (p. 25)

   a. Emotional reactions are likely to be under the control of the right brain hemisphere, whereas cognitive processes are predominantly the business of the left hemisphere (Cacioppo and Petty, 1981; Schwartz, Davidson, and Maer, 1975; Suberi and McKeever, 1977). This evidence is not strong, but it is very suggestive. In a recent review of work on lateralization, Tucker (1981) concluded that the two hemispheres do participate differentially in cognitive functions and in emotion, and that cognitive activity would not be possible without the independent neurophysiological processes that give rise to emotion.

   b. Emotional features of speech are apparently controlled by the right hemisphere, whereas semantic and lexical aspects are controlled by the left. Ross and Mesulam (1979) found a number of patients with lesions in the right hemisphere, directly across from Broca's area. All these patients produced intelligible speech, but it was speech totally devoid of emotional inflections and other affect-dependent prosodic parameters.

c. A *direct* pathway from the retina to the hypothalamus has been demonstrated in a large number of species (Nauta and Haymaker, 1969). On the basis of an extensive review, Moore (1973) concluded that "a retinal projection to the suprachiasmatic nuclei is a regular feature of the mammalian visual system" (p. 408). Since the hypothalamus plays a central role in the arousal and expression of emotion, the retinohypothalamic tract allows the organism to generate an emotional reaction from a purely *sensory* input. No mediation by higher mental processes is apparently required. Emotions could be only one synapse away. Thus, it is possible that rapidly changing light gradients, such as those that arise with looming objects, could generate fear reactions directly. Other studies show that direct aggression can be elicited by the electrical stimulation of the hypothalamus (Flynn, Edwards, and Bandler. 1971; Wasman and Flynn, 1962), and other efferent projections have been found issuing from the suprachiasmatic nuclei (Stephan, Berkley, and Moss, 1981). These findings would imply that pure sensory input requiring no transformation into cognition is capable of bringing about a full emotional response involving visceral and motor activity. There is no reason why subjective feeling could not follow as well. Only a specific form of activity at the retina is required; this could be produced by a looming object or by a rapidly changing illumination gradient. For many species, efficient stimuli exist that are capable of eliciting fixed action patterns by virtue of an automatic process that short-circuits even "global or spherical" perceptions. Extremely small changes in retinal excitation can produce these reactions (Goodale, 1982; Ingle, 1973). Newborn infants respond in this manner to a host of stimuli, and with over-learning, all sorts of other stimuli may acquire the ability of eliciting emotional reactions automatically, short-circuiting cognitive appraisal that initially may have been a necessary part of the emotional reaction.

d. Some olfactory and gustatory stimuli, when of sufficient amplitude, produce clear overt emotional reactions, and they produce them immediately and directly (Steiner, 1974). These responses are universal across cultures and require no learning.

3. *Appraisal and affect are often uncorrelated and disjoint.*

a. Affective judgments of persons are characterized by a primacy effect, whereas appraisal information [119] is more likely to display recency effect (Anderson and Hubert, 1963; Posner and Snyder, 1975).

b. Weights associated with trait adjectives that contribute to liking judgments of hypothetical individuals are uncorrelated with the recall of these adjectives (Dreben, Fiske, and Hastie, 1979).

c. Multidimensional space for preferences cannot be decomposed to reveal descriptive dimensions. The dimensions generated by similarity judgments of an array of objects (e.g., hues, soft drinks) are independent of the dimensions generated by comparisons of preferences among these objects (Cooper, 1973; Nakashima, 1909).

d.   If cognitive appraisal is a necessary determinant of affect, then changing appraisal should result in a change in affect. This is most frequently not so, and persuasion is one of the weakest methods of attitude change (Petty and Cacioppo, 1981).

4.   *New affective reactions can be established without an apparent participation of appraisal.*

    a.   Taste aversion can be established even when the possible association between food (CS) and the delayed nauseous UCS is obliterated by anesthesia (Garcia and Rusiniak, 1980). The UCS is administered and takes its effect when the animal is unconscious. Therefore, the appraisal, if it takes place at all, must make a rather remote connection between the ingested food and the nausea that occurred during anesthesia (and has probably been only vaguely registered). It is highly unlikely that any sort of appraisal process, even unconscious, could have been involved when the animal rejected the CS food following conditioning.

    b.   Lazarus and McCleary (1951) have found that subjects are able, without awareness, to make autonomic discriminations (GSR) among nonsense syllables. Lazarus insists that, in their experiment, *some* form of appraisal occurred prior to the emotional excitation, but there is no evidence that such was the case in fact. The argument is simply that appraisal occurred because, by definition, it must have occurred (Lazarus, 1982, p. 1021).

    c.   Preferences for stimuli (tones, polygons) can be established by repeated exposures, degraded to prevent recognition (Kunst-Wilson and Zajonc, 1980; Takenishi, 1982; Wilson, 1979). Interestingly, Mandler (personal communication) reported that he was unable to obtain the above effects. Yet, Seamon and his colleagues replicated the results more than once without difficulty (Seamon, Brody, and Kauff, 1983a, 1983b). In one of their first studies, they demonstrated that the affective discrimination, obtained in the absence of recognition memory, was subject to lateralization effects. Thus, affective preferences were best for stimuli presented in the right visual field, and recognition memory was best for stimuli shown in the left visual field. A subsequent study (Seamon et al., 1983b) has shown that affective discriminations in the absence of recognition memory can be made by the subject even when the test follows the initial exposure by as long as one week.

    d.   In blind tests, smokers are unable to identify the brand of cigarettes they customarily smoke, but when asked which cigarettes of those tasted they liked best, they unknowingly point to their own brand (Littman and Manning, 1954).

5.   *Affective states can be induced by noncognitive and nonperceptual procedures.*

    a.   Emotional excitation can be induced by drugs, hormones, or electrical stimulation of the brain. Individuals who are given valium concealed in their food will change their mood, whether they know about having ingested the drug or not. They may have all sorts of explanations for this change, and it is possible, as Schachter and Singer (1962) have shown, that some qualities of the valium-induced state may be altered by cognitive input. But in the final analysis, at least some very significant aspects of the change in the emotional state will be caused directly by the valium, regardless of what information the subjects are given and what justification they themselves offer afterwards.

b.   Ekman, Levenson, and Friesen (1983) have shown that the action of facial musculature unaccompanied by the subjective component of emotion produces distinctive autonomic reactions that correspond to the facial musculature patterns.

c.   A little-known theory advanced at the turn of the century by Waynbaum (1907) claimed to explain why particular emotional expressions and no others are associated with the particular emotional states. Why, Waynbaum asked, do we laugh in joy and cry in distress? His answer was that emotional reactions, in the form of muscle action, act as ligatures on veins and arteries regulating cerebral and facial blood flow. The altered blood flow and especially cerebral blood flow, was considered a sufficient condition for the elicitation of pleasurable and noxious states. Although it is probably wrong in several respects, Waynbaum's theory merits close attention. There are means today of testing Waynbaum's vascular theory of emotions, and several of its aspects will no doubt prove to be correct.

FACTS OR DEFINITION

These are facts, not conjectures, and they have to be somehow explained. If we require affect, by definition, to have cognitive appraisal as a necessary precondition, then we must discover for all the above findings and phenomena where and how cognition could possibly enter. Of all of these, Lazarus mentions only autonomic discrimination without awareness (Lazarus and McCleary, 1951). The effect is explained by assuming that "emotionally relevant meanings (connotations) [120] could be triggered by inputs whose full-fledged denotations had not yet been achieved" (p.1021). This argument may be quite correct, and one is tempted to suppose that some cognitive work took place because we deal with lexical material. But we must not prejudge the case. Marcel (1980) and Fowler, Wolford, Slade, and Tassinary (1981) have demonstrated that semantic features of words are accessible earlier than perceptions of physical stimulus properties of words, and they are accessible under viewing conditions so impoverished that even simple detection is at a chance level.

Experiments that use semantic material presented at levels that do not allow the subject to identify the stimuli, or even to detect them, may be questioned because we are tempted to assume that, in some unknown ways, the meaning of the stimuli becomes accessible to the subject *prior* to her or his affective reaction. But affective reactions are established without awareness to such stimuli as food (Garcia and Rusiniak, 1980), tone sequences (Wilson, 1979), Japanese nonsense words (Takenishi, 1982), or geometric figures (Kunst-Wilson and Zajonc, 1980; Seamon et al., 1983a, 1983b). Especially intriguing arc the Garcia-Rusiniak data described earlier, because, in their case, the conditioned stimulus was presented at optimal level while the noxious UCS was given much later and under anesthesia. The fact that the animal subsequently avoided the food in question (CS) is significant because it suggests that all sorts of cognitive appraisal processes must have been circumvented. Perhaps, if the experiment were conducted with humans, when asked why they refused the food, some of the subjects might have said that they did not find it appetizing in the first place. But we could not tell whether these appraisals came *before* rejecting the food and therefore caused rejection, or whether they came *afterwards* as a justification.

Nowhere in Lazarus's article is there any empirical evidence to suggest that cognitive appraisal *must* precede affect. The argument is based entirely on definition, and, as such, it becomes circular when applied to the explanation of the kinds of results that I discussed here and previously. Given Lazarus's definitional stance, there is no empirical evidence that can be marshaled to show that appraisal is *not* necessary. There is always the possibility that some appraisal took place, even if there is no evidence that it did.

INDEPENDENCE OF AFFECT OF COGNITION

If cognition is not a necessary condition for emotion, then there must be instances in which affective reactions are primary in the course of behavior. What are they?

The individual is never *without* being in some emotional state. Emotional reactions may have chronic (e.g., depression) or phasic character (e.g., mood), tonic character (e.g., jealousy), or acute character (e.g., surprise or mirth). The chronic state may be overlayed by the tonic arousal, and tonic state maybe altered by an acute reaction. No emotional reactions occur in a vacuum. They manifest themselves as changes in the emotional state characterizing the organism at the given time.

What are the first steps in the course of a change from one emotional state to another? Clearly, one such condition is cognitive activity. One may recall a sad event or be reminded of an impending unpleasant obligation. As a result, one's mood changes. But there are other reactions that cause people suddenly to change the focus of attention or to become generally alert. I have represented the course of such behavioral changes as having an early affective trigger (Zajonc, 1980, Figure 5). What makes the frog shift attention from a lily pad to a snake is not the perception of the snake itself. What shifts the frog's attention is a particular form of change in the environment, perhaps a change in the light pattern caused by a movement of the lily pad that differs from the patterns of the previous few minutes. There may have been perhaps a minute change in the ripple patterns of the water, or in a reflection that was sensed peripherally. A sensorimotor program is activated, muscles tense, and there is readiness for flight. Emotional state changes radically as a result of this minimal sensory input that needs not be transformed into meaningful information. The neuroanatomical structures necessary for such a cognition-free reaction are available and the relevant motor processes are also available (Goodale, 1982; Ingle, 1973). The retinohypothalamic fibers that lead from the retina project to the suprachiasmatic nucleus, and they can directly activate hypothalamic neurons (Moore, 1973). In turn, there are all sorts of projections from the hypothalamus and from the suprachiasmatic nucleus (Stephan et al., 1981) that participate in such typical emotional reactions as recruitment of carbohydrate from the liver, transfer of blood from the abdomen to the heart, lungs, and limbs; piloerection; and at the behavioral level, retraction of the lips, exposure of canines, or immobility.

CONCLUSION

The question of affective primacy must be settled on empirical grounds. If one insists that cognitive appraisal is always a precondition to emotion, one is forced to allow cognition to be reduced to such minimal processes as the firing of the retinal cells. Thus, if we accept Lazarus's position, all distinctions between cognition, perception, and sensation disappear.

Lazarus says that we do not need complete stimulus information to react emotionally. There can be no disagreement about that. However, the question [121] is not how much information the organism requires from the environment, but how little work it must do on this information to produce an emotional reaction. Lazarus insists that perceptions that are "global or spherical" will suffice. I ask what forms of cognition *will not* suffice? Lazarus must answer this question if he wishes to hold fast to the proposition that cognitive appraisal is a necessary condition for all emotional states. His argument cannot generate clear answers. He cannot declare that cognitive participation in emotion must allow for an appropriate emotional response, because that is simply begging the question. Nor can he assert that cognitive participation must allow for stimulus identification, because research (including Lazarus's own classic work) has shown that emotion can be generated without identification. Lazarus argues that, although there was no conscious identification, there was some form of unconscious identification. But we cannot be sure, can we?

It is a critical question for cognitive theory and for theories of emotion to determine just what is the minimal information process that is required for emotion. Can untransformed, pure sensory input directly generate emotional reactions? The answer is likely to be yes, because the pattern of various findings seems to point in that direction. Already in 16-week-old infants, the blink reflex is suppressed much more substantially when the child is exposed to smiling faces than to blank slides. Perrett, Rolls, and Caan (1982) have recently found a group of cells in the superior temporal sulcus of monkeys that respond only to faces. These neuronal cells produce evoked potentials to monkey faces and to human faces, but not to scrambled facial features or to other parts of human and monkey bodies, such as hands. The cells did not respond to faces shown in profile, and even a slight rotation decreased responding. Thus, these face detectors may act as sufficient triggers for the emotional arousal that is produced in response to faces. When areas in the brain that are in proximity to the temporal sulcus are damaged, there is a severe disruption in the emotional responding to faces (Kluever and Bucy, 1939). The disruption is especially severe when there is damage to the amygdala, and it is interesting in this respect that (a) heavy projections into the amygdala that lead from the superior temporal sulcus were found (Aggleton, Burton, and Passingham, 1980), and (b) there are also in the amygdala neurons that respond selectively to faces (Rolls, 1981; Sanghera, Rolls, and Roper-Hall, 1979). Given that the amygdala modulate the emotional response to faces, the organization of these systems suggests the possibility of processes whereby an emotional response to faces may occur directly to untransformed sensory information.

At the simplest level, any sufficiently intense physical stimulus produces an escape reaction. There is no doubt, therefore, that the organism is pre-programmed for particular classes of reactions (at the grossest level, for approach and avoidance) to particular classes of stimuli. Some property of afferent excitation, perhaps the extent of neural firing, selects between approach and avoidance reactions. If other stimuli or situations can acquire this property, they too will select between approach and avoidance, and the new process will become pre-programmed. Afferent excitation that acquired affective potential by virtue of cognitive processes, however complex, may become autonomous, and affective reactions may rid themselves of the cognitive mediators (Zajonc and Markus, 1982). Neutral stimuli that acquire emotional significance through an initially extensive cognitive process may eventually become able to select between approach and avoidance on the basis of a very rudimentary sensory process that involves no mental work. This sensory process short-circuits cognition and links the response to sensation in a most direct fashion. If it is possible to react emotionally on the basis of pure sensory input in one case, then it is possible to so react in other cases as well.

If cognitive appraisal must be involved in all affect, then a completely new view must be taken of a variety of phenomena that I have described here. The emotional system becomes subordinated to complete cognitive control. Such a system has a questionable adaptive value. It is emotional reactions that categorize the environment for us into safe and dangerous classes of objects and events. In contrast, if we assume that there may be conditions of emotional arousal that do not require cognitive appraisal, we shall dedicate our research to the questions of what these conditions are and how they differ from those that do require appraisal. Should it turn out that not all emotion depends on appraisal, we may wish to enquire about the precise role that appraisal plays in the natural history of emotional reactions. When does appraisal enter as a significant element of these reactions? What is its role in the three manifestations of emotional states: bodily process, overt expression, and subjective feeling?

REFERENCES

Aggleton. J.P., Burton. M.J., and Passingham, R.E. (1980). Cortical and subcortical afferents to the amygdala in the rhesus monkey (Macaca mulatta). *Brain Research, 190,* 347–368.

Anderson, N.H., and Hubert, S. (1963). Effects of concomitant verbal recall on order effects in personality impression formation. *Journal of Verbal Learning and Verbal Behavior, 2,* 379–391.

Cacioppo, J.T., and Petty, R.E. (1981). Lateral asymmetry in the expression of cognition and emotion. *Journal of Experimental Psychology: Human Perception and Performance, 7,* 333–341.

Cooper, L.G. (1973). A multivariate investigation of preferences. *Multivariate Behavior Research, 8,* 253–272.

Darwin, C.R. (1955). *Expression of the emotions in man and animals.* New York: Philosophical Library.

Dreben, E.K., Fiske, S.T. and Hastie, R. (1979). The independence of evaluative and item information: Impression and recall order [122] effects in behavior-based impression formation. *Journal of Personality and Social Psychology, 37,* 1758–1768.

Duncan, J., and Laird, J.D. (1977). Cross-modality consistencies in individual differences in self-attribution. *Journal of Personality, 45,* 191–196.

Ekman, P., Levenson, R.W., and Friesen, W.V. (1983). Autonomic nervous system activity distinguishes among emotions. *Science, 221,* 1208–1210.

Flynn, J.P., Edwards, S.B., and Bandler, R.J., Jr. (1971). Changes in sensory and motor systems during centrally elicited attack. *Behavioral Science, 16,* 1–19.

Fowler, C.A., Wolford, G., Slade, R., and Tassinary, L. (1981). Lexical access with and without awareness. *Journal of Experimental Psychology: General, 110,* 341–362.

Garcia, J., and Rusiniak, K.W. (1980). What the nose learns from the mouth. In D. Muller-Schwarze and R. M. Silverstein (Eds.), *Chemical signals* (pp. 141–156). New York: Plenum.

Goodale, M.A. (1982). Vision as a sensorimotor system. In T. E. Robinson (Ed.), *A behavioral approach to brain research* (pp. 41–61). New York: Oxford University Press.

Ingle, D. (1973). Two visual systems in the frog. *Science, 181,* 1053–1055.

Izard, C.E. (1971). *The face of emotion.* New York: AppletonCentury-Crofts.

Izard, C.E. (1977). *Human emotions.* New York: Plenum.

Izard, C.E. (1984). Emotion-cognition relationships and human development. In C. E. Izard, J. Kagan, and R. B. Zajonc (Eds.), *Emotions, cognition, and behavior* (pp. 17–37). New York: Cambridge University Press.

Kluever, H., and Bucy, P.C. (1939). Preliminary analysis of functions of the temporal lobes in monkeys. *Archives of Neurological Psychiatry, 42,* 979–1000.

Kunst-Wilson, W.R., and Zajonc, R.B. (1980). Affective discrimination of stimuli that cannot be recognized. *Science, 207,* 557–558.

Laird, J.D. (1974). Self-attribution of emotion: The effects of expressive behavior on the quality of emotional experience. *Journal of Personality and Social Psychology, 29,* 475–486.

Laird, J.D., Wegener, J.J., Halal, M., and Szegda, M. (1982). Remembering what you feel: The effects of emotion on memory. *Journal of Personality and Social Psychology, 42,* 646–657.

Lanzetta, J.T., and Orr, S.P. (1980). Influence of facial expressions on the classical conditioning of fear. *Journal of Personality and Social Psychology, 39,* 1081–1087.

Lazarus, R.S. (1982). Thoughts on the relations between emotion and cognition. *American Psychologist, 37,* 1019–1024.

Lazarus, R.S., and McCleary, R.A. (1951). Autonomic discrimination without awareness: A study of subception. *Psychological Review, 58,* 113–122.

Littman, R.A., and Manning, H.M. (1954). A methodological study of cigarette brand discrimination. *Journal of Applied Psychology, 38,* 185–190.

Marcel, T. (1980). Conscious and preconscious recognition of polysemous words: Locating the selective effects of prior verbal context. In R. S. Nickerson (Ed.), *Attention and performance VII* (pp. 435–457). Hillsdale, NJ: Erlbaum.

Moore, R.Y. (1973). Retinohypothalamic projection in mammals: A comparative study. *Brain Research, 49,* 403–409.

Nakashima, T. (1909). Contribution to the study of the affective processes. *American Journal of Psychology, 20,* 157–193.

Nauta, W.J.H., and Haymaker, W. (1969). Retino-hypothalamic connections. In W. Haymaker, E. Anderson, and W.J.H. Nauta (Eds.), *The hypothalamus* (pp. 187–189). Springfield, IL: Charles C Thomas.

O'Keefe, J., and Nadel, L. (1979). Precis of O'Keefe and Nadel "The hippocampus as a cognitive map" (and open peer commentary). *The Behavioral and Brain Sciences, 2,* 487–533.

Perrett, D.I., Rolls, E.T., and Caan, W. (1982). Visual neurones responsive to faces in the monkey temporal cortex. *Experimental Brain Research, 47,* 329–342.

Petty. R.E., and Cacioppo, J.T. (1981). *Attitudes and persuasion: Classic and contemporary approaches.* Dubuque, IA: Brown.

Posner, M.I., and. Snyder, C.R.R. (1975). Facilitation and inhibition in the processing of signals. In P. M. A. Rabbitt and S. Dornic (Eds.), *Attention and performance V* (pp. 669–682). New York: Academic Press.

Rhodewalt, F., and Comer, R. (1979). Induced-compliance attitude change: Once more with feeling. *Journal of Experimental Social Psychology, 15,* 35–47.

Rolls, E.T. (1981). Responses of amygdaloid neurons in the primate. In Y. Ben-Ari (Ed.). *The amygdaloid complex* (pp. 383–393). Amsterdam: Elsevier.

Ross, E.D., and Mesulam, M.M. (1979). Dominant language functions of the *right* hemisphere: Prosody and emotional gesturing. *Archives of Neurology, 36,* 144–148.

Sanghera, M.K., Rolls, E.T., and Roper-Hall, A. (1979). Visual responses of neurons in the dorsolateral amygdala of the alert monkey. *Experimental Neurology,* **63,** 610–626.

Schachter, S., and Singer, J. (1962). Cognitive, social, and physiological determinants of emotional state. *Psychological Review,* **65,** 379–399.

Schwartz, G.E., Davidson, R.J., and Maer, F. (1975). Right hemisphere lateralization for emotion in the human brain: Interaction with cognition. *Science,* **190,** 286–288.

Seamon, J.J., Brody, N., and Kauff, D.M. (1983a). Affective discrimination of stimuli that are not recognized: Effects of shadowing, masking, and cerebral laterality. *Journal of Experimental Psychology: Learning, Memory, and Cognition,* **9,** 544–555.

Seamon, J.J., Brody, N., and Kauff, D.M. (1983b). Affective discrimination of stimuli that are not recognized: II. Effect of delay between study and test. *Bulletin of the Psychonomic Society,* **21,** 187–189.

Simonov, P.V. (1972). On the role of the hippocampus in the integrative activity of the brain. *Acta Neurobiologiae Experimentalis,* **34,** 33–41.

Solomon, R.L. (1980). The opponent-process theory of acquired motivation: The costs of pleasure and the benefits of pain. *American Psychologist,* **35,** 691–712.

Steiner, J.E. (1974). Innate discriminative human facial expressions to taste and smell stimulation. *Annals of the New York Academy of Science,* **237,** 229.

Stephan, F.K., Berkley, K.J., and Moss, R.L. (1981). Efferent connections of the rat suprachiasmatic nucleus. *Neuroseience,* **6,** 2625–2641.

Suberi, M., and McKeever, W.F. (1977). Differential right hemispheric memory storage for emotional and non-emotional faces. *Neuropsychologia,* **15,** 757–768.

Takenishi, M. (1982). *Stimulus recognition plays some role in exposure effects.* Paper presented at the Meeting of the Japan Psychological Association, Kyoto.

Tomkins, S.S. (1962). *Affect, imagery, consciousness* (Vol. 1). New York: Springer.

Tucker, D.M. (1981). Lateral brain function, emotion, and conceptualization. *Psychological Bulletin,* **89,** 19–46.

Wasman, M., and. Flynn, J.P. (1962). Direct attack elicited from hypothalamus. *Archives of Neurology (Chicago),* **6,** 220–227.

Waynbaum, I. (1907). *La physionomie humaine: Son mecanisme et son role social.* Paris: Alcan.

Wilson, W.R. (1979), Feeling more than we can know: Exposure effects without learning. *Journal of Personality and Social Psychology,* **37,** 811–821.

Wundt, W. (1907). *Outlines of psychology.* Leipzig: Englemann.

Zajonc, R.B. (1980). Feeling and thinking: Preferences need no inferences. *American Psychologist,* **35,** 151–175.

Zajonc, R.B., and Markus, H. (1982). Affective and cognitive factors in preferences. *Journal of Consumer Research,* **9,** 123–131.

Zajonc, R.B., Pietromonaco, P., and Bargh, J. (1982). Independence and interaction of affect and cognition. In M.S. Clark and S.T. Fiske (Eds.), *Affect and cognition: The Seventeenth Annual Carnegie Symposium on Cognition* (pp. 211–227). Hillsdale, NJ: Erlbaum.

Zuckerman, M., Klorman, R., Larrance, D.T., and Spiegel, N.H. (1981). Facial, autonomic, and subjective components of emotion: The facial feedback hypothesis versus the externalizer-internalizer distinction. *Journal of Personality and Social Psychology,* **41,** 929–944. **[123]**

Chapter 16

Affect and Cognition: The Hard Interface*

R.B. Zajonc and Hazel Markus
University of Michigan

In contemporary psychology, cognitive and affective processes are treated within largely separate and distinct conceptual frameworks, and, with few exceptions (e.g., Lang, 1979; Mandler, 1975), scientific publications in one area of research do not cite those in the other. Yet both domains of research investigate processes that interact with one another constantly and vigorously. Even though most theories of emotion assume as necessary the extensive participation of cognitive functions (Lazarus, 1966; Mandler, 1975; Schachter and Singer, 1962), the precise nature of this participation has been seldom explicitly analyzed. And it is equally remarkable that, even though cognitive content is rarely processed without the participation of affect (Piaget, 1981), cognitive theories have no conceptual elements that reflect the contribution of affective factors (Zajonc, 1980). This conceptual isolation of affect and cognition is likely to persist unless we come to understand which elements of these two processes make contact with each other and how the influence of one process over the other is actually effected.

The interface of affect and cognition presents a considerable theoretical and experimental challenge because it is not clear just *how* and *where* the affect-cognition interface should best be studied. Both affect and cognition are complex and manifold processes sharing many subsystems of the organism (e.g., neural, visceral, muscular, glandular, mental) and deriving from a variety of common external and internal sources (e.g., biological states, sensory input, and subjective experiences). Traditionally, however, it has been thought that the contact between affect and cognition takes place primarily, or even exclusively, at the level of internal mental representations. Implicitly, research and theory have commonly held that for affect to influence information processing, some form of the

---

* This chapter was prepared as part of a research program supported by the National Science Foundation, Grant BS-8117977.

---

affective representation (say, the subjective experience of emotion) must make contact with a cognitive representation of the information being processed. Thus, the interaction of affective and cognitive elements is analyzed with a focus on the associative structures that represent both types of elements (Bower, 1981; Isen et al., 1978). **[73]***

In contrast, it is the premise of this chapter that associative structures are not the only form of representation, and that affect and cognition are, in fact, represented in multiple ways. This is most obvious with respect to affect. Feelings, emotions, and moods do result in specific sets of mental representations, but they are most readily identified by responses of the motor and visceral systems such as clenched fists, red faces, bulging veins, slumped postures, silly grins, pounding hearts, and queasy stomachs. The motor system is extensively engaged in affective processes, and it is reasonable that affect is at least partially represented by these somatic responses. Cognition, like affect, may also be represented in a variety of the organism's activities. For example, when observers are first exposed to a novel object, they do more than just orient their sensory apparatus so as to explore the various attributes and parts of the stimulus. They open their mouths, move their hands over their lips, and shift their weight from one foot to the other. The function of the motor system during nonperceptual tasks such as thinking, recalling, or imaging is even more striking. People engaged in an arithmetic problem often gnash their teeth, bite their pencils, scratch their heads, furrow their brows, or lick their lips. Why? Why do people who are angry, squint their eyes and tense their shoulders? Why do people who are thinking hard bite their lips and tap their feet? Are these actions just epiphenomena that accompany the core processes of feeling and thinking, or might they themselves be integral parts of these processes? Perhaps both affect and cognition avail themselves of the motor system for representational purposes to a significant degree. In this chapter, we will focus on this possibility and examine the motor system as a critical point of contact between affect and cognition. Our analysis is carried out in the expectation that the motor aspects of the affect-cognition interface can provide a rich database revealing affective and cognitive phenomena that can be directly observed, measured, and manipulated.

REPRESENTATION OF AFFECT

In the present context, we need not mean anything more by a "representation" than some event *within* the organism that *stands* for a particular referent, be it an external stimulus (concrete, verbal, or abstract) or an internal stimulus, such as proprioceptive experience or kinesthetic feedback. A representation, like a symbol, is "anything that denotes or refers to anything else" (Kolers and Smythe, 1979), and in the case of affect, the "something else" is some element, feature, or manifestation of affect. In representation of affect, as in language or in cognition generally, there need not be a one-to-one correspondence between a particular representation and its referent. The words *chair* and *table* stand for a variety of objects and meanings. Their meanings in the sentence "The chair may not be moved to the table" can be understood by knowing what information preceded and followed it, and they have quite different **[74]** meanings than in the sentence "The chair may not move to table a motion." Nor is it required that there be an isomorphism between the representation and its referent, because the representation of affect need not be an analog

---

* Bracketed bold numbers refer to original page numbers. Page numbers indicate where the original page ended.

or a map of its referent. Again, this is so also in language where, except for onomatopoeia, there is no analog correspondence between words and their referents. And the same is true of cognitive representations, such as propositions, categories, and cognitive structures.

REPRESENTATION OF AFFECT ACCORDING TO THEORIES OF EMOTION

There are two broad, partly overlapping classes of recent theories of emotion, and both would lead to similar conclusions about the nature of affective representations. One class—the cognitive theories of emotion—invokes cognition as a necessary factor (e.g., Lazarus, 1966; Mandler, 1975; Schachter and Singer, 1962). The motor system and expressive movements do not figure as significant elements in the cognitive theories of emotion. These elements are central in another class of theories: the somatic theories of emotion. This class of theories also considers cognitive processes to be involved in the generation of emotion, but in these theories the somatic processes play a more prominent role (e.g., Ekman and Friesen, 1975; Izard, 1977; Leventhal, 1980; Tomkins, 1962, 1963). These two classes of theories have generally different orientations and different purposes. The cognitive theories of emotion seek mainly to explicate the subjective manifestations of emotion: They are concerned with the emotional *experience* and with the phenomenology of emotion. The somatic theories of emotion, on the other hand, attempt mainly to describe the *expression* of emotion and to explicate the *perception* of emotional expressions. They are concerned with the universalities of expression of emotion, and they seek to identify the significant parameters of emotional expression so that the various forms of emotion can be identified and classified. Also, they attempt to specify those stimulus properties of emotional expression that allow one person to understand the emotion of another.

The cognitive theories of emotion assume that representation of affect is "imposed" by the individual. According to the Schachter-Singer position, individuals may construe representations of their emotions by combining perceptions of their internal states with those of external events. Thus, subjects who were injected with adrenaline were friendly in a friendly environment and hostile in a hostile environment. Persons' perceptions of their own behavior, too, may help them construct representations of their affective states, according to Bem's (1965) self-perception theory. And in the somatic theories of emotion, the representation of affect derives principally from kinesthetic and proprioceptive feedback that is generated by emotional arousal. In all theories of emotion, therefore, "representation of affect" is rather abstract, and it is [75] inferred by observing behavior and its antecedent conditions. It is invariably understood to be an abstract associative structure, erected from images, propositions, categories, or prototypes that stand for the external events that generated emotional arousal and for the internal states that correspond to that arousal. Its proof of existence rests entirely on inferences made from variations in behavior and their relationships to input. But we have no direct access to these representations and cannot observe them.

In both the cognitive and the somatic theories of emotion, the motor and somatic processes are also important elements in the generation of emotion. Nevertheless, in contemporary theories of emotion they are not considered *in themselves* as having significant representational and mnestic functions. Theories of emotion consider instead the kinesthetic *feedback* from muscular acts as the basis for the representation of affect. And, in order for this feedback to become representational, the kinesthetic and proprioceptive information must be encoded and processed by the individual in very much the same way as any other information that comes through the senses. This conception of affective representation is true even of motor theories of emotion such as that of Bull (1951), and, in fact, is true of all theories of emotion. In Izard's (1971, 1977) theory of emotion, it is the proprioceptive and kinesthetic feedback that is the basis for a direct representation of affect as "feeling," and it is feeling—the subjectively experienced emotion—that forms its cognitive representation.

Hard Representation of Affect

There is another, simpler route for affective representations than that mediated by subjective states that, in turn, are generated by kinesthetic and proprioceptive feedback. The motor movement can *in itself—without kinesthetic feedback and without a transformation of that feedback into cognition*—serve representational functions. Thus, the afferent reactions that are elicited by the organism's own motor behavior and not by the external stimulation—what von Holst (1954) called *reafference*—need not be integral parts of motor representations. When a dog withdraws a foreleg in response to a bell signaling an incipient shock, it is utterly reasonable to regard the leg flexion as a "representation" of the bell-shock configuration in itself, independently of its proprioceptive and kinesthetic feedback and certainly without an awareness of this feedback. On some future presentation of the bell, the "memory" of the bell-shock association will be *represented* by low amplitude motor activity in the same muscles of the foreleg that were involved in the flexion. Recall that according to the classic terminology, once conditioned, the response pattern becomes a "signaling system," a concept that is virtually synonymous with "representation." It is important to note that we actually consider the leg flexion *itself* as the representation of the affective episode. An "internal image" of the flexion, another form of a cognition about it, or the neural events that [76] produced the leg flexion can function as representations as well. Similarly, information about the commands controlling the effector system (Festinger and Canon, 1965) need not be part of the representational function of the motor system. But just because they can function in this manner is no reason to suppose that the representational capacity is exclusively theirs.

To be sure, the leg flexion is not the type of representation that has been commonly conceptualized in such terms as "proposition," "image," "category," and "cognitive structure." But, except for the fact that leg flexion is observable, its representational function is formally indistinguishable from representations given by associative structures, propositions, images, or scripts. It has all the critical representational properties. It has a fixed referent; it is symbolic in that it can substitute for that referent; it can be combined and interact with other representations; it can become a part of a larger "knowledge" or skill structure; and it can be retained, lost, suppressed, or retrieved. We shall call the representations provided by the motor system *hard* representations, mainly to distinguish them from the more abstract, verbal, prepositional, analog, or iconic forms of representations, which we will call *soft* representations.

It is obvious that some aspects and features of the motor processes in emotion must, in fact, be representational. Expressions of emotion have distinct meanings, readily grasped even by members of different linguistic and cultural communities (Ekman, 1971). These meanings, therefore, must be readily apprehended by individuals who produce these expressions. Theoretically, therefore, the representational and mnestic functions of the motor system in emotion are simply a matter of acknowledging the obvious. To avoid any misunderstanding, let us clearly acknowledge that all theories of emotion regard motor processes as having some *indirect* representational capacity. However, these theories endow the motor system with representational capacities only through cognitive mediation. That is, the motor output is thought to be important in emotional representation, but only when the organism perceives, and thereby obtains a soft representation of that motor output. With this view, motor output serves as a representation of affect only to the extent that the organism perceives it or registers its proprioceptive or kinesthetic feedback. In contrast, we are proposing that the motor responses in themselves—without a cognitive mediation—can serve representational and mnestic functions. The retention of these responses is a form of memory as valid as any other.

Needless to say, motor responses must have neural antecedents. And it may be asked, therefore, whether the neural events that activate a given motor response that acquires representational function may themselves be representational. These neural events, and others that are antecedents of soft representations, play a role in cognition and affect that is not easily established, given the current state of knowledge. The representational function of neural events that underlie soft and hard representations is problematic. We can only speculate. For any afferent or efferent act there is a corresponding neural [77] activity. However, there is a great deal of other simultaneous adjacent neural activity that has little to do with the figural afferent and efferent neural events. If the neural activity that is the correlate of particular information processing or affective event under examination is embedded in a noisy background, its representational usefulness would be limited. At times, however, neural events are more distinctive, whereas sensorimotor activity is diffuse and has no distinctive features that would be useful for representational purposes. Such states occur in dreams, for example. Under these conditions, neural processes may play a more significant representational and mnestic function.

From one point of view, however, it would seem that motor output cannot serve representational functions independently because, according to such views as the close-loop theory (Adams, 1971) or the schema theory (Schmidt, 1975), stable motor patterns are themselves controlled by cognitive programs. These theories require kinesthetic feedback to monitor the execution of the motor program or schema, because it is through such feedback that each successive subroutine is instantiated. Thus, if all recurring motor processes are *themselves* under the control of cognitive programs, their representational functions would be entirely redundant, superfluous, and not independent of the cognitive system. The earlier and the more recent studies on deafferentation, however, show that there is muscular "knowledge" *without kinesthetic feedback*. Taub (1980) severed the afferent fibers from both forelimbs of a monkey, and he blinded the animal to eliminate visual feedback. Yet even then the monkey could still perform previously acquired responses, with rather complex instrumental behavior patterns, "[running] off without requiring the support of sensory feedback of any kind" (p. 378). Thus, if muscular patterns, such as climbing and reaching, that entail extensive contact with particular features of the environment and, hence, an integration with other sensory input, need not be guided by kinesthetic or visual feedback, then motor patterns serving representational functions need such feedback even less, because these patterns are, for the most part, self-contained and seldom involve any features of the environment.

Other systems, too, such as the autonomic, glandular, or the visceral, can serve representational and mnestic functions in emotion. They, too, are hard representations of emotions. Thus, for example, Bull (1951) observed two distinct reactions when she hypnotized subjects to experience disgust: One was muscular in the form of an aversion to, or turning away from, the imagined source of stimulation, and the second was visceral in the form of nausea, as if the person was about to vomit. The gastrointestinal activity could well constitute a partial representation of disgust. But it must be only a partial representation in this case, because the muscular revulsion pattern is necessary to discriminate disgust from other states, such as seasickness. And recent work by Walker and Sandman (1981) suggests in a more subtle way that the cardiovascular system, too, has representational capacities. These workers found [78] systematic lateralization differences in evoked potentials elicited by visual stimuli during different cardiac events. Thus, potentials to a flash of light recorded from the right hemisphere were quite different when obtained during rapid heart rate and high carotid pulse pressure than when heart rate and pressure were low. No such differences were obtained from the potentials recorded from the left hemisphere. On the basis of these results, Walker and Sandman suggest that "afferent impulses from the cardiovascular system modulate the context with which the brain receives and processes information." These results can be taken to mean that the muscles of the heart have representational capacities for emotion. Thus, we shall assume for the present purposes that the somatic manifestations of emotion, and, in particular, *the motor manifestations,* have representational and mnestic capacity. The scream, the laugh, the shedding of tears, the rapid withdrawal of a burned finger, are, *in themselves,* all representations of the affective states.

Figure 16.1 illustrates diagrammatically affective representations. Because it is unnecessary to our illustration, we omit neural activity underlying emotion that was to be

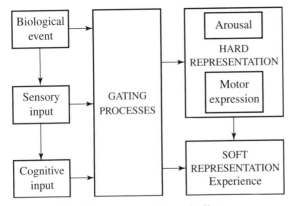

Figure 16.1   The representation of affect.

found in the thalamus according to earlier theories (Bard and Rioch, 1937; Cannon, 1929) and in the limbic system according to more recent views (MacLean, 1958; Pribram, 1981). We assume that an emotional state can be brought about by biological, sensory, or cognitive events. Thus, the injection of heroin produces temporary euphoria, the perception of a looming hawk elicits fright in the quail, and the memory of her husband's death elicits the widow's grief. Whether any of these events can actually generate the basic emotional state with its autonomic, visceral, and muscular correlates depends on a number of gating processes, including attention, ambient mood, the presence of competing emotional arousal that interferes with the elicitation of the new emotion, and competing muscular engagement. One cannot be roused from a depression into euphoria without some doing.

The generation of emotion is associated with three components. One is the *arousal* of autonomic and visceral activity. The second is the *expression* of emotion, which is mainly its motor manifestation. These two forms of discharge—the internal arousal processes and the manifest expression—constitute the basis of the *hard representation* of emotion. The third component is the *experience*[1] of emotion, which is the basis of its *soft representation*. The soft representation requires the mediation of the cognitive system. Thus, the soft representations of emotions are like any other abstract associative structures: They are in propositional or analog form, but in the case of affect, they derive from a transformation of sensory or kinesthetic input. In the present context, the experience of emotion is simply the cognition of having one. In the extreme case, only arousal is a necessary consequence of the generation of emotion. Neither experience nor expression need be part of the emotion process. The latter can be voluntarily suppressed—a skill taught to a high degree of proficiency in the English public school—or simulated even by poor **[79]** actors. And with regard to experience, the cognitions involved are sometimes not accessible to awareness, as in repressed guilt, for example.

In current research, the influence of affect on cognition is examined at the level of soft representation, because it is at this level that the critical causal contact whereby affect can influence cognition is thought to occur. How does fear or sadness, for example, influence cognition according to these views? These emotional states have, as their consequences, proprioceptive and kinesthetic stimulation. This stimulation, although internal, is perceived by the individual just as external stimuli are perceived. The soft representations (associative structures) that derive from the proprioceptive and kinesthetic feedback can thus interact with the associative structures representing the exposed stimuli (Bower, 1981; Isen et al., 1978), implicating processes such as spreading activation (Collins and Loftus, 1975).

Thus, when the affect-cognition interaction is viewed entirely at the soft representational level, we do not really analyze how emotion proper influences cognition, but only how one component of emotion influences cognition. We analyze instead how the *subjective (soft) representation of emotion* influences cognition, which is not altogether the same thing, because the problem reduces itself to the influence of one associative structure on another. **[80]**

---

[1] The term *experience of emotion* has been equated on occasion with the term *feeling* (e.g., Freud, 1948), and thus it was meant to include other correlates such as arousal. For our purposes, we retain the term *experience* exclusively to refer to cognitive (and perceptual) processes of emotion. Experience of emotion reflects primarily the subjective aspect of emotion. Experience, thus, should not be equated with "registration" because one can "experience" an emotion falsely, that is, without the antecedent arousal and expressive correlates.

THE ROLE OF HARD REPRESENTATIONS IN COGNITION

If we are to consider that cognition involves both soft and hard representations, their nature must be examined and specified. While the participation of motor processes is universally accepted as an integral part of emotion, their role in cognition is considerably more controversial. There have been, of course, several sporadic attempts to elevate the role of the motor system in the processing of information (see M.O. Smith, 1969, for a concise history). However, following the severe critique of the motor theory of speech perception (e.g., Neisser, 1967), there has been a marked hesitation in thinking of the motor system as having anything significant to contribute to higher mental processes. We attempt in this section to rehabilitate the representational and mnestic role of motor processes, for we fear that psychology may have abandoned the problem prematurely.

As noted earlier, affect and cognition share several subsystems of the organism. A given activity of the organism—muscular, visceral, glandular, or cardiovascular—may readily represent a cognitive element, an affective element or both simultaneously. *In themselves,* hard representations of affect and of cognition are not always distinguishable from each other. Data about the occasion and the origin of the given motor action (or bodily function) must be consulted when it cannot be determined on the basis of the topography of a motor action alone whether it represents a cognitive element, an affective element, or a mixture of both. But this is true of all behavior—its meaning cannot always be fully grasped without knowledge of its antecedents. The marathon runner may look down at his feet because he is depressed over the outcome of the race, or because his shoe is untied. In many cases, however, the parameters of the motor processes that represent pure information content can be distinguished from those that represent affect. These parameters have been identified fairly precisely in speech (e.g., Monrad-Krohn, 1963; Scherer, Koivumaki, and Rosenthal, 1972), although even in speech they are not *uniquely* identifiable: the parameters that represent affect in one language (e.g., rising pitch in English) may represent meaning in another (Chinese).

The Software and Hardware of Cognition: Extending the Computer Model

It is clear from the above that the conceptualization of the affect-cognition interface depends mainly on the role we are willing to assign to the motor processes in representational and mnestic functions of cognition. The tendency today is to regard motor processes that occur in association with information processing as secondary and derivative. For example, in the controversy about whether cognitive representations are in the form of propositions (Pylyshyn, [81] 1981) or images (Kosslyn, 1981), no mention was made at all of the possibility that they may have significant motor correlates. Nor is the possible role of motor representation listed by Norman (1980) among the most pressing issues that cognitive science must confront. The reluctance to consider somatic involvement in information processing is not accidental. The analysis of hard components of cognition is virtually incompatible with the type of computer model of information processing prevalent in contemporary psychology—a model that ignores some very important functions of the computer in drawing the analogy. The contents of the mind, according to this model, are regarded in terms analogous to computer memory, similar to patterns of electromagnetic charges on a tape or disk. For some reason, the computer model of information processing, however, came to ignore the multitude of electronic and mechanical events in the machine that produced the electromagnetic deposits. It focuses our conception of memory on the *product* of information processing; it makes us think of the software and ignore the hardware, so to speak. Yet human memory may be more akin to the *process* whereby electromagnetic charges are deposited on a tape than to the resulting patterns of these charges—the end product of this process.[2] The computer model prompts us to conceive of memory as a static store (short term or long term), with retrieval questions reducing themselves to the matter of computer-like search strategies (e.g., direct access vs. location). This form of memory "retains stimuli," their copies, traces, or analogs. In this form of memory, the individual's responses in themselves are not retained, nor are they significant components of the representation. It is only recently in computer simulation that a concern with responses and with the dynamic aspects of memory again becomes evident (Schank and Abelson, 1977; Simon, 1979).

Remembering Stimuli and Remembering Responses

Except for a few sporadic publications (e.g., Lang, 1978), the current view of memory is that we remember stimuli, not responses. It is the consequence of the language of the information-processing approach that the organism's memory functions are now viewed in terms of storing information. This view, of course, is a departure from the traditional stimulus-response approach in which the response figured as a much more significant conceptual element. Lang (1978) is a clear exception, for in his work, responses contribute quite considerably to all sorts of retrieval processes. This secondary role of the individual's responses promoted by the current views of memory is well illustrated in research on articulation effects. The logic of past research, because it considered motor involvement to be secondary and ancillary, focused on the advantage that was gained in cognitive activity through the addition of a motor process. The subject's responses themselves did not figure in the representational and mnestic process. The advantage was considered *as accruing* [82] *to the stimulus process.* Thus, for example, Murray (1965, 1966, 1967) compared the learning of letter lists by subjects who just looked at them, whispered them, or said them aloud. Loud reading resulted in best recall. Similar findings to those of Murray are reported by Wong and Blevings (1966). Other studies show that seeing one stimulus while saying another often reduces recall by more than one-half (Levy, 1971; Muensterberg, 1890; Murray, 1967; T.L. Smith, 1896; W.G. Smith, 1895). These studies form the basis for the inquiry, largely unresolved, into the role of the encoding and retrieval of acoustical (stimulus) and articulatory (response) properties of the material (Conrad, 1964; Hintzman, 1965, 1967; Levy, 1971; Levy and Murdock, 1968; Wickelgren, 1969). It is of some interest in the present context, therefore, that these authors stress the stimulus features as

---

[2] The computer model is misleading to some extent in the case of the "hardware-software" distinction. In the computer, the software and the hardware are perfectly correlated. There is no more in the one realm than in the other. And there is perfect access to both. This, however, is not the case in human information processing. Soft representations may be redundant with hard representations, but they are not fully redundant, and access to either is not yet possible in most instances.

critical factors in encoding and retrieval even in the case of articulation. The enhancement of recall by articulation is interpreted by invoking kinesthetic feedback that adds to the *enrichment of the stimulus* (Hintzman, 1967; Murray, 1965; Wong and Blevings, 1966). Thus, in the study of articulation effects, motor responses are viewed as serving an intermediary function: They only provide an opportunity for kinesthetic feedback, and it is the kinesthetic feedback that is actually encoded and retained. The articulatory responses *in themselves* are regarded as having no mnestic value. But it is clear that these findings could be very well interpreted by assuming that articulation provides for a more extensive participation of motor processes, since more intense and more extensive muscular action is involved in reading a word aloud than in reading it silently or in whispering it. Thus, these motor responses are able to provide a clearer and more stable representation: They are *motor representations of cognition* in very much the same way as flailing arms or thrashing legs are *affective representations of rage*.

Cognitive Hardware

Have we discarded the motor elements of cognitive processes prematurely? There is, of course, an enormous motor involvement during mental activity (Baddeley, Eldridge, and Lewis, 1981; Bills, 1937; Block, 1936; Courts, 1939; Jacobson, 1929; Sokolov, 1972). The clearest examples are to be found in attending and orienting. The active organism plays an especially important role in Gibson's theory (1966). People looking at a street scene or at a painting engage a complex set of orienting acts that expose them to different features of the stimulus. The head tilts at a proper angle, the lenses accommodate for the proper distance, and the eyes roam over the various parts of the stimulus. It is entirely possible that the orienting and attending responses have partial representational and mnestic functions. This possibility is strongly suggested by the studies of Held and his associates (e.g., Held and Hein, 1963) in which people or cats were exposed to a given environment, either by being allowed to move about on their own, or by being transported. In all cases, passive **[83]** visual experience alone, without the participation of the individual's own locomotor system, produced very inefficient spatial behavior. Even more dramatic results are reported by Dru, Walker, and Walker (1975) for rats with striate lesions. Only rats that were allowed actively to explore their environment recovered their visual functions. The rats remained functionally blind, however, when their experience involved only a passive exposure to the stimuli.[3]

Observers are anything but passive when they are exposed to stimuli. If it is a photograph, for example, they might smile if it is a photograph of a smiling face or frown if it is angry. It is quite easy to understand why it is that perceivers roam their eyes over the photograph or accommodate for the proper distance. But why do they open their mouths? And why do they smile? And what traces do these reactions leave?

The function of muscular activity present during cognitive tasks is quite puzzling and not well understood. Why do people scratch their heads and rub their chins when they try to remember something? Why does chess-playing require such an enormous

---

[3] Note that the role of motor activity in Gibson's (1966) perceptual theory emphasizes especially the orienting function. The active organism is viewed as better able to gain access to stimulus information than is an inactive organism. In our approach, however, the emphasis is on the role of motor responses as representational and mnestic devices, not as instrumentalities of orientation.

physical effort?[4] What is "going on in the mind" that requires muscular output? The arithmetical prodigy Truman Henry Safford is said to have engaged in rich and peculiar motor activity in the course of his rapid calculations.[5] "'What number is that which, being divided by the product of its digits, the quotient is 3; and if 18 be added, the digits will be inverted?' He flew out of his chair, whirled around, rolled up his eyes and said in about a minute. 24. 'Multiply in your head 365,365,365,365,365, by 365,365,365, 365,365,365.' He flew around the room like a top, pulled his pantaloons over the top of his boots, bit his hand, rolled his eyes in their sockets, sometimes smiling and talking, and then seeming to be in agony, until, in not more than one minute, said he, 133,491,850,208,566,925,016,658,299,941,583,225!'" (Scripture, 1891). When asked to suppress subvocalization, people find doing mental arithmetic impossible (Fryer, 1941) and reading comprehension suffers similarly (Baddeley, Eldridge, and Lewis, 1981).

The violinist Itzhak Perlman, in trying to play a difficult note, raises his eyebrows (if it is a high note) and keeps them raised until the note has been played. His face and body perform a rich program of varied movements. Why, again? With few exceptions (Piaget, 1954), it is generally believed that these motions are secondary and ancillary. But suppose that a good part of musical memory is in fact lodged in these peculiar movements. Suppose that they are significant. Looking at performing musicians, one is impressed with the possibility that they are engaged in a sort of matching process. It seems as if they had "*in* their eyebrows" or "*in* their tongue" a muscular representation of the ideal tone that they wish to produce. They seem to accommodate their hands, they adjust their bows over the strings of the instrument, and modulate finger pressure over the board seeking to attain the closest match between the output and that ideal. **[84]**

Thus, the issue that must be resolved is whether these movements are *generally* helpful (e.g., they rid the musician of excess energy or express emotion) or whether some of them, or some of their parameters, constitute essential and integral parts of the representation in memory of the music and its finer qualities. It is interesting in this respect that the raising of the eyebrows to high notes occurs *before* the note is actually played. And nobody raises eyebrows to a descending pitch. If the motor system is involved in learning a piece of music, it might also be implicated in learning a poem, in proving a theorem, in encoding a street scene, or in trying to recall a face of an old acquaintance. Surely, a person who tries to "mimic" a particular tree or even such an abstract stimulus as a number will register these items more efficiently and will remember them better than a person who remains passive.

Perhaps the head scratching and chin rubbing of people who are trying to solve a difficult problem or to remember something is in some way functional. It is certainly unlikely that these movements are "superstitious," since they occur with such an enormous uniformity in diverse cultures. And there is certainly no possibility that the scratching of the head will "release lost ideas." But it is possible that scratching one's head is a "resetting" action that modifies the individual's ambient muscular "attitude," changes motility, and discontinues a pattern of muscular processes that may have been interfering with a particular muscular pattern that *is* the memory that we seek.

---

[4] Note that an intense emotional reaction can be also physically exhausting. Recall your most recent domestic fight.

[5] We are grateful to Geoffrey Fong for drawing our attention to this article.

It is an obvious fact that mental processes are accompanied by overt and quasi-overt muscular activity. The overt activity is readily seen by any observer and the quasi-overt activity is revealed by electromyographic (EMG) studies (e.g., Cacioppo and Petty, 1981, 1981a; Jacobson, 1929; Lang, 1978; McGuigan, 1978; Schwartz et al., 1978; Sokolov, 1972). On the assumption that "the arms and fingers of the deaf are the locus of their oral, written and gestural speech," Max (1937) recorded EMG responses from the flexores digitorum of deaf and hearing subjects. Of the deaf subjects, 84% showed significant responses compared with only 31% of hearing subjects. Moreover, the average amplitudes for the two populations were 3.41 and 0.8 microvolts, respectively. The assumption here is that some of this muscular activity has significant representational and mnestic functions.

It is not difficult, thus, to demonstrate that muscular involvement can be advantageous in the encoding and retrieval of information. However, not all movement that occurs during thinking, recalling, or imaging is significant for affective or cognitive analysis. And in some cases, it will be quite difficult to separate the representational motor movements from motor movements that have no such function. It also will be difficult to establish for those movements that are, in fact, representational just what information they carry. But if we find conditions under which motor output can be demonstrated as significant in the acquisition and retrieval of information, a useful terrain for the study of the affect-cognition interface will have been found. [85]

EMPIRICAL RESEARCH ON THE HARD AFFECT–COGNITION INTERFACE: SOME POSSIBILITIES

The proposal to implicate hard representations in the study of the affect-cognition interface and thereby to gain greater knowledge about both processes is based mainly on the *potential* heuristic value of our approach. There is very little evidence at this time to support it directly, and judging by the past record of motor theories of perception and thought, this version will have a rough going as well. The most serious problem to overcome is that motor processes serve many masters. And because motor processes serve so many different functions of the organism, it will be certainly quite difficult to identify those processes that are significant for a particular act of information processing. Yet the multiple functions of the motor system are a fact of nature that the psychologist must accept. Motion, too, occurs in nature in terribly contaminated form, and the physicist had, therefore, to create experimental paradigms such as the vacuum or the inclined plane to observe it in its purified form. No one can predict the trajectory of a boulder tumbling down the side of a mountain. To examine the role of the motor system, it is necessary to discover or to create situations in which motor responses serve primarily representational and mnestic functions. To begin with, we have chosen the domains of face recognition, mood, attitudes, and emotional disturbance. Although a diverse set of problem areas, they are alike in their potential for suggesting paradigms that will be useful in designing investigations of hard representations.

Motor Reproducibility of Visual Input and Recognition Memory

In the initial phase of our research, we have chosen to examine the role of hard representations in the affect-cognition interface with respect to the perception and remembering of faces. Face perception seems to involve an extensive participation of affective processes. But it is particularly significant for our purposes because the subject's motor responses that are implicated in face recognition are probably *mainly* representational rather than otherwise instrumental.

It is useful in formulating the face recognition problem to make a distinction between two types of sensory input, a distinction that is highly correlated with sensory channels. Some sensory systems are what we may call *quasi-reproducible* and others are *nonreproducible.* Within some sensory systems, the organism can immediately produce the same or nearly the same physical stimulus energy that reached the sensorium. For other sensory systems, reproducibility is not possible without elaborate external support. Thus, for example, when one *hears* a dog bark, one can imitate it fairly well, as one heard it and, thus, *hear* the same stimulus once again. But when one *sees* a dog bark, one cannot produce a visual facsimile quite so readily. All sorts of auditory input can be [86] reproduced with some degree of accuracy—a feature that is much less true of the visual input and one that is profoundly involved in speech perception. Thus, we can approximate the sound of an automobile but not its sight. One could argue that we can actually produce visual images. But visual images have no radiant energy that impinges on the visual receptors. Nor can we reproduce odors, tastes, or temperatures.

There is one exception to the superiority of the auditory over the visual channel. This important exception is the visual perception of the human body and its parts, a crucial factor in the perception and recognition of some emotions (e.g., Ekman and Oster, 1979; Izard, 1971; Tomkins, 1980). People can imitate gestures and postures and view and feel their own imitations. The face and its expressions, like other parts of the body, can be partially reproduced by the organism. And it would appear that in the perception of persons, such a partial reproduction may, in fact, be going on. While there is no formal evidence, some preliminary observations in our laboratory indicate that perceivers do not necessarily mimic others' facial expressions to the full extent, but they do produce patterns of low amplitude muscle potentials that often correspond to the face that is seen. Sometimes these muscle potentials can only be revealed through EMG recordings. And, of course, people do not produce the visual stimulus of the perceived face and of its expressions that they themselves can see. But they do produce a fair analog which is readily translated into a visual image. Thus, changes in subjects' own expressions upon viewing photographs of faces (and certainly of actual faces) may play a significant role in encoding and retrieval, a fact that provides us with an opportunity for studying hard representations of affect and cognition. As in language learning and in many motor skills, production may turn out to be the key to efficient acquisition and retrieval (Liberman et al., 1967; Meyer and Gordon, in press).

A series of experiments carried out recently in our laboratory (Pietromonaco, Zajonc, and Bargh, 1981; Zajonc, Pietromonaco, and Bargh, 1982) illustrates how the role of hard representations can be explored in the study of the affect cognition interface. In one of these experiments, photographs of faces were shown during the study period, and subjects were tested for recognition memory in a subsequent session during which the original slides interspersed among an equal number of distractor items were presented for old-new judgments. During the study period, different tasks were assigned to subjects in different groups. Of interest here are three groups. In one group, the subjects were required to imitate the person in the photograph. Several points of focus were stressed. Specifically, the subjects were instructed to reproduce the direction of the person's gaze, the expression of the mouth and of the eyes, and the orientation of the head and shoulders. Another group viewed the slides while chewing bubble gum. In this group, we expected that the chewing would engage motor responses that would interfere with those that the subjects might have otherwise used in encoding the faces. The third group of subjects also [87] chewed gum, but, in addition, they had to make judgments about, but not imitate, the same features that the first group was asked to imitate. Thus, they had to decide whether the person in the photograph looked up or down, in what direction the head was turned, whether it was a smiling or a frowning face, and so on. All groups had an equal amount of time for studying the photographs.

The best performance was obtained by subjects who imitated the exposed faces (73% correct). The worst performance was that of the subjects chewing bubble gum (59% correct). The subjects who had to make judgments of the individual features but were prevented from using their facial musculature for representational purposes showed intermediate performance (70% correct).

It is perhaps in the ability to reproduce and mimic people's faces that an answer to the superior recognition memory for faces (Goldstein and Chance, 1970) may be found. Perhaps upside-down faces are so much harder to recognize than other upside-down objects (Ellis and Shepherd, 1975; Hochberg, 1968; Phillips and Rawles, 1979; Yin, 1969) precisely because one is denied the opportunity of mimicking them. It is interesting that people seem incapable of "mentally rotating" a face and then mimicking it. Even with training, the retention of upside-down faces is enormously difficult. It is a possibility that such mental rotation also involves a motor process, and that this process, involving the muscles of the face, perhaps around the eyes, interferes with muscular movements generating the representation of the face.

Our results indicate that motor processes are significant in encoding material, such as the human face, that has distinct affective elements and that cannot be processed without the participation of some, however minimal, affective reactions. It is, of course, not clear whether these results illustrate the role of hard representations of affect alone (i.e., the subject's emotional reaction to the photograph, such as attraction, empathy, or dislike), or just descriptive information (i.e., the shape of the face or direction of gaze), or, in fact, both. And it is up to future research to distinguish the features of the motor responses that serve as hard *affective* representations from those that serve as hard *cognitive* representations. Thus far, it is clear, however, that the musculature of the face serves a useful representational function.

Mood-Dependent Information Processing and Motor Cues

Recent studies on the antecedents and determinants of mood suggest that it also may be a useful domain for the exploration of hard representations in the affect-cognition interface. In recent experiments (Bower, 1981; Isen et al., 1978), mood is translated into a node in memory, as any other information would be translated. Mood effects are treated as a special case of state dependent learning (Ho, Richard, and Chute, 1978), with mood providing cues that become associated with the test items to be acquired and retained. Other studies, however, have revealed that mood is an ambient emotional state that has some

[88] distinct motor and visceral correlates. A person who is depressed has a different muscle tonus and motility than a person who feels utter delight (Whatmore and Kohli, 1968). It has been found, for example, that psychomotor speed is substantially decreased under a depressive state (Natale, 1977a, 1977b; Velten 1968) and that posture shows distinct changes (Bull, 1951). Subjects given the Velten mood induction procedure (Natale and Bolan, 1980; Velten, 1968) tend to hang their heads down and contract their corrugator muscles, a motor pattern that Darwin thought to be the paradigmatic expression of grief.

When stimuli that have an emotional content impinge on the individual, the muscular activity deriving from *their* affect must somehow interact with the muscular ambient state deriving from the subject's mood (Schwartz, Davidson, and Goleman, 1978). Miller (1926), for example, reports that reactions to electric shocks are markedly reduced when subjects are very relaxed. Both the speed and amplitude of their responses were found to be lowered by muscular relaxation, and the subjects indicated that the shocks felt less intense than under the normal state of motor readiness. Mood-dependent learning effects, therefore, can be interpreted in terms of the hard affect-cognition interface.

There is now also considerable evidence that the voluntary induction of a motor reaction that is normally associated with a particular emotion, say anger, results in significant cognitive consequences (Colby, Lanzetta, and Kleck, 1977; Duncan and Laird, 1977; Laird, 1974; Laird and Crosby, 1974; Laird et al., 1982; McArthur, Solomon. and Jaffe, 1980; Rhodewalt and Comer, 1979). As one subject in Laird's (1974) experiment said, "When my jaw was clenched and my brows down, I tried not to be angry but it just fit the position. I'm not in an angry mood, but I found my thoughts wandering to things that made me angry" (p. 480).

Why should interference and facilitation be associated with incongruence and congruence of muscular states? Take an agitated and excited individual whose muscles are active and tense. The person receives the word *CALM,* which he or she must encode. If some portion of the muscle pattern associated with the motor representation of *CALM* calls for relaxed muscles, there will be a direct *physical* conflict, as in Miller's (1926) research. Muscles cannot be both tense and relaxed. Washburn (1926) was quite explicit about this point. She wrote that the "normal attitude of a healthy individual is an attitude of cheerfulness. Now, an attitude of cheerfulness is an actual movement system involving certain innervations, and while it is maintained it will inhibit all incompatible innervations" (p. 224). Thus, a person in the attitude of cheerfulness may be temporarily incapable of generating the hard representations that may normally accompany a depressing thought, just as "he cannot pronounce t and g at the same time: the movements involved are incompatible" (p. 225). Note, in this respect, that the meaning of conflict and of limited capacity is quite clear when viewed at the level of hard representations. The same cannot be said for conflict viewed at the level of soft representations, however. It [89] appears that mood-dependent effects in particular and most state-dependent effects in general can be viewed as involving a conflict between ambient muscular state and hard representations of information items that the individual is asked to encode or retrieve. Thus, the hard representation of a given item is simply not the same physical configuration when the overall muscle tonus is changed. The individuals will be handicapped in their attempts, under the given ambient muscle tonus, to recall items that were acquired under another muscular state because the identical muscular representations cannot be faithfully reproduced. The role of muscle tonus in mood-dependent learning can be experimentally examined by varying the subjects' motility independently of their subjective representations of the mood-state dependency that had been suggested to them under hypnosis. In this way we would discover the independent contribution to mood-dependent effects of both the hard and the soft representations.

Motor Representations of Attitudes

Research on attitudes comprises another broad domain that can be fruitfully reexamined for the role of the motor system and hard representations. Typically, as is the case with mood effects, most attitude effects are assumed to result from an interplay of soft representations. The affective component of attitudes has usually been conceptualized as a mental component and is most often indicated by a mark on a rating scale. Social psychologists who have been the most prolific contributors to the attitude literature have been almost solely concerned with mental attitudes and have accorded little, if any, attention to the importance of the muscular or motor system in the determination and expression of attitudes.

This neglect of motor factors is particularly notable in light of the early history of the attitude concept, which reveals a strong and important emphasis on the motor component (cf. Fleming, 1967). Darwin (1872/1904), for example, defined attitude as an overt physical posture and used the term to mean motor expression. Sherrington (1906) also emphasized the motor component of attitudes and stressed that an attitude was the ordinary posture of the organism—"the steady tonic response" (p. 302).

Even the idea of a mental attitude derives from the concept of motor attitude and results from conceptualizing the mind as "assuming a stable posture, bracing itself in a determinate stance to receive the incoming signals so that the answer will be a resultant of posture and stimulus" (Fleming, 1967, p. 302). Washburn (1926) tried to reconcile the mental and motor aspects of attitudes and went so far as to suggest that all thought was accompanied by motor impulses. Every stimulus, even remembering a stimulus in the form of an image, "conduced to a slight actual performance of some movement" (p. 48). Equally radical are the views of Jousse (1925, 1974) and Wallon (1970). Subsequent work has focused almost exclusively on the mental nature of attitudes [90] and has largely ignored the possible contribution or involvement of the motor system.

A reconsideration of the involvement of the motor system could provide some additional and more comprehensive explanations of existing attitudinal effects and could suggest as well a set of mechanisms that would allow a more complete exploration of the affective nature of attitudes. Many recent approaches to attitudes have been criticized as being excessively "cold" and for failing to uncover significant data about the emotional nature, function, or consequences of attitudes. This, in part, may be due to the emphasis on soft representations of attitudes. It is entirely possible that attention to the hard representations of attitudes could reveal their affective aspect more precisely. For example, it is more than likely that approach and avoidance tendencies are associated with distinct skeletal and muscular "attitudes" toward the target (Bull, 1951). Galton observed these "attitudes" in social interaction, saying that "when two persons have an 'inclination' to one another, they visibly incline or slope together when sitting side by side or at a dinner table, and they throw the stress of their weights on the near legs of their chairs. It does not require much ingenuity to arrange a pressure gauge with an index and dial to indicate changes in stress" (quoted in Pearson, 1924, p. 270). The popular literature on "body language" may not be far off the mark in this respect, and clear motor differences in the face and other parts of the body are revealed in approach and avoidance reactions to tastes and odors, for example. Nodding and shaking one's head are nearly universal gestures indicating agreement and disagreement, gestures that have very powerful semantic content. It is quite difficult and awkward to say "you are absolutely right!" while shaking one's head or to say "that is absolutely wrong!" while nodding. Osgood (1962) assigned a particular role to the kinesthetic system in processing meaning. Wells and Petty (1980) had subjects make these movements, ostensibly to test the quality of the headphones through which the subjects heard editorial statements. Subsequent measures of agreement with these statements indicated definite effects associated with head movement. These motor "attitudes" of approach and avoidance are clearly identifiable in many animal species.

More specifically, it should be possible to conceptualize particular attitudinal effects, such as the mere exposure phenomenon in terms of affective motor preferences. Previous research on exposure indicates that when a stimulus object is presented on repeated occasions, the subjects' attitudes to that stimulus object will eventually become more positive. There are consistent findings in the literature showing that preference for objects increases with the logarithm of their frequency (Harrison, 1977; Matlin and Stang, 1978). Experiments of Kunst-Wilson and Zajonc (1980), Matlin (1971), Moreland and Zajonc (1977, 1979), and Wilson (1979) all show that this effect need not be mediated by the subjective feelings of familiarity that are generated by stimuli with which the subject had repeatedly been confronted. Even when the subject cannot **[91]** discriminate objectively old from objectively new stimuli, a clear preference for the old stimuli is obtained.

We do not know whether preference has a particular type of motor representation, but it is reasonable to assume that it has *some* type of motor representation. The first exposure of a stimulus generates an orienting pattern with its particular response topography and autonomic and visceral correlates. The body is tense and the limbs are poised for exploration, potential flight, or attack. Repeated exposures produce gradual habituation and the body relaxes and the autonomic arousal decreases. Galvanic skin response (GSR) measures to Turkish-like words were found to decrease with successive presentations (Zajonc, 1968). Thus, in making liking judgments of the stimuli that had been exposed, the subject makes use of the hard representations of his or her affective state that the stimuli elicit. In future studies, it should be possible to manipulate the involvement of the motor system during the exposure sequence as well as during the test sequence, much as was done in our face recognition studies, and thus investigate the contribution of the hard representations in the course of acquisition of positive affect for the exposed stimuli.

It was noted in a previous study (Zajonc, 1980) that attempts to change attitudes by means of persuasive communication are singularly unsuccessful, largely because persuasive communication does not reach the affective basis of the attitude. In the light of the present formulation, we can now specify why this is so. If motor responses are salient and significant in the affective system, then to change affective reactions from positive to negative one must also, and perhaps above all, change the motor aspects of these reactions.

Attitudes, because they contain strong affective elements, must also contain motor components (although these motor components may be primarily of low amplitudes). Given that the motor system is less amenable to change by means of verbal control than the abstract representational system, we should not be surprised that persuasive communications are unsuccessful in changing attitudes. The significance of the motor system in attitude change must have been appreciated in the practice of brainwashing because the method involves a massive assault on the body. The victim is very often starved, drugged, tortured, and emotionally agitated (Lifton, 1956). All these practices may result in a condition that makes it difficult to retrieve old thoughts and feelings and, at the same time, makes the motor system more receptive to new representational input.

Obsessional and Hysterical Syndromes and Tics

The role of the motor system has been given considerable thought in psychoanalysis and may provide yet another area for the exploration of the role of hard representations in the affect-cognition interface. The obsessional personality, for example, is characterized by meager expression of emotion and little awareness of affective arousal. These individuals seem to keep emotions [92] away, although they seem to be aware of the stimulus world around them that can bring about emotional reactions. The hysterical syndrome is just the opposite. The hysteric is overexpressive, exploding frequently with long and powerful motor outbursts. It is, therefore, interesting that the musculature and motility of these two types of pathologies is strikingly different. The obsessional personality is tense, holding his or her muscles under gripping control, lest an emotion be generated. The hysteric's muscle tonus and motility are either totally relaxed or in wild action.

The symptom of the psychogenic tic is paradigmatic for the interplay of hard and soft representations. The tic is thought to reveal the independence of the emotional motor impulses from the organized ego. In tics, the whole action of which the movement forms a part, has been repressed, and the repressed motor impulses return against the will of the ego (Fenichel, 1945). In the present language, the hard representations of some affective content thus appear to become separated from their soft representations and gain autonomy. According to psychoanalytic theory, the repressed tendencies whose *motor* intentions return in a tic are highly emotional. Most commonly repressed are instinctual temptations or punishments for warded-off impulses. "In tics, a movement that was once the concomitant sign of an affect (sexual excitement, rage, anxiety, grief, triumph, embarrassment) has become an equivalent of this affect, and appears instead of the warded-off affect" (Fenichel, 1945, p. 318). The tic may occur in several ways, all of which suggest disturbances in the links between the soft and the hard representations of a particular event or situation. For example, the tic may represent part of the original affective disposition whose real significance became inaccessible to awareness. The affective stimulus may have thus received hard representation when it originally occurred, but its soft representation was either never formed, distorted, or repressed. Thus, a facial tic was determined in one case to constitute an arrested act of crying because the patient had been trained never to show emotions (Fenichel, 1945, p. 319). It occurred whenever something came up that might have provoked crying. In another patient, the facial tic apparently constituted a suppressed act of laughter at the patient's own father.

Two other motor phenomena—stuttering and slips of the tongue—are also considered to result from disturbances in the expression of a particular affect. Stuttering is said to reveal a conflict between the expressions of two affects. The individual wishes to say something, and yet he does not wish to do so. According to the psychoanalytic view, stuttering arises when speaking itself acquires threatening significance or when the content of speech has a threatening meaning. Very often individuals begin to stutter when they wish to prove a point or when they are in the presence of an authority figure. Under these circumstances, a tic may arise from the blocking of hostility toward the authority figure. The latent expression of hostility—say an impulse to spit, to growl, or to bite—is incompatible with the motor responses required for the speech [93] production and stuttering occurs as a result. A slip of the tongue can be viewed in similar terms. Something disturbs the individual's hard representation of a particular stimulus. With a slip of the tongue, as opposed to stuttering, however, it is thought to be possible to explore the relationship between the actual utterance and the intended utterance. Thus, the underlying motive or emotion that interfered with the originally intended expression can, perhaps, be established.

CONCLUSION

Clearly, this chapter raises more questions than it answers. But many of the questions raised are empirical problems that have answers, some of which are now being obtained in our laboratory and elsewhere. And our approach allows us to formulate these questions quite readily and rather precisely. If the motor system indeed provides the organism with representational and mnestic functions, we should be able to specify them, measure them, observe them, interfere with them, or facilitate them. We could thus verify how they work and what contributions they make to cognitive and affective processes and to their interaction. Knowing these answers, our attempts to understand the nature of soft representations would be on a firmer ground. It is always better to start solving a system of equations after some of the unknowns have been eliminated.

It is not necessary for our purposes to deny or even to question the existence of soft representations, be they propositions (e.g., Pylyshyn, 1981) or analogs (Kosslyn, 1981). In fact, there must surely be a number of parallel representational systems of all kinds to allow for such a fabulous achievement as the acquisition of language by the child. It is, nevertheless, useful to discuss some of the presumed weaknesses of hard representations.

The Realities of Hard and Soft Representations

It is certainly the case that no research has ever demonstrated a strict one-to-one correspondence between neuromuscular activity and a particular image or a particular mental memory. There are some casual observations such as, for example, when we ask someone to describe a spiral and see the person make an overt hard representation with his or her hand, or when a person describes a particularly vile taste by reproducing the original facial expression. For the most part, however, no firm assertions can be made about the nature of this correspondence. But neither have images and associative structures been accessible to independent observation, manipulation, and verification. No research has thus far been able to generate information about the nature of soft representations, and there are doubts whether this information can ever be obtained (Anderson, 1978). There are doubts, furthermore, about whether soft representations of the form that is commonly postulated exist at all (Kolers and Smythe, 1979). Certainly, thus far, they are not available to inspection. At [94] best, it is possible to demonstrate a correspondence between some conditions of input and some parameters of output that are consistent with some of our theories about certain types of soft representations. For example, some forms of categorization (a cognitive activity) during input have been shown to influence retrieval in a systematic way, suggesting an organization that corresponds to these categories (Mandler, 1967). But this research has no *direct* evidence that anything internal—that is, soft—has actually happened in the course, or as a result, of the sorting or categorizing of the items. The findings suggest that *something soft* may have happened, but no one can be sure that it has and what it was. The entire effect could have resulted from the placement of one pile of cards farther to the right than another—a condition that involved distinct muscular patterns.

Motor Responses Are Too Diffuse to Serve Representational Functions

A criticism can perhaps be made that although the motor system might provide adequate representations of certain gross affective states, such as moods, for example, it is too diffuse to provide sufficient specificity to reflect faithfully the fine distinctions that are sometimes generated by the cognitive system. However, this limitation of the motor system must surely be illusory. The motor system is capable of extreme specificity. How else could we learn to *speak* a language? Because linguistic productions are readily understandable, even with a variety of subtle nuances, and because modern computer technology has nearly achieved speech recognition and speech identification, there can be hardly any question of motor specificity in language production. And if such specificity exists in language production, why does it not exist in other forms of motor output as well? The dancer, the gymnast, the skater, the sculptor, the diamond cutter, all require an enormous precision of motor output.

The Motor System Lacks Sufficient Variability

One criticism frequently voiced against the possible representational and mnestic function of the motor system is that it is simply too constrained and too limited to represent the enormous wealth of the stuff of the mind. There are two answers to this criticism. The first answer is that the motor system is virtually unlimited in its capacity to represent information, both content and affect. Consider the piano with its 88 keys. How many different melodies and each in how many different ways can be played with these 88 keys (disregarding the pedals that add another enormity of variations)? Now, the body has more than 200 bones and many more muscles. Let us just take a subset of these muscles, say 100, because all of them cannot function simultaneously (since when one contracts, its opposite must expand). Given 100 muscles, there are [95] 2^{100} different patterns possible for the *simultaneous* excitation of all the units. If we allow each muscle to be extended or contracted more than once, such that the motor process is allowed to be sequential (like a piece of music) rather than simultaneous, an infinite number of motor representations are possible. And the fact that these muscles may also vary in the amplitude of response, from a fraction of 1 microvolt to a massive contraction, expands the range of variations even more. The facial muscles can literally encode some 6,000 to 7,000 appearance changes (Izard, 1971).

The second answer to the question is that we have no way of knowing the capacity of the soft representational system and no basis for estimating it. Hence, we cannot compare hard and soft representations in this respect.

The Same Motor Response Seems to Represent Different Objects or Events

The answer to this criticism, which is similar to the criticism regarding the narrow variability of the hard process, is that this need not be so and seldom is so. One needs only to look at the brain activity in the various areas of the motor and premotor system and to make the obvious observation that it is easier to account for the responsiveness to differences than to similarities, because from one fraction of a second to the next, the pattern of activity changes radically.

Curarized Organisms Are Able to Acquire Information

That curarized animals are able to acquire information is often argued as a criticism of the motor theory of perception and thought. Two answers apply to this criticism. First, suppose that the curare evidence is absolutely incontrovertible. Thus, we would conclude that the organism can get along without the participation of the motor system in representing reality. But this would only mean that the motor system is unnecessary. It would not mean that it is insignificant. It could still be possible for the motor system to act as an accessory in representational and mnestic processes.

The second answer is a criticism of the curare studies themselves. Curare does not affect smooth muscles, and such organs as the heart and the lung retain their functions. Thus, if the only muscles available for representational and mnestic functions are the smooth ones, then it will be those, under these circumstances, that will process information presented to the organism. Moreover, curare experiments seldom if ever go "all the way," for fear of damaging the animal. Thus, it is possible that some low voltage potentials might still be detected in the muscles that are involved in the hard representation.

Many of the points raised in this chapter are, of course, not new. It is today taken, more or less for granted, that affect and cognition are represented in a **[96]** multitude of ways. Izard (1971) postulates central representations, Lang (1978) implicates both the stimulus and response in representational functions, and Leventhal (1980) speaks of innate, acquired (conditioned) and transformed (propositional) representations. It was our primary purpose, however, to draw attention to a neglected realm of representation of affect and cognition and point to an arena where they could be examined as one influences the other. In doing so, we have exaggerated the distinction between what we call "soft" and "hard" representations, and we did so deliberately.

Much of the opposition to the early concept of motor representations was brought about by the extreme position assumed by proponents of motor theories (e.g., Watson, 1914). The early statements of motor theory of thought made the muscular system a *necessary* and central condition for the cognitive process. Some recent positions are also equally categorical (e.g., Jousse, 1974; Wallon, 1970), and they are equally vulnerable to ready criticism. There is nothing in the relevant evidence or in the structure of cognitive theories to suggest that motor representations or, indeed, representations of any particular kind (subjective, prepositional, iconic, somatic, visceral, or neurophysiological) are in themselves *necessary* for cognition or for affect. It is more likely that there are a multitude of representational forms, partially independent and partially redundant, not one of which is absolutely necessary and each one of which is sufficient for some types of cognitive processes.

The proposal to rehabilitate some of the older ideas about the role of motor processes in cognition and affect (Jacobson, 1929), on the grounds that these processes are easy to observe, measure, and manipulate, must surely seem like looking for lost coins under a lamppost. And we admit that this is, in part, true. But a large number of coins—some of them quite valuable—were lost, and many must have rolled under the light.

REFERENCES

Adams, J.A. A close-loop theory of motor learning. *Journal of Motor Behavior,* 1971, **3**, 111–150, 411–418.

Anderson, J. R. Arguments concerning representations for mental imagery. *Psychological Review,* 1978, **85**, 249–277.

Baddeley, A., Eldridge, M., and Lewis, V. The role of subvocalisation in reading. *Quarterly Journal of Experimental Psychology,* 1981, **33A**, 439 454.

Bard, P., and Rioch, D. A study of four cats deprived of neocortex and additional portions of the forebrain. *Johns Hopkins Hospital Bulletin,* 1937, **60**, 73–147.

Bern, D.J. An experimental analysis of self-persuasion. *Journal of Experimental Social Psychology,* 1965, **1**, 199–218.

Bills, A.G. Facilitation and inhibition of mental work. *Psychological Bulletin,* 1937, **34**, 286–309.

Block, H. The influence of muscular exertion upon mental performance. *Archives of Psychology,* 1936, **No. 202**, 49.

Bower, G.H. Mood and memory. *American Psychologist,* 1981, **36**, 129–148.

Bull, N. The attitude theory emotion. *Nervous and Menial Disease Monographs,* 1951, **81**.

Cacioppo, J.T., and Petty, R.E. Electromyograms as measures of extent and affectivity of information processing. *American Psychologist,* 1981, **36**, 441–456. (a)

Cannon, W.B. *Bodily changes in pain, hunger, fear and rage.* New York: Appleton, 1929.

Colby, C.Z., Lanzetta, J.T., and Kleck, R.E. Effects of the expression of pain on autonomic and pain tolerance responses to subject-controlled pain. *Psychophysiology,* 1977, **14**, 537–540.

Collins, A.M., and Loftus, E.F. A spreading-activation theory of semantic processing. *Psychological Review,* 1975, **82**, 407–428.

Conrad, R. Acoustic confusions in immediate memorising. *British Journal of Psychology,* 1964, **55**, 75–84.

Courts, F.A. Relations between experimentally induced muscular tension and memorization. *Journal of Experimental Psychology,* 1939, **25**, 235–256.

Darwin, C. *The expression of emotions in man and animals.* London: Murray, 1904. (Originally published, 1872.)

Dru, D., Walker, J.P., and Walker, J.B. Self-produced locomotion restores visual capacity after striate lesions. *Science,* 1975, **187**, 265–267.

Duncan, J.W., and Laird, J.D. Cross-modality consistencies in individual differences in self-attribution. *Journal of Personality,* 1977, **45**, 191–206.

Ekman, P. Universal and cultural differences in facial expression of emotion. In J. K. Cole (Ed.), *Nebraska symposium on motivation,* vol. 19. Lincoln: University of Nebraska Press, 1971.

Ekman, P., and Friesen, W.V. *Unmasking the face.* Englewood Cliffs, N.J.: Prentice-Hall, 1975.

Ekman, P., and Oster, H. Facial expression of emotion. In M. R. Rosenzweig and L. W. Porter (Eds.), *Annual Review of Psychology,* 1979, **30**, 527–554.

Ellis, H.D., and Shepherd, J.W. Recognition of upright and inverted faces in the left and right visual fields. *Cortex,* 1975, **11**, 3–7.

Fenichel, O. *The psychoanalytic theory of neurosis.* New York: Norton, 1945.

Festinger, L., and Canon, L.K. Information about spatial location based on knowledge about efference. *Psychological Review,* 1965, **72,** 373–384.

Fleming, D. Attitude: The history of a concept. In D. Fleming and B. Bailyn (Eds.), *Perspectives in American history* (Vol. 1). Cambridge, Mass.: Charles Warren Center in American History, Harvard University, 1967.

Freud, S. The unconscious. In *Collected Papers* (Vol. 4). London: Hogarth Press, 1948. **[98]**

Fryer, D.H. Articulation in automatic mental work. *American Journal of Psychology,* 1941, **54,** 504–517.

Gibson. J.J. *The senses considered as perceptual systems.* Boston: Houghton Mifflin, 1966.

Goldstein, A., and Chance, J.E. Visual recognition memory for complex configurations. *Perception and Psychophysics,* 1970, **9,** 237–241.

Harrison, A.A. Mere exposure. In L. Berkowitz (Ed.), *Advances in experimental social psychology* (Vol. 10). New York: Academic Press. 1977.

Held, R., and Hein, A. Movement-produced stimulation in the development of visually guided behavior. *Journal of Comparative and Physiological Psychology,* 1963, **56,** 872–876.

Hintzman, D.L. Classification and aural coding in short-term memory. *Psychonomic Science,* 1965, **3,** 161–162.

Hintzman, D.L. Articulatory coding in short-term memory. *Journal of Verbal Learning and Verbal Behavior,* 1967, **6,** 312–316.

Ho, B.T., Richard, D.W., and Chute, D.L. *Drug discrimination and state dependent learning.* New York: Academic Press, 1978.

Hochberg, J. In the mind's eye. In R. Haber (Ed.), *Contemporary theory and research in visual perception,* pp. 309–331. New York: Holt, Rinehart and Winston, 1968.

Isen, A.M., Shalker, T.E., Clark, M., and Karp, L. Affect, accessibility of material in memory and behavior: A cognitive loop? *Journal of Personality and Social Psychology,* 1978, **36,** 1–12.

Izard, C.E. *The face of emotion.* New York: Appleton-Century-Crofts, 1971.

Izard, C.E. *Human emotions.* New York: Plenum, 1977.

Jacobson, E. *Progressive relaxation.* Chicago: University of Chicago Press, 1929.

Jousse, M. Études de psychologie linguistique: Le style oral rythmique et mnémotechnique chez verbo-moteurs. *Archives de Philosophie,* 1925, **2** (4), 429–676.

Jousse, M. *L'anthropologie du geste.* Paris: Gallimard, 1974.

Kolers, P.A., and Smythe, W.E. Images, symbols, and skills. *Canadian Journal of Psychology,* 1979, **33,** 158–184.

Kosslyn, S.M. The medium and the message in mental imagery: A theory. *Psychological Review,* 1981, **88,** 46–66.

Kunst-Wilson, W.R., and Zajonc, R.B. Affective discrimination of stimuli that cannot be recognized. *Science,* 1980, **207,** 557–558.

Laird, J.D. Self-attribution of emotion: The effects of expressive behavior on the quality of emotional experience. *Journal of Personality and Social Psychology,* 1974, **29,** 475–486.

Laird, J.D., and Crosby, M. Individual differences in the effects of engaging self-attribution of emotion. In H. London and R. Nisbett (Eds.), *Thinking and feeling: The cognitive alteration of feeling states.* Chicago: Aldine, 1974.

Laird, J.D., Wagener, J.J., Halal, M., and Szegda, M. Remembering what you feel: Effects of emotion on memory. *Journal of Personality and Social Psychology,* 1982, **42,** 646–657.

Lang, P.J. Emotional imagery: Theory and experiment on instructed somatovisceral control. In N. Birbaumer and H.D. Kimmel (Eds.), *Biofeedback and self-regulation.* Hillsdale, N.J.: Erlbaum, 1978.

Lang, P.J. Language, image and emotion. In P. Pliner, K. R. Plankstein, and I. M. Speigel (Eds.), *Perception of emotion in self and others* (Vol. 5). New York: Plenum, 1979.

Lazarus, R.S. *Psychological stress and the coping process.* New York: McGraw-Hill, 1966.

Leventhal, H. Toward a comprehensive theory of emotion. In L. Berkowitz (Ed.), *Advances in Experimental Social Psychology,* 1980, **13,** 139–207.

Levy, B.A. Role of articulation in auditory and visual short-term memory. *Journal of Verbal Learning and Verbal Behavior,* 1971, **10,** 123–132.

Levy, B.A., and Murdock, B.B. The effects of delayed auditory feedback and intralist similarity in short-term memory. *Journal of Verbal Learning and Verbal Behavior,* 1968, **7,** 887–894.

Liberman, A.M., Cooper, F.S., Shankweiler, D., and Studdert-Kennedy, M. Perception of the speech code. *Psychological Review,* 1967, **74,** 431–459. **[99]**

Lifton, R.J. "Thought reform" of Western civilians in Chinese Communist prisons. *Psychiatry,* 1956, **19,** 173–195.

MacLean, P.D. Contrasting functions of limbic and neocortical systems of the brain and their relevance to psychophysiological aspects of medicine. *American Journal of Medicine,* 1958, **25,** 611–626.

Mandler, G. Organization and memory. In K. W Spence and J. A. Spence (Eds.), *The psychology of learning and motivation* (Vol. 1). New York: Academic Press, 1967.

Mandler, G. *Mind and emotion.* New York: Wiley, 1975.

Matlin, M.W. Response competition, recognition, and affect. *Journal of Personality and Social Psychology,* 1971, **19**, 295–300.

Matlin, M.W., and Stang, D.J. *The Pollyanna principle: Selectivity in language, memory, and thought.* Cambridge, Mass.: Schenkman, 1978.

Max, L.W. Experimental study of the motor theory of consciousness: IV. Action-current responses in the deaf during awakening, kinaesthetic imagery and abstract thinking. *Journal of Comparative Psychology,* 1937, **21**, 301–344.

McArthur, L.Z., Solomon, M.R., and Jaffe, R.H. Weight and sex differences in emotional responsiveness to proprioceptive and pictorial stimuli. *Journal of Personality and Social Psychology,* 1980, **39**, 308–319.

McGuigan, F.J. Imagery and thinking: Covert functioning of the motor system. In G. E. Schwartz and D. Shapiro (Eds.), *Consciousness and self-regulation* (vol. 2). New York: Plenum, 1978.

Meyer, D.E., and Gordon, P.G. Dependencies between rapid speech perception and production: Evidence for a shared sensory-motor timing mechanism. In H. Bowma and D. Bouhuis (Eds.), *Attention and performance X,* (in press).

Miller. M. Changes in the response to electric shock produced by varying muscular conditions. *Journal of Experimental Psychology,* 1926, **9**, 26–44.

Monrad-Krohn, G.H. The third element of speech: Prosody and its disorders. In L. Halpern (Ed.), *Problems of dynamic neurology,* pp. 107–117. Jerusalem: Hebrew University Press, 1963.

Moreland, R.L., and Zajonc, R.B. Is stimulus recognition a necessary condition for the occurrence of exposure effects? *Journal of Personality and Social Psychology,* 1977, **35**, 191–199.

Moreland, R.L., and Zajonc, R.B. Exposure effects may not depend on stimulus recognition. *Journal of Personality and Social Psychology,* 1979, **37**, 1085–1089.

Muensterberg, H. Die Association successiver Vorstellungen. *Zeitschrift für Psychologie,* 1890, **1**, 99–107.

Murray, D.J. Vocalization-at-presentation and immediate recall, with varying presentation rates. *Quarterly Journal of Experimental Psychology,* 1965, **17**, 47–56.

Murray, D.J. Vocalization-at-presentation and immediate recall, with varying recall methods. *Quarterly Journal of Experimental Psychology,* 1966, **18**, 9–18.

Murray, D.J. The role of speech responses in short-term memory. *Canadian Journal of Psychology,* 1967, **21**, 263–276.

Natale, M. Effects of induced elation-depression on speech in the initial interview. *Journal of Consulting and Clinical Psychology,* 1977, **45**, 45–52. (a)

Natale, M. Induction of mood states and their effect on gaze behaviors. *Journal of Consulting and Clinical Psychology,* 1977, **45**, 960. (b)

Natale, M., and Bolan, R. The effect of Velten's mood-induction procedure for depression on hand movement and head-down posture. *Motivation and Emotion,* 1980, **4**, 323–333.

Neisser, U. *Cognitive psychology.* New York: Appleton-Century-Crofts, 1967.

Norman, D.A. Twelve issues for cognitive science. In D. A. Norman (Ed.), *Perspectives on cognitive science: Talks from the LaJolla Conference.* Hillsdale, N.J.: Erlbaum, 1980.

Osgood, C.E. Studies in the generality of affective meaning systems. *American Psychologist,* 1962, **17**, 10–28.

Pearson, K. *The life and labours of Francis Galton.* Cambridge: Cambridge University Press, 1924. **[100]**

Phillips, R.J., and Rawles, R.E. Recognition of upright and inverted faces: A correlational study. *Perception,* 1979, **8**, 557–583.

Piaget, J. *The construction of reality in the child.* New York: Basic Books, 1954.

Piaget, J. *Intelligence and affectivity: Their relationship during child development.* Palo Alto, Calif.: Annual Reviews, 1981.

Pietromonaco, P., Zajonc, R.B., and Bargh, J. *The role of motor cues in recognition memory for faces.* Paper presented al the Annual Convention of the American Psychological Association Los Angeles, 1981.

Pribram, K.H. Emotions. In S.B. Filskov and T.J. Boll (Eds.), *Handbook of clinical neuropsychology.* New York: Wiley, 1981.

Pylyshyn, Z.W. The imagery debate: Analogue media versus tacit knowledge. *Psychological Review,* **88**, 16–45.

Rhodewalt, F., and Comer, R. Induced-compliance attitude change: Once more with feeling. *Journal of Experimental Social Psychology,* 1979, **15**, 35–47.

Schachter, S., and Singer, J. Cognitive, social, and physiological determinants of emotional state. *Psychological Review,* 1962, **65**, 379–399.

Schank, R.C., and Abelson, R.P. *Scripts, plans, goals, and understanding.* Hillsdale, N.J.: Erlbaum, 1977.

Scherer, K.R., Koivumaki. J., and Rosenthal, R. Minimal cues in the vocal communication of affect: Judging emotions from content-masked speech. *Journal of Psycholinguistic Research,* 1972, **1**, 269–285.

Schmidt, R.A. A schema theory of discrete motor skill learning. *Psychological Review,* 1975, **82**, 225–260.

Schwartz, G.E., Davidson, R.J., and Goleman, J. Patterning of cognitive and somatic processes in the self-regulation of anxiety: Effects of meditation versus exercise. *Psychosomatic Medicine,* 1978, **40**, 321–328.

Schwartz, G.E., Fair, P.L., Mandel, M.R., Salt, P., Mieske, M., and Klerman, G.L. Facial electromyography in the assessment of improvement in depression. *Psychosomatic Medicine,* 1978, **40**, 355–360.

Scripture, E.W. Arithmetical prodigies. *American Journal of Psychology,* 1891, **4**, 1–59.

Sherrington, C.C. *The integrative action of the nervous system.* New York: Yale University Press, 1906.

Simon, H.A. Information processing models of cognition. In M. R. Rosenzweig and L. W. Porter (Eds.), *Annual Review of Psychology,* 1979, **30**, 363–396.

Smith, M.O. History of the motor theories of attention. *Journal of General Psychology,* 1969, **80**, 243–257.

Smith, T.L. On muscular memory. *American Journal of Psychology,* 1896, **7**, 453–490.

Smith. W.G. The relation of attention to memory. *Mind.* 1895, **4**, 47–73.

Sokolov, A.N. *Inner speech and thought.* New York: Plenum, 1972.

Taub, E. Somato-sensory deafferentiation research with monkeys: Implications for rehabilitation medicine. In L.P. Ince (Ed.), *Behavioral psychology and rehabilitation medicine: Clinical applications.* Baltimore: Williams and Wilkins, 1980.

Tomkins, S.S. *Affect, imagery, consciousness* (Vol. 1). New York: Springer-Verlag, 1962.

Tomkins, S.S. Affect as amplification: Some modifications in theory. In R. Plutchik and H. Kellerman (Eds.), *Emotion: Theory, research, and experience.* New York: Academic Press 1980.

Velten, E. A laboratory task for the induction of mood. *Behaviour Research and Therapy,* 1968, **6**, 473–482.

Walker, B.B., and Sandman, C.A. Visual evoked potentials change as heart rate and carotid pressure changed. *Psychophysiology,* 1982, **19**, 520–527.

Wallon, H. *De l'acte à la pensée.* Paris: Flammarion, 1970.

Washburn, M.F. *Movement and mental imagery: Outlines of a motor theory of the complexer mental processes.* Boston: Houghton Mifflin, 1926. **[101]**

Watson, J.B. *Behavior: An introduction to comparative psychology.* New York: Holt, 1914.

Wells, G.L. and Petty, R.E. The effects of overt head movement on persuasion: Compatibility and incompatibility of responses. *Basic and Applied Social Psychology,* 1980, **1**, 219–230.

Whatmore, G.B., and Kohli, D. Dysponesis: A neurophysiologic factor in functional disorders. *Behavioral Science,* 1968, **13**, 102–104.

Wickelgren, W.A. Auditory and articulatory coding in verbal short-term memory. *Psychological Review,* 1969, **76**, 232–235.

Wilson, W.R. Feeling more than we can know: Exposure effects without learning. *Journal of Personality and Social Psychology,* 1979, **37**, 811–821.

Wong, R., and Blevings, G. Presentation modes and immediate recall in children. *Psychonomic Science,* 1966, **5**, 381–382.

Yin, R. K. Looking at upside-down faces. *Journal of Experimental Psychology,* 1969, **81**, 141–145.

Zajonc, R.B. Attitudinal effects of mere exposure. *Journal of Personality and Social Psychology Monographs,* 1968, **9**(2, Part 2), 1–28.

Zajonc, R.B. Feeling and thinking: Preferences need no inferences. *American Psychologist,* 1980, **35**, 151–175.

Zajonc, R.B., Pietromonaco, P., and Bargh, J. Independence and interaction of affect and cognition. In M. S. Clark and S. T. Fiske (Eds.), *Affect and cognition: The seventeenth annual Carnegie symposium on cognition.* Hillsdale, N.J.: Erlbaum, 1982. **[102]**

Part Seven

Nonconscious Affect

Chapter 17

Affect, Cognition, and Awareness: Affective Priming with Optimal and Suboptimal Stimulus Exposures*

Sheila T. Murphy and R.B. Zajonc
University of Michigan

The affective primacy hypothesis (Zajonc, 1980) holds that affective reactions can be elicited with minimal stimulus input. This hypothesis challenges the cognitive appraisal viewpoint (Lazarus 1982), which maintains that affect cannot emerge without prior cognitive mediation. In this article, we provide evidence relevant to this debate and propose a theoretical model that describes how various stimuli can elicit an early affective reaction that may be sustained or diluted by subsequent cognitive operations.

Affective primacy was first suggested by a mere exposure experiment (Kunst-Wilson and Zajonc, 1980) in which subjects, by virtue of repeated exposures, developed affective preferences for previously novel Chinese ideographs. In that experiment, the ideographs were first presented under degraded viewing conditions. Later, when given direct recognition memory tests, subjects could not distinguish these old stimuli from new stimuli they had never seen. Yet, despite this lack of overt recognition, when asked which of two ideographs, old or new, they liked better, subjects consistently preferred the previously presented stimulus. Moreover, response time for the liking judgment was found to be significantly less than that for the direct recognition judgment (see Seamon, Brody, and Kauff, 1983, for an extension of these data).

* This research was supported by National Science Foundation Grants BNS-8505981 and BNS-8919734 to R. B. Zajonc. The early experiments were reported at the 96th Annual Convention of the American Psychological Association. New York. We are grateful to Tom Nelson. Phoebe Ellsworth, Shinobu Kitayama. Hazel Markus. Paula Niedenthal. Norbert Schwarz. Richard Petty, and Piotr Winkielman for their useful comments.

One way of interpreting these results is to allow for the possibility that gross affective discriminations can be made virtually without awareness, whereas cognitive discriminations require greater access to stimulus information. Indeed, the affective primacy hypothesis hinges on the assumption that the simple affective qualities of stimuli, such as good versus bad or positive versus negative, can be processed more readily than their nonaffective attributes. The mere exposure paradigm, however, provides only indirect evidence for this contention. Clearly, more direct evidence is needed.

The experimental paradigm of *priming,* in which the presentation of one stimulus, or prime, alters subjects' perceptions of a second target stimulus, may provide such evidence.[1] A priming paradigm that includes both extremely brief suboptimal and longer optimal exposures permits a sequential analysis of the effects of affect and cognition and, thus, lays an empirical basis for distinguishing between the two. If, as the affective primacy hypothesis suggests, global affective reactions are more immediate and less under voluntary control, we would expect that emotion-laden stimuli presented outside of conscious awareness may color our impressions and judgments to a degree unparalleled by other types of information. Consequently, if under degraded suboptimal conditions, affective priming is found to be superior to cognitive priming, then the affective primacy hypothesis will gain further support. Failure to find a systematic difference will call into question the assertion that affect can precede and, therefore, alter subsequent cognitions.

Precise definitions of the terms *affect* and *cognition* do not exist because definitive theories of these processes have yet to be formulated. Thus, different authors are prone to use these [723]* terms in different ways. Lazarus, (1982), for example, includes purely sensory processes in his definition of *cognitive* functions, whereas others reserve the term for symbolic processes that require some form of transformation of a past or present sensory input (see Zajonc, 1984, p. 118, for a more complete account of this position). Nevertheless, for present purposes, some definitional distinctions are necessary. Affective reactions are equated with expressions of preference and cognitive responses with such judgments as recognition memory, feature identification, categorization, and psychophysical judgments that deal with estimates of sensory and perceptual qualities (Zajonc, 1980). We do not require either affect or cognition to be accessible to consciousness.

Of course, in everyday experience, and even in the laboratory, a total separation between affect and cognition is rare (Zajonc, 1980). After all, many affective experiences involve some participation of cognitive processes, and virtually all cognitions have some affective qualities. Moreover, any priming stimulus may be capable of eliciting affective reactions because any stimulus can be conditioned to an emotional unconditioned stimulus. Thus, even though one can postulate a total separation between affect and cognition at the abstract level of conceptual analysis, one can only hope to approximate pure instances of affect and cognition at the empirical level.

It should also be noted that it is not the priming stimulus alone that inevitably determines the type of priming being investigated. Clearly, the distinction between affective and cognitive priming effects must also take into account the emotional elements in the

---

[1] Recent research in the general area of implicit memory (Roediger, 1990) uses the term *priming,* or *repetition priming,* for procedures where the stimulus sequence involves an optimal presentation followed by a presentation of the same stimulus in a degraded form, either for identification or stem completion (Tulving and Schacter, 1990). Here, we use the term *priming* mainly in its earlier meaning.

* Bracketed bold numbers refer to original page numbers. Page numbers indicate where the original page ended.

response that constitute the critical experimental outcome. For example, one could expose subjects to a highly emotional stimulus, say a grisly massacre scene, and ask them to make a purely cognitive response, for example, report the name of the street where it occurred. Or, one could present affectively neutral stimuli and require the subjects to indicate their preferences. Thus, regardless of what stimulus is shown or what response is measured in an experiment, a wealth of effects may be elicited so that the subject might experience a variety of affective and cognitive reactions that are not measured.

Hence, for experimental purposes, priming designated as affective should have a minimum of cognitive participation, and priming designated as cognitive should have a minimum of affective participation. The following experiments attempt to do just that. Priming stimuli had either strong affective content (e.g., faces expressing emotion) or emotionally bland content (e.g., large and small shapes). In all experiments, the primed target stimuli were Chinese ideographs. Stimulus access was manipulated by comparing extremely brief 4-ms suboptimal priming exposures with 1-s optimal priming exposures. By holding all other variables constant, these studies allow a comparison of the processing of affective and cognitive information and provide a more direct test of the primacy of affect hypothesis.

STUDY 1

To test the basic hypothesis that gross discriminations of positive and negative affect can be made outside of conscious awareness, and that they can precede and influence an individual's perceptions, a study was conducted in which subjects evaluated neutral stimuli, Chinese ideographs, that were preceded by either suboptimal or optimal affective primes.

Method

SUBJECTS   Thirty-two introductory psychology students (16 men and 16 women) participated in the following experiment in partial fulfillment of a course requirement. Half of the subjects were assigned to the optimal exposure condition and half to the suboptimal exposure condition.

MATERIALS AND APPARATUS   Male and female faces expressing happiness and anger were selected as affective primes. Emotionally charged words, commonly used in studies of nonconscious effects (i.e., McGinnies, 1949), were not used in the present study because they may require semantic encoding before they can instigate an affective process. Supporting this conjecture, Carr, McCauley, Sperber, and Parmelee (1982) found that pictures or images activate their meanings more rapidly than do words, which require a longer processing time. Among possible affective images, faces were selected because the facial configurations associated with happiness and anger have been found to be universally recognized as indicators of positive and negative affect (Ekman, 1972), thus reducing the possibility of idiosyncratic responses to the primes.

Each face was photographed against a black background with a black cloth covering any clothing that might otherwise be visible. Photographs of five male and five female faces were assembled for use in the present experiment. Each of these 10 faces was photographed twice, once smiling and once scowling, for a total of 20 photographs.

The target masks were Chinese ideographs, selected as being affectively bland, novel, and ambiguous (Niedenthal, 1987; Zajonc, 1968). Using a backward-masking procedure to more precisely control the duration of the prime, the facial primes were always presented immediately prior to a 2000-ms exposure of one of the target Chinese ideographs.

Three slide projectors, each outfitted with a Uniblitz shutter and a red filter, were used to project 45-cm × 60-cm images onto a screen at subjects' eye level at a distance of approximately 1.5 m. This presentation resulted in a 17° visual horizontal angle and 20° vertical angle. Luminance of the screen field was approximately 60 cd/m². The shutters, calibrated to be accurate to within 10% of the selected shutter speed, were controlled by two Uniblitz relay control boxes (Model SD-10). An IBM-XT microcomputer controlled the slide carousels as well as the sequencing of the Uniblitz shutters.

PROCEDURE   The cover story for the experiment was that the study dealt with snap judgments of novel stimuli. Subjects were told they would be presented with an assortment of Chinese characters that they were to rate on a 5-point Likert scale where 1 indicated they *did not like the ideograph at all,* and 5 indicated they *liked the ideograph quite a bit.* Subjects were then shown slides of 45 target Chinese ideographs.

Four priming conditions, two control and two experimental, were investigated. The series of 45 trials began with 5 control trials having no prime at all (subsequently referred to as the *no-prime control*). The remaining 40 trials consisted of 20 control trials that had random polygons as primes (subsequently referred to as the *irrelevant prime control*) interspersed with 20 experimental trials that had facial primes.[2] On the 20 experimental trials, 10 of the target ideographs were shown twice, once primed with positive affect (i.e., preceded by an image of an individual smiling) and once primed with negative affect (i.e., preceded by an image of the same individual scowling). Matching each of the 10 repeated ideographs with the same individual pictured for both [724] the positive and negative affective primes eliminates certain extraneous sources of variance, such as the relative attractiveness of both the Chinese characters and of the individual facial primes.[3] Moreover, this procedure allows us to compare the effects of positive and negative emotional primes *for the same target stimulus within the same subject.* Because subjects were unfamiliar with the ideographs, they were unaware that 10 of the 45 were repeated. Liking ratings of these 10 repeated ideographs, primed once by positive and once by negative affect, are the focus of the subsequent analyses.

In the degraded or suboptimal exposure condition, the primes were presented to subjects using a backward-pattern-masking technique, where the prime (a face) was presented for 4 ms, followed immediately by the subsequent presentation of a target stimulus (an ideograph) that also served as a backward mask. To ensure that subjects were attending to the screen during the brief suboptimal exposure, a fixation point was projected for 1000 ms at the center of the screen immediately prior to the prime, signaling the start of each trial. During the 20 experimental trials involving the 10 key ideographs, a slide of a face was flashed for 4 ms immediately prior to a Chinese character,

---

[2] It is important to note here, as well as in the following studies, that the "relevance" of any particular prime is contingent on the response we require from subjects. In the present study, the random polygons are considered *irrelevant primes* because it is predicted that they will have no effect on subjects' liking judgments of the ideographs. In a subsequent study, the same polygons became *relevant primes* because subjects were asked to make judgments of symmetry of geometric figures.

[3] There was, in fact, a significant rank-order correlation between the three independent judges' ratings of the attractiveness of the particular models smiling and the same individuals scowling.

for a stimulus-onset asynchrony (SOA) of 5 ms. On all trials, the Chinese ideograph appeared for 2000 ms, serving the dual function of pattern mask and target stimulus.

In the optimal viewing condition, the primes were shown to the subjects for a 1000-ms duration prior to the onset of the target ideographs, which were shown for a period of 2000 ms. Because subjects in this condition could clearly see the primes, they were told there would be two slides presented on each trial. To explain the presence of the primes, the experimenter alluded to "other experimental conditions" in which subjects would be asked to make different judgments involving the primes but stressed that subjects in this condition were to rate only the second slide or ideograph.

In both conditions, after subjects had rated the 45 ideographs, they were questioned as to whether they had noticed anything out of the ordinary and were encouraged to speculate as to the purpose of the experiment in which they had just participated.

FORCED-CHOICE TEST OF AWARENESS   A number of criticisms have been leveled at experiments reporting priming effects obtained for stimuli presented under degraded conditions. For the most part, these critics doubt that there actually is a total absence of conscious detection or identification (Eriksen, 1980; Holender, 1986; Purcell, Stewart, and Stanovitch, 1983). To ensure that the degraded 4-ms exposure used in the first phase of the experiment was, in fact, at a sufficiently suboptimal level, subjects in both the suboptimal and optimal conditions were given a forced-choice test of awareness following the 45 trials, as suggested by Eriksen (1960) and others (Brody, 1988; Cheesman and Merikle, 1986). In this test, subjects were informed that they would be given a series of trials in which faces would be presented briefly, immediately followed by an ideograph. As in the experiment itself, a focal point signaled a 4-ms exposure to a prime (a face) that was immediately followed by a 2000-ms exposure to a backward mask (an ideograph). Subjects were then presented for a period of 2000 ms with two test faces: an image of the actual prime on one side of the screen and an alternate face, or foil, on the other side of the screen. Subjects were then asked which of the two faces they thought was the prime.

The rationale underlying the forced-choice test is that if the subject truly cannot detect the prime, he or she should do no better than chance at recognizing it. Because it was hypothesized that affective information may be processed outside of conscious awareness, the emotional expression of the prime and of the foil was kept constant (i.e., both smiling or both angry).[4] Gender of the facial primes also remained constant. The primes and foils were also counterbalanced such that faces that served as primes for half of the subjects served as foils for the remainder, and vice versa. Each subject participated in 12 such forced-choice trials. At the conclusion of the forced-choice test of awareness, subjects were fully debriefed and thanked for their participation.

Results

No differences were found between male and female subjects. Subsequent analyses, therefore, ignore subject gender as a factor. A 2 × 2 analysis of variance (ANOVA) was

---

[4] The purpose of this forced-choice test of awareness was to determine whether subjects can somehow detect and therefore recognize the suboptimal prime. Holding constant the affect of the prime and the foil should not in any way impair the subjects' ability to perceive or detect the prime. An interesting point, however, is whether nonconscious processing of affect would enable subjects to perform at a level greater than chance when a prime and a foil are affectively inconsistent (i.e., one smiling and one scowling). This issue is taken up in Study 6.

performed comparing subjects' liking ratings of the 10 repeated ideographs across the within-subject affective priming conditions (positive vs. negative) and the between-subjects exposure conditions (optimal vs. suboptimal). The results revealed a significant Prime × Exposure Level interaction. $F(1, 30) = 24.96, p < .001$. The precise nature of the relationship between priming and exposure level is best explained through the following analyses.

Although no subject in the suboptimal condition reported being aware of the primes, affective suboptimal priming nevertheless had a significant influence on subjects' perceptions of the 10 key ideographs, as evident in Figure 17.1. A paired t test revealed that, when preceded by positive suboptimal primes (happy faces), target stimuli were rated significantly higher in likability than when preceded by negative suboptimal primes (angry faces of the same individuals). The mean liking of the 10 key ideographs following positive primes was 3.46, in contrast with a mean rating of 2.70 following negative primes, $t(15) = 4.87, p < .001$. As for the two control treatments in the suboptimal exposure condition, neither the polygons of the irrelevant prime control ($M = 3.06$), nor the absence of primes in the no-prime control ($M = 3.06$) caused ratings of the Chinese ideographs to depart significantly from the midpoint value of 3.0. Liking measures of Chinese ideographs preceded by positive and negative primes were both significantly different from those preceded by the irrelevant polygon controls, $t(15) = 2.23, p < .04$, and $t(15) = 2.31, p < .04$, respectively. The same pattern emerged between both positive and negative primes and the no-prime controls, $t(15) = 2.31, p < .04$, and $t(15) = 2.59, p < .02$, respectively. In short, the positive and negative suboptimal affective primes resulted in ratings of the target ideographs that were not only significantly different from one another, but also significantly different from the no-prime and irrelevant prime controls.

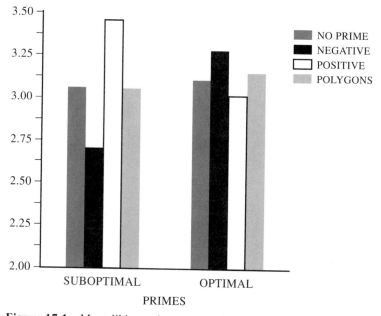

Figure 17.1   Mean liking ratings on a scale from 1 to 5 for the 10 key ideographs when preceded by positive as opposed to negative affective primes.

In contrast, optimally presented affective priming failed to produce a significant shift in subjects' liking of the 10 repeated ideographs, although there was an effect nearing significance in the opposite direction (3.02 for positive priming and 3.28 for negative priming), $t(15) = 1.96, p < .08$. In the optimal condition, irrelevant polygon controls and the absence of primes resulted in liking judgments of the Chinese ideographs that did not depart significantly from the midpoint value of 3.0 (3.15 **[725]** and 3.11, respectively). In fact, in the optimal condition no pair of means differed from one another at an acceptable level of statistical significance.

With regard to the forced-choice test of awareness, subjects were not able to select the prime from the incorrect alternative at a level greater than chance. Of 12 forced-choice trials, subjects correctly identified the prime on average only 5.78 times, which does not differ from the chance value of 6.0, $t(31) = 1.13$, *ns*. No subject scored above 8. Moreover, even though subjects were now informed of the presence of the degraded primes, they nevertheless still maintained that they were not aware of them.

Importantly, no significant differences emerged on this forced-choice test of awareness between subjects who had previously been in the optimal condition and those who had previously been in the suboptimal condition. The failure to find higher scores among subjects in the suboptimal exposure condition, who moments earlier had been exposed to 45 trials under identical viewing conditions (thus making the 12 forced-choice trials the 46th–57th such 4-ms exposures), suggests that no practice effects occurred.

Discussion

To summarize the first experiment, suboptimal affective primes—in the form of facial expressions presented for only 4 ms—generated significant shifts in subjects' preferences for the target ideographs, whereas the same primes presented at optimal exposure durations did not. This pattern of results replicates the somewhat anomalous results of earlier researchers (Fazio, Sanbonmatsu, Powell, and Kardes, 1986; Silverman and Weinberger, 1985; Smith, Spence, and Klein, 1959) in that the magnitude of the priming effect was inversely related to the length of exposure to the primes, with only suboptimal exposures producing any significant effects.

But why is it that the identical affective information seems more potent when presented at a level that *is not accessible to consciousness?* Relevant here are data reported by Seamon, Marsh, and Brody (1984), who found that the temporal advantage of affective discrimination over cognitive discrimination is reversed when the stimuli are exposed for longer durations. Their results show that people can make reliable affective discriminations given only minimal exposures, with preference for the previously exposed stimulus at about 60%. However, the level of this preference remains at 60% even when the exposures are extended to considerably longer durations. In contrast, recognition memory is unreliable at very short durations—less than 8 ms—but it continues to improve with longer exposures reaching levels above 80%.

Spence and Holland (1962) noted 30 years ago that conscious and nonconscious processes were commonly viewed as representing two different locations on a single continuum. "A response based on partial cues is on the same continuum with a response to a fully developed stimulus, but the former is a paler and less precise copy of the latter" (p. 163). Following this logic, increasing awareness should result in making information more accessible to the person and, thus, increasing the "fit" between stimulus and response. This view, Spence and Holland noted, is contradicted by findings that obtain stronger effects **[726]** with degraded stimuli (Eagle, 1959; Paul and Fisher, 1959; Smith et al., 1959). Spence and Holland argued that the "degree of awareness of a stimulus at the moment of input cannot be used to predict the extent of its effect on a response" (p. 164).[5]

Öhman, Dimberg, and Esteves (1989) also proposed a continuum model of consciousness. However, they allow emotion to enter the information-processing chain early, before more complex perceptual stimulus features are encoded. It would follow, then, that at very degraded exposure levels, affective influences might take place, giving rise to gross affective reactions. At very short exposures, these reactions are unencumbered by other more complex information that requires fuller access if it is to be appropriately encoded. At optimal exposures, the individual is capable of accessing not only the primitive and gross affective significance of the stimulus, but is also able to glean additional affective input from a more extensive cognitive appraisal. At longer exposures, then, the stimulus is likely to activate a complex network of associations allowing for feature identification and recognition. To the extent that the primitive and gross early emotional effects are consistent with the subsequent cognitive appraisal (Lazarus, 1982), no pronounced differences between suboptimal and optimal levels of exposure should be obtained. If, however, the subsequent information contradicts or dilutes the primary affective reaction, the possibility exists that the two sources of influence could nullify each other, thus canceling the priming effect. It may be the case that subjects in the suboptimal condition of the present study were only able to make gross positive or negative discriminations of the priming stimulus, (i.e., there was only the smile or the scowl). However, as exposure time increased to 1000 ms, more information about specific features of the face, such as attractiveness, hair color, and complexion, became available. These features, if inconsistent with the valence of the facial expression, may have diluted subjects' affective reactions and canceled the priming effect. Imagine, for example, the mixed messages evoked by a physically attractive but angry stranger.

Figures 17.2 and 17.3 show diagrammatically the theoretical predictions described by the above model. The unbroken curves in Figure 17.2 represent positive (A^+) and negative (A^-) affective reactions to the priming stimulus brought about by early direct access (i.e., the smile or scowl alone). However, an affective reaction based on a cognitive appraisal, that might involve more multifaceted feature identification and evaluation, would require considerably longer priming exposures. These cognitive appraisal elements, C^+ for positive and C^- for negative appraisal, are shown in broken curves and have a slower rise pattern than the A^- curves. Note that the differences between A^- and C^- curves are quite similar to those reported by Seamon et al. (1984).

We assume here that, in general, affective reactions are based on all available sources, including both early direct access and later cognitive appraisal. It can be further assumed that these sources combine. These cumulative affective reactions based on

---

[5] These authors spoke mainly of effects on the processing of cognitive content. When distinctions are made between affective and cognitive inputs, some of the contradictions disappear, as is later shown.

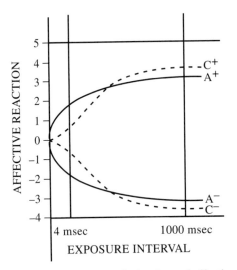

Figure 17.2   Theoretical values of affective reactions based on early affective (A⁺ and A⁻) and slower cognitive access (C⁺ and C⁻).

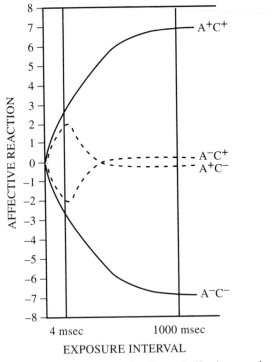

Figure 17.3   Theoretical values of affective reactions accumulating from early affective access (A⁺ and A⁻) and subsequent cognitive appraisal (C⁺ and C⁻). (Continuous curves represent accumulation when the two sources are consistent; broken curves represent inconsistent sources.)

early and late access are shown in Figure 17.3. Thus, if the early direct access source is positive and the subsequent cognitive appraisal leads to a positive evaluation as well (A^+C^+), we would expect generally positive priming. Alternatively, if the early direct access generates a positive affective reaction (perhaps due to a smiling face) and the later cognitive appraisal is negative (perhaps from a disheveled appearance, as in the curve marked A^+C^-), we would expect a dilution of the earlier reaction. The degree to which the initial affective reaction is diluted will depend on the valences of these two sources and on the weights each may be assigned in a given judgment. [727]

If the dilution explanation of the above results is correct, we would expect the responses of subjects in the optimal exposure condition to be a function of both the early affective cues, as well as those requiring a more extensive appraisal. More specifically, the strongest optimal priming effects should occur when the initial affective reaction coincides with secondary affective cues such as appearance (namely, scowling, unattractive primes or smiling, attractive primes). These are represented by the curves A^-C^- and A^+C^+.

To test this dilution hypothesis, three independent judges were invited to rank order the 10 positive and negative primes for attractiveness. The concordance in attractiveness rankings was .91 ($F = 20.50$, $p < .001$) for the 10 smiling faces and .90 ($F = 18.07$, $p < .001$) for the scowling faces. The data were then broken down by attractiveness within each valence, and the effects of the three primes judged most attractive were compared with the effects of the three primes judged least attractive. Ratings of the target ideographs that followed these selected primes were entered into a 2 (attractiveness: attractive vs. unattractive) × 2 (affect: positive vs. negative) within-subjects ANOVA run separately for the optimal and suboptimal exposure conditions.

As shown in Table 17.1, at optimal exposures, the three most attractive faces resulted in higher liking ratings of the Chinese ideographs than did the three least attractive faces (3.23 and 2.88, respectively), $F(1, 15) = 4.28$, $p < .06$. As predicted by Figure 17.3, the contrast was most pronounced between attractive smiling faces (A^+C^+), which resulted in an average rating of 3.25, and unattractive scowling faces (A^-C^-), which were associated with an average rating of 2.77. This difference was significant at $p < .01$, $t(15) = 3.15$. At

Table 17.1   Mean Liking Ratings for Ideographs Preceded by the Three Most Attractive and Three Least Attractive Facial Primes

Condition	Affect		Average
	Positive	Negative	
Optimal			
Attractive	3.25	3.21	3.23
Unattractive	2.98	2.77	2.88
Average	3.12	2.99	
Suboptimal			
Attractive	3.58	2.58	3.08
Unattractive	3.42	2.88	3.15
Average	3.50	2.73	

optimal exposures there was, however, no significant main effect for the affective valence of the primes. In other words, optimally presented smiling and angry faces were relatively ineffective in influencing subjects' liking of the ideographs (3.12 and 2.99, respectively), $F(1, 15) = 0.75, p < .40$.

In the suboptimal exposure condition, the opposite pattern of results emerged. When the primes were presented suboptimally, there was no significant main effect for attractiveness, with attractive primes producing a mean liking rating of 3.08 and unattractive primes producing a mean liking rating of 3.15, $F(1, 15) = 0.24, p < .63$. At the same time, the suboptimal primes did produce a significant main effect with regard to affect. Smiling faces yielded a mean liking rating of 3.50 in comparison with scowling faces, which resulted in a mean liking rating of 2.73, $F(1, 15)$ 21.59, $p < .001$.

Of course there are problems associated with this post hoc analysis. First, we must keep in mind that these faces were not initially selected on the basis of attractiveness. Moreover, the attractiveness of a particular face may have been correlated with the ability to produce an effective smile, thus confounding the analysis. The hypothesis that the attractiveness of a face operates primarily at higher levels of stimulus accessibility, however, is supported by the fact that under suboptimal conditions, ranked attractiveness had no effect on liking ratings whatsoever—a result that is consistent with the continuum hypothesis in Figure 17.3.

STUDY 2

There is, however, an alternative explanation for the failure in Study 1 of obtaining effects with primes presented at optimal exposures. In general, the subjects cannot be "wrong" when making evaluative judgments that reveal their own preferences. As beauty lies in the eye of the beholder, one's subjective liking for an object cannot possibly be incorrect. Perhaps subjects in the optimal exposure condition resented the faces looming in front of them, viewing them as a blatant attempt to sway their opinions. Perhaps, as a consequence, they sought to assert their independence and responded with reactance when judging the ideographs.

The first study was, therefore, replicated with the important modification that we now asked for an affective judgment of a more objective nature. Instead of asking subjects how well they liked the ideographs, we had them report whether they felt the ideographs represented "good" or "bad" objects. Now, any reactant behavior on the part of the subjects would, we hoped, be mitigated by the possibility that they could be wrong.[6]

Method

Study 2 used the identical procedure and apparatus as that used in Study 1, with one exception. Using the same experimental primes as in the liking study (happy and angry faces) and the same control primes, 32 subjects (16 men and 16 women) were asked to rate whether they felt each target ideograph represented a good or pleasant object by indicating a high score or an unpleasant or bad object by indicating a low score on a

---

[6] Similar good-bad judgments have been used previously with considerable success as proxies for affective reactions (Greenwald, Klinger, and Liu, 1989; Kunst-Wilson and Zajonc, 1980; Zajonc, 1968).

scale ranging from 1 to 5. It was stressed that each ideograph represented an actual object, the implication being that there was a correct answer. Half of the subjects took part in the optimal exposure condition and half in the suboptimal exposure condition.

Results

As in Study 1, a 2 × 2 ANOVA focusing on the effects of affective prime and exposure level on subjects' ratings of the 10 key ideographs was performed. These data revealed a main effect for affective prime, $F(1, 30) = 7.16$, $p < .01$, with positive primes being associated with higher good ratings than negative primes. Once more, exposure level did not yield a main effect, [728] $F(1, 30) = 0.34$, $p < .56$, but as in Study 1, there was a significant Prime × Exposure Level interaction, $F(1, 30)$ as 4.72, $p < .04$.

Once again, suboptimal affective priming had a significant impact on subjects' perceptions of the 10 key ideographs. As evident in Figure 17.4, when preceded by positive suboptimal affective primes, the target ideographs were rated higher than the same ideographs preceded by negative suboptimal primes (3.28 and 2.61, respectively), $t(15) = 2.70$, $p < .02$. Thus, in a situation where subjects' reactance could lead to errors, essentially the same results were obtained as when liking was used as the dependent measure. Priming with the irrelevant control primes, or polygons, resulted in a mean of 3.05 on the good-bad continuum that was virtually identical to the no-prime control (3.06). Neither of these controls were significantly different from the midpoint value of 3.0. Both positive and negative primes, however, were significantly different in their effects

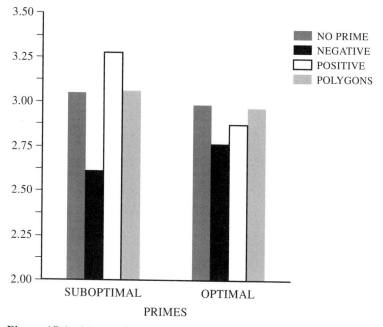

Figure 17.4   Mean ratings on the good-bad dimension for the 10 key ideographs when preceded by positive as opposed to negative affective primes.

on good-bad judgments from the effects of the polygons and the no-prime controls ($p <$ .05 for all comparisons).

Affective priming using full exposures, on the other hand, while showing a trend in the same direction, did not produce a significant shift in subjects' ratings of whether the ideographs represented a good or bad object. Following a positive prime, subjects gave the 10 key ideographs an average rating of 2.84, whereas the same ideographs following a negative prime received an average rating of 2.77, $t(15) = 0.57$, *ns*. It is important to note that this effect, although insignificant, was in the opposite direction from that obtained in the previous study using liking judgments. In other words, it appears that although subjects may resent being told what they like, they may be more open to suggestion regarding whether an ideograph refers to a good or bad object. Optimal priming with the irrelevant control polygons resulted in an average good-bad judgment of 2.97, and in the no-prime control the good-bad judgments had a mean of 2.99, both negligibly removed from the midpoint value of 3.0. No significant differences between any pair of means were found in the optimal condition.

Finally, subjects were not able to perform above a chance level on the forced-choice test of awareness. As in Study 1, primes effaces were presented suboptimally for 4 ms and then immediately masked by an ideograph. Subjects were then presented with two faces of the same gender expressing the same emotion and asked to indicate which they thought was the suboptimal prime. The mean accuracy level on this test was 5.72 out of a possible 12, very near the chance level of 6.0, $t(31) = 1.39$, *ns*.

Discussion

In contrast with the liking judgments of Study 1, subjects in the optimal condition of the present study, when faced with deciding whether an object referred to something good or something bad, tended to respond in a direction consistent with the affective primes. In other words, subjects reported the 10 key ideographs as more likely to represent pleasant objects when preceded by clearly visible smiling primes than when preceded by slides of the same individuals scowling. Although this trend [729] did not reach an acceptable level of statistical significance, it was nevertheless markedly different from the marginally significant contrast effect of the previous study where positive optimal primes led to lower liking ratings than negative optimal primes. This reversal may be due, in part, to subjects' belief that there was a correct answer. It may also be the case that liking is a unique sort of judgment in that one's preferences are in some sense sacred. Perhaps subjects in the present experiment did not experience the same reactance to a perceived attempt to influence their judgments of the meaning of Chinese ideographs. This discrepancy between the optimal conditions in Studies 1 and 2 heightens our suspicion that the nature of the judgment can constrain or substantially alter the influence of affective primes, at least those that are available to conscious awareness.

No inconsistency existed, however, for the suboptimal affective priming conditions in the first two studies. Regardless of whether subjects were reporting their preference for the ideographs or judging if the ideographs represented good or bad objects, the results were the same—positive suboptimal priming generated more positive ratings, whereas negative suboptimal priming led to lower ratings.

If the continuum of consciousness hypothesis is correct, and if the previously noted differences between optimal and suboptimal priming reflect the fact that early affective reactions are diluted by later incongruent information presented at longer exposures, then we would again expect the attractiveness of the primes to be a factor at optimal exposures. In other words, at optimal levels of accessibility, attractive smiling primes should elicit higher mean good responses than unattractive smiling primes. At degraded exposure levels, however, the attractiveness of the primes should make less difference.

To examine the continuum hypothesis in Study 2, a post hoc analysis of the three most attractive and the three least attractive primes, identical to that in Study 1, was conducted (see Table 17.2). Strong attractiveness effects were found in the optimal condition. There was an overall main effect for attractiveness, with the three most attractive primes resulting in significantly higher scores on the good-bad dimension than the three least attractive primes (3.28 vs. 2.81, respectively), $F(1, 15) = 9.47$, $p < .01$. Again, as in Study 1 and consistent with the predictions made in Figure 17.3, the most striking contrast was between attractive smiling faces (A^+C^+), which resulted in good-bad judgments of the target ideographs having a mean of 3.81, and unattractive angry faces (A^-C^-), which resulted in a mean of 2.31, $t(15) = 3.73$, $p < .01$. Unlike in Study 1, however, there was also a significant main effect for affect, with smiling faces resulting in higher mean good ratings (3.56) than angry faces (2.53), $F(1, 15) = 10.51$, $p < .01$.

As in Study 1, there was no effect for attractiveness of the primes among subjects in the suboptimal condition, suggesting that this information was not immediately accessible, $F(1, 15) = 0.06$, $p < .82$. Once again, suboptimal smiling primes resulted in higher ratings on the good-bad dimension than suboptimal angry primes (3.35 vs. 2.71), although this trend did not reach an acceptable level of statistical significance. $F(1, 15) = 1.90$, $p < .18$.

Table 17.2 Mean Good-Bad Ratings for Ideographs Preceded by the Three Most Attractive and Three Least Attractive Facial Primes

	Affect		
Condition	Positive	Negative	Average
Optimal			
Attractive	3.81	2.75	3.28
Unattractive	3.31	2.31	2.81
Average	3.56	2.53	
Suboptimal			
Attractive	3.46	2.54	3.00
Unattractive	3.23	2.88	3.06
Average	3.35	2.71	

STUDY 3

Although the findings of the first two studies confirm our expectations that some emotional stimuli of which we are unaware can color our judgments, they leave unanswered the question of whether nonconscious affect is unique in its ability to sway subsequent judgments. It may be the case that any relevant prime, regardless of whether it is emotional in nature, is more potent when presented suboptimally than when presented with full access to awareness. On the other hand, if affective information is processed faster and more efficiently than other types of information, as the affective primacy hypothesis suggests, then we would expect very weak or even nonexistent effects at the suboptimal level when cognitive judgments such as simple psychophysical decisions are primed by affectively bland but relevant stimuli.

Method

To test the above proposition, a third experiment was conducted using simple affectively bland primes—large and small circles and squares. Once again, Chinese ideographs served the dual role of target stimuli and pattern masks. Whereas the no-prime control condition was the same as in the previous studies, faces with relaxed, emotionally neutral expressions now served as irrelevant control primes.

SUBJECTS As in the previous studies, 32 introductory psychology students (16 men and 16 women) participated in the following experiment in partial fulfillment of a course requirement. Half of the subjects were assigned to the suboptimal and half to the optimal exposure condition.

PROCEDURE Subjects in this experiment, again ostensibly dealing with judgments of novel stimuli, were asked to rate 45 ideographs (the same as in Studies 1 and 2) with respect to size of the object each represented, where 1 indicated that a particular ideograph represented a relatively small object (like a bird or a mouse) and 5 indicated that an ideograph represented a relatively large object (like a tree or a house). The ideographs were all roughly equal in size. This time, the 10 critical repeated ideographs were preceded once by a relatively small prime (either a circle or square) and once by a larger version of the same shape. As in the previous studies, the first 5 trials had no primes at all. The remaining 40 trials consisted of 20 experimental trials showing circles and squares of different sizes and 20 irrelevant control trials showing neutral faces. The order of the trials was once again the same for all subjects.

At the conclusion of this phase of the experiment, subjects were informed of the true nature of the study and underwent a forced-choice test of awareness, as described in Study 1. Subjects in this test, however, were shown a series of 12 ideographs, each suboptimally primed by a 4-ms exposure to a large or small shape. They were then presented [730] with an image of the prime on one side of the screen and a foil (an image of the same shape but alternate size) on the other and asked to indicate which image was the suboptimal prime.

Results

Subjects' estimates of the size of the objects the 10 key ideographs represented were entered into a 2 (prime: small vs. large) × 2 (exposure level: suboptimal vs. optimal) ANOVA. These data revealed a significant main effect for the size of the prime, $F(1, 30) = 20.47$, $p < .001$, with larger primes generating increased size estimates of the object the ideograph represented. Level of exposure also produced a marginally significant main effect, $F(1, 30) = 3.56$, $p < .07$. As previously, there was also a strong Prime × Exposure Level interaction, $F(1, 30) = 16.47$, $p < .001$, with optimal primes producing far more substantial shifts in size ratings than suboptimal primes. Again, there were no gender differences in these results, and, consequently, this factor was ignored in subsequent analyses.

Size ratings of the target ideographs preceded by small suboptimal primes did not significantly differ from ratings of the same target ideographs when preceded by large suboptimal primes (3.87 and 3.93, respectively), $t(15) = 0.41$, ns. The irrelevant neutral faces (3.89) and no-prime controls (3.91) also had no effects under suboptimal exposure conditions, and there were no differences between the effects of these control primes and the experimental (large and small) primes. In short, none of the four types of suboptimal primes yielded ratings significantly different from one another.

In stark contrast with affective primes, optimally presented size primes did significantly influence subjects' perceptions of the identical ideographs, $t(15) = 4.47$, $p < .001$. Specifically, when an ideograph was preceded by a large, clearly visible prime, subjects rated the ideograph as representing a larger object than when the same ideograph was preceded by a small prime (4.01 vs. 3.05). As is apparent from Figure 17.5, ratings of the two control primes (3.51 for the irrelevant control primes and 3.80 for the no-prime controls) also differed from the two experimental primes ($p < .05$, with the exception of the planned comparison between large primes and no primes). In sum, whereas suboptimal size primes produced no significant effects, the same primes presented at optimal exposures showed distinct changes in subjects' size judgments of the ideographs.

In the forced-choice test of awareness, using large and small shapes, subjects once again failed to discriminate at a level greater than chance between the actual prime and a foil. On the average, only 5.97 out of 12 items (roughly a chance pattern) were correctly identified, $t(31) = 0.13$, ns.

STUDY 4

Unlike the affective primes of Studies 1 and 2, size primes produced no significant shifts in judgment at the suboptimal level, whereas the same primes presented at optimal exposures clearly influenced subjects' size judgments of the ideographs. This finding is consistent with the premise that affective information may be processed earlier than information, such as size, that is not generally affective in nature.

There is, however, an alternative explanation. Perhaps the results of the last study are in part due to the nature of the response required of the subjects. In Study 3, subjects were required to guess the *meaning* of a Chinese ideograph in terms of the size of the object it represented. This response was selected to retain a parallel with Study 2,

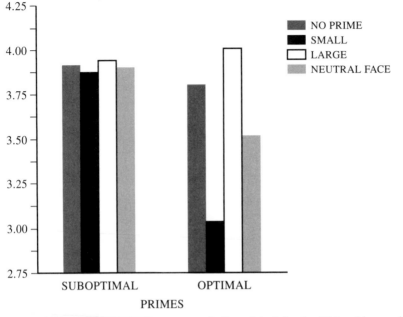

Figure 17.5 Mean size ratings on a scale from 1 to 5 for the 10 key ideographs when preceded by small as opposed to large primes.

where subjects had to report whether an ideograph referred to a good or bad object. Although during debriefing, some subjects were able to articulate a rule or heuristic they used in their judgments, many admitted that they were merely guessing. The question then arises as to whether the same results would be obtained in a domain where the subject believes himself or herself to be fully competent of making judgments. In other words, would we have obtained the same results if subjects did not feel as though they were guessing? Earlier research by Spence and Holland (1962) has shown that suboptimal primes can only produce effects on behavior if they are not in competition with other, more powerful conscious influences. Thus, it is plausible that if subjects were forced to concentrate on the objective features of the ideographs, they may no longer be susceptible to relevant primes at either the suboptimal or optimal level. To address this issue, a separate study was conducted using symmetric and asymmetric shapes as primes to determine whether these primes could influence subjects' judgments of the actual symmetry of the target ideographs.

Method

Thirty-two subjects (16 men and 16 women) participated in the experiment. Half were assigned to the 4-ms suboptimal condition and half to the 1000-ms optimal exposure condition. The symmetric primes were the large circles and squares from Study 3. The asymmetric primes were irregular polygons with jagged edges. Again, neutral faces served as irrelevant control primes. This time, subjects were asked to judge the symmetry of the actual ideographs themselves, as opposed to the objects they represented.

Results

A 2 × 2 ANOVA (Symmetric vs. Asymmetric Prime × Suboptimal vs. Optimal Exposure Level) was performed on subjects' symmetry ratings of the 10 key ideographs. Neither prime, nor exposure level produced a significant main effect, $F(1, 30) = 1.80$, $p < .19$, and $F(1, 30) = 0.33$, $p < .57$, respectively. There was, however, once more a significant Prime × Exposure Level interaction, $F(1, 30) = 4.06$, $p < .05$.

No effects were found for symmetric and asymmetric suboptimal primes (2.09 and 2.13, respectively), $t(1 5) = 0.43$, *ns*. Moreover, as indicated in Figure 17.6, no differences were found among any of the four suboptimal group means, including the control primes (2.19 for the irrelevant primes and 2.14 for the no-prime control).

However, as in Study 3, a significant difference emerged in subjects' ratings of the same ideographs following the 1000-ms presentation of primes. In the optimal condition, where they could clearly perceive the primes, subjects reported that the identical ideographs were more symmetrical following the symmetric primes than the asymmetric primes (2.28 and 2.09, respectively), $t(15) = 2.65$, $p < .02$. Also paralleling Study 3, the irrelevant neutral face control and the no-prime control fell in between the two extremes of symmetric and asymmetric primes (2.25 and 2.15, respectively). It is important to keep

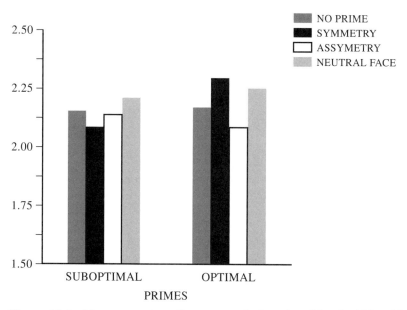

Figure 17.6   Mean symmetry ratings on a scale from 1 to 5 for the 10 key ideographs when preceded by symmetrical as opposed to asymmetrical primes.

in mind that in this experiment, subjects were not asked whether [731] the ideograph meant something symmetric or not, but whether it was, in fact, geometrically symmetric.

The subsequent forced-choice test of awareness, this time using symmetric and asymmetric shapes, revealed only chance level discrimination (6.15), $t(31) = 0.69$, *ns.* As in the previous studies, no systematic difference emerged on the forced-choice test between subjects in the suboptimal and optimal conditions, suggesting that no practice effects occurred.

Discussion

Subjects in the optimal condition of the present study, despite having access to the objective features of the ideographs, were nevertheless swayed by the presentation of clearly visible symmetric and asymmetric primes. It is interesting to note, however, that although statistically significant, the magnitude of this effect is substantially smaller than that of the previous study where subjects were asked to estimate the size of the objects the ideographs represented. This suggests that perhaps subjects' judgments of the symmetry of the ideographs may have been constrained by objective reality.

The suboptimal presentation of these same symmetric and asymmetric primes had absolutely no effect on subjects' judgments of the symmetry of the ideographs. This finding is consistent with the prediction that the suboptimal presentation of affectively neutral primes, namely, geometric shapes, would not produce the same shifts in judgment as affective primes. These results support a continuum theory of consciousness in which some forms of stimulation have access mainly at higher levels of exposure. In this particular case, the judgmental response to simple geometric shapes (represented by the C curves in Figure 17.2) seems to require a longer exposure than does an affective response to an emotional stimulus (represented by the A curves in Figure 17.2). Thus, the effects of simple geometric primes on nonevaluative cognitive judgments in Studies 3 (size) and 4 (symmetry), which showed significant optimal priming but no suboptimal priming, are the mirror image of the effects of emotional primes on evaluative judgments as seen in Studies 1 (liking) and 2 (good-bad).

STUDY 5

At least one plausible alternative explanation, other than the affective primacy hypothesis, might account for the findings presented thus far. It is important to note that the priming stimuli in Studies 3 and 4 differed in more than one way from those in Studies I and 2. The priming stimuli in Studies 3 and 4 (geometric shapes) were simple, abstract, and socially insignificant. In contrast, the priming stimuli in Studies 1 and 2 (faces) were complex, concrete, socially significant, and perhaps ones to which emotional reactions are "hard wired." It could be argued, therefore, that the perceptual response to human faces may have particular properties.

The theory that the face may be a unique stimulus has some support. Perrett, Rolls, and Caan (1982), for example, have located cells in the temporal sulcus of the monkey that respond to [732] the presentation of faces and only faces. Moreover, spontaneous mimicry of emotional expressions has been demonstrated in neonates as early as 36 hr after birth, suggesting that we may be innately prepared to perceive and respond to facial cues (Field, Woodson, Greenberg, and Cohen, 1982). Research by Dimberg (1982) further revealed that mimicry of facial expressions can take place involuntarily, outside of conscious awareness. It may be the case, therefore, that any information conveyed by a face, emotional or otherwise, holds a perceptual advantage. The question then is whether the suboptimal effects obtained in Studies 1 and 2 are dependent on the fact that faces were used as primes or rather on the fact that these faces elicited affect.

To examine this alternative explanation of the preceding results, another study was conducted using faces as primes but requiring a nonevaluative judgment from the subjects. This time, by presenting primes that consisted of male and female faces, we attempted to influence subjects' perceptions of whether an ideograph referred to a masculine or feminine object. Of course, even emotionally bland faces are not affectively bland stimuli. However, we now asked subjects to make a fairly nonevaluative discrimination based on nonaffective information conveyed by these faces. If both affective and nonaffective information conveyed by a face holds a perceptual advantage, then we would expect that, as in Study 1, the suboptimal presentation of male and female primes would influence subjects' perceptions of the ideographs, as in Studies 1 and 2. On the other hand, if the gender-related information contained in these faces is primarily cognitive and therefore processed further along the conscious access continuum, then the results should resemble those of Studies 3 and 4, showing no evidence of suboptimal priming.

Method

Thirty-two subjects (16 men and 16 women) in this experiment were asked to judge whether each of the 45 ideographs represented a feminine or masculine object on a scale from 1 to 5 where a rating of 1 indicated *masculine or not at all feminine* and 5 indicated *quite feminine*. In this study, the 10 repeated ideographs were preceded once by a female face and once by a male face. In an attempt to make the male and female primes as distinct from one another as possible, all male primes had short hair, whereas all female primes had hair shoulder length or longer. The faces expressed no emotional reactions other than a relaxed neutral aspect. Again, as in Studies 1 and 2, polygons served as irrelevant control primes, and there was also a no-prime control condition. Half of the subjects were exposed to these primes for only 4 ms and half for 1000 ms. and both exposures were immediately followed by an ideograph that appeared on the screen for 2000 ms.

Following the experiment proper, subjects were given a forced-choice discrimination task using neutral male and female faces as primes and foils.

Results

Femininity ratings of the 10 key ideographs were subjected to a 2 (prime: male vs. female face) × 2 (exposure level: suboptimal vs. optimal) ANOVA. The results indicate a significant main effect for the gender of the prime, $F(1, 30) = 9.16$, $p < .005$, with female primes producing higher ratings than male primes. **[733]** There was no significant main effect for exposure level, $F(1, 30) = 2.14$, $p < .15$. However, as in each of the preceding studies there was a robust Prime × Exposure Level interaction, $F(1\ 30) = 10.23$, $p < .003$.

The suboptimal primes of male and female faces had no significant effect on subjects' subsequent judgments of femininity (2.66 and 2.67, respectively; see Figure 17.7). Likewise, control prime conditions produced no distinct effects (2.63 for both the no-prime and irrelevant prime control). In the suboptimal condition, therefore, none of the four group means were significantly different from any other.

Optimally exposed primes, on the other hand, did significantly influence perceptions of femininity, with female primes producing higher ratings than male primes (3.19 vs. 2.74), $t(15) = 4.01$, $p < .001$. The control primes fell halfway between the masculine and feminine primes, with the irrelevant control primes (polygons) resulting in a mean femininity judgment of 2.93 and the no-prime condition resulting in a femininity judgment of 2.95. The pattern of results from this gender manipulation, then, was virtually identical to that of the size and symmetry manipulations, namely, ineffectual suboptimal priming and effective optimal priming.

The forced-choice test of awareness, using emotionally neutral faces of opposite gender, revealed only chance-level discrimination between the prime and the incorrect alternative, with an average score of 5.56 out of a possible 12, $t(31) = 1.62$, *ns*.

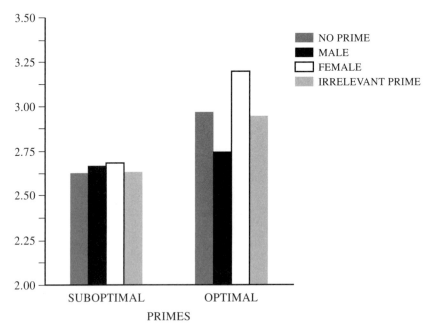

Figure 17.7   Mean femininity ratings on a scale from 1 to 5 for the 10 key ideographs when preceded by female as opposed to male primes.

Discussion

The pattern of results thus far agrees with the continuum model presented in Figures 17.2 and 17.3. Affective priming that used positive and negative facial expressions as primes shows effects under very brief exposures, whereas priming using nonaffective stimuli varying on such dimensions as size, symmetry, and gender shows effects primarily under lengthy exposure durations. As in Figure 17.2, A curves seem to have a faster rise time than C curves. It appears, therefore, that affective reactions may be evoked preattentively with extremely brief access to stimulus information (Kitayama, 1991). Because of this early access, affective reactions may have significant influence over how later information, even information regarding entirely unrelated and distinct stimuli, is processed and evaluated. Within the limits of these studies we have simply assumed that information accessed early and that accessed later combine. It is entirely possible that early affective reactions may interact in other important ways with subsequently accessed information. The precise nature of this interaction is of interest in its own right but is beyond the scope of this article.

STUDY 6

It is, however, within our power to examine the conditions of exposure in the aforementioned experiments. It follows from the previous findings that affective and cognitive reactions may under certain circumstances require different degrees, or perhaps even a different form, of access to awareness. Some evidence on this point comes from the forced-choice tests of awareness that were administered following each of the previous studies. Even after having been informed that suboptimal primes were being presented prior to each ideograph during this phase, subjects nevertheless maintained that they "couldn't see anything," [734] satisfying a subjective criterion of awareness (Cheesman and Merikle, 1986). Moreover, this denial of awareness was supported by subjects' subsequent failure to perform with better-than-chance accuracy on the objective forced-choice tests of awareness. The present studies, therefore, demonstrate the suboptimal influence of affect in conditions that meet both a subjective criterion of awareness (Cheesman and Merikle, 1986) and a more stringent objective criterion (Eriksen, 1960).

The failure of subjects to discriminate at a level greater than chance on the test of awareness raises an interesting theoretical point. Recall that in these forced-choice tests, the emotional valence of the prime and of the incorrect alternative or foil was kept constant: either both smiling or both scowling. Under these conditions, subjects were unable to correctly identify the suboptimal prime at a level greater than chance. Both the liking judgments of Study 1 and the good-bad judgments of Study 2, however, clearly indicate that gross positive and negative affective priming effects can be obtained even when subjects fail to show any objective or subjective awareness of the priming stimuli.

It follows, therefore, that subjects should be able to perform better than chance on a forced-choice test of awareness if they are asked to choose between faces that express affectively inconsistent emotions. Moreover, because the objective stimulus properties of the suboptimal primes (size, symmetry, and gender) did not influence subsequent nonevaluative judgments, subjects should not be able to discriminate between two faces that differ on an objective aspect such as gender. The following experiment tested this proposition.

Method

SUBJECTS   Sixty-four introductory psychology students (32 men and 32 women) participated in the experiment in partial fulfillment of a course requirement.

MATERIALS AND APPARATUS   Twelve pairs of photographs of male and female faces expressing happiness and anger were selected as affective primes. To make the gender of the primes easily distinguishable, all 6 male models had uniformly short hair, whereas all 6 female models wore their hair shoulder length or longer. Twelve Chinese ideographs from the previous studies served as masks. The apparatus that served to project stimuli and control luminance and exposure duration were the same as in the previous studies.

PROCEDURE   On arrival, subjects were informed that they would be exposed to a series of faces for intervals so short that they may not be aware of having seen anything. Nevertheless, on each trial they would be asked to guess which of two faces was, in fact, the face that was presented suboptimally. During each of the subsequent 12 trials, subjects were presented with a fixation point before a 4-ms exposure of a suboptimal facial prime, immediately followed by a 1000-ms exposure of a pattern mask (ideograph). Subjects were then presented for 2000 ms with a slide of the prime on one side of the screen and a slide of a face previously never shown (the foil) on the opposite side of the screen. They were asked to indicate which of the two faces they thought was the prime. The faces used as the suboptimal primes were the same for all subjects. The affective valence and gender of the foil, however, were orthogonally varied. Half of the subjects made forced-choice discriminations between slides with the same affective valence (i.e., both smiling or both scowling), and half discriminated between slides with the opposite affective valence (i.e., one smiling and one scowling). Gender consistency was likewise varied such that half of the subjects were presented with primes and foils that were of the same gender (i.e., both male or both female), whereas the remainder chose between two faces of the opposite gender (i.e., male and female). As in the previous forced-choice tests of awareness, the prime and incorrect alternative were counterbalanced such that stimuli that served as the prime for half of the subjects served as the foil for the remaining half, and vice versa.

Sixteen subjects were randomly assigned to each of the following four groups according to the properties of the pairs of stimuli presented: affective polarity and gender matched, affective polarity matched and gender opposite, affective polarity opposite and gender matched, and affective polarity and gender both opposite.

Results

No significant effects were found for the gender of the subject, so therefore the analysis of mean differences excluded this factor. A two-way ANOVA was performed on the subjects' choice data. As shown in Table 17.3, the combined inconsistent or opposite affect group had a mean accuracy of 7.19, which was significantly better than the chance level of 6.0. $t(62) = 6.26$. $p < .001$. There was no such main effect for gender consistency. Nor did gender consistency interact with affective consistency. The data can be summarized as follows: Primes shown as briefly as 4 ms can allow subjects to discriminate between faces that differ in emotional polarity. Distinct faces that do not differ in affective polarity, even if they differ in such obvious ways as gender, cannot be accurately discriminated from one another if they are exposed for only 4 ms.

GENERAL DISCUSSION AND CONCLUSIONS

In the previous studies, cognitive judgments, either categorical or psychophysical, responded to primes only at an optimal level of awareness. Judgments of size, symmetry, and gender were unaffected by their respective suboptimal primes, even when the priming stimulus was a face. In stark contrast, faces expressing affect used as suboptimal primes in Studies 1 and 2 produced significant shifts in subjects' ratings of liking and good-bad judgments. Moreover, subjects in the final study were able to make forced-choice discriminations at a level greater than chance between a prime and a foil only when the two faces were opposite in affective valence, namely, smiling and scowling. Subjects were unable to accurately discriminate between faces that did not differ in emotional polarity, even if they differed on other obvious dimensions, such as gender. Taken together, these findings further support the affective primacy hypothesis, suggesting that emotional reactions can occur with minimal stimulation and that they can therefore precede and alter subsequent cognitions (Zajonc, 1980).

   It is apparent that affect can be elicited without the participation of subjects' awareness. More interesting, however, is the **[735]** fact that the nonconscious priming of affective reactions under certain conditions can be more successful than when it is with the subjects' full awareness. What are the differences between conscious and nonconscious affect that might be relevant to our results? When affect is elicited at levels outside of conscious awareness, it is diffuse, and its origin and address are unspecified. So-called *free-floating anxiety* is a state in which the source and target are not accessible to the patient's awareness. The more an affective state is accompanied by cognitive correlates or appraisals, the clearer its origin and address. (They need not be correct, however, in the sense of corresponding to some objective reality.) The very fact that an

Table 17.3   Average Number Correct in Forced-Choice Test of Awareness Varying the Affect and Gender of the Foils

Condition	Affect		Average
	Consistent	Inconsistent	
Consistent	5.44	7.37	6.41
Inconsistent	5.50	7.00	6.25
Average	5.47	7.19	

address can be specified makes the affective reaction less likely to be displaced or diffused. Because of its diffuse quality, nonconscious affect can "spill over" onto unrelated
stimuli. The participation of directed cognitive correlates may impose constraints by
focusing affect onto specific targets, thus preventing its displacement. This is perhaps
the reason why suboptimal affective priming produced significant shifts in judgments
of novel target stimuli, whereas optimal affective priming did not.

The priming of nonevaluative responses, on the other hand, revealed a diametrically opposite pattern, with optimal primes resulting in significant shifts in judgment.
This intriguing result can be explained by allowing that different forms of information
can be processed with different degrees or perhaps even different forms of access to
awareness. Within this supposition, the processing of affective information seems, at
least, within the constraints of the present experiments, to have an earlier access than
the processing of information that is not affective in nature.

The present findings, then, are consistent with the theoretical model presented in
Figures 17.2 and 17.3 and with the continuum of consciousness model proposed by
Öhman et al. (1989) in which affect is processed early in the information-processing
chain. At longer exposure durations it is possible that new information overwhelms this
early subjectively felt affect. If the later information is congruent with affect in polarity, there is summation. Conversely, if the subsequent information is inconsistent with
the initial affective reaction, there is dilution. The results of the secondary analyses carried out in Studies 1 and 2 that separated the primes according to attractiveness support
this conjecture.

One could argue, however, that the present results could be explained within a cognitive mediation framework. Such a framework would suggest that priming is successful
because it makes categories accessible (Bargh, 1982; Collins and Loftus, 1975; Higgins,
Bargh, and Lombardi, 1985; Meyer and Schvaneveldt, 1971; Ratcliff and McKoon, 1988).
If one views the results of Studies 1 and 2 in terms of cognitive mediation, one could sur-
mise that the affective primes made the general categories of positive or negative objects
and events more accessible. This interpretation would not conflict with the finding that
affective priming is less effective at an optimal level if one further assumes that at a full
level of exposure, not only are gross positive and negative categories and their associative
nets activated, but many other categories are activated as well, such as gender, age, attractiveness, and so forth, perhaps overwhelming the more general affective reaction.

A strict cognitive mediation interpretation, however, would be hard-pressed to
explain the failure to produce suboptimal priming effects for such simple categories as
symmetry, size, and gender given the success of suboptimal affective priming under
identical experimental conditions. The fact that only the suboptimal affective primes
evoked a significant pattern of results suggests that the conceptualization of positive
and negative affect as being equivalent to any other category is inadequate.

Neuroanatomical Evidence: Structures and Processes
Allowing for Affective Primacy

The proposition that cognitive and affective processes, although continually interacting,
are basically independent (Zajonc, 1980, 1984) has received convergent support in the

form of recent neuroanatomical discoveries. For example, separation of affective processes on the one hand and recognition and categorization on the other is suggested in cases of prosopagnosia (PA). Many prosopagnosics are completely incapable of making even the most basic categorizations of faces, such as gender, race, and age (Bodamer, 1947; Pallis, 1955), although they retain their ability to make appropriate affective responses to distinct facial expressions (Ellis, 1986). In fact, PA patients, who suffer from bilateral cerebral lesions, are characterized by their inability to recognize the faces of persons with whom they are familiar. Interestingly, however, several studies have demonstrated that PA patients generate elevated skin conductance (galvanic skin response, or GSR) when presented with faces of persons they had previously known but cannot recognize (Bauer, 1984; Tranel and Damasio, 1985). As in the mere exposure phenomenon (Kunst-Wilson and Zajonc, 1980), prosopagnosics manifest a positive affective reaction to familiarity without the benefit of conscious recognition.

In interpreting these PA results, Bauer (1984) has proposed a model involving at least two anatomically and functionally distinct pathways. He has concluded that the prosopagnosics' bilateral lesions selectively impair the ventral visiolimbic pathway (implicated in object recognition) while sparing the dorsal visiolimbic connections. These spared visiolimbic connections allow for a preliminary, or "preattentive," analysis of emotional significance. In other words, prosopagnosics seem to retain their preferenda while losing their discriminanda (Zajonc, 1980).

Quite the opposite pattern is evident in patients suffering from prosopo-affective agnosia (PAA). PAA patients show deficits in discriminating specific emotions without suffering decrements in otherwise recognizing or categorizing faces in terms of their more "objective" properties. In a study by Kurucz and Feldmar (1979) PAA patients manifested no decrement in recognizing the photographed faces of both famous individuals and ward personnel. These same individuals, however, were severely impaired in their ability to discriminate between photographs of faces depicting happiness, anger, and sadness. Subjects' responses indicated that they failed to identify the appropriate emotion despite being able to perceive the features representative of the emotion. For example, typical PAA responses were "his face is wet, he is happy" or "he shows his teeth, he is sad" (Kurucz, Feldmar, and Werner, 1979, p. 94). The authors concluded that the ability to recognize faces is independent of the ability to process the affect conveyed by these faces. A similar dissociation between affect and cognition [736] is seen following an amygadalectomy that results in psychic blindness, or the Klüver-Bucy syndrome. Klüver and Bucy (1937) discovered that following a bilateral anterior lobectomy monkeys cease being threatened by stimuli that were previously threatening. They begin to eat raw meat and other previously shunned foods and show severe disturbance in sexual behavior. Nevertheless, these animals can be trained to make consistent discriminations among unfamiliar stimuli on the basis of physical characteristics such as size, shape, and color. One might suggest that for these animals, as for the PAA patients, objects lose their preferenda while retaining their discriminanda.

Even more definitive evidence on the separation of affective and cognitive processes has been recently contributed by Zola-Morgan, Squire, Alvarez-Royo, and Clower (1991). These researchers conducted tests of emotional reaction and memory function on four groups of monkeys: intact monkeys, monkeys whose amygdala had been removed, monkeys whose hippocampus—a structure heavily implicated in cognitive functions (LeDoux, 1987)—had been removed, and monkeys whose amygdala and hippocampus had both been removed. Monkeys with amygadalectomies performed well on memory tasks but lost their emotional reactions to emotion-inducing stimuli. In contrast, damage to the hippocampal formation resulted in memory deficits while leaving the emotional processes intact. Monkeys with lesions in both the hippocampus and the amygdala lost both their emotional reactivity and their ability to retain newly learned discriminations. These data agree with the notion of affective-cognitive independence.

A final converging line of neuroanatomical research reveals data supporting not only affective-cognitive independence but also affective primacy (Zajonc, 1984, 1989). It has been the common view that after registering stimuli, the sensory apparatus sends signals to the thalamus, which in turn relays them to the sensory areas of the neocortex for integration and analysis of meaning. This view is consistent with cognitive appraisal theory (Lazarus, 1982), which would require that all emotional reactions be mediated by neocortical activity. Yet LeDoux and his colleagues (Iwata, LeDoux, Meeley, Arneric, and Reis, 1986; Iwata, Chida, and LeDoux, 1987; LeDoux, 1986, 1987, 1990; LeDoux, Iwata, Cicchetti, and Reis, 1988) have found a direct pathway between the thalamus and the amygdala that is just one synapse long. This direct access from the thalamus to the amygdala allows the amygdala to respond faster to a stimulus event than the hippocampus, the latter being separated from the thalamus by several synapses. According to LeDoux, the response in the amygdala can occur as much as 40 ms faster. This neuroanatomical architecture thus allows us to like something even without knowing what it is.

Concluding Remarks

For brevity, priming was sometimes referred to as either cognitive or affective, depending on the priming stimuli. For clarity, however, it must again be noted that whether we categorize a form of priming as *cognitive* or *affective* depends not only on the type of priming stimulus used but also on the responses that constitute the dependent measures. Given these distinctions, we should expect that affective priming may show different patterns, depending on the priming stimuli and on the primed responses. For example, if affective priming must be induced by a prior cognitive process (e.g., by the presentation of affect-laden adjectives), we might expect effects similar to those obtained in semantic priming with stronger effects at optimal exposures than at suboptimal exposures. In the case of the priming of cognitive categories, for example, the typical finding is that when degree of accessibility is varied, stimuli with easier access have greater influence. Tversky and Kahneman's (1974) notion of availability proposes just that. There is, however, the possibility that early access to certain aspects of the semantic content of a word exists (Fowler, Wolford, Slade, and Tassinary, 1981; Marcel, 1983). If so, and if we assume that the dominant semantic factor of words is the evaluative factor that accounts for over 50% of the variance in meaning (Osgood, 1957), then longer exposures might result in dilution of the initial affect as seen in Studies 1 and 2. Of course, empirical evidence is required to verify this conjecture, and Studies 1 and 2 could be replicated using words as primes.

It is also necessary to explore whether affective stimuli other than faces, which may have very unique properties, replicate the present pattern of results. For example, would slides of snakes change preferences for Chinese ideographs only when presented suboptimally?

The present research raises other important theoretical questions. For instance, what are the implications of affective primacy on memory? How might the present results be integrated with current work on implicit memory (Roediger, 1990), indirect memory (Merikle and Reingold, 1991; Richardson-Klavehn and Bjork, 1988), repetition priming (Tulving and Schacter, 1990), and perceptual fluency (Jacoby and Dallas, 1981; Mandler, 1980)? The common feature of these extensive lines of research on memory is that by means of subtle tests they reveal memories of which the subject may not be aware. If subjects show preference for a stimulus that was preceded by a suboptimal prime of which they were not aware, can the expression of preference be considered simply as a more subtle indicator of memory (Merikle and Reingold, 1991)? Or could this be a distinct process, namely, affect? The present findings seem to support the second possibility. The diametrically opposite patterns of results we obtained did not depend on whether the tests were direct or indirect; they were all indirect. They depended only on whether the prime contained affective elements.[7] **[737]**

Another unanswered question involves the point of contact between early affective reactions and more specific emotions, such as anger or fear. Is it the case that greater emotional specificity is possible without the participation of cognitive processes? Would the subject attribute anger to Chinese ideographs preceded by an angry suboptimally presented face and fear to those preceded by a fearful face? Or would both angry and fearful suboptimal primes result in a gross negative affective reaction? A recent study (Murphy, 1990) examined subjects' ability to discriminate among six specific facial expressions (Ekman, 1972) at suboptimal levels of exposure. Subjects were only able to differentiate among emotions that differed in hedonic polarity. Happiness could be discriminated at a better-than-chance level from the negative emotions of anger, fear, disgust, and sadness. No reliable differentiation was observed among the four negative emotions. Also, surprise was not distinguished from any of the emotions, positive or negative. These findings suggest that the kinds of affective reactions we were able to induce with suboptimal stimulus input in Studies 1 and 2 may be limited to gross positive and negative influences. This implies that for more differentiated emotions, such as fear or anger, to emerge some sort of cognitive appraisal may be necessary.

---

[7] Interestingly, a reanalysis of our data from Study 1 and Study 2 shows that suboptimal affective primes had their most pronounced effect on the initial presentation of each of the 10 key ideographs. In other words, if a subject was first presented with an ideograph preceded by a positive prime (a smiling face), then the subsequent pairing of the same ideograph and a negative prime (a scowling face) was less effective. Consequently, the present experimental paradigm in which the identical ideographs were repeated twice may have had the inadvertent effect of dampening the overall magnitude of the priming. This pattern may have been due to subjects' becoming less susceptible to the suboptimal primes as the experiment wore on. However, this attenuation of effectiveness for subsequent priming might also suggest that subjects may possess some sort of residual memory trace of the individual ideographs that includes their initial affective evaluation. Importantly, no similar patterns emerged between the first and second presentations of the nonaffective primes in Studies 3–5. Coupled with other demonstrations of the subliminal memory traces of affective primes (Krosnick, Betz, Jussim, and Lynn, 1992) these findings provide indirect support for the early processing of affective information and point toward the relationship between information presented outside conscious awareness and memory as an intriguing arena for future inquiry.

Future research in this domain will, it is hoped, lead to a more systematic understanding of the dynamics of the interaction between affect and cognition. Above all, the methods presented here—namely, the comparisons between the effects of optimal and suboptimal primes—might stimulate future explorations of the degree to which cognitive processes available to consciousness participate in affective reactions and, conversely, how affective reactions of which the individual is not aware can modify perceptual and cognitive processes. However, there is clearly less doubt now that affective reactions may precede cognitive processes and may occur without conscious access to their eliciting stimuli.

REFERENCES

Bargh, J.A. (1982). Attention and automaticity in the processing of self-relevant information. *Journal of Personality and Social Psychology, 43*, 425–436.

Bauer, R.M. (1984). Autonomic recognition of names and faces in prosopagnosia: A neuropsychological application of the guilty knowledge test. *Neuropsychologia, 22*, 457–469.

Bodamer, J. (1947). Die Prosop-Agnosie [Prosopagnosia]. *Archiv der psychiatrichen Nervenkrankheiten, 179*, 6–53.

Brody, N. (1988). *Personality in search of individuality.* San Diego, CA: Academic Press.

Carr, T.H., McCauley, C., Sperber. R.D., and Parmelee, C.M. (1982). Words, pictures, and priming: On semantic activation, conscious identification, and the automaticity of information processing. *Journal of Experimental Psychology: Human Perception and Performance, 8*, 757–777.

Cheesman, J., and Merikle, P.M. (1986). Distinguishing conscious from nonconscious perceptual processes. *Canadian Journal of Psychology, 40*, 343–367.

Collins. A.M., and Loftus, E.F. (1975). A spreading activation theory of semantic processing. *Psychological Review, 82*, 407–428.

Dimberg, U. (1982). Facial reactions to facial expressions. *Psychophysiology, 19*, 643–647.

Eagle, M. (1959). The effects of subliminal stimuli of aggressive content upon conscious cognition. *Journal of Personality, 23*, 48–52.

Ekman, P. (1972). Universals and cultural differences in facial expressions of emotions. In J. Cole (Ed.). *Nebraska Symposium on Motivation* (Vol. 19). Lincoln: University of Nebraska Press.

Ellis. H.D. (1986). Processes underlying face recognition. In R. Bruyer (Ed.), *The neuropsychology of face perception and facial expression*, Hillsdale, NJ: Erlbaum.

Eriksen. C.W (1960). Discrimination and learning without awareness: A methodological survey and evaluation. *Psychological Review, 67*, 279–300.

Eriksen, C.W (1980). The use of a visual mask may seriously confound your experiment. *Perception and Psychophysics, 28*, 89–92.

Fazio, R.H., Sanbonmatsu, D.M., Powell, M.C., and Kardes. F.R. (1986). On the automatic activation of attitudes. *Journal of Personality and Social Psychology, 50*, 229–238.

Field, T.M., Woodson, R., Greenberg, R., and Cohen, D. (1982). Discrimination and imitation of facial expressions by neonates. *Science, 218*, 179–181.

Fowler, C.A., Wolford. G., Slade, R., and Tassinary, L. (1981). Lexical access with and without awareness. *Journal of Experimental Psychology: General, 30*, 289–447.

Greenwald, A.G., Klinger. M.R., and Liu, T.J. (1989). Unconscious processing of dichoptically masked words. *Memory and Cognition, 17*, 35–47.

Higgins, E.T., Bargh, J.A., and Lombardi, W. (1985). Nature of priming effects on categorization. *Journal of Experimental Psychology, 11*, 59–69.

Holender, D. (1986). Semantic activation without conscious identification in dichotic listening, parafoveal vision, and visual masking: A survey and appraisal. *Behavioral and Brain Sciences, 9*, 1–66.

Iwata, J., Chida, K., and. LeDoux, J.E. (1987). Cardiovascular responses elicited by stimulation of neurons in the central amygdaloid nucleus in awake but not anesthetized rats resemble conditioned emotional responses. *Brain Research, 418*, 183–188.

Iwata, J., LeDoux. J.E., Meeley, M. P., Arneric, S., and Reis, D.J. (1986). Intrinsic neurons in the amygdaloid field projected to by the medial geniculate body mediate emotional responses conditioned to acoustic stimuli. *Brain Research, 383*, 195–214.

Jacoby, L.L., and Dallas, M. (1981). On the relationship between autobiographical memory and perceptual learning. *Journal of Experimental Psychology: General, 110*, 306–340.

Kitayama, S. (1991). Impairment of perception by positive and negative affect. *Cognition and Emotion, 5*, 255–274.

Klüver, H., and Bucy, P.C. (1937). "Psychic blindness" and other symptoms following bilateral temporal lobectomy in Rhesus monkeys. *American Journal of Physiology, 19*, 352–353.

Kunst-Wilson. W.R., and Zajonc, R.B. (1980). Affective discrimination of stimuli that cannot be recognized. *Science, 207*, 557–558.

Kurucz, J., and Feldmar, G. (1979). Prosopo-affective agnosia as a symptom of cerebral organic disease. *Journal of the American Geriatrics Society, 27*, 225–230.

Kurucz, J., Feldmar, G., and Werner, W. (1979). Prosopo-affective agnosia associated with chronic organic brain syndrome. *Journal of the American Geriatrics Society, 27*, 91–95.

Lazarus, R.S. (1982). Thoughts on the relationship between emotion and cognition. *American Psychologist, 37*, 1019–1024.

LeDoux, J.E. (1986). Sensory systems and emotion. *Integrative Psychiatry, 4*, 237–248.

LeDoux, J.E. (1987). Emotion. In F. Plum, (Ed.), *Handbook of physiology*. 1: *The nervous system. Volume V: Higher functions of the brain* (pp. 419–460). Bethesda, MD: American Physiological Society. **[738]**

LeDoux. J.E. (1990). Information flow for sensation to emotion: Plasticity in the neural computation of stimulus values. In M. Gabriel and J. Moore (Eds.), *Neurocomputation and learning: Foundation and adaptive networks* (pp. 3–52). Cambridge, MA: MIT Press.

LeDoux. J.E., Iwata, J., Cicchetti, P. and Reis, D.J. (1988). Different projections of the central amygdaloid nucleus mediate autonomic and behavioral correlates of conditioned fear. *Journal of Neuroscience, 8*, 2517–2529.

Mandler, G. (1980). Recognizing: The judgment of previous occurrence. *Psychological Review, 87*, 252–271.

Marcel, P.M. (1983). Subliminal perception reaffirmed. *Canadian Journal of Psychology, 37*, 324–326.

McGinnies, E. (1949). Emotionality and perceptual defense. *Psychological Review, 56*, 244–251.

Merikle. P.M., and Reingold, E.M. (1991). Comparing direct (explicit) and indirect (implicit) measures to study unconscious memory. *Journal of Experimental Psychology: Learning, Memory, and Cognition, 17*, 224–233.

Meyer, D. and Schvaneveldt, R. (1971). Facilitation in recognizing pairs of words: Evidence of dependence between retrieval operations. *Journal of Experimental Psychology, 90*, 227–234.

Murphy, S.T. (1990). *The primacy of affect: Evidence and extension*. Unpublished doctoral dissertation, University of Michigan.

Niedenthal. P.M. (1987). *Unconscious affect in social cognition*. Unpublished doctoral dissertation, University of Michigan.

Öhman. A., Dimberg, U. and Esteves, F. (1989). Preattentive activation of aversive emotions. In T. Archer and L.G. Nilsson (Eds.), *Aversion, avoidance and anxiety: Perspectives on aversively motivated behavior*. Hillsdale, NJ: Erlbaum.

Osgood, C.E. (1957). Motivational dynamics of language behavior. In M.R. Jones (Ed.), *Nebraska Symposium on Motivation*. Lincoln: University of Nebraska Press.

Pallis, C.A. (1955). Impaired identification effaces and places with agosia for colour. *Journal of Neurology, Neurosurgery, and Psychiatry, 18*, 218–224.

Paul, I.H., and Fisher. C. (1959). Subliminal visual stimulation: A study of its influence on subsequent images and dreams. *Journal of Nervous and Menial Diseases, 129*, 315–340.

Perrett, D.I., Rolls, E.T., and Caan, W. (1982). Visual neurons responsive to faces in the monkey temporal cortex. *Experimental Brain Research, 47*, 342–392.

Purcell, D.G., Stewart, A.L., and Stanovitch, K.K. (1983). Another look at semantic priming without awareness. *Perception and Psychophysics, 34*, 65–71.

Ratcliff. R., and McKoon. G. (1988). A retrieval theory of pruning. *Psychological Review, 95*, 385–408.

Richardson-Klavehn, A., and Bjork, R.A. (1988). Measures of memory. *Annual Review of Psychology, 39*, 475–543.

Roediger. H.L. (1990). Implicit memory: Retention without remembering. *American Psychologist, 45,* 1043–1056.

Seamon, J.G., Brody. N., and Kauff. D.M. (1983). Affective discrimination of stimuli that are not recognized: Effect of delay between study and test. *Bulletin of the Psychonomic Society, 21,* 187–189.

Seamon, J.G., Marsh, R.L., and Brody, N. (1984). Critical importance of exposure duration for affective discrimination of stimuli that are not recognized. *Journal of Experimental Psychology: Learning, Memory, and Cognition, 10,* 465–469.

Silverman, L.H., and Weinberger, J. (1985). Mommy and I are one: Implications for psychotherapy. *American Psychologist,* 40, 1296–1308.

Smith, G.J., Spence. D.P., and Klein. G.S. (1959). Subliminal effects of verbal stimuli. *Journal of Abnormal and Social Psychology, 59,*167–177.

Spence, D.P., and Holland. B. (1962). The restricting effects of awareness: A paradox and explanation. *Journal of Abnormal Social Psychology,* 64, 163–174.

Tranel, D., and Damasio, A.R. (1985). Knowledge without awareness: An autonomic index of facial recognition by prosopagnosics. *Science, 228,* 1453–1454.

Tulving, E., and Schacter, D.L. (1990). Priming and human memory. *Science, 247,* 301–306.

Tversky, A., and Kahneman, D. (1974). Judgment under uncertainty: Heuristics and biases. *Science, 185,* 1124–1131.

Zajonc, R.B. (1968). Attitudinal effects of mere exposure. *Journal of Personality and Social Psychology* (Monograph] *9,* 1–27.

Zajonc, R.B. (1980). Feeling and thinking: Preferences need no inferences. *American Psychologist, 35,* 151–175.

Zajonc, R.B. (1984). On the primacy of affect. *American Psychologist, 39,* 117–124.

Zajonc, R.B. (1989). Bischofs gefühlvolle Verwirrungen über die Gefühle [Bischof's emotional fluster over the emotions]. *Psychologische Rundschau, 40,* 218–221.

Zola-Morgan, S., Squire. L.R., Avarez-Royo, P., and Clower, R.P. (1991). Independence of memory functions and emotional behavior: Separate contributions of the hippocampal formation and the amygdala. *Hippocampus, 1,* 207–220. **[739]**

Chapter 18

Mere Exposure: A Gateway to the Subliminal

R.B. Zajonc
Stanford University

Preferences constitute one of the fundamental sources of social and individual stability and change. They give our lives direction and our actions meaning. They influence ideological values, political commitments, the marketplace, kinship structures, and cultural norms. They are sources of attachment and antagonism, of alliance and conflict. No species would evolve if it could not actively discriminate between objects, events, and circumstances that are beneficial and those that are harmful.

Preferences are formed by diverse processes. Some objects, by their inherent properties, induce automatic attraction or aversion. Sucrose is attractive virtually at birth, whereas bitter substances—quinine, for example—are universally aversive. Preferences may also be established by classical or operant conditioning. If a child is rewarded when she sits in a particular corner of the crib, that corner will become a preferred location for her. An office worker whose colleagues notice his new tie will develop a preference for similarities. Preferences can also be acquired by virtue of imitation, a social process that emerges in fashions. Preferences also arise from conformity pressures. In economics, preference is regarded as the product of rational choice—a deliberate computation that weighs the pros and cons of alternatives.

But among the many ways in which preferences may be acquired, there is one that is absurdly simple, much simpler than rational choice. I discuss here this very primitive way—conscious and unconscious—of acquiring preferences, namely, the mere repeated exposure of stimuli, and I explain the process whereby repeated exposure leads to the formation of preferences.

Zajonc, R.B. (2001). Mere exposure: A gateway to the subliminal. *Current Directions in Psychological Science*, 10, 224–228.

THE MERE-REPEATED-EXPOSURE PHENOMENON

The repeated-exposure paradigm consists of no more than making a stimulus accessible to the individual's sensory receptors. There is no requirement for the individual to engage in any sort of behavior, nor is he or she offered positive or negative reinforcement. The exposures themselves are sometimes so degraded that the individual is not aware of their occurrence. Their effects are measured by the resulting changes in preference for the object. In contradiction to some early contentions (Birnbaum and Mellers, 1979; Lazarus, 1982), it can now be claimed that no cognitive mediation, rational or otherwise, is involved in these effects.

It is well known that words with positive meanings have a higher frequency of usage than words with negative meanings (Zajonc, 1968). The relationship holds over all parts of speech. Not only is *good* (5,122 occurrences in a random sample of 1,000,000 English words) more frequent than *bad* (1,001), and *pretty* (1,195) more frequent than *ugly* (178), but also *on* (30,224) is more frequent than *off* (3,644), *in* (75,253) is more frequent than *out* (13,649), and even *first* (5,154) is more frequent than *last* (3,517). In fact, the words in nearly every semantic category, and even letters and numbers, show a strong correlation between ratings for preference and frequency of usage, and not only words, but all kinds of stimuli have been found to increase **[224]*** in attractiveness with repeated exposures. This seemingly innocent finding (Zajonc, 1968) has stimulated decades of research on the relation between cognition and affect.

Obviously, the first question to ask is that of causality, that is, whether we are more likely to seek out positive than negative experiences, and therefore favor positive stimuli, or whether aspects of the world that we experience often acquire thereby positive valence. The finding that frequently occurring numbers and letters are better liked than less frequent numbers and letters favors the latter possibility. It has been demonstrated that the mere repeated exposure of a stimulus is entirely sufficient for the enhancement of preference for that stimulus. This mere-repeated-exposure effect is found in a variety of contexts, for a wide assortment of stimuli, using diverse procedures, and among both humans and nonhuman animals. In the extreme, an exposure effect was obtained prenatally (Rajecki, 1974). Tones of two different frequencies were played to two sets of fertile chicken eggs. When the hatched chicks were then tested for their preference for the tones, the chicks in each set consistently chose the tone that was played to them prenatally. Similarly, one group of rats was exposed to music by Schönberg and another to music by Mozart to see if they could acquire corresponding preferences. They did, slightly favoring the latter composer. And Taylor and Sluckin (1964) found that domestic chicks that were exposed either to their conspecific age peers or to a matchbox preferred the object to which they were previously exposed.

The earliest explanation of the effect was offered by Titchener. It proposed a virtual tautology, namely, that we like familiar objects because we enjoy recognizing familiar objects. But Titchener's hypothesis had to be rejected because in numerous studies, the enhancement of preferences for objects turned out not to depend on individuals' subjective impressions of how familiar the objects were (Wilson, 1979).

---

* Bracketed bold numbers refer to original page numbers. Page numbers indicate where the original page ended.

SUBLIMINAL INDUCTION OF AFFECT

The cumulative results lead to the inescapable conclusion that the changes in affect that accompany repeated exposures do not depend on subjective factors, such as the subjective impression of familiarity, but on the objective history of exposures (Zajonc, 2000). Even when exposures are subliminal, and subjects have no idea that any stimuli at all have been presented, those subliminal stimuli that are flashed frequently are liked better than those flashed infrequently (Murphy, Monahan, and Zajonc, 1995; Zajonc, 1980).[1] In fact, exposure effects are more pronounced when obtained under subliminal conditions than when subjects are aware of the repeated exposures.

ABSENCE OF AVERSIVE EVENTS AS AN UNCONDITIONED STIMULUS

Careful experiments have ruled out explanations of this phenomenon based on ease of recognition, an increased perceptual fluency, or subjective familiarity. But mere-exposure effects cannot take place in a total vacuum. What, then, is the process that induces preferences by virtue of exposures? One possibility that cannot be ruled out is that we have here a form of conditioning, unique to be sure, but nevertheless a form that features the essential conditioning factors. The classical paradigm of classical conditioning requires that the conditioned stimulus (CS) be followed by an unconditioned stimulus (US), preferably within 500 ms. The paradigm also requires that this joint occurrence be repeated several times in very much the same form. It is taken as given that the US has an innate capacity of eliciting the unconditioned response (UR). Thus, a dog will salivate (UR) when presented with food (UC), and if a bell is rung (CS) during the dog's feeding time, then after several repetitions of this joint event, the bell alone will make the dog salivate. The elicitation of salivation by the bell alone is evidence that conditioning has been successful, and salivation has become a conditioned response (CR). Although the connection between the response and the US is innate, the new relationship between the CS and the CR is acquired.

In the mere-repeated-exposure paradigm, the repeatedly exposed stimuli can be viewed as CSs. We can also think of the preference response as the CR. But where is the US? The mere-exposure paradigm requires that no positive or negative consequences follow exposures. And no response other than maintaining sensory access to the exposed stimulus is required of the participant. But just because the experimenter does not provide a US does not mean that there is no event that, from the point of view of the participant, could constitute a US. In fact, there is such an event. Contiguous with exposures (i.e., the presentations of the CS) are events characterized by a conspicuous absence of noxious or aversive consequences. Hence, the very absence of a noxious consequence could well act as a US. The absence of aversive consequences constitutes a safety signal that is associated with the CS. As in classi-

---

[1] The fact that the stimuli were actually below participants' awareness was tested by a forced-choice method developed by Eriksen (1980).

cal conditioning, after several CS-US occurrences, in which the US is simply the fact that the individual does not suffer any untoward experiences, the CR—an approach [225] tendency—becomes attached to the CS, now communicating that the current environment is safe.

On the initial presentations, when the stimulus is novel, both avoidance and approach responses are elicited, and the tendency to explore (approach) is tentative. But because the aftermath of the CS is invariably benign, avoidance and escape drop out to leave only approach responses. It is thus that positive affect can be attached to a stimulus by virtue of mere repeated exposures. Some forms of imprinting (Zajonc, 2000) can be conceptualized in the very same manner.

REPEATED EXPERIENCES AS A SOURCE OF POSITIVE AFFECT

How can we inquire into the dynamics of this conditioning paradigm in which even the CS is inaccessible to awareness and the very presence of the US is a matter of conjecture? We can assume that the absence of an aversive event that engenders approach behavior to the exposed object generates positive affect. Therefore, because a condition such as an absence of an aversive event is diffuse and unattached to any particular object in the immediate environment, not only should the exposed object become more attractive, but the overall affective state of the individual should become more positive. We should expect an enhancement of the individual's general affect and mood state just by virtue of the repeated exposures themselves. Monahan, Murphy, and I (Monahan, Murphy, and Zajonc, 2000) inquired into the effects of sheer stimulus repetition by subliminally exposing two groups to Chinese ideographs. One group was exposed to 5 ideographs, five times each in random order. The other group was exposed to 25 different ideographs, each shown but once. All exposures lasted 4 ms. Following the exposures, the participants in the repeated-exposures condition were in better moods and felt more positive than the participants who were exposed to 25 different ideographs.

Thus, repetitions of an experience in and of themselves are capable of producing a diffuse positive affective state. And if that is one of the consequences of repeated exposures, then the changed mood, although diffuse and unspecific, could well become attached to stimuli that are presented just afterward. Previous research has demonstrated that repeated exposures enhance preferences for the exposed stimuli. The exposures can also generate positive affect in response to additional stimuli that are similar in form or substance—even though they were not previously exposed. But if the affect generated by repetition of exposures is diffuse, and nonspecific, then any stimulus, if it follows a benign repetition experience, would become infused with positive affect. In a new experiment (Monahan et al., 2000), we again presented 5 stimuli five times each to one group of participants and 25 different stimuli once each to another group. Afterward, however, instead of measuring the participants' overall mood, we asked them to rate three categories of stimuli: Chinese ideographs that were previously shown, Chinese ideographs that were similar to those previously shown but novel, and totally distinct stimuli—random polygons. In all cases, the group that was exposed to repeated ideographs rated the stimuli more positively than the group exposed to 25 ideographs one time each. Also in all cases, the ratings of the repeated-exposure group were more positive than those obtained from a control group that had not experienced any prior exposures of the stimuli (see Figure 18.1).

THE INDEPENDENCE OF AFFECT AND COGNITION

This array of findings supports not only the proposition that affect may be elicited without a prior cognitive appraisal, but also the contention that affect and cognition may well be independent processes, because in the context of exposure effects, prototypical cognition is measured by recognition memory, whereas prototypical affect is measured by preference judgments. (For a more detailed discussion of the distinction, see Zajonc, 2000, pp. 46–47.) When I first published this hypothesis (Zajonc, 1980), claiming that affective reactions may precede cognitive reactions, and thus require no cognitive appraisal, there was no neuroanatomical or neurophysiological evidence to support it. Eventually, however, LeDoux (1996), Zola-Morgan, Squire, Alvarez-Royo, and Clower (1991), and other investigators published results confirming the original hypothesis that affect and cognition, although participating jointly in behavior, are separate psychological and neural processes that can be influenced independently of one another. Especially important is the work of Zola-Morgan and his colleagues, who have conducted experiments with monkeys, showing that lesions to the amygdala (a brain structure that is responsive to affective qualities of stimulation) impair emotional responsiveness but leave cognitive functions intact, whereas lesions to the hippocampus (a brain structure

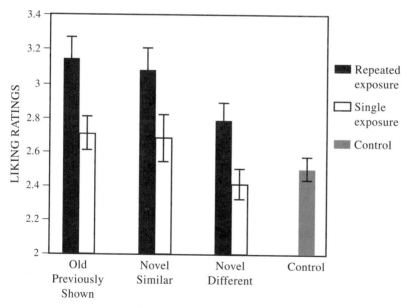

Figure 18.1   Preferences for diverse stimuli as a function of exposure condition.

SOURCE: Adapted from Monahan, Murphy, and Zajonc, 2000.

that plays an important role in memory) impair cognitive functions but leave emotional responsiveness intact.

Other neuroanatomical studies have confirmed that affect can be induced unconsciously. Thus, Elliott and Dolan (1998), taking PET (positron emission tomography) [226] measures, examined preference acquisition as a function of subliminal repeated exposures and inquired into the neuroanatomical correlates of these effects. They found that different regions of the brain were activated during subjects' affective reactions and memory judgments. Recognition judgments were localized in the frontopolar cortex and the parietal areas, whereas preference reactions showed right lateral frontal activation. This finding that recognition and preference are associated with different brain structures further supports the hypothesis that cognition and affect are independent systems.

Given the independence of affect, we can explain why it is that repeated-exposure effects are clearer and stronger when the exposures are subliminal than when subjects are aware of them. If a given process depends on cognitive appraisal, different individuals will access different cognitive content and attach different meanings to the same stimuli. Hence, the between-participants variability in reactions will be increased. If cognitive processes are not involved in a behavior, however, affective influences, which are necessarily less diverse than cognitive influences, will dominate the behavior, yielding a more homogeneous array of reactions.

CONCLUSION

The mere-exposure effect, when viewed as classical conditioning with the US consisting of the absence of aversive consequences, is a very simple, yet effective process for acquiring behavioral tendencies of adaptive value. The mere-exposure effect provides a flexible means of forming selective attachments and affective dispositions, with remarkably minimal investment of energy, even when exposures are not accessible to awareness.

The consequences of repeated exposures benefit the organism in its relations to the immediate animate and inanimate environment. They allow the organism to distinguish objects and habitats that are safe from those that are not, and they are the most primitive basis of social attachments. Therefore, they form the basis for social organization and cohesion—the basic [227] sources of psychological and social stability. Imprinting effects manifest substantial permanence. It remains to be demonstrated, however, how permanent are preferences induced by mere repeated exposures, under supra- and subliminal conditions. It is also not yet known if repeated-exposure effects are more readily established in younger than in older organisms, and what processes can reverse or extinguish them.

RECOMMENDED READING

Bornstein, R.F., Leone, D.R., and Galley, D.J. (1987). The generalizability of subliminal mere exposure effects: Influence of stimuli perceived without awareness on social behavior. *Journal of Personality and Social Behavior,* **53,** 1070–1079.

Harrison, A.A. (1977). Mere exposure. In L. Berkowitz (Ed.), *Advances in experimental social psychology* (Vol. 10, pp. 39–83). New York: Academic Press.

Jacoby, L.L. (1983). Perceptual enhancement: Persistent effects of an experience. *Journal of Experimental Psychology: Learning, Memory, and Cognition,* **9,** 21–38.

ACKNOWLEDGMENTS

I am grateful to Hazel Markus for her helpful suggestions.

REFERENCES

Birnbaum, M.H., and Mellers, B.A. (1979). Stimulus recognition may mediate exposure effects. *Journal of Personality and Social Psychology, 37,* 1090–1096.

Elliott, R., and Dolan, R.J. (1998). Neural response during preference and memory judgments for subliminally presented stimuli: A functional neuro-imaging study. *Journal of Neuroscience, 18,* 4697–4704.

Eriksen, C.W. (1980). Discrimination and learning without awareness: A methodological survey and evaluation. *Psychological Review, 67,* 279–300.

Lazarus, R.S. (1982). Thoughts on the relations between emotion and cognition. *American Psychologist, 46,* 352–367.

LeDoux, J. (1996). *The emotional brain.* New York: Simon and Schuster.

Monahan, J.L., Murphy, S.T., and Zajonc, R.B. (2000). Subliminal mere exposure: Specific, general, and diffuse effects. *Psychological Science, 11,* 462–466.

Murphy, S.T., Monahan, J.L., and Zajonc, R.B. (1995). Additivity of nonconscious affect: Combined effects of priming and exposure. *Journal of Personality and Social Psychology, 69,* 589–602.

Rajecki, D.W. (1974). Effects of prenatal exposure to auditory or visual stimulation on postnatal distress vocalizations in chicks. *Behavioral Biology, 11,* 525–536.

Taylor, K.F., and Sluckin, W. (1964). Flocking in domestic chicks. *Nature, 201,* 108–109.

Wilson, W.R. (1979). Feeling more than we can know: Exposure effects without learning, *Journal of Personality and Social Psychology, 37,* 811–821.

Zajonc, R.B. (1968). Attitudinal effects of mere exposures. *Journal of Personality and Social Psychology, 9* (2, Pt. 2), 1–27.

Zajonc, R.B. (1980). Feeling and thinking: Preferences need no inferences. *American Psychologist, 35,* 151–175.

Zajonc, R.B. (2000). Feeling and thinking: Closing the debate over the independence of affect. In J.P. Forgas (Ed.), *Feeling and thinking: The role of affect in social cognition* (pp. 31–58). Cambridge, England: Cambridge University Press.

Zola-Morgan, S., Squire, L.R., Alvarez-Royo, P., and Clower, R.P. (1991). Independence of memory functions and emotional behavior. *Hippocampus, 1,* 207–220.

Part Eight

Collective Phenomena

Chapter 19

Redundancy in Task Assignments and Group Performance*

R.B. Zajonc and William H. Smoke
University of Michigan

The problem of assessing determinants of group performance has been investigated from two different points of view. For the most part, studies in this area have been concerned with the effects of group variables, such as the presence of others [1, 2], cohesiveness [e.g., 8], leadership style [e.g., 5], and the like, on the performance of groups and of individuals working in groups. Recently, some attempts have been made to analyze the group product by means of a combinatorial analysis of individual abilities. Lorge and Solomon [4] performed such an analysis in the area of group problem solving, and Hays and Bush [3] have used it in group learning. In principle, this latter approach is analogous to that of Moore and Shannon in what they called the "crummy relay problem" [6], which refers to constructing reliable circuits out of unreliable relays. von Neumann [9] has shown that by using a number of components of limited unreliability a reliable machine may be constructed. Moore and Shannon have demonstrated that a reliable circuit may be designed by using arbitrarily unreliable relays. The increase in circuit reliability is obtained essentially by increasing the redundancy among relays. It would seem that the study of group performance in terms of redundancy among the abilities of individual members would hold considerable promise.

Consider, for example, a group of N individuals. Let H items of information be given to these individuals. The object is to recover this information from the group as a whole after some interval of time. For the present purposes it is irrelevant which individual remembers a particular item, although the item should be remembered by somebody in the group. There is evidence in **[361]**** the area of individual recall to the effect

---

* This work was done under the sponsorship of the Behavioral Sciences Division, Air Force Office of Scientific Research, Contract AF 49(630)-33.

** Bracketed bold numbers refer to original page numbers. Page numbers indicate where the original page ended.

Zajonc, R.B. & Smoke, W. (1959). Redundancy in task assignments and group performance. *Psychometrika*, 24, 361–370.

364

that the proportion of items recalled is inversely related to the number of items originally assigned [10]. Consequently, the probability that a given item is remembered by
a given individual is some inverse function of the number of items he was asked to
learn. On the other hand, the probability that at least one individual of those assigned
the given item remembers it increases with the number of individuals assigned the item.
The first consideration implies minimizing the number of items per individual, the second maximizing it. The problem then is to discover the optimal distribution of items
among individuals. The group as a whole is considered to remember an item when that
item is remembered by at least one individual.

CASE I

The following conditions are imposed on Case I.

(a) The probability $p(i, j)$ that item i is remembered by individual j is equal to the
constant p, $0 \leq p \leq 1$, or to zero according to whether or not item i is assigned to j.

(b) Each individual is assigned the same number, h, of items. Thus $\sum_i p(i, j) = hp$.

(c) Each item is assigned to an equal number, n, of individuals. Thus the probability, P, that a given item is recalled by at least one individual is given by

(1) $P = 1 - \prod_n (1 - p) = 1 - (1 - p)^n$,

the same for all items.

Under the conditions of Case I the problem is reduced to finding the assignment of
items which generates the greatest value of P, i.e., finding values of p and n that will max-
imize P. If it is assumed that one is dealing not with number of items (a discrete measure)
but with amount of material or amount of information (continuous measures), P may be
regarded as differentiable function of p. The necessary condition for P to be maximum as
a function of p is that $dP/dp = 0$. Since h is a differentiable function of p, and since by (b)
and (c) $Nh = Hn$, it follows that n is also a differentiable function of p. Thus, from (1)

(2) $\dfrac{dP}{dp} = 0 = -(1-p)^n \left[\dfrac{dn}{dp} \log(1-p) - \dfrac{n}{1-p} \right]$

Given $p \neq 1$, $dP/dp = 0$ only if the bracketed expression is zero, or

(3) $\dfrac{dn}{dp} \log(1-p) - \dfrac{n}{1-p} = 0$

Since $n = Nh/H$, **[362]**

(4) $\dfrac{dh}{dp} \log(1-p) - \dfrac{h}{1-p} = 0$

Thus far the function relating p to h has not been specified. However, the condition
in (4) holds for any *set* of values p and h which satisfy the relation $p = 1 - e^{k/h}$, for an
arbitrary constant k. Thus

$$P = 1 - [1 - (1 - e^{k/h})]^{Nh/H} = 1 - e^{Nk/H}$$

is a constant since all the terms in the expression are constants. Thus, if the probability of a given item being recalled by a given individual were given by $p = 1 - e^{k/h}$,
all assignments would be equally good. Under these conditions what is lost in p by

assigning more items to each individual is gained by increasing n, and consequently the probability that an item is remembered by the group as a whole is independent of the assignment of items to the group members.

If, however, the relation between p and h is not given by $p = 1 - e^{k/h}$ but by some other function $p = f(h)$, then in general not all assignments will be equally good. In fact, on the basis of empirical data available in this area [10] it would appear that the function is of the form $p = e^{-k^3h^3}$, for an empirical parameter k which depends on such factors as time, nature of the material, its organization, meaningfulness, or the like. This function fits data gathered by Oberly [7] with $k = .10$. Assuming $p = e^{-k^3h^3}$ and finding dh/dp,

(5) $(1 - p) \log (1 - p) - 2p \log p = 0,$

which is satisfied approximately for $p = .84$. Figure 19.1 shows the relation between P and p for selected values of k with $N/H = .01$.

Solving for h, $h = \sqrt{\log .84 / -k^2}$. Thus, the best assignment results when each individual is assigned $.42/k$ items. In terms of p, the maximum value of P obtains when each individual is given the number of items which would result in his forgetting about 16% of the material. Since the relationship between h, which denotes individual loads, and n, which reflects the amount of task-assignment redundancy, is known, the optimal amount of redundancy may be obtained. Thus, for Case I, $n = (.42/k)(N/H)$, the optimal amount of task-assignment redundancy.

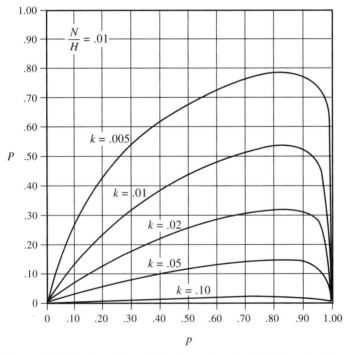

Figure 19.1   The relationship between P and p for different values of the constant k.

It is rather interesting to note that the result obtained is entirely independent of the size of the group, N, and the number of items, H, Thus for any given number of individuals and any given number of items, .42/k items per person represents the optimal assignment. Of course, the optimal amount of redundancy and consequently the maximum value of P vary with the ratio of individuals to items. The larger this ratio the higher the maximum possible value of P. Figure 19.2 represents the relationship between the maximum values of P and the N/H ratio for some selected values of the parameter k. [363]

The solution was obtained by assuming h to be a continuous variable. Given a group of N individuals and a collection of H discrete items, it will not be possible in general to assign the items to individuals in more than a small number of ways. Hence the assignments do not vary continuously. As a matter of fact, for given values of N and H only some of all the possible assignments satisfy the conditions (b) and (c). It can be demonstrated that if D is the greatest common divisor of N and H, the number of assignments of H items to N group members satisfying (b) and (c) is equal to D, given that two assignments are not considered distinct when they assign the same number of items to each individual.

CASE II

In Case II items of equal difficulties and individuals with equal recall capacities were considered. Now the case where there exist individual differences in recall will be examined.

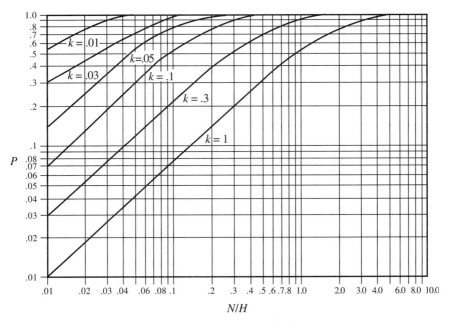

Figure 19.2   Maximum values of P as a Function of N/H.

Again a set of conditions is imposed.

(a) The probability, $p(i, j)$, that item i is remembered by individual j, is [364] equal to the constant p, $0 \le p \le 1$, or to zero according to whether or not item i is assigned to j.

(b) The number, h_j, of items assigned to individual j is such that $p = e^{-k_j^3 h_j^3}$ where k_j, is an empirical parameter obtained with respect to the individual j.

(c) The items are so distributed that for each item i the probability that i is remembered by at least one individual is equal to the constant $P' = 1 - \prod i \, [1 - p(i, j)]$, the same for all items.

Thus, the above conditions imply that different individuals will be assigned different numbers of items, depending on their individual abilities to remember them. The conditions also imply that each item i is assigned to the same number of individuals n, or that the redundancy is equal for all items. Hence

(6) $P' = 1 - \prod_i [1 - p(i, j)] = 1 - (1 - p)^n.$

Again, the necessary condition that P' be a maximum as a function of p is that $dP'/dp = 0$. Thus

(7) $\dfrac{dP'}{dp} = 0 = -(1 - p)^n \left[\dfrac{dn}{dp} \log(1 - p) - \dfrac{n}{1 - p} \right]$

If $p \ne 1$, then

(8) $(1 - p) \log(1 - p) \dfrac{dn}{dp} - n = 0$

In terms of the above conditions the number of assignments is equal to nH and to $\sum_j h_j$. Hence $nH = \sum_j h_j$. Thus

$$\frac{dn}{dp} = \frac{1}{H} \sum_j \frac{dh_j}{dp}$$

From restriction (b),

$$\frac{dp}{dp} = 1 = -2k_j^2 h_j \frac{dh_i}{dp} e^{-k_j^3 h_j^3} = -2k_j^2 h_j \frac{dh_j}{dp} p = (2p \log p) \frac{1}{h_i} \frac{dh_j}{dp}$$

Thus

$$h_j = (2p \log p) \frac{dh_j}{dp}$$

and [366]

$$\sum_j h_j = (2p \log p) \sum_j \frac{dh_j}{dp}$$

Therefore

$$\frac{dn}{dp} = \frac{1}{H} \sum_j \frac{dh_j}{dp} = \frac{1}{2p \log p} \left(\frac{1}{H} \right) \sum_j h_j = \frac{n}{2p \log p}$$

and

$$(1-p) \ \log(1-p) \frac{dn}{dp} - n = 1 - p \ \log(1-p) \frac{n}{2p \ \log p} - n \quad ,$$

or

(9) $(1 - p) \log (1 - p) - 2p \log p = 0$

Note that individual differences do not influence the solution, as (9) is satisfied for $p = .84$. However, the number of items, h_j, to be assigned to the different individuals will depend on their recall abilities which are reflected in the constants k_j. If the assignment of items to individuals satisfies (a) and (b), then for two individuals j_1 and j_2.

$$\exp(-k_{j_1}^2 h_{j_1}^2) = p = \exp(-k_{j_2}^2 h_{j_2}^2)$$

or

$$k_{j_1} h_{j_1} = k_{j_2} h_{j_2}$$

Thus

$$h_{j_2} = \frac{k_{j_1}}{k_{j_2}} h_{j_1}$$

and in general

$$h_{j_a} = \frac{k_{j_1}}{k_{j_a}} h_{j_1}$$

for each member j_a of the group. Since $\sum_j h_j = nH$,

$$nH = \sum_j \frac{k_{j_1}}{k_{j_a}} h_{j_a} = h_{j_1} k_{j_1} \sum_j \frac{1}{k_j}$$

Hence

$$h_{j_1} = \left(\frac{nH}{k_{j_1}}\right) \left(\frac{1}{\sum_j \frac{1}{k_j}}\right)$$

and in general [367]

(10) $h_{j_a} = \left(\dfrac{nH}{k_{j_a}}\right) \left(\dfrac{1}{\sum_j \dfrac{1}{k_j}}\right)$

for each individual j. In this case individual differences are exploited by assigning fewer items to less able members and more items to the capable individuals.

While the value $p = .84$ is optimal under the restrictions specified above, it remains to be determined whether a different solution is obtained by relaxing restriction (a) such that $p(i, j)$, is no longer required to be a constant across individuals.

CONCLUSIONS

The solutions presented provide a standard against which empirical results may be compared. Empirical tests must conform to the predictions, otherwise the restrictions imposed on the solutions could not have been met. Thus by careful experimental controls it can be discovered what variables determine the departures from the prediction.

For instance, the conditions imposed above require that $p(i, j)$, the probability of the individual j recalling the item i, be constant. This, of course, necessitates a complete independence of the recall probabilities in terms of the items, as well as in terms of individuals. The probability $p(i_1, j_2)$ must be independent of $p(i_1, j_2)$ and of $p(i_2, j_1)$. Therefore, the cases examined are valid not for groups of interacting members but for collections of individuals working independently of one another.

This requirement, however, is not at all a shortcoming. On the contrary, it allows one to study the effects of group interaction on individual and group performance in recall. The existence of group interaction would probably lower the value of the parameter k, and this effect can be evaluated readily by empirical tests. The difference between the values of the parameter k for individuals working together and for individuals working alone would provide information on the effect of group interaction on individual performance, and the difference between the corresponding values of P, information concerning the effect of group interaction on group performance.

It is noted that the model presented is not restricted to recall, and that it may, with slight modifications, be applied to other behaviors, such as learning, problem solving, or decision making.

REFERENCES

1. Allport, F.H. The influence of the group upon association and thought. *J. exp. Psychol*, 1920, **3**, 152–182.
2. Dashiell, J.F. An experimental analysis of some group effects. *J. abnorm. soc. Psychol.*, 1930, **25**, 190–199.
3. Hays, D.G. and Bush, R.R. A study of group action. *Amer. sociol. Rev.*, 1954, **19**, 693–701.
4. Lorge, I. and Solomon, H. Two models of group behavior in the solution of Eureka-type problems. *Psychometrika*, 1955, **20**, 139–148.
5. Maier, N.R.F. The quality of group decisions as influenced by the discussion leader. *Hum. Relat.*, 1950, **3**, 155 –174. **[368]**
6. Moore, E.F. and Shannon, C.E. Reliable circuits using less reliable relays. Part I. *J. Franklin Inst.*, 1956, **262**, 191–208.
7. Oberly, H.S. A comparison of the spans of "attention" and memory. *Amer. J. Psychol.*, 1928, **40**, 295–302.
8. Schachter, S., Ellertson, N., and Gregory, D. An experimental study of cohesiveness and productivity. *Hum. Relat.*, 1951, **4**, 229–238.
9. von Neumann, J. *Probabilistic logic*. Pasadena: California Inst. Technol., 1952.
10. Woodworth, R.S. *Experimental psychology*. New York: Holt, 1938. **[369]**

Chapter 20

Birth Order: Reconciling Conflicting Effects

R.B. Zajonc and Patricia R. Mullally
Stanford University

When a variable analyzed in one form explains 90% of variance of a given outcome, and in another equally justifiable form, the variable explains only 1%, we have a serious empirical contradiction. Such a contradiction emerges in the study of the role of birth order in intellectual test scores that this article seeks to resolve. In Figure 20.1, we present three secular trends for test scores that are characterized by a remarkably close correspondence with changes in the aggregate birth order.[1] In the first graph are quantitative Scholastic Assessment Test (SAT) scores, in the second, United Kingdom A-level data (taken there by 17-year-olds and similar to SATs in purpose but not in form), and in the third, the combined basic skills scores of Iowa elementary and high school children. Aggregate birth orders are calculated quite simply. The number of first children born in a given cohort year is multiplied by one, the number of second children is multiplied by two, third children by three, and so on, for all children born. The sum of these products is then divided by the total number of births in the given year, and a value of the average birth order is obtained. We see from the graphs that a child born in the United States in 1962, who took the SATs 18 years later in 1980, entered

---

[1] The SATs come from the official publications of the College Entrance Examination Board and Educational Testing Service. The A-level data are based on a report of the Manchester Centre for Education and Employment Research, kindly supplied by Alan Smithers, School of Education, Brunel University, Twickenham, United Kingdom. The Iowa data were supplied by Jim Gould of the State of Iowa Department of Education and Robert L. Brennan, Director of Iowa Testing Programs, whom we thank for their help. The current data were combined with an earlier data set (Zajonc, 1976), which was collected by W.E. Coffman, the former director of the Iowa Testing Programs. U.S. and Iowa birth orders were calculated from the *Natality Report* of the U.S. Bureau of the Census (1951–1991). The U.K. birth order was taken from the Office of Population Censuses and Surveys (1987), and it includes Wales, whereas the A-levels are only those from the United Kingdom. The Welsh population, however, constitutes only 5% of the combined birth cohort.

Zajonc, R.B. & Mullaly, P.R. (1997). Birth order: Reconciling conflicting effects. *American Psychologist*, 52, 685–699. Copyright © 1997 by the American Psychological Association. Reprinted with permission.

at birth a family that, on average, already had 2.05 children (that child's birth order was 3.05), whereas a child born in 1978 (who took the SATs last year) entered a family with only 1.02 siblings (this child's birth order was 2.02). The U.K. birth order figures also changed during this interval from 2.3 in 1962 (who took the A-levels in 1979) to 1.9 for children born in 1978 (who took their A-levels in 1995). Among others, a high

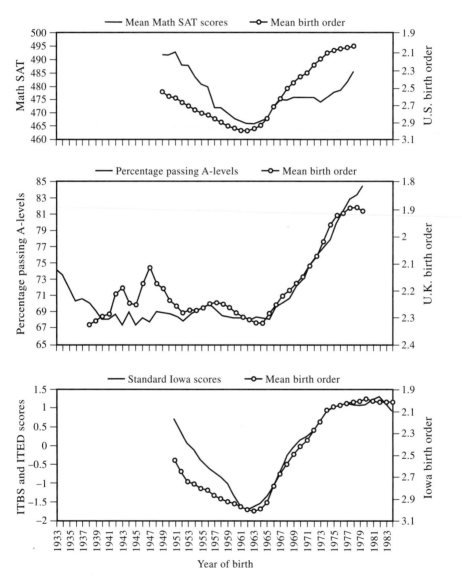

Note: The birth order data lag SAT scores by 18 years, the A-levels by 17 years, and the Iowa scores by 9-16 years. The birth order scale is inverted such that higher values represent lower birth ranks.

Figure 20.1 U.S. Math Scholastic Assessment Tests (SATs), U.K. A-Levels, and Iowa Basic Skills Scores for Iowa Children and Their Respective Birth Orders

aggregate birth order of a cohort means that the proportion of firstborns in that cohort is also relatively high—a factor that is significant, as we explain below, in understanding test score trends.

The correspondence between the test trends and family trends is remarkable. Regression equations showed that the aggregate birth order was, by far, the major source of variation in test scores, for it alone accounted for as much as 81% of variance in SATs, 86% in the A-levels, and 89% in the Iowa scores.[2] **[685]***

Cross-sectional studies also show a strong relationship between aggregate test scores and birth order (e.g., Belmont and Marolla, 1973; Breland, 1974; Davis, Cahan, and Bashi, 1977; Institut National d'Études Démographiques, 1973; Zajonc, 1976, 1983; Zajonc and Bargh, 1980b; Zajonc, Markus, and Markus, 1979). In these studies, temporal trends were not examined. Rather, the researchers compared average test scores of large numbers of individuals whose birth orders were known. The comparisons of average test scores classified according to the birth order of the test takers also yielded systematic differences, with as much as 96% variance in aggregate test scores accounted for by birth order (Zajonc and Bargh, 1980b). Yet similar studies in which individual test scores were examined for their correlation with the individual's particular birth order failed to account for more than 3% of variance in intellectual scores (Brackbill and Nichols, 1982; Ernst and Angst, 1983; Galbraith, 1982; Grotevant, Scarr, and Weinberg, 1977; Hauser and Sewell, 1983; Kessler, 1991; Olneck and Bills, 1979; Retherford and Sewell, 1991; Schooler, 1972; Steelman and Mercy, 1980; Svanum and Bringle, 1980; Zajonc and Bargh, 1980a; but see Zajonc, Markus, Berbaum, Bargh, and Moreland, 1991). In fact, in the Belmont and Marolla findings, aggregate birth order accounted for nearly 80% of all variance, but when analyzed individual-by-individual, birth order had only a negligible effect in the very same data set (Ernst and Angst, 1983).[3]

How can we reconcile these conflicting findings? Are the aggregate results "true" and the individually distributed analyses "false?" Or is it the other way around? The reader will see that both results are true, but they answer different questions. There are two ways of formulating the problem of birth order. Studies that report negative birth order results formulate the problem in terms of individual differences. These studies seek to explain all variance in test scores, and their research strategy is to examine as many factors as possible, birth order included, that influence individual test scores and compare their relative contributions to the total variance explained. And it is, indeed, the case that in comparison with such factors as parental education or socioeconomic

---

[2] All the F ratios of the regression analyses were significant well beyond the $p = .001$ level. The complete results of these regression analyses can be found in Zajonc (1996). The Iowa and U.K. test data were regressed only on aggregate birth order. However, the Quantitative SAT scores were regressed not only on birth order ($\beta = -3.12$, $SE = 0.63$) but on the proportion of men taking the test ($\beta = -0.25$, $SE = 0.22$), the proportion of Whites taking the test ($\beta = 1.52$, $SE = 0.59$), the proportion of the birth cohort taking the test ($\beta = -0.92$, $SE = 0.56$), and parental income ($\beta = 0.03$, $SE = 0.10$). SATs had a partial correlation with birth order equal to $-.79$.

* Bracketed bold numbers refer to original page numbers. Page numbers indicate where the original page ended.

[3] Differences in IQ associated with birth order are not trivial. For example, Belmont and Marolla (1973), in a study with nearly 400,000 18-year-old male participants, found a difference of about one fourth of a standard deviation in Raven scores (equivalent to four IQ points) between firstborns and fifthborns in families of five, and Breland (1974), in a study of nearly 800,000 National Merit candidates, showed, for the same comparison, a difference in IQ of nearly eight points (i.e., more than half of a standard deviation; p. 1013). As explained in the text, in the aggregate these differences are not small at all and have serious collective consequences.

status (SES), birth order alone is found in these individually distributed effects studies to contribute very little variance.

The problem of birth order can also be formulated by asking a different question: Other things being equal, to what extent are variations in birth order alone associated with variations in intellectual scores?[4] In other words, the focus is not on explaining all individually distributed variation in intellectual scores, but the focus is on birth order in particular and not on its role in comparison with other factors that have been identified as important sources of variation in test scores. In this article, we ask the derivative question, namely whether secular trends in aggregate test scores have any association with trends in birth order, an association that is clearly suggested by the data in Figure 20.1, and how this association can be explicated.

How is it possible for the same variable to account for almost all the variance in the criterion when analyzed in the aggregate (i.e., when averages of birth order are correlated with averages of test scores) and for a negligible amount of variance when correlations are computed between birth ranks of particular individuals and their particular scores? Belmont and Marolla (1973), in their study of 386,114 Dutch recruits, reported birth order differences, independent of family size, significant at $p < 10^{-13}$. The aggregate data yielded 77% of the variance explained by birth order alone (Zajonc and Bargh, 1980b). However, the same data set had a raw β, estimated by Marjoribanks and Walberg (1975), of only $-.078$, which translates into an increment in test scores of less than one tenth of a standard deviation per unit of birth order. Which of the two sets of figures quantify the birth order effect?

There may not be a meaningful answer to this question, because, as the reader shall see, both forms of analysis (distributed and aggregate) have their own interpretations and implications. But the distinction has profound empirical, methodological, and theoretical consequences because contradictory conclusions, often not acknowledged as such, have been drawn from both sources of analysis. There are several phenomena in which aggregate **[687]** and individually distributed analyses yield different outcomes, and quite often, similar controversies arise. For example, Mischel (1968) alarmed psychologists by stating that personality measures do not predict behavior, not to any respectable degree of validity. This conclusion was based on a review of individually distributed analyses in which a host of other factors that also determine behavior were not measured or controlled. However, Epstein (1986, 1990) showed that when outcomes are aggregated, a substantial relationship between personality and behavior is found. Smoking, too, shows strong consequences for lung cancer when analyzed in the aggregate, but shows little when individually distributed chances of lung cancer are calculated for smokers and nonsmokers. Accordingly, those who wish to deny the effects of smoking cite individually distributed data, and those who are opposed cite aggregate data. Ernst and Angst (1983), critics of birth order effects, took the very low β weight, estimated for individual data as the "true" evidence of the absence of birth order differences, and ignored systematic aggregate birth order differences reported by Belmont and Marolla (1973) and Breland (1974).

The statistical effects of aggregation can be estimated by an adaptation of the Spearman-Brown prophecy (Zajonc, 1962). The typical use for the Spearman-Brown

---

[4] Note that we do not regard birth order or family configuration to be the main or even partial causes of intellectual development. Rather, they are viewed here as quantifiable factors that show consistent correlations with test scores.

formula allows us to estimate an increment in test reliability when we increase the number of test items, provided all items have the same correlation with the criterion as the original set of items. However, the formula can be adapted for the distinct form of aggregation that is involved in birth order data. An example will be helpful. In one of the earliest experiments on group judgments, Gordon (1924) had 200 participants rank weights for their magnitude. Each participant's ranking of weights was compared with the true order, and Gordon obtained an average correlation of .41. But he then randomly constructed artificial groups of 5, 10, 20, and 50 individual judgments, with each group having its own average. When these average judgments were correlated with the true order, the correlations were .68, .79, .86, and .94 for averages of 5, 10, 20, and 50 randomly selected grouped judgments, respectively. Eysenck (1939) raised reliability of judgments from .47 to .98 simply by aggregating individual judgments into groups of 5, 10, 20, and 50. Note that the analyses that at one time explained 0.17% and at another 96% of the variance were performed on the very same data points, except for grouping or aggregating of the data. The first represents an average correlation, and the second represents the correlation of averages.[5] Thus, when birth order effects are evaluated on an individual-by-individual basis, the obtained relationship is essentially an average correlation. However, when researchers average, for any given trend, yearly birth orders and yearly test scores and calculate a correlation coefficient between them, the relationship obtained is the correlation of averages.[6] It is important to note in this respect, however, that although aggregate analysis will generally yield higher correlation coefficients, the

---

[5] The following approximation of the Spearman–Brown prophecy formula (Zajonc, 1962) estimates the correlation of averages, r_{xy}, from the average correlation, r_{xy}, where n is the number of observations in each unit or category of the aggregate.

$$r_{xy}^2 = \frac{nr_{xy}^2}{1+(n-1)r_{xy}^2}$$

The approximation assumes that $r_{xy}^2 = r_{yy}$, the average intercorrelation among participants. It follows from the approximation that given one entry per cell, as is the case in averaging individual correlations, $n = 1$, and given $r_{xy} = .1$, we obtain $r_{xy}^2 = .01$, the amount of variance typically accounted for an individual-difference approach to birth order that uses distributed analysis. However, if the number of observations in each unit of the aggregate (i.e., in each cohort) is increased thousandfold (i.e., $n = 1,000$) and if r_{xy}, remains equal to .1, we obtain a correlation of averages, r_{xy}, equal to .95.

[6] Note that when the prophecy formula is applied to estimate increments in test reliability by adding test items, it is a forgone conclusion that the reliability will increase. Such an increase in correlation between birth order and test scores will also be obtained when we aggregate within the entire unchanged n of observations, as, for example, in the distributed and the aggregated scores of the Belmont–Marolla (1973) data. But not all methods of aggregating will increase the reliability or correlation coefficient. In fact, the increment in a correlation coefficient deriving from the above form of aggregation can occur only if there is an underlying and pervasive relationship in the total n between the two variables. That not all forms of aggregation must necessarily result in increased correlation coefficients is shown by the following example in the SAT data. Within any cohort, individual SATs and the individual's parental income are correlated between .30 and .45. When we aggregate, say within the 1995 cohort, and examine the relationship between SAT scores and parental income, the correlation rises to .99. The same, of course, is obtained for the aggregated Belmont–Marolla data. But when we aggregate income differently, for example, over the 20-year secular trend (1975–1995), the relationship between the aggregate SATs and aggregate parental income drops from .35 to –.19! This means, of course, that the association between SATs and birth order in the three secular trends shown in Figure 20.1 is not simply or only a matter of aggregating individual scores. It means that there exists an underlying and pervasive relationship between the two variables.

power of the independent variable to make predictions for single individuals remains unchanged. **[688]** Even if the aggregate regression coefficient for birth order and SATs were over .90, the birth order of a single individual taken at random would still be a poor predictor of his or her SAT score. This point was clearly demonstrated by Ross and Nisbett (1991, pp. 102–108) in their cogent analysis of the Mischel-Epstein controversy. Of course, aggregate trends in birth order remain excellent predictors of aggregate trends in SATs.

WHY SHOULD BIRTH ORDER INFLUENCE TEST TRENDS?

Researchers often find trends that, quite accidentally, show close correlations with other unexpected factors. For these accidental correlations, subsequent studies eventually discover that they are either chance events or that both factors are actually influenced by a third one. But the parallels between the trends of birth orders and test scores are not fortuitous, given that over the 30 years there were over 3 million observations per birth order data point and over 1 million per SAT data point (and given that test scores consistently track birth order trends for three quite different populations and for different tests). More important, however, these trend data are entirely in agreement with a theory—the confluence model—published 20 years ago and are in fact predicted by the model (Zajonc, 1976). We discuss here the implications of the confluence model for understanding the test trends observed in Figure 20.1.

The basic idea of the confluence model is that intellectual growth of children can be enhanced or hindered by the immediate family circumstances, which, by virtue of their family position, are different even for children of the same family. This is evident by comparing some siblings for their linguistic experiences—experiences that have a profound influence on their later test scores (Huttenlocher, Haight, Bryk, and Seltzer, 1991). Compare, for example, the linguistic experiences of a firstborn son before the birth of his younger sibling with those of a girl who already has several younger brothers and sisters. During his presibling period, this firstborn interacts mainly with adults. He is exposed to a fairly sophisticated language, a rich vocabulary, and a variety of life's domains. He lives in an adult world. Just being surrounded by adults gives him auditory access to a pool of words, many of which he will be asked about in his SATs. However, the later-born girl who has several younger siblings hears a less diverse and more limited language, has less interactive access to her parents, and witnesses less often the process and product of abstract thought. She hears the language of toddlers because she lives in a toddler's world. The pool of words in which she is immersed is restricted, more primitive, contains very few low-frequency items, and does not afford the formation of complex sentences. In fact, Hart and Risley (1995) were able to quantify the pool of words in which children are immersed. They report that children of parents on welfare hear about 600 words per hour, children of working-class parents hear 1,200 words, and children of professional parents hear as many as 2,100.

The confluence model quantifies the way intellectual growth is influenced by the intellectual environment in the home, focusing on family configuration. But how can we quantify intellectual environment? Obviously, such a quantification requires a simplification, as all models do—a simplification that, in return, allows for precise formulation that produces testable and reliable estimates of the empirical data. Thus, we simply assume that the more intellectually mature that the people are who interact with the growing child, the more mature are the verbal, analytical, and conceptual experiences of the child. These experiences, we assume, will reveal themselves in the test scores of the child. Test scores may or may not measure what is popularly thought of as "intelligence," and it is true that the concept of intelligence itself needs better understanding (Neisser et al., 1996). But test scores represent a stark reality. Whatever they measure, one's life course can be significantly changed by what scores one manages to obtain.

A few simplified examples illustrate the major concepts that can be found in greater detail in prior publications (Zajonc, 1976, 1983; Zajonc and Bargh, 1980b; Zajonc et al., 1979). Consider the intellectual environment of the firstborn: Typically, the family environment consists of two mature adults and the newborn.[7] If we assign numerical values to this situation, say in mental-age units, such as those used in the Stanford Binet, we might be able to quantify in the abstract the quality of the family environment as it changes during the course of the child's development. We can assign, for instance, a value of 30 to each of the parents and 0 to the newborn child, take an average $(30 + 30 + 0)/3 = 20$, and consider this value as representing some approximation to the relative level of intellectual resources accessible to the newborn child, assuming all other things are constant.

Say, after four years, a new child is born into the above family. The second born's intellectual environment at birth is now $(30 + 30 + 4 + 0)/4 = 16$. And say that, after a lapse of three more years, there is a third offspring. The average value is reduced further: $(30 + 30 + 7 + 3 + 0)/5 = 14$. Thus, each successive sibling is born into a more "diluted" intellectual environment.

Note a few patterns:[8]

1. The individual whose score we are interested in predicting is also included in calculating the environment. In most analyses of environmental effects, the individual and the environment are treated as distinct entities. But here, because we are dealing with effects that occur over time, the person is treated as part of his or her own dynamically changing environment that influences him or her. The individual is part of that environment because, **[689]** like other family members, he or she influences it also and, as a result, is the target of a subsequent environmental influence in which he or she had some part. If A influences B at Time 1, and B influences A at a later Time 2, then A was influenced by A's own environment that A previously influenced. It is the case that parents have an influence over their children. But it works the other way too. Just observe the language of parents who have a new baby or listen to the speech of kindergarten teachers. For unspecified reasons, Ernst and Angst (1983), however, considered this feature of the model to be its

---

[7] Actually family patterns are rapidly changing and the proportion of single-parent households has grown substantially, especially in Europe.

[8] The confluence model does not use averages, as in the simplified examples, but root mean squares. Also, individual levels for a given age are calculated by assuming a growth function, $f(t) = 1 - e^{-k^2 t^2}$. See Zajonc and Bargh (1980b) for a complete discussion of the formal aspects of the model.

defect. Yet, if this theoretically compelling assumption is not made, empirical data cannot be fitted by the model.

2. Gaps between successive births are also important: For the last born, a gap of six years is better than a gap of two years, because he or she has an older sibling who knows more of what he or she needs to know.

3. Twins have a poorer environment because both have an immature sibling at birth: $(30 + 30 + 0 + 0)/4 = 15$. This is in accordance with data showing that the IQ of twins is about five points less than singly born children, and that of triplets is seven points less (Record, McKeown, and Edwards, 1970).

4. Children in one-parent families are also at a disadvantage because there is only one adult to contribute to the average level of intellectual environment (Carlsmith, 1964): $(30 + 0)/2 = 15$. Conversely, a larger number of adults (e.g., uncles, grandparents, child-care persons) provide an environment that is richer in intellectual resources.

5. Parental absolute scores remain unchanged at 30, assuming that by that age they have reached the typical asymptote. However, should the model be applied to populations for whom it can be assumed, for whatever reason, higher or lower adult intellectual levels, parental values can be adjusted accordingly (see, e.g., Zajonc and Bargh, 1980b), a procedure that elevates or reduces the absolute level of the predicted scores.

These illustrations specify the environment only at birth. One should not extrapolate from these illustrations, however, that the relative quality of the environment is constant over the entire growth period, such that it is always richer for the firstborn than for later borns. A subtle nontrivial inference follows from the confluence model, for the model predicts important changes, indeed a reversal of birth order effects that take place soon after the second child is born. In fact, in only a few years, the environment of the second born surpasses the first. This unexpected feature of growth patterns was revealed not by data, but by the mathematics of the confluence model, and it turned out subsequently to be empirically true. This is so because two factors interact over time. The environment of the firstborn, although superior at birth, when measured at age four—$(30 + 30 + 4 + 0)/4 = 16$—is, in fact, inferior to that of the second born when also measured at age four, which is $(30 + 30 + 8 + 4)/4 = 18$.

At the same time, however, according to the confluence model, another factor comes into play, a factor that has a positive developmental influence and that can more than compensate for the poorer environment of the firstborn in the early years of his or her life. There is a basic difference between the first and last-born child, affording the former an opportunity for growth enhancement that is denied to last and only children. The firstborn in a family of two or more often acts as a surrogate parent. His or her younger siblings ask questions about the meanings of words, they need help with various tasks (e.g., how to hold a bat), and they appeal to their older sibling to explain how things work or why they work in a certain way. In short, the firstborn child is in a way a "tutor" to the younger siblings, which has been shown to enhance mental growth and academic achievement (Bargh and Schul, 1980; Wagner, 1982; Whitman, 1988). However, since a one-year-old seldom requires an intellectual tutorial, older siblings do not begin to benefit from their teaching function until the younger sibling can begin to ask questions—perhaps after age 2—and can enter into an interaction in which some cognitive processes are involved. Eventually, the contribution of the teaching function overcomes the deficit of the firstborn's early environment, and it does so at about age 11 (± 2 years).

All children are last born for some period of time, and during that period of growth they do not benefit from the teaching function. The only child never has the opportunity to teach; he or she remains the last born at all times. And when measured past age 11 ± 2, that child's scores are generally lower than those of children in families of two.[9] It is a subtlety of the theory and of the empirical data that, when overlooked, may easily lead to discounting the birth order effect, for it turns out that test scores increase with birth order but only when measured past age 11 ± 2. Because some studies found positive test scores to increase with birth order, whereas others found them to decrease, the entire field of birth order research was declared by some (Ernst and Angst, 1983; Schooler, 1972) to be chaotic and inconsequential.[10] But, mirabile dictum, when age of testing is taken into account, very meaningful patterns emerge. A French survey (Tabah and Sutter, 1954) of national intellectual levels reported data of siblings in intact two-child families that showed that the IQ of the second born surpasses that of the firstborn for ages 6 and 7, is about the same for the ages 8 and 9, and falls below that of the firstborn afterwards. This pattern of data is replicated in 50 studies **[690]** that were analyzed more than a decade ago (Zajonc, 1983 Zajonc et al., 1979). We show below another example of the age dependence of birth order effects (see Figure 20.2). Perhaps inattention to this subtlety of birth order effects is one reason why the critics concluded that there are no birth order effects at all. Ernst and Angst (1983, pp. 43–69) ignored age dependence of birth order effects and cited as counterevidence to the model many studies of very young children (e.g., Svanum and Bringle, 1980) that failed to show birth order effects—studies that according to the confluence model should not show positive birth order effects in the first place.

The interaction of the two factors—the modulating effects of the "teaching function" and of the intellectual environment—explains many seemingly anomalous phenomena. Whereas the firstborn's situation is "diluted" by new siblings, he or she can eventually benefit from their presence by acting as a tutor to them. Because the only child can seldom assume a teaching function and, thus, benefit from it, his or her scores are generally lower than those of two-children families. This explains why the only child does not obtain the highest test scores and why, therefore, the family-size effect is often not monotone and is at a maximum for a two-child family (Zajonc, 1983; Zajonc et al., 1979). When measured past age 11, the only child has lower scores than one from a two- and sometimes even three-child family. In an analysis of six large data sets for the effects of aggregate birth order, populations tested at ages younger than 11 did not show the typical

---

[9] The preponderance of one-child families in China offers a very interesting population for an intensive study of family configuration effects on test scores.

[10] The effects of intervals between successive births are also age dependent, and they depend on birth rank as well. For example, when tested at age seven, the intellectual environment of the firstborn who has a sibling five years younger is not as rich as the firstborn who has a sibling only two years younger: $30 + 30 + 7 + 2 < 30 + 30 + 7 + 5$. The longer the interval is, the less the benefit. The reverse is true for the later-born child. When tested at seven, the second born with an interval of five years is better off than the second born with an interval of two years: $30 + 30 + 12 + 7 > 30 + 30 + 9 + 7$. The longer the interval is, the greater the benefit.

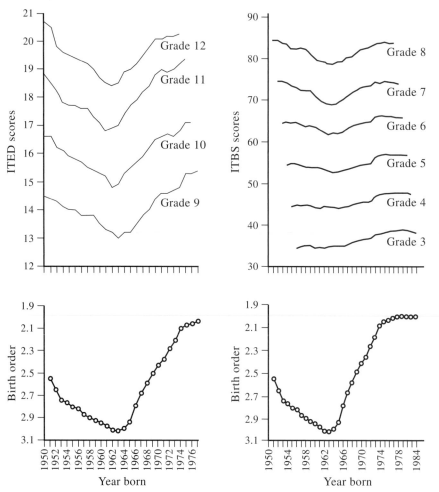

Figure 20.2   Iowa Test of Basic Skills (ITBS) and Iowa Test of Educational Development (ITED) Composite Standard Scores and Birth Order of Iowa Children in Grades 3–12

decline of scores with aggregate birth order (Zajonc and Bargh, 1980b). Only those tested at ages 17 and 18 featured the decline of scores with lower **[691]** aggregate birth orders.[11] When the Iowa scores plotted above are broken down by grades, a clear birth order effect is obtained only for children in grades higher than fifth, that is, older than 11 years (Figure 20.2). No other theory seeking to explicate birth order effects acknowledges the age dependence of these effects, let alone offers a conceptual analysis of these patterns.

---

[11] The partial correlation coefficients of aggregate test scores with aggregate birth order, when family size was held constant, for participants over 11 years of age were −.88 and −.90, whereas those for younger participants were both positive, .73 and .05. The respective standardized βs were −.53 and −.82 for the older participants and .27 and .02 for the younger participants (Zajonc and Bargh, 1980b).

ALTERNATIVES TO THE CONFLUENCE MODEL

There were some attempts to attribute birth order and family-size effects to a resource depletion process (Becker and Tomes, 1976; Blake, 1989; Gottfried, 1984; Lindert, 1977; Murnane, Maynard, and Ohls, 1981; Taubman and Behrman, 1986). The depletion theory posits that there is a fixed or nearly fixed inventory of resources (i.e., financial, affective, intellectual), resources that, when divided among an increasing number of siblings, leave a decreasing portion for each, which, researchers claim, explains why children from larger families have low test scores. Because there is less to draw on for each successive child, the depletion theory also claims to explain why test scores decrease with birth order.

The resource depletion theory encounters at least three serious contradictions. According to the resource depletion theory, only children should score the highest on intellectual performance tests. They do not (e.g., Breland, 1974; Zajonc et al., 1979). Second, the positive relationship between intellectual scores and birth order should be independent of age of testing. It is not (Tabah and Sutter, 1954; Zajonc et al., 1979). Third, according to the depletion model, the decline of scores with family size should be modulated by income. Children from families with higher SES levels should not show a drop in test scores with increasing family size because their resources are large enough to support more offspring, and later born children in high SES families, therefore, should not suffer substantial resource disadvantages. Yet, in contradiction to depletion theory, the relationship between family size and intellectual scores is the same for all socioeconomic levels (e.g., Breland, 1974; Zajonc, 1976). Of course, the absolute level of scores rises with SES or parental education. However, because the same developmental advantages and disadvantages among siblings, relative to each other, are constant, the patterns of differences in test scores among distinct birth orders also remain the same across the various SES levels, and differences in test scores associated with family size have the same patterns as well. Only the intercepts of these two functions change with SES.

THE CONFLUENCE MODEL CANNOT BE TESTED ON INDIVIDUALS

We have no practical means at present to test specific derivations from the confluence model on individual data points. During the course of the child's growth period, major changes occur when new siblings are born, or when some of them or any member of the household leaves the home. Some older children act intensively and extensively as tutors. Others participate marginally. Some parents relate to successive children in the same way, and others are more inconsistent. In some families, the standard of living may rise with the age of children, and in others it may decline. One child may have inspiring teachers or friends, whereas another lives in a dull neighborhood. Some parents love to read to their children, whereas others prefer to watch television. And a variety of traumatic events can have an impact on the development of the child. To take account of all these and similar conditions that may in some way influence test scores is virtually impossible in a sample of individual cases.

Moreover, a test of the confluence model, on the basis of individually distributed birth order effects, is simply impossible because the complexity of such a test goes well beyond even the most generous research means at researchers' disposal. Consider the task. Suppose we start modestly with no more than five siblings. If we wish to consider gender, we begin with 62 sibship categories (Male [M], Female [F], MM, MF, FM; FF, MMM, MMF, etc.). But the confluence model specifies birth intervals to be important also. Excluding multiple births, which could be studied separately, we may wish simply to examine differences only between short and long birth intervals. We now have 1,778 sibling categories and 8,258 participant categories. Thus, if we find a population that can generate 10 participants per cell, we need 100,000 participants, and probably many more, because some sibling categories will be very difficult to locate. We also know that the age of testing is important. The longitudinal approach would require repeated measures on these thousands of participants over a substantial period of time. And we have not begun to control for the host of other psychological, social, experiential, and economic factors that may contribute to the test scores, nor have we committed ourselves to observe the interactions between siblings and parents or among the siblings and record the tutorial help offered and received. Perhaps, there is only one test of the confluence model that approaches these requirements. It is a study of two-child families measuring both children's IQs at different ages (Tabah and Sutter, 1954). Consistent with the confluence model, this study clearly demonstrated the age dependence of birth order effects. Inferences consistent with the confluence model are therefore best examined on large samples, using aggregate analyses. Given a large sample and a classification of participants in which factors confounding birth order effects are allowed to be absorbed by the averaging process, strong aggregate effects of birth order are clearly and systematically revealed. That is the case when test trends are analyzed and when large samples are grouped according to family positions. Given that aggregate patterns **[692]** of birth order explain almost all the variance in test score trends means that, at the limit, birth order, even though obscured by extraneous noise, must be a meaningful factor at the individual level as well.[12]

In this sense, the problem of testing the confluence model is the same problem that is present in statistical mechanics. The motions of millions of individual particles cannot be recorded and measured simultaneously, and even though the theory of these aggregate motions derives from laws of motion of individual bodies, the outcomes are in aggregate form. The same is true of the confluence model. Even though it has been written for the individual case, it can, thus far, only have been examined on aggregate data.

MASSIVE GAINS IN IQ: THE FLYNN EFFECT

In contrast to the SATs, A-levels, and the Iowa scores time series, all of which had clear periods of decline, Flynn (1987) offered data showing that aggregate test scores have been steadily rising. These data, which came to be known as the Flynn effect, have received a variety of interpretations (Neisser et al., 1996). In general, however, the IQ averages are viewed as reflecting positive and desirable changes at the level of individual scores. That

---

[12] We are careful to say that they explain *trends,* or differences in aggregate scores of children in different positions in the family configuration, not absolute levels of scores.

is, taken individually, "people are becoming smarter" (Azar, 1996, p. 20), and they are becoming smarter at the rate of three to seven IQ points per decade.

There are three features of the Flynn (1987) data to be noted. For the most part, the rising trend was interpolated from a few data points, recorded in different countries, separated by varied intervals, and distributed over several decades. Many of the data points also came from populations of varied age. The U.S. data, for example, combined populations between 2 and 75 years of age. Yet the age of testing, as we pointed out above, is a crucial factor in test scores. It is likely, therefore, that the nonmonotonicity of the SATs, the A-levels, and the Iowa tests found in Figure 20.1 is probably concealed in Flynn's interpolated figures. Flynn (in press) proposed that SATs and IQ measure different proficiencies, but that would not explain why there are declines on tests that are highly related to the IQ measures (e.g., SATs) and why the minima on all the curves happen to occur precisely for 1962 ± 2 birth cohorts, which are the cohorts of the lowest aggregate birth order. Thus, instead of the three-fifths standard deviation increase that would be expected if there was, in fact, a three-point-per-decade rise, Quantitative SATs have yet to equal the high they reached 30 years ago. A-levels were also in a decline for the cohorts born between 1943 and 1953, from 74% to 67% passing the test (Figure 20.1).

There are two ways an average of a frequency distribution can change. When we say that the price of the average house has risen in 1996, this might mean that a comparable house bought in the previous year was less expensive. Or it might simply mean that the proportion of better houses sold in 1996 was greater than in 1995. The same holds for averages of test scores. This average can change over time when each or most of the scores of comparable individuals changed. That is, test takers may be smarter. Or it can change when the distribution of the scores is now different without anyone being more intelligent than students were previously. Of these two quite obvious possibilities, it is the first that is taken as the official or, at least, the attractive interpretation of the Flynn effect. Yet it is more likely that, at least in large part, average scores increased by virtue of changes in the proportion of earlier-born children in the cohort, a hypothesis left unexplored thus far.

Consider the following example that uses realistic figures. In 1962, Iowa recorded 14,964 first and 14,464 second births out of a total of 60,990. Thus, early borns represented 48.25% of all these births. One decade later, there were fewer total births in Iowa, namely 47,234. Of those, 16,892 were first and 12,746 were second births. Thus, the percentage of early births in Iowa in 1972 was considerably larger: 62.75%. It has been shown (Zajonc, 1976) that the proportion of SAT scores over 500 and the proportion of firstborns in the population are highly correlated. For the sake of argument, assume that, on the average, the overall aggregate Iowa IQ for the cohort born in 1962 was 100. Assume also, consistent with a variety of birth order data, that early borns scored, on the average, 105 on the IQ test. This must mean that the IQ of the later-born children was 95.3. What would the Iowa aggregate IQ be in 1972, given the changes in the birth order composition of the cohort but no changes in the test scores of early borns versus later borns? It can be computed as follows: $62.75(105) + 37.2(95.3) = 101.4$ (an increment of 1.4 only by virtue of recomposition of the Iowa cohort birth orders). The early borns were just as "smart" in 1972 as they were in 1962. Nor did the later borns change scores. There were just more early borns in 1972. Therefore, more often than not, the rise and decline in scores are better understood by examining changes in fertility patterns.

COLLECTIVE POTENTIATION OF BIRTH ORDER EFFECTS: A BONUS?

Note that the estimated figure of a 1.4 increase in IQ that was due to changes in the Iowa cohort composition alone (see previous page) is less than the three-point (and certainly less than the seven-point) increase per decade that was predicted by Flynn (1987). The fall and rise of SATs with birth order also exceeds the amount we would expect from static cross-sectional aggregate birth order effects (Zajonc and Bargh, 1980b). For example, the drop in Quantitative SATs seen in Figure 20.1 between birth cohorts in 1950 and in 1962 was one fourth of a standard deviation, whereas the increase in birth order figures was only on the order of half of a birth rank. But if we consult the cross-sectional analysis such as first offered by Belmont and Marolla (1973), a difference of half of a birth rank **[693]** corresponds to a difference of only one tenth of a standard deviation in intellectual test scores. Hence, the actual SAT drop for the above 12-year period was 2.5 times greater than we would expect from the corresponding birth order changes alone.

We might speculate, however, that the hypothetical 1.4-point Iowa rise that was due to recomposition of the cohorts birth order, as well as the large decline in SATs between 1950 and 1962 birth cohorts, could be accompanied by what might be a *collective potentiation* of birth order effects, that is, an increment in intellectual scores that is greater than one could derive from the average birth order changes alone. Consider the following argument. A year's generation of newborns with 20% of first births transfers this proportion to the classrooms and to the entire peer environment. If firstborns constitute 40% of the cohort, the typical classrooms will have a greater proportion of more advanced students who set higher standards and provide challenges to others, resulting in higher overall performance not just of firstborns, but of later borns as well. Thus, a cohort's average test scores may rise first because the cohort comprises a larger proportion of early borns who themselves score higher on intellectual tests, and second because their presence in the cohort recalibrates standards for all members of the cohort who now will develop faster and reach higher levels of proficiency.

Collective potentiation of individually distributed effects is a common phenomenon found in many domains, such as epidemiology, economics, and political behavior. It is manifest in protests, riots, revolutions, and other forms of mass movements (LeBon, 1895; Moscovici, 1985). In marketing, we see it in fashions and fads. The effect of popularity of a consumer item has an effect on individual preferences, but its combined aggregate effects, whereby popularity augments preferences and preferences increase popularity, are a clear bonus (Cooper, 1973). The dynamics of collective potentiation are clearly apparent in the fluctuations of the stock market. People tend to buy and sell a stock not only because they have some information—information of doubtful validity—that it will go up or down, but simply because other people, who are equally ill informed, are buying and selling that stock. In many cases, collective potentiation assumes significant, regional, national, and even international ramifications, leading to the emergence of institutional consequences in the form of organizations, parties, sects, dieting clubs, and doomsday groups.

The collective potentiation of birth order works in a similar fashion. Because the quality of our education depends to a great extent on our peers, a given year's offspring with a higher proportion of early borns has a "bonus": They will benefit from the higher standards of excellence throughout their schooling and advance more rapidly in the more challenging intellectual environment. However, not only students would be affected by a greater proportion of firstborns. Teachers, too, would advance their students more rapidly because they would be confronted with a more favorable distribution of grades than would be the case in a generation of students with few firstborns. The benefits of these collective programs carried out by a community of learners are extensively discussed by Bruner (1996) and by Brown and Campione (1990). Under these circumstances, it is not difficult to imagine that when birth order rises, the average national or state test scores would also rise by a quantity higher than estimated from individual birth order changes alone. The effects would rise not only because there are more firstborns in the cohort, but because all members of the cohort would benefit from collective potentiation provided by the school–peer environment. Here, then, is a case when, given a large proportion of firstborns in the classroom or in the peer group, the whole becomes greater than the sum of its parts.[13] At the same time, the collective potentiation of birth order effects is one of the important reasons why aggregate data are so much more robust than individually distributed birth order effects.

Creative products, be they in the realm of science, technology, sport, art, literature, music, or drama, are not randomly distributed over the globe or over the history of civilization. They emerge in a few highly concentrated times and locations. All but 1 of the 26 National Hockey League head coaches come from Canada. The finest string instruments come from Cremona. Brilliant theatrical productions are concentrated in London's West End and New York's Broadway. The best software comes from Silicon Valley. In these locations and in these times, a few highly talented individuals set high standards for others, invented new techniques, and propagated new approaches. They inspire others who build on examples set for them and, in turn, improve on previous products that challenge the original contributors to seek to achieve even higher standards.

In general, many group differences, especially those in test scores, might well derive from collective potentiation effects. A large proportion of low or high scores in a cohort will have potentiating effects on the entire cohort regardless of their origins. Thus, for example, if stereotype threat (Steele, 1997) depresses scores of individuals by an amount x, then the cohort will suffer by an amount $x + \varepsilon$, where ε is the collective potentiation of individual effects.

HOW LONG HAVE IQ SCORES BEEN RISING?

There is no doubt that the average scores have been rising somewhat. Certainly, a larger percentage of our population reaches a higher level of education today. The standard of living has increased enormously since 1918. And the SES of the average person has risen in most parts of the world, affording educational attainment to ever-increasing

---

[13] The collective potentiation of birth order effects could be readily estimated by comparing the scores of children in a given sibling size and a given birth rank who come from cohorts with a small proportion of firstborns with one with a high proportion of firstborns. Cohorts with a high frequency of firstborns should generally show higher scores for comparable sibling size and birth rank. In fact, the clearest results should be obtained for only children.

[694] segments of the population. The metacognitive environment that greets the 21st century is no doubt richer.

Together with these changes, however, there also have been natality changes that have had substantial impact on family configuration. In most countries, the birth rate has declined substantially during this century—by 50% in most Western countries. The Flynn effect has been illustrated by a linear increase of IQ from 1919 until 1990 (Azar, 1996; Horgan, 1996). Most people tested in 1919 were born about 1900, and those tested in 1990 were born in 1971. It is interesting, therefore, that over the 1900-1971 interval, birth rates dropped in Belgium from 28.9% to 14.4%, in Denmark from 29.7% to 15.2%, in France from 21.3% to 17.1%, in Italy from 33.0% to 16.8%, in the Netherlands from 31.6% to 17.2%, in the United Kingdom from 28.7% to 15.9%, and in the United States from 30.7% to 17.2%. And birth rates are correlated with the average orders of births. Because we saw a strong relationship between birth order and test scores in both the rise and the decline of these scores, there is no doubt that birth order itself contributed to the secular trend in intelligence. This assertion does not contradict the contribution of other factors, such as parental education or SES. But the three-point-per-decade increase cannot be documented as a continuous aggregate trend into the past, not only because we are still waiting for SATs to return to their 1969 record levels, but because we would have to suspect that our ancestors of only one century ago were morons.

SATS AND A-LEVELS INTO THE 21ST CENTURY

On the basis of the close association between birth order and test scores, some predictions of future test trends can be made because most of those who will be taking their SATs and A-levels in 17 or 18 years have been born, and we know their birth orders. On the basis of these data, it appears that if no other factors intervene, and if scores are not again recentered or restandardized, SATs will remain quite stable for the next two decades, whereas A-levels should begin to drop next year, will continue dropping slightly until the year 2000, and then will level off. This prediction, of course, holds only if more rigorous standards are not imposed on the exams in the meantime. But this prediction is made with some confidence, because taking account of birth order trends alone, an accurate prediction was made 20 years ago for SATs, forecasting a decline that would continue until 1980 followed by a rise thereafter (Zajonc, 1976). The confirmation of this prediction over 40 years is seen in Figure 20.1.

FAMILY ENVIRONMENT AND TEST SCORES

Given that test scores have tracked aggregate birth order yearly over several decades, in more than one country, on more than one test, and in populations of different ages, we must conclude, contrary to some recent views (Baumrind, 1993; Neisser et al., 1996; Rowe, 1994), that family environment factors are far from trivial in the analysis of test scores and test score trends. The recent work (Plomin and Daniels, 1987) that showed a correlation among siblings to be as low as that among random individuals seemed to support the view of the negligible effects that families have on their offspring. The work on differences among siblings, however, has not taken account of variations due to birth order. It is entirely possible that siblings are quite different from one another (Plomin and Daniels, 1987) because each grows up in a different environment that changes as new siblings are born and mature (Richardson, 1936).

ALTERNATIVE EXPLANATIONS OF THE LINK BETWEEN TEST TRENDS AND FAMILY TRENDS

Only 30 years ago, SATs went into free fall, as did A-levels 40 years ago. The decline was immediately met with a host of unsupported conjectures. Parents were not spending enough quality time with their offspring; TV was rotting their brains; schools were neglected by local governments; and crime, drugs, smoking, rock music, and, yes, eroding standards were often listed as serious contributing causes of the decline. But when SATs began to rise in the 1980s, President Reagan did not hesitate to take full credit. Each year, if the results of SAT tests or A-levels are down, school officials, governors, presidents, and the entire educational system get blamed for the decline. It is, therefore, not surprising that when the test scores are up, the same officials do not hesitate to take credit. Last year's SATs reached a 20-year high. Last year, also, the highest ever proportion of students in the United Kingdom passed A-levels. Predictably, the two countries reacted in their distinctive ways. The United Kingdom recoiled in shock that "standards were eroding" (Charter, 1996), whereas Americans were self-congratulatory. Experts affirmed with satisfaction that "more rigorous courses ... started to pay off" (Arenson, 1996).

Could we view the changes in the national SATs, the Iowa scores, and the A-levels as mediated by changes in standard of living, SES, expenditures per pupil, and so on?[14] None of these factors, even considering appropriate time lags, show either a minimum for the 1962 cohort, a decline before, or a rise after that year. It is obvious that one could not attribute the three aggregate test trends shown in Figure 20.1 to a changing SES of these populations. It suffices to consider the following example. In 1965, 1980, and 1995 (which correspond to the 1947, 1962, and 1977 birth cohorts), the average national Quantitative SAT scores were 493, 466, and 482, respectively. According to the Educational Testing Service, a 16-point difference in SATs corresponds to a difference of about \$10,000 in 1995 constant dollars of parental income. This would mean that the entire population of SAT takers **[695]** would had to have dropped in their family income by \$19,000 between 1965 and 1980 and then risen again by \$11,000 between 1980 and 1995. In fact, there was no low point for parental income of the national SAT takers in 1962. The correlation between aggregate Quantitative SATs and parental income was in fact −.19.

It is interesting in this respect that, at the individually distributed level, in contrast to birth order effects, SES explains a great deal of variance but is incapable of explaining secular test score trends. In the Broman, Nichols, and Kennedy (1975) study, of all

---

[14] The correlation between intellectual test scores and school expenditures per pupil is equal to .33, but there are glaring outliers. For example, North Dakota has the highest SATs in the nation (515 Verbal and 592 Quantitative), but it spends only \$4,636 per pupil. New York spends more than twice as much (\$9,300), but it ranks 42nd in SATs (419 Verbal and 473 Quantitative). See also footnote 6.

factors examined, the socioeconomic index, of which income was the most important component, contributed the largest proportion of variance to test scores. Most correlations between SES and test scores on individually distributed data fall between .25 and .50 (Jensen, 1969). Yet SES does not figure as a predictor of secular test score trends (see footnote 6). Variations in income are conspicuous and large at the individually distributed level and in comparing economically different regions, say counties of the United States. However, an average income of a country or a state does not change dramatically from year to year. And it is this lesser variability in SES, much restricted in its range, that cannot feature SES as a significant factor in SAT trends.

VERBAL SATS

Verbal SAT trends are somewhat different from Quantitative SATs. Even though, following the 1980 minimum, the Verbal SATs have a flatter curve than their Quantitative counterparts, they still show a partial correlation with birth order that is equal to −.79. The regression analysis reveals that factors other than birth order had additional and stronger influence on the Verbal SAT time series than was the case with Quantitative SATs. The standardized β coefficient for the proportion of White students taking SATs is considerably larger for Verbal SATs than for Quantitative SATs. The explanation of this difference might lie in the dramatic changes that occurred in the demographic composition of the SAT cohorts, especially in those born after 1967 (i.e., taking their SATs after 1985). In 1975, for example, the SAT takers comprised 7.9% African Americans, 1.4% Hispanic Americans, and 1.4% Asian Americans. In 1995, these percentages were 9.7%, 7.4%, and 7.6%, respectively, and were increasing at very different rates.

Important in this respect is the fact that the Asian American population, which has increased quite substantially in the percentage of SAT participants, has typically higher quantitative scores than the White population, but has lower verbal scores. For example, in 1995, Asian Americans scored 538 on the quantitative section, whereas Whites scored 498. But Asian Americans had only 418 on the Verbal SAT, whereas Whites scored 448. Both differences are equivalent to about one third of a standard deviation. In contrast, the African American and the Hispanic American groups showed differences between quantitative and verbal scores that were similar to those of the White students.

If verbal skills are more language dependent than quantitative skills, then quantitative scores would vary less with ethnic background than verbal scores. A quadratic equation is the same in Chinese, Spanish, and English. But a substantial proportion of students from some ethnic groups do not speak English as their first language. They are, therefore, at a disadvantage in terms of lexicon, idioms, local knowledge, associations, analogies, acquaintance with proverbs, popular similes, and all those other particular verbal resources that are required for quick answers to the Verbal SATs. Other changes in the composition of test takers included a drop among male test takers from 50% to 46% and an increase in the percentage of students in their cohorts taking the tests, from 23% to 32%. It is interesting, however, in this respect that the Verbal SAT scores of Whites were 500 in 1941 and dropped to 454 fifty years later, whereas their Quantitative SATs remained the same (Hayes et al., 1996). Clearly, the change in Verbal SATs cannot be explained by the demographic changes in the SAT population alone, and other factors, thus far not identified, must contribute to these variations in trends.

Another recent explanation of the disparity between Quantitative and Verbal trends focuses on schoolbook simplification (Hayes, Wolfer, and Wolfe, 1996). Hayes et al. examined samples of 800 elementary school readers for their lexical difficulty (Zakaluk and Samuels, 1988). Comparing readers published between 1919 and 1945 with those published between 1946 and 1962 and those published between 1963 and 1991, they found that there was a substantial decline in lexical difficulty. Hayes et al. attributed the pattern of verbal scores to lexical simplification of the reading materials. This hypothesis, of course, cannot apply to the Quantitative SATs, to A-levels, or to the Iowa data, all of which increased after 1980. Nor do they agree with the differential birth order effect in the Iowa scores when age of testing is taken into account (Figure 20.2). More important, the data for elementary and high school reading tests in the state of New York showed the same rise as the other time series for the cohort born past 1962 (Zajonc, 1976).

CAUTION

We must not draw premature conclusions about family planning on the basis of the confluence model and the data that it describes. Score differences between siblings and among families of different sizes are indeed small. But what are *small* differences? The 1% of variance explained by birth order found by Grotevant et al. (1977) was considered of trivial significance. Marjoribanks and Walberg's (1975) analysis of the Belmont and Marolla (1973) study that generated a β of $-.078$ for birth order is viewed by some as sufficient to disprove the confluence model (Ernst and Angst, 1983).

When the problem is formulated to describe all individually distributed effects on intellectual scores—that is, the investigation seeks to identify all the sources of variations that produce or are associated with individual differences in intellectual scores—birth order will be **[696]** found as a variable contributing relatively little variance. But, outside of parental education and SES, most other variables have only a negligible influence over test scores. Broman et al. (1975), examining 26,760 four-year-olds, were able to account for no more than 30% of variance altogether, even though they entered 27 variables in their regression analysis that included not only mother's education, but such factors as nystagmus, Apgar score, and neonatal hematocrit. Not surprising, because their participants were only four years old, they did not show consistent birth order effects.

But consider an example from epidemiology. An extensive study of 355,000 men screened in the early 1970s for cholesterol level (U.S. General Accounting Office, 1996) revealed that a difference in deaths from coronary heart disease (CHD) between those with a normal cholesterol level (i.e., 198 mg/dl) and those in the danger zone (226 mg/dl) was only .3%, with the former group having a risk of 4 in 1,000 deaths and the latter group 7 in 1,000. The corresponding survival figures for the two categories of risk were 99.6% and 99.3%, respectively, a difference that strikes us as negligible. And, accordingly, the relationship between cholesterol level and mortality six years after screening had a β of .00006! Yet major policy decisions are carried out with enormous sums of money invested in research, growing pharmaceutical profits, and patients' expenses, all justified by these risk figures. Note in this respect that in comparison with the U.S. General Accounting Office's raw β, the Marjoribanks and Walberg (1975) estimate of $-.078$ for birth order is more than 1,000 times greater than the comparable figure for cholesterol's role in CHD deaths. Of course, each β must be interpreted within its own context. However, it cannot be argued, on the strength of a few selected calculations that the influence of birth order is so weak as to be disregarded. Just as cholesterol is regarded as a risk factor, birth order can also be interpreted as a risk factor, a risk that may deny college entrance or a successful career. Hence, birth order trends characterized by fluctuations as large as 30 SAT points may have more significant consequences than it would at first appear. The implications of the above are especially important when researchers consider that the individually distributed analyses and aggregate-pattern analyses yield such distinctly different results: the first quite weak and the latter quite substantial, but both correct. The argument implies that family configuration factors can be invoked in large-scale and long-term policy planning, but are not very useful in understanding why Joe or Jill has low scores on the SAT. Yet if we know that Joe is a laterborn child and comes from a large family, whereas Jill is firstborn in a family of two, we could specify some differences in their risks of academic failure or success. And, although very small, these risks are more substantial than those associated with cholesterol.

Many factors, such as parental support, enthusiasm for one's teachers, effort, or, on the negative side, a neighborhood environment that derogates academic values, all contribute to a particular student's SATs. These factors are held constant when large aggregate data sets are analyzed. Moreover, test scores are not everything. Birth order and family size may contribute quite differently to psychological well-being and economic attainments than to test scores. For example, children from larger families might be more affiliative, more affectionate, good leaders, less prone to depression, or otherwise healthier. We simply have no data for these outcomes. We do know, however, from the work of Sulloway (1996) that when firstborn and later-born scientists are compared, the former are more likely to represent conservative positions and to cling to established theories whereas later borns are the revolutionaries. Darwin (the fifth of six children) and Copernicus (the last of three children) are classic examples.

TEST SCORE DIFFERENCES AND THEIR COLLECTIVE CONSEQUENCES

The differences associated with birth order when compared at the individually distributed level appear small indeed, as small as 1.5 IQ points per unit of birth order. But they are quite substantial when we inspect the secular trends. For instance, over a period of 12 years, between 1968 and 1980 (i.e., for the 1950 and 1962 birth cohorts), the Quantitative SATs dropped from 494 to 466 (see Figure 20.1). That amounts to one fourth of a standard deviation. The collective consequences of such differences are considerable. A community of 1,000 individuals with a mean IQ of 100 has 22 individuals who score below 70, that is, individuals who have to be cared for by the community, and 22 individuals who score above 130, that is, individuals who are most likely to contribute to the community's prosperity and progress. A one-fourth standard deviation shift in IQ, say a drop to a mean of 96, increases the number of those who have to be cared for to 41 and reduces the number of exceptionally gifted to 12. The changes in the intellectual resources of this community are enormous, even though a difference in IQ score of 4 points for a particular individual is within the range of measurement error.

PROMISE

The resolved paradox of analyses that explain little variance when using individually distributed data versus aggregate analyses that explain almost all variance does not apply uniquely to the birth order puzzle alone. It can be readily transferred to a variety of social psychological problems. Most commonly, scholars working at the individual level, particularly in the area of personality and developmental psychology, tend to ignore collective and cohort effects, and those working at the collective level tend to ignore the individual processes. This has certainly been the case with birth order effects. The separation of these approaches is not surprising given that some fields (e.g., anthropology, demography, economics, sociology, and political science) specialize in phenomena that take place mainly at the aggregate level, whereas psychology is preoccupied with individual phenomena. One branch [697] of psychology is ideally suited to bridge the individual collective chasm: social psychology. Ventures of this type, however, have been extremely rare, even in social psychology. The emergence of interdisciplinary initiatives between aggregate-focus and distributive-focus fields, such as economic psychology, cognitive anthropology, cultural psychology, and so on, is a promising reaction that will view phenomena from both an aggregate and a distributive perspective.

Although the SATs might be stable and may not drop, they are at miserably low levels. They were in the 490s for the cohort born in the mid-1940s. For the cohort born in 1962, the SATs were at their all-time low. Today they are at about 460 for the combined verbal and quantitative sections of the test. We cannot trust the Flynn effect to bail us out, given that extrapolation from the observed trends proves to be dangerous. Yet the scores can be higher. We have more and better means at our disposal now than at any other time in history.

Unlike the resource depletion model, which might advise reducing family size or increasing resources per family, the confluence model has some direct practical implications. We can change the scholastic experience of our children. One of the factors contributing to intellectual development is the tutorial function of the older children. Being a teacher or a tutor can substantially augment and accelerate mental growth. There are data showing that the teacher gains more than the learner in the process of teaching (Bargh and Schul, 1980; Kagan, 1992; McMahon and Goatley, 1995; Wagner, 1982; Whitman, 1988). Peer teaching can be easily implemented in our elementary and middle schools. For example, half of a class could be instructed about decimals. The other half could learn about the lowest common denominator. Then, after each has acquired some minimal understanding, they would teach each other. Impressive improvements in a variety of skills and domains have been achieved through such reciprocal teaching procedures (Bruce and Chan, 1991; Kelly, Moore, and Tuck, 1994; Moore, 1988). The key to the improvement is that the students are imbedded in a *metacognitive environment*—an environment in which items of knowledge are distributed over the community of learners (Bruner, 1996) who know who might know what and how well (Brown and Campione, 1990). The sharing of such knowledge and skills takes effect more rapidly than in a classroom conducted by a single teacher who is the sole source of knowledge and expertise.

The trends and changes in scores that we have analyzed here are a clear reflection of family patterns, confirming the important role of environmental factors and, especially, family and peer influences, which have been repeatedly downsized and outsourced in favor of genetic hypotheses. These diverse data support derivations from the confluence model—data that cannot be explained by alternative theories. Contrary to the prevailing doubts in its explanatory value, birth order is being rapidly reinstated as a salient factor in psychology.

REFERENCES

Arenson, K.W. (1996, August 23). Students continue to improve, College Board says. *The New York Times*, p. Al.

Azar, B. (1996, June). People are becoming smarter—Why? *The APA Monitor*, p. 20.

Bargh, J.A., and Schul, Y. (1980). On the cognitive benefit of teaching. *Journal of Educational Psychology*, **72**, 593–604.

Baumrind, D. (1993). The average expectable environment is not good enough: A response to Scarr. *Child Development*, **64**, 1299–1317.

Becker, G.S., and Tomes, N. (1976). Child endowments and the quantity and quality of children. *Journal of Political Economy*, **84**, S143–S162.

Belmont, L., and Marolla, F.A. (1973, December 14). Birth order, family size, and intelligence. *Science*, **182**, 1096–1101.

Blake, J. (1989). *Family size and achievement.* Berkeley: University of California Press.

Brackbill, Y., and Nichols, P.L. (1982). A test of the confluence model of intellectual development. *Developmental Psychology*, **18**, 192–198.

Breland, H.M. (1974). Birth order, family configuration, and verbal achievement. *Child Development*, **36**, 1011–1019.

Broman, S.H., Nichols, P.L., and Kennedy, W.A. (1975). *Preschool IQ: Prenatal and early developmental correlates.* Hillsdale, NJ: Erlbaum.

Brown, A.L., and Campione, J.C. (1990). Communities of learning and thinking: Or a context by any other name. *Contributions to Human Development*, **21**, 108–126.

Bruce. M.E., and Chan, L.K. (1991). Reciprocal teaching and transenvironmental programming: A program to facilitate the reading comprehension of students with reading difficulties. *Remedial and Special Education*, **12**, 44–54.

Bruner, J.S. (1996). *The culture of education.* Cambridge, MA: Harvard University Press.

Carlsmith, L. (1964). Effect of early father absence on scholastic aptitude. *Harvard Educational Review*, **34**, 3–21.

Charter, D. (1996, August 5). A-level record sparks standards row. *The London Times*, p. 1.

Cooper, L.G. (1973). A multivariate investigation of preferences. *Multivariate Behavioral Research*, **8**, 253–272.

Davis, D., Cahan, S., and Bashi, J. (1977). Birth order and intellectual development: The confluence model in the light of cross-cultural evidence. *Science*, **196**, 1470–1472.

Epstein, S. (1986). Does aggregation produce spuriously high estimates of behavior consistency? *Journal of Personality and Social Psychology*, **50**, 1199–1210.

Epstein, S. (1990). Comment on the effects of aggregation across and within occasions on consistency, specificity, and reliability. *Methodika*, **4**, 95–100.

Ernst, C., and Angst, J. (1983). *Birth order: Its influence on personality.* Berlin, Germany: Springer-Verlag.

Eysenck, H.J. (1939). The validity of judgments as a function of the number of judges. *Journal of Experimental Psychology*, **25**, 650–654.

Flynn, J.R. (1987). Massive IQ gains in 14 nations: What IQ tests really measure. *Psychological Bulletin,* **101,** 171–191.

Flynn, J.R. (in press). Intelligence on the rise? Secular changes in IQ and related measures. In U. Neisser (Ed.), *The rising curve.* Washington, DC: American Psychological Association.

Galbraith, R.C. (1982). Sibling spacing and intellectual development: A closer look at the confluence model. *Developmental Psychology,* **18,** 181–191.

Gordon, K.H. (1924). Group judgments in the field of lifted weights. *Journal of Experimental Psychology,* **3,** 398–400.

Gottfried, A.W. (Ed.). (1984). *Home environment and early cognitive development: Longitudinal research.* New York: Academic Press.

Grotevant, H.D., Scarr, S., and Weinberg, R.A. (1977). Intellectual development in family constellations with adopted and natural children: A test of Zajonc and Markus model. *Child Development,* **48,** 1699–1703.

Hart, B., and Risley, T.R. (1995). *Meaningful differences in the everyday experience of young American children.* Baltimore: P. H. Brookes.

Hauser, R.M., and Sewell, W.H. (1983). Birth order and education attainment **[698]** in full sibships (Working Paper No. 83-31). Madison: University of Wisconsin, Center for Demography and Ecology.

Hayes, D.P., Wolfer, L.T., and Wolfe, M.F. (1996). Schoolbook simplification and its relation to the decline in SAT—Verbal scores. *American Educational Research Journal,* **33,** 489–508.

Horgan, J. (1996, November). Get smart, take a test: A long-term rise in IQ scores baffles intelligence experts. *Scientific American,* pp. 12–24.

Huttenlocher, J., Haight, W., Bryk, A., and Seltzer, M. (1991). Early vocabulary growth: Relation to language input and gender. *Developmental Psychology,* **27,** 236–248.

Institut National d'Études Démographiques. (1973). *Enquête nationale sur le niveau intellectuel des enfants d'âge scolaire* [National survey of the intellectual level of school-age children]. Paris: Author.

Jensen, A.R. (1969). How much can we boost IQ and scholastic achievement? *Harvard Educational Review,* **39,** 1–123.

Kagan, S. (1992). *Cooperative learning.* San Juan Capistrano, CA: Resources for Teacher.

Kelly, M., Moore, D.W., and Tuck, B.F. (1994). Reciprocal teaching in a regular primary school classroom. *Journal of Educational Research,* **88,** 53–61.

Kessler, D. (1991). Birth order, family size, and achievement: Family structure and wage determination. *Journal of Labor Economics,* **9,** 413–426.

LeBon, G. (1895). *Psychologie des foules* [Psychology of crowds]. Paris: Olean.

Lindert, P.H. (1977). Sibling position and achievement. *Journal of Human Resources,* **12,** 198–219.

Marjoribanks, K., and Walberg, H.J. (1975). Birth order, family size, social class, and intelligence. *Social Biology,* **22,** 261–268.

McMahon, S.I., and Goatley, V.J. (1995). Fifth graders helping peers discuss texts in student-led groups. *Journal of Educational Research,* **59,** 23–34.

Mischel, W. (1968). *Personality and assessment.* New York: Wiley.

Moore, P.J. (1988). Reciprocal teaching and reading comprehension: A review. *Journal of Research in Reading,* **11,** 3–14.

Moscovici, S. (1985). *L'âge des foules.* Paris: Maison des Sciences de l'Homme.

Murnane, R.J., Maynard, R.A., and Ohls, J.C. (1981). Home resources and children's achievement. *Review of Economics and Statistics,* **63,** 369–377.

Neisser, U., Boodoo, G., Bouchard, T.J., Jr., Boykin, A.W., Brody, N., Ceci, S.J., Halpern, D.F., Loehlin, J.C., Perloff, R., Sternberg, R.J., and Urbina, S. (1996). Intelligence: Knowns and unknowns. *American Psychologist,* **51,** 77–101.

Office of Population Censuses and Surveys. (1987). *Birth statistics: Historical series of statistics from registrations of births in England and Wales, 1837–1983.* London: Her Majesty's Stationery Office.

Olneck, M.R., and Bills, D.B. (1979). Family configuration and achievement: Effects of birth order and family size in a sample of brothers. *Social Psychology Quarterly,* **2,** 135–148.

Plomin, R., and Daniels, D. (1987). Why are children in the same family so different from one another? *Behavioral and Brain Sciences,* **10,** 1–60.

Record, R.G., McKeown, T., and Edwards, J.H. (1970). The relation of measured intelligence to birth order and maternal age. *Annals of Human Genetics,* **34,** 61–69.

Retherford, R.D., and Sewell, W.H. (1991). Birth order and intelligence: Further tests of the confluence model. *American Sociological Review,* **56,** 141–158.

Richardson, S.K. (1936). The correlation of intelligence quotients of siblings at the same chronological age levels. *Journal of Juvenile Research,* **20,** 186–197.

Ross, L., and Nisbett, R.E. (1991). *The person and the situation: Perspectives of social psychology.* New York: McGraw-Hill.

Rowe, D.C. (1994). *The limits of family influence: Genes, experience, and behavior.* New York: Guilford Press.

Schooler, C. (1972) Birth order effects: Not here not now! *Psychological Bulletin,* **78,** 161–175.

Steele, C.M. (1997). A threat in the air: How stereotypes shape the intellectual identity and performance. *American Psychologist,* **52,** 613–629.

Steelman, L.C., and Mercy, J.A. (1980). Unconfounding the confluence model: A test of sibship size and birth order effects on intelligence. *American Sociological Review,* **45,** 571–582.

Sulloway, F. (1996). *Born to rebel.* Westminster, MD: Random House.

Svanum, S., and Bringle, R.G. (1980). Evaluation of confluence model variables on IQ and achievement test scores in a sample of 6- to 11-year-old children. *Journal of Educational Psychology,* **72,** 427–436.

Tabah, L., and Sutter, J. (1954). Le niveau intellectuel des enfants d'une même decrease famille [Intellectual level of children of the same family]. In *Le niveau intellectuel des enfants d'âge scolaire.* Paris: Presses Universitaires de France.

Taubman, P., and Behrman, J.R. (1986). Effects of number and position of siblings on child and adult outcomes. *Social Biology,* **33,** 22–34.

U.S. Bureau of the Census. (1951–1991). *Natality report.* Washington, DC: U.S. Government Printing Office.

U.S. General Accounting Office. (1996). *Cholesterol treatment: A review of clinical trials evidence.* Washington, DC: U.S. Government Printing Office.

Wagner, L. (1982). *Peer teaching.* Westport, CT: Greenwood Press.

Whitman, N.A. (1988). *Peer teaching.* College Station, TX: Association for the Study of Higher Education.

Zajonc, R.B. (1962). A note on group judgments and group size. *Human Relations,* **15,** 177–180.

Zajonc, R.B. (1976, April 16). Family configuration and intelligence. *Science,* **192,** 227–236.

Zajonc, R.B. (1983). Validating the confluence model. *Psychological Bulletin,* **93,** 457–480.

Zajonc, R.B. (1996, June). *Intellectual environment and intellectual performance.* Paper presented at the convention of the American Psychological Society, San Francisco.

Zajonc, R.B., and Bargh, J. (1980a). Birth order, family size, and decline of SAT scores. *American Psychologist,* **35,** 662–668.

Zajonc, R.B., and Bargh, J. (1980b). The confluence model: Parameter estimation in six divergent data sets on family factors and intelligence. *Intelligence,* **4,** 349–361.

Zajonc, R.B., Markus, G.B., Berbaum, M.L., Bargh, J.A., and Moreland, R.L. (1991). One justified criticism plus three flawed analyses equals two unwarranted conclusions: A reply to Retherford and Sewell. *American Sociological Review,* **56,** 159–165.

Zajonc, R.B., Markus, H., and Markus, G.B. (1979). The birth order puzzle. *Journal of Personality and Social Psychology,* **37,** 1325–1341.

Zakaluk, B., and Samuels, S.J. (1988). *Readability: Its past, present and future.* Newark, DE: International Reading Association. **[699]**

We are grateful to Hazel Markus for her valuable comments and to Kim Colwell for her help in the analysis of the data.

Chapter 21

The Zoomorphism of
Human Collective Violence

R.B. Zajonc
Stanford University

Sociobiology must be counted as one of the *big* ideas of our times. New understanding of some fundamental aspects of social behavior, such as cooperation, altruism, or dominance, came from the premises of sociobiology. These complex social phenomena are explained by invoking the concept of inclusive fitness, a force of nature that promotes the perpetuation of our genes—our own and that of our own species. Broad and profound scientific, philosophical, and pragmatic consequences were drawn from sociobiology. Its notions were absorbed not only by physiologists, geneticists, and molecular biologists but also by anthropologists, historians, political scientists, and, of course, psychologists. In fact, the fields of evolutionary psychology and evolutionary social psychology were spawned by the intellectual ferment created by the principles of inclusive fitness and reproductive success.

Based on these ideas, a number of bold implications deriving from the concepts of sociobiology and evolutionary psychology have been drawn in the scholarly domain—implications that were very rapidly echoed in the popular press and other media, most often in a simplified and vulgarized form. Thus, the Columbine High School shooting was explained in *Newsweek* by the genetically fixed urge to eliminate competitors for offspring, citing as culprit the cingulate gyrus, a brain structure that is apparently active in juvenile aggression (Begley, 1999). And in a recent book, Thornhill and Palmer (2000) treat rape as a *natural* phenomenon, merely an expression of the innate tendency to disperse the rapists' genes. Even genocide has become subject to sociobiological explanation. This chapter questions the widespread, and often uncritical, applications of sociobiological principles to the explanation of collective violence, which in the twentieth century alone produced by some estimates, over 100 million civilian deaths. It argues that the enthusiasm is at best premature and the evidence scant. **[222]***

---

* Bracketed bold numbers refer to original page numbers. Page numbers indicate where the original page ended.

Wrangham and Peterson (1996) draw a direct parallel between aggression in the chimpanzee and genocide, in particular, the Burundi genocide. These authors address the problem of aggression among males, which, of course, is virtually all of human aggression, from the following perspective:

> Aggression among males within a chimpanzee community happens most obviously at "election time" … when suddenly the old hierarchy is being challenged. Such times occur particularly when a young, low-ranking male whose physical and political power is growing develops a disrespectful attitude toward established authority, (p. 186)

The authors then go on to claim that the social dynamics in the chimpanzee community promise to help us understand what happened in Burundi 30 years ago:

> Burundi was not at peace…. In one month in 1972, Tutsi killed nearly every Hutu leader and any other Hutu who appeared literate…. The June elections produced Burundi's first Hutu president…. Melchior Ndadaye. But … an army tank rammed a hole in the white stucco wall of the presidential palace and radical Tutsi soldiers stabbed President Ndadaye to death…. They also assassinated a half dozen high officials. (p. 2)

"Elections" in both cases! The parallel seems irresistible. We read the following account, offered as a corresponding specimen of chimpanzee violence:

> On January 7, 1974, in Gombe National Park, Tanzania, a group of eight chimpanzees traveled purposefully … toward the border of their range…. Godi [an ordinary male] ate peacefully, alone in a tree…. By the time he saw the eight intruders they were already at his tree. Humphrey got to him first. Godi toppled at once. The other adult males pummeled his shoulder blades and back. After ten minutes Humphrey let go. The others stopped hitting him. (pp. 5–6)

In contrast to the chimpanzee raids at Gombe, which resemble what we observe during a high school or middle school recess, I cite a report by Iris Chang (1997) of what has become known as the Rape of Nanking. In 1931, the Japanese army occupied Manchuria. In 1937, Beijing, Tiensin, and Shanghai were taken. On December 13, 1937, Japanese troops entered Nanking (now Nanjing), at that time capital of Nationalist China. According to Iris Chang, the Japanese troops [223]

> began an orgy of cruelty seldom if ever matched in world history. Tens of thousands of young men were … mowed down by machine guns, used for bayonet practice, or soaked with gasoline and burned alive. For months the streets of the city were heaped with corpses…. Chinese men were used for decapitation contests. An estimated 20,000 to 80,000 Chinese women were raped….
>
> Not only did live burials, castration, carving of organs, and the roasting of people become routine, but more diabolical tortures were practiced, such

as hanging people by their tongues on iron hooks or burying people to their waists and watching them get torn apart by German shepherds, (p. 6)

One estimate counts as many as 300,000 noncombatants killed by the Japanese in just a few weeks. This figure is greater than four years of World War II military casualties of Great Britain (61,000), France (108,000), and Belgium (101,000) put together. Is it simply stretching the imagination to equate a chimpanzee beating with a massacre of 300,000 innocent civilians?

Sociobiological accounts of behavior have become much more strident, fueled by the recent discovery that we share as much as 98.5% of DNA with the chimpanzee (Gibbons, 1998). At the biological level, therefore, we humans are simply another ape. According to the views of the sociobiologists Dawkins (1989), Wilson (1975), and their followers (Barash, 1982) and predecessors (Morris, 1967), human social phenomena, such as cooperation and competition, aggression and affiliation, cruelty and kindness, monogamy and polygamy, heterosexuality and homosexuality, conformity and deviance, dominance and submission, and morality and decadence are all hardwired and can be explained by an appeal to the revised theory of evolution. There is at the same time a widening conviction that brain structures controlling these social processes will soon be identified.

The argument is that evolution worked for millions of years, whereas civilization had only a few thousand to overcome its influences (Morris, 1967). Hence, the analysis of animal behavior should give us clues, if not answers, to our own behavioral tendencies. The prototypical evolutionary position on aggression, which in sociobiology readily generalizes to phenomena of aggression among humans, is best represented by the Nobel laureate Konrad Lorenz (1966). It holds that these millions of years have endowed humans with the instinct (or whatever nativist term one wishes to substitute) for aggression, as they have endowed other species. Normally aggression remains dormant. Occasionally, however, under some specifiable circumstances, the inhibitions break down, and it is then that our "true" nature—our bestiality—emerges. We then descend to the level of our animal ancestors. We owe this view to Gustave LeBon (1995): **[224]**

> By the mere fact that he forms part of an organized crowd, a man
> descends several rungs in the ladder of civilization. Isolated he may be a
> cultivated individual; in a crowd, he is a barbarian—that is, a creature act-
> ing by instinct.
>   Impulsiveness, irritability, incapacity to reason, the absence of judg-
> ment.... the exaggeration of the sentiments, ... which are almost always
> observed in beings belonging to inferior forms of evolution. (pp. 52, 55–56)

Lorenz offered the concept of the *innate releasing mechanism,* a sort of hydraulic model (shown in Fig. 21.1), to represent aggression, which some could not resist calling the "flush toilet model." Two opposing forces describe the aggression process: the accumulation of aggression energy that seeks expression represented in the figure by the reservoir (ER) and inhibitions of natural and cultural origin represented by the restraining valve. The spring, which represents fears of punishment or guilt, makes the valve press against the **[225]** reservoir opening. When appropriate stimulus conditions

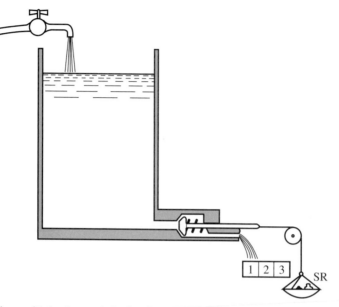

Figure 21.1   Lorenz's hydraulic model.

SOURCE: Reprinted by permission from Karl Lorenz, *The Foundations of Ethology*, p. 81. Translated by K.Z. Lorenz and R.W. Kickert. Copyright © 1981 by Springer.

arise, depending on their intensity (shown in kilogram weights), the valve is pulled back against the spring, and aggression (SR) is released.[1]

Note that the model features aggression as a compelling urge that accumulates constantly, putting an ever-increasing pressure on the inhibitory valve. Opposed to the building up of aggressive energy, the spring of restraints seems weak and inconsequential. One has the impression that the release of the aggressive urge is a matter of minimal force. And, in fact, the theory holds that the more intense, salient, and conspicuous the instigating stimulus (represented in the model by the counterweights), the more rapid and more complete is the release of the aggressive tendencies. This disinhibition model of aggression has been the pervasive, unquestioned view of aggression for centuries (Ardrey, 1961; Lorenz, 1966; Moyer, 1969; Storr, 1968). It is firmly imprinted on the intellectual discourse not only in science but also in the humanities. It is readily found in the literature. The Nobel laureate novelist Ivo Andric, in his epic about the

---

[1] Lorenz, who died in 1989, wrote the earliest version of the innate releasing mechanism (*angeborener Auslösemechanismus*) theory between 1944 and 1948, when he was a prisoner of war in Yerevan, Armenia. The material was edited by his daughter, Agnes von Cranach, and published in German in 1978 (Lorenz, 1978) and in English in 1981 (Lorenz, 1981). The exact statement reads as follows; "This phenomenon of *lowering of the threshold of releasing stimuli in proportion to the time elapsed since the last discharge of a motor pattern suggests the existence of some form of response-specific arousal energy. This would have to be continuously produced by the organism but used up by performance of the motor pattern specific to that response*" (Lorenz, 1981, p. 283 italics in the original). The 1981 publication features a modified version of the "old psycho-hydraulic" model, which he acknowledged was "much ridiculed" (p. 180). The new model, however, retains all the energy hydraulics that the old model required. It differs only in the variety of sources for that energy.

Ottoman history in the Balkans (1959), affirms unambiguously the disinhibition theory of aggression in his description of the outbreak of World War I:

> That wild beast, which lives in man and does not dare to show itself until the barriers of law and custom have been removed, was now set free. The signal was given, the barriers were down. As so often happens in the history of man, permission was tacitly granted for acts of violence and plunder, even for murder.... It is true that there had always been concealed enmities and jealousies and religious intolerance, coarseness and cruelty, but there had also been courage and fellowship and a feeling for measure of order, which restrained all these instincts. (pp. 282–283)

This theory of human violence is part of our common understanding, transmitted from one generation to the next in increasingly simplified form. We are exposed to it over and over again. It is uncontested, and it looms "true," "obvious," and "natural." The unprecedented rush to the fMRI laboratory is reminiscent of the early 1999 stock market rush to the technology shares that Allan Greenspan termed "irrational exuberance." Thus, for example, Hammer and Copeland (1998) write: "The emerging science of molecular biology has made startling discoveries that show beyond a doubt that genes are the single most important factor that distinguishes one person from another. We come in large part ready-made from the factory. We accept that we *look* like our parents and other blood relatives. We have a harder time with the idea that we *act* like them" (p. 11). Yet, more recently, voices of constraint have been heard. Paul Ehrlich (2000) firmly argued that genetic identity "does not necessarily produce identical natures, even when combined with substantially **[226]** identical environments" (p. 10), and that variation in behavior goes well beyond the mathematical limits of genetic variation (p. 4).

More specifically, there are good reasons why the current theory of aggression, that is merely a superficial modification of the original version, cannot begin to explain the 100 million casualties inflicted on unarmed civilians in the twentieth century alone.

1. Given the theory is true that human aggression is nothing but animal aggression, released when inhibitions are removed, we would expect the behavioral form of our own massacres to resemble those of lower animals. But the level of unspeakable atrocity seen in human massacres surpasses any animal aggression by many orders of magnitude, and its forms of brutality find no counterpart among any conspecific violence among the lower animals, even those closest to us.

2. Some massacres contradict the very principles of kin selection and reproductive success. Other cultural developments, for instance, contraception, also contradict the principle of reproductive success.

3. No animal kills on principle.

INNATE RELEASERS AND FIXED ACTION PATTERNS

Not only is the zoomorphic generalization a wild exaggeration, but the sociobiological theory of aggression is unsupported by empirical data, and in many instances it is contradicted by them. The sociobiology that formerly was practiced under the label of "ethology" held that the aggressive responses are evoked only if the individual confronts an appropriate stimulus in the environment, the "innate releaser." Thus the red cape is an innate releaser for a bull, for example, that elicits charging behavior. The innate releaser theory was challenged on a number of grounds, although its main tenets remain today intact. The innate releaser theory suffered because it featured a most inefficient dynamic system. It had to assume a continuous accumulation of energy for the aggressive response. The response had to be assumed sitting in readiness to be released when the restraining "valve" was removed. At the same time, the system required an equal amount of energy for the inhibition of the release, a most wasteful arrangement. Eventually, the term *innate releaser* was replaced by the *fixed action pattern* (Hinde, 1974), changing the original formulation so as not to require a continuous energy deployment, half for the incipient aggressive response and the other half for its restraint. But the notion that fixed action patterns are recruited by appropriate specific stimuli remained intact.

These ideas are perpetuated in textbooks, which ignore the fact that they are false. Note that both innate releaser and fixed action pattern theories are [227] very cumbersome in requiring very constraining assumptions. First, the organism must be capable of fairly precise identification of just the right eliciting stimuli. Second, the stimuli releasing the behavior are limited to a very specific type. For example, the schematic shape in Figure 21.2 is said to evoke flight behavior in the young gosling when moving overhead in one direction but not in the opposite direction because, ostensibly, the short-neck direction resembles a hawk, whereas the long-neck direction resembles a goose. Third, the theory holds that the more energy has accumulated to release the response, the less stimulus intensity is required for its release. Fourth, because the behavioral tendency is instinctive, it should not extinguish, even in the presence of negative reinforcement. Fifth, it should not habituate spontaneously. Sixth, it is a tendency that does not need to be learned, for it is given at birth. All of these presuppositions were contradicted by experimental data first reported by Hirsch, Lindley, and Tolman (1955) and confirmed in many subsequent experimental studies. Yet the original claim is cited frequently, whereas the contradictions are known by only a handful of scholars.

Figure 21.2   Schematic shape said to evoke flight behavior in goslings.

The classical documentation of the innate releaser (and fixed action pattern) theory is due to Tinbergen, with whom Lorenz shared the Nobel Prize. Tinbergen (1952) quite explicitly offered the releaser theory as explaining human behavior:

> To get light on the behavior of man, particularly his innate drives and conflicts, it is often helpful to study the elements of behavior in a simple animal. Here is a little fish that exhibits a complicated pattern of activities, all dependent on simple stimuli and drives. We have studied and analyzed its behavior by a large number of experiments, and have learned a good deal about why the [228] stickleback behaves as it does.... Let us begin with the stimulus that causes one stickleback to attack another. Early in our work we noticed that a male patrolling its territory would attack a red-colored intruder much more aggressively than a fish of some other color. Even a red mail van passing our windows at a distance of 1200 yards could make the males in the tank charge its glass side in that direction, (p. 23)

The stickleback lives in the shallow waters of muddy streams. In early spring the male leaves its school and seeks to stake out a territory. He does so by digging a nest in the form of a mound in the bottom of the stream, on which he piles up algae and coats it with a sticky secretion from his kidneys. He then bores a tunnel in the mound and is ready to mate. As soon as the nest is ready, he changes the color of his belly from inconspicuous gray to pink and then to brilliant scarlet. His back and eyes turn turquoise. Having achieved the conspicuous appearance, he attracts gravid females by zigzagging around them and guiding them to the nest. The gravid females are easy to spot, for they carry 50 to 100 large eggs. Once in the nest, the female lays eggs, with the male prodding her tail in a series of rhythmic thrusts. Once the eggs are laid, the male fertilizes them. When the first female leaves the nest, the male starts looking for another gravid female. Three to five gravid females are thus seduced into the male's nest. He then loses interest in females and also loses his bright coloring. Yet he guards the nest and fans the water to supply more oxygen to the hatching eggs. In the course of guarding his nest, he attacks other conspecifics, both males and females.

The sticklebacks' coloring is treated by Tinbergen as an innate releaser, and the aggression among sticklebacks is regarded as a reproductive fixed action pattern, for its function is to space out individuals so as to exploit the habitat most efficiently. Because the story has been perpetuated in psychology and biology textbooks and in the popular science press, few know that subsequent experimentation failed to confirm the theory. For instance, in thorough experiments by Peeke and his colleagues (Peeke, 1969; Peeke, Wyers, and Herz, 1969), models of fish that were colored totally red did not invite any more aggression than those that were colored less than 10%. In fact, no difference was found between colored models and models without any coloring at all. Ten out of 37 subjects did not display any aggressive responses. Moreover, when aggressive responses did occur, there was rapid habitation—a reaction that one would not expect from instinctive behavior. But not only models of fish, but a live stickleback as well, elicited responses that habituated very quickly.

The most damaging research, however, was carried out in France by Berthe Muckensturm (1965, 1969), and because it was published in a French journal, [229] it is largely unknown in the United States. Muckensturm used models colored not only red but also violet, gray, and yellow. Her results are striking because she tested her animals twice in individual trials and obtained consistent results over the repeated tests. Vast individual differences characterized the sticklebacks observed. The number of attacks at the models ranged from 1 to 141, similar over the repeated tests. We would not expect such extensive variability of instinctive behavior. The models colored red were not the most frequent targets. On the second test, 7 out of 15 did not attack the red target at all, and only 2 out of 15 fish attacked the red target most frequently. The most frequently attacked target, however, was the violet one. And, quite important, when the aquarium was illuminated by light that suppressed color, aggression did not stop.

Muckensturm noted that the males' coloring was reflective of the dominance structure—the leader being most brilliant. She also noted that the coloring changes only *after* the male acquires a nest. Before he acquires a nest, he must physically compete for his territory, and he does so by engaging in considerable combative behavior. Only *after* succeeding does he change his coloring, and then aggression wanes, both in the target and in his competitors. Since Tinbergen considered stickleback coloring and the aggression it elicited to be serving optimal distribution of the habitat's resources for healthy population growth, we would expect the coloring to appear *before,* not *after,* the stickleback has successfully set up a nest. Yet Muckensturm observed a great number of attacks before there was any coloring at all. In fact, it appeared that the coloring was the outcome of aggression rather than its cause or antecedent. The leader, which was the most brilliant fish, however, was seldom attacked. The main generalization that could be made from Muckensturm's data was that the sticklebacks attacked the unfamiliar targets. There is no yellow or violet in the sticklebacks' streams; these were the models most often attacked.

PRINCIPLES OF KIN SELECTION AND
INCLUSIVE FITNESS CONTRADICTED

According to the principles of inclusive fitness and kin selection, we are more likely to risk our lives trying to save our son or daughter than to save a cousin. Clearly, if we are interested in the propagation of our genes, the last thing we want to do is to kill our own. But we do kill our own. Large numbers of close relatives and neighbors were denounced to the Gestapo between 1933 and 1945. In Saarbrücken, a woman reported her own husband to the Gestapo for listening to the "enemy radio." In the former Yugoslavia, numerous instances of murder of members of one's own family were reported. And the following horrible account was published by Wole Soyinka (1998), the Nigerian dissident: [230]

> A Hutu, a leading citizen of a small Rwandan town, … felt personally indicted [when] an official accused the citizenry of being lax in the task of "bush clearing"—one of the many euphemisms for the task of eliminating the Tutsi. A day after his departure, the notable called a meeting of the villagers.… He began his address by revealing that, having taken to heart the rebuke …, he had decided to set an example, and thus slaughtered his Tutsi wife.

But that was only the first step.... they must eliminate every vestige of
Tutsi blood ... And in one stroke of his machete, he lopped off the head of
his oldest son. One by one, his three sons were led out of the hut ... and
slaughtered. (p. 11)

The principle that by force of nature all species seek to perpetuate their genes
makes aggression against virtual competitors a plausible derivation—a derivation also
attractive to economists who assume behavior to be dominated by self-interest. But
when applied to human aggression, where victims are counted in six- and seven-digit
numbers, the concept of a "selfish" gene is not compelling, theoretically or empirically.
We find in nature in profusion not only parasitic, antagonistic, and exploitative relations
among and within species but also symbiotic. Given some specifiable constraints, par-
asitism *and* symbiosis follow equally from the premise of inclusive fitness. In fact, it
was the difficulty that standard evolutionary theory had in explaining altruistic and
communal behavior that brought about the theory of inclusive fitness (Hamilton, 1964).
And the political theorist Francis Fukuyama (1992), rejecting the notion of the "selfish
gene," does not hesitate to argue for affiliation, cohesion, and communal order as the
basic forces of human nature.

RAPE IN SERVICE OF INCLUSIVE FITNESS

Another false application of the principle of inclusive fitness is a recent attempt by
Thornhill and Palmer (2000) to feature rape as a natural phenomenon whereby the
male simply increases the likelihood that his genes will be more extensively seeded.
Their work has been widely cited in the popular media. The intent of rape, they say, is
not just lust. Since the victims are mostly females of childbearing age, the main goal
of rape is to impregnate. What Thornhill and Palmer do not acknowledge, however, is
that the rapist very seldom stays around for 9 months to give protection to his offspring
and to make sure that it thrives. In fact, in one out of five cases there is quite severe
violence to the victim. Such violence does nothing but harm the carrier of the rapist's
genes and thus, as Barbara Ehrenreich (2000) aptly said, "It's a pretty dumb Darwinian
specimen who can't plant his seed without breaking the 'vessel' in the process" (p. 88).
And a substantial proportion of rape victims were prepubescent children, some less
than 8 years old. [231]

An example of rape that could not possibly serve the reproductive ambition of its
perpetrator is one that accompanied other atrocities when the Soviet army entered
Germany in 1945. The following, of which there are many parallels, is an eyewitness
testimony of one Hermann Sommer:

The victims had been beaten and stabbed.... A large number of bodies had
... the genitals stabbed through and were disemboweled.... A corporal
told me of a church where a girl and two soldiers had been found. The girl
had been actually crucified on the altar cross, the two soldiers strung up
on either side.... [T]he women were completely naked, raped and then
killed ... with stab wounds or rifle butt blows to the head. (De Zayas,
1993, pp. 40–41)

Similarly the Japanese soldiers entering Nanking in 1937 engaged in rape that was far from having a reproductive potential. Chang (1997) writes "Many soldiers went beyond rape to disembowel women, slice off their breasts, nail them alive to walls. Fathers were forced to rape their daughters and sons their mothers, as other family members watched" (p 6).

Of course, the significance of biological factors cannot be denied. We do know quite well that the hypothalamus is involved in suppression of violence, or that testosterone levels are important. But there is a gaping derivational chasm between these facts and the Rape of Nanking. During the last decade, neuroscience has celebrated many discoveries of brain regions that are associated with fairly specific functions. But we should not be prompted by these facts to apply this new knowledge to the massacre in Littleton, as was unabashedly done in a recent issue of *Newsweek*, proclaiming the birth of the new "science of teen violence." These are gross oversimplifications. A host of features occur in tandem with human collective violence that are not present among animals. These features give human massacres an entirely distinct character that calls for an analysis focusing on these unique features.

ANIMALS DON'T, BUT HUMANS DO KILL ON PRINCIPLE

It is true that we share 98.5% of our genetic variance with the chimpanzee. But the meager 1.5% of our unshared variance makes for an enormous chasm. The 98.5% of shared DNA allows the chimp to produce a grunt even several different grunts. But the 1.5% of unshared DNA allowed Mozart to write *The Magic Flute*. Our capacities for benign achievements, invention, and creation surpass those of the chimpanzee by many orders of magnitude But our capacities for malign achievements are also enormous. We have shown extraordinary creativity, originality, and ingenuity in killing and torturing our own conspecifics. There is no animal species that has committed atrocities on our **[232]** scale. In the measure of evil we stand alone. And the scale of atrocities in itself implies that there has to be elaborate organization, risk assessment, extensive planning, and preparation.

The attempt to construct an animal model of human collective violence faces so many discontinuities that only very superficial generalizations can be drawn. Of course, there is aggression among animals. Of course, animals protect their territory. Of course, we can locate brain structures in higher animals that correspond to ours and are activated in agonistic behavior. Of course, we can find collective animal aggression, such as among wolves. But human massacres are directed at our *conspecifics*. Animal aggression on the scale that would even remotely approximate any of the known massacres is never against conspecifics. And the scale of collective violence observed among humans surpasses that among animals by many orders of magnitude. Two million, which amounts to two out of every seven, Cambodians were killed between 1975 and 1978. During World War II, 6 million Jews, 3 million Poles, and millions of innocent civilians belonging to other ethnic groups lost their lives. Stalin's purges reach to nearly 15 million victims. In the Cultural Revolution in China, 43 million civilians lost their lives, many by starvation and disease, according to some estimates. And, as we have seen earlier, the ingenuity of mass murder and the level of atrocity accompanying some programs of genocide are never to be found among any animal species.

Above all, it is a deplorable but undeniable fact that most of the carnage of humans by other humans was the outcome of a deliberate, planned, and highly organized enterprise. In their work on violence, Wrangham and Peterson (1996) report a violent incident, cited previously, that started when "a group of eight chimpanzees traveled *purposefully* ... toward the border of their range" (p. 5; italics mine) and attacked a lone male. How would one know that the actions of these eight chimpanzees were driven by a *purpose,* that there was a plan to deliberately inflict harm on a particular individual or just any individual? There was nothing in the behavior of the group of eight that would indicate such a circumstance. Most conspecific aggression of the form that is reported in the animal literature is spontaneous and arises when there are disputes over access to resources such as nesting, prey, or mating priorities. And aggression so motivated is immediately preceded by a threat to these scarce resources—a threat that is patently conspicuous. There is no parallel to Wannsee Conference that decided on the Final Solution in 1942 and laid out plans, organization, and logistics for the extermination of millions of innocent conspecifics. To assume that these cataclysmic events belong to a common category with the beating that eight chimpanzees inflicted on one of theirs nears on obscenity. The term *bestiality* when characterizing human violence is an offense to the nonhuman species.

There is abundant evidence that human massacres are highly organized and previously planned. The Rwanda massacre of 1994, according to Gérard **[233]** Prunier (1995), was meticulously planned for years. Involved in the planning was the president's wife, Mme Agathe Habyarimana, and the circle of her loyal supporters known as the Clan de Madame. The major plans were developed in 1993 by Colonel Théoneste Bagosora. And only half an hour after the plane carrying President Habyarimana was shot down on April 6, 1994, atrocities began in a most methodical way. There was a clear order of targeting victims that started with the liberal members of the government, the president of the Constitutional Court, civil rights activists, priests, journalists, and others for whom deliberate lists with addresses arranged by priority and precedence were prepared. And 2 million machetes, bought from China, were freely distributed among the Hutu population. In 100 days, 800,000 Tutsi were killed.

We are tempted to believe that pogroms taking place in eastern Europe at the turn of the nineteenth century and later were spontaneous events, or that Kristallnacht was an impromptu outburst of violence. Yet both were planned and organized. As late as 1945, when only a handful of Jews remained in the Polish town of Kielce, violence erupted that was originally reported as a spontaneous riot. Yet, according to a recent historical account (Wiacek, 1992), the pogrom was well organized and well prepared. Wiacek cites the fact that the violence started when groups of perpetrators gathered in the town square, and each group was deployed to a separate section of town, known to be housing Jews. More important, on the previous day, Christian stores were boarded up and had crosses painted on their entrances.

But if human massacres are carefully and deliberately planned and highly organized campaigns, it is important to inquire what forces drive hundreds of thousands of ordinary men to commit extraordinary acts—acts of murder, mutilation, rape, expulsion, and total extermination. I have suggested elsewhere (Zajonc, under review) that, bizarre as it may seem, human collective violence is driven and justified on moral grounds. In all instances of extraordinary mass violence, the acts are endowed with the high purpose of a moral imperative. The doctrine of Manifest Destiny was invoked to justify the Philippine-American war of 1898, in which a quarter of a million were killed of disease or hunger. The bombings of Dresden, Hiroshima, and Nagasaki were justified on a moral principle. And so were the Holocaust, the Rwanda and Burundi genocides, China's Cultural Revolution, the slaughter of Native Americans, and the slaughter of the Herrero in 1904 by General Von Trotha. I was unable to find *any* accounts of massacres that were not viewed by their perpetrators as right and necessary.

It is true, however, that the subsequent generations sometimes accept the guilt of their forefathers, but it is also true that in only exceptional cases is there any punishment of the perpetrators. The standard outcome is nearly complete impunity. There is also a great deal of denial and distortion (App, 1973; Butz, 1976; Irving, 1977; Seidel, 1986; Stern, 1994;Vidal-Naquet, 1992). Shintaro Ishihara, the governor of Tokyo, denied the occurrence of the Nanjing **[234]** massacre altogether (French, 2000). Because of the wide diffusion of responsibility, it is difficult to assign guilt to particular individuals. Thus, even though the International Convention Against Genocide was signed in December 1948, the first trial for genocide took place not less than half a century later, against Dr. Milan Kovacevic.

SCIENTIFIC OBJECTIVITY AND THE STUDY OF MASSACRES

Massacres are extremely complex phenomena that will not be explained by a single factor, and no one discipline alone can explain the hundreds of massacres all over the globe. The task is novel and quite difficult. One important source of difficulty is our commitment to objectivity. Confronted with the scope and scale of atrocities that the twentieth century bestowed on our collective conscience, psychologists find themselves in a totally new setting of research. True: Pure and full objectivity is not to be found in *any* conventional research. After all, we *want* some research outcomes and not others. And we do hope for them. True: Empirical scientists introduce safeguards and control groups, counterbalance their experimental conditions, carry out independent replications, and invite opportunities for disconfirmation of their hypotheses. But, at the bottom, there lingers a wish, an expectation, a hope that things will turn out in a preferred way.

When we commit ourselves to the study of massacres, the criterion of objectivity becomes even more vulnerable. Two aspects of bias visit even the most impartial researcher. One is the revulsion against the unspeakable evil of the atrocities themselves. No one who has read historical accounts of the recent massacres and who has an ambition to understand these phenomena can formulate the problem without introducing one's own moral element into the study. In fact, Claude Lanzmann, the maker of the film *Shoah*, is adamant about the "obscenity of the very project of understanding [the Holocaust]" (Rosenbaum, 1998, p. 250). The analysis of massacres cannot be value-free. The point cannot be put more convincingly than in Langer's (1999) book on the Holocaust:

> Recently I was watching the testimony of a survivor of the Kovno ghetto.
> He spoke of the so-called *Kinderaktion,* when the Germans rounded up all
> the children (and many elderly) and took them to nearby Ninth Fort for
> execution. The witness was present in the room when an SS man entered

and demanded from a mother the one-year-old infant she was holding in her arms. She refused to surrender it, so he seized the baby by its ankles and tore the body in two before the mother's eyes.... I ask myself what we can do with such information, how we can inscribe it in the ... narratives that later will try to reduce to some semblance of order or pattern [235] the spontaneous defilement implicit in such deeds? How can we enroll such atrocities in the human community and identify them as universal tendencies toward evil inherent in all humankind? ...Well, we can't, (p. 3)

The other source of bias is our own ethnic, national, or racial identity. A Chinese scholar will look at the Rape of Nanking (Chang, 1997) differently than a Japanese scholar, and Germans and Jews will be predisposed to study the Holocaust from different perspectives. Because in each case there is a clearly identifiable group of perpetrators and a clearly identifiable group of victims, the researcher has little chance of giving equally impartial attention to both. This difficulty is exacerbated by the fact that scholars engaged in massacre research have more often than not some personal connection with the victims or the perpetrators. Can survivors' anger be put aside and an impartial, dispassionate analysis be put in place? Can descendants overcome their bewilderment upon learning that their parents or grandparents were killers or countenanced killing, rape, and plunder? Can those who were not witnesses or bystanders of past brutalities have legitimate insights into these horrid events? The revulsion bias and the engagement bias are both sources of partiality to which the researcher must be sensitive.

REFERENCES

Andric, I. (1959). *The bridge over the Drina*. London: Harvill.

App, A.J. (1973). *The six-million swindle: Blackmailing the German people for hard marks with fabricated corpses*. Tacoma Park, MD: St. Boniface Press.

Ardrey, R. (1961). *African genesis: A personal investigation into the animal origins and nature of man*. New York: Atheneum.

Barash, D.P. (1982). *Sociobiology and behavior* (2nd ed.). New York: Elsevier.

Begley, S. (1999, May 3). Why the young kill. *Newsweek*. **[236]**

Butz, A.R. (1976). *The hoax of the twentieth century: The case against the presumed extermination of European Jewry*. Torrance, CA: Institute for Historical Review.

Chang, I. (1997). *The rape of Nanking*. New York: Basic Books.

Dawkins, R. (1989). *The selfish gene*. Oxford: Oxford University Press.

De Zayas, A.M. (1983). *Zeugnisse der Vertreibung*. Krefeld, Germany: Sinus Verlag.

Ehrenreich, B. (2000, January 21). How "natural" is rape? *Time*, p. 88.

Ehrlich, P.R. (2000). *Human natures: Genes, cultures, and the human prospect*. Washington, DC: Island Press.

French, H.W. (2000, January 23). Japanese call '37 massacre a war myth, stirring storm. *New York Times*, p. A5.

Fukuyama. F. (1992). *The end of history and the last man*. New York: Free Press.

Gibbons, A. (1998). Which of our genes make us human: Comparison of primate DNA. *Science*. *281*, 1432.

Hamilton, W.D. (1964). The genetical evolution of social behaviour. *Journal of Theoretical Biology*, 7, 1–52.

Hammer, D., and Copeland, P. (1998). *Living with our genes: Why they matter more than you think*. New York: Doubleday .

Hinde, R.A. (1974). *Biological bases of human social behavior*. New York: McGraw-Hill.

Hirsch, J.U., Lindley, R.H., and Tolman, E.C. (1955). An experimental test of an alleged innate sign stimulus. *Journal of Comparative and Physiological Psychology, 48*, 278–280.

Irving, D. (1977). *Hitler's war*. New York: Avon.

Langer, L.L. (1999). *Preempting the Holocaust*. New Haven, CT: Yale University Press.

LeBon, G. (1995), *The crowd.* New Brunswick, NJ: Transaction.

Lorenz, K.Z. (1966). *On aggression.* London: Methuen.

Lorenz, K.Z. (1978). *Vergleichende Verhaltensforschung: Grundlagen der Etholgie* [Comparative study of behavior: The foundations of ethology]. Vienna: Springer.

Lorenz, K.Z. (1981). *The foundations of ethology* (K. Z. Lorenz andR. W. Kickert, Trans.). New York: Springer.

Morris, D. (1967). *The naked ape: A zoologist's study of the human animal.* New York: McGraw-Hill.

Moyer, K.E. (1969). Internal impulses to aggression. *Transactions of the New York Academy of Science, 31,* 104–114.

Muckensturm, B. (1965). Let nid et le territoire chez l'Epinoche *Gasterosteus aculeatus. Comptes Rendues d'Acedemie des Sciences, 260,* 4825.

Muckensturm, B. (1969). La signification de la livrée nuptiale de l'Epinoche. *Revue du Comportement Animal, 3,* 39–65.

Peeke, H.V. (1969). Habituation of conspecific aggression in the three-spined stickleback (*Gasterosteus aculeatus L.*). *Behaviour, 35,* 137–156.

Peeke, H.V., Wyers, E.J., and Herz, M.J. (1969). Waning of the aggressive response to male models in the three-spined stickleback (*Gasterosteus aculeatus L.*). *Animal Behaviour, 17,* 224–228.

Prunier, G. (1995). *The Rwanda crisis: History of genocide.* New York: Columbia University Press.

Rosenbaum, R. (1998). *Explaining Hitler: The search for the origins of his evil.* New York: Random House. **[237]**

Seidel, G. (1986). *The Holocaust denial: Antisemitism, racism and the New Right.* Leeds, Yorkshire: Beyond the Pale.

Soyinka, W. (1998, Oct. 4). Hearts of darkness. *New York Times Book Review*

Stern, K. (1994). *Holocaust denial.* New York: American Jewish Committee.

Storr, A. (1968). *Human aggression.* New York: Atheneum.

Thornhill, R., and Palmer, C.T. (2000). *A natural history of rape: Biological bases of sexual coercion.* Cambridge, MA: MIT Press.

Tinbergen, N. (1952). The curious behavior of the stickleback. *Scientific American, 187,* 22–26.

Vidal-Naquet, P. (1992). *Assassins of memory: Essays on the denial of the Holocaust.* New York: Columbia University Press.

Wiacek, T. (1992). Zabic zyda! Kulisy i tajemnice pogromu kieleckiego 1946. Kraków: Temax.

Wilson, E.O. (1975). *Sociobiology.* Cambridge, MA: Belknap Press of Harvard University Press.

Worchel, S. (1999). *Written in blood: Ethnic identity and the struggle for human harmony.* New York: Worth.

Wrangham, R., and Peterson, D. (1996). *Demonic males: Apes and the origins of human, violence.* Boston: Houghton Mifflin.

Zajonc, R.B. (under review). *Massacres: Mass murder in the name of moral imperatives.* **[238]**